CIVIL LIBERTIES AND THE FOREIGN INTELLIGENCE SURVEILLANCE ACT

DONALD J. MUSCH

Fourteenth Volume, Second Series
Terrorism: Documents of International & Local Control

James Walsh
General Editor

OCEANA PUBLICATIONS, INC. DOBBS FERRY, NEW YORK

Information contained in this work has been obtained by Oceana Publications from sources believed to be reliable. However, neither the Publisher nor its authors guarantee the accuracy or completeness of any information published herein, and neither Oceana nor its authors shall be responsible for any errors, omissions or damages arising from the use of this information. This work is published with the understanding that Oceana and its authors are supplying information, but are not attempting to render legal or other professional services. If such services are required, the assistance of an appropriate professional should be sought.

You may order this or any Oceana publication by visiting Oceana's website at http://www.oceanalaw.com.

Library of Congress Control Number: 2003109185

Terrorism: Documents of International and Local Control, Second Series
ISSN 1064-9352

ISBN 978-0-379-21503-8

© 2003 by Oceana Publications, Inc.

All rights reserved. No part of this publication may be reproduced or transmitted in any form or by any means, electronic or mechanical, including photocopy, recording, xerography, or any information storage and retrieval system, without permission in writing from the publisher.

OVERALL TABLE OF CONTENTS

THE FOREIGN INTELLIGENCE SURVEILLANCE ACT (FISA) 3
    The Historical Perspective—The Church Hearings and Beyond 11
    Executive Branch Practice & the FISC Decision 157

THE USA PATRIOT ACT OF 2001 203

THE DOMESTIC SECURITY ENHANCEMENT ACT OF 2003–PATRIOT II . . . 209

THE FOREIGN INTELLIGENCE COURT OF REVIEW DECISION,
November 18, 2002 295

TABLE OF CONTENTS

Introduction vii

THE FOREIGN INTELLIGENCE SURVEILLANCE ACT (FISA)

The Historical Perspective—The Church Hearings and Beyond

Commentary. 3

Summary of the Final Report of the Select Committee to Study Governmental Operations with Respect to Intelligence Activities, U.S. Senate, April 26, 1976 . 11

Testimony of Mr. Kenneth C. Bass, III before the Senate Judiciary Committee on "The USA Patriot Act in Practice: Shedding Light on the FISA Process," September 10, 2002 69

Foreign Intelligence Surveillance Act of 1978: S. Rep. No. 95-604 (Legislative History, P.L. 95-511). 79

Executive Branch Practice & the FISC Decision

Commentary 157

USA Patriot Act Amendments to FISA. 161

Foreign Intelligence Surveillance Court Decision, May 17, 2002 179

THE USA PATRIOT ACT OF 2001

Commentary 203

THE DOMESTIC SECURITY ENHANCEMENT ACT OF 2003–PATRIOT II

Commentary 209

Patriot Act II Draft Bill 213

ACLU Section-by-Section Analysis of Patriot II, February 14, 2003. 265

THE FOREIGN INTELLIGENCE COURT OF REVIEW DECISION
November 18, 2002

Commentary 297

Amici Curiae Brief filed September 19, 2002 by the ACLU in the United States Foreign Intelligence Surveillance Court of Review Decision 02-001 301

Foreign Intelligence Surveillance Court of Review Decision No. 02-001, November 18, 2002. 329

ACLU Petition for Writ of Certiorari to the U.S. Supreme Court of the Foreign Intelligence Surveillance Court of Review Decison 02-001 363

Cover Letters and Written Responses to Questions Regarding the Patriot Act As Submitted by the Department of Justice to the House Judiciary Committee Chairman, May 13, 2003 403

INTRODUCTION

It is well documented that government activities affecting personal rights escalate during times of crisis. Events since the attacks of 9/11 fit this practice. The Foreign Intelligence Surveillance Act (FISA) was enacted during the Cold War in the interest of national security to improve United States intelligence overseas and to provide better access to "foreign intelligence information." The FSIA specifically limits these surveillance activities within the United States. Passage of the FISA was a specific legislative pronouncement aimed at protecting against excessive government intrusion on personal liberties. Key to FISA was the creation of a Foreign Intelligence Surveillance Court (FISC), a secretive and specialized judicial tool which would ensure there was a check on the activities of the Executive Branch, most notably in the area of secret surveillance.

This work offers the reader an opportunity to revisit the actions and emotions which led to passage of the FISA, and the cataclysmic impact the attacks of 9/11 had on U.S. policy and its approach to the preservation of personal liberty. A distinct fear of a repeat of such attacks undoubtedly is driving the Administration to take very aggressive measures, not only to reconfigure the government's structure to cope with terrorism but to more closely align the legality of governmental actions with the concomitant dangers inherent in our 21st Century society. How far the pendulum swings towards the security argument will depend not so much on legislative oversight and initiative, but on the actual events which transpire in the near future. Put another way, relative quiet and peace from terrorists will likely precipitate increased pressure from the public to pull back from the more stringent authorities given the government. For example, freedom from violent acts will offer legislators a much easier opportunity to withdraw some of the Patriot Act authorities when the sunshine provisions come into effect in 2005.

To some extent, the public is still unaware of the degree of control and oversight which has been exercised by the FISC but, based on the required annual public reports submitted by the Attorney General to the Administrative Office of the U.S. Courts, there is clear evidence that the FISC has given virtually universal approval to the large number of government requests for electronic surveillance. The record for such applications shows:

Year	Approved	Disapproved
1997	749 approved	0 disapproved
1998	796 approved	0 disapproved
1999	886 approved	0 disapproved
2000	1012 approved	0 disapproved
2001	934 approved	0 disapproved
2002	1228 approved	0 disapproved

Actions of the Executive Branch, and two fundamental decisions by the FISC and its Foreign Intelligence Review Court (FIRC) brought to the fore many resurgent concerns advanced, most notably, by civil rights groups in the United States and in the press. Those actions of the Executive Branch were led with:

- forcefully pushing through the USA Patriot Act of 2001 (with admittedly minimal evaluation and discussion in Congress);
- changes in the procedures followed by the Executive Branch in fighting terrorism through the legal system;
- the filing of new procedures with the FISC and appealing the FISC decision (which agreed to such changes only with amendments) to the FIRC, and;
- the more recent circulation of broader legislative proposals aimed at improving the government's ability to fight terrorism.

More detailed coverage is given to the actions and arguments surrounding the FISC decision of May 17, 2002 because it effectively represented the first time FISC had actually refused to go along with a governmental request and the FISC decision, at least in the eyes of civil libertarians, drew a line over which the Executive could not venture while it claimed to be enforcing the FISA as originally passed and intended. The FISC decision was appealed to the FIRC whose decision was equally momentous for it found the governmental approach to be sound, and it laid the groundwork for either "more effective" or "continued egregious" governmental conduct, depending on one's point of view.

The proposed "Patriot II" legislation represents an Administration initiative which is valuable because it shows the outer limits (for the moment) which the government wishes to reach in fighting terrorism. Some speculate the draft was leaked to gauge the public reaction to the proposals—offering the Administration an opportunity to tailor a final product acceptable to the American public, and its legislators. Whatever the reason, the draft elicited intense (and mostly critical) comments from the press, advocacy groups, and legal scholars. To those having a natural antagonism towards the current Administration it is living proof that this Department of Justice knows "no limits" on power. On the other hand, for those who are striving to ensure continued security for this democracy (and chances are this includes most of those who are directly connected with the "war on terrorism") most of what is being proposed is viewed as effective and warranted—even if some aspects are a bitter pill to swallow!

Some of the material presented in this work originates from an advocacy group which is well known throughout the world—the American Civil Liberties Union (ACLU). The ACLU's petition for a writ of Certiorari to the U.S. Supreme Court was a unique filing. The comments the ACLU provided on Patriot II represent one of the few explanations of those provisions—the Administration has circulated nothing on the subject. Countering the advocacy perspective contained in the ACLU materials is the equally slanted material in Document Number 11 giving the Executive's answers to questions posed by Congress on FISA and Patriot I. And, throughout this volume, the reader will find examples of the commentary from a broad range of media—each contribution with its own point of view to forward. What the reader should be left with is not confusion, but hopefully a starting point for further inquiry into what is being proposed, what is being done, and what should be changed.

Donald J. Musch

August 5, 2003

THE FOREIGN INTELLIGENCE SURVEILLANCE ACT (FISA)
The Historical Perspective—The Church Hearings and Beyond

Commentary 3

Summary of the Final Report of the Select Committee to Study Governmental Operations with Respect to Intelligence Activities, U.S. Senate, April 26, 1976 . 11

Testimony of Mr. Kenneth C. Bass, III before the Senate Judiciary Committee on "The USA Patriot Act in Practice: Shedding Light on the FISA Process," September 10, 2002 69

Foreign Intelligence Surveillance Act of 1978. S. Rep. No. 95-604 (Legislative History, Ph. 95-511) 79

COMMENTARY

THE FOREIGN INTELLIGENCE SURVEILLANCE ACT (FISA)

The Historical Perspective—The Church Hearings and Beyond

Total disenchantment with governmental practices subsequent to Watergate led to the formation of the Senate Select Committee to Study Governmental Operations chaired by Senator Frank Church. The Committee was tasked "to conduct an investigation and study of governmental operations with respect to intelligence activities and of the extent, if any, to which illegal, improper, or unethical activities were engaged in by any agency of the Federal Government." Senate Resolution No. 21 included a comprehensive list of areas which the Committee was to address, and the ensuing 15-month investigation was perhaps the most comprehensive examination of intelligence operations conducted in the United States. In the area of civil liberties and the relationship of intelligence operations to domestic law enforcement agencies, the Committee confronted a broad range of issues dealing with electronic surveillance and other means for secretly obtaining information. As pointed out in the Committee Report issued on April 26, 1976:

> In the few years prior to the establishment of this Committee, however, the public's awareness of the need to examine intelligence issues was heightened. The series of allegations and partial exposure in the press and the congress provoked serious questions about the conduct of intelligence activities at home and abroad. The Watergate affair increased the public's concern about abuse of governmental power and caused greater attention to be paid to the need to follow and to strengthen the role of law to check such abuses . . . (Book I, page 11)

Addressing the question of warrantless electronic surveillance, the Committee reported:

> The courts have also not confronted intelligence issues. As the Supreme Court noted in 1972 in commenting on warrantless electronic surveillance, 'The practice has been permitted by successive presidents for more than a quarter of a century without 'guidance from the Congress or a definitive decision by the Court.' (Book I, page 11)

Though it was not a major topical area for consideration by the Committee, "coordination" of intelligence activities within the United States or involving American citizens (most particularly CIA-FBI coordination) was important and the Committee concluded: " . . . the Huston Plan episode illustrates the questions of propriety and legality which may arise in counterintelligence operations conducted in the United States or involving American citizens." (Book I, page 428). In the eyes of the Committee, Congress and the executive should pay more attention to this area of coordination because, among other reasons: "... counterintelligence has infringed on the rights and liberties of Americans." (Book I, page 440)

The Committee then issued as a "Major Finding," "The intelligence community has employed surreptitious collection techniques—mail opening, surreptitious entries, informants, and 'traditional' and highly sophisticated forms of electronic surveillance—to achieve its overly broad intelligence targeting and collection objectives..." adding later that the legal standards and procedures regulating their use have been insufficient. (Book II, page 183)

The extensive criticisms of governmental policy and practices within the Committee Report triggered diverse views, even among those who served on the Committee. Senator Baker, referred to a comment by former Director of Central Intelligence William Colby (as quoted from the *New York Times* which said:

> ... This year's excitement has made clear that the rule of law applies to all parts of the American Government, including intelligence. In fact, this will strengthen American intelligence. (Book I, page 595)

On the other hand, Senator Barry Goldwater stated in his separate comments to the Report:

> I have refused to sign the final report of the Select Committee on Intelligence Activities in the belief it will cause severe embarrassment, if not grave harm, to the Nation's foreign policy. (Book I, page 593)

But the balancing of acts which encroach on liberties to avoid other acts which can destroy the very fabric of our society permeates the hearings and the report, and the importance of its findings and deliberations were to focus attention on areas of immense importance which, heretofore, had been shielded by governmental secrecy, judicial inaction, and congressional complicity. And, in the end, in the relatively narrow field of laying down additional rules for domestic intelligence activities, the Report influenced the passage of the Foreign Intelligence Surveillance Act of 1978. The following excerpt from the Committee Report provides a valuable indication of the legal and executive branch actions which led up to the Watergate Hearings and the subsequent appointment and report of the Church Committee.

...

2. Gaps and Exceptions in the Law of Electronic Surveillance

Congress and the Supreme Court have both addressed the legal issues raised by electronic surveillance, but the law has been riddled with gaps and exceptions. The Executive branch has been able to apply vague standards for the use of this technique to particular cases as it has seen fit, and, in the case of NSA monitoring, the standards and procedures for the use of electronic surveillance were not applied at all.

When the Supreme Court first considered wiretapping, it held that the warrantless use of this technique was constitutional because the Fourth Amendment's warrant requirement applied only to physical trespass and did not extend to the seizure of conversation. This decision, the 1928 case of *Olmstead v. United States*, involved in a criminal prosecution, and left federal agencies free to engage in the unrestricted use of wiretaps in both criminal and intelligence investigations.[13]

Six years later, Congress enacted the Federal Communications Act of 1934, which made it a crime for "any person," without authorization, to intercept and divulge or publish the contents of wire and radio communications. The Supreme Court subsequently construed this section to apply to federal agents as well as to ordinary citizens, and held that evidence obtained directly or indirectly from the interception of wire and radio communications was not admissible in court.[14] But Congress acquiesced in the Justice Department's position that these cases prohibited only the divulgence of contents of wire communications outside the executive branch,[15] and Government wiretapping for intelligence purposes other than prosecution continued.

On the ground that neither the 1934 Act nor the Supreme Court decisions on wiretapping were meant to apply to "grave matters involving the defense of the nation," President Franklin Roosevelt authorized Attorney General Jackson in 1940 to approve wiretaps on "persons suspected of subversive activities against the Government of the United States, including suspected spies."[16] In the absence of any guidance from Congress or the Court for another quarter century, the executive branch first broadened this standard in 1946 to permit wiretapping in "cases vitally affecting the domestic security or where human life is in jeopardy,"[17] and then modified it in 1965 to allow wiretapping in "investigations related to the national security."[18] Internal Justice Department policy required the prior approval of the Attorney General before the FBI could institute wiretaps in particular cases,[19] but until the mid-1960's there was no requirement of periodic reapproval by the Attorney General.[20] In the absence of any instruction to terminate them, some wiretraps remained in effect for years.[21]

In 1967, the Supreme Court reversed its holding in the *Olmstead* case and decided that the Fourth Amendment's warrant requirement did apply to electronic surveillances.[22] It expressly declined, however, to extend this holding to cases involving the "national security."[22a] Congress followed suit the next year in the Omnibus Crime Control Act of 1968, which established a warrant procedure for electronic surveillance in criminal cases but included a provision that neither it nor the Federal Communications Act of 1934 "shall limit the constitutional power of the President."[23] Although Congress did not purport to define the President's power, the Act referred to five broad categories which thereafter served as the Justice Department's criteria for warrantless electronic surveillance and counterintelligence matters:

(1) to protect the Nation against actual or potential attack or other hostile acts of a foreign power;

(2) to obtain foreign intelligence information deemed essential to the security of the United States; and

(3) to protect the national security information against foreign intelligence activities.

The last two categories dealt with domestic intelligence interests:

> (4) to protect the United States against overthrow of the government by force or other unlawful means, or
>
> (5) against any other clear and present danger to the structure or existence of the government.

In 1972, the Supreme Court held in *United States v. United States District Court*,[23a] that the President did not have the constitutional power to authorize warrantless electronic surveillance to protect the nation from domestic threats.[24] The Court pointedly refrained, however, from any "judgment on the scope of the President's surveillance power with respect to the activities of foreign powers, within or without this country."[25] Only "the domestic aspects of national security" came within the ambit of the Court's decision.[26]

To conform with the holding in this case, the Justice Department thereafter limited warrantless wire tapping to cases involving a "significant connection with a foreign power, its agents or agencies."[27]

At no time, however, were the Justice Department's standards and procedures ever applied to NSA's electronic monitoring system and its "watch listing" of American citizens.[28] From the early 1960's until 1973, NSA complied a list of individuals and organizations, including 1200 American citizens and domestic groups, whose communications were segregated from the mass of communications intercepted by the Agency, transcribed, and frequently disseminated to other agencies for intelligence purposes.[29]

The Americans on this list, many of whom were active in the antiwar and civil rights movements, were placed there by the FBI, CIA, Secret Service, Defense Department, and NSA itself without prior judicial warrant or even the prior approval of the Attorney General. In 1970, NSA began to monitor telephone communications links between the United States and South America at the request of the Bureau of Narcotics and Dangerous Drugs (BNDD) to obtain information about international drug trafficking. BNDD subsequently submitted the names of 450 American citizens for inclusion on the Watch List, again without warrant or the approval of the Attorney General.[30]

The legal standards and procedures regulating the use of microphone surveillance have traditionally been even more lax than those regulating the use of wiretapping. The first major Supreme Court decision on microphone surveillance was *Goldman v. United States*, 316 U.S. 129 (1942), which held that such surveillance in a criminal case was constitutional when the installation did not involve a trespass. Citing this case, Attorney General McGrath prohibited the trespassory use of this technique by the FBI in 1952.[31] But two years later—a few weeks after the Supreme Court denounced the use of a microphone installation in a criminal defendant's bedroom[32]—Attorney General Brownell gave the FBI sweeping authority to engage in bugging for intelligence purposes. "... [C]onsiderations of internal security and the national safety are paramount," he wrote, "and, therefore, may compel the unrestricted use of this technique in the national interest."[33]

Since Brownell did not require the prior approval of the Attorney General for bugging specific targets, he largely undercut the policy that had developed for wiretapping. The FBI in many cases could obtain equivalent coverage by utilizing bugs rather than taps and would not be burdened with the necessity of a formal request to the Attorney General.

The vague "national interest" standards established by Brownell and the policy of not requiring the Attorney General's prior approval for microphone installations, continued until 1965, when the Justice Department began to apply the same criteria and procedures to both microphone and telephone surveillance.

Notes:

[13] *Olmstead v. United States*, 277 U.S. 438 (1928).

[14] *Nordone v. United States*, 302 U.S. 397 (1937); 308 U.S. 338 (1939).

[15] For example, letter from Attorney General Jackson to Rep. Hatton Summers, 3/19/41; See Electronic Surveillance Report: Sec. II.

[16] Memorandum from President Roosevelt to the Attorney General 5/21/40.

[17] Letter from Attorney General Tom C. Clark to President Truman, 7/17/46.

[18] Directive from President Johnson to Heads of Agencies, 6/30/65.

[19] President Roosevelt's 1940 order directed the Attorney General to approve wiretaps "after investigation of the need in each case." (Memorandum from President Roosevelt to Attorney General Jackson, 5/21/40.) However, Attorney General Francis Biddle recalled that Attorney General Jackson "turned it over to Edgar Hoover without himself passing on each case" in 1940 and 1941. Biddle's practice beginning in 1941 conformed to the President's order. (Francis Biddle, *In Brief Authority* (Garden City: Doubleday, 1962), p. 167.)

Since 1965, explicit written authorization has been required. (Directive of President Johnson 6/30/65.) This requirement however, has often been disregarded. In violation of this requirement, for example, no written authorizations were obtained from the Attorney General—or from any one else—for a series of four wiretaps implemented in 1971 and 1972 on Yeoman Charles Radford, two of his friends, and his father-in-law. See Electronics Surveillance Report: Sec. VI. The first and third of these taps were implemented at the oral instruction of Attorney General John Mitchell. (Memorandum from T.J. Smith E.S. Miller, 2/26/73.) The remaining taps were implemented at the oral request of David Young, and assistant to John Ehrlichman at the White House, who merely informed the Bureau that the requests originated with Ehrlichman and had the Attorney General's concurrence. (Memorandum from T.J. Smith to E.S. Miller, 6/14/73.)

[20] Attorney General Nicholas Katzenbach instituted this requirement in March 1965. (Memorandum from J. Edgar Hoover to the Attorney General, 3/3/65.)

[21] The FBI maintained one wiretap on an official of the Nation of Islam that had originally been authorized by Attorney General Brownell in 1957 for seven years until 1964 without any subsequent re-authorization. (Memorandum from J. Edgar Hoover to the Attorney General, 12/31/65, initialed "Approved: HB, 1/2/57.")

As Nicholas Katzenbach testified: "The custom was not to put a time limit on a tap, or any wiretap authorization. Indeed, I think the Bureau would have felt free in 1965 to put to tap on a phone authorized by Attorney General Jackson before World War II." (Nicholas Katzenbach testimony, 11/12/75, p. 87.)

[22] *Katz v. United States*, 389 U.S. 347 (1967).

[22a] The Court wrote: "Whether safeguards other than prior authorization by magistrate would satisfy the Fourth Amendment in a situation involving the national security is a question not presented by this case." 389 U.S. at 358 n. 23.

[23] 18 U.S.C. 2511 (3).

[23a] 407 U.S. 297 (1972).

[24] At the same time, the Court recognized that "domestic security surveillance" may involve different policy and practical considerations apart from the surveillance of 'ordinary crime,' 407 U.S. at 321, and thus did not hold that "the same type of standards and procedures prescribed by Title III [of the 1968 Act] are necessarily applicable to this case." (407 U.S. at 321.) The court noted:

"Given the potential distinctions between Title III criminal surveillance and those involving the domestic security, Congress may wish to consider protective standards for the latter which differ from those already prescribed for specified crime in Title III. Different standards may be compatible with the Fourth Amendment." (407 U.S. at 321.)

[25] 407 U.S. at 307.

[26] 407 U.S. at 320. *United States v. United States District Court* remains the only Supreme Court case dealing with the issue of warrantless electronic surveillance for intelligence purposes. Three federal circuit courts have considered this issue since 1972, however. The Third Circuit and the Fifth Circuit both held that the President may constitutionally authorize warrantless electronic surveillance for foreign counterespionage and foreign intelligence purposes. [*United States v. Butenko*, 494 F.2d 593 (3d Cir. 1974), *Cert. denied sub nom. Ivanov v. United States*, 419 U.S. 881 (1974); and *United States v. Brown*, 484 F.2d 418 (5th Cir. 1973). *Cert. denied* 415 U.S. 960 (1974).] The District of Columbia Circuit held unconstitutional the warrantless electronic surveillance of the Jewish Defense League, a domestic organization whose activities allegedly affected U.S. Soviet relations, but which was neither the agent of nor in collaboration with a foreign power. [*Zweibon v. Mitchell*, 516 F.2d 594 (D.C. Cir. 1975) (*en banc.*).]

[27] Testimony of Deputy Assistant Attorney General Kevin Maroney. Hearings before the Senate Subcommittee on Administrative Practice and Procedures, 6/29/72, p. 10. This language paralleled that of the Court in *United States v. United States District Court*, 407 U.S. at 309 n.8.

[28] Although Attorney General John Mitchell and Justice Department officials on the Intelligence Evaluation Committee apparently learned that NSA was making a contribution to domestic intelligence in 1971, there is no indication that the FBI told them of its submission of names of Americans for inclusion on a NSA "watch list." When Assistant Attorney General Henry Petersen learned of NSA practices in 1973, Attorney General Elliott Richardson ordered that they be terminated. (See Report on NSA; Sec. I, "Introduction and Summary.")

[29] See NSA Report: Sec. I, "Introduction and Summary."

[30] Memorandum from Iredell to Gayler, 4/10/70; See NSA Report: Sec. I. Introduction and Summary. BNDD originally requested NSA to monitor the South American link because it did not believe it had authority to wiretap a few public telephones in New York City from which drug deals were apparently being arranged. (Iredell testimony, 9/18/75, p. 99)

[31] Memorandum from the Attorney General to Mr. Hoover, 2/26/52.

[32] *Irvine v. California*, 347 U.S. 128 (1954).

[33] Memorandum from the Attorney General to the Director, FBI, 5/20/54.

A full summary of the Report is included as a document in this volume.

COMMENTARY: THE HISTORICAL PERSPECTIVE

FISA, affected by the events considered by the Church Committee and before, and as passed by Congress in 1978, was viewed as a major vehicle to control governmental activities which might impinge on private rights. As pointed out in the legislative history of the bill:

> As Attorney General Bell stated in testifying in favor of the bill:
>
>> I believe this bill is remarkable not only in the way it has been developed, but also in the fact that for the first time in our society the clandestine intelligence activities of our government shall be subject to the regulation and receive the positive authority of a public law for all to inspect. President Carter stated it very well in announcing this bill when he said that 'one of the most difficult tasks in a free society like our own is the correlation between adequate intelligence to guarantee our nation's security on the one hand, and the preservation of basic human rights on the other.' (P.S. 95-511, Legislative History, U.S. Cong. & Adm. News '78-30, page 3905).

Illustrating further what the Congress was trying to achieve, and the ills it was countering, the Legislative History points out that warrantless electronic surveillance abuses "illuminated in 1975 during the investigation of the Watergate break-in . . . ." and the subsequent conclusions of the Church Committee clearly identified numerous examples of illegal wiretaps without the benefit of judicial warrant.

Specific actions covered by FISA, and which were exempt from prior legislative restrictions, were electronic surveillance when done for "national security" but, as can be seen from governmental actions and judicial decisions post FISA, the FISA evolved (through amendments by the USA Patriot Act of 2001) into a valuable tool for governmental investigations, involving both criminal and foreign intelligence activities. The concern of many at the time FISA was enacted was that information would be circulated from electronic surveillance which did NOT involve foreign intelligence. As Ira R. Shapiro stated in the *Harvard Journal on Legislation* (Vol. 15, at page 202):

> But no similar qualms should block imposition of criminal penalties for improper retention or dissemination of information which is clearly not foreign intelligence information. Enactment of criminal sanctions would be a strong response to the revelations of the Church Committee. It would also allay public concern about the scope of the electronic surveillance permitted under the statute.

Mr. Shapiro concluded his note fully supporting passage of the FISA and stating:

> Every major provision of the bill has been written and reworked painstakingly, with careful attention to the concerns of both civil libertarians and the intelligence community. (at page 204)

FISA attempted to strike a balance between protecting the national security and protecting civil liberties by setting out a clear procedure for the use of electronic surveillance in gathering foreign intelligence. The law required the government to obtain a judicial warrant for such actions from any one of seven (now eleven) designated federal district court judges. The denial of an application could be appealed *by the government* to a special three judge court of appeals and from there *the government* could appeal to the U.S. Supreme Court. The new law also specifically eliminates the concept of Presidential "inherent power" as authority for authorizing electronic surveillance without a warrant.

Before a warrant will be issued by a judge, the Executive Branch must certify in writing that the information sought is "foreign intelligence information", as defined in the law. Within the Executive Branch, the Attorney General is required to make a finding that all requirements under the law have been met before the application is submitted to the judge.

According to the legislative history of the FISA:

> ... The bill does not impliedly authorize departure from the standard of criminality in other aspects of national security investigations or intelligence collection directed at Americans without the safeguards of judicial review and probably cause. It remains to determine, in fashioning a charter for the use of informants, physical surveillance and other investigative procedures, whether the departure from a criminal standard is an acceptable basis for investigating United States citizens on grounds of national security." (at page 3920) In discussing this "non criminal standard" topic, the legislative history notes that a number of Senators were opposed to approval of electronic surveillance in such instances but the Subparagraph was approved with the understanding the Administration would draft a revision in the espionage laws which might permit this non criminal standard to be repealed. (at page 3926).

One of the best expositions indicating what the legislators and the Executive Branch were trying to accomplish comes from the testimony of Mr. Kenneth C. Bass, III to the Senate Judiciary Committee on September 10, 2002. That testimony is included, in its entirety, in this volume.

SUMMARY OF THE FINAL REPORT OF THE SELECT COMMITTEE TO STUDY GOVERNMENTAL OPERATIONS WITH RESPECT TO INTELLIGENCE ACTIVITIES

U.S. SENATE
April 26, 1976*

A. Introduction

The purpose of the Senate Select Committee's inquiry into the intelligence activities of the United States has been to determine what secret governmental activities are necessary and how they best can be conducted under the rule of law. There is unquestioned need to build a new consensus between the executive and legislative branches concerning the proper scope and purpose of foreign and military intelligence activities. Allegations of abuse, revelations in the press, and the results of the Committee's 15 month inquiry have underlined the necessity to restore confidence in the integrity of our nation's intelligence agencies.

The findings and recommendations which follow are presented in that spirit. They are, in essence, an agenda for remedial action by both the legislative and executive branches of the United States Government. There is an urgency to completing this schedule of action. This task is no less important to safeguarding America's future than are intelligence activities themselves.

The Committee's investigation and the body of its report seek, within the limits of prudence, to perform the crucial task of informing the American people concerning the nature and scope of their Government's foreign intelligence activities. The fundamental issue faced by the Committee in its investigation was how the requirements of American democracy can be properly balanced in intelligence matters against the need for secrecy. Secrecy is essential for the success of many important intelligence activities. At the same time, secrecy contributed to many of the abuses, excesses and inefficiencies uncovered by the Committee. Secrecy also makes it difficult to establish a public consensus for the future conduct of certain intelligence operations.

Because of secrecy, the Committee initially had difficulty gaining access to executive branch information required to carry out the investigation. It was not until the Committee became responsible for investigating allegations of assassination plots that many of the obstacles were cleared away. The resulting access by the Committee was in some cases unprecedented. But the Committee's access to documents and records was hampered nonetheless in a number of other instances either because the materials did not exist or because the executive branch was unwilling to make them available.

---

*S. Rep. No. 94-755, pt. XVIII at 423 (1976)

Secrecy was also a major issue in preparing this report. In order to safeguard what are now agreed to be necessary intelligence activities, the Committee decided not to reveal publicly the full and complete picture of the intelligence operations of the United States Government. The recommendations as a whole have not been materially affected by the requirements of secrecy, but some important findings of the Committee must remain classified in accordance with the Committee's policy of protecting valid secrets. In this connection it should be noted that some information which in the Committee's opinion the American public should know remains classified and has been excluded from the report at the request of the intelligence community agencies. Only the Senate will receive the full version of the Committee's Final Report in accordance with the standing rules of the Senate.

In trying to reconcile the requirements of secrecy and open democratic processes, the Committee found itself with a difficult dilemma. As an investigating committee, it cannot take affirmative legislative action respecting some of the matters that came to its attention. On the other hand, because of necessary secrecy, the Committee cannot publicly present the full case as to why its recommendations are essential.

This experience underscores the need for an effective legislative oversight committee which has sufficient power to resolve such fundamental conflicts between secrecy and democracy. As stated previously, it is the Committee's view that effective congressional oversight requires the power to authorize the budgets of the national intelligence agencies. Without such authority, an oversight committee may find itself in possession of important secret information but unable to act effectively to protect the principles, integrity, and reputation of the United States.

The findings and recommendations which follow are organized principally by agency. There are, however, common themes in the recommendations which cut across agency lines. Some of these themes are: guarding against abuse of America's institutions and reputation; ensuring clear accountability for clandestine activities; establishing effective management of intelligence activities; and creating a framework of statutory law and congressional oversight for the agencies and activities of the United States intelligence community.

The Committee's recommendations fall into three categories: (1) recommendations that the Committee believes should be embodied in law; (2) recommendations to the executive branch concerning principles, practices, and policies which the Committee believes should be pursued within the executive's sphere of responsibilities; and (3) recommendations which should be taken into account by the executive branch in its relations with the intelligence oversight committee(s) of Congress.

B. General Findings

The Committee finds that United States foreign and military intelligence agencies have made important contributions to the nation's security, and generally have performed their missions with dedication and distinction. The

Committee further finds that the individual men and women serving America in difficult and dangerous intelligence assignments deserve the respect and gratitude of the nation.

The Committee finds that there is a continuing need for an effective system of foreign and military intelligence. United States interests and responsibilities in the world will be challenged, for the foreseeable future, by strong and potentially hostile powers. This requires the maintenance of an effective American intelligence system. The Committee has found that the Soviet KGB and other hostile intelligence services maintain extensive foreign intelligence operations, for both intelligence collection and covert operational purposes. These activities pose a threat to the intelligence activities and interests of the United States and its allies.

The Committee finds that Congress has failed to provide the necessary statutory guidelines to ensure that intelligence agencies carry out their missions in accord with constitutional processes. Mechanisms for, and the practice of, congressional oversight have not been adequate. Further, Congress has not devised appropriate means to effectively use the valuable information developed by the intelligence agencies. Intelligence information and analysis that exist within the executive branch clearly would contribute to sound judgments and more effective legislation in the areas of foreign policy and national security.

The Committee finds that covert action operations have not been an exceptional instrument used only in rare instances when the vital interests of the United States have been at stake. On the contrary, presidents and administrations have made excessive, and at times self-defeating, use of covert action. In addition, covert action has become a routine program with a bureaucratic momentum of its own. The long-term impact, at home and abroad, of repeated disclosure of U.S. covert action never appears to have been assessed. The cumulative effect of covert actions has been increasingly costly to America's interests and reputation. The Committee believes that covert action must be employed only in the most extraordinary circumstances.

Although there is a question concerning the extent to which the Constitution requires publication of intelligence expenditures information, the Committee finds that the Constitution at least requires public disclosure and public authorization of an annual aggregate figure for United States national intelligence activities. Congress' failure as a whole to monitor the intelligence agencies' expenditures has been a major element in the ineffective legislative oversight of the intelligence community. The permanent intelligence oversight committee(s) of Congress should give further consideration to the question of the extent to which further public disclosure of intelligence budget information is prudent and constitutionally necessary.

At the same time, the Committee finds that the operation of an extensive and necessarily secret intelligence system places severe strains on the nation's constitutional government. The Committee is convinced, however, that the competing demands of secrecy and the requirements of the democratic process—our Constitution and our laws—can be reconciled. The need to protect secrets must be balanced with the assurance that secrecy is not used as a means to hide the abuse of power or the failures and mistakes of policy. Means must and can be provided for lawful disclosure of unneeded or unlawful secrets.

The Committee finds that intelligence activities should not be regarded as ends in themselves. Rather, the nation's intelligence functions should be organized and directed to assure that they serve the needs of those in the executive and legislative branches who have responsibility for formulating or carrying out foreign and national security policy.

The Committee finds that Congress has failed to provide the necessary statutory guidelines to ensure that intelligence agencies carry out their necessary missions in accord with constitutional processes.

In order to provide firm direction for the intelligence agencies, the Committee finds that new statutory charters for these agencies must be written that take account of the experience of the past three and a half decades. Further, the Committee finds that the relationship among the various intelligence agencies and between them and the Director of Central Intelligence should be restructured in order to achieve better accountability, coordination, and more efficient use of resources.

These tasks are urgent. They should be undertaken by the Congress in consultation with the executive branch in the coming year. The recent proposals and executive actions by the President are most welcome.[1] However, further action by Congress is necessary.

C. The 1947 National Security Act and Related Legislation

The National Security Act of 1947[2] is no longer an adequate framework for the conduct of America's intelligence activities. The 1947 Act, preoccupied as it was with the question of military unification, failed to provide an adequate statement of the broad policy and purposes to be served by America's intelligence effort. The Committee found that the 1947 Act constitutes a vague and open-ended statement of authority for the President through the National Security Council. Neither espionage, covert action, nor paramilitary warfare is explicitly authorized by the 1947 Act. Nonetheless, these have come to be major activities conducted by the Central Intelligence Agency, operating at the direction of the President through the National Security Council. In contrast, the 1947 Act's specific charge to the Director of Central Intelligence (DCI) to coordinate national intelligence has not been effectively realized.

In addition to this broad concern, the Committee found that the 1947 Act does not provide an adequate charter for the Central Intelligence Agency. Moreover, no statutory charter exists for other key intelligence agencies: the National Security Agency and the Defense Intelligence Agency. Nor does the Act

---

[1] Executive Order 11905, 2/18/76.
[2] 50 U.S.C. 401 *et seq.*

create an overall structure for intelligence which ensures effective accountability, management control, and legislative and executive oversight.

Finally, the 1947 Act fails to establish clear and specific limits on the operation of America's intelligence organizations which will help ensure the protection of the rights and liberties of Americans under the Constitution and the preservation of America's honor and reputation abroad. The need for such limits is a need for legislation. The need is not satisfied by the President's recent proposals and Executive Order.

Recommendations[3]

1. The National Security Act should be recast by omnibus legislation which would set forth the basic purposes of national intelligence activities, and define the relationship between the Congress and the intelligence agencies of the executive branch. This revision should be given the highest priority by the intelligence oversight committee(s) of Congress, acting in consultation with the executive branch.

2. The new legislation should define the charter of the organizations and entities in the United States intelligence community. It should establish charters for the National Security Council, the Director of Central Intelligence, the Central Intelligence Agency, the national intelligence components of the Department of Defense, including the National Security Agency and the Defense Intelligence Agency, and all other elements of the intelligence community, including joint organizations of two or more agencies.

3. This legislation should set forth the general structure and procedures of the intelligence community, and the roles and responsibilities of the agencies which comprise it.

4. The legislation should contain specific and clearly defined prohibitions or limitations on various activities carried out by the respective components of the intelligence community.

D. The National Security Council and the Office of the President

The National Security Council (NSC) is an instrument of the President and not a corporate entity with authority of its own. The Committee found that in general the President has had, through the National Security Council, effective means for exerting broad policy control over at least two major clandestine activities—covert action[4] and sensitive technical collection. The covert American involvement in Angola and the operations of the *Glomar Explorer* are examples of that control in quite different circumstances, whatever conclusions one draws about the merits of the activities. The Central Intelligence Agency, in broad terms, is not "out of control."

---

[3] See recommendations on this subject in the Committee's Report on Intelligence Activities and Rights of Americans.

[4] See definition, p. 141.

The Committee found, however, that there were significant limits to this control:

1. Clandestine Activities

The degree of control and accountability exercised regarding covert action and sensitive collection has been a function of each particular President's willingness to use these techniques.

The principal NSC vehicle for dealing with clandestine activities, the 40 Committee and its predecessors, was the mechanism for reviewing and making recommendations regarding the approval of major covert action projects. However, this body also served generally to insulate the President from official involvement and accountability in the approval process until 1974.[5]

As high-level government officials, 40 Committee members have had neither the time nor inclination to adequately review and pass judgment on all of the literally hundreds of covert action projects. Indeed, only a small fraction of such projects (those which the CIA regards as major or sensitive) are so approved and/or reviewed. This problem is aggravated by the fact that the 40 Committee has had virtually no staff, with only a single officer from the Clandestine Services acting as executive secretary.

The process of review and approval has been, at times, only general in nature. It sometimes has become *pro forma*, conducted over the telephone by subordinates.

The President, without consulting any NSC mechanism, can exercise personal direction of clandestine activities as he did in the case of Chile in 1970.

There is no systematic White House-level review of either sensitive foreign espionage or counterintelligence activities. Yet these operations may also have a potential for embarrassing the United States and sometimes may be difficult to distinguish from covert action operations. For example, a proposal to recruit a high foreign government official as an intelligence "asset" would not necessarily be reviewed outside the Central Intelligence Agency at the NSC level, despite the implications that recruitment might pose in conducting American foreign relations. Similarly, foreign counterintelligence operations might be conducted without any prior review at the highest government levels. The Committee found instances in the case of Chile when counterintelligence operations were related to, and even hard to distinguish from, the program of covert action.

---

[5] Appendix D. Senate Select Committee Hearings, Vol. 7, p. 230.

In 1974 the Hughes-Ryan Amendment (22 USC, 2422, section 662) was enacted. It provides that no funds appropriated under the Foreign Assistance Act or any other act may be expended by or on behalf of CIA foreign operations other than for obtaining necessary intelligence "unless and until the President finds that each such operation is important to the national security of the United States and reports, in a timely fashion, a description and scope of such operation to the appropriate committees of the Congress . . ."

The President's proposals to upgrade the 40 Committee into the Operations Advisory Group and to give explicit recognition to its role in advising the President on covert activities are desirable. That upgrading, however, will strain further the Group's ability to conduct a systematic review of sensitive clandestine operations. Under the new structure, the Group members are cabinet officers who have even less time than their principal deputies, who previously conducted the 40 Committee's work. The Group's procedures must be carefully structured, so that the perspective of Cabinet officers can in fact be brought to bear.

2. Counterintelligence

There is no NSC-level mechanism for coordinating, reviewing or approving counterintelligence activities in the United States, even those directed at United States citizens, despite the demonstrated potential for abuse. Both the FBI and the CIA are engaged in counterintelligence, with the CIA operating primarily abroad. The Committee found frictions between the two agencies over the last thirty-five years. The so-called Huston Plan, discredited because of its excessive scope and patent illegalities, was justified in part as a response to the need for improved CIA–FBI coordination. At the same time, the Huston Plan episode illustrates the questions of propriety and legality which may arise in counterintelligence operations conducted in the United States or involving American citizens.

3. Coordination and Resource Allocation

The Director of Central Intelligence has been assigned the function of coordinating the activities of the intelligence community, ensuring its responsiveness to the requirements for national intelligence, and for assembling a consolidated national intelligence budget. Until the recent establishment of the Committee on Foreign Intelligence (CFI), there was no effective NSC-level mechanism for any of these purposes. The Committee believes that the CFI is a step in the right direction and is to be commended. However, the language of the Presidential Order is such that much will depend on how the order is in fact implemented. "Manage" and "coordinate" are terms that are general in nature and have proven to be so in matters of intelligence. Because the CFI was formed only recently, questions remain about its operation and its relation to the DCI's current responsibilities and to the existing authority of the Secretary of Defense.

Moreover, the Committee notes that a major collector and consumer of intelligence information, the Department of State, is not represented on the CFI. It should be. Other agencies with an important stake in intelligence, such as the Department of the Treasury, the Energy Resources Development Administration, and the Arms Control and Disarmament Agency should play an appropriate role in the CFI on an ad hoc basis.

4. Executive Oversight

The Committee finds that Presidents have not established specific instruments of oversight to prevent abuses by the intelligence community. In essence, Presidents have not exercised effective oversight.

The President's Foreign Intelligence Advisory Board (PFIAB) has served Presidents as a useful "Kitchen Cabinet" for intelligence and related matters. It has carried out studies that have resulted in useful changes in procedure and emphasis within the intelligence community, as well as in the adoption of new technologies and techniques. At the same time, the Committee has found that any expectations that PFIAB would serve as an independent watchdog have been mistaken. The PFIAB has been given neither statutory nor Presidential authority to serve such a function. For instance, when the Board became aware of the Huston Plan, it asked the Attorney General and the Director of the FBI for a copy of the plan. That request was refused, and the Board did not pursue the matter with the White House.

The Committee finds the President's recent establishment of the Intelligence Oversight Board to be long overdue. In the Committee's opinion, however, this does not eliminate the need for vigorous congressional oversight. Moreover, the Order is broadly phrased and at some points ambiguous. The effectiveness of the Oversight Board, as well as the rest of the President's reforms, will depend in large measure on the details of their implementation.

The Committee makes the following recommendations concerning the National Security Council and the Office of the President. These recommendations are designed to support and extend the measures taken recently by the President.

Recommendations

5. By statute, the National Security Council should be explicitly empowered to direct and provide policy guidance for the intelligence activities of the United States, including intelligence collection, counterintelligence, and the conduct of covert action.

6. By statute, the Attorney General should be made an advisor to the National Security Council in order to facilitate discharging his responsibility to ensure that actions taken to protect American national security in the field of intelligence are also consistent with the Constitution and the laws of the United States.

7. By statute, the existing power of the Director of Central Intelligence to coordinate the activities of the intelligence community should be reaffirmed. At the same time, the NSC should establish an appropriate committee—such as the new Committee on Foreign Intelligence—with responsibility for allocating intelligence resources to ensure efficient and effective operation of the national intelligence community. This committee should be chaired by the DCI

and should include representatives of the Secretary of State, the Secretary of Defense, and the Assistant to the President for National Security Affairs.[6]

8. By statute, an NSC committee (like the Operations Advisory Group) should be established to advise the President on covert action. It would also be empowered, at the President's discretion, to approve *all* types of sensitive intelligence collection activities. If an OAG member dissented from an approval, the particular collection activity would be referred to the President for decision. The Group should consist of the Secretary of State, the Secretary of Defense, the Assistant to the President for National Security Affairs, the Director of Central Intelligence, the Attorney General, the Chairman of the Joint Chiefs of Staff, and the Director of OMB, as an observer. The President would designate a chairman from among the Group's members.

9. The chairman of the Group would be confirmed by the Senate for that position if he were an official not already subject to confirmation. In the execution of covert action and sensitive intelligence collection activities specifically approved by the President, the chairman would enter the chain of command below the President.

10. The Group should be provided with adequate staff to assist in conducting thorough reviews of covert action and sensitive collection projects. That staff should not be drawn exclusively from the Clandestine Service of the CIA.

11. Each covert action project should be reviewed and passed on by the Group. In addition, the Group should review all on-going projects at least once a year.

12. By statute, the Secretary of State should be designated as the principal administration spokesman to the Congress on the policy and purpose underlying covert action projects.

13. By statute, the Director of Central Intelligence should be required to fully inform the intelligence oversight committee(s) of Congress of each covert action[7] prior to its initiation. No funds should be expended on any covert action unless and until the President certifies and provides to the congressional intelligence oversight committee(s) the reasons that a covert acton is required by extraordinary circumstances to deal with grave threats to the national security of the United States. The congressional intelligence oversight committee(s) should be kept fully and currently informed on all covert action projects, and the DCI should submit a semi-annual report on all such projects to the committee(s).

14. The Committee recommends that when the Senate establishes an intelligence oversight committee with authority to authorize the national intelligence budget, the Hughes-Ryan Amendment (22 USC, 2422) should be

---

[6] In effect, this recommendation would establish the President's proposed Committee on Foreign Intelligence in law but would include a representative of the Secretary of State. It would also empower the DCI to establish intelligence requirements. See Recommendation #16, p. 434.

[7] A covert action would consist of either a major project, or an aggregation of smaller projects meeting the standards of this paragraph.

amended so that the foregoing notifications and presidential certifications to the Senate are provided only to that committee.

15. By statute, a new NSC counterintelligence committee should be established, consisting of the Attorney General as chairman, the Deputy Secretary of Defense, the Director of Central Intelligence, the Director of the FBI, and the Assistant to the President for National Security Affairs. Its purpose would be to coordinate and review foreign counterintelligence activities conducted within the United States and the clandestine collection of foreign intelligence within the United States, by both the FBI and the CIA. The goal would be to ensure strict conformity with statutory and constitutional requirements and to enhance coordination between the CIA and FBI.[8] This committee should review the standards and guidelines for all recruitments of agents within the United States for counterintelligence or positive foreign intelligence purposes, as well as for the recruitment of U.S. citizens abroad. This committee would consider differences between the agencies concerning the recruitment of agents, the handling of foreign assets who come to the United States, and the establishment of the bona fides of defectors. It should also treat any other foreign intelligence or counterintelligence activity of the FBI and CIA which either agency brings to that forum for presidential level consideration.

EXECUTIVE COMMAND AND CONTROL/INTELLIGENCE ACTIVITIES

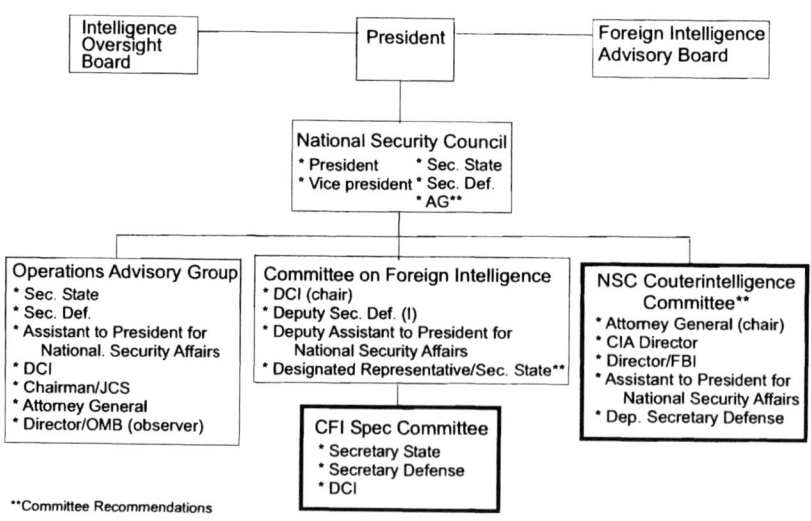

---

[8] See related legislative proposals in the Committee's Report on Intelligence Activities and the rights of Americans.

E. The Director of Central Intelligence

The 1947 National Security Act gave the DCI responsibility for "coordinating the intelligence activities of the several Government departments and agencies in the interest of national security." In addition, the DCI as the President's principal foreign intelligence adviser was given responsibility for coordinating and producing national intelligence for senior policymakers. However, the Committee found that these DCI responsibilities have often conflicted with the particular interests and prerogatives of the other intelligence community departments and agencies. They have not given up control over their own intelligence operations, and in particular the Department of Defense and the military services, which allocate 80 percent of the direct costs for national intelligence, have insisted that they must exercise direct control over peacetime intelligence activities to prepare for war. Thus, while the DCI was given responsibility under the 1947 act for intelligence community activities, he was not authorized to centrally coordinate or manage the overall operations of the community.

1. Coordinator of the Intelligence Community

The Committee has found that the DCI in his coordinator role has been unable to ensure that waste and unnecessary duplication are avoided. Because the DCI only provides guidance for intelligence collection and production, and does not establish requirements, he is not in a position to command the intelligence community to respond to the intelligence needs of national policymakers. Where the DCI has been able to define priorities, he has lacked authority to allocate intelligence resources—either among different systems of intelligence collection or among intelligence collection, analysis and finished intelligence production.

The Committee supports President Ford's objectives of enhancing the stature of the DCI and establishing a mechanism such as the Committee on Foreign Intelligence (CFI) with the DCI as chairman to control the allocation of national intelligence programs resources. The Committee questions, however, whether the CFI can be effective without some appropriate modification of the peacetime authority of the Secretary of Defense. In order to strike an appropriate balance between the requirements of national and tactical intelligence, the intelligence collected by national means should be readily available to the military commanders and vice versa, and the Secretary of Defense and the military services should retain direct control over the operations of tactical military intelligence. Nonetheless, the DCI needs the right to review tactical military intelligence operations in order to make budget choices between tactical and national intelligence activities. Moreover, to carry out his coordinating role, the DCI needs to retain control over major technical intelligence collection systems which service both tactical and national intelligence requirements.

2. Producer of National Intelligence

In the area of providing finished intelligence, the Committee discovered that the DCI, in his role as intelligence adviser, has faced obstacles in ensuring that his national intelligence judgments are objective and independent of department and agency biases. The Committee has been particularly concerned with pressures from both the White House and the Defense Department on the DCI to alter his intelligence judgments. One example of such pressure investigated by the Committee occurred in the fall of 1969 when the DCI modified his judgment on the capability of the Soviet SS–9 system when it conflicted with the public position of Secretary of Defense Laird. After a meeting with staff of the Office of the Secretary of Defense, Director Helms deleted a paragraph from the draft of the National Intelligence Estimate on Soviet strategic forces which stated that within the next five years it was "highly unlikely" that the Soviets would attempt to achieve "a first strike capability, i.e., a capability to launch a surprise attack against the United States with assurance that the U.S.S.R. would not itself receive damage it would regard as unacceptable."

The Committee believes that over the past five years the DCI's ability to produce objective national intelligence and resist outside pressure has been reduced with the dissolution of the independent Board of National Estimates and the subsequent delegation of its staff to the departments with responsibility for drafting the DCI's national intelligence judgments.

In the end, the DCI must depend on his position as the President's principal intelligence adviser or on his personal relationship with the President to carry out his various responsibilities and to withstand pressures to compromise his intelligence judgments. Consequently, the Committee has been concerned that the DCI's proximity and access to the President has diminished over the years. Since 1969, at least until the confirmation of Mr. Bush, the DCI has rarely seen the President except at NSC meetings. The influence a DCI could have from a close relationship with the President has generally been lacking.

While President Ford's Executive Order is a step in the right direction, the Committee believes that the DCI's responsibility over intelligence community activities should be enhanced and spelled out clearly and in detail in statute. The Executive should not continue defining these responsibilities alone as it has done since 1947 through Executive Orders and National Security Council Intelligence Directives (NSCIDs).

The Committee believes that the Congress, in carrying out its responsibilities in the area of national security policy, should have access to the full range of intelligence produced by the United States intelligence community. The Committee further believes that it should be possible to work out a means of ensuring that the DCI's national intelligence judgments are available to the appropriate Congressional committees on a regular basis without compromising the DCI's role as personal adviser to the President.

Finally, the Committee has found concern that the function of the DCI in his roles as intelligence community leader and principal intelligence adviser to the President is inconsistent with his responsibility to manage one of the intelligence community agencies—the CIA. Potential problems exist in a number of areas. Because the DCI as head of the CIA is responsible for human clandestine collection overseas, interception of signals communication overseas, the development and interception of technical collection systems, there is concern that the DCI as community leader is in "a conflict of interest" situation when ruling on the activities of the overall intelligence community.

The Committee is also concerned that the DCI's new span of control—both the entire intelligence community and the entire CIA—may be too great for him to exercise effective detailed supervision of clandestine activities.

Recommendations

16. By statute, the DCI should be established as the President's principal foreign intelligence adviser, with exclusive responsibility for producing national intelligence for the President and the Congress. For this purpose, the DCI should be empowered to establish a staff directly responsible to him to help prepare his national intelligence judgments and to coordinate the views of the other members of the intelligence community. The Committee recommends that the Director establish a board to include senior outside advisers to review intelligence products as necessary, thus helping to insulate the DCI from pressures to alter or modify his national intelligence judgments. To advise and assist the DCI in producing national intelligence, the DCI would also be empowered to draw on other elements of the intelligence community.

17. By statute, the DCI should be given responsibility and authority for establishing national intelligence requirements, preparing the national intelligence budget, and providing guidance for United States national intelligence program operations. In this capacity he should be designated as chairman of the appropriate NSC committee, such as the CFI, and should have the following powers and responsibilities:

a. The DCI should establish national intelligence requirements for the entire intelligence community. He should be empowered to draw on intelligence community representatives and others whom he may designate to assist him in establishing national intelligence requirements and determining the success of the various agencies in fulfilling them. The DCI should provide general guidance to the various intelligence agency directors for the management of intelligence operations.

b. The DCI should have responsibility for preparing the national intelligence program budget for presentation to the President and the Congress.[9] The definition of what is to be included within that national intelligence program should be established by Congress in consultation with the Executive. In this capacity, the Director of Central Intelligence should be involved early in the budget cycle in preparing the budgets of the respective intelligence community agencies. The Director should have specific responsibility for choosing among the programs of the different collection and production agencies and departments and to insure against waste and unnecessary duplication. The DCI should also have responsibility for issuing fiscal guidance for the allocation of all national intelligence resources. The authority of the DCI to reprogram funds within the intelligence budget should be defined by statute.[10]

c. In order to carry out his national intelligence responsibilities the DCI should have the authority to review all foreign and military intelligence activities and intelligence resource allocations, including tactical military intelligence which is the responsibility of the armed forces.[11]

d. The DCI should be authorized to establish an intelligence community staff to support him in carrying out his managerial responsibilities. This staff should be drawn from the best available talent within and outside the intelligence community.

e. In addition to these provisions concerning DCI control over national intelligence operations in peacetime, the statute should require establishment of a procedure to insure that in time of war the relevant national intelligence operations come under the control of the Secretary of Defense.

18. By statute, the position of Deputy Director of Central Intelligence for the intelligence community should be established as recommended in Executive Order 11905. This Deputy Director should be subject to Senate confirmation and would assume the DCI's intelligence community functions in the DCI's absence. Current provisions regarding the status of the DCI and his single deputy should be extended to cover the DCI and both deputies. Civilian control of the nation's intelligence is important; only one of the three could be a career military officer, active or retired.

---

[9] [The DCI] shall: Ensure the development and submission of a budget for the National Foreign Intelligence Program to the CFI. (Executive Order 11905, Sec. 3(d)iii.)

[10] "Reprogramming" means shifting money previously approved for one purpose to another use; for instance, from clandestine human collection to technical collection or covert action.

[11] In contrast to President Nixon's 1971 letter to Director Helms which asked the DCI to plan and review ". . . all intelligence activities including tactical intelligence and the allocation of all intelligence resources," President Ford's Executive Order 111905 states that ". . . neither the DCI nor the CFI shall have responsibility for tactical intelligence."

19. The Committee recommends that the intelligence oversight committee(s) of Congress consider whether the Congress should appropriate the funds for the national intelligence budget to the DCI, rather than to the directors of the various intelligence agencies and departments.

20. By statute, the Director of Central Intelligence should serve at the pleasure of the President but for no more than ten years.

21. The Committee also recommends consideration of separating the DCI from direct responsibility over the CIA.[12]

F. The Central Intelligence Agency

1. The Charter for Intelligence Activities: Espionage, Counterintelligence and Covert Action

The Committee finds that the CIA's present charter, embodied in the National Security Act of 1947, the CIA Act of 1949, and the 1974 Hughes-Ryan amendments to the Foreign Assistance Act, is inadequate in a number of respects.

While the legislative history of the 1947 Act makes clear that the CIA's mandate would be limited to "foreign intelligence," the Act itself does not so specify. Covert action, in the past a major CIA activity, is not mentioned in the 1947 Act, although the Act contains a vague and open-ended authorization for the National Security Council to direct the CIA to undertake "such other functions and duties related to the intelligence affecting the national security as the NSC may from time to time direct."[13] No explicit authority even to collect intelligence is provided the Agency.

The restrictions on domestic activities in the 1947 Act were not clearly defined, nor was the potential conflict between these limits and the Director's authority to protect "sources and methods" of intelligence gathering resolved. Neither did the 1947 Act set forth the Agency's role in conducting counterintelligence and in collecting foreign intelligence.

The Congress' confusing and ill-defined charge to the Agency in these areas resulted in conflicts of jurisdiction with other government agencies. The lack of legislative specificity also opened the way to domestic activities such as Operation CHAOS[14] which clearly went beyond Congress' intent in enacting and amending the National Security Act. In sum, the Committee finds that a clear statutory basis is needed for the Agency's conduct abroad of covert action, espionage, counterintelligence and foreign intelligence col-

---

12   See discussion on pp. 449–450.
13   Appendix B, Hearings, Vol. 7, p. 210.
14   See the Committee's detailed report on Project CHADS.

lection and for such counterespionage operations within the United States as the Agency may have to undertake as a result of the activities abroad.[15]

Foreign Espionage

Espionage is often equated with the slightly broader category of "clandestine human collection." Although "clandestine human collection" may include collection of public information by a covert source, espionage centers on recruiting and handling agents to acquire "protected" or "denied" information.

Espionage on behalf of the United States Government is primarily the responsibility of the Central Intelligence Agency's Clandestine Service which operates on a world-wide basis. The Clandestine Service—officially, the Directorate of Operations—is responsible for CIA clandestine human collection, espionage, covert action, paramilitary operations and counterintelligence. The CIA also has special responsibilities for coordinating the military services' limited espionage activities abroad.

By CIA doctrine, espionage should be aimed at securing information others wish to conceal and not at collecting information available through diplomatic channels or from public sources, such as the press, television and radio.

The Clandestine Service regards espionage, rather than covert action and other such activities, as the essence of its mission. Indeed, the Committee found that clandestine human intelligence collection is often considered a prerequisite as well as a precursor of successful covert action, paramilitary activity, and counterintelligence.

Espionage targets vary, covering political, military and economic information wherever we perceive a national interest. Espionage involves a variety of techniques, ranging from technical surveillance, break-ins and theft, to human reporting by controlled agents, paid and unpaid of protected information. It is generally illegal in the countries against which it is aimed, but its widespread practice by nation states makes the status of espionage under international law ambiguous.

Covert action, which is designed to have an impact, differs from clandestine collection and classic espionage, which are designed to obtain intelligence without affecting the source or revealing the fact that the information has been collected. In practice, however, covert action and espionage overlap, since they rely on the same CIA officers, foreign intermediaries, and sources of information.[16]

---

[15] See the Committee's Report on Domestic Intelligence, Part IV, for recommended limitations on such activity.

[16] Senate Select Committee, "Covert Action in Chile," p. 6ff.

The Committee believes that the United States cannot forego clandestine human collection and expect to maintain the same quality of intelligence on matters of the highest importance to our national security. Technical collection systems do not eliminate the usefulness of espionage in denied areas (essentially the communist countries). Agent intelligence can help provide valuable insight concerning the motivations for activities or policies of potential adversaries, as well as their future intentions.

Nevertheless, the Committee found that there are certain inherent limitations to the value of clandestine sources. Espionage information tends to be fragmentary, and there is always some question as to the trustworthiness and reliability of the source.

The Committee found that over the last decade, the size of the Clandestine Service has been reduced significantly, particularly in the field. However, there remains the question of whether the complements abroad and at headquarters have been reduced sufficiently.

The Committee found that the CIA's clandestine collection effort has been reoriented towards denied areas and away from internal political and security developments in the Third World. The Committee believes that this changed emphasis is desirable and welcomes it.

The Committee found that while internal supervision of espionage within the CIA appears sufficient, there is inadequate external review and control over CIA espionage activities. There is no effective machinery to ensure that the Secretaries of States and Defense and the Assistant to the President for National Security Affairs, who are knowledgeable about the value and limitations of espionage, systematically participate directly in decisions concerning such issues as how large our espionage effort should be, the relative priorities, risk assessments, and possible duplication of effort between overt and clandestine human collection.

The Committee notes that the duplication between the CIA's Clandestine Service and the State Department's overt Foreign Service reporting appears to have diminished in recent years. However, William Colby when he was DCI voiced concern that the problem had not been solved. The Committee notes that increased collection efforts regarding economic issues may aggravate the overlap problem.

Foreign Intelligence Collection in the United States

The CIA engages in both overt and clandestine activity within the United States for the purpose of foreign intelligence collection. The Domestic Collection Division (DCD) is responsible primarily for overt collection, while the Foreign Resources Division (FRD) manages clandestine collection of foreign intelligence. Both divisions are currently within the Directorate of Operations. Formerly run and staffed by the Directorate of Intelligence, the DCD was moved to Operations in 1973 and now has many clandestine services officers assigned to it.

The Domestic Collection Division openly collects foreign intelligence information from American citizens on a wide variety of subjects, primarily of an economic and technological nature. The Domestic Collection Division currently maintains contact with tens of thousands of American citizens who, on a confidential basis, volunteer information of intelligence value to the United States. The Committee notes that the Central Intelligence Agency is *overtly* in contact with many members of the American academic community to consult with them on the subjects of their expertise. On occasion, at the request of the academic concerned, these contacts are confidential.

The Committee believes there are significant benefits to both the government and the universities in such contacts and that they should not be discouraged. The Committee sees no danger to the integrity of American academic institutions in continuing such overt contacts.

The Domestic Collection Division operates from 38 offices around the United States and lists itself in local telephone directories, although it conducts its business as discretely as possible.

The Foreign Resources Division (FRD) performs its functions in a more traditional operational manner much as it is done overseas; foreign nationals of special interest, located in the United States, are enlisted to cooperate secretly with the CIA abroad. FRD's activity, which takes place throughout the United States, is carried out by some of CIA's very best personnel. In the performance of its job, FRD maintains contact with a large number of Americans who are witting of its mission and willing to be cooperative. There are also a number of Americans who are not aware that they are participating in such CIA activities.[17]

The Committee believes that the activities of the Foreign Resources Division and the Domestic Collection Division make an important and useful contribution to the overall intelligence effort; however, there are significant problems.

The Committee found that the Domestic Collection Division, subsidiary to its overt role, supports the clandestine components of the CIA. It provides such services as re-settling defectors, and, by drawing on DCD's extensive contacts in the U.S., reports leads regarding foreign nationals who could prove useful abroad or U.S. firms whose offices abroad could help the CIA.

The Committee is concerned that this kind of assistance provided by the Domestic Collection Division, if not closely watched, could lead to an exploitation of cooper-

---

[17] For explanation of italics, see footnote, p. 179.

ating Americans beyond that which they, themselves, envisioned or beyond these limited CIA objectives.[18]

The Committee notes that due to the recent revelations about CIA activities, some foreign intelligence sources are shying away from cooperation with the Domestic Collection Division, thus impeding this division's most important function, namely, the overt collection of foreign intelligence.

The Committee also questions the recruiting, for foreign espionage purposes, if immigrants desiring American citizenship, because it might be construed as coercive.

Foreign Counterintelligence[19]

Counterintelligence is defined quite broadly by the CIA. It includes the knowledge needed for the protection and preservation of the military, economic, and productive strength of the United States, as well as the government's security in domestic and foreign affairs, against or from espionage, sabotage, and subversion designed to weaken or destroy the United States.

Counterintelligence (CI) is a special form of intelligence activity, aimed at discovering hostile foreign intelligence operations and destroying their effectiveness. It involves protecting the United States Government against infiltration by foreign agents, as well as controlling and manipulating adversary intelligence operations. An effort is made to discern the plans and intentions of enemy intelligence services and to deceive them about our own.

The Committee finds that the threat from hostile intelligence services is real. In the United States alone, well over a thousand Soviet officials are on permanent assignment. Among these, over 40 percent have been identified as members of the KGB or GRU, the Soviet civilian and military intelligence units, respectively. Estimates for the number of *unidentified* Soviet intelligence officers raise this figure to over 60 percent and some defector sources have estimated that 70 percent to 80 percent of Soviet officials in the United States have some intelligence connection.

Furthermore, the number of Soviets with access to the United States his tripled since 1960, and is still increasing. In 1974, for example, over 200 Soviet ships with a total crew complement of 13,000 officers and men visited this country. Some 4,000 Soviets entered the United States as commercial or exchange visitors in 1974. In 1972–1973, for example, approximately one third of the Soviet exchange students here for the academic year under the East-West student exchange program were cooperating with the KGB, according to the Central Intelligence Agency.

---

[18] *Ibid.*
[19] See also the Select Committee Report on CHAOS and the counterintelligence recommendations in the committee's Report on Domestic Intelligence Activities and the Rights of Americans, Part IV.

Other areas of counterintelligence concern include the sharp increase in the number of Soviet immigrants to the United States (4,000 in 1974 compared to fewer than 500 in 1972); the rise in East-West commercial exchange visitors (from 641 in 1972 to 1,500 in 1974); and the growing number of officials in this country from other Communist bloc nations (from 416 in 1960 to 798 in 1975).

Both the FBI and the CIA are engaged in counterintelligence work. The CIA operates primarily abroad. Within the United States the counterintelligence mission is conducted by the FBI, except when the CIA, in consultation with the FBI, continues activities begun abroad.

Defectors are an important source of counterintelligence. Within the United States, the interrogation of defectors is primarily the responsibility of the FBI, though the CIA may also participate. Sometimes, however, the bona fides of a defector are disputed between the CIA and the FBI and there is no established interagency mechanism for settling such disputes—which may last for years. An incident in which a defector was held in so-called "incommunicado interrogation" for two years was, in part, a result of the lack of such a mechanism.[20]

Liaison among the various U.S. Government counterintelligence units at home is particularly important, because counterintelligence—with all its intricacies and deceptions—requires coordination among agencies and sharing of records. Unlike the totally unified KGB organization, the American intelligence service is fragmented and depends upon liaison to make operations more effective.

Coordination between CIA and FBI counterintelligence units is especially critical. The history of CIA–FBI liaison has been turbulent, though a strong undercurrent of cooperation has usually existed at the staff level since 1952 when the Bureau began sending a liaison person to the CIA on a regular basis. The sources of friction between the CIA and FBI in the early days revolved around such matters as the frequent unwillingness of the Bureau to collect positive intelligence for the CIA within the United States or to help recruit foreign officials in this country.

In 1970 an essentially minor incident resulted in an order from FBI Director Hoover to discontinue FBI liaison with the Central Intelligence Agency. Although informal communications between CIA and FBI staff personnel continued, it was not until the post-Hoover era that formal liaison relations were reestablished. Today, there is still a need for closer coordination of FBI and CIA counterintelligence efforts.

The Committee believes that counterintelligence requires the direct attention of Congress and the executive for three reasons: (1) two distinct and partly incompatible approaches to counterintelligence have emerged and

---

[20] Recommendation 14 is based, in part, on these findings.

demand reconciliation; (2) recent evidence suggests that FBI counterespionage results have been less than satisfactory; and (3) counterintelligence has infringed on the rights and liberties of Americans.

Disagreement over the approach to counterintelligence affects all aspects of this activity—compartmentation, method of operation, security, research priorities, deception activities, and liaison. The Committee found that there has been no high-level executive branch review of the classified issues surfaced in this important disagreement.

The Committee also found that there is no system of clearance outside the CIA or FBI for sensitive counterespionage operations, despite the difficulty of distinguishing some of these operations from covert action.

On the FBI contribution to counterintelligence, testimony before the Committee reveals that the Bureau has given insufficient priority to discovering and controlling foreign agents within the United States. Insufficient manpower in the counterintelligence field, especially highly trained analysts, appears to be part of the problem.

Recommendations

22. By statute, a charter should be established for the Central Intelligence Agency which makes clear that its activities must be related to foreign intelligence. The Agency should be given the following missions:

- The collection of denied or protected foreign intelligence information.[21]
- The conduct of foreign counterintelligence.[22]
- The conduct of foreign covert action operations.
- The production of finished national intelligence.

23. The CIA, in carrying out foreign intelligence missions, would be permitted to engage in relevant activities within the United States so long as these activities do not violate the Constitution nor any federal, state, or local laws within the United States.[23] The Committee has set forth in its Domestic Recommendations proposed restrictions on such activities to supplement restrictions already contained in the 1947 National Security Act. In addition, the Committee recommends that by statute the intelligence oversight committee(s) of Congress and the proposed counterintelligence committee of the National Security Council be re-

---

[21] This would not preclude the NSC from assigning appropriate overt collection functions to the CIA.

[22] The CIA would be excluded from any law enforcement or criminal investigation activities. (See the Committee's Report on Domestic Intelligence Activities and the Rights of Americans, Part IV.)

[23] Ibid.

quired to review, at least annually, CIA foreign intelligence activities conducted within the United States.[24]

24. By statute, the Attorney General should be required to report to the President and to the intelligence oversight committee(s) of Congress any intelligence activities which, in his opinion, violate the Constitutional rights of American citizens or any other provision of law and the actions he has taken in response. Pursuant to the Committee's Domestic Recommendations, the Attorney General should be made responsible for ensuring that intelligence activities do not violate the Constitution or any other provision of law.

25. The Committee recommends the establishment of a special committee of the Committee on Foreign Intelligence to review all foreign human intelligence collection activities. It would make recommendation activities. (See the committee's Report on Domestic Intelligence Activities and the Rights of Americans, Part IV.)

U.S. clandestine human collection operations and choices between overt and clandestine human collection. This committee would be composed of a representative of the Secretary of State as chairman, the other statutory members of the CFI, and others whom the President may designate.

26. The intelligence oversight committee(s) of Congress should carefully examine intelligence collection activities of the Clandestine Service to assure that clandestine means are used only when the information is sufficiently important and when such means are necessary to obtain the information.

27. The intelligence oversight committee(s) should consider whether:

- the Domestic Collection Division (overt collection operations) should be removed from the Directorate of Operations (the Clandestine Service), and returned to the Directorate of Intelligence;
- the CIA's regulations should require that the DCD's overt contacts be informed when they are to be used for operational support of clandestine activities;
- the CIA's regulations should prohibit recruiting as agents immigrants who have applied for American citizenship.

28. The President of the United States, in consultation with the intelligence oversight committee(s) of Congress, should undertake a classified review of current issues regarding counterintelligence. This review should form the basis for a classified Presidential statement on national counterintelligence policy and objectives, and should closely examine the following issues: compartmentation, operations, security, research, ac-

---

[24] For recommended review requirements for covert action operations, see p. 26 ff.

countability, training, internal review, deception, liaison and coordination, and manpower.

2. CIA Production of Finished Intelligence

Intelligence production refers to the process (coordination, collation, evaluation, analysis, research, and writing) by which "raw" intelligence is transformed into "finished" intelligence for senior policymakers. The finished intelligence product includes a daily report and summaries, as well as longer analytical studies and monographs on particular topics of policy interest. In the CIA, finished intelligence is produced by the Directorate of Intelligence and the Directorate of Science and Technology.

Certain problems and issues in the area of CIA intelligence production have come to the Committee's attention. The Committee believes thees problems deserve immediate attention by both the executive branch and future congressional intelligence oversight bodies. These problems bear directly on the resources allocated to the production of finished intelligence, the personnel system, and the organizational structure of intelligence production.

The Committee recognizes that it is not the primary purpose of intelligence to predict every world event. Rather, the principal function of intelligence is to anticipate major foreign developments and changes in policies which bear on United States interests. Intelligence should also provide a deeper understanding of the behavior, processes, and long-term trends which may underlie sudden military and political developments.

The Committee wishes to emphasize that there is an important difference between an intelligence failure and a policy failure. The United States had intelligence on the possibility of a Turkish invasion of Cyprus in 1974. The problem of taking effective action to prevent such an invasion was a policy question and not an intelligence failure.

The Committee has received evidence that on some subjects, such as the current capability of the strategic and conventional forces of potential adversaries, U.S. intelligence is considered excellent. But in other areas, U.S. finished intelligence is viewed by policymakers as far from satisfactory in light of the total resources devoted to intelligence. On balance, the Committee found that the quality, timeliness, and utility of our finished intelligence is generally considered adequate, but that major improvement is both desirable and possible.

One issue examined by the Committee is whether intelligence community elements responsible for producing finished intelligence receive adequate attention and support. Production is, in the words of one observer, "the stepchild of the intelligence community." Since finished intelligence is a principal purpose of all United States intelligence activities, the Committee finds that this neglect of finished intelligence is unacceptable for the future.

Intelligence resources are overwhelmingly devoted to intelligence collection. The system is inundated with raw intelligence. The individual analysts responsible for producing finished intelligence has difficulty dealing with the sheer volume of information. Policymakers want the latest reports, and producers of finished intelligence often have to compete with the producers of raw intelligence for policymakers' attention. In a crisis situation, analysts tend to focus on the latest piece of evidence at the expense of a longer and broader view. Intelligence Community staff saw this tendency as one reason why the Cyprus coup in July 1974 was not foreseen.

The Intelligence Community staff in its postmortem on the 1974 Cyprus crisis noted another general analytical problem which was involved in the failure to anticipate the Cyprus coup and the Arab attack on Israeli forces in October of 1973: "the perhaps subconscious conviction (and hope) that, ultimately, reason and rationality will prevail, that apparently irrational moves (the Arab attack, the Greek sponsored coup) will not be made by essentially rational men."

An additional area of the Committee's concern is that analysts are often not informed in a timely way of national policies and programs which affect their analyses and estimates. In its examination of cases involving Cambodia and Chile in the 1970s, the Committee encountered evidence that the analysts were so deprived.

Another issue uncovered by the Committee is whether the highest quality personnel are recruited into the CIA analytical staff. Among the problems raised:

- Analysts tend to be hired early in their careers, and stay in the Agency throughout their careers. The nature of their work tends to insulate them from other useful experiences.

- The analysts career pattern rewards most analyst by promoting them to supervisory positions thereby reducing the time available to utilize their analytical skills.

- Some analysts complain that there are too many steps in the process for reviewing finished intelligence—too much bureaucratic "layering" in the analytical components. With each successive level of review, the analysis and commentary tend to become increasingly derivative.

- There has been little lateral entry of established analysts and intelligence experts into CIA ranks to leaven the outlook, interests and skills of the Agency's intelligence analysts.[25]

A final issue raised by the Committee's investigation of intelligence production is whether the new organizational structure proposed by the President will assure the appropriate stature for the Directorate of Intelligence to help overcome existing problems in the production of finished intelligence. Instead of reporting directly to the DCI (who is still to be the President's chief intelligence adviser), CIA analysts may well report through the Deputy for the CIA. Experience indicates that the new Deputy will need to devote the bulk of his time to managing the Clandestine Services and the Directorate for Science and Technology. At the same time, the DCI may be preoccupied with greater community-wide management responsibilities. Without some further restructuring, the Committee believes that the production of finished intelligence may be lost in the shuffle.

Recommendations

29. By statute, the Director of the Directorate of Intelligence (DDI) should be authorized to continue to report directly to the Director of Central Intelligence.

30. The Committee recommends that a system be devised to ensure that intelligence analysts are better and more promptly informed about United States policies and programs affecting their respective areas of responsibility.

31. The Central Intelligence Agency and the intelligence oversight committee(s) of Congress should reexamine the personnel system of the Directorate of Intelligence with a view to providing a more flexible, less hierarchical personnel system. Super-grade positions should be available on the basis of an individual's analytical capabilities.

32. The Directorate for Intelligence should seek to bring more established analysts into the CIA at middle and upper grade levels for both career positions and temporary assignments.

33. Greater emphasis should be placed on stimulating development of new tools and methods of analysis.

34. Agency policy should continue to encourage intelligence analysts to assume substantive tours of duty on an open basis in other agencies (State, Defense, NSC staff) or in academic institutions to broaden both their analytical outlook and their appreciation for the relevance of their analysis to policymakers and operators within the Government.

---

[25] In FY 1975, only 18 out of 105 analysts hired by the DDI from outside the CIA were at grades GS–12 to GS–15.

3. Covert Action and Paramilitary Operations

Covert action is the attempt to influence the internal affairs of other nations in support of United States foreign policy in a manner that conceals the participation of the United States Government. Covert action includes political and economic action, propaganda and paramilitary activities.

The basic unit of covert action is the project. Covert action "projects" can range from single assets, such as a journalist placing propaganda, through a network of assets working in the media, to major covert and military intervention such as in Laos. The Agency also maintains what it terms an "operational infrastructure" of "stand-by" assets (agents of influence or media assets) who can be used in major operations—such as in Chile. These "stand-by" assets are also part of on-going, most often routine, projects. There are no inactive assets.

Covert Action

The Committee has found that the CIA has conducted some 900 major or sensitive covert action projects plus several thousand smaller projects since 1961. The need to maintain secrecy shields covert action projects from the rigorous public scrutiny and debate necessary to determine their compatibility with established American foreign policy goals. Recently, a large-scale covert paramilitary operation in Angola was initiated without any effort on the part of the executive branch to articulate, and win public support for, its overall policy in Africa. Only public disclosure has allowed the nation to apply its standards of success or failure to covert action projects and then only in retrospect, often without the benefit of the details prompting the original choice of covert rather than overt action.

The secrecy covert action requires means that the public cannot determine whether such actions are consistent with established foreign policy goals. This secrecy also has allowed covert actions to take place which are inconsistent with our basic traditions and values.

Some covert operations have passed restrospective public judgments, such as the support given Western European democratic parties facing strong communist opposition in the late 1940s and 1950s. Others have not. In the view of the Committee, the covert harassment of the democratically elected government of Salvador Allende in Chile did not command U.S. public approval.

Even if the short-term consequences of covert action are consistent with stated policy and accepted standards, the Committee has found that the continued use of covert action techniques within or against a foreign society can have unintended consequences that sometimes subvert long-term goals. For instance, extended covert support to foreign political leaders, parties, labor unions, or the media has not always accomplished the intended objective of strengthening them against the communist challenge. In some cases, it has both encouraged a debilitating dependence on United States covert support, and made those receiving such support vulnerable to repudiation in their own society when their covert ties are exposed. Furthermore, prolonged covert relations and the resulting dependence of recipients on continued CIA support seem to encourage the CIA to extend its ties to means of controlling the recipients in other respects. Covert actions also have, over time, developed a bureaucratic momentum of their own that often surpasses the original need for covert action.

Paramilitary Operations

Covert paramilitary operations are a special, extreme form of covert action. These operations most often consist of covert military assistance and training, but occasionally have involved actual combat activities by American advisers.

Because military assistance involves foreign policy commitments, it is, with one exception, authorized by the Congress. That exception is *covert* military assistance which is channeled through the CIA without being authorized or approved by the Congress as a whole.

Covert U.S. paramilitary combat operations frequently amount to making war, but they do not come under the War Powers Act since they usually do not involve *uniformed* U.S. military officers. American military officers engaged in CIA-sponsored paramilitary operations are "sheep-dipped" for paramilitary duty—that is, they appear to resign from the military yet preserve their place for reactivation once their tour as civilian in paramilitary operations has ended.

The Committee finds that major paramilitary operations have often failed to achieve their intended objective. Most have eventually been exposed. Operations, as in Angola, recently, and Indonesia in the late 1950s are examples of such paramilitary failures. Others, such as Laos, are judged successes by the CIA and officials within the executive branch. The "success" in Laos, however, must be seen against the larger American involvement in Indochina which failed.

Paramilitary operations often have evolved into large-scale programs with a high risk of exposure (and thus embarrassment and/or failure). In some cases, the CIA has been used to undertake paramilitary operations simply because the Agency is less accountable to the public for highly visible "secret" military operations. In all cases considered by the Committee, command and control within the executive branch was rigorous. However, all such operations have been conducted without direct congressional authority or public debate. In recent years, some have been continued in the face of strong congressional disapproval.

Recently, however—apart from Angola—United States paramilitary activities have been at a very low level. The capability for these actions, residing jointly in the CIA and the Department of Defense, consists of a cadre of trained officers, stockpiles of military equipment, logistic networks and small collections of air and maritime assets.

Review and Approval of Covert Action

Given the open and democratic assumptions on which our government is based, the Committee has given serious consideration to the option of proposing a total ban on all forms of covert activity. The Committee has concluded, however, that the United States should maintain the capability to react through covert action when no other means will suffice to meet extraordinary circumstances involving grave threats to U.S. national security. Nevertheless, covert action should be considered as an exception to the normal process of government action abroad, rather than a parallel but invisible system in which covert operations are routine.

Absent some means of assuring public participation in assessing each covert action, the mechanisms of executive branch review and control and of legislative intelligence oversight must serve as the restricted arenas in which such standards are applied to covert action. The Committee's examination of the covert action record over the last 25 years has underscored the necessity for legislative reinforcement of the executive branch's internal review process. This is necessary to assure that all covert action projects are reviewed, and to establish a system of formal accountability within the executive accessible to congressional intelligence oversight bodies.

The CIA has not been free, however, to carry out covert action as it sees fit. The Committee's investigation revealed that on the whole, the Agency has been responsive to internal and external review and authorization requirements. Most of the significant covert operations have been approved by the appropriate NSC committee. At the same time, the Committee notes that approval outside the Agency does not solve all problems since the NSC committees have approved (and in some cases *initiated*) projects that involved highly improper practices or were inconsistent with declared foreign policies.

Approximately three-fourths of all covert action projects are never reviewed or approved by a high level body outside the CIA.[26] These projects which are not brought before the NSC for review are so-called "non-sensitive" projects, or part of what the CIA calls its "operational infrastructure." The Committee found that a single small project, though not reviewed by the NSC, still can be of great importance (e.g. QJWIN, the CIA "executive

---

[26] Since 1974, the President has had to certify all covert actions as important to the national security—treating smaller projects by certain broad categories.

action" assassination capability, and AMLASH, the Cuban officer being groomed to kill Fidel Castro). Moreover, a cluster of small projects can be aggregated to form a program of significance (e.g., Chile).

Until recently, Congress, through its committees, has failed to effectively oversee CIA covert action. Much of this flowed from the legitimate desire of the congressional oversight committees to maintain the security of covert action projects, but it also resulted from a hesitancy to challenge the President or to become directly involved in projects he deemed necessary. Covert paramilitary operations pose a special problem, since they cut across several functions (and committee jurisdictions) of Congress—namely, granting military assistance and making war.

Members of the congressional oversight committees are almost totally dependent on the executive branch for information on covert operations. The secrecy needed for these covert operations allows the executive to limit the information provided to the Congress and to use covert actions to avoid the open scrutiny and debate of the normal foreign policy procedures. While the Committee believes that the executive should continue to have the initiative in formulating covert action, it also strongly believes that the appropriate oversight bodies of Congress should be fully informed prior to the initiation of such actions.

Congressional power over the purse can serve as the most effective congressional oversight tool if there is the courage and the will to exercise it. In addition to the regular budget for covert action, the Agency draws on a Contingency Reserve Fund for unanticipated projects. Any withdrawals from this fund require approval from the Office of Management and Budget and notification, within 48 hours, to the appropriate congressional committees. The Committee believes that the Contingency Fund can also provide one of the mechanisms by which Congress can effectively control covert action.

Recommendations

35. The legislation establishing the charter for the Central Intelligence Agency should specify that the CIA is the only U.S. Government agency authorized to conduct covert actions. The purpose of covert actions should be to deal with grave threats to American security. Covert actions should be consistent with publicly-defined United States foreign policy goals, and should be reserved for extraordinary circumstances when no other means will suffice. The legislation governing covert action should require executive branch procedures which will ensure careful and thorough consideration of both the general policies governing covert action and particular covert action projects; such procedures should require the participation and accountability of highest level policymakers.

36. The Committee has already recommended, following its investigation of alleged assassination attempts directed at foreign leaders, a statute to forbid such activities. The Committee reaffirms its support for such a statute and further recommends prohibiting the following covert activities by statute:

- All political assassinations.[27]

- Efforts to subvert democratic governments.

- Support for police or other internal security forces which engage in the systematic violation of human rights.

37. By statute, the appropriate NSC committee (e.g., the Operations Advisory Group) should review every covert action proposal.[28]

The Committee recommends that the Operations Advisory Group review include:

- A careful and systematic analysis of the political premises underlying the recommended actions, as well as the nature, extent, purpose, risks, likelihood of success, and costs of the operation. Reasons explaining why the objective cannot be achieved by overt means should also be considered.

- Each covert action project should be formally considered at a meeting of the OAG, and if approved, forwarded to the President for final decision. The views and positions of the participants would be fully recorded. For the purpose of OAG, presidential, and congressional considerations, all so-called non-sensitive projects should be aggregated according to the extraordinary circumstances or contingency against which the project is directed.

38. By statute, the intelligence oversight committee(s) of Congress should require that the annual budget submission for covert action programs be specified and detailed as to the activity recommended. Unforeseen covert action projects should be funded from the Contingency Reserve Fund which could be replenished only after the concurrence of the oversight and any other appropriate congressional committees. The congressional intelligence oversight committees should be notified prior to any withdrawal from the Contingency Reserve Fund.

39. By statute, any covert use by the U.S. Government of American citizens as combatants should be preceded by the notification required for all covert actions. The statute should provide that within 60 days of such notifi-

---

[27] The Committee endorses Executive Order 11905, of February 18, 1976, which states: "No employee of the United States Government shall engage in, or conspire to engage in, political assassination."

[28] Executive Order 11905, 2/18/76, established the Operations Advisory Group and directed it to "consider and develop a policy recommendation, including any dissents, for the President prior to his decision on each special activity [e.g., covert operations] in support of national foreign policy objectives."

cation such use shall be terminated unless the Congress has specifically authorized such use. The Congress should be empowered to terminate such use at any time.[29]

40. By statute, the executive branch should be prevented from conducting any covert military assistance program (including the indirect or direct provision of military material, military or logistics advice and training, and funds for mercenaries) without the explicit prior consent of the intelligence oversight committee(s) of Congress.

G. Reorganization of the Intelligence Community

1. The Position of the DCI

The Committee recommendations regarding the Director of Central Intelligence (pages 43–45) would, if implemented, increase his authority over the entire intelligence community. Given such increased authority, the Committee believes that both the executive branch and the intelligence oversight committee(s) of Congress should give careful consideration to removing the DCI from direct management responsibility for the Central Intelligence Agency. This would free the DCI to concentrate on his responsibilities with regard to the entire intelligence community and would remove him from any conflict of interest in performing that task. It might also increase the accountability of the Central Intelligence Agency by establishing a new and separate senior position—a Director of the Central Intelligence Agency—responsible for only the CIA.

2. The Structures of the CIA

The Committee believes that several important problems uncovered in the course of this inquiry suggest that serious consideration also be given to major structural change in the CIA—in particular, separating national intelligence production and analysis from the clandestine service and other collection functions. Intelligence production could be placed directly under the DCI, while clandestine collection of foreign intelligence from human and technical sources and covert operations would remain in the CIA.

The advantages of such a step are several:

- The DCI would be removed from the conflict of interest situation of managing the intelligence community as a whole while also directing a collection agency.

- The concern that the DCI's national intelligence judgments are compromised by the impulse to justify certain covert action operations or by the close association of the analysts with the clandestine service would be remedied.

---

[29] This recommendation parallels the current provisions of the War Powers Resolution which could be so amended. (Appendix C, Hearings, Vol. 7, p. 226.)

- The problem, seen by some in the intelligence community, of bias on the part of CIA analysts toward the collection resources of the CIA would be lessened.
- It would facilitate providing the intelligence production unit with greater priority and increased resources necessary for improving the quality of its finished intelligence.
- Tighter policy control of the Clandestine Service by the National Security Council and the Department of State would be possible.
- The Director would be able to focus increased attention on monitoring Clandestine Services.
- Internal reorganization of the Directorate for Intelligence and the remainder of the CIA could be facilitated.

There are potential drawbacks as well:

- The Director of Central Intelligence might lose the influence that is part of having command responsibility for the clandestine services.
- The increasing, though still not extensive, contact between national intelligence analysts and the Clandestine Service for the purpose of improving the espionage effort might be inhibited.
- The DCI would have managerial responsibility over the former CIA analysts which might place him in a conflict-of-interest situation in regard to the production of intelligence.
- The increased number of independent agencies would increase the DCI's coordination problems.
- If the clandestine services did not report to the DCI, there would be the problem of establishing an alternative chain of command to the President.
- The Clandestine Service might be downgraded and fail to secure adequate support.

Nonetheless, on balance, the Committee believes such a separation of functions and consequent possible realignments in authority within the intelligence community medit serious consideration.

Recommendations

41. The intelligence oversight committee(s) of Congress in the course of developing a new charter for the intelligence community should give consideration to separating the functions of the DCI and the Director of the CIA and to dividing the intelligence analysis and production functions from the clandestine collection and covert action functions of the present CIA.

H. Relations with United States Institutions and Private Citizens

In the immediate postwar period, as the communists pressed to influence and to control international organizations and movements, mass communications, and cultural institutions, the United States responded by involving American private institutions and individuals in the secret struggle over minds, institutions, and ideals. In the process, the CIA subsidized, and even helped develop "private" or non-government organizations that were designed to compete with communists around the world. The CIA supported not only foreign organizations, but also the international activities of United States student, labor, cultural, and philanthropic organizations.

These covert relationships have attracted public concern and this Committee's attention because of the importance that Americans attach to the independence of these institutions.

The Committee found that in the past the scale and diversity of these covert actions has been extensive. For operational purposes, the CIA has:

- Funded a special program of a major American business association;

- Collaborated with an American trade union federation;

- Helped to establish a research center at a major United States university;

- Supported an international exchange program sponsored by a group of United States universities;

- Made widespread use of philanthropic organizations to fund such covert action programs.

The Committee's concern about these relationships is heightened by the Agency's tendency to move from support to use of both institutions and individuals. For example, the initial purpose of the Agency's funding of the National Student Association was to permit United States students to represent their own ideas, in their own way, in the international forums of the day. Nevertheless, the Committee has found instances in which the CIA moved from general support to the "operational use" of individual students.[30] Contrary to the public's understanding, over 250 United States students were sponsored by the CIA to attend youth festivals in Moscow, Vienna and Helsinki and used for missions such as reporting on Soviet and Third World personalities or observing Soviet security practices. The CIA also used National Student Association Summer International Seminars in the United States in the 1950s and 1960s to identify and screen new leaders whom they would eventually support at the national NSA Convention.

When the CIA's relationship to NSA was publicly revealed in 1967, the Johnson Administration established the Katzenbach Committee, with a limited mandate to investigate the relationship of the CIA to "U.S. educational and private voluntary organizations which operate abroad." The Katzenbach

---

[30] Operational use, according to CIA directives, means performing services in support of the CIA Operations Directorate, and may include the recruitment, utilization, or training of any individual for such purposes as providing cover and collecting intelligence.

Committee recommended that it should be the policy of the United States Government not to provide any "covert financial assistance or support, direct or indirect, to any of the nation's educational or private voluntary organizations."

The Committee found that the CIA not only carried out this Katzenbach recommendation but also terminated support for a number of other U.S.-based organizations such as publishing houses. Nevertheless, the CIA, with the approval of the appropriate NSC committee, insured the continuation of a number of high priority operations by either moving them overseas or encouraging private and non-CIA government support of domestically-based operations. More importantly, however, the CIA shifted its operational interest from institutional relationships to individuals in, or affiliated with, private institutions.

The Committee inquiry has been particularly concerned about the current operational use of United States citizens as individuals. Some academics now help the CIA by providing leads and, on occasion, making introductions to potential sources of foreign intelligence. American academics and freelance writers are occasionally used abroad to assist the CIA's clandestine mission.

1. Covert Use of the U.S. Academic Community

The Central Intelligence Agency is now using several hundred American academics,[31] *who in addition to providing leads and sometimes making introductions for intelligence purposes, occasionally write books and other material to be used for propaganda purposes abroad. Beyond these, an additional few more are used in an unwitting manner for minor activities.*

These academics are located in over 100 American colleges, universities, and related institutes. At the majority of institutions, no one other than the individual academic concerned is aware of the CIA link. At the others, at least one university official is aware of the operational use made of academics on his campus. In addition, there are several American academics abroad who serve operational purposes, primarily the collection of intelligence.

The CIA gives a high priority to obtaining leads on potential foreign intelligence sources especially those from communist countries. This Agency's emphasis reflects the fact that many foreign nationals in the United States are in this category. The Committee notes that American academics provide valuable assistance in this activity.[32]

The Committee is concerned, however, that American academics involved in such activities may undermine public confidence that those who train our youth are upholding the ideals, independence, and integrity of American universities.

---

[31] "Academics" includes administrators, faculty members, and graduate students engaged in teaching.

[32] For explanation of italics, see footnote, p. 79.

Government Grantees

CIA regulations adopted in 1967 prohibit the "operational" use of certain narrow categories of individuals. The CIA is prohibited from using teachers, lecturers, and students receiving grants from the Board of Foreign Fellowships under the Fulbright-Hayes Act.[33] There is no prohibition on the use of individuals participating in any other federally funded exchange programs. For example, the CIA may use those grantees—artists, specialists, athletes, leaders, etc.—who do not receive their grants from the Board of Foreign Scholarships. The Committee is concerned that there is no prohibition against exploiting such open federal programs for clandestine purposes.[34]

2. The Covert Use of Books and Publishing Houses

The Committee has found that the Central Intelligence Agency attaches a particular importance to book publishing activities as a form of covert propaganda. A former officer in the Clandestine Service stated that books are "the most important weapon of strategic (long-range) propaganda." Prior to 1967, the Central Intelligence Agency sponsored, subsidized, or produced over 1,000 books; approximately 25 percent of them in English. In 1967 alone, the CIA published or subsidized over 200 books, ranging from books on African safaris and wildlife to translations of Machiavelli's *The Prince* into Swahili and works of T. S. Eliot into Russian, to a competitor to Mao's little red book, which was entitled *Quotations from Chairman Liu*.

The Committee found that an important number of the books actually produced by the Central Intelligence Agency were reviewed and marketed in the United States:

- A book about a young student from a developing country who had studied in a communist country was described by the CIA as "developed by [two areas divisions] and produced by the Domestic Operations Division . . . and has had a high impact in the United States as well as in the [foreign area] market." This book, which was produced by the European outlet of a United States publishing house was published in condensed form in two major U.S. magazines.[35]

- Another CIA book, *The Penkovsky Papers*, was published in United States in 1965. The book was prepared and written by witting agency assets who drew on actual case materials and publication rights to the manuscript were sold to the publisher through a trust fund which was established for the purpose. The publisher was unaware of any U.S. Government interest.

---

[33] CIA regulations also prohibit the operational use of members of ACTION and officials, employees, and grantees of the Ford, Rockefeller, and Carnegie Foundations.

[34] For explanation of italics, see footnote, p. 79.

[35] CBS commentator Eric Sevareid, in reviewing this book, spoke a larger truth than he knew when he suggested that "our propaganda services could do worse than flood [foreign] university towns with this volume."

In 1967, the CIA stopped publishing within the United States. Since then, the Agency has published some 250 books abroad, most of them in foreign languages. The CIA has given special attention to publication and circulation abroad of books about conditions in the Soviet Bloc. Of those targeted at audiences outside the Soviet Union and Eastern Europe, a large number has also been available in English.

3. Domestic "Fallout"

The Committee finds that covert media operations can result in manipulating or incidentally misleading the American public. Despite efforts to minimize it, CIA employees, past and present, have conceded that there is no way to shield the American public completely from "fallout" in the United States from Agency propaganda or placements overseas. Indeed, following the Katzenbach inquiry, the Deputy Director for Operations issued a directive stating: "Fallout in the United States from a foreign publication which we support is inevitable and consequently permissible."

The domestic fallout of covert propaganda comes from many sources: books intended primarily for an English-speaking foreign audience; CIA press placements that are picked up by an international wire service; and publications resulting from direct CIA funding of foreign institutes. For example, a book written for an English-speaking foreign audience by one CIA operative was reviewed favorably by another CIA agent in the *New York Times. The Committee also found that the CIA helped create and support various Vietnamese periodicals and publications. In at least one instance, a CIA supported Vietnamese publication was used to propagandize the American public and the members and staff of both houses of Congress. So effective was this propaganda that some members quoted from the publication in debating the controversial question of United States involvement in Vietnam.*

The Committee found that this inevitable domestic fallout was compounded when the Agency circulated its subsidized books in the United States prior to their distribution abroad in order to induce a favorable reception overseas.

The Covert Use of U.S. Journalists and Media Institutions on February 11, 1976, CIA Director George Bush announced new guidelines governing the Agency's realtionship with United States media organizations:

> Effective immediately, CIA will not enter into any paid or contractual relationship with any full-time or part-time news correspondent accredited by any U.S. news service, newspaper, periodical, radio or television network or station.[36]

---

[36] According to the CIA, "accredited" applies to individuals who are "formally authorized by contract or issuance of press credentials to represent themselves as correspondents." (For explanation of italics, see footnote, p. 179.)

Agency officials who testified after the February 11, 1976, announcement told the Committee that the prohibition extends to non-Americans accredited to specific United States media organizations.

The CIA currently maintains a network of several hundred foreign individuals around the world who provide intelligence for the CIA and at times attempt to influence opinion through the use of covert propaganda. These individuals provide the CIA with direct access to a large number of newspapers and periodicals, scores of press services and news agencies, radio and television stations, commercial book publishers, and other foreign media outlets.

Approximately 50 of the assets are individual American journalists or employees of U.S. media organizations. Of these, fewer than half are "accredited" by U.S. media organizations and thereby affected by the new prohibitions on the use of accredited newsmen. The remaining individuals are non-accredited freelance contributors and media representatives abroad, and thus are not affected by the new CIA prohibition.

More than a dozen United States news organizations and commercial publishing houses formerly provided cover for CIA agents abroad. A few of these organizations were unaware that they provided this cover.

The Committee notes that the new CIA prohibitions do not apply to "unaccredited" Americans serving in media organizations such as representatives of U.S. media organizations abroad or freelance writers. Of the more than 50 CIA relationships with United States journalists, or employees in American media organizations, fewer than one half will be terminated under the new CIA guidelines.

The Committee is concerned that the use of American journalists and media organizations for clandestine operations is a threat to the integrity of the press. All American journalists, whether accredited to a United States news organization or just a stringer, may be suspects when any are engaged in covert activities.[37]

4. Covert Use of American Religious Personnel

The Committee has found that over the years the CIA has used very few religious personnel for operational purposes. The CIA informed the Committee that only 21 such individuals have ever participated in either covert action projects or the clandestine collection of intelligence. On February 11, 1976, the CIA announced:

> CIA has no secret paid or contractual relationships with any American clergyman or missionary. This practice will be continued as a matter of policy.

The Committee welcomes this policy with the understanding that the prohibition against all "paid or contractual relationships" is in fact a prohibition against any operational use of all Americans following a religious vocation.

---

[37] For explanation of italics, see footnote, p. 179.

Recommendations

In its consideration of the recommendations that follow, the Committee noted the Central Intelligence Agency's concern that further restriction on the use of Americans for operational purposes will constrain current operating programs. The Committee recognizes that there may be at least some short-term operational losses if the Committee recommendations are effected. At the same time, the Committee believes that there are certain American institutions whose integrity is critical to the maintenance of a free society and which should therefore be free of any unwitting role in the clandestine service of the United States Government.

42. The Committee is concerned about the integrity of American academic institutions and the use of individuals affiliated with such institutions for clandestine purposes. Accordingly, the Committee recommends that the CIA amend its internal directives to require that individual academics used for operational purposes by the CIA, together with the President or equivalent official of the relevant academic institutions, be informed of the clandestine CIA relationship.[38]

43. The Committee further recommends that, as soon as possible, the permanent intelligence oversight committee(s) of Congress examine whether further steps are needed to insure the integrity of American academic institutions.

44. By statute, the CIA should be prohibited from the operational use of grantees who are receiving funds through educational and/or cultural programs which are sponsored by the United States Government.

45. By statute, the CIA should be prohibited from subsidizing the writing, or production for distribution within the United States or its territories, of any book, magazine, article, publication, film, or video or audio tape unless publicly attributed to the CIA. Nor should the CIA be permitted to undertake any activity to accomplish indirectly such distribution within the United States or its territories.

46. The Committee supports the recently adopted CIA prohibitions against any paid or contractual relationship between the Agency and U.S. and foreign journalists accredited to U.S. media organizations. The CIA prohibitions should, however, be established in law.

47. The Committee recommends that the CIA prohibitions be extended by law to include the operational use of any person who regularly contributes material to, or is regularly involved directly or indirectly in the editing of material, or regularly acts to set policy or provide direction to the activities of U.S. media organizations.

---

[38] This recommendation is consistent with and would extend section 4(b)(9) of E.O. 11905 which states that CIA sponsorship of classified or unclassified research must be "known to appropriate senior officials of the academic institutions and to senior project officials."

48. The Committee recommends that the Agency's recent prohibition on covert paid or contractual relationship between the Agency and any American clergyman or missionary should be established by law.

I. Proprietaries and Cover

1. Proprietary Organizations

CIA proprietaries are business entities wholly-owned by the Agency which do business, or only appear to do business, under commercial guise. They are part of the "arsenal of tools" of the CIA's Clandestine Services. They have been used for espionage as well as covert action. Most of the larger proprietaries have been used for paramilitary purposes. The Committee finds that too often large proprietaries have created unwarranted risks of unfair competition with private business and of compromising their cover as clandestine operations. For example, Air America, which at one time had as many as 8,000 employees, ran into both difficulties.

While internal CIA financial controls have been regular and systematic, the Committee found a need for even greater accountability both internally and externally. Generally, those auditing the CIA have been denied access to operational information, making management-oriented audits impossible. Instead, audits have been concerned only with financial security and integrity.

The Committee found that the CIA's Inspector General has, on occasion, been denied access to certain information regarding proprietaries. This has sometimes inhibited the ability of the Inspector General's office to serve the function for which it was established. Moreover, the General Accounting Office has not audited these operations. The lack of review, by either the GAO or the CIA Inspector General's office, means that, in essence, there has been no outside review of proprietaries.

One of the largest current proprietaries is an insurance-investment complex established in 1962 to provide pension annuities, insurance and escrow management for those who, for security reasons, could not receive them directly from the U.S. Government. The Committee determined that the Congress was not informed of the existence of this proprietary until "sometime" after it had been made operational and had invested heavily in the domestic stock markets—a practice the CIA has discontinued. Moreover, once this proprietary was removed from the Domestic Operations Division and placed under the General Counsel's office it received no annual CIA project review.

The record establishes that on occasion the insurance-investment complex had been used to provide operational support to various covert action projects. The Inspector General, in 1970, criticized this use of the complex because it threatened to compromise the security of the complex's primary insurance objectives.

In general, the Committee found that when the CIA sought to dispose of or dissolve a proprietary, considerable effort was made to avoid conflicts of interest. However, pressures were sometimes unsuccessfully brought to bear on the CIA from without, and on one or more occasions from high level Agency officials to do a favor by disposing of an entity in a manner that would benefit a particular party. In this connection, the Committee notes that the CIA is not subject to the provisions of the Federal Disposal of Property Act which ordinarily guards against such pressures.

Management and control of proprietaries frequently required, and still do, what is termed "cooperative interface" with other goverment agencies, such as the SEC and the IRS. The Committee found no evidence that these relationships involved circumventing statutory or regulatory requirements. Their purpose appears to be to enable the Agency to comply with other agencies' requirements in a secure manner. However, the nature and extent of such "interfacing" has not always been completely recorded in the CIA, making it difficult to ensure the propriety of such relationships.

2. Cover

The Committee examined cover because it is an important aspect of all CIA clandestine activities. Its importance is underscored by the tragic murder of a CIA Station Chief in Greece, coupled with continuing disclosures of CIA agents' names. The Committee sought to determine what, if anything, has been done in the past to strengthen cover, and what should be done in the future.

The Committee found conflicting views about what constitutes cover, what it can do, and what should be done to improve it. A 1970 CIA Inspector General report termed the Agency's concept and use of cover to be lax, arbitrary, uneven, confused, and loose. The present cover staff in the CIA considered the 1970 assessment to be simplistic and overly harsh. There is no question, however, that some improvements and changes are needed.

The Committee finds that there is a basic tension between maintaining adequate cover and effectively engaging in overseas intelligence activities. Almost every operational act by a CIA officer under cover in the field—from working with local intelligence and police to attempting to recruit agents—reveals his true purpose and chips away at his cover. Some forms of cover do not provide concealment but offer a certain degree of deniability. Others are so elaborate that they limit the amount of work an officer can do for the CIA. In carrying out their responsibilities, CIA officers generally regard the maintenance of cover as a "nuisance."

The situation of the Athens Station Chief, Richard Welch, illustrates the problem of striking the right balance between cover and operations, and also the transparency of cover. As the Chief of the CIA's Cover Staff stated, by the time a person becomes

Chief of Station, "there is not a great deal of cover left.[39] *The Chief of the Cover Staff identified terrorism as a further security problem for officers overseas, one that is aggravated by the erosion of cover.*[40]

Recommendations

49. By statute, the CIA should be permitted to use proprietaries subject to external and internal controls.

50. The Committee recommends that the intelligence oversight committee(s) of Congress require at least an annual report on all proprietaries. The report should include a statement of each proprietary's nature and function, the results of internal annual CIA audits, a list of all CIA intercessions on behalf of its proprietaries with any other United States Government departments, agencies or bureaus, and such other information as the oversight committee deems appropriate.

51. The intelligence oversight committee(s) of Congress should require that the fiscal impact of proprietaries on the CIA's budget be made clear in the DCI's annual report to the oversight committee. The Committee should also establish guidelines for creating large proprietaries, should these become necessary.

52. By statute, all returns of funds from proprietaries not needed for its operational purposes or because of liquidation or termination of a proprietary, should be remitted to the United States Treasury as Miscellaneous Receipts.

The Department of Justice should be consulted during the process of the sale or disposition of any CIA proprietary.

53. By statute, former senior government officials should be prohibited from negotiating with the CIA or any other agency regarding the disposal of proprietaries. The intelligence oversight committee(s) of Congress should consider whether other activities among agencies of the intelligence community, the CIA, and former officials and employees, such as selling to or negotiating contracts with the CIA, should also be prohibitied as is the case regarding military officials under 18 U.S.C. 207.

J. Intelligence Liaison

Throughout the entire period of the CIA's history, the Agency has entered into liaison agreements with the intelligence services of foreign powers.

---

[39] For example, the CIA was concerned about the fact that the home that Mr. Welch moved into had been previously publicly identified as belonging to the former Station Chief. CIA officials have testified that the Agency has no evidence that the recent congressional inquiries into intelligence activities had any adverse impact on Mr. Welch's cover or any relationship to his tragic death. (George Bush testimony, 4/8/76, p. 41.)

[40] For explanation of italics, see footnote, p. 179.

Such arrangements are an extremely important and delicate source of intelligence and operational support. Intelligence channels can also be used to negotiate agreement outside the field of intelligence. The Committee notes that all treaties require the advice and consent of the Senate, and executive agreements must be reported to the Foreign Relations Committee of the Senate. Because of the importance of intelligence liaison agreements to national security, the Committee is concerned that such agreements have not been systematically reviewed by the Congress in any fashion.

Recommendations

54. By statute, the CIA should be prohibited from causing, funding, or encouraging actions by liaison services which are forbidden to the CIA. Furthermore, the fact that a particular project, action, or activity of the CIA is carried out through or by a foreign liaison service should not relieve the Agency of its responsibilities for clearance within the Agency, within the executive branch, or with the Congress.

55. The intelligence oversight committee(s) of Congress should be kept fully informed of agreements negotiated with other governments through intelligence channels.

K. The General Counsel and Inspector General

The General Counsel, as chief legal officer of the Central Intelligence Agency, has a special role in insuring that CIA activities are consistent with the Constitution and laws of the United States. The Committee found that, in the past, the participation of the General Counsel in determining the legality or propriety of CIA activities was limited; in many instances the General Counsel was not consulted about sensitive projects. In some cases the Director's investigative arm, the Inspector General, discovered questionable activities that often were not referred to the General Counsel for a legal opinion. Moreover, the General Counsel never had general investigatory authority.

The Inspector General not only serves as the Director's investigative arm, but he also aids the Director in attempts to increase the efficiency of Agency activities. Inspector General investigations of various Agency offices (component surveys) have been an important management tool often leading to the discovery of questionable practices. These component surveys were halted in 1973 but have recently been reinstituted.

The Committee found that there were problems with the component surveys. In some situations the Inspector General was denied access to essential information. The surveys often failed to effectively cover sensitive programs cutting across component boundaries or raising issues which affected the Agency as a whole. Finally, the Inspector General's recommendations were often disregarded particularly when the directorate being investigated opposed their implementation.

Under the President's recently issued Executive Order, the Inspector General and the General Counsel are required to report to the Intelligence Oversight Board any activities that come to their attention which raise questions of legality or propriety. The Director of the CIA is charged with assuring that those officials will have access to the information necessary to fulfill their duties under the Executive Order.

The Committee also found that while both the General Counsel and Inspector General provided valuable assistance to the Director, neither had authority to provide assistance to the congressional oversight bodies.

The Committee believes that the intelligence oversight committee(s) of Congress should examine the internal review mechanisms of foreign and military intelligence agencies and consider the feasibility of applying recommendations such as those suggested for the CIA.

Recommendations

56. Any CIA employee having information about activities which appear illegal, improper, outside the Agency's legislative charter, or in violation of Agency regulations, should be required to inform the Director, the General Counsel, or the Inspector General of the Agency. If the General Counsel is not informed, he should be notified by the other officials of such reports. The General Counsel and the Inspector General shall, except where they deem it inappropriate, be required to provide such information to the head of the Agency.[41]

57. The DCI should be required to report any information regarding employee violations of law related to their duties and the results of any internal Agency investigation to the Attorney General.[42]

58. By statute, the Director of the CIA should be required to notify the appropriate committees of the Congress of any referrals made to the Attorney General pursuant to the previous recommendation.[43]

---

[41] The General Counsel and Inspector General should have authority to pass the information to the Attorney General without informing the head of the Agency in extraordinary circumstances, if the employee providing the information so requests and if the General Counsel or the Inspector General deems it necessary.

The Inspector General should also regularly inform Agency employees about grievance procedures.

[42] See 28 U.S.C. 535.

[43] Should the General Counsel or Inspector General determine that it would be inappropriate to notify the Director of an activity that appeared illegal, improper, outside the Agency's legislative charter, or in violation of Agency regulations, the General Counsel or Inspector General would be required to notify the appropriate committees of the Congress.

59. The Director of the CIA should periodically require employees having any information on past, current, or proposed Agency activities which appear illegal, improper, outside the Agency's legislative charter, or in violation of the Agency's regulations, to report such information.

60. By statute, the General Counsel and the Inspector General should have unrestricted access to all Agency information and should have the authority to review all of the Agency activities.

61. All significant proposed CIA activities should be reviewed by the General Counsel for legality and constitutionality.

62. The program of component inspections conducted by the Inspector General should be increased, as should the program of surveys of sensitive programs and issues which cut across component lines in the Agency.[44]

63. The Director shall, at least annually, report to the appropriate committees of the Congress on the activities of the Office of the General Counsel and the Office of the Inspector General.[45]

64. By statute, the General Counsel should be nominated by the President and confirmed by the Senate.

65. The Agency's efforts to expand and strengthen the staffs of the General Counsel and Inspector General should be continued.[46]

---

[44] The Inspector General's component surveys should consider not only the effectiveness of the component but should also examine the component's compliance with the legislative charter of the Agency, Agency regulations, and the law. The Director should be required to inform the Inspector General as to what actions have been taken on the recommendations made by the Inspector General.

[45] The report should include: (a) a summary of all Agency activities that raise questions of legality or propriety and the General Counsel's findings concerning these activities; (b) a summary of the Inspector General's investigations concerning any of these activities; (c) a summary of the practices and procedures developed to discover activities that raise questions of legality or propriety; (d) a summary of each component, program or issue survey, including the Inspector General's recommendations and the Director's decisions; (e) a summary of all other matters handled by the Inspector General.

The report should also include a discussion of (a) major legal problems facing the Agency; (b) the need for additional statutes; (c) any cases referred to the Department of Justice.

[46] Efforts to recruit lawyers for the Office of General Counsel from outside the CIA should be increased. Efforts should also be made to provide for rotation of the attorneys in the General Counsel's Office to other governmental positions.

The Inspector General's Office should be staffed by outstanding, experienced officers drawn from inside and outside the Agency. Consideration should be given to establishing a greater number of permanent positions within the Office. Individuals rotated into the Inspector General's Office from another Agency office should not be involved in surveys of offices to which they might return.

The work of both offices would benefit from regular inspections from outside.

66. The General Counsel should be promoted to, and the Inspector General should continue to hold executive rank equal to that of the Deputy Directors of the CIA.

L. The Department of Defense

The intelligence agencies of the Department of Defense make a major contribution to the development, management, and operation of intelligence systems and to the production of military and technical intelligence information. Additionally, the Department, with its major responsibility for the nation's defense is a major user of finished intelligence. The Committee's inquiry into the Department of Defense intelligence agencies focused on the Department's intelligence budget which comprises over 80 percent of the direct national United States intelligence budget.

The Committee also examined the Defense Intelligence Agency (DIA), the National Security Agency (NSA), and the intelligence activities of the military services. That portion of the investigation of NSA which centered on potential abuses is presented in detail in the Domestic Section of the Committee's report.

1. General Findings and Conclusions

The Committee finds that despite the magnitude of the tasks and the complexity of the relationships, most of the important collection activities conducted by the Defense Department (the reconnaissance and SIGINT systems) are managed relatively efficiently and are generally responsive to the needs of the military services as well as to the policymakers on the national level.

Defense intelligence must respond to a range of consumers—policymakers in Washington, defense and technical analysts, and operational commanders in the field—yet the primary mission of defense intelligence is to supply the armed services with the intelligence necessary for their operations. This overriding departmental requirement creates a major problem in the overall allocation of intelligence resources throughout the intelligence community. In promulgating Executive Order 11905, the Administration has decided on a greater centralization of authority in the Director of Central Intelligence. The Committee notes that this will require some changes in the Secretary of Defense's authority over allocating defense intelligence resources. With regard to intelligence resources management within the Department of Defense, the Committee found that the establishment of a Deputy Secretary of Defense for Intelligence should enable more effective management of defense intelligence resources and help the Defense Department play an appropriate role in the new centralized interagency structure under the Director of Central Intelligence.

Increasingly, technological intelligence systems have grown capable of serving both the interests of national policymakers and planners and of field commanders. Thus, it is often difficult to distinguish between "national" and "tactical" intelligence assets, collection, or production. It is the Committee's view that while the effect of the President's Executive Order giving the DCI more authority will be to bring national intelligence assets and budgets under the DCI's control and guidance, the defense intelligence programs which are tactical in nature and integral to the military's operational commands should remain under the control of the Secretary of Defense. The precise line drawn between the tactical and military intelligence at any given time will have a significant impact on the definition of national intelligence and on the purview of any oversight committee(s) of Congress.

2. The Defense Intelligence Agency

Even though the Defense Intelligence Agency has been the principal agency for the production of intelligence in the Defense Department, Secretaries of Defense and other key DOD officials have frequently looked to other intelligence sources rather than to DIA. For example, Robert McNamara relied heavily on the CIA; Melvin Laird sought analyses from the Defense Department's Directorate of Defense Research and Engineering; and James Schlesinger used a special Net Assessment Group. This tendency of Secretaries of Defense to rely on analytic resources outside of DIA is partly but not entirely, related to dissatisfaction with DIA's performance (see the detailed report on DIA). Another factor is the obvious difference between the role of the Defense Department as *manager* of military intelligence collection systems and the role of the Secretary of Defense as a *consumer* of intelligence products. For example, the Secretary's requirements for political and economic intelligence are considerably different from the intelligence needs of the operating forces and the Joint Chiefs of Staff, who are the primary military customers of DIA.

Historically, DOD has managed the bulk of all technical intelligence collection systems, but the CIA has managed many important national technical collection systems and has been in charge of much of the analytic function and is the primary producer of *national* intelligence. The largest proportion of intelligence needed by the military establishment, however, is *tactical*. Therefore, national intelligence is a secondary mission of DIA. Much of DIA's effort is directed toward producing intelligence needed by the JCS, the Unified and Specified Commands, and force planners and technical analysts in the services. The Secretary of Defense, on the other hand, is equally or more concerned with national intelligence. In this context, it is not surprising that DOD's civilian leadership has complemented DIA's product with analyses from sources in other agencies.

The Committee is of the view that the Secretary of Defense has a continuing need for a strong analytical intelligence capability within the Department of Defense. The Committee found that DIA has met this need better than the service intelligence organizations which preceded it, but that DIA has not fulfilled expectations that it would provide a coordinating mechanism for all defense intelligence activities and information.

The essential problem of the Defense Intelligence Agency was summed up in one study commissioned by the executive branch as "too many jobs and too many masters."[47] These problems have not been solved by the reorganizations undertaken thus far, nor has the DIA's existence led to a diminution in the size of the separate military intelligence services that was hoped for.

The Committee finds that the Defense Intelligence Agency faces serious impediments to improving the quality of, and opportunities for, its civilian and military staff. The Agency's personnel and command structure, its lack of high-level grades, and the relatively short tours for military officers are factors which make it difficult for DIA to develop and retain the high-quality analytic personnel essential for a high-quality finished product.

3. The National Security Agency

The National Security Agency is one of the largest and most technically oriented components of the United States intelligence community. Its basic function is collecting and processing foreign communications and signals for intelligence purposes. NSA is also responsible for creating and supervising the cryptography of all United States Government agencies, and has a special responsibility for supervising the military services' cryptologic agencies. Another major responsibility is protecting the security of American communications.

The Committee regards these functions as vital to American security. NSA's capability to perform these functions must be preserved. The Committee notes that despite the fact that NSA has been in existence for several decades, NSA still lacks a legislative charter. Moreover, in its extensive investigation, the Committee has identified intelligence community abuses in levying requirements on NSA and abuses by NSA itself in carrying out its functions. These abuses are detailed in the domestic portion of the Committee report. The Committee finds that there is a compelling need for an NSA charter to spell out limitations which will protect individual constitutional rights without impairing NSA's necessary foreign intelligence mission.

---

[47] The Report to the President and Secretary of Defense on the Department of Defense by the Blue Ribbon Defense Panel (Fitzhugh Report), 7/1/70.

4. Civilian or Military Leadership

DIA and NSA have always been headed by professional military officers. In the case of DIA, Deputy Directors have also been military. This past practice should not stand in the way of appointment of any individuals, whether civilian or military, best qualified to administer these sensitive agencies.

5. Special Issues

Several important issues concerning NSA have been revealed during the course of the Committt's investigation which require regular reviews by both the intelligence oversight committee(s) of Congress and by the executive branch.

- How can the risks involved in the operations of collection systems be balanced against the value of positive intelligence information acquired through those operations?

- How far in the research/development process of collection systems should the competition between agencies continue before it leads to unwarranted duplication? Should those who develop a system also manage its acquisition and subsequent operation, or should all operations be consolidated, for example, under the Department of Defense?

- How can the technology of advanced intelligence collection systems be better utilized to assist the civilian and domestic agencies of the Government without compromising the principal mission or security of these intelligence systems, or the open character of these portions of American government?

Recommendations

67. In order to implement the Committee's and the President's recommendations for expanding the DCI's resource-allocation responsibility appropriate adjustments should be made in the Secretary of Defense's general authority regarding Defense intelligence activities and in the Department's internal budgeting procedures. At the same time, there should be provision for the transfer to the Secretary of Defense of responsibilities, particularly tasking intelligence agencies, in the event of war.

68. By statute, the intelligence oversight committee(s) of Congress, in consultation with the Executive, should establish a charter for the Defense Intelligence Agency which would clearly define its mission and relationship to other intelligence agencies. The Committee recommends that the charter include the following provisions:

> A. In order to encourage close coordination between consumers and producers of national intelligence, DIA should be a part of the Office of the Secretary of Defense, and should report directly to the Deputy Secre-

tary of Defense for Intelligence. A small J-2 staff should be reconstituted to provide intelligence support, primarily of an operational nature, to the Joint Chiefs of Staff. The Secretary of Defense should ensure full coordination and free access to information between the two groups.

B. The Director of the DIA should be appointed by the President and subject to Senate confirmation. Either the Director or Deputy Director of the Agency should be a civilian.

C. The Congress must relieve DIA from certain Civil Service regulations in order to enable the quality of DIA personnel to be upgraded. In addition, more supergrade positions must be provided for civilians in DIA.

69. By statute, a character for the National Security Agency should be established which, in addition to setting limitations on the Agency's operations (see Domestic Subcommittee Recommendations), would provide that the Director of NSA would be nominated by the President and subject to confirmation by the Senate. The Director should serve at the pleasure of the President but not for more than ten years. Either the Director or the Deputy Director should be a civilian.

70. The Department of Defense should centralize the service counterintelligence and investigative activities within the United States in the Defense Investigative Service (DIS) in order to reduce wasteful duplication.

The Department of State and the Foreign Service have an important role in the intelligence operations of the United States Government. Because of its responsibilities in formulating and conducting U.S. foreign policy, the State Department is a principal customer for intelligence. Abroad, the Foreign Service, operating overtly, is the principal collector of political intelligence and is a major collector of economic intelligence.[48]

Because of its foreign policy responsibilities and its worldwide complex of diplomatic and consular installations, the Department of State is the only Washington agency potentially able to oversee other U.S. Government activities abroad—including those of the CIA. In the field, this responsibility clearly falls on the Ambassador by law. Indeed, Ambassadors are the sole mechanism available outside of the CIA itself to assure that NSC decisions are appropriately carried out by the Clandestine Service. The Committee found that the role of the Department of State and the Ambassadors constitute a central element in the control and improvement in America's intelligence operations overseas. However, the Committee also found that Ambassadors are often reluctant to exercise their authority in intelligence matters. The Department has not encouraged them to do so, and the ad-

---

[48] The Department has often indicated in budget documents relating to intelligence as having a budget of $10 million, particularly for the Bureau of Intelligence and Research. However, the intelligence community staff estimates the costs attributable to the function of overt intelligence collection by the Foreign Service at $80 million.

ministration has not issued directives to implement existing law covering the authority of Ambassadors.

The Committee found that in general the Department of State exercised substantial high-level influence over decisions to undertake major covert action programs. In the field, Ambassadors are generally knowledgeable and often involved in significant covert activities projects. There were, however, notable exceptions, such as the effort to prevent Salvador Allende from coming to power in Chile by means of a military coup which was concealed from the Department, the Secretary of State and the American Ambassador to Chile.

In contrast to covert action, the Committee found that neither the State Department nor U.S. Ambassadors are substantially informed about espionage or counterintelligence activities directed at foreign governments. Such coordination as exists in this respect is at the initiative of the Central Intelligence Agency and is infrequent. The Committee found that there is no systematic assessment outside the CIA of the risks of foreign espionage and counterespionage operations and the extent to which those operations conform with overall foreign policy.

In general, Ambassadors in the field are uninformed about specific espionage activities within their countries of assignment. Unlike the case of covert action, Ambassadors are not asked to appraise the risks of espionage activities, nor to assess their benefits. Often Ambassadors do not want to know the specifics of such operations, and what coordination as exists in their cases is based on a general injunction from them to the Station Chiefs that they not be confronted with any "surprises."

That is not always enough if an Ambassador wishes to participate in policy decisions. For example, a shift of resources toward recruitment of internal targets in a Western country was under consideration between Washington and the field, and the U.S. Ambassador had not been informed. In this connection, the Committee believes it would be unrealistic to use clandestine recruitment to try to establish the kind of intimate relationship with political elites in friendly countries which we have enjoyed as a result of the shared experience of WWII and its aftermath.

The Committee finds that more than a year after enactment of a statute making Ambassadors responsible for directing, coordinating, and supervising all U.S. Government employees within their country of assignment,[49] instructions implementing this law have still not been issued by any quarter of the executive branch. A former Under Secretary of State told the Committee that the law, in effect, had been "suspended" in view of

---

[49] 22 U.S.C. 2680a. The instructions prepared by the State Department and forwarded to the NSC have been opposed by the CIA on the grounds that the CIA still has a responsibility to protect sources and methods from unauthorized disclosure. The NSC has not acted on the proposed instructions.

Presidential inaction. Moreover, the CIA has not modified its practices pursuant to this law. The Committee finds this thwarting of the United States law unacceptable.

The Committee finds that Ambassadors cannot effectively exercise their legal responsibilities for a wide variety of intelligence activities within their jurisdiction without State Department assistance on the Washington aspects of the activities. Such support is particularly important in the case of intelligence operations aimed at a third country. An Ambassador may be able to judge the local risks of an espionage effort, but if it is directed toward a third country the Ambassador may not be able to assess the importance or value of the effort without Washington support.

In the past, the Department of State, at least, has not had a parallel responsibility nor the right of access to information necessary to enable it to provide support to an Ambassador seeking to exercise his statutory responsibility over CIA espionage and counterespionage operations. The Committee notes section 4 in Executive Order No. 11905 of February 18, 1976 which may be intended to provide such State Department back-up for Ambassadors.

At present, the CIA handles both State Department and its own communications with overseas posts. Under this arrangement, the Ambassador's access to CIA communications is at the discretion of the CIA. The Committee finds that this is not compatible with the role assigned to the Ambassador by law; the Ambassador cannot be sure that he knows the full extent and nature of CIA operations for which he may be held accountable.

The Committee finds that Ambassadors' policies governing intelligence activities have sometimes been interpreted in a manner which vitiated their intent. For example, one Ambassador prohibited any electronic surveillance by his Embassy's CIA component. The head of the CIA component interpreted this to proscribe only CIA electronic surveillance and believed that such surveillance could be conducted in cooperation with local security services.

The Committee found evidence that CIA Station Chiefs abroad do not always coordinate their intelligence reporting on local developments with their Ambassadors. The Committee does not believe that Ambassadors should be able to block CIA field reports. However, it found that there was no standard practice for Ambassadors to review and comment on intelligence reporting from the field.

The Committee finds that the Foreign Service is the foremost producer in the United States Government of intelligence on foreign political and economic matters. The Committee believes, however, that the State Department does not adequately train Foreign Service personnel, particularly in political reporting. Nor does the Department fund their collection operations, nor manage their activities so as to take full advantage of this extremely important intelligence capability. In effect, the Department, despite being a major source of intelligence, considers this function secondary to its principal task of diplomatic representation and negotiations.

From discussions in nearly a dozen foreign service posts, the Committee established that there is inadequate funding for Foreign Service reporting officers to carry out their responsibilities. The funds available are considered "representation funds" and must be shared with the administration and consular sections of most embassies. Such representation funds have been a favorite target for congressional cuts in the State Department budget.

Recommendations

71. The National Security Council, the Department of State, and the Central Intelligence Agency should promptly issue instructions implementing Public Law 93–475 (22 U.S.C. 2680a). These instructions should make clear that Ambassadors are authorized recipients of sources and methods information concerning all intelligence activities, including espionage and counterintelligence operations. Parallel instructions from other components of the intelligence community should be issued to their respective field organizations and operatives. Copies of all these instructions should be made available to the intelligence oversight committee(s) of Congress.

72. In the exercise of their statutory responsibilities, Ambassadors should have the personal right, which may not be delegated, of access to the operational communications of the CIA's Clandestine Service in the country to which they are assigned. Any exceptions should have Presidential approval and should be brought to the attention of the intelligence oversight committee(s) of Congress.

73. By statute, the Department of State should be authorized to take the necessary steps to assure its ability to provide effective guidance and support to Ambassadors in the execution of their responsibilities under Public Law 93–475 (22 U.S.C. Sect. 2680a).

74. Consideration should be given to increasing and earmarking funds for Foreign Service overt collection of foreign political and economic information. These funds might be administered jointly by the State Department's Bureau of Intelligence and Research and the Bureau of Economic Affairs.

75. The NSC should review the question of which U.S. Government agency should control and operate communications with overseas diplomatic and consular posts, including the CIA, and other civilian agencies operating abroad.

76. The Department of State should establish specific training programs for political reporting within the Foreign Service Institute, and place greater emphasis on economic reporting.

N. Oversight and the Intelligence Budget

The Committee finds that a full understanding of the budget of the intelligence community is required for effective oversight. The secrecy surrounding the budget, however, makes it impossible for Congress as a whole to make use of this valuable oversight tool.

Congress as a body has never explicitly voted on a "budget" for national intelligence activities. Congress has never voted funds specifically for CIA, NSA, and other national intelligence instrumentalities of the Department of Defense.[50]

The funding levels for these intelligence agencies are fixed by subcommittees of the Armed Services and Appropriations Committees of both Houses. Funds for these agencies are then concealed in the budget of the Department of Defense. Since this Departmental budget is the one Congress approves, Congress as a whole, and the public, have never known how much the intelligence agencies are spending or how much is spent on intelligence activities generally. Neither Congress as a whole, nor the public can determine whether the amount spent on intelligence, or by the intelligence agencies individually, is appropriate, given the priorities.

Because the funds for intelligence are concealed in Defense appropriations, those appropriations are thereby inflated. Most members of Congress and the public can neither determine which categories are inflated nor the extent to which funds in the inflated categories are being used for purposes for which they are approved.

Finally, the Committee believes there is serious question as to whether the present system of complete secrecy violates the constitutional provision that:

> No Money shall be drawn from the Treasury but in Consequence of Appropriations made by Law; and a regular Statement and Account of the Receipts and Expenditures of all public Money shall be published from time to time.[51]

The Committee believes that the overall figure for national intelligence activities can be made public annually without endangering national security or revealing sensitive programs.[52] The Committee carefully examined the possible impact of such disclosure on the sources and methods of intelligence gathering and believes it to be minimal. The Committee found that

---

[50] Funds for the intelligence activities of the Department of State, ERDA, and the FBI are reviewed by the appropriate congressional committees and are voted upon by Congress as a whole, when Congress appropriates funds for these agencies.

[51] United States Constitution, Art. I. Sec. 9 Cls. 7.

[52] The Committee noted that the Special Senate Committee to Study Questions Related to Secret and Confidential Government Documents, chaired by Senators Mansfield and Scott concluded that the aggregate figure for each intelligence agency should be made public.

the primary concern about this level of disclosure was that it would lead to pressure for even more detailed revelation which would compromise vital intelligence programs.

The Committee believes that disclosure of an aggregate figure for national intelligence is as far as it is prudent to go at this stage in reconciling the nation's constitutional and national security requirements. Public speculation about overall intelligence costs would be eliminated, the public would be assured that funds appropriated to particular government agencies were in fact intended for those agencies, and both Congress and the public would be able to assess overall priorities in governmental spending.

The Committee's analysis indicated that _____ billion constitutes the direct costs to the United States for its national intelligence program for FY 1976. This includes the total approved budgets of CIA, DIA, NSA and the national reconnaissance program.[53] If the cost of tactical intelligence by the armed services and indirect support costs[54] which may be attributed to intelligence and intelligence-related activities is added, the total cost of U.S. Government intelligence activities would be twice that amount. This represents about three percent of the total federal budget, and about eight percent of controllable federal spending.

It should be stressed that this larger estimate represents a full cost and includes activities which also fulfill other purposes. Thus the entire amount could not be "saved" if there were no intelligence activities funded by or through the Defense Department.

The CIA's budget for the fiscal year is contained in the Defense Department budget. The Committee found that the CIA spends approximately 70 percent more than it is appropriated, with the additional funds coming from advances and transfers from other agencies. These transfers and advances are made with the knowledge and approval of OMB and the appropriate congressional committees. The use of advances and transfers between agencies is a common governmental practice. In this case the CIA receives funds as the contracting agent for agencies in the Defense Department as well as other intelligence community agencies.

Recommendations

77. The intelligence oversight committee(s) of Congress should authorize on an annual basis a "National Intelligence Budget," the total amount of which would be made public. The Committee recommends that the oversight committee consider whether it is necessary, given the Constitutional

---

[53] The direct costs of the intelligence activities of the ERDA, FBI, and State Department are contained in their respective budgets.

[54] Indirect support costs include costs for personnel, operations and maintenance which support intelligence activities. Examples are the operation of training facilities, supply bases, and commissaries.

requirement and the national security demands, to publish more detailed budgets.

78. The intelligence oversight committee(s) of Congress should monitor the tactical and indirect support accounts as well as the national activities of intelligence agencies in order to assure that they are kept in proper perspective and balance.

79. At the request of the intelligence oversight committee(s) of Congress and as its agent, staff members of the General Accounting Office should conduct full audits, both for compliance and for management of all components of the intelligence community. The GAO should establish such procedures, compartmentation and clearances as are necessary in order to conduct these audits on a secure basis. In conducting such audits, the GAO should be authorized to have full access to all necessary intelligence community files and records.

O. Chemical and Biological Agents and the Intelligence Community

The Committee investigated the testing and use of chemical and biological agents by agencies within the intelligence community. The testing programs originated in response to fears that countries hostile to the United States would use chemical and biological agents against Americans or our allies. Initially, this fear led to defensive programs. Soon this defensive orientation became secondary as the possibility of using these chemical and biological agents to obtain information from, or to gain control of, enemy agents, became apparent.

The Committee found that United States intelligence agencies engaged in research and development programs to discover materials which could be used to alter human behavior. As part of this effort, testing programs were instituted, first involving witting human subjects. Later, drugs were surreptitiously administered to unwitting human subjects.

The Agency considered the testing programs highly sensitive. The Committee found that few people within the agencies knew about them; there is no evidence that Congress was informed about them. These programs were kept from the American public because, as the Inspector General of the CIA wrote, "the knowledge that the Agency is engaging in unethical and illicit activities would have serious repercussions in political and diplomatic circles and would be detrimental to the accomplishment of its [CIA's] mission."

The research and development program and particularly the testing program involving unwitting human subjects involved massive abridgements of the rights of individuals, sometimes with tragic consequences. The deaths of two Americans resulted from these programs; other participants in the testing programs still suffer residual effects. While some controlled testing for defensive purposes might be defended, the nature of the tests, their scale, and the fact that they were continued for years after it was known that the surreptitious administration of LSD to unwitting subjects was dangerous, indicate a disregard for human life and liberty.

The Committee's investigation of the testing and use of chemical and biological agents also raised serious questions about the adequacy of command and control procedures within the CIA. The Committee found that the Director waived the CIA's normal administrative controls for this development and testing program in order to assure its security. According to the head of the CIA's Audit Branch, the waiver produced "gross administrative failures." The waiver prevented the internal review mechanisms of the Agency—the Office of the General Counsel, the Inspector General, and the Audit Staff—from exercising adequate supervision of the program. The waiver had the paradoxical effect of providing looser administrative controls and less effective internal review of this controversial and highly sensitive project than existed for normal Agency activities.

The Committee found that the security of the program was protected not only by the waiver but also by a high degree of compartmentation within the CIA. This resulted in excluding the CIA's Medical Staff from the principal research and testing program involving the effect of chemical and biological agents on human subjects.

The Committee also found that within the intelligence community there were destructive jurisdictional conflicts over drug testing. Military testers withheld information from the CIA, ignoring their superiors' suggestions for coordination. The CIA similarly failed to provide information on its programs to the military. In one case the military attempted to conceal its overseas operational testing of LSD from the CIA and the CIA attempted surreptitiously to discover the details of the military's program.

Recommendations

80. The CIA and other foreign and foreign military intelligence agencies should not engage in experimentation on human subjects utilizing any drug, device or procedure which is designed, intended, or is reasonably likely to harm the physical or mental health of the human subject, except with the informed consent in writing, witnessed by a disinterested third party, of each human subject, and in accordance with the guidelines issued by the National Commission for the Protection of Human Subjects for Biomedical and Behavioral Research. Further, the jurisdiction of the Commission should be amended to include the Central Intelligence Agency and the other intelligence agencies of the United States Government.

81. The Director of the Central Intelligence Agency and the Secretary of Defense should continue to make determined efforts to locate those individuals involved in human testing of chemical and biological agents and to provide follow-up examinations and treatment, if necessary.

P. General Recommendations

82. *Internal Regulations*—Internal CIA directives or regulations regarding significant Agency policies and procedures should be waived only with the explicit written approval of the Director of Central Intelligence. Waiver of any such regulation or directive should in no way violate any law or infringe on the constitutional right and freedom of any citizen. If the DCI approves the waiver or amendment of any significant regulation or directive, the NSC and the appropriate congressional oversight committee(s) should be notified immediately. Such notification should be accompanied by a statement explaining the reasons for the waiver or amendment.

83. *Security Clearances*—In the course of its investigation, the Committee found that because of the many intelligence agencies participating in security clearance investigations, current security clearance procedures involve duplication of effort, waste of money, and inconsistent patterns of investigation and standards. The intelligence oversight committee(s) of Congress, in consultation with the intelligence community, should consider framing standard security clearance procedures for all civilian intelligence agencies and background checks for congressional committees when security clearances are required.

84. *Personnel Practices*—The Committee found that intelligence agency training programs fail to instruct personnel adequately on the legal limitations and prohibitions applicable to intelligence activities. The Committee recommends that these training programs should be expanded to include review of constitutional, statutory, and regulatory provisions in an effort to heighten awareness among all intelligence personnel concerning the potential effects intelligence activities may have on citizens' legal rights.

85. *Security Functions of the Intelligence Agencies*—The Committee found that the security components of intelligence agencies sometimes engaged in law enforcement activities. Some of these activities may have been unlawful. Intelligence agencies' security functions should be limited to protecting the agencies' personnel and facilities and lawful activities and to assuring that intelligence personnel follow proper security practices. (See the Committee's Final Report on Domestic Intelligence, section on Intelligence Activities and the Rights of American Citizens, p. 304.)

86. *Secrecy and Authorized Disclosure*—The Committee has received various administration proposals that would require persons having access to classified and sensitive information to maintain the secrecy of that information. The Committee recommends that the issues raised by these proposals be considered by the new legislative intelligence oversight committee(s) of Congress and that, in recasting the 1947 National Security Act and in consultation with the executive branch, the oversight committee(s) consider

the wisdom of new secrecy and disclosure legislation. In the view of the Committee any such consideration should include carefully defining the following terms:

• national secret;

• sources and methods;

• lawful and unlawful classification;

• lawful and unlawful disclosure.

The new legislation should provide civil and/or criminal penalties for unlawful classification and unlawful disclosure. The statute should also provide for internal departmental and agency procedures for employees who believe that classification and/or disclosure procedures are being improperly or illegally used to report such belief. There should also be a statutory procedure whereby an employee who has used the Agency channel to no avail can report such belief without impunity to an "authorized" institutional group outside the agency. The new Intelligence Oversight Board is one such group. The intelligence oversight committee(s) of Congress would be another. The statute should specify that revealing classified information in the course of reporting information to an authorized group would not constitute unlawful disclosure of classified information.

87. *Federal Register for Classified Executive Orders*—In the course of its investigation, the Committee often had difficulty locating classified orders, directives, instructions, and regulations issued by various elements of the executive branch. Access to these orders by the intelligence oversight committee(s) of Congress is essential to informed oversight of the intelligence community.

The Committee recommends that a Federal Register for classified executive orders be established, by statute. The statute should require the registry, under appropriate security procedures, of all executive orders—however they are labeled—concerning the intelligence activities of the United States. Among the documents for which registry in the Classified Federal Register should be required are all National Security Council Intelligence Directives (NSCIDs), and all Director of Central Intelligence Directives (DCIDs). Provision should be made for access to classified executive orders by the intelligence oversight committee(s) of Congress. Classified executive orders would not be lawful until filed with the registry, although there should be provision for immediate implementation in emergency situations with prompt subsequent registry required.

TESTIMONY OF MR. KENNETH C. BASS, III
SENIOR COUNSEL
STERNE, KESSLER, GOLDSTEIN, & FOX
BEFORE THE SENATE JUDICIARY COMMITTEE

September 10, 2002

The USA Patriot Act in Practice: Shedding Light on the FISA Process

The Delicate—and Difficult—Balance of Intelligence and Criminal Prosecution Interests in the Foreign Intelligence Surveillance Act

Mr. Chairman and Member of the Committee, I appreciate the invitation to appear before the Committee to discuss an issue of considerable significance to our Nation: how should we balance the differing, and often overlapping, goals of protecting national security from hostile acts of foreign powers and enforcing criminal laws. My goal is to share with the Committee the Department of Justice's perspective at the time of the enactment and implementation of the Foreign Intelligence Surveillance Act of 1978, to review the evolution of that perspective over the past two decades and to discuss what this Committee, the Department of Justice and the Foreign Intelligence Surveillance Court should do in post-9/11 environment.

I want to caveat my remarks with an essential fact. Any evaluation of what "should" be done must be based on a thorough understanding of what "has" been done in the past. The legal and policy principles at the heart of the current debate reflect years of secret activity in the implementation of FISA. I was personally aware of that activity for only a few years preceding and immediately following passage of FISA. I have endeavored to stay informed about these issues since I left the Department in 1981, but I have not had access to the most critical facts that remain within the classified written and unwritten history of FISA as reflected in FISA applications, hearings, FISC orders and executive deliberations. I am aware that this Committee is, to some extent, burdened with the same limitations. It is entirely possible that my views on what ought to be done now would change if I had access to the full historical record. Despite that limitation, I believe any consideration by the Committee should include the "original understanding." I hope today to convey that understanding and provide suggestions based on that history in light of recent events.

I. The Original Understanding

The perspective that surrounded the passage and initial implementation of FISA was significantly influenced by the events that lead to the creation of the Office of Intelligence Policy and Review and the passage of FISA itself. For many years the Executive Branch had engaged in electronic surveillance of certain targets without a judicial warrant and in reliance on an assertion of the inherent authority of the President as Commander-in-Chief to take acts necessary to protect national security. During the Vietnam War that established practice was invoked to undertake warrantless surveillance of a number of anti war individuals and groups on a belief that their activities threatened national security. In some cases those surveillance targets were domestic groups with no provable ties to any foreign interest. One such surveillance came before the Supreme Court in United States v. United States District Court, 407 U.S. 297 (1972). In that case, commonly referred to as the Keith decision, the Court held that the Nixon Administration's warrantless surveillance "to protect the nation from attempts of domestic organizations to attack and subvert the existing structure of Government" violated the Fourth Amendment. Id. at 300, emphasis added. The Court eschewed a "precise definition" but stated that term "domestic organization" meant "a group or organization (whether formally or informally constituted) composed of citizens of the United States and which has no significant connection with a foreign power, its agents or agencies." Id. at 309, n.8, emphasis added. The Keith decision and subsequent revelations during the Watergate investigations lead to an effort that began in the Ford Administration to create a Foreign Intelligence Surveillance Court to issue judicial warrants for national security investigations.

When I joined the Department of Justice in the Carter Administration as a senior lawyer in the Office of Legal Counsel, I assumed responsibilities for certain "national security" functions that soon resulted in the creation of the Office of Intelligence Policy and Review that I headed. The Administration was committed to enactment of what became FISA. We took the Keith case as our fundamental guidance on the limits of any warrantless national security surveillance.

During our tenure the Department learned that a Vietnamese citizen in the United States was sending packages to Paris through a courier who happened to be a CIA agent. In Paris the documents were delivered to an official of the Vietnamese government. We were asked to approve a warrantless search of one of the packages. On the basis of the information then available to us, we declined to advise the Attorney General that we should invoke the foreign intelligence exception and engage in warrantless physical searches of the packages if there was a reasonable expectation of privacy. We did, however, conclude that the specific package in the courier's possession was not protected by any reasonable privacy expectation and a search even in the context of a criminal investigation would not require a warrant. We thus authorized the courier to open the package and inspect its contents. That inspection revealed that classified government documents were indeed being transferred to a Vietnamese official in Paris. On the basis of that information and other investigations, we subsequently advised the Attorney General to obtain the President's personal approval of subsequent searches of packages that were, in our opinion, protected by a reasonable expectation of privacy. In addition to those physical search authorizations, the Attorney General approved installation of a wiretap of the individual's phone. Eventually we learned that the source of the classified documents was a U.S. citizen employed by the United States Information Agency. The Attorney General also approved installation of covert television surveillance of the citizen's USIA office.

Throughout investigation, the Criminal Division was informed of its status. Eventually the President accepted Attorney General Bell's advice that we should prosecute the Vietnamese individual and the U.S. citizen. They were arrested and indicted in January 1978. Their trial lawyers challenged the legality of the initial package inspection as well as the subsequent Presidential authorizations for physical searches and electronic surveillance. The District Court held an evidentiary hearing and ruled that the initial package inspection was constitutional because there was no reasonable expectation of privacy and that subsequent searches and surveillance authorized by the President did not violate the Fourth Amendment under the Keith test. However, the District Court also found, on the basis of certain Criminal Division memoranda, that the investigation became "primarily a criminal investigation" on July 20, 1977 and suppressed evidence obtained from warrantless searches and surveillance after that date.

Both defendants were convicted and appealed. They contended that the original package inspection was unconstitutional and that the President did not have inherent authority to approve the subsequent searches and surveillance. I argued on appeal that the District Court correctly upheld the validity of the early searches, but had erroneously adopted the "primary purpose" test to suppress evidence obtained after July 20. The Fourth Circuit characterized our position as contending "that, if surveillance is to any degree directed at gathering foreign intelligence, the executive may ignore the warrant requirement of the Fourth Amendment." United States v. Troung Dinh Hung, 629 F.2d 908, 915 (1980). The defendants argued that the foreign intelligence exception to the warrant requirement could not be invoked unless the search was conducted "solely" for foreign policy purposes. The Court of Appeals rejected both arguments and affirmed the District Court's reliance on the "primary purpose" test.

FISA was enacted during the pendency of the Troung appeal. As passed, the Act included a requirement that "an executive branch official . . . designated by the President from among those executive branch officers employed in the area of national security [certify] that the purpose of the [FISA] search is to obtain foreign intelligence information." 50 U.S.C. § 1823(a)(7), as originally enacted.

Over the years the language of the Act and the Troung decision evolved into the adoption of a "primary purpose" test in the administration of FISA that resulted in the creation in 1995 of a "wall" of separation between intelligence and law enforcement. That wall in turn lead to the amendments in the PATRIOT Act changing the relevant language from "the purpose" to "a significant purpose."

I am not privy to all the actions that led the Department, the FBI and the FISC to implement that "wall." I am confident, however, that the post-1995 strict separation was not consistent with the view we held in the beginning. I also believe the "wall" reflects an erroneous view of the 1978 Act and the court decisions.

The Troung decision involved searches and surveillances undertaken without any prior judicial approval. Since passage of FISA, similar searches have been authorized by an Article III judge under the FISA procedures. That critical different was, in my view, overlooked in the creation of the "wall." The Troung court was concerned with the limits of warrantless surveillance in a prosecution context. That concern is absent whenever a FISA order has been issued. Thus the basis for concern about the "primary purpose" of an FBI surveillance is not present when a FISA order has been obtained. For me the FISA order is a warrant within the meaning of the Fourth Amendment, as long as the purpose of the surveillance is to obtain foreign intelligence, as that term is defined in FISA itself.

The evolution of the "primary purpose" test reflects confusion between the purpose of the surveillance and the motivating cause of the surveillance. Admittedly we were never faced with a terrorist environment like today's post 9/11 concerns. We did have international terrorist cases, but those cases rarely involved any threat of criminal activities in the United States. Our focus was on international terrorist organizations whose violent activities were directed to foreign targets and also engaged in fund-raising and other activities in the United States. As the Committee knows, the term "foreign intelligence" in FISA was intentionally drafted to include information about criminal and non-criminal activities of agents of foreign powers. That information would normally be of interest to the national security/foreign affairs community. To the extent that information implicated criminal concerns, it was overwhelmingly in the arena of espionage, not terrorism.

Against that backdrop we never engaged in any analysis of the "primary purpose" of a FISA surveillance. We were totally comfortable with an understanding that if the purpose for undertaking the surveillance was to gather information about the activities of agents of foreign powers that was not otherwise obtainable, then "the purpose" of the surveillance was to gather foreign intelligence. The subsequent use of that information, at least insofar as it concerned U.S. persons, was governed by the minimization procedures. Dissemination and use of the information for criminal law enforcement purposes was expressly authorized by FISA and that use did not, to us, affect "the purpose" of the surveillance. This view did not, however, mean that we would have authorized a FISA application that had its origin entirely within the law enforcement community with no prior involvement of an official in the intelligence community, had such a case ever arisen.

For me the key provision in FISA is not the "purpose" language, but the certification language that restricts authority to Executive Branch officials "employed in the area of national security." Given the background of FISA, particularly the Supreme Court's Keith decision, that provision was a clear indication that the FISA authority was to be exercised when an official with national security responsibilities certified that there was a national security reason to undertake the surveillance. The delegations of authority by successive Presidents have always included the top officials in what we all recognize as the intelligence/national security community. The problem arises because of the counterintelligence and law enforcement responsibilities of the FBI. Because the Bureau has both responsibilities, the Director is both an intelligence official and a law enforcement official.

Although FISA does not explicitly limit certifications by the FBI Director to exercises of his "intelligence" responsibilities, we had always understood the fundamental purpose of FISA surveillances to be limited by the Keith principle. Thus a "pure law enforcement" investigation was to be handled using traditional law enforcement authorities, such as Title III. We never viewed FISA as an alternative to Title III for such cases. At the same time we never believed that FISA precluded applications where the ultimate use of the information gathered would be criminal prosecution. As long as the investigation related to a matter of concern to the national security community and the information sought met the FISA definition of foreign intelligence, the statutory requirements were met.

Thus for us the phrase "purpose" referred to the goal of the surveillance itself, not the goal of the broader investigation. By definition, at least during the Carter Administration, counterintelligence investigations of U.S. persons always contemplated a possible criminal prosecution. But that reality did not mean that the purpose of the FISA surveillance was law enforcement. The purpose was to gather foreign intelligence information about the activities of the U.S. person. That purpose remained the same throughout the course of surveillance, even if there was a decision to undertake a criminal prosecution instead of a non-prosecutorial solution such as a false-flag or "turning" operation.

II. Evolution of "the Primary Purpose" Concern

It is now apparent that our original understanding has not been followed in recent times. Until the past few years when the Lee/Bellows investigation and other disclosures have brought the issue forward, the evolving attitudes remained hidden from public view. There were several judicial decisions upholding FISA surveillances, and a few of them made reference to the "purpose" or "primary purpose" of FISA surveillances. It is now clear that the Department and the FISC read those decisions as requiring creation of a "wall" between the intelligence and the law enforcement responsibilities of the FBI and the Department. As I read those decisions, none of them required the adoption of the 1995 procedures. Certainly the Supreme Court never addressed the issue and there was a clear divergence of views among the circuits. For reasons that remain hidden in the classified FISA files and the institutional memory of the participants, what emerged was the July, 1995 directive from the Attorney General that sharing of FISA information with law enforcement officials of the FBI and the Criminal Division must not "inadvertently result in ether the fact or the appearance of the Criminal Division's directing or controlling the FI or FCI investigation toward law enforcement objectives." Those procedures also mandated the inclusion in FISA renewal applications of a disclosure to the FISC of "any contacts among the FBI, the Criminal Division, and a U.S. Attorney's Office, in order to keep the FISC informed of the criminal justice aspects of the ongoing investigation."

The reasons for that directive remain a mystery. But for me the 1995 directive was not required either by FISA as it was originally enacted or by the reported decisions of any court. It is unclear whether the 1995 procedures originated with the Department, the FISC or some other institution. It is, however, clear that the directive was not subsequently followed, that numerous instances of that failure were disclosed to the FISC, that the FISC became quite concerned about these violations, that a senior FBI official was disciplined and that the FISC has now refused to approve the Department's effort to change those procedures as the Department believes it need to do.

Based on the public materials, I see no basis in FISA or judicial decisions for imposing the 1995 limitations. There may well be valid policy reasons or specific classified DOJ or FISC actions that led the Department to adopt the 1995 procedures. The Committee should, I believe, try to determine precisely why the procedures were adopted. But regardless of those reasons, it is clear to me that the 1995 procedures reflect an understanding of FISA's requirements that is far more restrictive than our original understanding.

III. The PATRIOT Act Response

Congress changed the FISA language from "the purpose" to "a significant purpose" in two subsections of FISA. It did not, however, change all occurrences of the phrase and that action has contributed to the current FISC/DOJ impasse. Moreover, the atmosphere surrounding passage of the PATRIOT Act and its sparse legislative history makes it difficult to be confident about any correct legal interpretation of the effect of that Act on the 1995 procedures. The Department believes that the change justifies tearing down the 1995 wall and authorizes FISA surveillances where "the primary purpose" is criminal law enforcement. The FISC, on the other hand, unanimously concluded that the amendments did not justify eliminating the 1995 restrictions.

From my observation of the PATRIOT Act's passage, it appears there is support in the legislative debates for the Department's view. However, the specific issues involved in the Department's appeal to the Court of Review do not appear to have been fully understood or addressed by the Congress. It is plain beyond debate that Congress intended to facilitate increased information-sharing between the intelligence and law enforcement communities. It is equally plain that Congress intended to eliminate the "primary purpose" gloss that had encrusted FISA over the years. It is not at all clear that Congress intended to change the process to the extent the Department now seeks.

IV. Recommendations

With full awareness of the limitations on my knowledge of the classified facts, I advance a few specific recommendations:

A. Obtain More Information and Make it Public

The Committee should ensure that t has a full and complete understanding of the reasons that led to the promulgation of the 1995 procedures and the pre- and post-1995 incidents with the FISC that led to the FISC decision to bar future appearances before it of a particular FBI agent.

The Committee needs to learn whether the present DOJ appeal to the Court of Review was based on an actual impairment of the FBI's ability to protect the national security or a more abstract concern about the proper interpretation of the PATRIOT Act. For that reason the Committee, either directly or through the Intelligence Committee, needs access to an unredacted version of the Department's brief on appeal.

The Committee should also meet with one or more judges of the FISC to obtain their perspective on how the 1995 procedures and the "wall" developed. I understand that the FISC may be concerned about such a meeting because of separation of powers concerns. It is entirely appropriate for traditional courts to address the other branches solely through published opinions and thus decline a congressional request to meet to discuss legal issues that tribunal has decided. But the FISC is not a traditional court that publishes opinions. It works, and properly so, in a classified environment. There are no published opinions that explain what the FISC believes the "primary purpose" principle requires a wall between the intelligence and law enforcement functions. There is no public opinion explaining the numerous departures from the 1995 procedures that lead to the FISC's order barring the FBI agent from appearing before it. Finally, it appears that the FISC has not been precluded by separation of powers concerns from full and open communications and meetings with the executive branch. Given the unique business of that court and the congressional need to obtain a complete perspective on this issue, the Committee and the FISC should find some means for a full and frank dialogue.

To the fullest possible extent, the Committee should make this information public, recognizing legitimate concerns about disclosing case-specific information, but erring on the side of disclosure rather than continued secrecy.

B. Introduce Elements of an Adversarial Process for FISA

I have previously advocated appointment of counsel to serve as a "devil's advocate" for U.S. persons who are targets of FISA applications. I believe any process that departs from our normal adversary proceedings is subject to increased risk of error. When there is no counsel on "the other side," the court finds itself in an uncomfortable position of being critic as well as judge. I believe the May 17, 2002 amended decision and order of the FISC reflects the built-up tension in that Court's role, a tension exacerbated by the total absence of an adversarial process.

I do not suggest that counsel for the target be used in non-U.S. person cases, nor even in all U.S.-person cases. Nor would I have counsel communicate with the target. Indeed it might be possible to eliminate certain target-identifying information from the pleadings disclosed to cleared counsel. But I believe the FISA process would be enhanced if the FISC in certain cases appointed a lawyer with the requisite background to review the FISA filing and interpose objections as appropriate. I think the FISC, as an Article III court has the inherent authority to make such appointments now. But Congress could facilitate that outcome by specific authorizing amendments to FISA.

I had hoped that the Court of Review would appoint counsel to serve as amicus curiae to defend the FISC order and decision in the present appeal. I am aware that petitions to intervene were filed by public interest organizations. Unfortunately the Court of Review proceeded to hear arguments yesterday in a closed proceeding. The secrecy of that hearing and the absence of any meaningful adversary process diminished the quality—as well as the public acceptability—of the Court's ultimate decision.

C. Insure that the Office of Intelligence Policy and Review Remains Fully Involved

One of the less-well-publicized aspects of the FISC May 17 order is the preservation of the role of OIPR as a full participant in the exchange of information between the intelligence and law enforcement components. The Department's public disclosures on this aspect of their proposed new procedures provide absolutely no explanation for the change. The Department has deleted every part of its argument on this point in its redacted brief.

OIPR has played an important role throughout FISA as part of the internal "checks and balances" to offset features of FISA that depart from the criminal search warrant standards. The Department has not stated publicly why OIPR's role needs to be changed. I understand that they have stated "off the record" that it is "administratively difficult or inconvenient" to require OIPR's presence under the 1995 procedures and the FISC's amendment to the new procedures. That justification, if it is indeed the reason, is unpersuasive. Here again there may be legitimately classified reasons to support the Department's position. If so, this Committee should obtain access to those reasons and make an independent evaluation of the validity of the proposed change. If there is in fact some limitation of human or physical resources that led to the proposed curtailing of OIPR's role, Congress should provide the needed resources to insure the Office continues to function both as advocate for FISA applications and as watchdog.

D. Do Not Change the FISA "Agent of a Foreign Power" Definition

As noted earlier, the Keith "agent of a foreign power" principle was the overriding jurisprudential concept on which FISA was based. In essence, if activities were being undertaken on behalf of a foreign power, they were appropriate for consideration by the national security/intelligence components of the government, but if there was no such agency, the matter was one for domestic law enforcement and not an assertion of inherent Commander-in-Chief authority. Domestic law enforcement surveillances were to be left to Title III warrants, while national security/intelligence surveillances were to proceed using FISA warrants.

In the aftermath of 9/11 there have been some proposals to amend FISA to delete the "agent of a foreign power" limitation, at least with regard to non-U.S. persons. That proposal would fundamentally change the basic concept of FISA and transform it from a foreign affairs/national security intelligence tool to a criminal intelligence tool. That change would, in my opinion, unnecessarily blur the already difficult line between the intelligence and law enforcement communities. It would also institutionalize an alienage-based distinction of considerable significance.

In a given case where there is no basis to allege that a particular individual is acting as an agent of a foreign power, the matter is rarely going to be of concern to the National Security Council, the Department of State and the Department of Defense. Absent an interest from one of those components, there is no legitimate foreign intelligence interest and no reason to authorize FISA surveillance.

E. Change FISC Rule 11

In April 2002 the FISC adopted Rule 11 requiring all FISA applications to include "informative descriptions of any ongoing criminal investigations of FISA targets, as well as the substance of any consultations between the FBI and criminal prosecutors at the department of Justice or a United States Attorney's Office. I believe that requirement is unsound and goes well beyond any appropriate role of the FISC.

I recognize the FISC has a duty to oversee the implementation of minimization procedures. That duty properly includes reports of dissemination of information obtained through FISA surveillances and searches. But Rule 11 is not limited to dissemination of FISA-derived information. Rule 11 requires comprehensive reporting on all aspects of any criminal investigation involving a FISA target. That requirement injects the FISC far too deeply into criminal investigations. It amounts to a comprehensive contemporaneous oversight of certain criminal investigations and prosecutorial decisions. That is not an appropriate role for an Article III court. Investigation and prosecution of crimes is an executive, not judicial, function. Rule 11 should accordingly be substantially revised to limit any reports to those needed to monitor implementation of minimization procedures.

FOREIGN INTELLIGENCE SURVEILLANCE ACT OF 1978

LEGISLATIVE HISTORY
P.L. 95-511*

SENATE REPORT NO. 95-604—PART 1

Nov. 15, 22, 1977 [To accompany S. 1566]

The Committee on the Judiciary, to which was referred the bill (S. 1566) to amend title 18, United States Code, to authorize applications for a court order approving the use of electronic surveillance to obtain foreign intelligence information, having considered the same, reports favorably thereon with amendments and recommends that the bill, as amended, do pass.

Purpose of Amendments

The amendments to S. 1566 are designed to clarify and make more explicit the statutory intent, as well as to provide further safeguards for individuals subjected to electronic surveillance pursuant to this new chapter. Certain amendments are also designed to provide a detailed procedure for challenging such surveillance, and any evidence derived therefrom, during the course of a formal proceeding.

Finally, the reported bill adds an amendment to Chapter 119 of title 18, United States Code (Title III of the Omnibus Crime Control and Safe Streets Act of 1968, Public Law 90-351, section 802). This latter amendment is technical and conforming in nature and is designed to integrate certain provisions of Chapters 119 and 120. A more detailed explanation of the individual amendments is contained in the section-by-section analysis of this report.

History of the Bill

The "Foreign Intelligence Surveillance Act of 1977", S. 1566, was introduced by Senator Kennedy on May 18, 1977 to provide a statutory procedure for the authorization of applications for a court order approving the use of electronic surveillance to obtain foreign intelligence information. The bill, cosponsored by seven other Senators (Mr. Bayh, Mr. Eastland, Mr. Inouye, Mr. McClellan, Mr. Mathias, Mr. Nelson and Mr. Thurmond), was referred to and considered by the Committee on the Judiciary.

---

*Legislative History, U.S. Cong. & Adm. News '78-30 at 3904.

S. 1566 has its origin in S. 3197, "The Foreign Intelligence Surveillance Act of 1976", 94th Cong. 2d Sess. (1976). That legislation, also introduced by Senator Kennedy with broad, bipartisan support, including that of the Ford Administration, was the subject of Senate hearings by both the Subcommittee on Criminal Laws and Procedures of the Committee on the Judiciary and the Select Committee on Intelligence. S. 3197 was reported favorably by both Senate Committees by a combined vote of 24 ayes to 2 nays, but the Session ended before the full Senate could act on the legislation.

S. 1566 picks up where S. 3197 left off. Following the introduction of the measure, two days of hearings were held by the Subcommittee on Criminal Laws and Procedures, chaired by Senator Kennedy at the request of Senator McClellan. Eight witnesses testified, and a number of other individuals submitted statements for the hearing record. Among those testifying were Attorney General Griffin B. Bell; Director of the FBI, Clarence Kelley; Director of the Central Intelligence Agency, Stansfield Turner; Secretary of Defense Harold Brown; John Shattuck of the American Civil Liberties Union; and Morton H. Halperin of the Center for National Security Studies.

Broad-based support was voiced for S. 1566 throughout the hearing, with the Administration indicating its support of the bill.

S. 1566 as reported, however, has been amended in relative minor respects to respond to the constructive criticisms and suggestions elicited in the hearings. As amended, the bill was approved by the Subcommittee on Criminal Laws and Procedures with a unanimous recommendation for favorable action.

Position of the Administration

The Administration supports the enactment of S. 1566 and has supported its swift passage. As Attorney General Bell stated in testifying in favor of the bill:

> I believe this bill is remarkable not only in the way it has been developed, but also in the fact that for the first time in our society the clandestine intelligence activities of our government shall be subject to the regulation and receive the positive authority of a public law for all to inspect. President Carter stated it very well in announcing this bill when he said that "one of the most difficult tasks in a free society like our own is the correlation between adequate intelligence to guarantee our nation's security on the one hand, and the preservation of basic human rights on the other." It is a very delicate balance to strike, but one which is necessary in our society, and a balance which cannot be achieved by sacrificing either our nation's security or our civil liberties. In my view this bill strikes the balance, sacrifices neither our security nor our civil liberties, and assures that the abuses of the past will remain in the past and that the dedicated and patriotic men and women who serve this country in intelligence positions, often under substantial hardships and even danger, will have the affirmation of Congress that their activities are proper and necessary.[1]

---

[1] Hearing before the Subcommittee on Criminal Laws and Procedures of the Senate Committee on the Judiciary, Foreign Intelligence Surveillance Act of 1977, 95th Cong., 1st sess., p. 13 (1977) (hereinafter cited as "Senate Judiciary Hearings").

General Statement

I. Summary of the Legislation

The bill reported by the Judiciary Committee amends title 18, United States Code, by adding a new chapter after chapter 119, entitled "Electronic Surveillance Within the United States for Foreign Intelligence Purposes." The purpose of the bill is to provide a procedure under which the Attorney General can obtain a judicial warrant authorizing the use of electronic surveillance in the United States for foreign intelligence purposes. If enacted, this legislation would require a judicial warrant authorizing the following for foreign intelligence purposes:

(a) The acquisition of a wire or radio communication sent to or from the United States by intentionally targeting a known United States person in the United States under circumstances in which the person has a reasonable expectation of privacy and a warrant would be required for law enforcement purposes.

(b) A wiretap in the United States to intercept a wire communication, such as a telephone or telegram communication;

(c) The acquisition of a private radio transmission in which all of the communicants are located within the United States; or

(d) The use in the United States of any electronic, mechanical or other surveillance device to acquire information other than a wire communication or radio communication under circumstances in which the person has a reasonable expectation of privacy and a warrant would be required for law enforcement purposes.

S. 1566 authorizes the Chief Justice of the United States to designate seven district court judges, any one of whom may hear applications for and grant orders approving electronic surveillance for foreign intelligence purposes. The bill further provides that the Chief Justice shall designate three judges from the United States district courts or courts of appeals to sit as a special Court of Appeals to hear appeals by the United States from denials of applications made by any one of the seven district court judges. The United States may further appeal from this special court to the Supreme Court.

Under S. 1566, a judge may issue a warrant authorizing electronic surveillance within the United States only if he finds that: the President has authorized the Attorney General to approve applications for such electronic surveillance; the application has been approved by the Attorney General; on the basis of the facts submitted to the court, there is probable cause to believe that the target of the surveillance is a foreign power or an agent of a foreign power; the place at which the surveillance is directed is being used or about to be used by that foreign power or agent; minimization procedures to be followed are reasonably designed to minimize the acquisition and retention of information relating to Americans that is not foreign intelligence information; Executive certification that the information sought is foreign intelligence information which cannot reasonably be obtained by normal investigative techniques; and, if the target of the surveillance is a United States person, such certification is not clearly erroneous. The order may approve the electronic surveillance for no longer than 90 days with respect to all natural persons and some foreign powers, but extensions of up to 90 days may be granted upon an application and after the same findings as required for the original order. With respect to official "foreign powers", as defined in the legislation, the approval may be for as long as one year.

In the event that an emergency arises and resort to a court is not possible, the Attorney General is authorized to approve electronic surveillance. Such an emergency surveillance cannot continue for more than 24 hours without a judge's approval; a judge must be immediately notified of the emergency surveillance; and an application must be made to the judge within 24 hours of approval of that emergency surveillance.

The bill would limit the use of information concerning United States citizens and lawful resident aliens acquired from electronic surveillances to matters properly related to foreign intelligence and the enforcement of criminal law. No information obtained from an electronic surveillance could be used or disclosed against any person except for lawful purposes. A judge may order the notification of a person under electronic surveillance if an emergency surveillance was authorized but subsequently disapproved by a judge.

S. 1566 provides for annual reports by the Attorney General to the Congress and the Administrative Office of the United States Courts containing statistical information relating to surveillances during the preceding year.

The bill does not provide statutory authorization for the use of any technique other than electronic surveillance, and, combined with chapter 119 of title 18, it constitutes the exclusive means by which electronic surveillance, as defined, and the interception of domestic wire and oral communications may be conducted; the bill recognizes no inherent power of the President in this area.

In three major respects S. 1566 increases the protections for United States citizens and lawful resident aliens over those contained in S. 3197. First, the definition of electronic surveillance has been expanded to include the targeting of United States persons in their international communications.

This is specifically aimed at eliminating one of the abuses identified by the Senate Select Committee to Study Governmental Operations With Respect to Intelligence Activities and largely implements one of that Committee's recommendations. (Book II, Intelligence Activities and the Rights of Americans, S. Rept. 94–755, 94th Cong., 2d Sess. 309 (1976).) Second, when a United States citizen or lawful resident alien is the target of an electronic surveillance, the judge is required to review the Executive Branch certification to determine if it is clearly erroneous. No review of the certification was allowed in S. 3197. Finally, S. 1566 spells out that the Executive cannot engage in electronic surveillance within the United States without a prior judicial warrant. This is accomplished by repealing the so-called executive "inherent power" disclaimer clause currently found in section 2511(3) of Title 18, United States Code, S. 1566 provides instead that its statutory procedures (and those found in chapter 119 of title 18) "shall be the exclusive means" for conducting electronic surveillance, as defined in the legislation, in the United States. The highly controversial disclaimer has often been cited as evidence of a congressional ratification of the President's inherent constitutional power to engage in electronic surveillance in order to obtain foreign intelligence information essential to the national security. Despite the admonition of the Supreme Court that the language of the disclaimer was "neutral" and did not reflect any such congressional recognition of inherent power, the section has been a major source of controversy. By repealing section 2511(3) and expressly stating that the statutory warrant procedures spelled out in the law must be followed in conducting electronic surveillance in the United States, this legislation ends the eight-year debate over the meaning and scope of the inherent power disclaimer clause.

II. Statement of Need

The Federal Government has never enacted legislation to regulate the use of electronic surveillance within the United States for foreign intelligence purposes. Although efforts have been made in recent years by Senator Kennedy, Senator Nelson, Senator Mathias, and former Senator Philip A. Hart to circumscribe the power of the executive branch to engage in such surveillance, and the Senate came very close to enacting such legislation during the 94th Congress, the fact remains that such efforts have never been successful.[2] The hearings held this year on S. 1566 were the sixth set of hearings on warrantless wiretapping in as many years.[3] The Committee believes that S. 1566 is a measure which can successfully break this impasse

---

[2] See, e.g., S. 3197, *Foreign Intelligence Surveillance Act of 1976*, 94th Cong., 2d sess. (1976); S. 743, *National Security Surveillance Act of 1975*, 94th Cong., 1st sess. (1975); S. 2820, *Surveillance Practices and Procedures Act of 1973*, 93rd Cong., 1st sess. (1973); S. 4062, *Freedom from Surveillance Act of 1974*, 93rd Cong., 2d sess. (1974).

[3] See, e.g., Hearings before the Subcommittee on Criminal Laws and Procedures of the Senate Committee on the Judiciary, *Foreign Intelligence Surveillance Act of 1976*, 94th Cong., 2d sess. (1976); Senate Select Committee on Intelligence, *Foreign Intelligence Surveillance Act of 1976*, 94th

and provide effective, reasonable safeguards to ensure accountability and prevent improper surveillance. S. 1566 goes a long way in striking a fair and just balance between protection of national security and protection of personal liberties. It is a recognition by both the Executive Branch and the Congress that the statutory rule of law must prevail in the area of foreign intelligence surveillance.

The need for such statutory safeguards has become apparent in recent years. This legislation is in large measure a response to the revelations that warrantless electronic surveillance in the name of national security has been seriously abused. These abuses were initially illuminated in 1973 during the investigation of the Watergate break-in. Since that time, however, the Senate Select Committee to Study Government Operations with Respect to Intelligence Activities, chaired by Senator Church (hereafter referred to as the Church Committee), has concluded that every President since Franklin D. Roosevelt asserted the authority to authorize warrantless electronic surveillance and exercised that authority. While the number of illegal or improper national security taps and bugs conducted during the Nixon administration may have exceeded those in previous administrations, the surveillances were regrettably by no means atypical. In summarizing its conclusion that surveillance was "often conducted by illegal or improper means," the Church committee wrote:

> Since the 1930's, intelligence agencies have frequently wiretapped and bugged American citizens without the benefit of judicial warrant. . . . [P]ast subjects of these surveillances have included a United States Congressman, Congressional staff member, journalists and newsmen, and numerous individuals and groups who engaged in no criminal activity and who posed no genuine threat to the national security, such as two White House domestic affairs advisers and an anti-Vietnam War protest group. (vol. 2, p. 12)

The application of vague and elastic standards for wiretapping and bugging has resulted in electronic surveillances which, by any objective measure, were improper and seriously infringed the Fourth Amendment Rights of both the targets and those with whom the targets communicated. The inherently intrusive nature of electronic surveillance, moreover, has enabled the Government to generate vast amounts of information—unrelated to any legitimate government interest—about the personal and political lives of American citizens. The collection of this type of information

---

Cong., 2d sess. (1976); Subcommittee on Surveillance of the Senate Committee on Foreign Relations and the Subcommittee on Administrative Practice and Procedure of the Senate Committee on the Judiciary, *Warrantless Wiretaping and Electronic Surveillance*, 94th Cong., 1st sess. (1975); Joint Hearings before the Subcommittee on Administrative Practice and Procedure and the Subcommittee on Constitutional Rights of the Senate Committee on the Judiciary, *Warrantless Wiretapping and Electronic Surveillance*, 93d Cong., 2d sess. (1974); Hearings before the Subcommittee on Administrative Practice and Procedure of the Senate Committee on the Judiciary, *Warrantless Wiretapping*, 92d Cong., 2d sess. (1972). In the joint report of the Subcommittees on Surveillance and Administrative Practice and Procedure issued in 1975, findings were made that "there are not adequate written standards or criteria within the executive branch to govern the warrantless electronic surveillance of either Americans or foreigners. There is a gap in the statutes, the case, and in administrative regulation on the use of warrantless wiretaps or bugs by executive branch agencies for alleged 'national security' purposes."

has, in turn, raised the danger of its use for partisan political and other improper ends by senior administration officials. (vol. 3, p. 32.)

Also formidable—although incalculable—is the "chilling effect" which warrantless electronic surveillance may have on the constitutional rights of those who were not targets of the surveillance, but who perceived themselves, whether reasonably or unreasonably, as potential targets. Our Bill of Rights is concerned not only with direct infringements on constitutional rights, but also with government activities which effectively inhibit the exercise of these rights. The exercise of political freedom depends in large measure on citizens' understanding that they will be able to be publicly active and dissent from official policy, within lawful limits, without having to sacrifice the expectation of privacy that they rightfully hold. Arbitrary or uncontrolled use of warrantless electronic surveillance can violate that understanding and impair that public confidence so necessary to an uninhibited political life.

S. 1566 is designed, therefore, to curb the practice by which the Executive Branch may conduct warrantless electronic surveillance on its own unilateral determination that national security justifies it. At the same time, however, this legislation does not prohibit the legitimate use of electronic surveillance to obtain foreign intelligence information. As the Church committee pointed out:

> Electronic surveillance techniques have understandably enabled these agencies to obtain valuable information relevant to their legitimate intelligence missions. Use of these techniques has provided the Government with vital intelligence, which would be difficult to acquire through other means, about the activities and intentions of foreign powers and has provided important leads in counterespionage cases. (vol. 2, p. 274)

Safeguarding national security against the intelligence activities of foreign agents remains a vitally important Government purpose. Few would dispute the fact that we live in a dangerous world in which hostile intelligence activities in this country are still carried on to our detriment.

Striking a sound balance between the need for such surveillance and the protection of civil liberties lies at the heart of S. 1566. As Senator Kennedy stated in introducing S. 1566:

> The complexity of the problem must not be underestimated. Electronic surveillance can be a useful tool for the Government's gathering of certain kinds of information; yet, if abused, it can also constitute a particularly indiscriminate and penetrating invasion of the privacy of our citizens. My objective over the past six years has been to reach some kind of fair balance that will protect the security of the United States without infringing on our citizens' human liberties and rights.[4]

The committee believes that the Executive Branch of Government should have, under proper circumstances and with appropriate safeguards, authority to acquire important foreign intelligence information by means of electronic surveillance. The committee also believes that the past record

---

[4] 123 Cong. Rec. S7857 (daily ed., May 18, 1977).

and the state of the law in the area make it desirable that the Executive Branch not be the sole or final arbiter of when such proper circumstances exist. S. 1566 is designed to permit the Government to gather necessary foreign intelligence information by means of electronic surveillance but under limitations and according to procedural guidelines which will better safeguard the rights of individuals.

III. Background

The bipartisan congressional support for S. 1566 and the constructive co-operation of the Executive Branch toward the legislation signifies a constructive change in the ongoing debate over electronic surveillance. That debate has centered around the power of the President to acquire information necessary for the national security and the constitutionality of warrantless electronic surveillance. This is not surprising since the United States Supreme Court has never expressly decided the issue of whether the President has constitutional authority to authorize warrantless electronic surveillance in cases concerning foreign intelligence. Whether the President has so-called "inherent power" to engage in or authorize warrantless electronic surveillance and, if such power exists, what limitations, if any, restrict the scope of that power, are issues which have troubled constitutional scholars for decades.

The history of warrantless electronic surveillance offers support to both proponents and critics of the concept of "inherent power" and clearly highlights the need for passage of S. 1566.

In 1928, the Supreme Court in *Olmstead* v. *United States*[5] held that wiretapping was not within the coverage of the Fourth Amendment. Three years later, Attorney General William D. Mitchell authorized telephone wiretapping, upon the personal approval of bureau chiefs, of syndicated bootleggers and in "exceptional cases where the crimes are substantial and serious, and the necessity is great and [the bureau chief and the Assistant Attorney General] are satisfied that the persons whose wires are to be tapped are of the criminal type." These general guidelines governed the Department's practice through the thirties and telephone wiretapping was considered to be an important law enforcement tool.[6]

---

[5] 277 U.S. 438, 48 S.Ct. 564, 72 L.Ed. 944.

[6] The history of the practice of the Department of Justice which follows in this Report is derived from Attorney General Edward H. Levi's testimony before the Church committee on Novmber 6, 1975 and the final report of that committee. The relevant portions of the report include Book I, *Foreign and Military Intelligence,* chapter IX, "Counterintelligence;" Book II, *Intelligence Activities and the Rights of Americans,* chapter II, "The Growth of Domestic Intelligence," finding C, "Excessive Use of Intrusive Techniques," and finding E, "Political Abuse of Intelligence Information"; Book III, *Supplementary Detailed Staff Reports on Intelligence Activities and the Rights of Americans,* "Dr. Martin Luther King, Jr., Case Study," "Warrantless FBI Electronic Surveillance," Warrantless Surreptitious Entries," "Domestic CIA and FBI Mail Open-

Congress placed the first restrictions on wiretapping in the Federal Communications Act of 1934, which made it a crime for any person "to intercept and divulge or publish the contents of wire and radio communications."[7] The Supreme Court construed this section to apply to Federal agents and held that evidence obtained from the interception of wire and radio communications, and the fruits of that evidence, were inadmissible in court.[8] However, the Justice Department did not interpret the Federal Communications Act or the *Nardone* decision as prohibiting the interception of wire communications *per se*; rather only the interception and divulgence of their contents outside the Federal establishment was considered to be unlawful. Thus, the Justice Department found continued authority for its national security wiretaps.

In 1940, President Roosevelt issued a memorandum to the Attorney General stating his view that electronic surveillance would be proper under the Constitution where "grave matters involving defense of the nation" were involved. The President authorized and directed the Attorney General "to secure information by listening devices [directed at] the conversation or other communications of persons suspected of subversive activities against the Government of the United States, including suspected spies." The Attorney General was requested "to limit these investigations so conducted to a minimum and to limit them insofar as possible as to aliens."[9]

This practice was continued in successive administrations. In 1946, Attorney General Tom C. Clark sent President Truman a letter informing him of President Roosevelt's directive. Clark's memorandum, however, omitted the portion of President Roosevelt's directive limiting wiretaps "insofar as possible to aliens." Instead, he recommended that the directive "be continued in force" in view of the "increase in subversive activities" and "a very substantial increase in crime." President Truman approved.[10]

In the early fifties, however, Attorney General J. Howard McGrath took the position that he would not approve or authorize the installation of microphone surveillances by means of trespass. This policy was quickly reversed by Attorney General Herbert Brownell in 1954 in a sweeping memorandum to FBI Director Hoover instructing him that the Bureau was indeed

---

ing," National Security Agency Surveillance Affecting Americans," and "National Security, Civil Liberties, and the Collection of Intelligence: A Report on the Huston Plan"; Book IV, *Supplementary Detailed Staff Reports on Foreign and Military Intelligence*, "Intelligence and Technology."

[7] 47 U.S.C. 605 (1964 ed.), 48 Stat. 1103.

[8] *Nardone v. United States*, 302 U.S. 379, 58 S.Ct. 275, 82 L.Ed. 314 (1937); 308 U.S. 338, 60 S.Ct. 266, 84 L.Ed. 307 (1939).

[9] III Church committee 297.

[10] II Church committee 60. In 1950, aides to President Truman discovered Clark's incomplete quotation, and the President considered returning to the terms of the original 1940 authorization. However, the 1946 directive was never rescinded.

authorized to conduct such trespassory surveillances regardless of the fact of surreptitious entry, and without the need to first acquire the Attorney General's authorization. Such surveillance was simply authorized whenever the Bureau concluded that the "national interest" so required. The Brownell memorandum is instructive:

> It is my opinion that the department should adopt that interpretation which will permit microphone coverage by the FBI in a manner most conducive to our national interest. I recognize that for the FBI to fulfill its important intelligence function, considerations of internal security and the national interest are paramount; and, therefore, may compel the unrestricted use of this technique in the national interest.[11]

From the relatively limited authorization of warrantless electronic surveillance under President Roosevelt, then, the mandate for the FBI was quickly expanded to the point where the only criterion was the FBI's subjective judgment that the "national interest" required the electronic surveillance.

The practice of the Bureau during the fifties was also described in a memorandum from Director Hoover to the Deputy Attorney General on May 4, 1961:

> [I]n the internal security field, we are utilizing microphone surveillances on a restricted basis even though trespass is necessary to assist in uncovering the activities of Soviet intelligence agents and Communist party leaders. In the interests of national safety, microphone surveillances are also utilized on a restricted basis, even though trespass is necessary, in uncovering major criminal activities. We are using such coverage in connection with our investigations of the clandestine activities of top hoodlums and organized crime. From an intelligence standpoint, this investigative technique has produced results unobtainable through other means. The information so obtained is treated in the same manner as information obtained from wiretaps, that is, not from the standpoint of evidentiary value but for intelligence purposes.[12]

The policy of the Department of Justice was stated publicly in 1966 by the Solicitor General in a supplemental brief to the Supreme Court in *Black v. United States*.[13] Referring to the general delegation of authority by Attorneys General to the Director of the Bureau, the Solicitor stated:

> An exception to the general delegation of authority has been prescribed, since 1940, for the interception of wire communications, which (in addition to being limited to matters involving national security or danger to human life) has required the specific authorization of the Attorney General in each instance. No similar procedure existed until 1965 with respect to the use of devices such as those involved in the instant case, although records of oral and written communications within the Department of Justice reflect concern by Attorneys General and the Director of the Federal Bureau of Investigation that the use of listening

---

[11] III Church committee 297.
[12] III Church committee 297.
[13] 385 U.S. 26, 87 S.Ct. 190, 17 L.Ed.2d 26, on remand 282 F.Supp. 35 (1966).

devices by agents of the Government should be confined to a strictly limited category of situations.

Under departmental practice in effect for a period of years prior to 1963, and continuing until 1965, the Director of the Federal Bureau of Investigation was given authority to approve the installation of devices such as that in question for intelligence (and not evidentiary) purposes which required in the interests of internal security or national safety, including organized crime, kidnappings and matters wherein human life might be at stake. . . .

Present departmental practice, adopted in July 1965 in conformity with the policies declared by the President on June 30, 1965, for the entire Federal establishment, prohibits the use of such listening devices (as well as the interception of telephone and other wire communications) in all instances other than those involving the collection of intelligence affecting the national security. The specific authorization of the Attorney General must be obtained in each instance when this exception is invoked.

In *Katz v. United States*, 389 U.S. 347 (1967)[1], the Supreme Court finally discarded the *Olmstead* doctrine and held that the Fourth Amendment's warrant provision did apply to electronic surveillance. The Court explicitly declined, however, to extend its holding to cases "involving the national security." 389 U.S. at 358, n. 23. The next year, Congress followed suit: responding to the *Katz* case, Congress enacted the Omnibus Crime Control and Safe Streets Act (18 U.S.C. sections 2510–2520).[14] Title III of that Act established a procedure for the judicial authorization of electronic surveillance for the investigation and prevention of specified types of serious crimes and the use of the product of such surveillance in court proceedings. It prohibited wiretapping and electronic surveillance by persons other than duly authorized law enforcement officers, personnel of the Federal Communications Commission, or communication common carriers monitoring communications in the normal course of their employment.

---

[1] 88 S.Ct. 507, 19 L.Ed.2d 576.

Title III, however, disclaimed any intention of legislating in the national security area. The Act contained a proviso in section 2511(3) stating:

Nothing contained in this chapter or in section 605 of the Communications Act of 1934 (48 Stat. 1143; 47 U.S.C. 605) shall limit the constitutional power of the President to take such measures as he deems necessary to protect the Nation against actual or potential attack or other hostile acts of a foreign power, to obtain foreign intelligence information deemed essential to the security of the United States, or to protect national security information against foreign intelligence activities. Nor shall anything contained in this chapter be deemed to limit the constitutional power of the President to take such measures as he deems necessary to protect the United States against the overthrow of the Government by force or other clear and present danger to the structure or existence of the Government.

---

14 See also, S. Rept. 1097, *Senate Committee on the Judiciary, Omnibus Crime Control and Safe Streets Act of 1967*; 90th Cong., 2d sess. (1968).

Against this background the Supreme Court decided the *Keith*[15] case in 1972. While the issue was narrowly drawn—"the delicate question of the President's power, acting through the Attorney General, to authorize electronic surveillance in internal security matters without prior judicial approval" (407 U.S. at 301)—the court's opinion inevitably shed some light on the deeper problem of balancing conflicting interests in national security cases (407 U.S., at 320–321):

> 1. The Court took notice of the long-standing Justice Department policy of warrantless electronic surveillance. It also recognized the "elementary truth" that "unless Government safeguards its own capacity to function and to preserve the security of its people, society itself could become so disordered that all rights and liberties would be endangered."[16]

> 2. In balancing the constitutional rights involved against the governmental objectives, the Court noted the "convergence of First and Fourth amendment values not ordinarily present in cases of "ordinary" crime."[17] The Court went on to pose the issue: "If the legitimate need of the Government to safeguard domestic security requires the use of electronic surveillance the question is whether the needs of citizens for privacy and free expression may not be better protected by requiring a warrant before such surveillance is undertaken. We must also ask whether a warrant requirement would unduly frustrate the efforts of Government to protect itself from acts of subversion and overthrow directed against it."[18]

> 3. In concluding that a warrant was required in domestic security surveillance cases, the Court emphasized the traditional reasons for requiring a warrant:[19]

>> These fourth amendment freedoms cannot properly be guaranteed if domestic security surveillances may be conducted solely within the discretion of the Executive Branch. The Fourth Amendment does not contemplate the executive officers of Government as neutral and disinterested magistrates. Their duty and responsibility are to enforce the laws, to investigate, and to prosecute. * * * But those charged with this investigative and prosecutorial duty should not be the sole judges of when to utilize constitutionally sensitive means in pursuing their tasks. The historical judgment, which the Fourth Amendment accepts, is that unreviewed executive discretion may yield too readily to pressures to obtain incriminating evidence and overlook potential invasions of privacy and protected speech.

---

[15] *United States v. United States District Court*, 407 U.S. 297, 92 S.Ct. 2125, 32 L.Ed.2d 752 (1972).
[16] 407 U.S., at 312.
[17] 407 U.S., at 313.
[18] 407 U.S., at 315.
[19] 407 U.S., at 316–317.

4. The Court then went on to consider and reject the Government's argument that the disclosure of information in a warrant application posed the serious danger of leaks and the Government's argument that "internal security matters are too subtle and compex for judicial evaluation."[20] The Court observed that "[c]ourts regularly deal with the most difficult issues of our society. There is no reason to believe that Federal judges will be insensitive to or uncomprehending of the issues involved in domestic security cases."[21] As to the secrecy claim, the Court observed the "[t]he investigation of criminal activity has long involved imparting sensitive information to judicial officers who have respected the confidentialities involved."[22]

5. Finally, the Court rejected the distinction, stressed by the Government, between surveillance for law enforcement purposes and surveillance designed to obtain intelligence relating to domestic threats to national security. The Court responded that official surveillance, whether its purpose is criminal investigation or ongoing intelligence gathering, risks infringement of constitutionally protected privacy and speech.

However, the Court emphasized that "this case involves only the domestic aspects of national security. We have not addressed, and expressed no opinion as to, the issues which may be involved with respect to activities of foreign powers or their agents."[23]

And, in construing the effect of the title III presidential disclaimer the court wrote:[24]

> Section 2511(3) certainly confers no power, as the language is wholly inappropriate for such a purpose. It merely provides that the Act shall not be interpreted to limit or disturb such power as the President may have under the Constitution. In short, Congress simply left presidential powers where it found them.... [W]e therefore think the conclusion inescapable that Congress only intended to make clear that the Act simply did not legislate with respect to national security surveillances.

Since the *Keith* case, three circuit courts of appeals have addressed the question the Supreme Court reserved. The Fifth Circuit in *United States* v. *Brown*, 484 F.2d 418 (5th Cir. 1973), cert. denied, 415 U.S. 960 (1974), upheld the legality of a surveillance in which the defendant, an American citizen, was incidentally overheard as a result of a warrantless wiretap authorized by the Attorney General for foreign intelligence purposes. The court found that on the basis of "the President's constitutional duty to act for the

---

[20] 407 U.S., at 320.
[21] 407 U.S., at 320.
[22] 407 U.S., at 320–321.
[23] 407 U.S., at 321–322.
[24] 407 U.S., at 303, 306.

United States in the field of foreign affairs, and his inherent power to protect national security in the conduct of foreign affairs ... the President may constitutionally authorize warrantless wiretaps for the purpose of gathering foreign intelligence."[25]

In *United States v. Butenko,* 494 F.2d 593 (3d Cir. 1974) (en banc), cert. denied sub nom. *Ivanov v. United States,* 419 U.S. 881 (1974), the Third Circuit similarly held that electronic surveillance conducted without a warrant would be lawful so long as the primary purpose was to obtain foreign intelligence information. The court found that such surveillance would be reasonable under the Fourth Amendment without a warrant even though it might involve the overhearing of conversations.

However, in *Zweibon v. Mitchell,* 516 F.2d 594 (D.C. Cir. 1975), cert. denied, 425 U.S. 944 (1976)[2], the Circuit Court of Appeals for the District of Columbia, in the course of an opinion requiring that a warrant must be obtained before a wiretap is installed on a domestic organization that is neither the agent of, nor acting in collaboration with, a foreign power, questioned whether any national security exception to the warrant requirement would be constitutionally permissible.

---

[2] 96 S.Ct. 1684, 48 L.Ed.2d 187.

Although the holding of *Zweibon* was limited to the case of a domestic organization without ties to a foreign power, the plurality opinion of the court—in legal analysis closely patterned on *Keith*—concluded "that an analysis of the policies implicated by foreign security surveillance indicates that, absent exigent circumstances, all warrantless electronic surveillance is unreasonable and therefore unconstitutional."[26]

Thus, after almost 50 years of case law dealing with the subject of warrantless electronic surveillance, and despite the practice of warrantless foreign intelligence surveillance sanctioned and engaged in by nine administrations, constitutional limits on the President's powers to order such surveillances remains an open question. This legislation would provide the secure framework by which the Executive Branch may conduct legitimate electronic surveillance for foreign intelligence purposes within the context of this Nation's commitment to privacy and individual rights.

---

[25] 484 F.2d at 426.

[26] 516 F.2d at 613–614. Neither *Brown* nor *Butenko* provide a systematic analysis of the problem within the framework indicated by the Supreme Court decision in *Keith,* i.e., whether the requirement of a warrant would unduly frustrate the exercise of the President's responsibility in the area of national security. The court's opinion in *Brown* simply confirmed the President's inherent power to authorize foreign intelligence collection through, among other things, electronic surveillance without a warrant. The *Butenko* opinion offers a sightly more extensive analysis of the problem. On the other hand, the *Zweibon* opinion, insofar as it considered and rejected the arguments for the existence of an inherent power by applying the analytical framework used by the Supreme Court in *Keith,* was a plurality opinion.

IV. Conclusion

S. 1566 would alter the current debate arising out of the uncertainty of the present law by completing an exclusive charter for the conduct of electronic surveillance in the United States. It would relegate to the past the wire-tapping abuses brought to light during the committee hearings by providing, for the first time, effective substantive and procedural statutory controls over foreign intelligence electronic surveillance.[27]

The basis for this legislation is the understanding—concurred in by the Attorney General—that even if the President has an "inherent" constitutional power to authorize warrantless surveillance for foreign intelligence purposes, Congress has the power to regulate the exercise of this authority by legislating a reasonable warrant procedure governing foreign intelligence surveillance.[28]

The bill provides external and internal checks on the executive. The external check is found in the judicial warrant procedure which requires the executive branch to secure a warrant before engaging in electronic surveillance for purposes of obtaining foreign intelligence information. Such surveillance would be limited to a "foreign power" and "agent of a foreign power." United States citizens and lawful resident aliens could be targets of electronic surveillance only if they are: (1) knowingly engaged in "clandestine intelligence activities which involve or will involve a violation" of the criminal law; (2) knowingly engaged in activities "that involve or will involve sabotage or terrorism for or on behalf of a foreign power"; or (3) "pursuant to the direction of an intelligence service or intelligence network of a foreign power" are knowingly or secretly collecting or transmitting foreign intelligence in a manner harmful to the security of the United States. All other persons—such as illegal aliens or foreign visitors—could also be targets if they are: (1) either officers or employees of a

---

[27] The Church committee concluded that, in many cases, surveillance was based on the belief that groups or individuals were directed, financed or otherwise controlled by a hostile foreign power. Some of the surveillances were directed against citizens or organizations whose activities, while not necessarily violent, were thought to be sufficiently subversive to pose a danger to the security of the country. (III, pp. 316–317.) However, from this "subversive activities" standard it was, according to the committee, relatively easy to justify and order electronic surveillance against American citizens and organizations, not primarily because of their own activities, but because they were believed to be adversely influenced, whether consciously or not, by persons acting under the direction of foreign power. The electronic surveillance of Martin Luther King was justified not because King himself posed any threat to national security, but because of the possibility that two of King's advisers were associated with the Communist party. (III, p. 318.)

The infinite elasticity of the "national security" criteria unrestrained by any judicial or external check, has been dramatically underscored in recent years by a series of surveillance s directed against Government employees and journalists for the avowed purposes of identifying the sources of "leaks" of classified information. (III. p. 321.)

[28] Cf. See *Youngstown Sheet & Tube Co. v. Sawyer,* 343 U.S. 579, 72 S.Ct. 863, 96 L.Ed. 1153 (1952) (Jackson, J. concurring).

foreign power; or (2) are "knowingly engaging in clandestine intelligence activities for or on behalf of a foreign power under circumstances which indicate that such activities would be harmful to the security of the United States." For such surveillance to be undertaken, a judicial warrant must be secured on the basis of a showing of "probable cause" that the target is a "foreign power" or an "agent of a foreign power." Thus the courts for the first time will ultimately rule on whether such foreign intelligence surveillance should occur.

Before a warrant can be requested, a designated Executive Branch official must first certify in writing to the court that the information sought to be obtained is "foreign intelligence information" as defined, and that the purpose of the surveillance is to obtain such information. Moreover the Attorney General is required to make a finding that the requirements for a warrant application have been met before he authorizes the application. These provisions provide an internal check on applications for electronic surveillance by establishing a method of written accountability within the Executive Branch.

Other procedural safeguards assure that the Government will not engage in illegitimate eavesdropping or misuse of information so acquired. The bill requires that each order include a detailed procedure to minimize the extraneous or irrelevant information that might otherwise be obtained; information acquired concerning United States citizens or lawful resident aliens can be used and disclosed only for foreign intelligence purposes or in connection with the enforcement of the criminal law; even if the target is not a United States citizen or lawful resident alien information acquired can only be used for "lawful purposes"; detailed provisions safeguard the right of the criminal defendant to challenge the validity and propriety of the surveillance; if the target is an individual or specified types of foreign powers the application for a warrant must state the means by which the surveillance will be effected; when the target is an "official" foreign power, as defined, the application must still designate the type of electronic surveillance to be used and whether or not physical entry will be used to effect the surveillance; finally, the Attorney General is required to transmit to the Congress annually certain statistics concerning the surveillances engaged in during the preceding year.

Most importantly, the disclaimer in 18 U.S.C. § 2511(3) is replaced by provisions that assure that this bill, together with chapter 119, will be the *exclusive* means by which electronic surveillance covered by this bill, and the interception of wire and oral communications, may be conducted.

A difficult issue posed during committee deliberations was whether foreign intelligence electronic surveillance should be limited to situations involving the commission of a crime. S. 1566 provides four limited situations in which natural persons may be made the target of an electronic surveillance without a probable cause showing of criminal activity. The first and least problematic involves persons who are neither citizens nor permanent resident aliens but who are officers or employees of a "foreign power". This provision is primarily designed to cover foreigners who are employed in diplomatic and consular offices in the United States. It is unchanged from the provisions in S. 3197.

The second situation, which constitutes a major change from S. 3197, involves an alien (other than an alien who has been admitted for permanent resident) who "knowingly engages in clandestine intelligence activities for or on behalf of a foreign power under circumstances which indicate that such activities would be harmful to the security of the United States." S. 3197 made no such distinction between aliens and United States citizens in the application of the noncriminal standard. S. 1566, however, broadens the noncriminal standard of S. 3197 in cases involving nonresident aliens.

The third situation involves a United States citizen or permanent resident alien who, "pursuant to the direction of an intelligence service or intelligence network of a foreign power, knowingly collects or transmits information or material to an intelligence service or intelligence network of a foreign power in a manner intended to conceal the nature of such information or material or the fact of such transmission or collection, under circumstances which indicate the transmission of such information or material would be harmful to the security of the United States, or that lack of knowledge by the United States of such collection or transmission would be harmful to the security of the United States." This standard was also present in S. 3197 except for the addition of "collection" to the activities which would justify surveillance.

The last situation, and the one most disturbing to some members of the committee, is the change from S. 3197 allowing electronic surveillance of one who conspires with or aids or abets another engaged in the noncriminal activities described in the second and third situations. While the Committee feels this is justified, it should be emphasized that the aider or abetter cannot be an unknowing dupe. The bill requires that he know that the person he is aiding is engaged in the described activities.

S. 3197 did not extend the doctrine of conspiracy to the non-criminal standard. Thus, insofar as S. 1566 loosens the language of the non-criminal standard for certain aliens, and permits the application of conspiracy to that standard in all cases, the bill posed problems to some members of the committee.

Although there is precedent for departing from a strict criminal standard in the issuance of search warrants deemed compatible with the fourth amendment, *see e.g., Camara v. Municipal Court*, 387 U.S. 523 (1967)[3]; *Almeida-Sanchez v. United States*, 413 U.S. 266[4] (1973); *cf. United States v. Martinez-Fuerte*, 428 U.S. 543 (1976)[5], (no warrant required at all), those decisions did not involve national security surveillance. It should also be pointed out, however, that in the *Keith* case, *supra*, the Supreme Court noted that the reasons for domestic security surveillance may differ from those justifying surveillance for domestic crimes and that, accordingly, "different standards may be compatible with the Fourth Amendment if they are reasonable both in relation to the legitimate needs of Government for intelligence information and the protected rights of our citizens. For the warrant application may vary according to the governmental interest to be enforced and the nature of citizens rights deserving protection."[29] As indicated in the section-by-section analysis, this departure from the general principle that such surveillance must be linked to criminal activity is intended to be a narrow, circumscribed one, reflecting the deep concern of the committee. This bill authorizes electronic surveillance in a limited number of non-criminal situations only under the twin safeguards of an independent review by a neutral judge and his application of a "probable cause standard".

---
[3] 87 S.Ct. 1727, 18 L.Ed.2d 930.
[4] 93 S.Ct. 2535, 37 L.Ed.2d 596.
[5] 96 S.Ct. 3074, 49 L.Ed.2d 1116.

It is important to note that the committee's favorable recommendation of this legislation in no way reflects any judgment that it would also be appropriate to depart from the standard of criminal activity as the basis for using other intrusive investigative techniques. The bill does not impliedly authorize departure from the standard of criminality in other aspects of national security investigations or intelligence collection directed at Americans without the safeguards of judicial review and probable cause. It remains to determine, in fashioning a charter for the use of informants, physical surveillance and other investigative procedures, whether the departure from a criminal standard is an acceptable basis for investigating United States citizens on grounds of national security.

Conforming amendments in S. 1566 integrate existing electronic surveillance provisions in title III of the Omnibus Crime Control and Safe Streets Act with the new provisions of the bill.

Section-by-Section Analysis

Section 1 of the bill provides that the Act may be cited as the "Foreign Intelligence Surveillance Act of 1977".

Section 2 of the bill amends title 18, United States Code, by adding a new chapter 120 composed of sections 2521–2527 as follows:

Section 2521

Subsection (a) provides that except for those terms specifically defined in this section the definitions of chapter 119, relating to the interception of wire and oral communications, apply to this chapter as well.

---
[29] 407 U.S. at 322; see also, *Zweibon v. Mitchell*, 516 F.2d at 669.

A. "Foreign Power"

Subsection (b)(1) defines "foreign power" in six separate ways:

(1) "A foreign government or any component thereof, whether or not recognized by the United States." This category would include foreign embassies and consulates and similar "official" foreign governmental establishments which are located in the United States.

(2) "A faction of a foreign nation or nations, not substantially composed of permanent resident aliens or citizens of the United States." This category is intended to include factions of a foreign nation or nations which are in a contest for power over, or control of the territory of, a foreign nation or nations. The faction must be foreign-based and controlled from abroad. Specifically excluded from this category is any faction of a foreign government or government which is substantially composed of permanent resident aliens or citizens of the United States.

(3) "An entity, which is openly acknowledged by a foreign government or governments to be directed and controlled by such foreign government or governments." This is a category which was not specifically delineated in S. 3197. Certain changes have been made in the S. 3197 warrant requirements with respect to specific foreign powers which generally require less information to be given to the judge and allow the surveillance to be continued for a longer period of time without the need for reauthorization. This decision to treat certain "foreign powers" differently in terms of warrant requirements was made at the insistence of the Administration. The Committee is satisfied, however, that the distinction is sufficiently limited so as not to pose any threat of abuse. Thus, it is only with respect to "entities" openly acknowledged by a foreign government to be directed and controlled by such foreign government—those which are clearly arms of a government or governments and not privately controlled—that are subject to the extended warrants granted on a lesser showing. Such "official" entities are treated in the same manner as the government they serve.

(4) "A foreign-based terrorist group." This category refers to a foreign-based group whose activities involve "terrorism", as defined. The committee recognizes that many international terrorist groups have members from various nations, and may not in fact have any clearly definable "base." Nevertheless, under this definition the group must be "foreign-based;" that is, it must not be based in the United States, although it may carry out terrorist acts in this country. It is the Committee's belief that a domestic terrorist group should be subjected to electronic surveillance only pursuant to Title III. Where, however, a group is not domestically based, but derives strength and

refuge by organizing, planning, and preparing its terrorist activities outside the jurisdiction of the United States, then that group is a legitimate target for intelligence surveillance under this bill no matter what the citizenship of its members.

(5) "A foreign-based political organization, not substantially composed of permanent resident aliens or citizens of the United States." This category is intended to include, for example, those foreign political parties which are mere instrumentalities of a foreign government and which are not substantially composed of Americans. This category clearly does not include organizations comprised of Americans of Greek, Irish, Jewish, Chinese or other extraction, who have joined together out of interest in or concern for the country of their ethnic origin.

(6) "An entity, which is directed and controlled by a foreign government or governments." This category, found verbatim in S. 3197, would include an entity which appears to be a legitimate commercial establishment but which is actually being utilized by a foreign government as a cover for espionage activities. A law firm, public relations firm, or other legitimate concern which merely represents a foreign government or its interests is not, by definition, an entity under this category. The question of whether a group, commercial enterprise, or organization comes within the scope of this definition is one for the court to determine on the basis of a probable cause standard.

B. "Agent of a Foreign Power"

Subsection (b)(2) defines an "agent of a foreign power" in two separate ways. Subparagraph (A)(i) includes officers or employees of foreign powers who are not United States citizens or aliens lawfully admitted for permanent residence. The definition is framed in this way because it is presumed that nonresident aliens who are officers or employees of a foreign power are likely sources of foreign intelligence information. Given the tenuous relationship of foreign officers or employees with the United States and their close relationship with a foreign power, this standard is considered by the Committee to be reasonable in light of the Government's legitimate need for foreign intelligence information and the nature of the interests upon which the search would intrude. The reference to employees of a foreign power is meant to include those persons who have a normal employee-employer relationship.[30] The subparagraph is not intended to encompass such foreign visitors as professors, lecturers, ex-

---

[30] This bill is not intended, of course, to repeal or abrogate the Vienna Convention on Diplomatic Relations, which was ratified by the Senate and came into effect in the United States on December 13, 1972. The Convention provides that diplomatic agents, their residences (article 30(1)), and their missions (article 22 (1) and (3)), as well as their official correspondence (Article 27(2) and 30(2)), are "inviolable." The obligations of the Convention are reciprocal; when another nation has failed to maintain the inviolability of American diplomatic commu-

change students, performers, or athletes, even if they are receiving remuneration or expenses from their home government in such capacity.

Subparagraphs (A) (ii), (iii) and (B) of subsection (b)(2) comprise the second definition of "agent of a foreign power." They define an agent in terms of the activities in which he is engaged for or on behalf of a foreign power.

Subparagraph (A)(ii) defines an agent of a foreign power as a person who is not a citizen or resident alien of the United States who "knowingly engages in clandestine intelligence activities for or on behalf of a foreign power under circumstances which indicate that such activities would be harmful to the United States." This category could potentially include illegal aliens, foreign terrorists, exchange visitors, foreign businessmen, foreign students, and foreign seamen. While it is expected that in most cases such foreigners would, even under this standard, be violating United States criminal laws, and would certainly be subject to deportation (see, e.g., 8 U.S.C. § 1251(a)(7)), there is no specific requirement that the activity providing the justification for the surveillance constitute a Federal crime. This separate non-criminal standard for foreigners is a significant change from S. 3197. In favorably reporting S. 3197 during the 94th Congress, the Committee accepted the need for a narrower noncriminal standard applicable to *all* persons within the United States. S. 1566, however, while retaining the S. 3197 noncriminal standard largely intact for United States citizens and lawful resident aliens, alters it substantially when other persons—not United States citizens or resident aliens—are the targets of the surveillance.

For example, no reference is made to the requirement of "direction" from a foreign power's "intelligence service or intelligence network", nor is there any requirement of "collection" or "transmission" in a secret manner. Because it eliminates such requirements when foreign visitors—and only when foreign visitors—are involved, the bill has been criticized by some members of the Committee. The Fourth Amendment to the Constitution speaks in terms of protecting all "persons"—not just United States citizens and law resident aliens—yet the bill establishes a different standard for illegal aliens and foreign visitors.

Proponents of the change, however, point out that where there are compelling considerations of national security, alienage distinctions are clearly

---

nications, this country is free under international law to act similarly towards representatives of that nation (article 47(2a)). The bill does not affect nor does the Committee intend to affect, the legal interpretations of the Vienna Convention under which the Executive Branch has made those treaty obligations effective within the United States.

lawful.[31] The Director of the FBI testified in support of the different standard. He pointed out that large numbers of temporary aliens visit the United States and that many of these aliens are working for foreign intelligence networks. The Select Committee on Intelligence Activities similarly identified the problem, pointing out that one quarter of the Soviet exchange students coming to the United States in a ten-year period were found to be intelligence officers.[32] This Committee is aware *that less intrusive investigative techniques may not be able to obtain sufficient information about persons visiting here only for a limited time:* the additional showing required for United States citizens and permanent resident aliens, therefore, may simply not be possible. Weighing these findings, recommendations, and considerations, as well as the recognized, bipartisan goal of enacting statutory safeguards in this area, the Committee has concluded that this distinction between United States citizens, lawful resident aliens and other aliens should be permitted.

It is clear, however, that this standard—unlike that in subparagraph (A)(i)—is not one which allows surveillance on the basis of the alien's status *per se*. The alien must be engaged in "clandestine intelligence activities" for or on behalf of a foreign power, and while these clandestine activities need not involve criminal violations (as they must for United States citizens and permanent resident aliens), they must be occurring under circumstances which indicate that the activities would be harmful to the security of the United States. Additionally, of course, the determination that sufficient justification exists to conduct electronic surveillance of a foreign visitor or a nonresident alien will be made by a judge, and not a member of the Executive Branch.

Subparagraph (B)(i) is unchanged from the comparable provision S. 3197 and allows surveillance of any person, including a United States citizen or permanent resident alien, who is knowingly engaged in clandestine intelligence activities for or on behalf of a foreign power, which activities involve or will involve a violation of the criminal statutes of the United States. Under this standard the person to be surveilled must be shown to have a knowing and substantial connection with the foreign power for whom he is working. There must be a principal-agent relationship under which the alleged agent has undertaken to provide services for his foreign principal. The agent must also be knowingly engaged in "clandestine intelligence activities" which involve or will involve violations of federal criminal law. It is anticipated that most of the persons surveilled under this section will be violating the criminal espionage laws (Title 18, U.S. Code, sections 792–799, 951; title 42, U.S. Code, section 2272–2278b; and title 50, U.S. Code, section 855).

---

[31] See, e.g., *Hampton v. Mow Sun Wong*, 426 U.S. 88, 115, 96 S.Ct. 1895, 48 L.Ed.2d 495 (1976).
[32] Book I, at 163–164.

C. "Clandestine Intelligence Activities"

The term "clandestine intelligence activities" as used in the bill is directed primarily toward those traditional activities associated with "spying," that is gathering information in a clandestine manner or conducting covert operations for a foreign power.

In addition to those activities which fall within the substantive statutory crimes of spying are activities directly related to spying which are criminal within the meaning of the conspiracy, attempt, and aiding and abetting statutes. Examples would include maintaining a "safehouse" for secret meetings, servicing "letter drops" or "dead drops" to facilitate covert transmission of instructions or information, recruiting new agents, or infiltrating and exfiltrating agents under deep cover to and from the United States.

In addition to conventional "spying," that is, the gathering of information, the intelligence agencies of foreign powers also engage in covert action designed to influence events in this country. Under subparagraph (b)(i), if such political action is covert, involves a violation of federal criminal law, such as the bribery of a public official, and is undertaken directly on behalf of a foreign power, it would be encompassed by this subparagraph. The bill does not authorize electronic surveillance when the activities, even though not public and conducted for a foreign power, involve *lawful* acts such as lobbying or the use of confidential contacts to influence public officials, directly or indirectly, through the dissemination of information. Individuals exercising their right to lobby public officials or to engage in political dissent from official policy may well be in contact with representatives of foreign governments and groups when the issues concern foreign affairs or international economic matters.

They must continue to be free to communicate about such issues and to obtain information or exchange views with representatives of foreign governments or with foreign groups, free from any fear that such contact might trigger the Government's power to conduct electronic surveillance. The intent of the bill is to exclude from the definition of "clandestine intelligence activities" any activity which involves the lawful exercise of first amendment rights of speech, petition, assembly, and association. In no event may lawful political activity within the ambit of the protections afforded by the first amendment be the basis, or form any part of the basis, for finding that any individual is engaged in "clandestine intelligence activities." As a corollary, even the lawful gathering of information done in a confidential manner which is a part of lawful political activity—such as gathering "intelligence" about the political strength and plans of proponents or opponents of a particular policy—would not constitute "clandestine intelligence activity" under this section, where such information gathering is a normal ancillary part of lobbying, organizing political protest, and other political activity protected by the first amendment. Clandestine collection of information regarding the business plans or trade secrets of an American company which merely might provide a competitive advantage to foreign firms, for example, in bidding on a contract with a third country would also not be "clandestine intelligence activity" under subsection (b)(i) unless the foreign disclosure of such financial or business information involved or would involve a violation of federal criminal law. Classified information held by private firms is covered in this way.

And, in the case of an organization whose leaders are engaged in clandestine intelligence activity, such activity cannot be attributed to every member of the group. There must be probable cause that a particular member is himself engaged in such activity, or is conspiring with or knowingly aiding and abetting those who are, before electronic surveillance directed against him may be authorized under this chapter.

Whatever the nature of the activity in question, there must be a clandestine aspect. The statute requires that the alleged foreign agent not only be working for or on behalf of a foreign power or its agent, but also, as a separate requirement, that he be engaged in *clandestine* intelligence activity.

There must also be an effort to obtain information which is being kept secret and is not generally available to the public, or not available to the general public. Therefore, the collection, for whatever purpose, of information within the public domain such as that contained in books, magazines, scientific journals, or newspapers would never constitute "clandestine intelligence activity."[33]

Finally, the word "involve" as used in subparagraph (b)(i) is not intended to encompass any individuals who are not actually engaged in a violation of federal law. It is intended to encompass a violation of federal law which is an integral part of the clandestine intelligence activity even though the clandestine intelligence activity itself might fall between the cracks of the espionage laws. For instance, foreign intelligence agents might be collecting sensitive industrial or technological information. While this collection may not violate the espionage laws, the agents may have to transport the material across state lines, thereby violating federal laws which proscribe the interstate transportation of stolen property. The phrase "will involve", which also appears in this subparagraph, is likewise in no way intended to diminish or dilute the nature of the criminal activity to be established. Its

---

[33] It should be noted that even failing to comply fully with the Foreign Agents Registration Act (22 U.S.C. 611, et seq.) in and of itself is not intended to be clandestine intelligence activity merely because the agent seeks to lobby Congress or influence public opinion on matters relating to the national defense or foreign affairs. If, however, foreign intelligence services hide behind the cover of some person or organization in order to influence American political events and deceive Americans into believing that the opinions or influence is of domestic origin and initiative and such deception is willfully maintained in violation of the Foreign Agents Registration Act, then electronic surveillance might be justified under subsection (b)(i) of S. 1566 if all the other statutory criteria were met.

only purpose is to permit electronic surveillance at some point prior to the time when the actual crime sought to be prevented, for example the actual passage of classified documents, actually occurs. The Committee recognizes that an argument can be made that a person could be surveilled for an inordinate period of time. That is clearly not the intention. Indeed, even upon an assertion by the government that an informant has claimed that someone has been instructed by a foreign power to go into "deep cover" for several years before actually commencing his espionage activities, such facts would not necessarily be encompassed by the immediacy of the phrase "will involve." Under the extension provisions of section 2525(c), discussed *infra*, the judge can insist on examining the fruits of any earlier surveillance when it is necessary to determine whether there is probable cause to believe that the individual will be involved in clandestine intelligence activities.

Subparagraph (B)(ii) includes any person who knowingly engages in activities that involve or will involve sabotage or terrorism for or on behalf of a foreign power. The terms "sabotage" and "terrorism" are defined and require a showing of criminal activity. Again, the nature of the knowledge and agency relationship are the same as required under subparagraph (B)(i). In no event may mere sympathy for, identity of interest with, or vocal support for the goals of a foreign group, even a foreign terrorist group, be sufficient. The terms "involve" and "will involve" are intended to encompass activities directly supportive of some act of terrorism, *e.g.*, the purchase or surreptitious importation into the United States of explosives for use in a terrorist incident, or the planning for an assassination.

D. *The Noncriminal Standard*

Subparagraph (B)(iii) is the so-called non-criminal standard applicable to United States citizens and resident aliens. The only substantive change from the similar provision in S. 3197 is the inclusion—at the Administration's request—of "collection" among the activities justifying the surveillance. This change makes sense. Actual transmission of information to a foreign intelligence service may not yet be completed or may not be detected, yet, given the other criteria under this subparagraph, collection alone should be sufficient to justify the surveillance.

During the course of the hearings on S. 1566, testimony was elicited from various witnesses as to the precise contours of the noncriminal standard. All witnesses agreed that the phrase would, with limited exception for certain activity, refer to activity constituting a Federal or State crime. On the basis of testimony of, and discussions with, the Department of Justice, the committee agreed to include language covering certain narrowly circumscribed intelligence activities closely related to criminal espionage but not presently constituting an offense under Federal law. Such a decision was made despite serious reservations voiced by various members of the Committee. In introducing S. 1566, Senator Kennedy stated that he had "never been altogether satisfied with the explanations offered by the Department of Justice as to why a noncriminal standard is necessary at all."[34] This view continues to be shared by many Committee members. However, for various reasons—perhaps the most important being the desire of the Committee to at long last enact important statutory safeguards in this area and to avoid the acrimony of past fruitless efforts—the Committee has again agreed to include in S. 1566 a narrow, carefully circumscribed, noncriminal standard. *The Administration has agreed, however, to draft a revision of the espionage laws which might enable this narrow noncriminal standard to be repealed.*[35] In the interim, the Committee believes that this subparagraph contains standards sufficiently stringent as to be incapable of abuse.

Although the Administration is committed to using the criminal standards wherever possible, there are several situations where this subparagraph may be necessary. For example, the situation where the information being collected or transmitted is not "information relating to the national defense," as defined by the courts. *Gorin v. United States*, 312 U.S. 19 (1941)[6]; *United States v. Heine*, 151 F.2d 813 (2d Cir. 1945) (L. Hand, J.), cert. denied, 328 U.S. 833 (1946)[7]. The example is also cited where Federal agents have witnessed a series of "meets" or "drops" between a hostile foreign intelligence officer and a citizen, information is being passed, but the federal agents have been unable to determine precisely what information is being transmitted. A third example referred to is where personally damaging information is being gathered about persons for purposes of blackmailing them into becoming foreign agents. This may or may not be a crime, depending on whether the technical requirements of the blackmail or extortion statutes have been satisfied, but the national security could be threatened, and electronic surveillance may enable the government to protect the victim from such attempts. Another example is where a foreign intelligence service is targeting the installations or personnel of a foreign government in the United States. There still must be a nexus to our national security, but such nexus may well exist where the foreign government is an ally of the United States and a compromise of the former's secrets to an adversary nation may endanger our own security.[36]

---
[6] 61 S.Ct. 429, 85 L.Ed. 488.
[7] 66 S.Ct. 975, 90 L.Ed. 1608.

---

[34] 123 Cong. Rec. S7857 (daily ed., May 18, 1977).
[35] *Senate Judiciary Hearings*, testimony of Attorney General Griffin Bell, pp 12–46 (June 13, 1977).
[36] Of course, nothing in this subparagraph would allow electronic surveillance of those engaged in protests demonstrations, or other such lawful activity directed against a third country, even if carried out at the direction of a foreign power.

Because of this range of cases, which may or may not fall within the ambit of the espionage laws, but do involve Americans working for a foreign intelligence service under circumstances dangerous to the national security, the Committee has chosen to include this limited non-criminal standard for Americans. The bill permits, in this subparagraph, the surveillance of any person if the Government can establish that there is probable cause to believe that:

(1) Said person was acting pursuant to the direction of a foreign intelligence service;

(2) Said person was knowingly either collecting or transmitting information or material to a foreign intelligence service in a manner intended to conceal either the nature of the information or material or the fact that it was being collected or transmitted; and

(3) The circumstances indicate that the transmission of the information or material would harm the security of the United States, or that lack of knowledge by the United States government about what is being transmitted would harm the security of the United States.

E. "Pursuant to the Direction of an Intelligence Service or Intelligence Network of a Foreign Power"

Perhaps the most important phrase in the subparagraph is the requirement that the target of the surveillance be acting "pursuant to the direction of an intelligence service or intelligence network of a foreign power." This language means that a person must be acting under the direction and control of such power.

There must be a principal-agency relationship under which the alleged agent has undertaken to do the bidding of his foreign principal. This subparagraph, therefore, would not authorize electronic surveillance of United States citizens or permanent resident aliens, whatever the nature of their alleged activities, unless there was probable cause to believe they are acting pursuant to the direction of a foreign intelligence service or network. It does not authorize electronic surveillance under any circumstances for the class of individuals included by the Supreme Court within the scope of the *Keith* decision requiring judicial warrants for alleged threats to security of a domestic nature. It is the intent of this requirement that even if there is some substantial contact between domestic groups or individual citizens and a foreign power, as defined in this bill, no electronic surveillance under this subparagraph may be authorized unless the American is acting under the direction of an intelligence service of a foreign power.

For example, Americans of Greek, Jewish, Irish, or Chinese extraction legitimately may seek to influence United States policy toward the country of their ethnic origin. In the process, such Americans are likely to be in communication with representatives of the governments of those countries in order to learn about particular situations or problems. If an American formulates lobbying efforts in part on the basis of such advice or suggestions he could, in one sense, be said to be following the "direction" of a foreign power. But this subparagraph requires that the agent act pursuant to the "direction of intelligence service or network of a foreign power". Thus, such "direction" from personnel of a foreign power which are not connected with an intelligence service or network would not be a basis for electronic surveillance under this subparagraph. There would have to be additional information specifically indicating the Americans had undertaken to do the bidding of an intelligence service or network, or its agents, rather than merely acting because of an affinity for the same concerns as that foreign power. The key legal doctrine is that of agency; mutual goals or common concerns are not sufficient.

Another example of Americans having contact with foreign powers is the case of Americans who were active in the protest against United States involvement in Vietnam. Some of them may have attended international conferences at which there were representatives of foreign powers, as defined in the bill, or may have been directly in communication with foreign governments concerning this issue. There may have been an exchange of information about activities protesting the Vietnam war. But if there merely had been evidence that an American was coordinating the dates of planned peace demonstrations in the United States to coincide with similar activities abroad in order to maximize worldwide public attention, that would not have sufficed to find probable cause that the American was acting under the direction of a foreign intelligence service as required by this subparagraph. Additional evidence would have been required indicating that the American had undertaken to follow the instruction of a foreign intelligence service or network, rather than simply trying to coordinate his independent effort with related activities abroad.

For both of these two illustrations, it should be emphasized that even if there was probable cause to believe an American was acting pursuant to the direction of a foreign intelligence service, the court would also have to find probable cause to believe that the American was engaged in the secret collection or transmission of information or material to a foreign power. This is a separate and distinct requirement.

Further, an organization substantially composed of Americans, whether residing in the United States or abroad, would not come within the definition of acting pursuant to the direction of a foreign intelligence service merely because it was part of a worldwide confederation of national organizations. Even if a domestic organization were found to be acting through its leaders at the direction of a foreign intelligence service, an individual's mere membership in that organization, without more information about his own undertaking to do so, would not constitute probable cause to believe that that particular member was acting pursuant to the direction of a foreign intelligence service for purposes of this subparagraph.

Finally, it is necessary that the person be *aware* he is acting on behalf of a foreign power. An American might be secretly collecting information about important technology, for example, and have been misled into the belief he was acting for a research institute or a multi-national corporation. Therefore it would not suffice to establish probable cause that the American is, *in fact*, engaged in a covert activity at the direction of a foreign power; the government must establish probable cause that the American knows his efforts are on behalf of a foreign power's intelligence activities.

It also follows, of course, that evidence a foreign power is trying to recruit an American as an agent does not suffice to establish probable cause to believe he has agreed to do the foreign power's bidding and is engaged on its behalf. Before electronic surveillance could be directed against the American, the court would have to find probable cause that the American had responded positively to the recruitment effort and it is now acting as a member of that power's intelligence network.

In applying these various tests, the judge is expected to take all the known circumstances into account, e.g., who the American is, where he is employed, whether he has access to classified or other sensitive information, the nature of the clandestine meetings (whether it is merely in an out-of-the-way restaurant as opposed to a hidden location in a distant city), the method of transmission (handing over a sealed envelope in a public place, as opposed to using a "drop"), and whether there are any other reasonable explanations for the behavior. It is clear, moreover, that the circumstances must not merely be suspicious, but must be sufficient support for a finding of probable cause that the security of the United States would be harmed.

This subparagraph also recognizes that there are certain rare situations where, for example, a citizen who has access to classified information is clandestinely meeting with a known intelligence officer of a hostile foreign power, and it is, therefore, essential that the United States find out what is transpiring between them. In such a rare case, lack of knowledge by the U.S. Government about what is being transmitted might, by definition, harm the security of the United States. In such a situation, if the judge concludes that there is probable cause to believe that such "lack of knowledge would be harmful to the security of the United States," an American could also be targeted.

The Committee emphasizes that this narrow inclusion for electronic surveillance without probable cause to believe that the targets are engaged in criminal activity is, of course, not intended to provide a bootstrap for even broader authority to investigate noncriminal activity of Americans absent the safeguards in this bill. The Committee emphasizes that S. 1566 establishes a legislative scheme to deal only with electronic surveillance; the use of other investigative techniques do not fall within the scope of this bill.

F. "Conspires or Aids and Abets"

Subparagraphs (A)(iii) and (B)(iv) are provisions which allow electronic surveillance of persons who knowingly conspire with or aid or abet persons who could otherwise be subjected to electronic surveillance under the provisions discussed above. Insofar as the doctrines of conspiracy and aiding and abetting have been made applicable to the noncriminal standards of S. 1566—a change from S. 3197—some members of the Committee are concerned. They feel that the safeguards and protections found in the narrow, carefully circumscribed language of the noncriminal standards (especially in the non-criminal standard applicable to United States citizens) can be abused through the use of the conspiracy and aiding and abetting language.

Under (A)(iii) non-resident aliens can be subjected to electronic surveillance by conspiring with or aiding or abetting another non-resident alien, knowing that person is engaged in clandestine intelligence activities for or on behalf of a foreign power. Under (B)(iv) a person can be subjected to electronic surveillance if he conspires with or aids or abets a person knowing that person is engaged in the activities described in subparagraphs (B)(i) through (iii). Under both (A)(iii) and (B)(iv) the Government would have to establish probable cause that the prospective target knew both that the person with whom he was conspiring or whom he was aiding or abetting was engaging in the described activities as an agent of a foreign power and that his own conduct was assisting or furthering such activity. The knowledge requirement is therefore applicable to both the status of the person being aided by the proposed subject of the surveillance and the nature of the activity being promoted. The innocent dupe who unwittingly aids a foreign intelligence officer cannot be targeted under this provision.[37]

An illustration of the "knowing" requirement is provided by the case of Dr. Martin Luther King. Dr. King was subjected to electronic surveillance on "national security grounds" when he continued to associate with two advisers whom the Government had apprised him were suspected of being American Communist party members and, by implication, agents of a foreign power. Dr. King's mere continued association and consultation with those advisers, despite the Government's warnings, would clearly not have been a sufficient basis under this bill to target Dr. King as the subject of electronic surveillance.

---

[37] In the case of a person alleged to be knowingly aiding or abetting those engaged in terrorist activities on behalf of a foreign power, such a person might be assisting a group engaged in both lawful political activity and unlawful terrorist acts. In such a case, it would be necessary to establish probable cause that the individual was aware of the terrorist activities undertaken by the group and was knowingly furthering them, and not merely that he was aware of and furthering their lawful activity.

Indeed, even if there had been probable cause to believe that the advisers alleged to be Communists were engaged in criminal clandestine intelligence activity for a foreign power within the meaning of this section, and even if there were probable cause to believe Dr. King was aware they were acting for a foreign power, it would also have been necessary under this bill to establish probable cause that Dr. King was knowingly engaged in furthering his advisers' criminal clandestine intelligence activities. Absent one or more of these required showings, King could not have been found to be one who knowingly aids or abets a foreign agent.[38]

Subsection (b)(3) defines "terrorism" as criminal activities which are violent or dangerous to human life. The purpose of the activities must be either the forceful intimidation of the civilian population, the intimidation of national leaders in order to force a significant change in governmental policy, or the affecting of Governmental conduct by assassination or kidnaping. Examples of such activities would be the detonation of bombs in a metropolitan area, the kidnapping of a high-ranking government official, the hijacking of an airplane in a deliberate and articulated effort to force the government to release a certain class of prisoners or to suspend aid to a particular foreign country, or the deliberate assassination of persons to strike fear into others to deter them from exercising their rights.

Subsection (b)(4) defines "sabotage" as activities which would constitute crimes under chapter 105 of title 18, United States Code, if conducted against the United States. In S. 3197 only actual violations of chapter 105 were included in the definition of sabotage. But by its terms, chapter 105 makes criminal only acts of sabotage against United States government facilities. S. 1566 has expanded the definition of sabotage to include similar acts when committed against a State or another nation's facilities and materials relating to defense. Thus, sabotage directed against State and local police facilities and equipment, or against the defense facilities of foreign nations, would constitute sabotage under this definition.[39] Of course, electronic surveillance under this chapter could be undertaken only if such sabotage was knowingly con-

---

[38] Mere membership in the United States Communist Party is not sufficient under this bill to establish probable cause that a person is acting under the direction and control of a foreign power or that he is engaged in clandestine intelligence activities.

Moreover, even if additional information established probable cause to believe some members of the party were acting under the direction and control of a foreign power, neither efforts to collect information about the plans and program of the civil rights movement or other political protests, nor efforts to stimulate or shape them would constitute clandestine intelligence activity within this section. Gathering information about the movement would neither be criminal espionage nor the kind of economic or technical information relating to the national security whose collection might satisfy the noncriminal standard. Similarly, since the civil rights protest movement itself involved constitutionally protected rights of association, speech and petition for redress of grievances, efforts by a foreign power to involve itself in such a movement are intended to be specifically excluded from the definition of clandestine intelligence activity.

[39] Under 18 U.S.C. 956, it is a Federal crime for persons within the United States to conspire to injure or destroy property located in and owned by a foreign government.

ducted for or on behalf of a foreign power and was related to foreign intelligence as defined. The Committee agrees with the Administration that where persons are knowingly engaged in sabotage of State or foreign facilities for or on behalf of a foreign power, such persons should be subjected to foreign intelligence electronic surveillance in this country even before there is probable cause to believe that they will engage in sabotage against Federal facilities.

G. "Foreign Intelligence Information"

Subsection (b)(5) defines "foreign intelligence information" to include five types of information, which, while not mutually exclusive, tend to be distinguishable. Subparagraph (A) of this subsection is defined as information deemed necessary for the United States to protect itself against actual or potential attack or other similarly grave hostile acts of foreign power or its agents. This category is intended to encompass information which relates to foreign military capabilities and intentions, as well as acts of force or aggression which would have serious adverse consequences to the national security of the United States. The term "hostile acts" must be read in the context of the subparagraph which is keyed to actual or potential attack on the United States. Thus, only the most "grave" types of "hostile acts" would be envisioned as falling within this provision.[40]

Subparagraph (B) of this subsection includes information which because of its importance is deemed essential (i) to the national defense or the security of the Nation or (ii) to the conduct of the foreign affairs of the United States. This subparagraph also requires that the information sought involve "information with respect to foreign powers or territories", and would therefore not include information about the views or planned statements or activities of Members of Congress, executive branch officials, or private citizens concerning the foreign affairs of the United States.

It is anticipated that the types of "foreign intelligence information" defined in subparagraphs (A) and (B) will be the types most often sought when an electronic surveillance is instituted against a foreign power as defined in

---

[40] In testifying last year in the House Hearings on S. 3197, Attorney General Levi confirmed this interpretation:

"Mr. Kastenmeier. How do you understand the term other hostile acts of a foreign power? Is there enough precedent or other language so that we understand precisely what the hostile acts constitute, whether a criticism of our participation in the Vietnam war would be a hostile act? Or attempting to board an American ship on the high seas is a more classical case. How broad is the hostile acts?

"Attorney General Levi. I certainly wouldn't think that hostile acts involved criticism. I would assume—I don't know that we can get a better definition. But it does after all say, 'against actual or potential attack or other hostile acts.' So that it is the actual or potential attack which really gives the flavor to what is meant.

"Mr. Kastenmeier. In other words, it must be seen in a broader context, and therefore be much more limited?

"Attorney General LEVI. I would think so." (House Hearings 10-11, emphasis added.)

Section 2521(b)(1) (A), (B), (C), and (E), or against most foreign agents as defined in Section 2521(b)(2)(A)(i).

Subparagraph (C) of this subsection includes information which is deemed necessary for the United States to protect against terrorism by a foreign power or foreign agent. It is anticipated that the type of information described in this subparagraph will be the type sought when an electronic surveillance is instituted against the type of foreign power defined in Section 2521(b)(1)(D), or against the type of foreign agent defined in Section 2521(b)(2)(B)(ii).

Subparagraph (D) of this subsection includes information which is deemed necessary for the United States to protect against sabotage by a foreign power or foreign agent.

Subparagraph (E) of this subsection includes information which is deemed necessary to the ability of the United States to protect against the clandestine intelligence activities of an intelligence service or network of a foreign power or a foreign agent. This subparagraph encompasses classic counterintelligence information; that is, information deemed necessary to the nation's ability to discover and protect against the activities of clandestine intelligence services of foreign powers in the United States. This subsection is not intended to encompass information sought about dissident political activity by United States citizens allegedly "necessary" to determine the nature and extent of any possible involvement in those activities by the intelligence services of foreign powers. Such a dragnet approach to counterintelligence has been the basis for past improper investigations of citizens and is not intended to be included as a permissible avenue of "foreign intelligence" collection under this subparagraph. Nor does this subparagraph include efforts to prevent "news leaks" or to prevent publication of such leaked information in the American press, unless there is reason to believe that such publication is itself being done by an agent of a foreign intelligence service and that such publication would harm the national security.

Most importantly, all five subparagraphs set out standards establishing a nexus between the information sought and the desired end. Subparagraph (B) requires that the information sought be "essential" while the other subparagraphs establish a standard of "necessary."

Where the term "necessary" is used, the Committee intends to require more than a showing that the information would be useful or convenient. When the term "essential" is used, the Committee intends to require a showing that the information is important and required but not that it is of utmost importance or indispensable.

The use of these standards is intended by the committee to mandate that a significant degree of need be demonstrated by those seeking the surveillance. For example, it is often contended that the intelligence analyst, if not the policymaker himself, must have every possible bit of information about a subject because it might prove an important piece of the larger picture. In that sense, any information relating to the specified purposes might be called "necessary" but such a reading is clearly not intended.

"Essential" is used in subparagraph (B) because of the more amorphous nature of the information which can be acquired under this subparagraph. While subparagraph (A) deals with positive foreign intelligence involving actual or potential attack or comparable hostile acts and subparagraphs (C), (D), and (E) cover terrorist, sabotage, and counterintelligence information, subparagraph (B) potentially brings within the definition of foreign intelligence information a broader range of material dealing with the national defense and foreign affairs of the United States.

In addition, information about a United States citizen's private affairs shall not be deemed "foreign intelligence information" unless it directly relates to his activities on behalf of a foreign power. This interest is achieved by including in each subsection of the foreign intelligence definition the requirement that the information sought actually "relates to" the type of information deemed necessary or essentional. For example, the government could not seek purely personal information about a United States citizen or permanent resident alien, who is a suspected spy, upon a theory that it might learn something which would be "compromising." Instead, the bill makes clear that the only information about United States citizens or permanent resident aliens which may be sought must not only be necessary to the ability of the U.S. to protect against clandestine intelligence activities, but must also "relate to" the activities themselves. This restriction might not always be fully applicable to agents of foreign powers as defined in Section 2521(b)(2)(A)(i), because information about their private lives may itself be foreign intelligence information. For example, such information might identify their true status or reveal the intentions or activities of the foreign power of which they are officers or employees.

H. "Electronic Surveillance"

Paragraph (6) defines "electronic surveillance" to include four separate types of activities.

Subparagraph (A) makes a major improvement over the language of S. 3197 by protecting United States citizens and resident aliens in the United States from being targeted in their international communications without a judicial warrant no matter where the surveillance is being carried out. Under S. 3197 such targeting did not fall within the confines of the bill; this provision is, therefore, a significant extension of the protections afforded United States citizens and lawful resident aliens. The subparagraph specifically brings within the procedures of S. 1566 the acquisition of the contents of a wire or radio communication of United States citizens and permanent resident aliens in the United States by intentionally targeting that particular, known United States citizen or resident alien, under circumstances in which a person has a reasonable expectation of privacy and a warrant would be required for law enforcement purposes. Thus, for example, the "watch-listing" activities of the National Security Agency, if directed against United States citizens in the United States, would require a warrant under this regulation.

Subparagraph (B) includes the acquisition, by an electronic, mechanical, or other surveillance device, of the contents of a wire communication without the consent of any party thereto when such acquisition occurs in the United States while the communication is being transmitted by wire. As this subdefinition makes clear, the location of the parties to the wire communication is immaterial if the acquisition occurs within the United States. Thus, either a wholly domestic telephone call or an international telephone call can be the subject of electronic surveillance under this subdefinition if the acquisition of the content of the call takes place in this country and if such acquisition occurs "while the communication is being transmitted by wire." This second qualifier is necessary because the definition of "wire communication" under 18 U.S.C. 2510(1) includes any communication "made in whole or in part" through wire facilities. Because most telephonic and telegraphic communications are transmitted at least in part by microwave radio transmissions, subdefinition (B) is meant to apply only to those surveillance practices which are effected by tapping into the wire over which the communication is being transmitted. The interception of the microwave radio transmission is meant to be covered by subdefinition (C) if the sender and all intended recipients are located within the United States, or by subdefinition (A) if it is done through the targeting of a United States citizen or resident alien in the United States.

Subparagraph (C) includes the intentional acquisition by an electronic, mechanical, or other surveillance device of the contents of a radio communication, without the consent of any party thereto, made with a reasonable expectation of privacy and under circumstances where a warrant would be required for law enforcement purposes, where both the sender and all intended recipients are located within the United States, *i.e.*, a totally domestic radio communication. This part of the definition would reach not only the acquisition of communications made wholly by radio but also the acquisition of "wire communications" by means of intercepting the radio transmitted portion of those communications within the United States. The territorial limits of this subdefinition are not dependent on the point of acquisition, as is the case with subdefinition (B), but on the locations of the communicants. Thus, the acquisition of radio communications outside the territorial limits of the United States would be covered if all of the communicants were located within the United States. Only acquisition of those domestic radio communications made with a reasonable expectation of privacy where a warrant would be required for law enforcement purposes would be included in the term "electronic surveillance." This would exclude, for example, commercial broadcasts, as well as ham radio and citizen band radio broadcasts (cf. 47 U.S.C. section 605); *United v. Hall*, 488 F.2d 193 (9th Cir. 1973).

Only "intentional" acquisitions of domestic communications are within this subdefinition because, by their very nature, radio transmissions may be intercepted anywhere in the world, even though the sender and all intended recipients are in the United States. Thus, intelligence collection may be targeted against foreign or international communications but accidently and unintentionally acquire communications intended to be totally domestic. It is the Committee's understanding that these communications are immediately destroyed. Absent the word "intentional", however, these accidental interceptions, even if the contents are immediately destroyed, could leave these agencies open to civil or criminal liability for failing to secure a judicial warrant.

The effect of subparagraphs (A), (B) and (C) of Section 2521 (b)(6), therefore, is to include within the term "electronic surveillance" the nonconsensual acquisition of all domestic radio communications made with a reasonable expectation of privacy, the nonconsensual acquisition within the United States of all wire communications, as defined in 18 U.S.C. Section 2510(1), except those international wire communications which are acquired by intercepting the radio transmitted portions of the communications, and the targeting of particular United States citizens or resident aliens in the United States in order to acquire international communications made with a reasonable expectation of privacy.

The reason for excepting from the definition of "electronic surveillance" the acquisition of international radio transmissions, including international wire communications when acquired by intercepting radio transmissions when not accomplished by targeting a particular United States person in the United States, is to exempt from the procedures of the bill certain signals intelligence activities of the National Security Agency.

Although it is desirable to develop legislative controls in this area, the Committee has concluded that these practices are sufficiently different from traditional electronic surveillance techniques, both conceptually and technologically, that, except when they target particular United States citizens or resident aliens in the United States, they should be considered separately by the Congress.[41] The fact that this bill does not bring these activities within its purview, however, should not be viewed as congressio-

---

[41] The nature of National Security Agency activities, the purposes of such activities and the technological problems associated with such activities have been carefully documented by the Church committee in vol. III, pages 733 *et seq*. See also, II Church committee 58–60, 108 and 308–311.

nal authorization of such activities. This committee merely recognizes that this particular signals intelligence activity is not covered by the procedures outlined in this bill. In any case, the requirements of the Fourth Amendment would, of course, continue to apply to this type of communications intelligence activity.[42]

Subparagraph (D) brings within the definition of "electronic surveillance" the acquisition of information, not transmitted as a wire communication or radio communication, by the installation or use of an electronic, mechanical, or other surveillance device for monitoring in the United States under circumstances in which a person has a reasonable expectation of privacy and a warrant would be required for law enforcement purposes. This is intended to include the acquisition of oral communications made by a person exhibiting an expectation that such utterances are not subject to acquisition, under circumstances justifying such expectation. In addition, it is meant to include the installation of beepers and "transponders," if a warrant would be required in the ordinary criminal context. *United States v. Holmes*, 537 F.2d 227 (5th Cir. 1976). It could also include miniaturized television cameras and other sophisticated devices not aimed merely at communications.

This part of the definition is meant to be broadly inclusive, because the effect of including a particular means of surveillance is not to prohibit it but to subject it to judicial oversight. It is not meant to include, however, the acquisition of those international radio transmissions or international wire communications, when acquired by intercepting radio transmissions, which are not acquired by targeting a particular United States person in the United States. Nor, as earlier indicated, is it meant to require a court order in any case where a search warrant would not be required in an ordinary criminal context.

It has been held, for example, that Fourth Amendment protections do not extend to activities undertaken in the open where a participant could reasonably anticipate that his activities might be observed.[43] But two persons in a public park, far from any stranger, would not reasonably anticipate that their conversations could be overhead from a far through a directional microphone, and so would retain their right of privacy. Of course, law enforcement officials may, if they wish, continue to obtain an ordinary search warrant or chapter 119 court order if the facts and circumstances so justify it.

The definition of "electronic surveillance" comprising the interception of wire communications and radio transmissions has an explicit exception where any party has consented to the interception. This is intended to per-

---

[42] The Committee notes with approval, however, that broadscale electronic surveillance of American citizens while abroad has been limited in part by both the President's Executive Order applicable to the foreign intelligence agencies and Department of Justice directives to the intelligence community. See Executive Order No. 11905. February 18, 1976; testimony of Attorney General Edward H. Levi before the Church Committee, November 6, 1975, p. 15. Thus, the surveillance of journalists, such as in the Joseph Kraft case, would be prohibited.

[43] *Air Pollution Variance Board v. Western Alfalfa Corp.*, 416 U.S. 861, 94 S.Ct. 2114, 40 L.Ed.2d 607 (1974).

petuate the existing law regarding consensual interceptions found in 18 U.S.C. section 2511(2)(c) and in the case law interpreting 47 U.S.C. section 605.[44] Whether consent may be inferred in a particular case will depend on the facts and circumstances.

That part of the definition of "electronic surveillance" regarding the installation of a device requires that the acquisition of information be under circumstances in which a person has a constitutionally protected right of privacy. There is no such right in those situations where the interception is consented to by at least one party to the conversation. For instance, a body microphone placed on an informer with his consent is an installation of a device to acquire information, but a person speaking to the informer has no justifiable expectation that the informer will not repeat, record, or even transmit by a miniature transmitter what the person voluntarily tells the informer. By telling the informer something, the person has, with respect to that information, surrendered his expectation of privacy vis-a-vis the informer. Such a situation is not, of course, limited to body microphones. Telephone conversations to which one of the parties has consented and microphones installed with consent would be functionally equivalent. What is important is the consent. So long as one party to the conversation has consented to the surveillance, the other party has no justifiable expectation of privacy in that which he voluntarily reveals to the party who has consented to the surveillance.[45]

Thus the absence of a reasonable expectation of privacy where one party consents to the surveillance is the equivalent of the explicit consent provision in 18 U.S.C. section 2511(2)(c).

I. "Attorney General"

Paragraph (7) defines "Attorney General" to mean the Attorney General of the United States, the Acting Attorney General, or the Deputy Attorney General. Under S. 3197 only the Attorney General or the Acting Attorney General could approve an application. The Administration had urged the Committee to permit a specially designated Assistant Attorney General to approve an application for surveillance. The Administration cites as the reason for the delegation of this authority to a specially designated assistant Attorney General the need to lessen the administrative burden of the Attorney General which would be perpetuated even after this bill has established the safeguards of a judicial warrant procedure.[46]

Some members of the Committee were troubled that the delegation of this authority as suggested by the Administration would not provide the tight con-

---

[44] *Lopez v. United States*, 373 U.S. 427, 83 S.Ct. 1381, 10 L.Ed.2d 462 (1963); *Rathbun v. United States*, 355 U.S. 197 (1957).
[45] *United States v. White*, 401 U.S. 745, 91 S.Ct. 1122, 28 L.Ed.2d 453 (1971).
[46] *Senate Judiciary Hearings*, Testimony of Attorney General Bell, pp. 18-19 (June 13, 1977).

trol and objective methods that should be required in the foreign intelligence area. These Committee members distinguish Title III applications, for which authority may be delegated, by pointing out that: (1) Such applications are made in conjunction with specific criminal investigations and are, therefore, more capable of objective determination; and (2) that when it comes to foreign intelligence electronic surveillance it is more likely that the heads of various agencies, such as the Secretary of Defense or the Director of the FBI, will intercede directly in the application process, thus placing more pressure on the Attorney General's designate to approve the warrant request. These Committee members believe that, in the last analysis, only the Attorney General could withstand such official pressure and decide the issue in an objective manner.

Senator Kennedy maintained during the hearings on S. 1566 that since administrative inconvenience was not cited by the Ford Administration as a reason for delegating authority to review the applications, the present Department of Justice should not depart from the previous Administration's commitment.[47]

With the assurance of Attorney General Bell in his testimony during the hearings on S. 1566 that he would personally continue to approve applications under the bill until standards of review have been well established,[48] the Committee adopted a modified version of the Administration's proposal. It provides authority for the Attorney General (or the Acting Attorney General) or the Deputy Attorney General—rather than a specially designated Assistant Attorney General—to approve applications for an electronic surveillance order under this chapter.

J. "Minimization"

Paragraph (8) deals with "minimization", i.e., procedures which are designed to limit the acquisition, retention, and dissemination of information that is not foreign intelligence information and which relates to United States citizens or permanent resident aliens. The paragraph defines "minimization procedures" as procedures reasonably designed to minimize the acquisition and retention, and prohibit the dissemination, except as provided in subsections 2526 (a) and (b), of any information concerning United States persons not related to foreign intelligence. Specifically, information concerning Americans must be related to the ability of the United States to protect itself against actual or potential attack or other grave hostile acts of a foreign power or agent of a foreign power, to provide for the national defense or security of the Nation, to provide for the conduct of the foreign affairs of the United States, to protect against terrorism or sabotage by foreign powers or their agents, or to protect against the clandestine intelligence activities of a foreign intelligence service or an agent of a foreign power.

---

[47] *Senate Judiciary Hearings*, pp. 18-20.
[48] *Senate Judiciary Hearings*, Testimony of Attorney General Bell, p. 20 (June 13, 1977).

The minimization requirement of this paragraph is meant generally to parallel the minimization provision in existing law. (18 U.S.C. 2518 (5)) As the courts have noted in construing that section, "It is . . . obvious that no electronic surveillance can be so conducted that innocent conversations can be totally eliminated."[49] In assessing the minimization effort, the court's role is to determine whether "on the whole, the agents have shown a high regard for the right of privacy and have done all they reasonably could to avoid unnecessary intrusion."[50] Absent a charge that the minimization procedures have been completely disregarded, the test of compliance is "whether a good faith effort to minimize was attempted."[51]

Among the factors to be considered in evaluating the reasonableness of the agents' conduct will be the scope of the enterprise under investigation, the location and operation of the subject telephone (or microphone), the Government's expectations of the character of and parties to the calls, the degree of judicial supervision, and the length or brevity of the monitored conversations.[52] Minimization procedures may differ from case to case depending on the nature of the agency relationship, the individuals using the facilities or place to be surveilled, the type of foreign intelligence information sought, and other similar factors. Minimization procedures might also include restrictions on the use of surveillance to times when foreign intelligence information is likely to be obtained, directions that the surveillance cease if it does not produce results of the specified type, requirements that conversations not involving the named target be deleted from the records at an appropriate time, and other requirements specified by the judge. For example, if a citizen or permanent resident alien were using facilities of a foreign agent that were the target of the surveillance, the government would be required to minimize the acquisition and retention of any information that did not relate to foreign intelligence information.

The definition of minimization speaks in terms of *acquistion, retention* and *dissemination*.

By minimizing acquisition the committee envisions, for example, that in a given case, where A is the target of a wiretap, after determining that A's wife is not engaged with him in clandestine intelligence activities, the interception of her calls on the tapped phone, to which A was not a party, would be discontinued as soon as it was realized that she rather than A was the party. In other cases, however, primarily for sophisticated technological reasons, it may not be possible to avoid acquiring all conversations. In these situations minimizing *retention* and *dissemination* becomes most

---

[49] *United States v. Bynum*, 485 F.2d 490, 500 (2nd Cir. 1973), cert. denied 423 U.S. 1005 (1975).
[50] *United States v. Tortorello*, 480 F.2d 764, 784, (2nd Cir.), cert. denied 414 U.S. 886 (1973).
[51] *United States v. Armocida*, 515 F.2d 29, 44 (3d Cir. 1975).
[52] *United States v. Armocida, supra: United States v. James*, 494 F.2d 1007 (D.C. Cir. 1974), cert. denied 419 U.S. 1020 (1975); *United States v. Bynum, supra*.

important. By minimizing retention, the committee intends that information acquired, which does not relate to the approved purposes justifying the warrant, be destroyed. For example, after determining that A's wife is not engaged with her husband in clandestine intelligence activities, her communications, acquired and retained in order to make this determination, would be destroyed. Indeed, even A's communications which are not relevant to his clandestine intelligence activities should be destroyed. In certain cases destruction would take place almost immediately while in other cases the information might be retained for a reasonable period in order to determine whether it did indeed relate to one of the approved purposes. Procedures governing minimization—particularly how long information should be retained and how it should be destroyed once it is deemed irrelevant—are to be fashioned by the court and are, of course, subject to judicial supervision.

The Committee amendment to the minimization definition makes explicit the intent that information not related to an approved purpose not be disseminated. The only exceptions to this prohibition recognized by the Committee are for one of the purposes authorized in Section 2521(b)(8), or for the enforcement of the criminal law under the provisions of Section 2526 (a) and (b). Under the dissemination phrase, information being held to determine relevancy would not be disseminated until the determination was made (or would only be disseminated to those who could determine its relevancy.) It could also mean that, even with respect to information relevant to an approved purpose, dissemination would be restricted to those officials with a need for such information. And, again, the judge, in fashioning the minimization order, could place specific restrictions on the retrieval of such information.

In short, the committee believes that the definition of minimization procedures authorizes and requires that information concerning American citizens and lawful resident aliens be handled in such a way as to assure that it is used only for the purposes specified in the definition and that it cannot be used for any other purpose. Some have suggested that the statutory definition is too general. The committee recognizes, however, that minimization requirements must differ from case to case and that minimization restrictions which are appropriate for some surveillances would be inappropriate for others. A certain flexibility in the statute is, therefore, necessary with careful judicial scrutiny of a particular application the best protection against abuse. But the definition does not give *carte blanche* to the judge. It requires that the procedures be designed to limit the acquisition, retention, and dissemination of information concerning American citizens and lawful resident aliens to that information which is related to one of the approved purposes; in addition, the procedures must provide that the information obtained by the surveillance will not be *used* for an unrelated purpose (other than for enforcement of the criminal law, see section 2526(a), *infra*).

Of course, minimization only applies to information known to concern United States persons. Where communications are encoded or otherwise not processed so the contents of a communication are not known, it would not be possible to minimize the acquisition, retention and dissemination of information concerning United States persons. Nevertheless, the minimization procedures can be structured to apply to other agencies of the Government, so that if an agency different from the intercepting agency decodes or processes the communication, it could be required to minimize the retention and prohibit the dissemination of information therein concerning United States persons.

It should be noted that this provision contains one significant change from the minimization provisions in chapter 119. Section 2518(8)(a) requires that all interceptions be recorded, if possible, and that the tapes not be edited or destroyed for ten years. In a criminal context the maintenance of such tapes and files under court seal ensures that the interceptions will be retained in their original state so that when criminal prosecutions are undertaken it is clear that the evidence is intact and has not been tampered with. Although there may be cases in which information acquired from a foreign intelligence surveillance will be used as evidence of a crime, these cases are expected to be relatively few in number, unlike Title III interceptions the very purpose of which is to obtain evidence of criminal activity. The Committee believes that in light of the relatively few cases in which information acquired under this chapter may be used as evidence, the better practice is to allow the destruction of information that is not foreign intelligence information or evidence of criminal activity. This course will more effectively safeguard the privacy of individuals, ensuring that irrelevant information will not be filed. The committee believes that existing criminal statutes relating to obstruction of justice will defer any efforts to tamper with evidence acquired under this chapter. Such destruction should occur, of course, only pursuant to procedures approved by the court. Destruction insures that the information cannot be used to "taint" a civil or criminal proceeding; accordingly, there is no requirement to index, for purposes of 18 U.S.C. § 3504, interceptions which are destroyed.

The committee is concerned that the surveillance authorized under this chapter not result in the acquisition and retention of information which would adversely affect the exercise of first amendment rights. Nor should any dissemination of the information obtained so affect those rights. Such abuses occurred with distressing frequency in the past. Information relating to the lawful political activity of American citizens or resident aliens is, by definition, not foreign intelligence information and may not be acquired, retained, or disseminated under the provisions of this legislation.

In addition to the general minimization requirements discussed above, there are two specific requirements aimed at particular types of surveillance.

The first requires that appropriate steps be taken to prevent foreign intelligence information, which relates solely to the conduct of foreign affairs, from being maintained in a way that would permit retrieval by reference to the name of a United States citizen or lawful resident alien who is a party to the intercepted communication. This requirement is intended to strike a balance between individual rights and government needs in the delicate situation where American citizens are overheard in conversations which contain information solely related to the conduct of foreign affairs.

In a hypothetical case, for example, an ambassador from an important neutral nation, speaking to a United States Senator, tells the Senator that his country has been secretly approached by a foreign nation concerning a planned attack on the United States. Assuming that the surveillance was initiated against the ambassador and approved in accordance with the procedures of this chapter, there should be no doubt that the information could be retained and used because of its importance and relationship "to the ability of the United States to protect itself against actual or potential attack." At the same time, however, the constitutional rights of speech, association, and privacy of the Senator are implicated. He is plainly not the target of the surveillance, nor could he be, since he is not the "agent of a foreign power." Still he is overheard. The functioning of democratic Government can be impaired if its representatives are deterred from discussing important issues with representatives of other countries for fear that their conversations will be overheard and retained.

There is no perfect solution to the problem. As long as the surveillance was instituted lawfully, the Senator's conversation may be overheard. Given the subject matter of the conversation, it should not be excluded by minimization procedures. If the subject matter is foreign intelligence information, the information should be retained. The alternative—a blanket rule depriving the Government of the right to retain foreign intelligence information, regardless of its importance, because an American citizen was incidentally overheard—is unacceptable. Similarly, it would not be advisable to obligate the Government to render the conversation senseless by deleting all portions of the statements in the conversation made by the Senator.

The Committee believes, however, that every effort should be made to minimize the "chilling effect" that retention of such conversations of Americans will have. No file should be started or maintained under the name of the American citizen when the information relates solely to the conduct of foreign affairs.

The second requirement provides special protections for permanent resident aliens and citizens of the United States who are employed by an entity controlled and directed by a foreign government or governments, which is the target of electronic surveillance and which is not substantially composed of officers or employees of a foreign government or individuals who are agents of a foreign power as defined in Section 2521(b)(2)(B). In such cases, the government must, in addition to the general procedures required by this paragraph present a statement of procedures to prevent the acquisition, retention, and dissemination of communications of permanent resident aliens and United States citizens who are not officers or executives of the entity responsible for activities which involve foreign intelligence information.

K. "United States Person"

Section 2521(b)(9) defines a "United States person" to include a citizen of the United States, an alien lawfully admitted for permanent residence, an unincorporated association of which a substantial number of members are citizens of the United States or permanent resident aliens, and a corporation incorporated in the United States, but not including corporations or associations which are "foreign powers." This definition is new to S. 1566 since S. 3197 made no distinction in its provisions between different types of "persons." As already indicated, this new section has proven troublesome. As Senator Kennedy stated when he introduced S. 1566:

> Another major question mark concerning the bill involving the decision of the Justice Department to grant less protections and safeguards to illegal aliens or foreign visitors. This disquieting feature of the bill was absent from S. 3197. When it comes to illegal aliens or foreign visitors today's legislation provides an expanded noncriminal standard, does not allow the court to look behind the executive branch certification and allows the government to use the information obtained as a result of the surveillance for whatever purpose it deems necessary. The Fourth Amendment of the Constitution speaks in terms of protecting all "persons"—not just American citizens and lawful resident aliens—and to the extent that this bill establishing different standards and procedures for illegal aliens and temporary foreign visitors, it is open to criticism.[53]

Proponents of the change correctly point out, however, that this new distinction in S. 1566 is, in large part, the result of an Administration decision to confer additional statutory protections, over and above those found in S. 3197, for American citizens and lawful resident aliens. Thus, for example, in cases involving American citizens or lawful resident aliens S. 1566 allows the court to look behind the Executive branch certification and also expands the definition of electronic surveillance. The Committee recognizes these distinct improvements over S. 3197 and is aware of the Administration's reluctance to extend these safeguards across the board to all persons.

The term "members" with respect to unincorporated associations is not intended, of course, to be limited to formal, card-carrying members. For in-

---

[53] Congressional Record S7857 (daily ed. May 18, 1977).

stance, an unincorporated commercial establishment's employees would be members under this definition. Corporations or groups which are within the definitions of a foreign power in Section 2521(b)(1) (C), (D), or (F) would continue to be foreign powers notwithstanding incorporation in the United States or the presence of a substantial number of American members.

Section 2521(b)(10) offers a new definition of "United States" for geographic purposes. Evidence publicized last year of CIA bugging in Micronesia led the Administration to propose this change which makes explicit that S. 1566 covers electronic surveillance in all areas under the territorial sovereignty of the United States (the United States and its territories) as well as the Canal Zone and Micronesia. The term "territorial sovereignty" does not include United States embassies, military bases and other installations abroad. The Commonwealth of the Northern Marianas is intended to be covered by this definition after its severance from the Trust Territory of the Pacific Islands. The remainder of the Trust Territory of the Pacific Islands is intended to be covered so long as the Trust is in effect and thereafter only if the political status agreements with the United States provide for territorial sovereignty of the United States in a manner similar to that of the Northern Mariana Islands, Puerto Rico or Guam.

Section 2522

Section 2522 authorizes the submission of applications to a judge for a court order approving the use of electronic surveillance under this chapter. Applications may be submitted only if the President has, by prior written authorization, empowered the Attorney General to approve the submission. This section does not require the President to authorize each specific application; he may authorize the Attorney General generally to seek applications under this chapter or upon such terms and conditions as the President wishes so long as the terms and conditions are consistent with this chapter.

Section 2523

Subsection (a) provides for the public designation by the Chief Justice of seven United States district court judges, any one of whom may hear applications and grant orders under this chapter. Each judge shall have nationwide jurisdiction, and the Committee contemplates that there will be some geographic dispersion among them.

The subsection provides that none of the designated judges shall have jurisdiction to hear an application for electronic surveillance if that same application has been previously denied by another of the designated district judges. This provision is intended to make clear that if the government desires to pursue an application after a denial, it must seek review in the special court of review established in subsection (b); it cannot apply to another district judge. Obviously, where one judge has asked for additional information before approving an application, and that judge is unavailable when the Government comes forward with such additional information, the Government may seek approval from another judge. It would, however, have to inform the second judge about the first application (see Section 2524(a)(9), *infra*).

Similarly, where an application is made and then withdrawn, perhaps because of a change in circumstances makes the electronic surveillance no longer technically feasible, the Government may seek approval from another judge if the application is subsequently reinstated.

The subsection further provides that a designated district judge who denies an application for electronic surveillance shall provide a complete written statement of the reasons for the denial, and, if the Government seeks review of the decision, forward that statement and other documents comprising the record to the special court of review. This ensures that the special court of review will have the full record of the proceedings of the district court in reviewing the case.

Subsection (b) provides for the public designation by the Chief Justice of three judges from the Federal courts of appeals or district courts who shall sit together as a special court of review having jurisdiction to review denials of applications made to the individual judges designated in subsection (a). One of the three is to be publicly designated as the presiding judge. If the special court of review determines that an application was properly denied, it shall provide a written statement of the reasons for its decision and, on petition of the government for a writ of certiorari, forward the complete record to the Supreme Court, which will have jurisdiction to review the decision.

Subsection (c) provides for the expeditious handling of all proceedings under this chapter and also states that the Chief Justice, in consultation with the Attorney General and the Director of Central Intelligence, shall establish security measures under which applications made and orders granted shall be maintained. The Committee contemplates that the record of applications made, information provided, and orders granted by the several judges designated under this chapter shall be maintained in such a way that the judges designated under this chapter shall have access to the records of actions taken by the other judges similarly designated.

Section 2524

This section is patterned after 18 U.S.C. section 2518 (1) and (2), and specifies what information must be included in the application. Applications must be made in writing and under oath or affirmation by a federal officer. If the officer making the application is unable to verify personally the accuracy of the information or representations upon which the application is based, the application must also include affidavits by investigative or other officers who are able to provide such personal verification. Thus, for example, if the applicant was an attorney in the Department of Justice who had not personally gathered the information contained in the application, it would be necessary that the application also contain an affidavit by the investigating officer personally attesting to the status and reliability of any informants or other covert sources of information. By this means the source of all information contained in the application and its accuracy will have been sworn to by a named official of the United States Government and a chain of responsibility established for judicial review.

Each application must be approved by the Attorney General, who may grant such approval if he finds that the appropriate procedures have been followed. The Attorney General shall also state in writing his belief that the facts and circumstances relied upon for the application would justify a judicial finding of probable cause that the target is an agent of a foreign power and that the facilities or place at which the electronic surveillance is directed are being used, or about to be used, by an agent of a foreign power, and that all other statutory criteria have been met. In addition, the Attorney General must personally be satisfied that the certification has been made pursuant to statutory requirements.

Paragraph (1) of subsection (a) requires that the application identify the Federal officer making the application; that is, the name of the person who actually presents the application to the judge.

Paragraph (2) requires that the application contain evidence of the authority of the applicant to make this application. This would consist of the presidential authorization to the Attorney General and the Attorney General's approval of the particular application.

Paragraph (3) requires the identity or description of the person who is the target of the electronic surveillance. The word "person" is used in its juridical sense to mean the individual or entity that is the target of the surveillance. However, care must be taken in framing the order authorizing such surveillance (and minimization procedures) that surveillance against one individual does not lead to the interception of communications of an entire group or organization of United States citizens, thus violating constitutional rights of association and privacy.

Paragraph (4) requires a statement of the facts and circumstances justifying the applicant's belief that the target of the electronic surveillance is a foreign power or an agent of a foreign power and that the facilities or place at which the surveillance is directed are being used or are about to be used by that power or agent. These requirements parallel existing law. (18 U.S.C. 2518(1)(b)(ii) and (iv)).

Paragraph (5) requires a statement of the proposed minimization procedures.

The statement of procedures required under this paragraph should be full and complete and subject to the closest judicial scrutiny. These procedures may differ from case to case, depending on the type of foreign agent involved, the individuals using the facilities or place to be surveilled, the type of foreign intelligence information sought, and other similar factors. Minimization procedures should normally include such elements as methods to avoid the acquisition of irrelevant information at the time of intercept, restrictions on the use of surveillance to times when foreign intelligence information is likely to be obtained, and requirements for deletion of information obtained which is not foreign intelligence information.

For example steps should be taken to prevent unnecessary invasion of the privacy of a target's family caused by a twenty-four hour tap on the family phone when it is known that the target is out of town or at the office. Similarly, conversations unrelated to foreign intelligence should not be retained or, of course, disseminated.

Paragraph (6) calls for a factual description of the nature of the information sought by the electronic surveillance, except where the surveillance is of a foreign power as defined in section 2521(b)(1) (A), (B), or (C). The description should be as specific as possible and sufficiently detailed so as to state clearly what the Government seeks. A simple designation of which subdefinition of "foreign intelligence information" is involved will not suffice.

Such a description is not required where a target is one of the "official" foreign powers defined in Section 2521(b)(1) (A), (B), or (C). Where these types of powers are the targets, a designation of a particular subcategory of the definition of "foreign intelligence information" will suffice. The reason for this distinction is, that with respect to such "official" targets, the sensitivity of the surveillance is greatly multiplied while the risk of a fruitless surveillance which will not obtain any foreign intelligence information is greatly reduced. Therefore the Administration maintains that such applications should not require as much detailed information to be presented as in cases involving American citizens or other individual targets.

Paragraph (7) requires a certification or certifications by the Assistant to the President for National Security Affairs or by an appropriate executive official appointed by the President with the advice and consent of the Senate. The certification would be made by the official having ultimate responsibility for the collection of the information—normally the Assistant to the President for National Security Affairs, the Director of the Central Intelligence Agency, the Director of the Federal Bureau of Investigation, or the Secretary of Defense—or such other officer, appointed with the advice and consent of the Senate, who has full knowledge of the case. The possibility of additional certifications is provided to insure that a detailed and complete certification is presented to the judge.

The certification shall state that the information sought is foreign intelligence information, that the purpose of the surveillance is to obtain foreign intelligence information, and that such information cannot feasibly be obtained by normal investigative techniques. It shall include a designation of what type of foreign intelligence information is sought and where the target is not a foreign power as defined in section 2521(b)(1) (A), (B), or (C) a reasoned statement of the basis for certifying that the information sought is foreign intelligence information and that such information cannot feasibly be obtained by other investigative techniques.

The requirement that the information sought be "foreign intelligence information" is designed to insure that a high-level official with responsibility in the area of national security, will review and, where the target is not a foreign power as defined in section 2521(b)(1) (A), (B) or (C), explain the Executive Branch determination that the information sought is in fact foreign intelligence information. The requirement that this judgment be explained is to ensure that those making certifications carefully consider the cases before them and avoid the temptation to simply sign off on certifications which consist largely of boilerplate language. The committee does not intend that the certification be vague generalizations or standardized assertions. The designated official must similarly explain that the purpose of the surveillance is to obtain the described foreign intelligence information. This requirement is designed to prevent the practice of targeting one individual for electronic surveillance when the true purpose of the surveillance is to gather information about another individual. It is also designed to make explicit that the sole purpose of such surveillance is to secure foreign intelligence information and not to obtain information for any other purpose. The designated official must similarly explain in his affidavit why the information cannot be obtained through less intrusive techniques. This requirement is particularly important in those cases when United States citizens or resident aliens are the target of the surveillance.

Finally, where the target of the surveillance is one of the special class of "official" foreign powers (defined in sections 2521(b)(1) (A), (B) or (C)), the certification shall include a statement of the period of time for which the surveillance is required. With respect to surveillances of this special class of foreign powers, this statement is placed in the certification since the reviewing court does not have the power to control the length of the surveillance within the 90-day period otherwise applicable in the bill. This provision—a major change from the blanket 90-day limitation in S. 3197—has been criticized by some members of the committee who object to the likelihood of lengthy, ongoing wiretaps being conducted without adequate judicial supervision.

Paragraph (8) requires the application to contain a statement of the means by which the surveillance will be effected where it is not targeted against the special class of foreign powers. Unlike S. 3197, where the target is one of the special classes of foreign powers listed in section 2521(b)(1) (A), (B), or (C), the Administration has insisted that only a designation of the type of surveillance according to the categories of the definition of electronic surveillance be required. It will generally be sufficient in such cases if the application merely indicates whether the information will be acquired by means of a wiretap, a microphone installation, the interception of a radio signal or some other means. The Administration maintains that less specificity in describing the means of the surveillance is required for the special class of foreign powers because of the extreme importance and sensitivity of the information sought. However, if such a surveillance requires physical entry of the property of a non-consenting person, a statement to that effect is required.[54]

Paragraph (9) parallels 18 U.S.C. Section 2518(1)(e) and requires a statement concerning all previous applications dealing with the same persons, facilities, or places and the disposition of each such previous application.

Paragraph (10) parallels 18 U.S.C. Section 2518(1)(d) and requires a statement as to the period of time for which the surveillance is necessary in those cases where the special class of foreign powers is not the target. If the surveillance order is not to terminate automatically when the particular information sought has been obtained, the applicant must provide additional facts supporting his belief that additional information of the same type will be obtained thereafter.

Subsection (b) allows the Attorney General to require other executive officers to provide information to support the application.

Subsection (c) enables the judge to require the applicant to furnish further information as may be necessary to make the required determinations. It parallels existing law, 18 U.S.C. Section 2518(2). Such additional proffers would, of course, be made part of the record and would be subject to the security safeguards applied to the application and order.

Section 2525

Subsection (a) of this section is patterned after 18 U.S.C. Section 2518(3) and specifies the findings the judge must make before he grants an order approving the use of electronic surveillance for foreign intelligence purposes. While the issuance of an order is mandatory if the judge finds that

---

[54] Some members of the Committee have expressed concern that the failure of S. 1566 to require a statement of means in cases involving the special class of foreign powers is part of a disquieting pattern, a pattern that results in less oversight of warrant applications by both the Department of Justice and the judiciary. Thus, insofar as (1) the Attorney General can delegate his authority to review warrant applications (2521(b)(7), *supra*), (2) the court has no supervisory role over the length of surveillance of "official" foreign powers (2524(a)(7)(F), *supra*), and (3) the Government need not give a statement of the means by which the surveillance of "official" foreign powers will be effected, there is obviously a marked lessening of the statutory safeguards found in S. 3197. The opportunity for abuse obviously increases. Some members of the Committee have gone along with these changes with the greatest reluctance and only because they view S. 1566—in its entirety—as a major improvement over existing law.

all of the requirements of this section are met, the judge has the discretionary power to modify the order sought, such as with regard to the period of authorization (except where the special class of foreign powers is the target) or the minimization procedures to be followed.

Paragraph (1) of this subsection requires the judge to find that the President has authorized the Attorney General to approve such applications.

Paragraph (2) requires the judge to find that the Attorney General has approved the application being submitted and that the application has been made by a federal officer.

Paragraph (3) requires a finding that there is "probable cause" to believe that the target of the electronic surveillance is a foreign power or an agent of a foreign power and that the facilities or place at which the surveillance is directed are being used or are about to be used by that power or agent.

In determining whether probable cause exists under this section, the court must consider the same requisite elements which govern such determinations in the traditional criminal context. Such elements include, for example, the issue of any informant's reliability, the circumstances under which the informant was able to learn about the alleged activity of the individual who is the subject of the warrant, the length of time which has passed since the information relied upon was acquired, and the degree to which information corroborating an informant must relate to the essential conduct on which the application is premised and not merely to incidental details.

In addition, in order to find "probable cause" to believe the subject of the surveillance is an "agent of a foreign power" under subsection 2521(b)(2)(A) (ii), (iii), or (B), the judge must, of course, find that the Government has established probable cause that each and every element of that status exists. For example, if a United States citizen or resident alien is alleged to be acting on behalf of a foreign entity, the judge must first find probable cause to believe that the entity is a "foreign power" as defined in section 2521. There must also be probable cause to believe the person is acting for or on behalf of that foreign power and probable cause to believe that the efforts undertaken by the person on behalf of the foreign power constitute sabotage, terrorism or other proscribed activities as defined in section 2521.

Similar findings of probable cause are required for each element necessary to establish that a United States citizen is conspiring with or aiding and abetting someone engaged in sabotage, terrorism, or clandestine intelligence activities at the direction of a foreign power.

A judicial determination that a person is an agent of a foreign power as defined in section 2521(b)(2)(B)(iii) requires other findings: that the person is acting pursuant to the direction of a foreign intelligence service or network; that the person is knowingly collecting or transmitting information or material to that service or network in a covert manner; and that the circumstances surrounding the activity taken together are so compelling that they indicate that the information or material transmitted to the network harm the security of the United States, or that lack of knowledge of the collection or transmission would harm our national security. Thus, the nature of the activity, its relationship to the national security, and the status of the target are all vital to the judicial determination. The required finding must be made by the judge, on the basis of the information and explanation provided by the Government. In order to determine whether the requisite probable cause has been established, the judge may request such additional information as is necessary in light of the facts and circumstances to make the required determination.

Paragraph (4) requires the judge to find that the procedures described in the application to minimize the acquisition, retention, and dissemination of certain information or communications relating to United States citizens or lawful resident aliens fit the definition of minimization procedures. The committee contemplates that the court would give these procedures most careful consideration. If it is not convinced that they will be effective, the application should be denied or the procedures modified. The committee realizes that total minimization may not be possible. Therefore, the bill's requirement is phrased in terms of minimization procedures being "reasonably designed." Thus, for example, where irrelevant information cannot be erased from part of a tape, minimization procedures should prohibit dissemination of the tape. In addition, where it cannot immediately be determined whether a certain piece of information is irrelevant, minimization procedures should require that within a specified time such a determination be made and the irrelevant matter expunged.

Paragraph (5) requires that the judges find that the application contains the description and certification or certifications specified in section 2524(a)(7). If the application meets the requirement of those sections, the court is not permitted to substitute its judgment for that of the executive branch officials, except where a United States person is the target of a surveillance. In such a case, the judge must review the certifications to determine whether they are clearly erroneous. This authority of the court to "look behind" the certifications and reject them if "clearly erroneous" is recognized by the committee as a major improvement over S. 3197 (which did not provide for any judicial review of the certifications.) The "clearly erroneous" standard of review is not, of course, comparable to a probable cause finding by the judge. Nevertheless, S. 1566 does provide a workable procedure for judicial review (and possible rejection) of Executive branch certifications.

Despite the fact that the court is not allowed to "look behind" the certification in cases not involving United States persons there are several checks against the possibility of arbitrary executive action. First, the court, not the Executive branch, makes the finding of whether probable cause exists that the target of surveillance is a foreign power or its agent. It is this finding that constitutes a fundamental safeguard for the civil liberties of the individual. It is also an effective external control on arbitrary executive action. Second, the certification procedure assures written accountability within the Executive branch for the decision made to engage in such surveillance. This constitutes an internal check on executive branch arbitrariness.

Moreover, it should be noted that if the description and certification do not fully comply with sections 2524(a)(7), they can and must be rejected by the court. Thus, the court could invalidate the certification if it were not properly signed by the President's designee, did not designate the type of information sought, or did not state that the information sought is foreign intelligence information, that the purpose of the surveillance is to obtain foreign intelligence information, and that such information cannot feasibly be obtained by normal investigative techniques. Further, if the certification did not present an explanation of why the information sought is foreign intelligence information which cannot be obtained through normal investigative techniques, the judge could (if surveillance was not targeted against the special class of foreign powers) reject the application or defer approval until an adequate certification was supplied.

Subsection (b) specifies what the order approving the electronic surveillance must contain. It must include the identity or a description of the person or persons targeted by the electronic surveillance. The order must specify the place or facilities against which the surveillance is directed. The order must also specify the type of information sought, or where the special class of foreign powers is the target, a specific definition of "foreign intelligence information." These requirements are designed to satisfy the Fourth Amendment's requirements that warrants describe with particularity and specificity the person, place, and objects to be searched or seized. The order must, in addition to the Fourth Amendment's requirements, specify the means by which the surveillance will be effected (where the target is one of the special class of foreign powers, however, only a specific definition of "electronic surveillance" is required). In addition, the order must specify the period of time during which the surveillance is approved.

The order shall direct that minimization procedures will be followed. It is intended that the court shall monitor compliance with the minimization procedures in much the same way as has been done pursuant to chapter 119. Failure to abide by the minimization procedures may be treated as contempt of court.

The order may also direct that a common carrier, landlord, custodian, contractor or other specified person furnish information, facilities or technical assistance necessary to accomplish the electronic surveillance successfully and with a minimum of interference to the services provided by such person to the target of the surveillance. If this is done, the court shall direct that the person rendering the assistance maintain under security procedures approved by the Attorney General and the Director of the Central Intelligence Agency any records concerning the surveillance which the person wishes to retain. If the judge directs such assistance, he shall also direct that the applicant compensate the person for such assistance. These provisions generally parallel 18 U.S.C. 2518(4).

This directive provision must be read in conjunction with the bill's conforming amendment to 18 U.S.C. 2511(2)(a)(ii), contained in section 4(b) of this bill. That amendment requires that before a communication common carrier or its agent provides such information, facilities or technical assistance to an investigative or law enforcement officer, that officer is required to furnish to the carrier either an order signed by the authorizing judge certifying that a court order directing such assistance has been issued or, in the case of surveillance undertaken under chapter 119 or 120 in which a prior order is not required, such as an emergency surveillance, a certification under oath by the officer requesting the assistance that the applicable statutory requirements have been met.

Subsection (c) allows an order approving electronic surveillance under this chapter against any person or entity other than a special foreign power as defined in Section 2521(b)(1) (A), (B), or (C) to be effective for the period necessary to achieve its purposes or for 90 days, whichever is less. In the Committee's view 90 days is the maximum length of time during which a surveillance of these persons or entities for foreign intelligence purposes should continue without new judicial scrutiny. This period of time is not as long as some have wished but longer than others desired. It is considered to be a reasonable condition in the foreign intelligence context.[55]

When the special class of "official" foreign powers is targeted, however, the surveillance may last as long as one year. Moreover, the Executive determines the necessary length of the surveillance of these special foreign powers (not to exceed one year without re-authorization), and this determination is not subject to the court's review or approval. As already indicated, this is a substantial change from S. 3197 which has provoked widespread criticism from some members of the Committee. The Administration, however, offers considerable arguments for the change: First, the determination that an entity is within the definition of Section 2521(b)(1) (A), (B), or (C) is not likely to be erroneous. Unlike a person suspected of being a foreign agent, whether an entity fits one of the three special classes of foreign powers—such as a foreign embassy or consulate—will usually be self-evident. Second, the likelihood of obtaining valuable foreign intelli-

---

[55] *United States v. United States District Court*, 407 U.S. 297 at 323, 92 S.Ct. 2125, 32 L.Ed.2d 752 (1972).

gence information from these entities is very high. Third, surveillance against such official powers, because of their continuing presence in the United States, is likely to be required for much longer periods of time. Although such surveillance could be accomplished by successive 90 day court renewals, the Administration cites the generation of four times the amount of required paperwork with the attendant increased possibility of a compromise as well as the administrative burden which would result, as reasons for exempting these foreign powers from the 90 day limitation. Given these considerations and the unique status of the targets involved, the Administration feels that one year is not an excessive period of time.

Others disagree, maintaining that excessive paperwork and administrative inconvenience are not sufficient reasons to extend such surveillance to as long as one year without judicial approval (and with the possibility that the Attorney General will not even personally be reviewing the foreign power warrant application). Nevertheless, the Committee has acceded to the Administration's position and has granted the change from S. 3197 in the limited situation of special foreign powers as defined in section 2521(b)(1) (A), (B), or (C).

In coming to this conclusion, however, the Committee emphasizes that, in order for United States citizens to be adequately protected in such cases, this provision must not be interpreted to bar judicial review of the effectiveness of the minimization procedures. United States citizens may be overheard talking to employees of such a "special" foreign power. As already indicated, the court has the power to review minimization during the course of the surveillance as it does now under Chapter 119. This applies regardless of the type of target and remains an important protection.

As under chapter 119, extensions of an order may be sought and granted on the same basis as the original order. A new application, including a new certification pursuant to section 2524(a)(7), would therefore be required, updating the information previously provided. Before the extension should be granted, however, the court would again have to find probable cause that the target is a foreign power or its agent. To aid the judge in making this determination anew, it is expected that the court would evaluate the success or failure of any previous surveillances and the facts and circumstances surrounding such surveillance. The court, however, in considering a renewal involving a foreign power as defined in section 2521(b)(1) (A), (B), or (C), cannot order the government to submit any information actually obtained as a result of the original surveillance or previous extension. This change from S. 3197 was made at the request of the Administration and reflects its concern with the sensitive nature of the information obtained from special foreign powers.

Subsection (d) authorizes the Attorney General to approve an emergency electronic surveillance prior to judicial authorization under certain limited circumstances. First, the Attorney General must determine that an emergency situation exists which requires the employment of electronic surveillance before an order authorizing such surveillance can with due diligence be obtained. In addition, the factual basis for the issuance of an order under this chapter must be present.

The procedures under which such an emergency surveillance is authorized are considerably stricter than those of the comparable provision in chapter 119, 18 U.S.C. section 2518(7). First, only the Attorney General (as defined) may authorize such emergency surveillance, whereas in 18 U.S.C. section 2518(7) the Attorney General may designate "any investigative or law enforcement officer" to authorize emergency interceptions under that subsection. Second, the Attorney General or his designee must contemporaneously notify one of the designated judges that an emergency surveillance has been authorized. There is no comparable requirement in 18 U.S.C. section 2518(7). Third, an application for an order approving the surveillance must be made to that judge within 24 hours; 18 U.S.C. section 2518(7) requires the application to be made within 48 hours. Fourth, the emergency surveillance cannot continue beyond 24 hours without the issuance of an order; under 18 U.S.C. section 2418(7) the emergency surveillance may continue indefinitely until the judge denies the application. Fifth, the Attorney General must order that minimization procedures required by this chapter for the issuance of a judicial order be followed during the period of the emergency surveillance. There is no comparable provision under 18 U.S.C. section 2518(7). This last provision is designed to ensure that as much as possible be done to eliminate the acquisition, retention and dissemination of information which is not foreign intelligence information. The Committee's intent is to place the Attorney General in the role of the court during the 24 hour emergency period. He must examine the minimization procedures as the court would normally do under paragraph (a)(4) of this section, and order that the appropriate procedures be followed just as if he were the court granting a judicial order.

The committee wishes to emphasize that the application must be made for judicial approval even if the surveillance is terminated within the twenty-four hour period and regardless of whether the information sought is obtained. This requirement ensures that all emergency surveillance initiated pursuant to this chapter will receive judicial review and that judicial approval or denial will be forthcoming *nunc pro tunc*. Thus, the termination of an emergency surveillance before the expiration of the twenty-four hour period shall not be a basis for the court failing to enter an order approving or disapproving the subsequent application. It is necessary for both the Department of Justice and Congressional oversight committees to have available a complete record both of the bases for such emergency surveillance authorization and of the judicial determinations of their legality under the statutory standard.

This provision for emergency authorization of surveillance by the Attorney General may not be utilized pending an appeal under section 2523, following the denial of an application for a judicial order. Under such circumstances, the Attorney General could not reasonably determine that "the factual basis for the issuance of an order under this chapter to approve such surveillance exists," as required by this subsection.

If the application is subsequently denied, or if the surveillance is terminated without an order eventually being sought (which, as already indicated, would constitute an unlawful act under this subsection), no information obtained or evidence derived from the surveillance shall be received, used or disclosed by the Government in any trial hearing or other proceeding before any court, grand jury, department, office, agency, regulatory body, legislative committee or other Federal, State or local authority. This exclusionary provision is designed to be absolute.

A denial of the application may be reviewed in the same manner as a denial of an original application under section 2523.

Section 2526

This section sets forth the permissible uses which may be made of information acquired by means of electronic surveillance conducted pursuant to this chapter. The fact that effective minimization may be more difficult in the foreign intelligence area than in the more traditional criminal area, and that this chapter contains certain less restrictive procedures than does chapter 119 (for example, 90 days of surveillance per order rather than 30 days), mandates that the uses to be made of the information acquired by means of this chapter be carefully restricted. This section, therefore, places more stringent restrictions on use and dissemination than does the corresponding provision of Title III, 18 U.S.C. 2517. The extent to which the Government should be required to surrender to the parties in a criminal trial the underlying documentation used to justify electronic surveillance raises delicate problems and competing interests. On the one hand, broad rights of access to the documentation and subsequent intelligence information can threaten the secrecy necessary to effective intelligence practices. However, the defendant's constitutional guarantee of a fair trial could seriously be undercut if he is denied the materials needed to present a proper defense. The Committee believes that a just, effective balance has been struck in this section.

Subsection (a) requires that information concerning United States persons acquired from electronic surveillance conducted pursuant to this chapter may be used by Federal officers and employees only for purposes relating to the ability of the United States to protect itself against actual or potential attack or other grave hostile acts of a foreign power or foreign agent; to provide for the national defense or security of the nation; to provide for the conduct of foreign affairs; to protect against the terrorist or sabotage activities of a foreign power or an agent of a foreign power; to protect against the clandestine intelligence activities of an intelligence service or network of a foreign power or an agent of a foreign power; or for the enforcement of the criminal law. Thus the lawful uses of foreign intelligence information concerning United States citizens and resident aliens gathered pursuant to this chapter are carefully restricted to actual foreign intelligence purposes and the enforcement of the criminal law.

A major change from S. 3197 has, however, been made in this section at the insistence of the Administration. Whereas in S. 3197 this section applied to all persons, whether or not they were American citizens, S. 1566 limits the protections of section 2526(a) to United States persons. Information concerning non-United States persons (who indeed may be foreigners not even in the United States) is not subject to the same restrictions as information concerning United States persons. For example, the information obtained might be used to deport an illegal alien even though such use of the information is not for foreign intelligence purposes and is not for the purpose of enforcing the criminal law.

This differentiation between United States persons and other persons was sufficiently troublesome to the Committee to result in an important amendment to section 2526(a). By limiting the subsection to United States persons, the possibility existed that information obtained by surveillance could be used in a variety of illegal ways against, for example, foreign visitors and students. The Committee has amended this subsection to make clear that no information acquired pursuant to this chapter may be used or disclosed for other than "lawful purposes". The committee does not intend nor does the bill permit that information gathered about a foreign visitor be used to blackmail him into becoming an agent against his country. S. 1566, as amended, now requires that in those cases where the government wishes to use foreign intelligence information against non-United States persons, beyond the specific purposes listed in section 2526(a), it do so in a lawful manner and for lawful purposes.

There is no specific restriction in the bill as to whom Federal officers may disclose information concerning United States persons acquired pursuant to this chapter (although specific minimization procedures might require specific restrictions in particular cases). First, the Committee believes that dissemination should be permitted to state and local law enforcement officials. If Federal agents monitoring a foreign intelligence surveillance authorized under this chapter were to overhear information relating to a violation of state criminal law, such as homicide, the agents could hardly be expected to conceal such information from the appropriate local officials. Second, the Committee can conceive of situations where disclosure should be made outside of government channels. For example, Federal agents may learn of a terrorist plot to kidnap a business executive. Certainly in such cases they should be permitted to disclose such information to the executive and his company in order to provide for the executive's security. Finally, the Committee believes that foreign intelligence information relating to crimes, espionage activities, or the acts and intentions of foreign powers may, in some circumstances, be appropriately disseminated to cooperating intelligence services of other nations. So long as all the procedures of this chapter are followed by the Federal officers, including minimization and the limitations on dissemination, this cooperative relationship should not be terminated by a blanket prohibition on dissemination to foreign intelligence services. The Committee wishes to stress, however, that any such dissemination be carefully reviewed to ensure that there is a sufficient reason why disclosure to foreign intelligence services is in the interests of the United States.

Disclosure, in compelling circumstances, to local officials for the purpose of enforcing the criminal law, and to foreign intelligence services under the circumstances described above are generally the only exceptions to the rule that dissemination should be limited to Federal officials.

It is recognized that these strict requirements only apply to information known to concern United States persons. Where the information in the communication is encoded or otherwise not known to concern United States persons, only the requirement that the information be disclosed for lawful purposes applies. There is no requirement that before disclosure can be made information be decoded or otherwise processed to determine whether information concerning United States persons is indeed present. Of course, the restrictions on use and disclosure apply to the entire Government, so that if any agency received coded information from the intercepting agency, were it to break the code, the limitations on use and disclosure would apply to it.

Section 2526(a) also states that foreign intelligence information obtained may be used to enforce the criminal law "if its use outweighs the possible harm to the national security." This new language, which did not appear in S. 3197, states the obvious. The Department of Justice always has the option of deciding whether to proceed with a criminal prosecution or forego it in the interests of national security. For example, the Department of Justice may decline to prosecute rather than disclose the names of important witnesses and key informants. Whether to go forward with a criminal prosecution remains in the exclusive hands of the Executive Branch and nothing in section 2526(a) changes that fact.

This subsection also notes that no otherwise privileged communication obtained in accordance with or in violation of this chapter shall lose its privileged character. This provision is identical to 18 U.S.C. 2517(4) and is designed, like its Title III predecessor, to change existing law as to the scope and existence of privileged communications only to the extent that it provides that otherwise privileged communications do not lose their privileged character because they are intercepted by a person not a party to the conversation.

Subsection (b) must be read in conjunction with the minimization requirements of section 2521(b)(8) and with the preceding subsection (a). As previously noted, the minimization procedures mandated by the court are designed to restrict the acquisition of information obtained by means of electronic surveillance to information related to foreign intelligence. However, even the most thorough minimization efforts may result in the acquisition of some information which is not foreign intelligence information. This subsection states that such incidentally acquired information which is evidence of a crime may be retained and disclosed for law enforcement purposes. Such disclosure would, of course, be restricted by the provisions of subsection (a).

The requirement that such criminal evidence be acquired incidentally logically connotes that it must be acquired lawfully. This requires that there be a good faith effort to minimize.[56]

Thus for example, if monitoring agents choose to disregard the minimization standards and thereby acquire evidence of a crime against an overheard party whose conversation properly should have been minimized, that evidence would be acquired in violation of this chapter and would properly be suppressed if offered at any official proceeding.

Disclosure for law enforcement purposes must be accompanied by a statement that such evidence, or any information derived therefrom, may only be used in a criminal proceeding with the advance authorization of the Attorney General. This provision is designed to eliminate circumstances in which a local prosecutor has no knowledge that evidence was obtained through foreign intelligence electronic surveillance. In granting approval of the use of the evidence the Attorney General would alert the prosecutor to the surveillance and he, in turn, would alert the court in accordance with subsection (c).

Subsections (c), (d) and (e) set forth the procedures under the bill whereby information acquired by means of electronic surveillance may be received in evidence or otherwise used or disclosed in any trial, hearing or other Federal or State proceeding. Although the primary purpose of electronic surveillance conducted pursuant to this chapter will not be the gathering of criminal evidence, it is contemplated that such evidence will be acquired and this subsection and the succeeding one establish the procedural mechanisms by which such information may be used in formal proceedings.

---

[56] *United States v. Armocida*, 515 F. 2d 29 (3rd Cir. 1975).

At the outset the committee recognizes that nothing in subsection (c) abrogates the rights afforded a criminal defendant under *Brady v. Maryland*,[57] and the Jencks Act.[58] These legal principles inhere in any such proceeding and are wholly consistent with the procedures detailed here. Furthermore, nothing contained in this section is intended to alter the traditional principle that the Government cannot use material at trial against a criminal defendant, and then withhold from him such material at trial.[59]

Subsection (c) states that no information acquired pursuant to this chapter may be used unless, prior to the trial, hearing, or other proceeding, or at a reasonable time prior to an effort to disclose the information or submit it in evidence, the government notifies the court that such information was acquired by means of electronic surveillance conducted pursuant to this chapter. This provision has been broadened in S. 1566 over its counterpart in S. 3197 by including non-judicial proceedings. In instances in which the government intends to disclose surveillance information in such a non-judicial forum, subsection (c) would require that the United States district court in the district in which the disclosure is to take place be notified of the proposed disclosure or use.

Subsection (d) parallels 18 U.S.C. 2518(10)(a) and provides a separate statutory vehicle by which a person who has been a subject of electronic surveillance and against whom evidence derived therefrom is to be or has been introduced or otherwise used or disclosed in any trial, hearing or proceeding may move to suppress the contents of any communication acquired by, or evidence derived from, such electronic surveillance. The grounds for such a motion would be that (a) the communication was unlawfully acquired, or (b) the surveillance was not made in conformity with the order of authorization or approval.

The "subject" of electronic surveillance means an individual who was a party to the intercepted communication or was a person against whom the interception was directed. Thus the word is defined to coincide with the definition of "aggrieved person" in section 2510 of title III.[60]

One situation in which such a motion might be presented would be that in which the court orders disclosed to the party the court order and accompanying application under subsection (e) prior to ruling on the legality of the surveillance. Such motion would also be appropriate, however, even after the court's finding of legality if, in subsequent trial testimony, a Government witness provides evidence that the electronic surveillance may have been authorized or conducted in violation of the court order. The most common circumstance in which such a motion might be appropriate

---

[57] 373 U.S. 83, 83 S.Ct. 1194, 10 L.Ed.2d 215 (1963).
[58] 18 U.S.C. 3500 *et seq.*
[59] *United States v. Andolschek*, 142 F. 2d 503 (2nd Cir. 1944).
[60] See also, *Alderman v. United States*, 394 U.S. 165 (1967).

would be a situation in which a defendant queries the government under 18 U.S.C. 3504 and discovers that he has been intercepted by electronic surveillance even before the government has decided whether evidence derived from that surveillance will be used in the presentation of its case. In this instance, under the appropriate factual circumstances, the defendant might move to suppress such evidence under this subsection even without having seen any of the underlying documentation.

A motion under this subsection shall be made before the trial, hearing, or proceeding unless there was no opportunity to make such motion or the movant was not aware of the grounds for the motion, the only change in subsection (d) from S. 3197 is to remove as a separate, independent basis for suppression the fact that the order was insufficient on its face. This is not a substantive change, however, since communications acquired pursuant to an order insufficient on its face would be unlawfully acquired and therefore subject to suppression under paragraph (1).

Subsection (e) states in detail the procedure the court shall follow when it receives a notification under subsection (c) or a suppression motion is filed under subsection (d). This procedure applies, for example, whenever an individual makes a motion pursuant to subsection (d) or 18 U.S.C. 3504, or any other statute or rule of the United States to discover, obtain or suppress evidence or information obtained or derived from electronic surveillance conducted pursuant to this chapter (for example, Rule 12 of the Federal Rules of Criminal Procedure). Although a number of different procedures might be used to attack the legality of the surveillance, it is this procedure "notwithstanding any other law" that must be used to resolve the question. The Committee wishes to make very clear that the procedures set out in subsection (e) apply whatever the underlying rule or statute referred to in the motion. This is necessary to prevent the carefully drawn procedures in subsection (e) from being bypassed by the inventive litigant using a new statute, rule or judicial construction.

The special procedures in subsection (e) cannot be invoked until they are triggered by a Government affidavit that disclosure or an adversary hearing would harm the national security of the United States. If no such assertion is made, the Committee envisions that mandatory disclosure of the application and order, and discretionary disclosure of other surveillance materials, would be made to the defendant, as is required under Title III.[61] When the procedure is so triggered, however, the Government must make available to the court a copy of the court order and accompanying application upon which the surveillance was based.

The court must then conduct an *ex parte, in camera* inspection of these materials as well as any other documents which the Government may be ordered to provide, to determine whether the surveillance was authorized

---

[61] 18 U.S.C. 2518 (9) and (10).

and conducted in a manner which did not violate any constitutional or statutory right of the person against whom the evidence is sought to be introduced. The subsection further provides that in making such a determination, the court may order disclosed to the person against whom the evidence is to be introduced the court order or accompanying application, or portions thereof, or other materials relating to the surveillance, only if it finds that such disclosure is necessary to make an accurate determination of the legality of the surveillance. Thus, this subsection deals with the procedure to be followed by the trial court in determining the legality (or illegality) of the surveillance.

The question of how to determine the legality of an electronic surveillance conducted for foreign intelligence purposes has never been decided by the Supreme Court. As Justice Stewart noted in his concurring opinion in *Giordano v. United States*, "Moreover, we did not in *Alderman, Butenko* or *Ivanov*, and we do not today, specify the procedure that the District Courts are to follow in making this preliminary determination [of legality.]" 394 U.S. 310, 314 (1968); see also, *Taglianetti v. United States*, 394 U.S. 316 (1968).[8] The committee views the procedures set forth in this subsection as striking a reasonable balance between an entirely *in camera* proceeding which might adversely affect the defendant's ability to defend himself, and mandatory disclosure, which might occasionally result in the wholesale revelation of sensitive foreign intelligence information.

---
[8] 89 S.Ct. 1099, 22 L.Ed.2d 302.

The decision whether it is necessary to order disclosure to a person is for the court to make after reviewing the underlying documentation and determining its volume, scope and complexity. The committee has noted the reasoned discussion of these matters in the opinion of the Court in *United States v. Butenko, supra*. There, the court, faced with the difficult problem of determining what standard to follow in balancing national security interests with the right to a fair trial stated:

> The distinguished district court judge reviewed *in camera* the records of the wiretaps at issue here before holding the surveillances to be legal . . . Since the question confronting the district court as to the second set of interceptions was the legality of the taps, not the existence of tainted evidence, it was within his discretion to grant or to deny Ivanov's request for disclosure and a hearing. The exercise of this discretion is to be guided by an evaluation of the complexity of the factors to be considered by the court and by the likelihood that adversary presentation would substantially promote a more accurate decision. (494 F.2d at 607)

Thus, in some cases, the court will likely be able to determine the legality of the surveillance without any disclosure to the defendant.

In other cases, however, the question may be more complex because of, for example, indications of possible misrepresentation of fact, vague identification of the persons to be surveilled or surveillance records which includes a significant amount of nonforeign intelligence information, calling into question compliance with the minimization standards contained in the order. In such cases, the committee contemplates that the court will likely decide to order disclosure to the defendant, in whole or in part since such disclosure "is necessary to make an accurate determination of the legality of the surveillance."[62]

Cases may arise, of course, where the court believes that disclosure is necessary to make an accurate determination of legality, but the Government argues that to do so, even given the court's broad discretionary power to excise certain sensitive portions, would damage the national security. In such situations the Government must choose—either disclose the material or forego the use of the surveillance-based evidence. Indeed, if the Government objects to the disclosure, thus preventing a proper adjudication of legality, the prosecution would probably have to be dismissed, and, where the court determines that the surveillance was unlawfully authorized or conducted, the court would, "in accordance with the requirements of law," suppress that evidence which was unlawfully obtained.[63]

Where the court determines that the surveillance was lawfully authorized and conducted, it would, of course, deny any motion to suppress. In addition, the Committee emphasizes that, once a judicial determination is made that the surveillance was lawful, a motion for discovery of evidence

---

[62] Cf. *Alderman v. United States*, 394 U.S. 165, 182 n. 14 (1968); *Taglianetti v. United States, supra* at 317.

[63] The Committee has deliberately chosen the general phrase "in accordance with the requirements of law" to avoid dealing with the very complex problem of what procedures are to be followed in those cases where the trial court determines that the surveillance was either unlawfully authorized or conducted or the Government's refusal to disclose the underlying documentation to the defendant prevents the court from making that determination. The evidence obtained would not, of course, be admissible during the trial. But beyond this is the question of whether, in the case of an illegal surveillance, the Government is constitutionally mandated to surrender to the defendant all the records of the surveillance in its possession in order for the defendant to make an intelligent motion on the question of taint. The Supreme Court opinion in *Alderman v. United States, supra,* clearly answers this question in the affirmative. In the *Alderman* case, the Court held that, once a defendant claiming evidence against him was the fruit of unconstitutional electronic surveillance has established the illegality of such surveillance (and his "standing" to object), he *must* be given confidential materials in the Government's files to assist him in establishing the existence of "taint." The Court rejected the Government's contention that the trial court could be permitted to screen the files *in camera* and give the defendant only material which was "arguably relevant" to his claim, saying such screening would be sufficiently subject to error to interfere with the effectiveness of adversary litigation of the question of "taint."

Alderman, however, was a pre-title III case (which, in section 2518(10)(a) confers discretion on the court to deal with the issue of "taint" in "the interest of justice") and both this committee and the Department of Justice have maintained that *Alderman* was an exercise of the Supreme Court's supervisory jurisdiction over the lower federal courts and not a constitutional interpretation. *Senate Committee on the Judiciary, S. Rept. 91–617, Organized Crime Control Act of 1970,* 91st Cong., 2d sess., 64–70 (1970). However, the Supreme Court has refused to reconsider the *Alderman* rule and, in fact, reasserted its validity in its *Keith* decision. (*United States v. United States District Court, supra,* at 393.)

must be denied unless disclosure or discovery is required by the requirements of due process.

Subsection (f) provides for notice to be served on United States citizens and permanent resident aliens who were targets of an emergency surveillance and, in the judge's discretion, on other citizens and resident aliens who are incidentally overheard, where a judge denies an application for an order approving an emergency electronic surveillance. Such notice shall be limited to the fact that an application was made, the period of the emergency surveillance, and the fact that during the period information was or was not obtained. This notice may be postponed for a period of up to ninety days upon a showing of good cause to the judge. Thereafter the judge may forego the requirement of notice upon a second showing of good cause.

The fact which triggers the notice requirement—the failure to obtain approval of an emergency surveillance—need not be based on a determination by the court that the target is not an agent of a foreign power engaged in clandestine intelligence activities, sabotage, or terrorist activities or a person aiding such agent. Failure to secure a warrant could be based on a number of other factors, such as an improper certification. A requirement of notice in all cases would have the potential of compromising the fact that the Government had focused an investigation on the target. Even where the target is not, in fact, an agent of a foreign power, giving notice to the person may result in compromising an on-going foreign intelligence investigation because of the logical inferences a foreign intelligence service might draw from the targeting of the individual. For these reasons, the Government is given the opportunity to present its case to the judge for initially postponing notice. After ninety days, during which time the Government may be able to gather more facts, the Government may seek the elimination of the notice requirement altogether.

It is the intent of the Committee that if the Government can initially show that there is a reason to believe that notice might compromise an ongoing investigation, or confidential sources or methods, notice should be postponed. Thereafter, if the Government can show a likelihood that notice would compromise an ongoing investigation, or confidential sources or methods, notice should not be given.

Section 2527

Section 2527 requires the submission of annual reports to both the Congress and the Administrative Office of the United States Courts containing statistical information relating to electronic surveillance under this chapter. Specifically, the reports must include the total number of applications made for orders and extensions and the total number of orders or extensions granted, modified, and denied. The statistics in these reports should present a quantitative indication of the extent to which surveillance under this chapter are used.

The requirements in S. 3197 for the public reporting of certain additional statistics have been altered due to the introduction in S. 1566 of two different types of warrant (creating a 90 day warrant for one class of target, and a one year warrant for "official" foreign powers). The reporting requirements in S. 3197, if reenacted verbatim in S. 1566, would obviously give foreign intelligence networks significant information concerning the number and duration of surveillances of "official" foreign powers. Changes have been made, therefore, in the public reporting requirements of S. 3197 so as to avoid the compromising of sensitive information.

The statistics reported pursuant to this section will provide a basis for further inquiry by appropriate oversight committees of the Congress.

Such congressional oversight is particularly important in monitoring the operation of this statute. By its very nature foreign intelligence surveillance must be conducted in secret. This bill reflects the need for such secrecy; judicial review is limited to a select panel and routine notice to the target is avoided. In addition, unlike the statutory scheme in Title III, it is not contemplated that most electronic surveillance conducted pursuant to this chapter will result in criminal prosecution.

For these reasons, the Committee believes it important that congressional oversight play an important role in the proper implementation of the statute. In that regard section 2527 must be read in the context of other congressional enactments mandating intelligence oversight.[64] This Committee contemplates that the Department of Justice and intelligence agencies will provide such information to those committees as is required by their independent oversight mandate. Indeed, it is expected that some form of Congressional oversight will be written into S. 1566 itself by the Senate Intelligence Committee when the bill is referred to that Committee. Such oversight would be seriously hampered if congressional committees were denied access to the information found in the application record, such as the underlying affidavits and documentation, requests for extensions, the appeal record, orders and decisions of the court.

In addition, in the exercise of its oversight function, the Senate Committee on the Judiciary shall consult with members of the Department of Justice and the intelligence community concerning the proper implementation of the act.

Section 3

Section 3 delays the effective date of the act until 90 days following the designation of the first judge pursuant to section 2523 of this chapter. The

---

[64] See, e.g., S. Res. 400, 95th Cong., 2d Sess. (1976).

purpose of this delay is to allow time for the development of the applications required under this bill and of security measures governing the submission of these applications to the courts. The 90 day delay will also prevent the situation where one judge will be forced to handle all of the applications.

Conforming Amendments

Section 4 serves the important purpose of integrating the new chapter 120 with the current electronic surveillance law found in chapter 119 of title 18, United States Code. Various provisions of chapter 119 are applicable to the electronic surveillance engaged in under the new bill and the conforming amendments in this section of S. 1566 are designed to make changes reflecting this fact. In addition, where certain provisions of chapter 119 should not encompass the surveillance procedures in S. 1566, conforming amendments so limit such sections:

(a)(1) and (2). These amendments are designed to establish the same criminal penalties for violations of this chapter as apply to violations of chapter 119. As amended, these sections will make it a criminal offense to engage in electronic surveillance except as otherwise specifically provided in chapters 119 and 120. This amendment also provides, however, that "with respect to techniques used by law enforcement officers" which do not involve the actual interception of wire or oral communications, yet do fall within the literal definition of electronic surveillance in chapter 120—such as the use of a pen register—the procedures of chapter 120 do not apply. In such cases criminal penalties will not attach simply because the government fails to follow the procedures in chapter 120 (such penalties may, of course, attach if the surveillance is commenced without a search warrant or in violation of a court order.) In all cases involving electronic surveillance for the purpose of obtaining foreign intelligence information, however, the prohibitions of 18 U.S.C. 2511 would apply.

(a) (3), (4), (5), and (6). These amendments make clear that the prohibitions in chapter 119 concerning disclosure and use of information, obtained through the interception of wire or oral communications in sections 2511(1)(c) and (d), also apply to disclosure and use of information obtained through electronic surveillance as defined in chapter 120.

The statute calls for a fine of not more than $10,000 or imprisonment for not more than five years, or both, for each violation.

(b)(1) This amendment adds radio communication to wire communication and extends the meaning of intercept to include "or otherwise acquire" in section 2511(2)(a)(i), which permits communication common carriers to engage in certain activities.

(b)(2) This amendment, when read in conjunction with section 2525(b)(2)(B), makes explicit the fact that a court order obtained under chapter 120 may direct an officer, employee or agent of a communication common carrier to provide certain assistance to the government agents implementing the order. The nature and scope of such assistance is intended to be identical to that which may be directed under section 2518(4)(e) of chapter 119. The amendment further provides that before the carrier may provide such information or assistance, whether under chapter 119 or 120, the government agent must furnish the carrier with an order signed by the court (but not necessarily the same order as authorizes the actual surveillance) if an order has been acquired, or a sworn statement by the agent that all statutory requirements have been met if the surveillance is being conducted pursuant to the provisions of section 2518(7) of chapter 119 or sections 2525(d) of chapter 120. The document so furnished must also set forth the period of time for which the surveillance is authorized and a description of the facilities from which the communication is to be intercepted. Any violation of this subsection by a carrier or its representative will render the carrier liable for the civil damages provided for in section 2520, subject, of course, to the good faith reliance defense contained therein.

(c)(1) This amendment makes explicit that an employee of the Federal Communications Commission may engage in electronic surveillance as well as intercept a wire or oral communication in the discharge of monitoring responsibilities exercised by the Commission.

(c)(2) This amendment makes clear that it is legal to engage in electronic surveillance, as well as intercept a wire or oral communication, if a party consents.

(c)(3) This amendment: (1) provides statutory authorization for the government to conduct tests of equipment which may result in electronic surveillance as defined in section 2521(b)(6); (2) authorizes the conduct of "sweeps" to discover illegal taps and bugs, which "sweeps" may result in "electronic surveillance" as defined in section 2521(b)(6); and (3), makes explicit that chapter 119 and 120 are the "exclusive means by which electronic surveillance, as defined in Section 2521(b)(6) of chapter 120, and the interception of domestic wire and oral communications may be conducted."

All tests conducted pursuant to this provision must be in the normal course of official business by the government agent conducting the test and must be designed solely for determining the capability of equipment used for foreign intelligence gathering purposes. In addition, the test period shall be limited to that necessary to determine such capability and shall in no instance exceed ninety days without the express approval of the Attorney General. The contents of any communication acquired as a result of the test shall be disclosed only to those officials conducting the test and shall be used and retained by them only for the purpose of the test. At the completion of the testing period, the contents so acquired shall be destroyed.

The Committee contemplates that in all cases such testing will be approved by a senior official prior to the commencement of the testing period.

"Sweeps" to discover the existence and capability of electronic surveillance equipment in violation of 18 U.S.C. section 2511 or 47 U.S.C. section 605 do not have a specific time limit, but are limited in time to that "necessary to determine the existence and capability of such equipment".

The Department of Defense, in a letter to the Committee, has characterized these activities as follows:

> These activities, commonly called technical surveillance countermeasures surveys, are for the purpose of determining if a particular sensitive area has been penetrated by electronic surveillance devices installed by a foreign power or other hostile forces. In some cases, these surveys are conducted on a continuous basis. Since these activities are strictly defensive in nature and are for the sole purpose of detecting and neutralizing the illegal efforts of hostile powers, a time limit does not seem appropriate.

Information acquired pursuant to such "sweeps" may be used only to enforce chapter 119 or section 605 of the Communications Act of 1934 or to protect information from being subject to unlawful electronic surveillance. The provision is not an authorization to target a person known to be, or suspected of, engaging in unlawful electronic surveillance, even where the purpose is to determine the existence and capability of that person's electronic surveillance equipment. If the person engaged in the unlawful electronic surveillance is an agent of a foreign power, he should be targeted under the applicable provisions of chapter 120. This provision is designed to confer statutory authority on the Government's effort to locate and analyze unlawful electronic surveillance activity.

A new paragraph (f) is added to section 2511(2) by this conforming amendment, which must be read in conjunction with the conforming amendment contained in paragraph (d) which repeals section 2511(3) of Title 18, United States Code, the so-called "National Security disclaimer" of Title III of the 1968 Omnibus Crime Control and Safe Streets Act. The effect of these two conforming amendments is to establish Chapter 120 as the exclusive congressional statement on the question of the Executive's power to order electronic surveillance.

This new paragraph states that nothing in chapter 119 or section 605 of the Communications Act of 1934 shall be deemed to affect the acquisition of foreign intelligence information by a means other than electronic surveillance, as defined in chapter 120. The purpose of this prefactory phrase is twofold. First, it sets forth the sections of the United States Code which regulate the procedures by which electronic surveillance may be conducted within the United States and the statutory controls for the use and dissemination of information so acquired. If enacted, this chapter will constitute the sole and exclusive statutory authority under which electronic surveillance of a foreign power or its agent to obtain foreign intelligence information may be conducted within the United States. It will complement chapter 119, which deals with electronic surveillance for law enforcement purposes and section 605 of the Communications Act of 1934, as amended, which restricts the dissemination of certain information transmitted by wire or radio. Second, the language of this amendment exempts from section 605 and chapter 119 foreign intelligence gathering by means of an electronic, mechanical or other surveillance device if the acquisition does not come within the definition of "electronic surveillance" contained in section 2521(b)(6). Specifically, this provision is designed to make clear that the legislation does not deal with international signals intelligence activities as currently engaged in by the National Security Agency and electronic surveillance conducted outside the United States. As to methods of acquisition which come within the definition of "electronic surveillance" in this bill, the Congress has declared that this statute, not any claimed presidential power, controls.

The activities of the National Security Agency pose particularly difficult conceptual and technical problems which are not dealt with in this legislation. Although many on the Committee are of the opinion that it is desirable to enact legislative safeguards for such activity, the committee adopts the view expressed by the Attorney General during the hearings that enacting statutory controls to regulate the National Security Agency and the surveillance of Americans abroad raises problems best left to separate legislation.[65] This language insures that certain electronic surveillance activities targeted against international communications for foreign intelligence purposes will not be prohibited absolutely during the interim period when these activities are not regulated by chapter 120 and charters for intelligence agencies and legislation regulating international electronic surveillance have not yet been developed.

Paragraph (f) continues by stating that with respect to electronic surveillance, as defined in Section 2521(b)(6), and the interception of domestic wire and oral communications, the procedures of chapter 119 and chapter 120 shall be the "exclusive means by which electronic surveillance . . . may be . . . conducted." This statement puts to rest the notion that Congress recognizes an inherent Presidential power to conduct such surveillances in the United States outside of the procedures contained in chapters 119 and 120.

It is clear that the Supreme Court has recognized that Congress may legislate in areas, where, absent such legislation, a constitutional power of the executive may be found to exist. *Youngstown Sheet and Tube v. Sawyer*, 343 U.S. 579 (1952)[9]. In that landmark case the Supreme Court rejected President Truman's argument that he had inherent constitutional authority to seize the steel mills to prevent strikes and in-

---

[65] For a discussion of NSA activities and proposed legislative controls, see II Church committee 58–60, 108 and 308–311. The problems posed by electronic surveillance of Americans overseas can be found at pages 305 and 306; see, also III Church committee 733, *et seq.*

sure continued steel production needed for the war effort. The decision was influenced in large measure by the fact that Congress, by passing the Taft-Hartley Act, had explicitly rejected seizure of the steel mills and enacted a legislative alternative to curb labor unrest. In his concurring opinion Justice Jackson wrote:

> When a President takes measures incompatible with the express or implied will of Congress, his power is at the lowest ebb, for then he can rely only upon his own constitutional power minus any Constitutional power of Congress over the matter. Courts can sustain exclusive presidential control in such a case only by disabling the Congress from acting upon the subject. (343 U.S. at 637.)

---

[9] 72 S.Ct. 863, 96 L.Ed. 1153.

(d) This amendment repeals section 2511(3) of chapter 119 eliminating any congressional recognition or suggestion of inherent Presidential power with respect to electronic surveillance.

(e) This amendment brings any electronic surveillance as defined in chapter 120 under the same statutory exclusionary rule as applies to chapter 119. This section imposes an evidentiary sanction for failure to comply with the provisions of the chapter. It makes explicit that not only is the communication itself excluded but also any information obtained from electronic surveillance.

(f) This amendment makes explicit that the requirements for an application enumerated in subsection 2518(1) apply only to surveillance conducted pursuant to chapter 119, since chapter 120 contains its own requirements.

(g) This amendment makes explicit that the necessary elements of an order set forth in subsection 2518(4) apply only to surveillance conducted pursuant to chapter 119, since chapter 120 contains its own requirements.

(h) This amendment makes explicit that the procedures for disclosure of the application and accompanying application under this subsection apply only to surveillances conducted pursuant to chapter 119, since chapter 120 contains its own requirements.

(i) This amendment makes explicit that the provision for a statutory suppression motion contained in this subsection applies only to surveillances conducted pursuant to chapter 119, since chapter 120 contains its own requirements.

(j) This amendment makes explicit that the reporting requirements of the Administrative Office of the United States Courts contained in this subsection apply only to surveillances conducted pursuant to chapter 119 since chapter 120 contains its own requirements.

(k) These amendments are designed to authorize the recovery of civil damages for violations of chapter 120 in the same manner and amounts as already provided for violations of chapter 119. The only category of individuals who would be exempted from the provisions of this section are foreign powers and agents of a foreign power as defined in section 2521(b)(1) and (b)(2)(A) of chapter 120.

Cost Estimate of Congressional Budget Office

October 13, 1977.

Hon. James O. Eastland,
Chairman, Committee on the Judiciary,
U.S. Senate, Washington, D.C.

Dear Mr. Chairman: Pursuant to section 403 of the Congressional Budget Act of 1974, the Congressional Budget Office has reviewed S. 1566, the Foreign Intelligence Surveillance Act of 1977, as ordered reported by the Senate Committee on the Judiciary, October 5, 1977.

Based on this review, it appears that no additional cost to the government would be incurred as a result of enactment of this bill.

Sincerely,

Alice M. Rivlin, *Director.*

MINORITY VIEWS OF SENATOR JAMES ABOUREZK

After giving careful consideration to S. 1566, the Foreign Intelligence Surveillance Act of 1977, I have reluctantly decided that I cannot support this legislation in its present form.

I have reached this decision with great hesitancy, because I endorse the goals of S. 1566—to bring electronic surveillance for foreign intelligence purposes under the rule of law and to put to rest once and for all the myth of some "inherent executive power" which, it has been alleged, superseded the clear mandate of the fourth Amendment to the Constitution.

As to the latter point, S. 1566 is clearly superior to S. 3197, its predecessor from the 94th Congress. For years, Congress has struggled with the question of a supposed inherent Presidential power in the foreign intelligence sphere. Every recent administration has claimed such a power and Congress explicitly recognized the possibility of such an inherent power when it incorporated the "national security disclaimer" in title III of the Omnibus Crime Control and Safe Streets Act of 1968.[66]

When the Ford administration proposed legislation to cover foreign intelligence electronic surveillance in 1976, it nevertheless sought to retain some vestige of this inherent power. Although the Judiciary Committee substantially amended the "Presidential Power" section of S. 3197, the bill as reported by the committee last year did reflect the demand of the Ford Administration that the proposed legislation not completely foreclose the possibility of the President exercising this supposed "constitutional power" in a narrow range of exceptional circumstances. As was noted at that time:

> It is worth emphasizing, as the congressional report indicates, that section 2528 does not constitute either a conferral or a recognition of any Presidential power to conduct warrantless electronic surveillance for foreign national security purposes. Section 2528 simply disclaims congressional intent to mandate the bill's warrant procedures in two possible situations involving surveillance by electronic, mechanical or other technical devices.

> Given their exclusion from the warrant requirement of this legislation, the President may ultimately be found to have power to authorize each of these kinds of surveillance without judicial warrant. But even if such warrantless surveillances were constitutional in the absence of congressional action, Congress could impose a similar warrant procedure as the required mode of conducting them, just as this bill mandates procedures for the forms of surveillance it covers. For now, however, S. 3197 defers the exercise of congressional power in regard to these additional areas of intelligence gathering.

> In this subsection, S. 3197 stops short of asserting the regulatory power of Congress to its fullest extent.[67]

---

[66] 18 U.S.C. 2511(3).

[67] Rept. 94–1035, "Senate Committee on the Judiciary, Foreign Intelligence Surveillance Act of 1976, Additional Views of Senators Abourezk, Hart and Mathias," 94th Cong., 2d sess., 76 (1976).

I am pleased to note that the Judiciary Committee has, this year, asserted its power to the fullest extent as regards electronic surveillance within the United States. The committee has adopted statutory language, with the full support of the Carter administration, which makes it clear that, if enacted, the Congress does not recognize any claim of inherent executive power to engage in electronic surveillance within the United States and that S. 1566 and title III of the 1968 act represent "the exclusive means" by which such activities can be conducted.

I regard this as a very positive action and commend President Carter and Attorney General Bell for their farsighted efforts in this regard.

This is not the only improvement which S. 1566 makes over S. 3197. As the committee report points out, this year's bill also brings within its scope certain targeting activities of the National Security Agency which were not covered by S. 3197. It also allows for a limited degree of judicial review of the executive certifications relating to United States citizens and resident aliens.

Again, I believe that the committee has acted wisely in adopting these improvements to the legislation.

Yet despite these positive features, I believe that S. 1566 is fatally defective in one important respect. It is the inclusion of this fiawed provision that prevents me from supporting the Foreign Intelligence Surveillance Act.

I am referring, of course, to the so-called, noncriminal standard contained in subsection 2521(b)(2)(B)(iii).

For the second year in a row, the Justice Department has prevailed on the committee to include in this legislation a provision that would allow U.S. citizens and resident aliens who were not violating any federal law to be targeted for foreign intelligence electronic surveillance. This year's provision is, in fact, slightly broader than the one finally adopted by the Senate Intelligence Committee last year in that "collection" activities have been added to the definition in S. 1566.

During the committee hearings on the bill, I questioned the Attorney General closely about the need for this noncriminal standard. In addition, in response to a written inquiry he supplied me with six hypothetical cases which, he asserted, pointed up the necessity of this provision.[68]

After carefully reviewing both the oral testimony and written submissions on the question, however, I have not been convinced that this controversial provision is necessary, wise, or, most importantly, consistent with the Constitution.

---

[68] As an appendix, I have attached both the Justice Department's hypotheticals and an analysis of each prepared by the Washington Office of the American Civil Liberties Union.

Let me make it clear that my opposition does not stem from a belief that this noncriminal standard is overly broad. Nor do I believe that its inclusion will result in the wholesome abuses of electronic surveillance that have occurred in the past.

It is clear from any fair reading of subsection 2521(b)(2)(B)(iii) that it has been drafted as narrowly as possible.

Yet, the fact remains that this provision is in direct conflict with my belief that the 4th Amendment requires a showing of probable cause that a criminal offense has been, or is about to be, committed before an American citizen can be subjected to the pervasive type of search which electronic surveillance entails. I believe, as the Church committee found, that "as a matter of principle . . . an American ought not to be targeted for surveillance unless there is probable cause to believe that he may violate the law."[69]

Exposing Americans to such risk should be limited to situations where the alleged activity is sufficiently harmful to the national security to have been made a Federal offense.

It was principally this provision which prevented me from supporting S. 1566 in the Judiciary Committee. I believe that there is some cause for hope, however, that before this bill is scheduled for action by the full Senate, some compromise may be reached on this issue.

Attorney General Bell has already indicated that the Justice Department intends to propose statutory revisions to the espionage law intended to cover those types of intelligence activities which are designed to be covered by the non-criminal standard of S. 1566. If this were done, of course, there would be no need for subsection 2511(b)(2)(B)(iii).

A more likely short-term solution, however, might involve revising that provision of the bill so that it provides the flexibility needed by our intelligence agencies while at the same time protecting the constitutional liberties of our citizens.

I believe that such a formulation—some middle ground which will serve both purposes—can be found.

For my part, I intend to work toward that end. At the committee markup of S. 1566 on October 5, I withdrew my amendment to strike the noncriminal standard in order to provide a more neutral framework for continued discussions with representatives of the Justice Department on this matter. It is my hope that the Attorney General will be responsive to this invitation and will join us in attempting to reach some accommodation on this difficult and important issue.

---

[69] Report 94–755 "Senate Select Committee to Study Governmental Operations With Respect to Intelligence Activities, Final Report, Book II, Intelligence Activities and the Rights of Americans," 94th Congress, 2d Session, 325 (1976).

THE FOREIGN INTELLIGENCE SURVEILLANCE ACT (FISA)
Executive Branch Practice & the FISC Decision

Commentary 157
USA Patriot Act Amendments to FISA 161
Foreign Intelligence Surveillance Court Decision, May 17, 2002 179

Executive Branch Practice & the FISC Decision

"The underlying premise of the legislation (FISA) is that, in certain situations, the use of electronic surveillance to gather foreign intelligence is justified and should be permitted..." (Ira R. Shapiro in *The Harvard Journal of Legislation*, December, 1977, at page 203). Since 1978 there has been a chain of events which has affected the ultimate latitude deemed acceptable for FISA electronic searches. At issue over the years has been the question of the nature and extent of the cooperation authorized between law enforcement agencies (most notably the FBI) and the intelligence community. This issue was framed most often in the context of the warrants FISA authorizes for electronic surveillance.

For over twenty years, governmental offices and individuals attempted to abide by rules and procedures which would comply with the original intentions of FISA. Throughout this period the government operated as if there was a requirement that FISA approvals for electronic surveillance were only available when the "primary purpose" of those actions was foreign intelligence. In part, this practice was adopted because it was thought to be consistent with judicial decisions such as *United States v. Truong*, 629 F. 2d 908 (4th Cir. 1980). Testimony from FBI representatives, and from federal prosecutors clearly indicates a belief that a "wall" existed which restricted the degree of cooperation between law enforcement and intelligence collectors and that such a "wall" was dictated by judicial decisions and Executive Branch practice.

As stated in the Staff Study of the Permanent Select Committee on Intelligence of the House of Representatives dated April 9, 1996 (IC21 Intelligence Community in the 21st Century, at page 286):

> ... The Truong-Humphrey case (4th Cir.) requires that FCI investigations maintain an intelligence focus. When the focus shifts from FCI to criminal, then investigators can not use FCI techniques. Evidence obtained through the use of FCI techniques after the focus shifts to criminal investigation would be suppressed.

In testimony before the Senate Select Committee on Intelligence on September 20, 2002, Michael E. Rolince, representing the FBI, said:

> At times, criminal investigators are also frustrated by a "wall" procedure imposed by the Foreign Intelligence Surveillance Court (FISC). In a class by itself, FISA information is controlled by statute. Although the statute does not preclude the passing of information to criminal investigators, there are restrictions on the use of the information. The FISC and the Department of Justice have been cautious through the years of permitting intelligence and criminal investigators to become closely associated for fear their cooperation would be interpreted as an attempt to circumvent the criminal process.

Mr. Rolince went on to describe the changes under the Patriot Act which permitted much closer cooperation and stated that criminal agents "cannot control the FISA or the FISA process."

At another level, a field representative of the FBI, testifying before the Senate Select Committee on Intelligence on September 20, 2002 stated:

> Briefly, "The Wall" and implied, interpreted, created or assumed restrictions regarding it (cooperation between law enforcement and intelligence community), prevent myself and other FBI agents working a criminal case out of the New York Field Office from obtaining information from the Intelligence Community, regarding Khalid Al-Mihdhar and Nawaf Al-Hazmi in a meeting on June 11, 2001 ... FBI HQ representatives said that FBI New York was compelled to open an "intelligence case" and that I nor any of the other "criminal case" investigators assigned to track Al-Qaeda could attempt to locate him ...

And the view of a federal prosecutor testifying before the joint Intelligence Committee on October 8, 2002 is of note:

> This leads me to another point about information sharing, but in the other direction. If I were to single out one significant concern that I had about our counterterrorism efforts prior to September 11th (dating from at least 1995), it was that I feared we could be hampered in our efforts to detect and prevent terrorist attacks because of the barriers between the intelligence side and the law enforcement side of our government. Some of these barriers were (and perhaps still are) statutory; some were (and perhaps still are) cultural; some were (and still are) court-imposed; some were (and may still be) voluntarily imposed by the agencies by way of guidelines to assure compliance with all legal requirements and to make an adequate record of such compliance ...

> Much of the information gathered by law enforcement as evidence of a terrorist related plot is also most often foreign intelligence information relevant to the national security. And yet ... that evidence, if gathered on the intelligence side, could not be shared with prosecutors unless and until a decision was made in the Justice Department, that it was appropriate to pass that information "over the wall" to prosecutors ... **the requirements of FISA (prior to its amendment) requiring, in the view of some, that "the primary purpose" of every FISA search had to be for national security purposes impeded the FBI in its foreign counter intelligence function.** (emphasis supplied)

The Attorney General, in a memorandum dated March 6, 2002, asserted that amendments to the FISA mean the Act can now "be used *primarily*" for a law enforcement purpose, so long as a significant foreign intelligence purpose remains." This memorandum also detailed new "minimization" procedures which would be followed by the Department of Justice in processing FISA matters. In *In Re All Matters Submitted to the Foreign Intelligence Surveillance Court* (May 17, 2002) the FISC decided that the steps being advocated by the Attorney General had, essentially, broken the "wall" which the Court believed was imposed between the intelligence and criminal prosecution functions. It then went on to determine that the new procedures being submitted would increase the role of criminal prosecutors to such an extent they would be "**directing FISA surveillance and searches from start to finish in counterintelligence cases having overlapping intelligence and criminal investigations or interests ...** " and added this is consistent with the government's contention that the FISA has been amended to allow FISA to be used PRIMARILY for a law enforcement purpose.

The Court went on to state that what the government wished to do was to use FISA to obtain evidence for law enforcement purposes rather than foreign intelligence purposes, thereby substituting the more restrictive rules under Title III electronic surveillances and Rule 41 search with the less rigid FISA standards. Finding "that parts of Section II.B. of the minimization procedures submitted with the Government's motion are NOT reasonably designed, in light of their purposes and technique, consistent with the need of the United States to obtain, produce, or disseminate foreign intelligence information . . ." the Court granted the Government's motion BUT MODIFIED the Government procedures by requiring safeguards in coordination between the FBI and other organizations, prohibited law enforcement officials from making recommendations to intelligence officials concerning the initiation, operation, continuation or expansion of FISA searches or surveillance, and also stated that law enforcement officers could not direct or control the use of FISA procedures to enhance criminal prosecution. It closed its ruling with the statement:

> The purpose of minimization procedures as defined in the Act (FISA), is not to amend the statute, but to protect the privacy of Americans in these highly intrusive surveillances and searches. 'consistent with the need of the United States to obtain, produce, and disseminate foreign intelligence information.

The Government refused to accept the ruling of the Court, and appealed its decision to the Foreign Intelligence Surveillance Court of Review.

USA PATRIOT ACT AMENDMENTS TO FISA

P.L. 107-56
[H.R. 3162]

The following provisions of the USA Patriot Act of 2001 include those which directly affect the FISA and some provisions which expand or elaborate on governmental authority to conduct counter-terrorism activities.

* * *

TITLE II—ENHANCED SURVEILLANCE PROCEDURES

SEC. 201. AUTHORITY TO INTERCEPT WIRE, ORAL, AND ELECTRONIC COMMUNICATIONS RELATING TO TERRORISM.

Section 2516(1) of title 18, United States Code, is amended—

(1) by redesignating paragraph (p), as so redesignated by section 434(2) of the Antiterrorism and Effective Death Penalty Act of 1996 (Public Law 104-132; 110 Stat. 1274), as paragraph (r); and

(2) by inserting after paragraph (p), as so redesignated by section 201(3) of the Illegal Immigration Reform and Immigrant Responsibility Act of 1996 (division C of Public Law 104-208; 110 Stat. 3009-565), the following new paragraph:

'(q) any criminal violation of section 229 (relating to chemical weapons); or sections 2332, 2332a, 2332b, 2332d, 2339A, or 2339B of this title (relating to terrorism); or'.

SEC. 203. AUTHORITY TO SHARE CRIMINAL INVESTIGATIVE INFORMATION.

(a) AUTHORITY TO SHARE GRAND JURY INFORMATION-

(1) IN GENERAL—Rule 6(e)(3)(C) of the Federal Rules of Criminal Procedure is amended to read as follows:

'(C)(i) Disclosure otherwise prohibited by this rule of matters occurring before the grand jury may also be made—

'(I) when so directed by a court preliminarily to or in connection with a judicial proceeding;

'(II) when permitted by a court at the request of the defendant, upon a showing that grounds may exist for a motion to dismiss the indictment because of matters occurring before the grand jury;

'(III) when the disclosure is made by an attorney for the government to another Federal grand jury;

'(IV) when permitted by a court at the request of an attorney for the government, upon a showing that such matters may disclose a violation of State criminal law, to an appropriate official of a State or subdivision of a State for the purpose of enforcing such law; or

'(V) when the matters involve foreign intelligence or counterintelligence (as defined in section 3 of the National Security Act of 1947 (50 U.S.C. 401a)), or foreign intelligence information (as defined in clause (iv) of this subparagraph), to any Federal law enforcement, intelligence, protective, immigration, national defense, or national security official in order to assist the official receiving that information in the performance of his official duties.

'(ii) If the court orders disclosure of matters occurring before the grand jury, the disclosure shall be made in such manner, at such time, and under such conditions as the court may direct.

'(iii) Any Federal official to whom information is disclosed pursuant to clause (i)(V) of this subparagraph may use that information only as necessary in the conduct of that person's official duties subject to any limitations on the unauthorized disclosure of such information. Within a reasonable time after such disclosure, an attorney for the government shall file under seal a notice with the court stating the fact that such information was disclosed and the departments, agencies, or entities to which the disclosure was made.

'(iv) In clause (i)(V) of this subparagraph, the term 'foreign intelligence information' means—

'(I) information, whether or not concerning a United States person, that relates to the ability of the United States to protect against—

'(aa) actual or potential attack or other grave hostile acts of a foreign power or an agent of a foreign power;

'(bb) sabotage or international terrorism by a foreign power or an agent of a foreign power; or

'(cc) clandestine intelligence activities by an intelligence service or network of a foreign power or by an agent of foreign power; or

'(II) information, whether or not concerning a United States person, with respect to a foreign power or foreign territory that relates to—

'(aa) the national defense or the security of the United States; or

'(bb) the conduct of the foreign affairs of the United States.'.

(2) CONFORMING AMENDMENT—Rule 6(e)(3)(D) of the Federal Rules of Criminal Procedure is amended by striking '(e)(3)(C)(i)' and inserting '(e)(3)(C)(i)(I)'.

(b) AUTHORITY TO SHARE ELECTRONIC, WIRE, AND ORAL INTERCEPTION INFORMATION—

(1) LAW ENFORCEMENT—Section 2517 of title 18, United States Code, is amended by inserting at the end the following:

'(6) Any investigative or law enforcement officer, or attorney for the Government, who by any means authorized by this chapter, has obtained knowledge of the contents of any wire, oral, or electronic communication, or evidence derived therefrom, may disclose such contents to any other Federal law enforcement, intelligence, protective, immigration, national defense, or national security official to the extent that such contents include foreign intelligence or counterintelligence (as defined in section 3 of the National Security Act of 1947 (50 U.S.C. 401a)), or foreign intelligence information (as defined in subsection (19) of section 2510 of this title), to assist the official who is to receive that information in the performance of his official duties. Any Federal official who receives information pursuant to this provision may use that information only as necessary in the conduct of that person's official duties subject to any limitations on the unauthorized disclosure of such information.'.

(2) DEFINITION—Section 2510 of title 18, United States Code, is amended by—

(A) in paragraph (17), by striking 'and' after the semicolon;

(B) in paragraph (18), by striking the period and inserting '; and'; and

(C) by inserting at the end the following:

'(19) 'foreign intelligence information' means—

'(A) information, whether or not concerning a United States person, that relates to the ability of the United States to protect against—

'(i) actual or potential attack or other grave hostile acts of a foreign power or an agent of a foreign power;

'(ii) sabotage or international terrorism by a foreign power or an agent of a foreign power; or

'(iii) clandestine intelligence activities by an intelligence service or network of a foreign power or by an agent of a foreign power; or

'(B) information, whether or not concerning a United States person, with respect to a foreign power or foreign territory that relates to—

'(i) the national defense or the security of the United States; or

'(ii) the conduct of the foreign affairs of the United States.'.

(c) PROCEDURES—The Attorney General shall establish procedures for the disclosure of information pursuant to section 2517(6) and Rule 6(e)(3)(C)(i)(V) of the Federal Rules of Criminal Procedure that identifies a United States person, as defined in section 101 of the Foreign Intelligence Surveillance Act of 1978 (50 U.S.C. 1801)).

(d) FOREIGN INTELLIGENCE INFORMATION—

(1) IN GENERAL—Notwithstanding any other provision of law, it shall be lawful for foreign intelligence or counterintelligence (as defined in section 3 of the National Security Act of 1947 (50 U.S.C. 401a)) or foreign intelligence information obtained as part of a criminal investigation to be disclosed to any Federal law enforcement, intelligence, protective, immigration, national defense, or national security official in order to assist the official receiving that information in the performance of his official duties. Any Federal official who receives information pursuant to

this provision may use that information only as necessary in the conduct of that person's official duties subject to any limitations on the unauthorized disclosure of such information.

(2) DEFINITION—In this subsection, the term 'foreign intelligence information' means—

(A) information, whether or not concerning a United States person, that relates to the ability of the United States to protect against—

(i) actual or potential attack or other grave hostile acts of a foreign power or an agent of a foreign power;

(ii) sabotage or international terrorism by a foreign power or an agent of a foreign power; or

(iii) clandestine intelligence activities by an intelligence service or network of a foreign power or by an agent of a foreign power; or

(B) information, whether or not concerning a United States person, with respect to a foreign power or foreign territory that relates to—

(i) the national defense or the security of the United States; or

(ii) the conduct of the foreign affairs of the United States.

SEC. 206. ROVING SURVEILLANCE AUTHORITY UNDER THE FOREIGN INTELLIGENCE SURVEILLANCE ACT OF 1978.

Section 105(c)(2)(B) of the Foreign Intelligence Surveillance Act of 1978 (50 U.S.C. 1805(c)(2)(B)) is amended by inserting ', or in circumstances where the Court finds that the actions of the target of the application may have the effect of thwarting the identification of a specified person, such other persons,' after 'specified person'.

SEC. 207. DURATION OF FISA SURVEILLANCE OF NON-UNITED STATES PERSONS WHO ARE AGENTS OF A FOREIGN POWER.

(a) DURATION—

(1) SURVEILLANCE—Section 105(e)(1) of the Foreign Intelligence Surveillance Act of 1978 (50 U.S.C. 1805(e)(1)) is amended by—

(A) inserting '(A)' after 'except that'; and

(B) inserting before the period the following: ', and (B) an order under this Act for a surveillance targeted against an agent of a foreign power, as defined in section 101(b)(1)(A) may be for the period specified in the application or for 120 days, whichever is less'.

(2) PHYSICAL SEARCH—Section 304(d)(1) of the Foreign Intelligence Surveillance Act of 1978 (50 U.S.C. 1824(d)(1)) is amended by—

(A) striking 'forty-five' and inserting '90';

(B) inserting '(A)' after 'except that'; and

(C) inserting before the period the following: ', and (B) an order under this section for a physical search targeted against an agent of a foreign power as defined in section 101(b)(1)(A) may be for the period specified in the application or for 120 days, whichever is less'.

(b) EXTENSION—

(1) IN GENERAL—Section 105(d)(2) of the Foreign Intelligence Surveillance Act of 1978 (50 U.S.C. 1805(d)(2)) is amended by—

(A) inserting '(A)' after 'except that'; and

(B) inserting before the period the following: ', and (B) an extension of an order under this Act for a surveillance targeted against an agent of a foreign power as defined in section 101(b)(1)(A) may be for a period not to exceed 1 year'.

(2) DEFINED TERM—Section 304(d)(2) of the Foreign Intelligence Surveillance Act of 1978 (50 U.S.C. 1824(d)(2) is amended by inserting after 'not a United States person,' the following: 'or against an agent of a foreign power as defined in section 101(b)(1)(A),'.

SEC. 208. DESIGNATION OF JUDGES.

Section 103(a) of the Foreign Intelligence Surveillance Act of 1978 (50 U.S.C. 1803(a)) is amended by—

(1) striking 'seven district court judges' and inserting '11 district court judges'; and

(2) inserting 'of whom no fewer than 3 shall reside within 20 miles of the District of Columbia' after 'circuits'.

SEC. 209. SEIZURE OF VOICE-MAIL MESSAGES PURSUANT TO WARRANTS.

Title 18, United States Code, is amended—

(1) in section 2510—

(A) in paragraph (1), by striking beginning with 'and such' and all that follows through 'communication'; and

(B) in paragraph (14), by inserting 'wire or' after 'transmission of'; and

(2) in subsections (a) and (b) of section 2703—

(A) by striking 'CONTENTS OF ELECTRONIC' and inserting 'CONTENTS OF WIRE OR ELECTRONIC' each place it appears;

(B) by striking 'contents of an electronic' and inserting 'contents of a wire or electronic' each place it appears; and

(C) by striking 'any electronic' and inserting 'any wire or electronic' each place it appears.

SEC. 214. PEN REGISTER AND TRAP AND TRACE AUTHORITY UNDER FISA.

(a) APPLICATIONS AND ORDERS—Section 402 of the Foreign Intelligence Surveillance Act of 1978 (50 U.S.C. 1842) is amended—

(1) in subsection (a)(1), by striking 'for any investigation to gather foreign intelligence information or information concerning international terrorism' and inserting 'for any investigation to obtain foreign intelligence information not concerning a United States person or to protect against international terrorism or clandestine intelligence activities, provided that such investigation of a United States person is not conducted solely upon the basis of activities protected by the first amendment to the Constitution';

(2) by amending subsection (c)(2) to read as follows:

'(2) a certification by the applicant that the information likely to be obtained is foreign intelligence information not concerning a United States person or is relevant to an ongoing investigation to protect against international terrorism or clandestine intelligence activities, provided that such investigation of a United States person is not conducted solely upon the basis of activities protected by the first amendment to the Constitution.';

(3) by striking subsection (c)(3); and

(4) by amending subsection (d)(2)(A) to read as follows:

'(A) shall specify—

'(i) the identity, if known, of the person who is the subject of the investigation;

'(ii) the identity, if known, of the person to whom is leased or in whose name is listed the telephone line or other facility to which the pen register or trap and trace device is to be attached or applied;

'(iii) the attributes of the communications to which the order applies, such as the number or other identifier, and, if known, the location of the telephone line or other facility to which the pen register or trap and trace device is to be attached or applied and, in the case of a trap and trace device, the geographic limits of the trap and trace order.'.

(b) AUTHORIZATION DURING EMERGENCIES—Section 403 of the Foreign Intelligence Surveillance Act of 1978 (50 U.S.C. 1843) is amended—

(1) in subsection (a), by striking 'foreign intelligence information or information concerning international terrorism' and inserting 'foreign intelligence information not concerning a United States person or

information to protect against international terrorism or clandestine intelligence activities, provided that such investigation of a United States person is not conducted solely upon the basis of activities protected by the first amendment to the Constitution'; and

(2) in subsection (b)(1), by striking 'foreign intelligence information or information concerning international terrorism' and inserting 'foreign intelligence information not concerning a United States person or information to protect against international terrorism or clandestine intelligence activities, provided that such investigation of a United States person is not conducted solely upon the basis of activities protected by the first amendment to the Constitution'.

SEC. 215. ACCESS TO RECORDS AND OTHER ITEMS UNDER THE FOREIGN INTELLIGENCE SURVEILLANCE ACT.

Title V of the Foreign Intelligence Surveillance Act of 1978 (50 U.S.C. 1861 et seq.) is amended by striking sections 501 through 503 and inserting the following:

'SEC. 501. ACCESS TO CERTAIN BUSINESS RECORDS FOR FOREIGN INTELLIGENCE AND INTERNATIONAL TERRORISM INVESTIGATIONS.

'(a)(1) The Director of the Federal Bureau of Investigation or a designee of the Director (whose rank shall be no lower than Assistant Special Agent in Charge) may make an application for an order requiring the production of any tangible things (including books, records, papers, documents, and other items) for an investigation to protect against international terrorism or clandestine intelligence activities, provided that such investigation of a United States person is not conducted solely upon the basis of activities protected by the first amendment to the Constitution.

'(2) An investigation conducted under this section shall—

'(A) be conducted under guidelines approved by the Attorney General under Executive Order 12333 (or a successor order); and

'(B) not be conducted of a United States person solely upon the basis of activities protected by the first amendment to the Constitution of the United States.

'(b) Each application under this section—

'(1) shall be made to—

'(A) a judge of the court established by section 103(a); or

'(B) a United States Magistrate Judge under chapter 43 of title 28, United States Code, who is publicly designated by the Chief Justice of the United States to have the power to hear applications and grant orders for the production of tangible things under this section on behalf of a judge of that court; and

'(2) shall specify that the records concerned are sought for an authorized investigation conducted in accordance with subsection (a)(2) to obtain foreign intelligence information not concerning a United States person or to protect against international terrorism or clandestine intelligence activities.

'(c)(1) Upon an application made pursuant to this section, the judge shall enter an ex parte order as requested, or as modified, approving the release of records if the judge finds that the application meets the requirements of this section.

'(2) An order under this subsection shall not disclose that it is issued for purposes of an investigation described in subsection (a).

'(d) No person shall disclose to any other person (other than those persons necessary to produce the tangible things under this section) that the Federal Bureau of Investigation has sought or obtained tangible things under this section.

'(e) A person who, in good faith, produces tangible things under an order pursuant to this section shall not be liable to any other person for such production. Such production shall not be deemed to constitute a waiver of any privilege in any other proceeding or context.

'SEC. 502. CONGRESSIONAL OVERSIGHT.

'(a) On a semiannual basis, the Attorney General shall fully inform the Permanent Select Committee on Intelligence of the House of Representatives and the Select Committee on Intelligence of the Senate concerning all requests for the production of tangible things under section 402.

'(b) On a semiannual basis, the Attorney General shall provide to the Committees on the Judiciary of the House of Representatives and the Senate a report setting forth with respect to the preceding 6-month period—

'(1) the total number of applications made for orders approving requests for the production of tangible things under section 402; and

'(2) the total number of such orders either granted, modified, or denied.'.

SEC. 216. MODIFICATION OF AUTHORITIES RELATING TO USE OF PEN REGISTERS AND TRAP AND TRACE DEVICES.

(a) GENERAL LIMITATIONS—Section 3121(c) of title 18, United States Code, is amended—

(1) by inserting 'or trap and trace device' after 'pen register';

(2) by inserting ', routing, addressing,' after 'dialing'; and

(3) by striking 'call processing' and inserting 'the processing and transmitting of wire or electronic communications so as not to include the contents of any wire or electronic communications'.

(b) ISSUANCE OF ORDERS—

(1) IN GENERAL—Section 3123(a) of title 18, United States Code, is amended to read as follows:

'(a) IN GENERAL—

'(1) ATTORNEY FOR THE GOVERNMENT—Upon an application made under section 3122(a)(1), the court shall enter an ex parte order authorizing the installation and use of a pen register or trap and trace device anywhere within the United States, if the court finds that the attorney for the Government has certified to the court that the information likely to be obtained by such installation and use is relevant to an ongoing criminal investigation. The order, upon service of that order, shall apply to any person or entity providing wire or electronic communication service in the United States whose assistance may facilitate the execution of the order. Whenever such an order is served on any person or entity not specifically named in the order, upon request of such person or entity, the attorney for the Government or law enforcement or investigative officer that is serving the order shall provide written or electronic certification that the order applies to the person or entity being served.

'(2) STATE INVESTIGATIVE OR LAW ENFORCEMENT OFFICER—Upon an application made under section 3122(a)(2), the court shall enter an ex parte order authorizing the installation and use of a pen register or trap and trace device within the jurisdiction of the court, if the court finds that the State law enforcement or investigative officer has certified to the court that the information likely to be obtained by such installation and use is relevant to an ongoing criminal investigation.

'(3)(A) Where the law enforcement agency implementing an ex parte order under this subsection seeks to do so by installing and using its own pen register or trap and trace device on a packet-switched data network of a provider of electronic communication service to the public, the agency shall ensure that a record will be maintained which will identify—

'(i) any officer or officers who installed the device and any officer or officers who accessed the device to obtain information from the network;

'(ii) the date and time the device was installed, the date and time the device was uninstalled, and the date, time, and duration of each time the device is accessed to obtain information;

'(iii) the configuration of the device at the time of its installation and any subsequent modification thereof; and

'(iv) any information which has been collected by the device.

To the extent that the pen register or trap and trace device can be set automatically to record this information electronically, the record shall be maintained electronically throughout the installation and use of such device.

'(B) The record maintained under subparagraph (A) shall be provided ex parte and under seal to the court which entered the ex parte order authorizing the installation and use of the device within 30 days after termination of the order (including any extensions thereof).'.

(2) CONTENTS OF ORDER—Section 3123(b)(1) of title 18, United States Code, is amended—

(A) in subparagraph (A)—

(i) by inserting 'or other facility' after 'telephone line'; and

(ii) by inserting before the semicolon at the end 'or applied'; and

(B) by striking subparagraph (C) and inserting the following:

'(C) the attributes of the communications to which the order applies, including the number or other identifier and, if known, the location of the telephone line or other facility to which the pen register or trap and trace device is to be attached or applied, and, in the case of an order authorizing installation and use of a trap and trace device under subsection (a)(2), the geographic limits of the order; and'.

(3) NONDISCLOSURE REQUIREMENTS—Section 3123(d)(2) of title 18, United States Code, is amended—

(A) by inserting 'or other facility' after 'the line'; and

(B) by striking ', or who has been ordered by the court' and inserting 'or applied, or who is obligated by the order'.

(c) DEFINITIONS—

(1) COURT OF COMPETENT JURISDICTION—Section 3127(2) of title 18, United States Code, is amended by striking subparagraph (A) and inserting the following:

'(A) any district court of the United States (including a magistrate judge of such a court) or any United States court of appeals having jurisdiction over the offense being investigated; or'.

(2) PEN REGISTER—Section 3127(3) of title 18, United States Code, is amended—

(A) by striking 'electronic or other impulses' and all that follows through 'is attached' and inserting 'dialing, routing, addressing, or signaling information transmitted by an instrument or facility from which a wire or electronic communication is transmitted, provided, however, that such information shall not include the contents of any communication'; and

(B) by inserting 'or process' after 'device' each place it appears.

(3) TRAP AND TRACE DEVICE—Section 3127(4) of title 18, United States Code, is amended—

(A) by striking 'of an instrument' and all that follows through the semicolon and inserting 'or other dialing, routing, addressing, and signaling information reasonably likely to identify the source of a wire or electronic communication, provided, however, that such information shall not include the contents of any communication;'; and

(B) by inserting 'or process' after 'a device'.

(4) CONFORMING AMENDMENT—Section 3127(1) of title 18, United States Code, is amended—

(A) by striking 'and'; and

(B) by inserting ', and 'contents' after 'electronic communication service'.

(5) TECHNICAL AMENDMENT—Section 3124(d) of title 18, United States Code, is amended by striking 'the terms of'.

(6) CONFORMING AMENDMENT—Section 3124(b) of title 18, United States Code, is amended by inserting 'or other facility' after 'the appropriate line'.

SEC. 218. FOREIGN INTELLIGENCE INFORMATION.

Sections 104(a)(7)(B) and section 303(a)(7)(B) (50 U.S.C. 1804(a)(7)(B) and 1823(a)(7)(B)) of the Foreign Intelligence Surveillance Act of 1978 are each amended by striking 'the purpose' and inserting 'a significant purpose'.

SEC. 219. SINGLE-JURISDICTION SEARCH WARRANTS FOR TERRORISM.

Rule 41(a) of the Federal Rules of Criminal Procedure is amended by inserting after 'executed' the following: 'and (3) in an investigation of domestic terrorism or international terrorism (as defined in section 2331 of title 18, United States Code), by a Federal magistrate judge in any district in which activities related to the terrorism may have occurred, for a search of property or for a person within or outside the district'.

SEC. 220. NATIONWIDE SERVICE OF SEARCH WARRANTS FOR ELECTRONIC EVIDENCE.

(a) IN GENERAL—Chapter 121 of title 18, United States Code, is amended—

(1) in section 2703, by striking 'under the Federal Rules of Criminal Procedure' every place it appears and inserting 'using the procedures described in the Federal Rules of Criminal Procedure by a court with jurisdiction over the offense under investigation'; and

(2) in section 2711—

(A) in paragraph (1), by striking 'and';

(B) in paragraph (2), by striking the period and inserting '; and'; and

(C) by inserting at the end the following:

'(3) the term 'court of competent jurisdiction' has the meaning assigned by section 3127, and includes any Federal court within that definition, without geographic limitation.'.

(b) CONFORMING AMENDMENT—Section 2703(d) of title 18, United States Code, is amended by striking 'described in section 3127(2)(A)'.

SEC. 224. SUNSET.

(a) IN GENERAL—Except as provided in subsection (b), this title and the amendments made by this title (other than sections 203(a), 203(c), 205, 208, 210, 211, 213, 216, 219, 221, and 222, and the amendments made by those sections) shall cease to have effect on December 31, 2005.

(b) EXCEPTION—With respect to any particular foreign intelligence investigation that began before the date on which the provisions referred to in subsection (a) cease to have effect, or with respect to any particular offense or potential offense that began or occurred before the date on which such provisions cease to have effect, such provisions shall continue in effect.

TITLE V—REMOVING OBSTACLES TO INVESTIGATING TERRORISM

SEC. 504. COORDINATION WITH LAW ENFORCEMENT.

(a) INFORMATION ACQUIRED FROM AN ELECTRONIC SURVEILLANCE—Section 106 of the Foreign Intelligence Surveillance Act of 1978 (50 U.S.C. 1806), is amended by adding at the end the following:

'(k)(1) Federal officers who conduct electronic surveillance to acquire foreign intelligence information under this title may consult with Federal law enforcement officers to coordinate efforts to investigate or protect against—

'(A) actual or potential attack or other grave hostile acts of a foreign power or an agent of a foreign power;

'(B) sabotage or international terrorism by a foreign power or an agent of a foreign power; or

'(C) clandestine intelligence activities by an intelligence service or network of a foreign power or by an agent of a foreign power.

'(2) Coordination authorized under paragraph (1) shall not preclude the certification required by section 104(a)(7)(B) or the entry of an order under section 105.'.

(b) INFORMATION ACQUIRED FROM A PHYSICAL SEARCH—Section 305 of the Foreign Intelligence Surveillance Act of 1978 (50 U.S.C. 1825) is amended by adding at the end the following:

'(k)(1) Federal officers who conduct physical searches to acquire foreign intelligence information under this title may consult with Federal law enforcement officers to coordinate efforts to investigate or protect against—

'(A) actual or potential attack or other grave hostile acts of a foreign power or an agent of a foreign power;

'(B) sabotage or international terrorism by a foreign power or an agent of a foreign power; or

'(C) clandestine intelligence activities by an intelligence service or network of a foreign power or by an agent of a foreign power.

'(2) Coordination authorized under paragraph (1) shall not preclude the certification required by section 303(a)(7) or the entry of an order under section 304.'.

TITLE VIII—STRENGTHENING THE CRIMINAL LAWS AGAINST TERRORISM

SEC. 802. DEFINITION OF DOMESTIC TERRORISM.

(a) DOMESTIC TERRORISM DEFINED—Section 2331 of title 18, United States Code, is amended—

(1) in paragraph (1)(B)(iii), by striking 'by assassination or kidnapping' and inserting 'by mass destruction, assassination, or kidnapping';

(2) in paragraph (3), by striking 'and';

(3) in paragraph (4), by striking the period at the end and inserting '; and'; and

(4) by adding at the end the following:

'(5) the term 'domestic terrorism' means activities that—

'(A) involve acts dangerous to human life that are a violation of the criminal laws of the United States or of any State;

'(B) appear to be intended—

'(i) to intimidate or coerce a civilian population;

'(ii) to influence the policy of a government by intimidation or coercion; or

'(iii) to affect the conduct of a government by mass destruction, assassination, or kidnapping; and

'(C) occur primarily within the territorial jurisdiction of the United States.'.

(b) CONFORMING AMENDMENT—Section 3077(1) of title 18, United States Code, is amended to read as follows:

'(1) 'act of terrorism' means an act of domestic or international terrorism as defined in section 2331;'.

SEC. 817. EXPANSION OF THE BIOLOGICAL WEAPONS STATUTE.

Chapter 10 of title 18, United States Code, is amended—

(1) in section 175—

(A) in subsection (b)—

(i) by striking 'does not include' and inserting 'includes';

(ii) by inserting 'other than' after 'system for'; and

(iii) by inserting 'bona fide research' after 'protective';

(B) by redesignating subsection (b) as subsection (c); and

(C) by inserting after subsection (a) the following:

'(b) ADDITIONAL OFFENSE—Whoever knowingly possesses any biological agent, toxin, or delivery system of a type or in a quantity that, under the circumstances, is not reasonably justified by a prophylactic, protective, bona fide research, or other peaceful purpose, shall be fined under this title, imprisoned not more than 10 years, or both. In this subsection, the terms 'biological agent' and 'toxin' do not encompass any biological agent or toxin that is in its naturally occurring environment, if the biological agent or toxin has not been cultivated, collected, or otherwise extracted from its natural source.';

(2) by inserting after section 175a the following:

'SEC. 175b. POSSESSION BY RESTRICTED PERSONS.

'(a) No restricted person described in subsection (b) shall ship or transport interstate or foreign commerce, or possess in or affecting commerce, any biological agent or toxin, or receive any biological agent or toxin that has been shipped or transported in interstate or foreign commerce, if the biological agent or toxin is listed as a select agent in subsection (j) of section 72.6 of title 42, Code of Federal Regulations, pursuant to section 511(d)(l) of the Antiterrorism and Effective Death Penalty Act of 1996 (Public Law 104-132), and is not exempted under subsection (h) of such section 72.6, or appendix A of part 72 of the Code of Regulations.

'(b) In this section:

'(1) The term 'select agent' does not include any such biological agent or toxin that is in its naturally-occurring environment, if the biological agent or toxin has not been cultivated, collected, or otherwise extracted from its natural source.

'(2) The term 'restricted person' means an individual who—

'(A) is under indictment for a crime punishable by imprisonment for a term exceeding 1 year;

'(B) has been convicted in any court of a crime punishable by imprisonment for a term exceeding 1 year;

'(C) is a fugitive from justice;

'(D) is an unlawful user of any controlled substance (as defined in section 102 of the Controlled Substances Act (21 U.S.C. 802));

'(E) is an alien illegally or unlawfully in the United States;

'(F) has been adjudicated as a mental defective or has been committed to any mental institution;

'(G) is an alien (other than an alien lawfully admitted for permanent residence) who is a national of a country as to which the Secretary of State, pursuant to section 6(j) of the Export Administration Act of 1979 (50 U.S.C. App. 2405(j)), section 620A of chapter 1 of part M of the Foreign Assistance Act of 1961 (22 U.S.C.

2371), or section 40(d) of chapter 3 of the Arms Export Control Act (22 U.S.C. 2780(d)), has made a determination (that remains in effect) that such country has repeatedly provided support for acts of international terrorism; or

'(H) has been discharged from the Armed Services of the United States under dishonorable conditions.

'(3) The term 'alien' has the same meaning as in section 1010(a)(3) of the Immigration and Nationality Act (8 U.S.C. 1101(a)(3)).

'(4) The term 'lawfully admitted for permanent residence' has the same meaning as in section 101(a)(20) of the Immigration and Nationality Act (8 U.S.C. 1101(a)(20)).

'(c) Whoever knowingly violates this section shall be fined as provided in this title, imprisoned not more than 10 years, or both, but the prohibition contained in this section shall not apply with respect to any duly authorized United States governmental activity.'; and

(3) in the chapter analysis, by inserting after the item relating to section 175a the following:

'175b. Possession by restricted persons.'.

TITLE IX—IMPROVED INTELLIGENCE

SEC. 901. RESPONSIBILITIES OF DIRECTOR OF CENTRAL INTELLIGENCE REGARDING FOREIGN INTELLIGENCE COLLECTED UNDER FOREIGN INTELLIGENCE SURVEILLANCE ACT OF 1978.

Section 103(c) of the National Security Act of 1947 (50 U.S.C. 403-3(c)) is amended—

(1) by redesignating paragraphs (6) and (7) as paragraphs (7) and (8), respectively; and

(2) by inserting after paragraph (5) the following new paragraph (6):

'(6) establish requirements and priorities for foreign intelligence information to be collected under the Foreign Intelligence Surveillance Act of 1978 (50 U.S.C. 1801 et seq.), and provide assistance to the Attorney General to ensure that information derived from electronic surveillance or physical searches under that Act is disseminated so it may be used efficiently and effectively for foreign intelligence purposes, except that the Director shall have no authority to direct, manage, or undertake electronic surveillance or physical search operations pursuant to that Act unless otherwise authorized by statute or Executive order;'.

SEC. 905. DISCLOSURE TO DIRECTOR OF CENTRAL INTELLIGENCE OF FOREIGN INTELLIGENCE-RELATED INFORMATION WITH RESPECT TO CRIMINAL INVESTIGATIONS.

(a) IN GENERAL—Title I of the National Security Act of 1947 (50 U.S.C. 402 et seq.) is amended—

(1) by redesignating subsection 105B as section 105C; and

(2) by inserting after section 105A the following new section 105B:

'DISCLOSURE OF FOREIGN INTELLIGENCE ACQUIRED IN CRIMINAL INVESTIGATIONS; NOTICE OF CRIMINAL INVESTIGATIONS OF FOREIGN INTELLIGENCE SOURCES

'SEC. 105B. (a) DISCLOSURE OF FOREIGN INTELLIGENCE—(1) Except as otherwise provided by law and subject to paragraph (2), the Attorney General, or the head of any other department or agency of the Federal Government with law enforcement responsibilities, shall expeditiously disclose to the Director of Central Intelligence, pursuant to guidelines developed by the Attorney General in consultation with the Director, foreign intelligence acquired by an element of the Department of Justice or an element of such department or agency, as the case may be, in the course of a criminal investigation.

'(2) The Attorney General by regulation and in consultation with the Director of Central Intelligence may provide for exceptions to the applicability of paragraph (1) for one or more classes of foreign intelligence, or foreign intelligence with respect to one or more targets or matters, if the Attorney General determines that disclosure of such foreign intelligence under that paragraph would jeopardize an ongoing law enforcement investigation or impair other significant law enforcement interests.

'(b) PROCEDURES FOR NOTICE OF CRIMINAL INVESTIGATIONS—Not later than 180 days after the date of enactment of this section, the Attorney General, in consultation with the Director of Central Intelligence, shall develop guidelines to ensure that after receipt of a report from an element of the intelligence community of activity of a foreign intelligence source or potential foreign intelligence source that may warrant investigation as criminal activity, the Attorney General provides notice to the Director of Central Intelligence, within a reasonable period of time, of his intention to commence, or decline to commence, a criminal investigation of such activity.

'(c) PROCEDURES—The Attorney General shall develop procedures for the administration of this section, including the disclosure of foreign intelligence by elements of the Department of Justice, and elements of other departments and agencies of the Federal Government, under subsection (a) and the provision of notice with respect to criminal investigations under subsection (b).'.

(b) CLERICAL AMENDMENT—The table of contents in the first section of that Act is amended by striking the item relating to section 105B and inserting the following new items:

'Sec. 105B. Disclosure of foreign intelligence acquired in criminal investigations; notice of criminal investigations of foreign intelligence sources.

'Sec. 105C. Protection of the operational files of the National Imagery and Mapping Agency.'.

TITLE X—MISCELLANEOUS

SEC. 1003. DEFINITION OF 'ELECTRONIC SURVEILLANCE'.

Section 101(f)(2) of the Foreign Intelligence Surveillance Act (50 U.S.C. 1801(f)(2)) is amended by adding at the end before the semicolon the following: ', but does not include the acquisition of those communications of computer trespassers that would be permissible under section 2511(2)(i) of title 18, United States Code'.

FOREIGN INTELLIGENCE SURVEILLANCE COURT DECISION

May 17, 2002

FILED
KAREN E. SUTTON, CLERK
MAY 17 2002
U.S. Foreign Intelligence Surveillance Court

UNITED STATES
FOREIGN INTELLIGENCE SURVEILLANCE COURT

IN RE ALL MATTERS SUBMITTED TO THE FOREIGN INTELLIGENCE SURVEILLANCE COURT

Docket Numbers: Multiple

MEMORANDUM OPINION (AS CORRECTED AND AMENDED)

I

The Department of Justice has moved this Court to vacate the minimization and "wall" procedures in all cases now or ever before the Court, including this Court's adoption of the Attorney General's July 1995 intelligence sharing procedures, which are not consistent with new intelligence sharing procedures submitted for approval with this motion. The Court has considered the Government's motion, the revised intelligence sharing procedures, and the supporting memorandum of law as required by the Foreign Intelligence Surveillance Act (hereafter the FISA or the Act) at 50 U.S.C. §1805(a)(4) and §1824(a)(4) (hereafter omitting citations to 50 U.S.C.) to determine whether the proposed minimization procedures submitted with the Government's motion comport with the definition of minimization procedures under §1801(h) and §1921(4) of the Act. The Government's motion will be GRANTED, EXCEPT THAT THE PROCEDURES MUST BE MODIFIED IN PART.

The Court's analysis and findings are as follows:

JURISDICTION. Section 1803 of the FISA which established this Court provides that the Court "shall have jurisdiction to hear applications for and grant orders approving electronic surveillance anywhere within the United States under the procedures set forth in this Act." The comparable provision added when the FISA was amended to include physical searches appears in §1822(c) entitled "Jurisdiction of Foreign Intelligence Surveillance Court," and says

> The Foreign Intelligence Surveillance Court shall have jurisdiction to hear applications for and grant orders approving a physical search *for the purpose of obtaining foreign intelligence information* anywhere in the United States under the procedures set forth in this subchapter. (emphasis added)

Examination of the text of the statute leaves little doubt that the collection of foreign intelligence information is the *raison d'etre* for the FISA. Starting with its title, foreign intelligence information is the core of the Act.

- foreign intelligence information is defined in §1801(e);

- minimization procedures to protect the privacy rights of Americans, defined in §1801(h), and §1821(4), must be reasonably designed and consistent with the need of the United States to obtain, produce, and disseminate foreign intelligence information;

- section 1802(b) which authorizes the Government to file applications for electronic surveillance with this Court, empowers the judges of this Court to grant orders "approving electronic surveillance of a foreign power or agent of a foreign power *for the purpose of obtaining foreign intelligence information.*" (emphasis added);

- applications for electronic surveillance and physical search must contain a certification from a senior Executive Branch official (normally the FBI Director in U.S. person cases) that "the information sought is foreign intelligence information," that "a significant purpose of the surveillance is to obtain foreign intelligence information," that "such [foreign intelligence] information cannot reasonably be obtained by normal investigative techniques," and "designates the type of foreign intelligence information being sought." (§1804(a)(7)) Comparable requirements apply in applications for physical searches. (§1923(a)(7)).

- Applications for physical searches must contain a statement of the facts and circumstances relied on by the FBI affiant to justify his or her belief that the premises or property to be searched contains foreign intelligence information and a statement of the nature of the foreign intelligence information being sought. (§1823(a)(4)(B) and §1823(a)(6).

Additionally, the two Presidential Executive orders empowering the Attorney General to approve the filing of applications for electronic surveillances and physical searches, and granting the FBI Director and other senior executives the power to make the certifications required under the Act, specify "*the purpose of obtaining foreign intelligence information.*" (emphasis added) E.O. 12139, May 23, 1979, and E.O. 12949, February 9, 1995). Clearly this Court's jurisdiction is limited to granting orders for electronic surveillances and physical searches for the collection of foreign intelligence information under the standards and procedures prescribed in the Act.[47]

SCOPE. Our findings regarding minimization apply only to communications of or concerning U.S. persons as defined in §1801(i) of the act: U.S. citizens and permanent resident aliens whether or not they are the named targets in the electronic surveillances and physical searches. Conversely, this opinion does not apply to communications of foreign powers defined in §1801(a), nor to non-U.S. persons.

METHODOLOGY. The analysis and findings in this opinion are based on traditional statutory construction of the FISA's provisions. The question before the Court involves straightforward application of the FISA as it pertains to minimization procedures, and raises no constitutional questions that need be decided. Discretion to evaluate proposed minimization procedures has been vested in the Court by the Congress expressly in the Act, (§1805(a)(4) and §1824(a)(4)). The Court's determinations are grounded in the plain language of the FISA, and where applicable, in its legislative history. The statute requires the Court to make the necessary findings, to issue orders "as requested or modified," for electronic surveillances and physical searches, as well as to "assess compliance" with minimization procedures for information concerning U.S. persons. (§1805 and §1824 of the Act).

CONSIDERATION OF THE ISSUE. Prior to May of 1979, when the FISA became operational, it was not uncommon for courts to defer to the expertise of the Executive Branch in matters of foreign intelligence collection. Since May 1979, this Court has often recognized the expertise of the government in foreign intelligence collection and counterintelligence investigations of espionage and international terrorism, and accorded great weight to the government's interpretation of FISA's standards. However, this Court, or on appeal the Foreign Intelligence Surveillance Court of Review having jurisdiction "to review the denial of any application," is the arbiter of the FISA's terms and requirements. (§1803(b)) The present seven members of the Court have reviewed and approved several thousand FISA applications, including many hundreds of surveillances and searches of U.S. persons. The members bring their specialized knowledge to the issue at hand, mindful of the FISA's preeminent role in preserving our national security, not only in the present national emergency, but for the long term as a constitutional democracy under the rule of law.

II

We turn now to the government's proposed minimization procedures which are to be followed in all electronic surveillances and physical searches past, present, and future. In addition to the Standard Minimization Procedures for a

U.S. Person Agent of a Foreign Power that are filed with the Court, which we continue to approve, the government has submitted new supplementary minimization procedures adopted by the Attorney General and promulgated in the form of a memorandum addressed to the Director of the FBI and other senior Justice Department executives and dated March 6, 2002. (hereafter the Attorney General's memorandum or the 2002 procedures). The Attorney General's memorandum is divided into three sections entitled:

"I. INTRODUCTION AND STATEMENT Of GENERAL PRINCIPLES,"[48]

"II. INTELLIGENCE SHARING PROCEDURES CONCERNING THE CRIMINAL DIVISION," AND "III. INTELLIGENCE SHARING PROCEDURES CONCERNING A USAO."

The focus of this decision is sections II and III which set out supplementary procedures affecting the acquisition, retention, and dissemination of information obtained through electronic surveillances and physical searches of U.S. persons to be approved as part of the government's applications and incorporated in the orders of this Court.

Our duty regarding approval of these minimization procedures is inscribed in the Act, as is the standard we must follow in our decision making. Where Congress has enacted a statute like the FISA, and defined its terms, we are bound to follow those definitions. We cannot add to, subtract from, or modify the words used by Congress, but must apply the FISA's provisions with fidelity to their plain meaning and in conformity with the overall statutory scheme. The FISA is a statute of unique character, intended to authorize electronic surveillances and physical searches of foreign powers and their agents, including U.S. Persons. "Further, as a statute addressed entirely to 'specialists,' it must as Mr. Justice Frankfurter observed, 'be read by judges with the minds of *** specialists'."[49]

The Attorney General's new minimization procedures are designed to regulate acquisition, retention, and dissemination of information involving the FISA (i.e., disseminating information, consulting, and providing advice) between FBI counterintelligence and counterterrorism officials on the one hand, and FBI criminal investigators, trial attorneys in the Justice Department's Criminal Division, and U.S. Attorney's Offices on the other hand. These new minimization procedures supersede similar procedures issued by the Attorney General in July 1995 (hereafter the 1995 procedures) which were augmented in January 2000 and then in August 2001 by the current Deputy Attorney General. The Court has relied on the 1995 procedures, which have been followed by the FBI and the Justice Department in all electronic surveillance and physical searches of U.S. persons since their promulgation in July 1995. In November 2001, the court formally adopted the 1995 procedures, as augmented, as minimization procedures defined in §1801(h) and §1821(4), and has incorporated them in all applicable orders and warrants granted since then.

The 2002 procedures have been submitted to the Court pursuant to §1804(a)(5) and §1823(a)(5) to supplement the Standard Minimization Procedures for U.S. Person Agents of Foreign Powers. Both sets of procedures are to be applied in past and future electronic surveillances and physical searches subject to the approval of this Court. Pursuant to §1805(a) and §1824(a) the Court has carefully considered the 2002 intelligence sharing procedures. The Court finds that these procedures 1) have been adopted by the Attorney General, 2) are designed to minimize the acquisition and retention, and prohibit the dissemination, of nonpublicly available information concerning unconsenting United States persons, and 3) are, therefore, minimization procedures as defined in §1801(h) and §1821(4).

The standard we apply in these findings is mandated in §1805(a)(4) and §1824(a)(4), which state that "the proposed minimization procedures meet the definition of minimization procedures under §101(h), [§1801(h) and §1821(4)] of the Act." The operative language of each section to be applied by the Court provides that minimization procedures must be reasonably designed in light of their purpose and technique, and mean—

> specific procedures, which shall be adopted by the Attorney General, that are reasonably designed in light of the purpose and technique of the particular surveillance, [search] to minimize the acquisition and retention, and prohibit the dissemination, of nonpublicly available information concerning unconsenting United States persons consistent with the need of the United States to obtain, produce, and disseminate foreign intelligence information. §1801(h)(1) and §1821(4)(A).

Thus in approving minimization procedures the Court is to ensure that the intrusiveness of foreign intelligence surveillances and searches on the privacy of U.S. persons is "consistent" with the need of the United States to collect foreign intelligence information from foreign powers and their agents.

Our deliberations begin with an examination of the first part of §1801(h) and §1821(4) involving the acquisition, retention and dissemination of U.S. person information. Most of the rules and procedures for minimization are set forth in the Standard Minimization Procedures which will continue to be applied along with the 2002 procedures, and permit exceptionally thorough acquisition and collection through a broad army of contemporaneous electronic surveillance techniques. Thus, in many U.S. person electronic surveillances the FBI will be authorized to conduct, simultaneously, telephone, microphone, call phone, e-mail and computer surveillance of the U.S. person target's home, workplace and vehicles. Similar breadth is accorded the FBI in physical searches of the target's residence, office, vehicles, computer, safe deposit box and U.S. mails where supported by probable cause. The breadth of acquisition is premised an the fact that clandestine intelligence activities and activities in preparation for international terrorism are undertaken with considerable discretion and support from sophisticated intelligence services of nation states and well-financed groups engaged in international terrorism.

The intrusiveness of the FBI's electronic surveillances and sophisticated searches and seizures is sanctioned by the following practices and provisions in the FISA:

- a foreign intelligence standard of probable cause instead of the more traditional criminal standard of probable cause;
- having to show only that the place or facility to be surveilled or searched is being used or about to be used without the need of showing that it is being used in furtherance of the espionage or terrorist activities;
- surveillances and searches are conducted surreptitiously without notice to the target unless they are prosecuted;
- surveillances and now searches arc authorized for 90 days, and may continue for as long as one year or more in certain cases;
- large amounts of information are collected by automatic recording to be minimized after the fact;
- most information intercepted or seized has a dual character as both foreign intelligence information and evidence of crime (e.g., the identity of a spy's handler, his/her communication signals and deaddrop locations; the fact that a terrorist is taking flying lessons, or purchasing explosive chemicals) differentiated primarily by the persons using the information;[50]
- when facing criminal prosecution, a target cannot obtain discovery of the FISA applications and affidavits supporting the Court's orders in order to challenge them because the FISA mandates in camera, ex parte review by the district court "if the Attorney General files an affidavit under oath that disclosure or an adversary hearing would harm the national security." §1806(f))and §1825(g)

It is self evident that the technical and surreptitious means available for acquisition of information by electronic surveillances and physical searches, coupled with the scope and duration of such intrusions and other practices under the FISA, give the government a powerful engine for the collection of foreign intelligence information targeting U.S. persons.

Retention under the standard minimization procedures is also heavily weighted toward the government's need for foreign intelligence information. Virtually all information seized, whether by electronic surveillance or physical search, is minimized hours, days, or weeks after collection. The principal steps in the minimization process are the same for electronic surveillances and physical searches:

- information is reduced to an intelligible form: if recorded it is transcribed, if in a foreign language it is translated, if in electronic or computer storage it is accessed and printed, if in code it is decrypted and if on film or similar media it is developed and printed;

- once the information is understandable, a reviewing official, usually an FBI case agent, makes an informed judgment as to whether the information seized is or might be foreign intelligence information related to clandestine intelligence activities or international terrorism;
- if the information is determined to be, or might be, foreign intelligence, it is logged into the FBI's records and filed in a variety of storage systems from which it can be retrieved for analysis, for counterintelligence investigations or operations, or for use at criminal trial;
- if found not to be foreign intelligence information, it must be minimized, which can be done in a variety of ways depending upon the format of the information: if recorded the information would not be indexed, and thus become non-retrievable, if in hard copy from facsimile intercept or computer print-out it should be discarded, if on re-recordable media it could be erased, or if too bulky or too sensitive, it might be destroyed.

These same principles of minimization are applied to all information collected, whether by electronic surveillance or physical search. The most critical step in retention is the analysis in which an informed judgment is made as to whether or not the communications or other data seized is foreign intelligence information. To guide FBI personnel in this determination the Standard Minimization Procedures for U.S. Person Agent of a Foreign Power in Section 3(a)(4) Acquisition/Interception/Monitoring and Logging provide that "communications of or concerning United States persons that could not be foreign intelligence information or are not evidence of a crime . . . may not be logged or summarized." (emphasis added). Minimization is required only if the information "could not be" foreign intelligence. Thus, it is obvious that the standard for retention of FISA-acquired information is weighted heavily in favor of the government.

This brings us to the third and perhaps most complex part of minimization practice, the dissemination and use of FISA- acquired information. Recognizing the broad sweep of acquisition allowed under FISA's definition of electronic surveillance (and, subsequently, physical searches), coupled with the low threshold for retention in the "could not be foreign intelligence" standard, Congress has provided guidance for the Court in the FISA's legislative history:

> On the other hand, given this degree of latitude the committee believes it is imperative that with respect to information concerning U.S. persons which is retained as necessary for counterintelligence or counter terrorism purposes, *rigorous and strict controls* be placed on the retrieval of such identifiable information and its dissemination or use *for purposes other than counterintelligence or counter terrorism.* (emphasis added)[51]
>
> The judge has the *discretionary power to modify* the order sought, such as with regard to the period of authorization . . . or the *minimization procedures* to be followed. (emphasis added)[52] The Committee contemplates that the court would

give these procedures most careful consideration. If it is *not* of the opinion that they will be *effective*, the procedures should be modified. (emphasis added)[53]

Between 1979 when the FISA became operational and 1995, the government relied on the standard minimization procedures described herein to regulate all electronic surveillance. In 1995, following amendment of the FISA to permit physical searches, comparable minimization procedures were adopted for foreign intelligence searches. On July 19, 1995, the Attorney General issued *Procedures for Contracts Between the FBI and Criminal Division Concerning FI and Foreign Counterintelligence Investigations*, which in part A regulated "Contacts During an FI or FCI Investigation in Which FISA Surveillance or Searches are Being Conducted" between FBI personnel and trial attorneys of the Department's Criminal Division. The Court was duly informed of these procedures and has considered them an integral part of the minimization process although they were not formally submitted to the Court under §1804 (a)(5) or §1823(a)(5). In January, 2000 the Attorney General augmented the 1995 procedures to permit more information sharing from FISA cases with the Criminal Division, and the current Deputy Attorney General expanded the procedures in August 2001. Taken together, the 1995 Procedures, as augmented, permit substantial consultation and coordination as follows:

a. reasonable indications of significant federal crimes in FISA cases are to be reported to the Criminal Division of the Department of Justice;

b. The Criminal Division may then consult with the FBI and give guidance to the FBI aimed at preserving the option of criminal prosecution, but may not direct or control the FISA investigation toward law enforcement objectives;

c. the Criminal Division may consult further with the appropriate U.S. Attorney's Office about such FISA cases;

d. on a monthly basis senior officials of the FBI provide briefings to senior officials of the Justice Department, including OIPR, and the Criminal Division, about intelligence cases, including those in which FISA is or may be used;

e. all FBI 90-day interim reports and annual reports of counterintelligence investigations, including FISA cases, are being provided to the Criminal Division, and must now contain a section explicitly identifying any possible federal criminal violations;

f. all requests for initiation or renewal of FISA authority must now contain a section devoted explicitly to identifying any possible federal criminal violations;

g. the FBI is to provide monthly briefings directly to the Criminal Division concerning all counterintelligence investigations in which there is a reasonable indication of a significant federal crime;

h. prior to each briefing the Criminal Division is to identify (from FBI reports) those intelligence investigations about which it requires additional information and the FBI is to provide the information requested; and

i. since September 11, 2001, the requirement that OIPR be present at all meetings and discussions between the FBI and Criminal Division involving certain FISA cases has been suspended; instead, OIPR reviews a daily briefing book to inform itself and this Court about those discussions.

The Court came to rely on these supplementary procedures, and approved their broad information sharing and coordination with the Criminal Division in thousands of applications. In addition, because of the FISA's requirement (since amended) that the FBI Director certify that "the purpose" of each surveillance and search was to collect foreign intelligence information, the Court was routinely apprised of consultations and discussions between the FBI, the Criminal Division, and U.S. Attorney's offices in cases where there were overlapping intelligence and criminal investigations or interests. This process increased dramatically in numerous FISA applications concerning the September 11th attack on the World Trade Center and the Pentagon.

In order to preserve both the appearance and the fact that FISA surveillances and searches were not being used *sub rosa* for criminal investigations, the Court routinely approved the use of information screening "walls" proposed by the government in its applications. Under the normal "wall" procedures, where there were separate intelligence and criminal *investigations*, or a single counter-espionage investigation with overlapping intelligence and criminal *interests*, FBI criminal investigators and Department prosecutors were not allowed to review all of the raw FISA intercepts or seized materials lest they become defacto partners in the FISA surveillances and searches. Instead, a screening mechanism, or person, usually the chief legal counsel in a FBI field office, or an assistant U.S. attorney not involved in the overlapping criminal investigation, would review all of the raw intercepts and seized materials and pass on only that information which might be relevant evidence. In unusual cases such as where attorney-client intercepts occurred, Justice Department lawyers in OIPR acted as the "wall." In significant cases, involving major complex investigations such as the bombings of the U.S. Embassies in Africa, and the millennium investigations, where criminal investigations of FISA targets were being conducted concurrently, and prosecution was likely, this Court became the "wall" so that FISA information could not be disseminated to criminal prosecutors without the Court's approval. In some cases where this Court was the "wall," the procedures seemed to have functioned as provided in the Court's orders; however, in an alarming number of instances, there have been troubling results.

Beginning in March 2000, the government notified the Court that them had been disseminations of FISA information to criminal squads in the FBI's New York field office, and to the U.S. Attorney's Office for the Southern District of Now York, without the required authorization of the Court as the"wall" in four or five FISA cases. Subsequently, the government filed a notice with the Court about its unauthorized disseminations.

In September 2000, the government came forward to confess error in some 75 FISA applications related to major terrorist attacks directed agaiinst the United States. The errors related to misstatements and omissions of material facts. including:

> a. an erroneous statement in the FBI Director's FISA certification that the target of the FISA was not under criminal investigation;
>
> b. erroneous statements in the FISA affidavits of FBI agents concealing the separation of the overlapping intelligence and criminal investigations, and the unauthorized sharing of FISA information with FBI criminal investigators and assistant U.S. attorneys;
>
> c. omissions of material facts from FBI FISA affidavits relating to a prior relationship between the FBI and a FISA target, and the interview of a FISA target by an assistant U.S. attorney.

In November of 2000, the Court held a special meeting to consider the troubling number of inaccurate FBI affidavits in so many FISA applications. After receiving a more detailed explanation from the Department of Justice about what went wrong, *but not why*, the Court decided not to accept inaccurate affidavits from FBI agents whether or not intentionally false. One FBI agent was barred from appearing before the Court as a FISA affiant. The Court decided to await the results of the investigation by the Justice Department's Office of Professional Responsibility before taking further action.

In March of 2001, the government reported similar misstatements in another series of FISA applications in which there was supposedly a "wall" between separate intelligence and criminal squads in FBI field offices to screen FISA intercepts, when in fact all of the FBI agents were on the same squad and all of the screening was done by the one supervisor overseeing both investigations.

To come to grips with this problem, in April of 2001, the FBI promulgated detailed procedures governing the submission of requests to conduct FISA surveillances and searches, and to review draft affidavits in FISA applications, to ensure their accuracy. These procedures are currently in use and require careful review of draft affidavits by the FBI agents in the field offices who are conducting the FISA case investigations, as well as the supervising agents at FBI headquarters who appear before the Court and swear to the affidavits.

In virtually every instance, the government's misstatements and omissions in FISA applications and violations of the Court's orders involved information sharing and unauthorized disseminations to criminal investigators and prosecutors. These incidents have been under investigation by the FBI's and the Justice Department's Offices of Professional Responsibility for more than one year to determine how the violations occurred in the field offices, and how the misinformation found its way into the FISA applications and remained uncorrected for more than one year despite procedures to verify the accuracy of FISA pleadings. As of this date, no report has been published, and how these misrepresentations occurred remains unexplained to the Court.

As a consequence of the violations of its orders, the Court has taken some supervisory actions to assess compliance with the "wall" procedures. First, until September 15, 2001, it required all Justice Department personnel who received certain FISA information to certify that they understood that under "wall" procedures FISA information was not to be shared with criminal prosecutors without the Court's approval. Since then, the Court has authorized criminal division trial attorneys to review all FBI international terrorism case files, including FISA case files and required reports from FBI personnel and Criminal Division attorneys describing their discussions of the FISA cases. The government's motion that the Court rescind all "wall" procedures in all international terrorism surveillances and searches now pending before the Court, or that has been before the Court at anytime in the past, was deferred by the Court until now at the suggestion of the government, pending resolution of this matter.

Given this history in FISA information sharing, the Court now turns to the revised 2002 minimization procedures. We recite this history to make clear that the Court has long approved, under controlled circumstances, the sharing of FISA information with criminal prosecutors as well as consultations between intelligence and criminal investigations where FISA surveillances and searches are being conducted. However, the proposed 2002 minimization procedures eliminate the bright line in the 1995 procedures prohibiting direction and control by prosecutors on which the Court has relied to moderate the broad acquisition retention, and dissemination of FISA information in overlapping intelligence and criminal investigations. Paragraph A.6 of the 1995 procedures provided in part:

> Additionally, the FBI and the Criminal Division should ensure that advice intended to preserve the option of a criminal prosecution does not inadvertently result in either the fact or the appearance of the Criminal Division's *directing or controlling* the FI or FCI investigation toward law enforcement objectives. (emphasis added)

As we conclude the first part of our statutory task, we have determined that the extensive acquisition of information concerning U.S. persons through secretive surveillances and searches authorized under FISA, coupled with broad powers of retention and information sharing with criminal prosecutors, weigh heavily on one side of the scale which we must balance to ensure that the proposed minimization procedures are consistent with the need of the United States to obtain, produce, and disseminate *foreign intelligence information*. (§1805(a)(4) and §1824(a)(4))

III

The 2002 minimization rules set out in sections II and III, "Intelligence Sharing Procedures Concerning the Criminal Division" and "Intelligence Sharing Procedures Concerning a USAO," continue the existing practice approved by this Court of in-depth dissemination of FISA infomation to Criminal Division trial attorneys and U.S. Attorney's Offices (*hereafter criminal prosecutors*). These new procedures apply in two kinds of counterintelligence cases in which *FISA is the only effective tool available* to both counterintelligence and criminal investigators:

> 1) those cases in which separate intelligence and criminal investigations of the same U.S. person FISA target are conducted by different FBI agents (*overlapping investigations*), usually involving international terrorism, and in which separation can easily be maintained, and

> 2) those cases in which one investigation having a U.S. person FISA target is conducted by a team of FBI agents which has both intelligence and criminal interests (*overlapping interests*) usually involving espionage and similar crimes in which separation is impractical.

In both kinds of counterintelligence investigations where FISA is being used, the proposed 2002 minimization procedures authorize extensive consultations between the FBI and criminal prosecutors "to coordinate efforts to investigate or protect against" actual or potential attack, sabotage, international terrorism and clandestine intelligence activities by foreign powers and their agents as now expressly provided in §1806(k)(1) and §1825(k)(1), These consultations propose to include:

> II. A. "*Disseminating Information*," which gives criminal prosecutors access to "all information developed" in FBI counterintelligence investigations, including FISA acquired information, as well as annual and other reports, and presumably ad hoc reporting of significant events (e.g., incriminating FISA intercepts or seizures) to criminal prosecutors.

> II. B. "*Providing Advice*," where criminal prosecutors are authorized to consult extensively and provide advice and recommendations to intelligence officials about "all issues necessary to the ability of the United States to investigate or protect against foreign attack, sabotage, terrorism, and clandestine intelligence activities." Recommendations may include advice about criminal investigation and prosecution as well as the strategy and goals for investigations, the law enforcement and intelli-

gence methods to be used in investigations, and the interaction between intelligence and law enforcement components of investigations.

Last, but most relevant to this Court's finding, criminal prosecutors are empowered to advise FBI *intelligence officials* concerning *"the initiation, operation, continuation, or expansion of FISA searches and surveillance."* (emphasis added). This provision is designed to use this Court's orders to enhance criminal investigation and prosecution, consistent with the government's interpretation of the recent amendments that FISA may now be "used *primarily* for a law enforcement purpose."

In section III, "Intelligence Sharing Procedures Concerning a USAO," U.S. attorneys are empowered to "engage in consultations to the same extent as the Criminal Division under parts II. A and II. B of these procedures," in cases involving international terrorism.

A fair reading of those provisions leaves only one conclusion—under sections II and III of the 2002 minimization procedures, criminal prosecutors are to have a significant role *directing* FISA surveillances and searches from start to finish in counterintelligence cases having overlapping intelligence and criminal investigations or interests, guiding them to criminal prosecution. The government makes no secret of this policy, asserting its interpretation of the Act's new amendments which "allows FISA to be used *primarily* for a law enforcement purpose."

Given our experience in FISA surveillances and searches, we find that these provisions in sections II.B and III, particularly those which authorize criminal prosecutors to advise FBI intelligence officials on the initiation, operation, continuation or expansion of FISA's intrusive seizures, are designed to enhance the acquisition, retention and dissemination of *evidence for law enforcement purposes, instead* of being consistent with the need of the United States to "obtain, produce, and disseminate *foreign intelligence information* (emphasis added) as mandated in §1801(h)and §1821(4). The 2002 procedures appear to be designed to amend the law and substitute the FISA for Title III electronic surveillances and Rule 41 searches. This may be because the government is unable to meet the substantive requirements of these law enforcement tools, or because their administrative burdens are too onerous. In either case, the FISA's definition of minimization procedures has not changed, and these procedures cannot be used by the government to amend the Act in ways Congress has not. We also find the provisions in section II.B and III. wanting because the prohibition in the 1995 procedures of criminal prosecutors *"directing or controlling"* FISA cases has been revoked by the proposed 2002 procedures. The government's memorandum of law expends considerable effort justifying deletion of that bright line, but the Court is not persuaded.

The Court has long accepted and approved minimization procedures authorizing in-depth information sharing and coordination with criminal prosecutors as described in detail above. In the Court's view, the plain meaning of consultations and coordination now specifically authorized in the Act is based on the need to adjust or bring into alignment two different but complementary interests—intelligence gathering and law enforcement. In FISA cases this presupposes separate intelligence and criminal investigations, or a single investigation with intertwined interests, which need to be brought into harmony to avoid dysfunction and frustration of either interest. If criminal prosecutors direct both the intelligence and criminal investigations, or a single investigation having combined interests, *coordination becomes subordination* of both investigations or interests to law enforcement objectives. The proposed 2002 minimization procedures require the Court to balance the government's use of FISA surveillances and searches against the government's need to obtain and use evidence for criminal prosecution, determining the "need of the United States to obtain, produce, and disseminate foreign intelligence information" as mandated by §1801(h) and §1821(4).

Advising FBI intelligence officials on the initiation, operation, continuation or expansion of FISA surveillances and searches of U.S. persons means that criminal prosecutors will tell the FBI when to use FISA (perhaps when they lack probable cause for a Title III electronic surveillance), what techniques to use, what information to look for, what information to keep as evidence and when use of FISA can cease because there is enough evidence to arrest and prosecute. The 2002 minimization procedures give the Department's criminal prosecutors every legal advantage conceived by Congress to be used by U.S. intelligence agencies to collect foreign intelligence information, including:

- a foreign intelligence standard instead of a criminal standard of probable cause;
- use of the most advanced and highly intrusive techniques for intelligence gathering; and
- surveillances and searches for extensive periods of time;

based on a standard that the U.S. person is only using or about to use the places to be surveilled and searched, without any notice to the target unless arrested and prosecuted, and, if prosecuted, no adversarial discovery of the FISA applications and warrants. All of this may be done by use of procedures intended to minimize collection of U.S. person information, consistent with the need of the United States to obtain and produce foreign intelligence information. If direction of counterintelligence cases involving the use of highly intrusive FISA surveillances and searches by criminal prosecutors is necessary to obtain and produce foreign intelligence information, it is yet to be explained to the Court.

THEREFORE, because

- the procedures implemented by the Attorney General govern the minimization of electronic surveillances and searches of U.S. persons;

- such intelligence and criminal investigations both target the same U.S. person;
- the information collected through FISA surveillances and searches is both foreign intelligence information and evidence of crime, depending upon who is using it;
- there are pervasive and invasive techniques for electronic surveillances and physical searches authorized under the FISA;
- surveillances and searches may be authorized for extensive periods of time;
- notice of surveillances and searches is not given to the targets unless they prosecuted;
- the provisions in FISA constrain discovery and adversary hearings and require ex parte, in camera review of FISA surveillances and searches at criminal trial;
- the FISA, as opposed to Title III and Rule 41 searches, is the only tool available in these overlapping intelligence and criminal investigations;
- there are extensive provisions in the minimization procedures for dissemination of FISA intercepts and seizures to criminal prosecutors and for consultation and coordination with intelligence officials using the FISA;
- criminal prosecutors would, under the proposed procedures, no longer be prohibited from "directing or controlling" counterintelligence investigations involving use of the FISA toward *law enforcement objectives*; and
- criminal prosecutors would, under the proposed procedures, be empowered to direct the use of FISA surveillances and searches *toward law enforcement objectives* by advising FBI intelligence officials on the initiation, operation, continuation and expansion of FISA authority from this Court,

The Court FINDS that parts of section II.B of the minimization procedures submitted with the Government's motion are NOT reasonably designed, in light of their purpose and technique, "consistent with the need of the United States to obtain, produce, or disseminate foreign intelligence information" as defined in §1801(h) and §1821(4) of the Act.

THEREFORE, pursuant to this Court's authority under §1805(a) and §1824(a) to issue ex parte orders for electronic surveillances and physical searches *"as requested or as modified,"* the Court herewith grants the Governments motion BUT MODIFIES the pertinent provisions of sections II.B. of the proposed minimization procedures as follows:

> The second and third paragraphs of section II.B shall be deleted, and the following paragraphs substituted in place thereof:
>
>> The FBI, the Criminal Division, and OIPR may consult with each other to coordinate their efforts to investigate or protect against foreign attack or other grave hostile acts, sabotage, international terrorism or clandestine intelligence activities by foreign powers or their agents. Such consultations and co-

ordination may address, among other things, exchanging information already acquired, identifying categories of information needed and being sought, preventing either investigation or interest from obstructing or hindering the other, compromise of either investigation, and long term objectives and overall strategy of both investigations in order to ensure that the overlapping intelligence and criminal interests of the United States are both achieved. Such consultations and coordination may be conducted directly between the components, however, OIPR shall be invited to all such consultations, and if they are unable to attend, OIPR shall be apprised of the substance of the consultations forthwith in writing so that the Court may be notified at the earliest opportunity.

Notwithstanding the foregoing, law enforcement officials shall not make recommendations to intelligence officials concerning the initiation, operation, continuation or expansion of FISA searches or surveillances. Additionally, the FBI and the Criminal Division shall ensure that law enforcement officials do not direct or control the use of the FISA procedures to enhance criminal prosecution, and that advice intended to preserve the option of a criminal prosecution does not inadvertently result in the Criminal Division's directing or controlling the investigation using FISA searches and surveillances toward law enforcement objectives.

These modifications are intended to bring the minimization procedures into accord with the language used in the FISA, and reinstate the bright line used in the 1995 procedures, on which the Court has relied. The purpose of minimization procedures as defined in the Act, is not to amend the statute, but to protect the privacy of Americans in these highly intrusive surveillances and searches, "consistent with the need of the United States to obtain, produce, and disseminate foreign intelligence information.

A separate order shall issue this date.

All seven judges of the Court concur in the Corrected and Amended Memorandum Opinion.

ROYCE C. LAMBERTH
Presiding Judge

DATE: 5-17-02 6:40 p.m.

FILED
KAREN E. SUTTON, CLERK
MAY 17 2002
U.S. Foreign Intelligence
Surveillance Court

UNITED STATES
FOREIGN INTELLIGENCE SURVEILLANCE COURT

IN RE ALL MATTERS SUBMITTED TO THE FOREIGN INTELLIGENCE SURVEILLANCE COURT

Docket Numbers: Multiple

ORDER (AS AMENDED)

Motion having been made by the United States of America, by James A. Baker, Counsel for Intelligence Policy, United States Department of Justice, for the Court to approve proposed minimization procedures entitled *Intelligence Sharing Procedures for Foreign Intelligence and Foreign Counterintelligence Investigations Conducted by the FBI*, to be used in electronic surveillances and physical searches authorized by this Court, as well as a supporting memorandum of law, and a supplemental memorandum, which filing was approved by the Attorney General of the United States, and full consideration having been given to the matters set forth therein, the Court finds:

1. The President has authorized the Attorney General of the United States to approve applications for electronic surveillance and physical search for foreign intelligence purposes. 50 U.S.C. §1805(a)(1) and §1824(a)(1);

2. The motion has been made by a Federal officer and approved by the Attorney General, 50 U.S.C. §1805(a)(2) and §1824(a)(2);

3. The proposed minimization procedures entitled *Intelligence Sharing Procedures for Foreign Intelligence and Foreign Counterintelligence Investigations Conducted by the FBI* as modified herein, meet the definition of minimization procedures under §1801(h) and §1821(4)of the Act, 50 U.S.C. §1805(a)(4) and §1824(a)(4).

WHEREFORE IT IS ORDERED,

A. The aforementioned minimization procedures are herewith modified, pursuant to this Court's authority under 50 U.S.C. §1805(a) and (c) and 50

U.S.C. §1824(a) and (c), to delete the second, third, and fourth paragraphs from Section I of the proposed minimization procedures. A revised statement of "General Principles" that is not inconsistent with the Court's opinion may be included in the Attorney General's memorandum.

B. The aforementioned minimization procedures are further modified, pursuant to this Court's authority under 50 U.S.C. §1805(a) and (c) and 50 U.S.C. §1824(a) and (c), to delete the second and third paragraphs from Section II.B and substitute the following paragraphs in place thereof:

> The FBI, the Criminal Division, and OIPR may consult with each other to coordinate their efforts to investigate or protect against foreign attack or other grave hostile acts, sabotage, international terrorism, or clandestine intelligence activities by foreign powers or their agents. Such consultations and coordination may address, among other things, exchanging in information already acquired; identifying categories of information needed and being sought; preventing either investigation or interest from obstructing or hindering the other; compromise of either investigation: and long term objectives and overall strategy of both investigations in order to ensure that the overlapping intelligence and criminal interests of the United States are both achieved. Such consultations and coordination may be conducted directly between the components; however, OIPR shall be invited to all such consultations, and if they are unable to attend, OIPR shall be apprized of the substance or the meetings forthwith in writing so that the Court may be notified at the earliest opportunity."

> "Notwithstanding the foregoing, law enforcement officials shall not make recommendations to intelligence officials concerning the initiation, operation, continuation or expansion of FISA searches or surveillances. Additionally, the FBI and the Criminal Division shall ensure that law enforcement officials do not direct or control the use of the FISA procedures to enhance criminal prosecution, and that advice intended to preserve the option of a criminal prosecution does not inadvertently result in the Criminal Division's directing or controlling the investigation using FISA searches and surveillances toward law enforcement objectives.

C. Use of the aforementioned minimization procedures as modified, in all *future* electronic surveillance and physical searches shall be subject to the approval of the Court in each electronic surveillance and physical search where their use is proposed by the Government pursuant to 50 U.S.C. §1804(a)(5)) and §1823(a)(5).

WHEREFORE, IT IS FURTHER ORDERED, pursuant to the authority conferred on this Court by the Foreign Intelligence Surveillance Act, that the motion of the United States to use the aforementioned minimization procedures as modified, in all electronic surveillances and physical searches already approved by the Court, as described in the Government's motion is GRANTED AS MODIFIED herein.

A separate Memorandum Opinion bas been filed this date. The motion of the United States has been considered by all of the judges of this Court, all of whom concur in the Memorandum Opinion and in the Order. The

Court has also adopted a new administrative rule to monitor compliance with this Order as follows:

Rule 11. Criminal Investigations in FISA Cases

All FISA applications shall include informative descriptions of any ongoing criminal investigations of FISA targets, as well as the substance of any consultations between the FBI and criminal prosecutors at the Department of Justice or a United States Attorney's Office.

All seven judges of the Court concur in this Amended Order.

ROYCE C. LAMBERTH
Presiding Judge,
United States Foreign Intelligence
Surveillance Court

Signed 5-17-02 6:40 p.m. E.S.T.

FILED
KAREN E. SUTTON, CLERK
MAY 17 2002
U.S. Foreign Intelligence
Surveillance Court

UNITED STATES
FOREIGN INTELLIGENCE SURVEILLANCE COURT

IN RE ALL MATTERS SUBMITTED TO THE FOREIGN INTELLIGENCE SURVEILLANCE COURT
Docket Numbers: Multiple

ORDER

Motion having been made by the United States of America, by James A. Baker, Counsel for Intelligence Policy, United States Department of Justice, for the Court to clarify its order of April 22, 2002 in the above captioned matter, and full consideration having been given to the matters set forth therein, the motion to clarify is granted and the Court's order and memorandum opinion of April 22, 2002 in this matter are amended as follows:

1. The language of the Court's order and memorandum opinion of April 22, 2002 are amended to include the following substitute sentence in the second paragraph of the modified minimization procedures to read: "Additionally, the FBI and the Criminal Division shall ensure that law enforcement officials do not direct or control the use of the FISA procedures to enhance criminal prosecution, and that advice intended to preserve the option of a criminal prosecution does not inadvertently result in the Criminal Division's directing or controlling the investigation using FISA searches and surveillances toward law enforcement objectives."

2. The government also asks that the Court clarify whether its use of the term "law enforcement officials" in the substitute minimization language adopted by the Court "applies to FBI agents as well as to prosecutors." The Court's own opinion states as follows:

The Attorney General's new minimization procedures are designed to regulate the acquisition, retention and dissemination of information involving the FISA (i.e., disseminating information, consulting, and providing advice) between FBI counterintelligence and counter-terrorism officials on the one hand, and FBI *criminal investigators*, trial attorneys in the Justice

Department's Criminal Division, and U.S. Attorney's Offices on the other hand. (emphasis added) (Opinion, 6-7).

The Court uses, and intended to use, the term "law enforcement officials" in conjunction with the source and context from which it originated, i.e., the recent amendment to the FISA in which Congress expressly authorized consultations and coordination between federal officers who conduct electronic surveillances and physical searches to acquire foreign intelligence information and "Federal law enforcement officers." (50 U.S.C. §1806(k) and §1825(k). The new minimization procedures apply to the minimization process in FISA electronic surveillances and physical searches, and to those involved in the process—including both FBI agents and criminal prosecutors.

Contrary to the assumption made in the government's motion, all of the judges of this Court concurred in both the opinion and order of April 22, 2002.

> ROYCE C. LAMBERTH
> Presiding Judge
> United States Foreign Intelligence
> Surveillance Court

Date: 5-17-02 6:40 p.m.

CONCURRING IN THE ORDER:

Honorable William H. Stafford, Jr.
Judge, United States Foreign
Intelligence Surveillance Court

Honorable Stanley S. Brotman
Judge, United States Foreign
Intelligence Surveillance Court

Honorable Harold A. Baker
Judge, United States Foreign
Intelligence Surveillance Court

Honorable Michael J. Davis
Judge, United States Foreign
Intelligence Surveillance Court

Honorable Claude M. Hilton
Judge, United States Foreign
Intelligence Surveillance Court

Honorable Nathaniel M. Gorton
Judge, United States Foreign
Intelligence Surveillance Court

ENDNOTES

[47] On April 17, 2002 the Government filed a supplemental memorandum of law in support of its March 7, 2002 motion. The supplemental memorandum misapprehends the issue that is before the Court. That issue is whether the FISA authorizes electronic surveillances and physical searches *primarily for law enforcement purposes* so long as the Government also has "a significant" foreign intelligence purpose. The Court is not persuaded by the supplemental memorandum, and its decision is not based an the issue of its jurisdiction but on the interpretation of minimization procedures.

[48] The Attorney General's memorandum of March 6, 2002 asserts its interpretation of the recent amendments to the FISA to mean that the Act can now "be used *primarily* for a law enforcement purpose, so long as a significant foreign intelligence purpose remains." The government supports this argument with a lengthy memorandum of law which we have considered. However, the Court has decided this matter by applying the FISA's standards for minimization procedures defined in §1801(h) and §1821(4) of the Act, and does not reach the question of whether the FISA may be used primarily for law enforcement purposes. We leave this question for another day.

[49] *Cheng Fan Kwok* v. *Immigration and Naturalization Service*, 392 U.S. 206, S.Ct. 1970 (1968).

[50] Sections §1801(h)(3) and §1821(4)(C) require that the minimization procedures must allow retention and dissemination of evidence of a crime which has been, is being, or is about to be committed. Such crimes are not related to the target's intelligence or terrorist activities, and the information would have to be discarded otherwise because it is not necessary to produce foreign intelligence information. Such retention and dissemination is not relevant to the issues considered in this opinion. Foreign Intelligence Surveillance Act of 1978, H.R. 7308, 95th Congress, 2nd Session, Report 95-1283, Pt. 1, p.62.

[51] Id. at 59.

[52] Id at 78.

[53] Id. at 80.

THE USA PATRIOT ACT OF 2001
Commentary 203

THE USA PATRIOT ACT OF 2001

There was little controversy over the passage of the Uniting and Strengthening America by Providing Appropriate Tools Required to Intercept and Obstruct Terrorism (USA PATRIOT ACT) Act of 2001 only a few weeks after the terrorist attacks on September 11th, 2001. As pointed out by Clarence Page in *The Washington Times* of April 26, 2003,

> I don't know that 5 percent of the people who voted for that bill (the USA Patriot Act)" David Keene, president of the American Conservative Union quipped at a recent panel on the act held by the American Civil Liberties Union. "You're always an optimist", quipped former Rep. Bob Barr, Georgia Republican . . . But public comment on the Act was relatively muted with the exception of statements from some human rights organizations which objected both to the speedy passage (with its lack of discussion and evaluation) and to the potential for infringing on private rights contained in the Act.

Yet, as stated in the *Congressional Quarterly Weekly* on September 22, 2001 regarding the new legislative initiative, "Next to authorizing the use of military force, some of the most important decisions Congress will now have to make involve striking a new balance between law enforcement powers and civil liberties." What is clear is that the Administration (and Congress after September 11th) recognized that drastic steps were required to protect against future terrorist attacks and that a war footing might not succeed against an elusive terrorist mindset without giving up something in the arena of private rights.

An excellent article in *The Washington Post* of October 27, 2003 by Robert O'Harrow Jr. gives a realistic and riveting portrayal of the evolution of the Patriot Act by focusing on the Executive and Legislative Branch participants who were operating in the shadow of this nation's most gruesome tragedy. In the Senate, Senator Patrick Leahy as Chairman of the Senate Judiciary Committee played a crucial role in fashioning "sunset" provisions as a *quid pro quo* for provisions which diminished personal freedoms. Another Democrat, Senator Russell Feingold, was, according to O'Harrow, unable and unwilling to accept the new legislative initiatives, and Feingold is quoted as saying on the floor of the Senate:

> There is no doubt . . . that if we lived in a police state, it would be easier to catch terrorists. If we lived in a country where the police were allowed to search your home at any time for any reason; if we lived in a country where the government was entitled to open your mail, eavesdrop on your phone conversations, or intercept your e-mail communications . . . the government would probably discover and arrest more terrorists, or would-be terrorists . . . But that would not be a country in which we would want to live.

From the Executive side, White House Deputy Counsel Timothy Flanigan is pictured as having fought consistently to have the Bush/Ashcroft provisions passed, and mention is also made that civil libertarians were given little opportunity to contribute their thoughts to the process. On the House side, there was constant disagreement between the Ashcroft proposals and Representative Bob Barr who, according to the *Congressional Quarterly Weekly* article on September 29, 2001, felt the laundry list of changes being proposed represented a wide range of tactics which had, in the past, been proposed by the Justice Department unsuccessfully and which would now, in light of 9/11, be considered in an atmosphere of shock and fear.

Though the O'Harrow article cited above captures the personal infighting, and the give and take of negotiating new legislation, an objective retrospective appraisal of what took place would recognize that this comprehensive and key legislation was passed expeditiously, giving the President and Executive branch broad tools to fight terrorism while offering elected leaders the chance to point to something concrete that they had done to meet the expanding threats. Passage of this new Act could be viewed as the initial major step which changed the fight against terrorism from the prior "reaction" approach (investigate what has happened and convict those responsible) to the "prevention" approach (gather information and perform investigations to head off the attack before it happens). The latter is much broader in coverage, encompassing new powers regarding financial transactions, a tightening of controls over personal transactions, and an expansion of Executive Branch authority in the field of information collection. *The Economist* on March 3rd, 2003 described the change in the following words:

> Two big changes mark the government's anti-terrorism policy. The first is to focus not on catching and punishing terrorists after an attack—the usual goal of law enforcement—but on preventing one from taking place. The second is to consider terrorism no longer primarily as a threat from abroad. In the past, despite their howls about congressional oversight, American spies abroad have been freer in what they can do than their domestic equivalents. Now the idea is for more of the same powers to be wielded domestically.

George H. Pike, writing in *Information Today*, published December 1, 2002, said the Patriot Act is a reaction to a cataclysmic and damaging event and its passage reflects the "willingness by the public, courts, and legislatures to curtail civil liberties (when national security is endangered) . . . " And Pike appears perfectly correct in stating that the 9/11 attacks "impacted this country's 'national well-being' at a level that we haven't seen since World War II and perhaps before." Pike, and many others quickly follow with the admonition that Americans must guard against going too far in protecting security and infringing on civil liberties. As described by Senator Leahy in his comments prior to a Senate Judiciary Committee Hearing (on "Protecting Constitutional Freedoms in the Face of Terrorism") on October 3, 2001 (only days before passage of the Patriot Act):

> We must improve our ability to find and punish the evildoers who attacked innocent people on September 11 and to prevent similar tragedies from occurring

in the future. But we should not compromise the civil rights of our citizens in the process.

In the very next month, after passing the Patriot Act, Senator Leahy opened a second session by the Senate Judiciary Committee on November 28, 2001 (with the same subject) by remarking:

> ... we empowered the Justice Department with new and more advanced ways to track terrorists ... The separate but complementary roles of these two branches of government, working together and sharing a unity of purpose made that bill (the Patriot Act) a better law than either could have made through unilateral initiative.

At that same hearing, Michael Chertoff, Assistant Attorney General reflected the Administration's satisfaction with the new legislation and the broader "preventive" approach to the problem, stating:

> ... as we are currently doing, we can pursue a comprehensive and systematic investigate approach, informed by all-source intelligence, that aggressively uses every available legally permissible investigative technique to try to identify, disrupt, and, if possible incarcerate or deport sleepers and other persons who pose possible threats to our national security.

The Patriot Act passed 98-1 in the Senate and 357-66 in the House after limited hearings and discussion in Congress. Key provisions of the new law are included as a Document in this volume. President Bush signed the Patriot Act (PL 107-56) into law on October 26, 2001 with a number of striking new authorities:

- It incorporated a wide-ranging law on money-laundering associated with terrorist organizations and activities.
- It expanded authority for searches and seizures without notifying the suspect.
- It amended the Foreign Intelligence Surveillance Act (FISA) by promoting increased cooperation between law enforcement and intelligence actions.
- It introduced criminal penalties for individuals to possess harmful biological agents and toxins in large quantities.
- It included a sunset provision requiring Congressional action to extend provisions of the Act beyond the year 2004.
- Wiretaps can move with a suspect.
- Prosecutors can release secret grand jury testimony and wiretap information to intelligence agencies.

But the Spring of 2003 was NOT the same as October of 2001 and the public, including elected officials, had seen how the Act operates and what frailties or dangers it might possess. Predictably, the numerous and detailed evaluations of what happened on 9/11, the quest to find the weaknesses in our personnel and programs (care is taken NOT to say blame will be established), and the mere passage of time which tends to cushion the initiative seen immediately after 9/11, all have a bearing on what is now transpiring. In the area of privacy, the authority for the government to gather information about the personal life of individuals prompted verbally violent reactions from the educational community. Those same provisions have sparked expressions of dismay, disagreement, and downright refusal to cooperate, from a number of local authorities.

- The American Library Association. According to *The Washington Post* on April 10, 2003:

  ... the American Library Association ... formally denounced the Patriot Act provision (giving Federal authorities authority to examine all book and computer records at libraries—and prohibits the libraries from informing patrons that their computer practices or reading are being monitored) and passed a resolution urging Congress to repeal it.

- Local Jurisdictions. Arcata, California is only one of the numerous local jurisdictions which objects to the new legislation, and it has taken the unusual step of passing a resolution which urges officials and the public to refuse requests by Federal authorities if they believe they violate an individual's personal rights. They then added, as pointed out by Evelyn Nieves in *The Washington Post* on April 21st, 2003, a specific Ordinance outlawing voluntary compliance with the Patriot Act. According to *The Post* article: "89 cities have passed resolutions condemning the Patriot Act, with at least a dozen more in the works and a statewide resolution against the act close to being passed in Hawaii."

Other areas of concern (covered in more detail elsewhere in this Volume) included:

- The impact of the Patriot Act amendments to the Foreign Intelligence Surveillance Act (FISA) and the operation of the Foreign Intelligence Surveillance Court and its Appellate Court have attracted widespread attention in the general public and within the civil rights community.

- The surfacing of the new draft Domestic Security Enhancement Act of 2003 (Patriot Act II) with its far reaching additional amendments to the Patriot Act generated additional fervor amongst personal liberty advocates and is prompting more careful examinations of the Patriot Act operation.

The full text of the USA Patriot Act of 2001 can be found in *Terrorism: Documents of International and Local Control*, Volume 29. Oceana Publications, Inc., Dobbs Ferry, New York.

THE DOMESTIC SECURITY ENHANCEMENT ACT OF 2003–PATRIOT II

Commentary 209
Patriot Act II Draft Bill 213
ACLU Section-by-Section Analysis of Patriot II, February 14, 2003. 265

THE DOMESTIC SECURITY ENHANCEMENT ACT OF 2003–PATRIOT II

Perhaps nothing proposed since 9/11 has precipitated the chorus of critical comment which has been generated by the highly publicized Patriot II. Its surfacing was itself controversial, unexpected, and in the view of many, a clumsy birth for a highly complex and volatile series of policies.

Patriot II was first revealed by the Center for Public Integrity which placed the entire draft (marked "not for distribution" and dated January 9, 2002) on its website. According to the release which circulated the document, a Justice spokesperson indicated he knew nothing about the draft, adding "This is all news to me. I have never heard of this." Staff of the Senate Judiciary Committee provided the same response. After the draft was placed on the website the Justice Department distributed a release in which they indicated no final proposals had been presented to the Attorney General and that it would be "... premature to speculate on any future decisions." However, there were indications in the documentation that the draft was circulated to the Vice President. All these factors led to immediate speculation of the Administration's intentions and, of course, led some media representatives to suggest the draft was actually leaked to the Public Integrity group. Whether it should be viewed as a monumental expansion of the Patriot Act and an aggressive move by the Administration, or as a test to see what reactions might be is unknown. If it is a test case, there is the possibility the Administration will tailor the final version to make it more acceptable—half a loaf is better than none! An editorial dated March 13, 2003 in the *Buffalo News* states: "The fundamental changes in America envisioned by the draft version of "Patriot II" legislation prepared by the Justice Department seemingly have triggered enough protest to drive this misguided attempt at police-state powers underground ... "

Patriot II (which is reproduced in full as a document in this volume) would, among other things, permit the government to create a DNA database of people not convicted of a crime, strip citizens of their citizenship in certain circumstances, permit speedy deportation of legal immigrants based on suspicions, permit government access to personal information without judicial oversight, and, last but not least, prohibit individuals from releasing information on certain environmental hazards.

What does this new initiative say? In most instances it would be possible to circulate a detailed description of each provision provided by the sponsor. Failing this, it is possible to use such material provided by other sources. In this case, the memorandum circulated by the American Civil Liberties Union is instructive (though undoubtedly it represents an ACLU prejudice).

According to the ACLU (in a memo placed on their website and dated February 14, 2003:

> Among its most severe problems, the bill
>
> *Diminishes personal privacy by removing checks on government power, specifically by*
>
> - Making it easier for the government to initiate surveillance and wiretapping of U.S. citizens under the authority of the shadowy, top-secret Foreign Intelligence Surveillance Court. (Sections 101, 102 and 107)
> - Permitting the government, under certain circumstances, to bypass the Foreign Intelligence Surveillance Court altogether and conduct warrantless wiretaps and searches. (Sections 103 and 104)
> - Sheltering federal agents engaged in illegal surveillance without a court order from criminal prosecution if they are following orders of high Executive Branch officials. (Section 106)
> - Creating a new category of "domestic security surveillance" that permits electronic eavesdropping of entirely domestic activity under looser standards than are provided for ordinary criminal surveillance under Title III. (Section 122)
> - Using an overbroad definition of terrorism that could cover some protest tactics such as those used by Operation Rescue or protesters at Vieques Island, Puerto Rico as a new predicate for criminal wiretapping and other electronic surveillance. (Sections 120 and 121)
> - Providing for general surveillance orders covering multiple functions of high tech devices, and by further expanding pen register and trap and trace authority for intelligence surveillance of United States citizens and lawful permanent residents. (Sections 107 and 124)
> - Creating a new, separate crime of using encryption technology that could add five years to any sentence for crimes committed with a computer. (Section 404)
> - Expanding nationwide search warrants so they do not have to meet even the broad definition of terrorism in the USA PATRIOT Act. (Section 125)
> - Giving the government secret access to credit reports without consent and without judicial process. (Section 126)
> - Enhancing the government's ability to obtain sensitive information without prior judicial approval by creating administrative subpoenas and providing new penalties for failure to comply with written demands for records. (Sections 128 and 129)
> - Allowing for the sampling and cataloguing of innocent Americans' genetic information without court order and without consent. (Sections 301-306)
> - Permitting, without any connection to anti-terrorism efforts, sensitive personal information about U.S. citizens to be shared with local and state law enforcement. (Section 311)
> - Terminating court-approved limits on police spying, which were initially put in place to prevent McCarthy-style law enforcement persecution based on political or religious affiliation. (Section 312)
> - Permitting searches, wiretaps and surveillance of United States citizens on behalf of foreign governments—including dictatorships and human rights abusers—in the absence of Senate-approved treaties. (Sections 321-22)

http://www.aclu.org/news/NewsPrint.cfm?ID=11835&c=206

Patriot II confirms the direction the Administration is taking in the terrorism field. It is a broad brush initiative covering a multiplicity of areas and having a significant impact on a wide range of actions.

PATRIOT ACT II DRAFT BILL

A BILL

To enhance the domestic security of the United States of America, and for other purposes.

Be it enacted by the Senate and House of Representatives of the United States of America in Congress assembled,

SECTION 1. SHORT TITLE; TABLE OF CONTENTS.

(a) SHORT TITLE.—This Act may be cited as the "Domestic Security Enhancement Act of 2003."

(b) TABLE OF CONTENTS.—The table of contents of this Act is as follows:

Sec. 1. Short Title; Table of Contents.

TITLE I—ENHANCING NATIONAL SECURITY AUTHORITIES

Subtitle A: Foreign Intelligence Surveillance Act Amendments

Sec. 101. Individual Terrorists as Foreign Powers.

Sec. 102. Clandestine Intelligence Activities by Agent of a Foreign Power.

Sec. 103. Strengthening Wartime Authorities Under FISA.

Sec. 104. Strengthening FISA's Presidential Authorization Exception.

Sec. 105. Law Enforcement Use of FISA Information.

Sec. 106. Defense of Reliance on Authorization.

Sec. 107. Pen Registers in FISA Investigations.

Sec. 108. Appointed Counsel in Appeals to FISA Court of Review.

Sec. 109. Enforcement of Foreign Intelligence Surveillance Court Orders.

Sec. 110. Technical Correction Related to the USA PATRIOT Act.

Sec. 111. International Terrorist Organizations as Foreign Powers.

Subtitle B: Enhancement of Law Enforcement Investigative Tools

Sec. 121. Definition of Terrorist Activities.

Sec. 122. Inclusion of Terrorist Activities as Surveillance Predicates.

Sec. 123. Extension of Authorized Periods Relating to Surveillance and Searches in Investigations of Terrorist Activities.

Sec. 124. Multi-function Devices.

Sec. 125. Nationwide Search Warrants in Terrorism Investigations.

Sec. 126. Equal Access to Consumer Credit Reports.

Sec. 127. Autopsy Authority.

Sec. 128. Administrative Subpoenas in Terrorism Investigations.

Sec. 129: Strengthening Access to and Use of Information in National Security Investigations.

TITLE II—PROTECTING NATIONAL SECURITY INFORMATION

Sec. 201. Prohibition of Disclosure of Terrorism Investigation Detainee Information.

Sec. 202. Distribution of "Worst Case Scenario" Information.

Sec. 203. Information Relating to Capitol Buildings.

Sec. 204. Ex Parte Authorizations Under Classified Information Procedures Act.

Sec. 205. Exclusion of United States Security Requirements from Gross Income of Protected Officials.

Sec. 206. Grand Jury Information in Terrorism Cases.

TITLE III—ENHANCING INVESTIGATIONS OF TERRORIST PLOTS

Subtitle A: Terrorism Identification Database

Sec. 301. Short Title.

Sec. 302. Collection and Use of Identification Information from Suspected Terrorists and Other Sources.

Sec. 303. Establishment of Database to Facilitate Investigation and Prevention of Terrorist Activities.

Sec. 304. Definitions.

Sec. 305. Existing Authorities.

Sec. 306. Conditions of Release.

Subtitle B: Facilitating Information Sharing and Cooperation

Sec. 311. State and Local Information Sharing.

Sec. 312. Appropriate Remedies with Respect to Law Enforcement Surveillance Activities.

Sec. 313. Disclosure of Information.

Subtitle C: Facilitating International Terrorism Investigations

Sec. 321. Authority to Seek Search Warrants and Orders to Assist Foreign States.

Sec. 322. Extradition Without Treaties and for Offenses Not Covered by an Existing Treaty.

TITLE IV—ENHANCING PROSECUTION AND PREVENTION OF TERRORIST CRIMES

Subtitle A: Increased Penalties and Protections Against Terrorist Acts

Sec. 401. Terrorism Hoaxes.

Sec. 402. Providing Material Support to Terrorism.

Sec. 403. Weapons of Mass Destruction.

Sec. 404. Use of Encryption to Conceal Criminal Activity.

Sec. 405. Presumption for Pretrial Detention in Cases Involving Terrorism, Firearms, Explosives, or Serious Violent Felonies.

Sec. 406. "Mass Transportation Vehicle" Technical Correction.

Sec. 407. Acts of Terrorism Transcending National Boundaries.

Sec. 408. Postrelease Supervision of Terrorists.

Sec. 409. Suspension, revocation, and denial of certificates for civil aviation or national security reasons.

Sec. 410. No Statute of Limitations for Terrorism Offenses.

Sec. 411. Penalties for Terrorist Murders.

Subtitle B: Incapacitating Terrorism Financing

Sec. 421. Increased Penalties for Terrorism Financing.

Sec. 422. Money Laundering Through Hawalas.

Sec. 423. Suspension of Tax-Exempt Status of Designated Terrorist Organizations.

Sec. 424. Denial of Federal Benefits to Terrorists.

Sec. 425. Corrections to Financing of Terrorism Statute.

Sec. 426: Terrorism-Related Specified Activities for Money Laundering.

Sec. 427: Assets of Persons Committing Terrorist Acts Against Foreign Countries or International Organizations.

Sec. 428: Technical and Conforming Amendments Relating to the USA PATRIOT ACT.

TITLE V—ENHANCING IMMIGRATION AND BORDER SECURITY

Sec. 501. Expatriation of Terrorists.

Sec. 502. Enhanced Criminal Penalties for Violations of Immigration and Nationality Act.

Sec. 503. Inadmissibility and Removability of National Security Aliens or Criminally Charged Aliens.

Sec. 504. Expedited Removal of Criminal Aliens.

Sec. 505. Clarification of Continuing Nature of Failure-to-Depart Offense, and Deletion of Provisions on Suspension of Sentence.

Sec. 506. Additional Countries of Removal.

TITLE I: ENHANCING NATIONAL SECURITY AUTHORITIES

Subtitle A: Foreign Intelligence Surveillance Act Amendments

SEC. 101. INDIVIDUAL TERRORISTS AS FOREIGN POWERS.

Section 101(a)(4) of the Foreign Intelligence Surveillance Act of 1978 (50 U.S.C. 1801(a)(4)) is amended by inserting "or individual" after "group".

SEC. 102. CLANDESTINE INTELLIGENCE ACTIVITIES BY AGENT OF A FOREIGN POWER.

Section 101(b)(2)(A) and (B) of the Foreign Intelligence Surveillance Act of 1978 (50 U.S.C. 1801(b)(2)(A) and (B)) are each amended by striking ", which" and all that follows through "States".

SEC. 103. STRENGTHENING WARTIME AUTHORITIES UNDER FISA.

Sections 111, 309, and 404 of the Foreign Intelligence Surveillance Act of 1978 (50 U.S.C. 1811, 1829, and 1844) are each amended by inserting after "Congress" the following: ", the enactment of legislation authorizing the use of military force, or an attack on the United States, its territories or possessions, or its armed forces creating a national emergency.".

SEC. 104. STRENGTHENING FISA'S PRESIDENTIAL AUTHORIZATION EXCEPTION.

Section 102(a)(1)(A)(ii) of the Foreign Intelligence Surveillance Act of 1978 (50 U.S.C. 1802(a)(1)(A)(ii)) is amended by striking ", other than the spoken communications of individuals,".

SEC. 105. LAW ENFORCEMENT USE OF FISA INFORMATION.

Sections 106(b), 305(c), and 405(b) of the Foreign Intelligence Surveillance Act of 1978 (50 U.S.C. 1806(b), 1825(c), and 1845(b)) are each amended by striking "the Attorney General" and inserting "the Attorney General, the Deputy Attorney General, the Associate Attorney General, or an Assistant Attorney General designated by the Attorney General".

SEC. 106. DEFENSE OF RELIANCE ON AUTHORIZATION.

(a) Section 109 of the Foreign Intelligence Surveillance Act of 1978 (50 U.S.C. 1809(b)) is amended by inserting after "jurisdiction" the following: "or was authorized by and conducted pursuant to the authorization of the President or the Attorney General".

(b) Section 307(b) of the Foreign Intelligence Surveillance Act of 1978 (50 U.S.C. 1827(b)) is amended by inserting after "jurisdiction" the following: "or was authorized by and conducted pursuant to the authorization of the President or the Attorney General".

SEC. 107. PEN REGISTERS IN FISA INVESTIGATIONS.

Section 402(a)(1) of the Foreign Intelligence Surveillance Act of 1978 (50 U.S.C. 1842(a)(1)) is amended by striking "not concerning" and all that follows through "intelligence activities".

SEC. 108. APPOINTED COUNSEL IN APPEALS TO FISA COURT OF REVIEW.

Section 103(b) of the Foreign Intelligence Surveillance Act of 1978 (50 U.S.C. 1803(b)) is amended by inserting after the first sentence the following: "The court of review in its discretion may appoint counsel, with appropriate security clearance, to defend the denial of the application, and such counsel shall be compensated as provided for representation in an appellate court case under section 3006A(d) of title 18, United States Code.".

SEC. 109. ENFORCEMENT OF FOREIGN INTELLIGENCE SURVEILLANCE COURT ORDERS.

Section 103 of the Foreign Intelligence Surveillance Act of 1978 (50 U.S.C. 1803) is amended by—

(1) redesignating subsection (d) as subsection (e); and

(2) inserting after subsection (c) the following:

"(d) Enforcement of court's orders.

"The court established by subsection (a) shall have the same authority as a United States district court to enforce its orders, including the authority to punish any disobedience of such orders as contempt of court.".

SEC. 110. TECHNICAL CORRECTION RELATED TO THE USA PATRIOT ACT.

Section 224(a) of Pub. L. 107–56 is amended by inserting "204," before "205".

SEC. 111. INTERNATIONAL TERRORIST ORGANIZATIONS AS FOREIGN POWERS.

(a) Section 101(i) of the Foreign Intelligence Surveillance Act of 1978 (50 U.S.C. 1801(i)) is amended by striking "or (3)" and inserting "(3), or (4)".

(b) Section 105(e) of the Foreign Intelligence Surveillance Act of 1978 (50 U.S.C. 1805(e)) is amended—

(1) in paragraph (1), by striking "or (3)" and inserting "(3), or (4)"; and

(2) in paragraph (2), by striking "or against a foreign power as defined in section 101(a)(4) that is not a United States person,".

(c) Section 304(d) of the Foreign Intelligence Surveillance Act of 1978 (50 U.S.C. 1824(d)) is amended—

(1) in paragraph (1), by striking "or (3)" and inserting "(3), or (4)"; and

(2) in paragraph (2), by striking "or against a foreign power, as defined in section 101(a)(4), that is not a United States person,".

Subtitle B: Enhancement of Law Enforcement Surveillance Tools

SEC. 121. DEFINITION OF TERRORIST ACTIVITIES.

(a) Section 2510 of title 18, United States Code, is amended—

(1) by redesignating paragraphs (20) and (21) as paragraphs (22) and (23) respectively; and

(2) by inserting after paragraph (19) the following:

"(20) 'terrorist activities' means an offense described in section 2332b(g)(5)(B), an offense involved in or related to domestic or international terrorism as defined in section 2331, or a conspiracy or attempt to engage in such conduct;

"(21) 'criminal investigation' includes any investigation of terrorist activities;".

(b) Section 3127(1) of title 18, United States Code, is amended by inserting "'terrorist activities', 'criminal investigation'," after "service',".

SEC. 122. INCLUSION OF TERRORIST ACTIVITIES AS SURVEILLANCE PREDICATES.

(a) Section 2516 of title 18, United States Code, is amended—

(1) in subsection (1)—

(A) in paragraph (c)—

(i) by inserting before "section 1992 (relating to wrecking trains)" the following: "section 37 (relating to violence at international airports), section 930(c) (relating to attack on federal facility with firearm), section 956 (conspiracy to harm persons or property overseas),"; and

(ii) by inserting before "a felony violation of section 1028" the following: "section 1993 (relating to mass transportation systems),".

(B) in paragraph (q), by striking all that follows the semicolon;

(C) by redesignating paragraph (r) as paragraph (s); and

(D) by inserting after paragraph (q) the following:

"(r) terrorist activities; or"; and

(2) in subsection (2)—

(A) by inserting "or activities" before "as to which"; and

(B) by inserting "terrorist activities or" before "the commission".

(b) Section 2518(7)(a) of title 18, United States Code, is amended—

(1) by redesignating subparagraphs (ii) and (iii) as subparagraphs (iii) and (iv) respectively; and

(2) by inserting after subparagraph (i) the following:

"(ii) terrorist activities,".

(c) Section 3123(b)(1)(D) of title 18, United States Code, is amended by inserting "or activities" after "offense".

(d) Section 3125(a)(1) of title 18, United States Code, is amended—

(1) in subparagraph (A), by striking "or" at the end;

(2) by redesignating subparagraph (B) as subparagraph (D); and

(3) by inserting after subparagraph (A) the following:

"(B) terrorist activities;

"(C) conspiratorial activities threatening the national security interest; or".

(f) Section 3127(2)(A) of title 18, United States Code, is amended to read as follows:

"(A) any district court of the United States (including a magistrate judge of such a court) or any United States court of appeals that—

"(i) has jurisdiction over the offense or activities being investigated;

"(ii) is in or for a district in which the provider of wire or electronic communication service is located; or

"(iii) is in or for a district in which a landlord, custodian, or other person subject to section 3124(a) or (b) is located; or".

SEC. 123. EXTENSION OF AUTHORIZED PERIODS RELATING TO SURVEILLANCE AND SEARCHES IN INVESTIGATIONS OF TERRORIST ACTIVITIES.

(a) Section 2518 of title 18, United States Code, is amended—

(1) in subsection (5)—

(A) in the first sentence, by inserting "or, in the case of an interception relating to terrorist activities, ninety days" after "thirty days";

(B) in the second sentence, by striking "Such thirty-day period begins" and inserting "These periods begin";

(C) in the fourth sentence, by inserting "or, in the case of an interception relating to terrorist activities, ninety days" after "thirty days"; and

(D) in the fifth sentence—

(i) by striking "practicable," and inserting "practicable and"; and

(ii) by striking ", and must terminate" and all that follows through "thirty days."; and

(2) in subsection (6), by inserting in the second sentence after "require" the following: "so long as no interval is less than thirty days in the case of an interception relating to terrorist activities".

(b) Section 2705(a)(2)(A) and (b)(1) of title 18, United States Code, are amended by inserting "or the national security" after "individual".

(c) Section 3123(c)(1) and (2) of title 18, United States Code, are amended by inserting after "or, in an investigation of terrorist activities, 120 days" after "sixty days".

SEC. 124. MULTI-FUNCTION DEVICES

(a) Section 2518(4) of title 18, United States Code, is amended by inserting at the end the following: "Where a communication device to be monitored under an order authorizing the interception of a wire, oral, or electronic communication is capable of performing multiple functions, communications transmitted or received through any function performed by the device may be intercepted and accessed unless the order specifies otherwise and, upon a showing as for a search warrant, the order may authorize the retrieval of other information (whether or not constituting or derived from a communication whose interception the order authorizes) from the device.".

(b) Section 2703 of title 18, United States Code, is amended—

(1) in subsection (a), by striking "court with jurisdiction over the offense under investigation or equivalent State warrant" and inserting "court in a district in which the provider is located or that has jurisdiction over the offense or activities under investigation or equivalent State warrant or pursuant to a court order issued under section 2518"; and

(2) in subsections (b)(1)(A) and (c)(1)(A), by striking "court with jurisdiction over the offense under investigation or equivalent State warrant" and inserting "court in a district in which the provider is located

or that has jurisdiction over the offense or activities under investigation or equivalent State warrant or a court order issued under section 2518".

(c) Section 3123(b) of title 18, United States Code, is amended by inserting at the end the following as a flush last sentence: "Where the order relates to a communication device capable of performing multiple functions, a pen register or trap and trace device may be used with respect to communications transmitted or received through any function of the device unless the order specifies otherwise.".

SEC. 125. NATIONWIDE SEARCH WARRANTS IN TERRORISM INVESTIGATIONS.

Rule 41(a)(3) of the Federal Rules of Criminal Procedure is amended—

(1) by inserting "or of an offense listed in 18 U.S.C. § 2332b(g)(5)(B))" after "2331)"; and

(2) by inserting "or offense" after "the terrorism".

SEC. 126. EQUAL ACCESS TO CONSUMER CREDIT REPORTS.

Section 1681b(a)(1) of title 15, United States Code is amended by striking "grand jury" and inserting "grand jury, or the request of a law enforcement officer upon his certification that the information will be used only in connection with his duties to enforce federal law, in which case the disclosure to such law enforcement officer will not be disclosed to the consumer to whom such report relates without further order of a federal court".

SEC. 127. AUTOPSY AUTHORITY.

(a) Chapter 31 of title 28, United States Code, is amended by adding at the end the following:

"§ 530C. Autopsy authority in criminal investigations

"Notwithstanding any other provision of law, the Attorney General may, when deemed necessary or appropriate in the conduct of a criminal investigation, take custody of, and order an autopsy and related scientific or medical tests to be performed on the body of, a deceased person. To the extent consistent with the needs of the autopsy or of specific scientific or medical tests, the Attorney General shall take such steps as necessary to respect the provisions of any applicable law protecting religious beliefs of the deceased person or the deceased persons family. Before ordering an autopsy or related tests under this section, the Attorney General shall endeavor to inform the family of the deceased person, if known, that the autopsy shall be performed. After the autopsy and any related tests have been performed, the remains of the deceased person shall be returned as soon as practicable to that deceased person's family, if known.".

(b) The table of sections for chapter 31 of title 28, United States Code, is amended by inserting at the end: "530C. Autopsy authority in criminal investigations.".

SEC. 128. ADMINISTRATIVE SUBPOENAS IN TERRORISM INVESTIGATIONS.

(a) IN GENERAL—Chapter 113B of title 18, United States Code, is amended by inserting after section 2332e the following:

"Sec. 2332f. Administrative subpoenas in terrorism investigations.

"(a) AUTHORIZATION OF USE—In any investigation with respect an offense listed in section 2332b(g)(5)(B) or an offense involved in or related to international or domestic terrorism as defined in section 2331, the Attorney General may subpoena witnesses, compel the attendance and testimony of witnesses, and require the production of any records (including books, papers, documents, electronic data, and other tangible things that constitute or contain evidence) that he finds relevant or material to the investigation. A subpoena under this section shall describe the records or items required to be produced and prescribe a return date within a reasonable period of time within which the records or items can be assembled and made available. The attendance of witnesses and the production of records may be required from any place in any State or in any territory or other place subject to the jurisdiction of the United States at any designated place of hearing; except that a witness shall not be required to appear at any hearing more than 500 miles distant from the place where he was served with a subpoena. Witnesses summoned under this section shall be paid the same fees and mileage that are paid to witnesses in the courts of the United States.

"(b) SERVICE—A subpoena issued under this section may be served by any person designated in the subpoena as the agent of service. Service upon a natural person may be made by personal delivery of the subpoena to him or by certified mail with return receipt requested. Service may be made upon a domestic or foreign corporation or upon a partnership or other unincorporated association that is subject to suit under a common name, by delivering the subpoena to an officer, to a managing or general agent, or to any other agent authorized by appointment or by law to receive service of process. The affidavit of the person serving the subpoena entered by him on a true copy thereof shall be sufficient proof of service.

"(c) ENFORCEMENT—In the case of the contumacy by, or refusal to obey a subpoena issued to, any person, the Attorney General may invoke the aid of any court of the United States within whose jurisdiction the investigation is carried on or the subpoenaed person resides, carries on business, or may be found, to compel compliance with the subpoena. The court may issue an order requiring the subpoenaed person, in accordance with the subpoena, to appear, to produce records, or to give testimony touching the matter under investigation. Any failure to obey the order of the court may be punished by the court as contempt thereof. Any process under this subsection may be served in any judicial district in which the person may be found.

"(d) NON-DISCLOSURE REQUIREMENTS—No person shall disclose to any other person that a subpoena was received or records provided pursuant to this section, other than to (i) those persons to whom such disclosure is necessary in order to comply with the subpoena, (ii) an attorney to obtain legal advice with respect to testimony or the production of records in response to the subpoena, and (iii) other persons as permitted by the Attorney General. Any person who receives a disclosure under this subsection shall be subject to the same prohibition of disclosure.

"(e) IMMUNITY FROM CIVIL LIABILITY—Any person, including officers, agents, and employees, who in good faith produce the records or items requested in a subpoena shall not be liable in any court of any State or the United States to any customer or other person for such production or for non-disclosure of that production to the customer or other person, in compliance with the terms of a court order for non-disclosure.".

(b) TECHNICAL AND CONFORMING AMENDMENT—The analysis for chapter 113B of title 18, United States Code, is amended by inserting after the item relating to section 2332e the following:

"Sec. 2332f. Administrative subpoenas in terrorism investigations".

SEC. 129. STRENGTHENING ACCESS TO AND USE OF INFORMATION IN NATIONAL SECURITY INVESTIGATIONS.

(a) VIOLATION OF NONDISCLOSURE PROVISIONS FOR NATIONAL SECURITY LETTERS AND COURT ORDERS.—Section 1510 of title 18, United States Code, is amended by adding at the end the following:

"(e) Whoever violates section 2709(c) or 2332f(d) of this title, section 625(d) or 626(c) of the Fair Credit Reporting Act, section 1114(a)(3) or (5)(D) of the Right to Financial Privacy Act, section 802(b) of the National Security Act of 1947, or section 501(d) of the Foreign Intelligence Surveillance Act of 1978, shall be imprisoned for not more than one year, and if the violation is committed with the intent to obstruct an investigation or judicial proceeding, shall be imprisoned for not more than five years.".

(b) JUDICIAL ENFORCEMENT OF NATIONAL SECURITY LETTERS.—Chapter 113B of title 18, United States Code, is amended—

(1) in the chapter analysis, by inserting before the item relating to section 2333 the following:

"2332g. Enforcement of requests for information."; and

(2) by inserting before section 2333 the following:

"§ 2332g. Enforcement of requests for information

"In the case of a refusal to comply with a request for records, a report, or other information made to any person under section 2709(b) of this title, section 625(a) or (b) or 626(a) of the Fair Credit Reporting Act, section 1114(a)(5)(A) of the Right to Financial Privacy Act, or section 802(a) of the National Security Act of 1947, the Attorney General may invoke the aid of any court of the United States within whose jurisdiction the investigation is carried on or the person resides, carries on business, or may be found, to compel compliance with the request. The court may issue an order requiring the person to comply with the request. Any failure to obey the order of the court may be punished by the court as contempt thereof.

Any process under this section may be served in any judicial district in which the person may be found.".

(c) USE OF NATIONAL SECURITY LETTERS IN THE INVESTIGATION OF TERRORIST ACTIVITIES.—(1) Section 2709(b)(1) and (2) of title 18, United States Code, are each amended by striking "international terrorism" and inserting "terrorist activities (as defined in section 2510)".

(2) Sections 625(a), (b), and (c) and 626(a) of the Fair Credit Reporting Act (15 U.S.C. 1681u(a), (b), and (c) and 1681v(a)) are each amended by striking "international terrorism" and inserting "terrorist activities (as defined in section 2510 of title 18, United States Code)".

(3) Section 1114(a) of the Right to Financial Privacy Act (12 U.S.C. 3414(a)) is amended—

(A) in paragraph (1)(C), by striking "international terrorism" and inserting "terrorist activities (as defined in section 2510 of title 18, United States Code)"; and

(B) in paragraph (5)(A), by striking "for foreign counter intelligence purposes to protect against international terrorism" and inserting "to protect against terrorist activities".

(d) SHARING OF INTELLIGENCE AMONG FEDERAL AGENCIES.—(1) Section 2709(d) of title 18, United States Code, is amended by striking "for foreign" and all that follows through "such agency".

(2) Section 625(f) of the Fair Credit Reporting Act (15 U.S.C. 1681u(f)) is amended by striking "not" and all that follows through "investigation." and inserting the following: "disseminate information obtained pursuant to this section only as provided in guidelines approved by the Attorney General.".

(3) Section 626(a) of the Fair Credit Reporting Act (15 U.S.C. 1681v(a)) is amended by striking "conduct or such investigation, activity or analysis" and inserting the following: "conduct of such investigation, activity or analysis, and such government agency may disclose the contents of that report or information to another government agency authorized to engage in such investigation, activity or analysis".

(4) Section 1114(a)(5)(B) of the Right to Financial Privacy Act (12 U.S.C. 3414(a)(5)(B)) is amended by striking "for foreign" and all that follows through "such agency".

(5) Section 802(e)(3) of the National Security Act of 1947 (50 U.S.C. 436(e)(3)) is amended by striking "clearly".

TITLE II: PROTECTING NATIONAL SECURITY INFORMATION

SEC. 201. PROHIBITION OF DISCLOSURE OF TERRORISM INVESTIGATION DETAINEE INFORMATION.

Notwithstanding section 552 of title 5, United States Code, or any other provision of law, no officer, employee, or agency of the United States shall disclose, without the prior determination of the Attorney General or the Director of Central Intelligence that such disclosure will not adversely impact the national security interests of the United States, the names or other identifying information relating to any alien who is detained within the United States, or any individual who is detained outside the United States, in the course of any investigation of international terrorism until such time as such individual is served with a criminal indictment or information.

SEC. 202. DISTRIBUTION OF "WORST CASE SCENARIO" INFORMATION.

(a) SHORT TITLE. This section may be cited as the "Community Protection from Chemical Terrorism Act."

(b) FINDINGS. Congress finds that—

(1) the nationwide threat of terrorist attacks has greatly increased since September 11, 2001;

(2) government-mandated publicly available information on worst-case scenario accidents at chemical facilities provides a blueprint that terrorists may use to plan and carry out terrorist attacks;

(3) improved protections are necessary to prevent terrorists from using information described in paragraph (2) to target and attack local communities; and

(4) while communities have a right to know about the use of chemicals in their communities, communities also have the right not to allow terrorists to use such information to destroy the communities.

(c) SAFE USAGE OF CHEMICAL INFORMATION. Section 112(r)(7) of the Clean Air Act (42 U.S.C. 7412(r)(7)) is amended by deleting subparagraph (H) and inserting in lieu thereof:

"(H) ACCESS TO OFF-SITE CONSEQUENCE ANALYSIS INFORMATION

"(i) DEFINITIONS—In this subparagraph:

"(I) CRIMINAL RELEASE—The term 'criminal release' means an emission of a regulated substance into the ambient air from a stationary source that is caused, in whole or in part, by a criminal act.

"(II) DISTANCE TO ENDPOINT—The term 'distance to endpoint' means the radius of the area of an accidental release or a criminal release.

"(III) MEMBER OF THE PUBLIC—The term 'member of the public' means—

"(aa) an individual who is not an official user; and

"(bb) an official user who is not carrying out an official use.

"(IV) OFFICIAL USE—The term 'official use' means an action of a Federal, State, or local government agency, or an entity referred to in subclause (V)(ee), that is intended to carry out a function necessary to prevent, plan for, or respond to an accidental release or a criminal release.

"(V) OFFICIAL USER—The term 'official user' means—

"(aa) an officer or employee of the United States;

"(bb) an officer or employee of an agent or contractor of the United States;

"(cc) an officer or employee of a State or local government;

"(dd) an officer or employee of an agent or contractor of a State or local government; and

"(ee) an officer or employee or an agent or contractor of an entity that has been given, by a State or local government, responsibility for preventing, planning for, or responding to accidental releases or criminal releases.

"(VI) OFF-SITE CONSEQUENCE ANALYSIS INFORMATION—The term 'off-site consequence analysis information' means—

"(aa) any information in a risk management plan, including in the executive summary of the plan, that consists of, identifies, or describes or identifies, with respect to a worst-case or alternative release scenario for a toxic release or flammable release—

"(AA) the name, physical state, or concentration of a chemical;

"(BB) the quantity released, release rate, or duration of the release;

"(CC) the topography, whether urban or rural;

"(DD) the distance to endpoint;

"(EE) the estimated residential population, public receptors, or environmental receptors within the distance to endpoint;

"(FF) any map or other graphic depiction used to illustrate a scenario; and

"(GG) the prevention program designed to prevent or mitigate the release; and "(bb) any information derived from the information described in item (aa) (including any statewide or national ranking of stationary sources derived from the information described in item (aa)) that is not publicly available from a source other than a risk management plan.

"(VII) READ-ONLY ACCESS—The term 'read-only access' means access that—

"(aa) allows the reading of information; but

"(bb) does not allow removal, mechanical reproduction, or other duplication (including notetaking) of information.

"(VIII) RISK MANAGEMENT PLAN—The term 'risk management plan' means a risk management plan registered with the Administrator by an owner or operator of a stationary source under subparagraph (B)(iii).

"(IX) STATE OR LOCAL OFFICIAL USER—The term 'State or local official user' means an official user described in any of items (cc) through (ee) of subclause (V).

"(ii) AVAILABILITY UNDER FREEDOM OF INFORMATION ACT—

"(I) IN GENERAL—Off-site consequence analysis information shall not be made available under section 552 of title 5, United States Code.

"(II) APPLICABILITY—Subclause (I) applies to off-site consequence analysis information obtained or developed by the Administrator before, on, or after the date of enactment of this subparagraph.

"(iii) ACCESS BY MEMBERS OF THE PUBLIC TO OFF-SITE CONSEQUENCE ANALYSIS INFORMATION—Except as provided in this clause, notwithstanding any other provision of law, no member of the public shall have access to off-site consequence analysis information. The Administrator, in consultation with the Attorney General, shall establish procedures to allow a member of the public read-only access to off-site consequence analysis information that does not disclose the identity or location of any facility or any information from which the identity or location of any facility could be deduced.

"(iv) ACCESS BY STATE OR LOCAL OFFICIAL USERS TO OFF-SITE CONSEQUENCE ANALYSIS INFORMATION—The Administrator shall allow access by a State or local official user, for official use, to off-site consequence analysis information relating to stationary sources located in the State or local official user's State or in a contiguous State, or in any case where the off-site consequence analysis indicates that release would require, under existing mutual aid agreements, a response by that State or local jurisdiction.

"(v) PROHIBITION ON DISCLOSURE BY OFFICIAL USERS—

"(I) IN GENERAL—

"(aa) PROHIBITION—No official user shall knowingly disclose off-site consequence analysis information in any form to any member of the public, except to the extent that such disclosure is for official use or is otherwise authorized under this subparagraph.

"(bb) EXTENT OF DISCLOSURE FOR OFFICIAL USE—Under item (aa), an official user may disclose for official use only the quantity of off-site consequence analysis information that is necessary for the purpose of preventing, planning for, or responding to accidental releases or criminal releases.

"(II) CRIMINAL PENALTIES—Notwithstanding section 113, a violation of subclause (I) shall be punished as a Class A misdemeanor under section 3559 of title 18, United States Code.

"(III) NOTICE—The Administrator shall provide to each official user who receives off-site consequence analysis information—

"(aa) notice of the definition of official use and examples of actions that do and actions that do not fall within that definition; and

"(bb) notice of the prohibition established by subclause (I) and the penalties established by subclause (II).

"(vi) EFFECT ON STATE OR LOCAL LAW—

"(I) IN GENERAL—Subject to subclause (II), this subparagraph supersedes any provision of State or local law that is inconsistent with this subparagraph.

"(II) AVAILABILITY OF INFORMATION UNDER STATE LAW—Nothing in this subparagraph precludes a State from making available data on the off-site consequences of chemical releases collected in accordance with State law.

"(IV) AVAILABILITY OF INFORMATION—Information that is developed by the Attorney General, or requested by the Attorney General and received from a covered stationary source, for the purpose of preparing the report or conducting the review under this clause, shall not be disclosed or released under the Freedom of Information Act (5 U.S.C. 552).

"(vii) AUTHORIZATION OF APPROPRIATIONS—There are authorized to be appropriated to the Administrator and the Attorney General such sums as are necessary to carry out this subparagraph, to remain available until expended.".

SEC. 203. INFORMATION RELATING TO CAPITOL BUILDINGS

Notwithstanding section 552 of title 5, United States Code, or any other provision of law, information provided by the Office of Compliance or the Architect of the Capitol to any officer, employee or agency of the Executive Branch of government relating to the United States Capitol and related buildings, shall not be disclosed under section 552(a) of title 5 United States Code, by such Executive Branch officer, employee or agency.

SEC. 204. EX PARTE AUTHORIZATIONS UNDER CLASSIFIED INFORMATION PROCEDURES ACT.

Section 4 of the Classified Information Procedures Act (18 U.S.C. App. 3) is hereby amended by deleting the "may" in the second sentence and inserting "shall".

SEC. 205. EXCLUSION OF UNITED STATES SECURITY REQUIREMENTS FROM GROSS INCOME OF PROTECTED OFFICIALS

The Internal Revenue Code of 1986 is amended—

(a) by redesignating section 140 as section 141, and

(b) by inserting after section 139 the following:

"§ 140 Personnel security interests of the United States

"Gross income shall not include any amount expended from appropriated funds that the Secretary of the Treasury, the Attorney General, and the Director of Central Intelligence, or their designees, shall jointly determine is required to provide for the security of officers or employees of the United States and otherwise in the interests of the United States. The Secretary of the Treasury, the Attorney General and the Director of Central Intelligence, acting jointly, may determine the scope of protective services required by class of official or otherwise, and such determinations shall not be publicly disclosed."

SEC. 206. GRAND JURY INFORMATION IN TERRORISM CASES.

Rule 6(e)(2)(B) of the Federal Rules of Criminal Procedure is amended—

(1) in clause (vi), by striking "or" at the end;

(2) in clause (vii), by striking the period at the end and inserting "; or"; and

(3) by inserting at the end the following:

"(viii) a witness or a person to whom a subpoena is directed, if there is reason to believe that otherwise there may result a danger to the national security or to the life or physical safety of an individual, flight from prosecution, destruction of or tampering with evidence, intimidation of a potential witness, or other serious jeopardy to an investigation and if the witness or person is notified of the prohibition of disclosure. Such a witness or person may consult with counsel prior to testifying before the grand jury or responding to the subpoena and shall notify such counsel of the prohibition of disclosure, and such counsel shall be subject to the same prohibition of disclosure.".

TITLE III: ENHANCING INVESTIGATIONS OF TERRORIST PLOTS
Subtitle A: Terrorism Identification Database

SEC. 301. SHORT TITLE.

This Subtitle may be cited as the "Terrorist Identification Database Act of 2003."

SEC. 302. COLLECTION AND USE OF IDENTIFICATION INFORMATION FROM SUSPECTED TERRORISTS AND OTHER SOURCES.

(a) COLLECTION AND RECEIPT OF DNA SAMPLES, FINGERPRINTS, AND OTHER INFORMATION.—

(1) COLLECTION FROM SUSPECTED TERRORISTS IN CUSTODY OR UNDER SUPERVISION OR ON CONDITIONAL RELEASE.—

(A) DEPARTMENT OF JUSTICE.—The Attorney General, and any other official or agency designated by the Attorney General, shall have the authority to collect DNA samples, fingerprints, and other identification information from any suspected terrorist who is in the custody of the Attorney General, the United States Marshal Service, the Bureau of Prisons, or the Immigration and Naturalization Service. A Federal official or agency so designated by the Attorney General shall collect DNA samples, fingerprints, and other identification information from any such person as directed by the Attorney General.

(B) PROBATION OFFICERS.—Upon the request of the Attorney General, the probation office responsible for the supervision under Federal law of an individual on probation, parole, or supervised release shall collect DNA samples, fingerprints, and other identification information from any suspected terrorist.

(C) DEPARTMENT OF DEFENSE.—The Secretary of Defense, and any other official or agency within the Department of Defense designated by the Secretary, shall have the authority to collect DNA samples, fingerprints, and other identification information from any suspected terrorist who is in the custody of, or being detained by, the Department of Defense. A Federal official or agency so designated by the Secretary shall collect DNA samples, fingerprints, and other identification information from any such person as directed by the Secretary.

(D) COLLECTION PROCEDURES.—Any official authorized under paragraph (A), (B), or (C) to collect a DNA sample from a suspected terrorist may use or authorize the use of such means as are reasonably necessary to collect a DNA sample from any such suspected terrorist who refuses to cooperate in the collection of the sample.

(E) CRIMINAL PENALTY.—An individual from whom the collection of a DNA sample is authorized under subsection (a)(1) who fails to cooperate in the collection of that sample shall be—

(i) guilty of a class A misdemeanor; and

(ii) punished in accordance with title 18, United States Code.

(2) COLLECTION OR RECEIPT OF OTHER IDENTIFICATION INFORMATION.—The Attorney General, the Secretary of Defense, or other designated official or agency, may also collect and receive, either directly or from another Federal, State, local, or foreign government agency, or other appropriate source—

(A) DNA samples, fingerprints, and other identification information of any suspected terrorist, regardless of whether he or she is in custody or under supervision, where such samples or information are voluntarily provided by the suspected terrorist or otherwise lawfully acquired from any source;

(B) DNA samples, fingerprints, and other identification information that have been recovered from the scenes of terrorist activities, including unidentified human remains, or that have been recovered from any item that may have been handled by a suspected terrorist; and

(C) DNA samples, fingerprints, and other identification information of any person, where such samples or information are voluntarily provided by the person and may assist in the investigation and identification of terrorists and the prevention of terrorism.

(b) COLLECTION, ANALYSIS, STORAGE, AND MAINTENANCE OF DNA SAMPLES, FINGERPRINTS, AND OTHER INFORMATION.—

(1) ANALYSIS AND USE OF SAMPLES.—The Attorney General shall have the authority to analyze DNA samples, fingerprints, and other information collected or received under subsection (a) or that has been lawfully acquired under any other source of law. Any such analysis of DNA samples shall be conducted in conformity with the quality assurance standards issued by the Director of the Federal Bureau of Investigation under section 210303 of the Violent Crime Control and Law Enforcement Act of 1994 (42 U.S.C. 14131).

(2) AGREEMENTS WITH OTHER ENTITIES CONCERNING DNA SAMPLES.—The Attorney General may enter into agreements with Federal agencies, with units of State or local government, or with private entities, to assist in the collection, analysis, storage, or maintenance of the DNA samples described in paragraph (1).

SEC. 303. ESTABLISHMENT OF DATABASE TO FACILITATE INVESTIGATION AND PREVENTION OF TERRORIST ACTIVITIES.

(a) DATABASES.—

(1) The Attorney General may establish one or more databases of DNA records, fingerprints, and other identification information—

(A) that was collected or received under section 2(a);

(B) that was obtained as a result of any analysis conducted under section 2(b); and

(C) that is information of the kind described in section 2(a) or 2(b), but which may have been collected or received before the effective date of this Act.

(2) Any federal agency, including the Department of Defense and any probation office, shall provide to the Attorney General, for inclusion in such databases as may be established, any DNA records, fingerprints, and other identification information described in paragraph (1). As directed by the Attorney General, any DNA records, fingerprints, and other identification information described in paragraph (1) shall be included in the databases authorized by this section.

(b) USES.—

(1) GENERALLY.—The Attorney General may use DNA records, fingerprints, and other identification information contained in the databases described in subsection (a) for the purposes of detecting, investigating, prosecuting, preventing, or responding to terrorist activities, or other criminal or unlawful activities by suspected terrorists, and may share the information with other Federal, State, local, or foreign agencies only for these purposes. In addition, the Attorney General may use and disclose the information for other purposes and to other entities and persons to the extent permitted by law.

(2) DATABASE SEARCHES.—The Attorney General may search information in the databases described in subsection (a) against the national DNA index established by section 210304 of the Violent Crime Control and Law Enforcement Act of 1994 (42 U.S.C. 14132), the Integrated Automated Fingerprint Identification System of the Federal Bureau of Investigation, other databases maintained by Federal, State, or local law enforcement agencies, and other appropriate databases as determined by the Attorney General. Authorized searches of any such DNA, fingerprint, law enforcement, or other appropriate database as determined by the Attorney General may also be made against the databases described in subsection (a).

(3) POPULATION STATISTICS DATABASE.—If personally identifiable information is removed, the DNA records maintained in the da-

tabases described in subsection (a) may be used and disclosed for quality control and protocol development purposes and for a population statistics database.

(c) RELATION TO OTHER LAWS.—

(1) IN GENERAL.—Except as provided in paragraph (2), DNA samples and records and other information described in this section may be used and disclosed in conformity with this section, notwithstanding any limitation on the use or disclosure of such samples, records, or information under the DNA Identification Act of 1994 (42 U.S.C. 14131–14134), the DNA Analysis Backlog Elimination Act of 2000 (42 U.S.C. 14135-14135e), or any other law.

(2) RELATION TO THE PRIVACY ACT.—

(A) The databases established under this section shall be deemed to be systems of records within the full scope of the exemption in subsection (j)(2) of section 552a of title 5, United States Code (the Privacy Act), and therefore exempt from any provisions of such section other than those specifically enumerated in such subsection (j)(2).

(B) Section 552a of title 5, United States Code, is amended—

(i) in subsection (a)(8)(B)—

(I) by striking "or" at the end of subparagraph (vii);

(II) by adding "or" at the end of subparagraph (viii); and

(III) by adding at the end the following new subparagraph:

"(ix) matches performed pursuant to section 3 of the Terrorist Identification Database Act of 2002;"; and

(ii) in subsection (b)(7)—

(I) by striking "to another" and inserting "(A) to another";

(II) by striking "sought;" and inserting "sought; or"; and

(III) by adding at the end the following new paragraph:

"(B) pursuant to section 3 of the Terrorist Identification Database Act of 2002;".

SEC. 304. DEFINITIONS.

As used in this Act.

(1) The term "DNA sample" means a tissue, fluid, or other bodily sample of an individual on which a DNA analysis can be carried out.

(2) The term "DNA analysis" means analysis of the deoxyribonucleic acid (DNA) identification information in a bodily sample.

(3) The term "suspected terrorist" means any person as to whom the Attorney General or the Secretary of Defense, as appropriate, has determined that there is reason to believe—

(A) has engaged in terrorism as defined in section 2331(1) or 2331(5) of title 18, United States Code, or has committed an offense described in section 2332b(g)(5)(B) of such title, or who has conspired or attempted to do so;

(B) is an enemy combatant, a prisoner of war, or other battlefield detainee;

(C) is a member of a terrorist organization designated as such pursuant to section 219 of the Immigration and Nationality Act;

(D) is an alien who is described in section 212(a)(3)(A)(i), 212(a)(3)(A)(iii), 212(a)(3)(B), 212(a)(3)(F), 237(A)(4)(a)(i), 237(a)(4)(iii), or 237(a)(4)(B) of the Immigration and Nationality Act, or who is engaged in any other activity that endangers the national security of the United States.

SEC. 305. EXISTING AUTHORITIES.

The authorities granted under this Act are in addition to any authorities that may exist under any other source of law. Nothing in this Act shall be construed to preclude the receipt, collection, analysis, maintenance, or dissemination of evidence or information pursuant to any other source of law.

SEC. 306. CONDITIONS OF RELEASE.

(a) CONDITIONS OF PROBATION.—Section 3563(a)(9) of title 18, United States Code, is amended by striking the period at the end and inserting "or section 3 of the Terrorist Identification Database Act of 2002.".

(b) CONDITIONS OF SUPERVISED RELEASE.—Section 3583(d) of title 18, United States Code, is amended by striking the period after "the DNA Analysis Backlog Elimination Act of 2000" and inserting "or section 3 of the Terrorist Identification Database Act of 2002.".

(c) CONDITIONS OF PAROLE.—Section 4209 of title 18, United States Code, insofar as such section remains in effect with respect to certain individuals, is amended by inserting before "or section 1565 of title 10." the following: ", section 3 of the Terrorist Identification Database Act of 2002,".

(d) CONDITIONS OF RELEASE GENERALLY.—If the collection of a DNA sample from an individual under any form of supervision or conditional release is authorized pursuant to section 2(a) of this Act, the individual shall cooperate in the collection of a DNA sample as a condition of that supervision or conditional release.

Subtitle B: Facilitating Information Sharing and Cooperation

SEC. 311. STATE AND LOCAL INFORMATION SHARING.

(a) CONSUMER INFORMATION.—Section 626(a) of the Fair Credit Reporting Act (15 U.S.C. 1681v(a)) is amended by adding at the end the following: "The recipient of that consumer report or information may further disclose the contents of that report or information to law enforcement personnel of a State or political subdivision of a State (including the chief executive officer of that State or political subdivision who has the authority to appoint or direct the chief law enforcement officer of that State or political subdivision) to assist the official receiving that information in the performance of the official duties of that official. Any chief executive officer or law enforcement personnel of a State or political subdivision of a State who receives information pursuant to this subsection shall only use that information consistent with such guidelines as the Attorney General shall issue to protect confidentiality.".

(b) VISA INFORMATION.—Section 222(f) of the Immigration and Nationality Act (8 U.S.C. 1202 (f)) is amended—

(1) in paragraph (1), by striking the period at the end and inserting a semicolon;

(2) by redesignating paragraph (2) as paragraph (3); and

(3) by inserting after paragraph (1) the following:

"(2) the Secretary of State may provide copies of any record of the Department of State and of diplomatic and consular offices of the United States pertaining to the issuance or refusal of visas or permits to enter the United States, or any information contained in those records, to law enforcement personnel of a State or political subdivision of a State (including the chief executive officer of that State or political subdivision who has the authority to appoint or direct the chief law enforcement officer of that State or political subdivision) to assist the official receiving that information in the performance of the official duties of that official, and any chief executive officer or law enforcement personnel of a State or political subdivision of a State who receives information pursuant to this paragraph shall only use that information consistent with such guidelines as the Attorney General shall issue to protect confidentiality; and".

(c) EDUCATIONAL RECORDS INFORMATION.—Section 444(j)(1)(B) of the General Education Provisions Act (20 U.S.C. 1232g(j)(1)(B)) and section 408(c)(1)(B) of the National Education Statistics Act of 1994 (20 U.S.C. 9007(c)(1)(B)) are each amended—

(1) by inserting after "disseminate" the following: "(including disclosure of such reports, records, and information to law enforcement personnel of a State or political subdivision of a State, including the chief executive officer of that State or political subdivision who has

the authority to appoint or direct the chief law enforcement officer of that State or political subdivision, to assist the official receiving that information in the performance of the official duties of that official)"; and

(2) by adding at the end the following: "Any chief executive officer or law enforcement personnel of a State or political subdivision of a State who receives information pursuant to this paragraph shall only use that information consistent with those guidelines.".

SEC. 312. APPROPRIATE REMEDIES WITH RESPECT TO LAW ENFORCEMENT SURVEILLANCE ACTIVITIES

(a) Requirements for relief.—

(1) Prospective relief.—

(A) Prospective relief in any civil action with respect to law enforcement surveillance activities shall extend no further than necessary to correct the current and ongoing violation of the Federal right of a particular plaintiff or plaintiffs. The court shall not grant or approve any prospective relief unless the court finds that such relief is narrowly drawn, extends no further than necessary to correct the violation of the Federal right, and is the least intrusive means necessary to correct the violation of the Federal right. The court shall give substantial weight to any adverse impact on national security, public safety, or the operation of a criminal justice system caused by the relief.

(B) The court shall not order any prospective relief that requires a government official to refrain from exercising his authority under applicable law, unless—

(i) Federal law requires such relief to be ordered;

(ii) the relief is necessary to correct the violation of a Federal right; and

(iii) no other relief will correct the violation of the Federal right.

(C) Nothing in this section shall be construed to authorize the courts, in exercising their remedial powers, to repeal or detract from otherwise applicable limitations on the remedial powers of the courts.

(2) Preliminary injunctive relief.—In any civil action with respect to law enforcement surveillance activities, to the extent otherwise authorized by law, the court may enter a temporary restraining order or an order for preliminary injunctive relief. Preliminary injunctive relief must be narrowly drawn, extend no further than necessary to cor-

rect the harm the court finds requires preliminary relief, and be the least intrusive means necessary to correct that harm. The court shall give substantial weight to any adverse impact on public safety or the operation of a criminal justice system caused by the preliminary relief and shall respect the principles of comity set out in paragraph (1)(B) in tailoring any preliminary relief. Preliminary injunctive relief shall automatically expire on the date that is 90 days after its entry, unless the court makes the findings required under subsection (a)(1) for the entry of prospective relief and makes the order final before the expiration of the 90-day period.

(b) Termination of relief.—

  (1) Termination of prospective relief.—

    (A) In any civil action with respect to law enforcement surveillance activities in which prospective relief is ordered, such relief shall be terminable upon the motion of any party or intervener—

      (i) 2 years after the date the court granted or approved the prospective relief;

      (ii) 1 year after the date the court has entered an order denying termination of prospective relief under this paragraph; or

      (iii) in the case of an order issued before September 11, 2001, immediately.

    (B) Nothing in this section shall prevent the parties from agreeing to terminate or modify relief before the relief is terminated under subparagraph (A).

  (2) Immediate termination of prospective relief.—In any civil action with respect to law enforcement surveillance activities, a defendant or intervener shall be entitled to the immediate termination of any prospective relief if the relief was approved or granted in the absence of a finding by the court that the relief is narrowly drawn, extends no further than necessary to correct a current and ongoing violation of the Federal right, and is the least intrusive means necessary to correct the violation of the Federal right.

  (3) Limitation.—Prospective relief shall not terminate if the court makes written findings based on the record that prospective relief remains necessary to correct a current and ongoing violation of the Federal right, extends no further than necessary to correct the violation of the Federal right, and that the prospective relief is narrowly drawn and the least intrusive means to correct the violation.

  (4) Termination or modification of relief.—Nothing in this section shall prevent any party or intervener from seeking modification or termination before the relief is terminable under paragraph (1) or (2),

to the extent that modification or termination would otherwise be legally permissible.

(c) Settlements.—

(1) Consent decrees.—In any civil action with respect to law enforcement surveillance activities, the court shall not enter or approve a consent decree unless it complies with the limitations on relief set forth in subsection (a).

(2) Private settlement agreements.—

(A) Nothing in this section shall preclude parties from entering into a private settlement agreement that does not comply with the limitations on relief set forth in subsection (a), if the terms of that agreement are not subject to court enforcement other than the reinstatement of the civil proceeding that the agreement settled.

(B) Nothing in this section shall preclude any party claiming that a private settlement agreement has been breached from seeking in State court any remedy available under State law.

(d) State law remedies.—The limitations on remedies in this section shall not apply to relief entered by a State court based solely upon claims arising under State law.

(e) Procedure for motions affecting prospective relief.—

(1) Generally.—The court shall promptly rule on any motion to modify or terminate prospective relief in a civil action with respect to law enforcement surveillance activities. Mandamus shall lie to remedy any failure to issue a prompt ruling on such a motion.

(2) Automatic stay.—Any motion to modify or terminate prospective relief made under subsection (b) shall operate as a stay during the period—

(A)(i) beginning on the 30th day after such motion is filed, in the case of a motion made under paragraph (1) or (2) of subsection (b); or

(ii) beginning on the 180th day after such motion is filed, in the case of a motion made under any other law; and

(B) ending on the date the court enters a final order ruling on the motion.

(3) Postponement of automatic stay.—The court may postpone the effective date of an automatic stay specified in subsection (e)(2)(A) for not more than 60 days for good cause. No postponement shall be permissible because of general congestion of the court's calendar.

(4) Order blocking the automatic stay.—Any order staying, suspending, delaying, or barring the operation of the automatic stay described in paragraph (2) (other than an order to postpone the effective date of the automatic stay under paragraph (3)) shall be treated as an order refusing to dissolve or modify an injunction and shall be appealable pursuant to section 1292(a)(1) of title 28, United States Code, regardless of how the order is styled or whether the order is termed a preliminary or a final ruling.

(f) Definitions.—As used in this section—

(1) the term "consent decree" means any relief entered by the court that is based in whole or in part upon the consent or acquiescence of the parties but does not include private settlements;

(2) the term "civil action with respect to law enforcement surveillance activities" means any civil proceeding arising under Federal law with respect to the use of investigative methods by Federal, State, and local law enforcement officials, including (but not limited to) overt surveillance; covert surveillance; electronic surveillance; intelligence gathering; undercover operations; the use of informants; and the recording, filing, retention, indexing or dissemination of information obtained through these methods, including the dissemination of such information to other Federal, state, or local law enforcement officials.

(3) the term "private settlement agreement" means an agreement entered into among the parties that is not subject to judicial enforcement other than the reinstatement of the civil proceeding that the agreement settled;

(4) the term "prospective relief" means all relief other than compensatory monetary damages (but not including relief necessary to remedy discrimination based on race, color, religion, sex, or national origin in violation of a Federal right);

(5) the term "relief" means all relief in any form that may be granted or approved by the court, and includes consent decrees but does not include private settlement agreements;

(6) "State" means a State, the District of Columbia, and any commonwealth, territory, or possession of the United States.

SEC. 313. DISCLOSURE OF INFORMATION.

Notwithstanding any other law, a commercial or business entity, and any employee or agent of such a commercial or business entity, shall not be subject to civil liability in any court for the voluntary provision or disclosure of information to a Federal law enforcement agency, based on a reasonable belief that the information may assist in the investigation or prevention of terrorist activities (as defined in section 2510 of title 18, United States Code).

Subtitle C: Facilitating International Terrorism Investigations

SEC. 321. AUTHORITY TO SEEK SEARCH WARRANTS AND ORDERS TO ASSIST FOREIGN STATES.

Section 1782 of title 28, United States Code, is amended—

(1) in the first sentence, by deleting "thing" and inserting in lieu thereof "thing, or may issue a warrant for the seizure of evidence under Federal Rule of criminal Procedure 41 or an order permitting the use of a trap and trace or pen register technology under 18 U.S.C. 3121, et seq.,", and

(2) by adding at the end thereof, "An order authorizing a search or the use of trap and trace or pen register technology may be issued only in accordance with the procedures established by the statutes and rules applicable to United States criminal prosecutions.".

SEC. 322. EXTRADITION WITHOUT TREATIES AND FOR OFFENSES NOT COVERED BY AN EXISTING TREATY.

(a) Chapter 209 of title 18, United States Code, is amended by adding at the end the following:

"Sec. 3197. Extradition for Offenses Not Covered by an Existing Treaty.

"(a) The provisions of this Chapter shall also be construed to permit the extradition of any person, regardless of nationality, to any country with which an extradition treaty or convention remains in force, and the procedures set forth in this Chapter and in the treaty or convention shall apply, even if the offense for which extradition is requested is not expressly included in a list of extraditable crimes in such treaty or convention, if

"(1) the offense for which extradition is sought is punishable by more than one year's imprisonment in the requesting state;

"(2) the conduct with which the person is charged or convicted, had it occurred in the United States, would constitute an offense punishable by more than one year's imprisonment; and

"(3) the requesting state affirms, through the diplomatic channel, that it would grant reciprocal extradition for similar conduct in response to a request made by the United States."

(b) Chapter 209 of title 18, United States Code, is amended by adding at the end the following:

"Sec. 3198. Extradition absent a treaty

"(a) SERIOUS OFFENSE DEFINED—In this section, the term 'serious offense' means conduct that would be—

"(1) an offense described in any multilateral treaty to which the United States is a party that obligates parties—

"(A) to extradite alleged offenders found in the territory of the parties; or

"(B) submit the case to the competent authorities of the parties for prosecution; or

"(2) conduct that, if that conduct occurred in the United States, would constitute

"(A) a crime of violence (as defined in section 16);

"(B) the distribution, manufacture, importation or exportation of a controlled substance (as defined in section 201 of the Controlled Substances Act (21 U.S.C. 802);

"(C) bribery of a public official; misappropriation, embezzlement or theft of public funds by or for the benefit of a public official;

"(D) obstruction of justice, including payment of bribes to jurors or witnesses;

"(E) the laundering of monetary instruments, as described in section 1956, if the value of the monetary instruments involved exceeds $100,000;

"(F) fraud, theft, embezzlement, or commercial bribery if the aggregate value of property that is the object of all of the offenses related to the conduct exceeds $100,000;

"(G) counterfeiting, if the obligations, securities or other items counterfeited, have an apparent value that exceeds $100,000;

"(H) a crime against children under chapter 109A or section 2251, 2251A, 2252, or 2252A; or

"(I) a conspiracy or attempt to commit any of the offenses described in any of subparagraphs (A) through (H), or aiding and abetting a person who commits any such offense.

"(b) AUTHORIZATION OF FILING—

"(1) IN GENERAL—If a foreign government makes a request for the extradition of a person who is charged with or has been convicted of an offense within the jurisdiction of that foreign government, and no extradition treaty is in force between the United States and the foreign government, the Attorney General may authorize the filing of a complaint for extradition pursuant to subsections (c) and (d).

"(2) FILING AND TREATMENT OF COMPLAINTS—

"(A) IN GENERAL—A complaint authorized under paragraph (1) shall be filed pursuant to section 3184.

"(B) PROCEDURES—With respect to a complaint filed under paragraph (1), procedures of sections 3184 and 3186 shall be followed as if the offense were a 'crime provided for by such treaty' as described in section 3184.

"(c) CRITERIA FOR AUTHORIZATION OF COMPLAINTS—The Attorney General may authorize the filing of a complaint described in subsection (b) only upon a certification—

"(1) by the Attorney General, that in the judgment of the Attorney General—

"(A) the offense for which extradition is sought is a serious offense; and

"(B) submission of the extradition request would be important to the law enforcement interests of the United States or otherwise in the interests of justice; and

"(2) by the Secretary of State, that in the judgment of the certifying official, based on information then known—

"(A) submission of the request would be consistent with the foreign policy interests of the United States;

"(B) the facts and circumstances of the request, including humanitarian considerations, do not appear likely to present a significant impediment to the ultimate surrender of the person if found extraditable; and

"(C) the foreign government submitting the request is not submitting the request in order to try or punish the person sought for extradition primarily on the basis of the race, religion, nationality, or political opinions of that person.

"(d) LIMITATIONS ON DELEGATION AND JUDICIAL REVIEW—

"(1) DELEGATION BY ATTORNEY GENERAL; JUDICIAL REVIEW—The authorities and responsibilities of the Attorney General under subsection (c) may be delegated only to the Deputy Attorney General.

"(2) DELEGATION—The authorities and responsibilities of the Secretary of State set forth in this subsection may be delegated only to the Deputy Secretary of State.

"(3) LIMITATION ON JUDICIAL REVIEW—The authorities and responsibilities set forth in this subsection are not subject to judicial review.

"(e) CASES OF URGENCY—

"(1) IN GENERAL—In any case of urgency, the Attorney General may, with the concurrence of the Secretary of State and before any formal certification under subsection (c), authorize the filing of a complaint seeking the provisional arrest and detention of the person sought before the receipt of documents or other proof in support of a formal request for extradition.

"(2) FILING OF COMPLAINTS; ORDER BY JUDICIAL OFFICER—

"(A) FILING—A complaint filed under this subsection shall be filed in the same manner as provided in section 3184.

"(B) ORDERS—Upon the filing of a complaint under subparagraph (A) and a finding that the facts recited in the complaint constitutes probable cause to believe that a serious crime was committed by the person sought, the appropriate judicial officer may issue an order for the provisional arrest and detention of the person.

"(C) RELEASES—If, not later than 45 days after the arrest, the formal request for extradition and documents in support of that are not received by the Department of State, the appropriate judicial officer may order that a person detained pursuant to this subsection be released from custody.

"(f) HEARINGS—

"(1) IN GENERAL—Subject to subsection (h), upon the filing of a complaint for extradition and receipt of documents or other proof in support of the request of a foreign government for extradition, the appropriate judicial officer shall hold a hearing to determine whether the person sought for extradition is extraditable.

"(2) CRITERIA FOR EXTRADITION—Subject to subsection (g) in a hearing conducted under paragraph (1), the judicial officer shall find a person extraditable if the officer finds—

"(A) probable cause to believe that the person before the judicial officer is the person sought in the foreign country of the requesting foreign government;

"(B) probable cause to believe that the person before the judicial officer committed the offense for which that person is sought, or was duly convicted of that offense in the foreign country of the requesting foreign government;

"(C) that the conduct upon which the request for extradition is based, if that conduct occurred within the United States, would be a serious offense punishable by imprisonment for more than 10 years under the laws of—

"(i) the United States;

"(ii) the majority of the States in the United States; or

"(iii) of the State in which the fugitive is found; and

"(D) no defense to extradition under subsection (f) has been established.

"(g) LIMITATION OF EXTRADITION—

"(1) IN GENERAL—A judicial officer shall not find a person extraditable under this section if the person has established that the offense for which extradition is sought is—

"(A) an offense for which the person is being proceeded against, or has been tried or punished, in the United States; or

"(B) a political offense.

"(2) POLITICAL OFFENSES—For purposes of this section, a political offense does not include—

"(A) a murder or other violent crime against the person of a head of state of a foreign state, or of a member of the family of the head of state;

"(B) an offense for which both the United States and the requesting foreign government have the obligation pursuant to a multilateral international agreement to—

"(i) extradite the person sought; or

"(ii) submit the case to the competent authorities for decision as to prosecution; or

"(C) a conspiracy or attempt to commit any of the offenses referred to in subparagraph (A) or (B), or aiding or abetting a person who commits or attempts to commit any such offenses.

"(h) LIMITATIONS ON FACTORS FOR CONSIDERATION AT HEARINGS

"(1) IN GENERAL—At a hearing conducted under subsection (a), the judicial officer conducting the hearing shall not consider issues regarding—

"(A) humanitarian concerns;

"(B) the nature of the judicial system of the requesting foreign government; and

"(C) whether the foreign government is seeking extradition of a person for the purpose of prosecuting or punishing the person because of the race, religion, nationality or political opinions of that person.

"(2) CONSIDERATION BY SECRETARY OF STATE—The issues referred to in paragraph (1) shall be reserved for consideration exclusively by the Secretary of State as described in subsection (c)(2).

"(3) ADDITIONAL CONSIDERATION—Notwithstanding the certification requirements described in subsection (c)(2), the Secretary of State may, within the sole discretion of the Secretary—

"(A) in addition to considering the issues referred to in paragraph (1) for purposes of certifying the filing of a complaint under this section, consider those issues again in exercising authority to surrender the person sought for extradition in carrying out the procedures under section 3184 and 3186; and

"(B) impose conditions on surrender including those provided in subsection (i).

"(i) CONDITIONS OF SURRENDER; ASSURANCES—

"(1) IN GENERAL—The Secretary of State may—

"(A) impose conditions upon the surrender of a person sought for extradition under this section; and

"(B) require such assurances of compliance with those conditions, as the Secretary determines to be appropriate.

"(2) ADDITIONAL ASSURANCES—In addition to imposing conditions and requiring assurances under paragraph (1), the Secretary shall demand, as a condition of the extradition of the person that is sought for extradition—

"(A) in every case, an assurance the Secretary determines to be satisfactory that the person shall not be tried or punished for an offense other than the offense for which the person has been extradited, absent the consent of the United States; and

"(B) in a case in which the offense for which extradition is sought is punishable by death in the foreign country of the requesting foreign government and is not so punishable under the applicable laws in the United States, an assurance the Secretary determines to be satisfactory that the death penalty—

"(i) shall not be imposed; or

"(ii) if imposed, shall not be carried out.".

(c) Chapter 309 of title 18, United States Code, is amended—

(1) in section 3181, by inserting ", other than sections 3197 and 3198," after "The provisions of this chapter" each place that term appears; and

(2) in section 3186, by striking "or 3185" and inserting ", 3185, 3197 or 3198".

(d) The table of sections for chapter 209 of title 28, United States Code, is amended by inserting at the end the following:

"3197. Extradition for offenses not covered by an existing treaty."

"3198. Extradition absent a treaty.".

TITLE IV: ENHANCING PROSECUTION AND PREVENTION OF TERRORIST CRIMES

Subtitle A: Increased Penalties and Protections Against Terrorist Acts

SEC. 401. TERRORISM HOAXES.

(a) PROHIBITION ON HOAXES—Chapter 47 of title 18, United States Code, is amended by inserting after section 1036 the following:

"Sec. 1037. False information and hoaxes

"(a) CRIMINAL VIOLATION—Whoever engages in any conduct, with intent to convey false or misleading information, under circumstances where such information may reasonably be believed and where such information concerns an activity which would constitute a violation of section 175, 229, 831, or 2332a, shall be fined under this title or imprisoned not more than 5 years, or both.

"(b) CIVIL ACTION—Whoever engages in any conduct, with intent to convey false or misleading information, under circumstances where such information concerns an activity which would constitute a violation of section 175, 229, 831, or 2332a, is liable in a civil action to any party incurring expenses incident to any emergency or investigative response to that conduct, for those expenses.

"(c) REIMBURSEMENT—The court, in imposing a sentence on a defendant who has been convicted of an offense under subsection (a), shall order the defendant to reimburse any person or entity incurring any expenses incident to any emergency or investigative response to that conduct, for those expenses. For the purpose of this provision, a State or local government, or private not-for-profit organization that provides fire or rescue services that is dispatched and responds to such an emergency shall be entitled to the greater of actual costs of response or $1,000. A person ordered to make reimbursement under this subsection shall be jointly and severally liable for such expenses with each other person, if any, who is ordered to make reimbursement under this subsection for the same expenses. An order of reimbursement under this subsection shall, for the purposes of enforcement, be treated as a civil judgment.".

(b) CLERICAL AMENDMENT—The table of sections at the beginning of chapter 47 of title 18, United States Code, is amended by adding after the item for section 1036 the following: "1037. False information and hoaxes.".

SEC. 402. PROVIDING MATERIAL SUPPORT TO TERRORISM.

(a) Section 2339A(a) of title 18, United States Code, is amended by—

(1) designating the first sentence as paragraph (1);

(2) designating the second sentence as paragraph (3);

(3) inserting after "for life." the following:

"(2) Whoever, in or affecting interstate or foreign commerce, or while outside the United States and a national of the United States (as defined in section 1203(c)) or a legal entity organized under the laws of the United States (including any of its States, districts, commonwealth, territories or possessions), provides material support or resources or conceals or disguises the nature, location, source, or ownership of material support or resources, knowing or intending that they are to be used in preparation for, or in carrying out, an act of international or domestic terrorism (as defined in section 2331), or in the preparation for, or in carrying out, the concealment or escape from the commission of any such act, or attempts or conspires to do so, shall be punished as provided under paragraph (1)."; and

(4) by inserting "act or" after "underlying".

(b) Section 2331(1)(B) and (5)(B) of title 18, United States Code, are each amended by inserting "by their nature or context" after "appear".

(c) Section 2339A(b) of title 18, United States Code, is amended by adding at the end the following: "The term 'training' means instruction or teaching designed to impart a specific skill.".

(d) Section 2339B(g)(4) of title 18, United States Code, is amended to read as follows:

"(4) the term 'material support or resources' has the same meaning as in section 2339A (including the definition of 'training' in that section), except that no person may be prosecuted under this section in connection with the term 'personnel' unless that person has knowingly provided, attempted to provide, or conspired to provide a terrorist organization with one or more individuals (which may be or include himself) to work in concert with the organization or under its direction or control;".

SEC. 403. WEAPONS OF MASS DESTRUCTION.

(a) EXPANSION OF JURISDICTIONAL BASES AND SCOPE. Section 2332a of title 18, United States Code, is amended by

(1) amending paragraph (a)(2) to read as follows:

"(2) against any person or property within the United States, and

"(A) the mail or any facility of interstate or foreign commerce is used in furtherance of the offense;

"(B) such property is used in interstate or foreign commerce or in an activity that affects interstate or foreign commerce;

"(C) any perpetrator travels in or causes another to travel in interstate or foreign commerce in furtherance of the offense; or

"(D) the offense, or the results of the offense, affect interstate or foreign commerce, or, in the case of a threat, attempt, or conspiracy, would have affected interstate or foreign commerce;";

(2) in paragraph (a)(3), deleting the comma at the end and inserting "; or";

(3) in subsection (a), adding the following at the end:

"(4) against any property within the United States that is owned, leased, or used by a foreign government,";

(4) in paragraph (c)(1), deleting "and" at the end;

(5) in paragraph (c)(2), deleting the period at the end and inserting "; and"; and

(6) in subsection (c), inserting the following at the end:

"(3) the term 'property' includes all real and personal property.".

(b) RESTORATION OF THE COVERAGE OF CHEMICAL WEAPONS. Section 2332a of title 18, United States Code, as amended by subsection (a), is further amended by

(1) in the caption, deleting "certain";

(2) in subsection (a), deleting "(other than a chemical weapon as that term is defined in section 229F)"; and

(3) in subsection (b), deleting "(other than a chemical weapon (as that term is defined in section 229F))".

(c) CONFORMING AMENDMENT TO NEW SELECT AGENT REGULATIONS.—(1) Section 175b(a)(1) of title 18, United States Code, is amended by striking "as a select agent in Appendix A" and all that follows and inserting the following: "as a non-overlap or overlap select biological agent or toxin in [sections 73.4 and 73.5] of title 42, Code of Federal Regulations, pursuant to section 351A of the Public Health Service Act, and is not exempted under [section 73.6] of title 42, Code of Federal Regulations.".

(2) The amendment made by paragraph (1) shall take effect at the same time that [sections 73.4, 73.5, and 73.6] of title 42, Code of Federal Regulations, become effective.

SEC. 404. USE OF ENCRYPTION TO CONCEAL CRIMINAL ACTIVITY.

(a) Part I of title 18, United States Code, is amended by inserting after chapter 123 the following:

"CHAPTER 124—ENCRYPTED WIRE OR ELECTRONIC COMMUNICATIONS AND STORED ELECTRONIC INFORMATION

"Sec. 2801. Unlawful use of encryption

"(a) Any person who, during the commission of a felony under Federal law, knowingly and willfully encrypts any incriminating communication or information relating to that felony—

"(1) in the case of a first offense under this section, shall be imprisoned not more than 5 years, fined under this title, or both; and

"(2) in the case of a second or subsequent offense under this section, shall be imprisoned not more than 10 years, fined under this title, or both.

"(b) The terms 'encrypt' and 'encryption' refer to the scrambling (and descrambling) of wire communications, electronic communications, or electronically stored information, using mathematical formulas or algorithms in order to preserve the confidentiality, integrity, or authenticity of, and prevent unauthorized recipients from accessing or altering, such communications or information."

(b) The table of Chapters is amended by inserting after to Chapter 123, the following:

"Chapter 124—Encrypted Wire or Electronic Communications and Stored Electronic Information"

SEC. 405. PRESUMPTION FOR PRETRIAL DETENTION IN CASES INVOLVING TERRORISM.

Section 3142 of title 18, United States Code, is amended—

(1) in subsection (e)—

(A) by inserting "or" before "the Maritime"; and

(B) by striking ", or an offense under section 924(c), 956(a), or 2332b of title 18 of the United States Code" and inserting ", an offense under section 924(c), or an offense described in section 2332b(g)(5)(B)"; and

(2) in subsections (f)(1)(A) and (g)(1), by inserting "or an offense described in section 2332b(g)(5)(B)" after "violence".

SEC. 406. "MASS TRANSPORTATION VEHICLE" TECHNICAL CORRECTION.

(a) Section 1993 of title 18, United States Code, is amended—

(1) in paragraph (7), by deleting "and" at the end;

(2) in paragraph (8), by deleting the period at the end in inserting in lieu thereof "; and"; and

(3) by inserting at the end thereof the following:

> "(9) The term 'vehicle' means any carriage or other contrivance used, or capable of being used, as a means of transportation on land, water, or throughout the air.".

(b) The title of chapter 97 of title 18, United States Code, is amended to read "RAILROADS AND OTHER MASS TRANSPORTATION SYSTEMS".

(c) The table of chapters for Part I of title 18, United States Code, is amended in the item relating to chapter 97 by amending the title to read "Railroads and other mass transportation systems".

(d) The title of section 1993 of title 18, United States Code, is amended by adding "on land, water, or through the air" after "systems".

(e) The table of sections for chapter 97 of title 18, United States Code, is amended in the item relating to section 1993 by adding "on land, water, or through the air" after "systems".

SEC. 407. ACTS OF TERRORISM TRANSCENDING NATIONAL BOUNDARIES.

(a) Section 2332b of title 18, United States Code, is amended—

(1) in subsection (a)(1), by inserting "in a case" before "involving";

(2) in subsection (b)(1)(A), by inserting "any person travels in interstate or foreign commerce or" before "the mail"; and

(3) in subsection (g)—

(A) by amending paragraph (1) to read as follows:

"(1) the term 'conduct transcending national boundaries' means conduct engaged in—

> "(A) by the defendant or another person outside of the United States, in addition to conduct occurring in the United States;

> "(B) at the instigation of a foreign power or of a person outside of the United States; or

"(C) in furtherance of an objective of a foreign power or of a person outside of the United States.";

(B) in paragraph (4), by striking "and" at the end;

(C) in paragraph (5), by striking the period at the end and inserting "; and"; and

(D) by inserting at the end the following:

"(6) the term 'foreign power' has the meaning given that term in section 101 of the Foreign Intelligence Surveillance Act of 1978 (50 U.S.C. 1801).".

(b) Section 1958 of title 18, United States Code, is amended—

(1) in subsection (a), by striking "facility in" and inserting "facility of"; and

(2) in subsection (b)(2), by inserting "or foreign" after "interstate".

SEC. 408. POSTRELEASE SUPERVISION OF TERRORISTS.

Section 3583 of title 18, United States Code, is amended—

(1) in subsection (e)(3), by inserting "on any such revocation" after "required to serve";

(2) in subsection (h), by striking "that is less than the maximum term of imprisonment authorized under subsection (e)(3)"; and

(3) in subsection (j)—

(A) by striking ", the commission" and all that follows through "person,"; and

(B) by inserting "and the sentence for any such offense shall include a term of supervised release of at least 10 years" before the period.

SEC. 409. SUSPENSION, REVOCATION, AND DENIAL OF CERTIFICATES FOR CIVIL AVIATION OR NATIONAL SECURITY REASONS.

Chapter 447 of title 49, United States Code, is amended—

(1) in the chapter analysis, by inserting at the end the following:

"44727. Suspension, revocation, and denial of certificates for civil aviation or national security reasons."; and

(2) by inserting at the end the following:

"§ 44727. Suspension, revocation, and denial of certificates for civil aviation or national security reasons

"(a) Suspension of Certificate.—

"(1) Notification of Initial Threat Determination.—The Under Secretary of Transportation for Security or designee shall notify the Administrator of the Federal Aviation Administration of the identity of—

"(A) any holder of a certificate issued by the Administrator under this chapter on whom the Under Secretary or designee has served an initial determination that the certificate holder poses a threat to civil aviation or national security; or

"(B) any holder of a certificate issued by the Administrator under this chapter on whom the Under Secretary or designee has served an initial determination that an individual who has a controlling or ownership interest in the certificate holder poses a threat to civil aviation or national security by virtue of that interest.

"(2) Suspension.—The Administrator of the Federal Aviation Administration shall issue an order suspending any certificate identified by the Under Secretary or designee pursuant to paragraph (1)(A) or (B). The Administrator's order of suspension shall be immediately effective and remain effective until—

"(A) the Administrator withdraws the order; or

"(B) the Administrator issues an order revoking the certificate.

The Administrator's order of suspension is not subject to administrative or judicial review.

"(3) Opportunity to Respond to Initial Threat determination.—The Under Secretary or designee shall afford certificate holders and persons with a controlling or ownership interest identified in paragraph (1)(A) or (B) notice and an opportunity to respond to an initial determination that the certificate holders or persons pose a threat to civil aviation or national security prior to the issuance of a final threat determination.

"(4) Judicial Review of Initial Threat Determination.—The initial determination by the Under Secretary or designee that a certificate holder or person with a controlling or ownership interest identified in subsection (a)(1)(A) or (B) poses a threat to civil aviation or national security is not subject to judicial review.

"(b) Revocation of Certificate.—

"(1) Notification of Final Threat Assessment.—The Under Secretary or designee shall notify the Administrator of the identity of any certificate holder described in subsection (a)(1)(A) or (B) on whom—

"(A) a withdrawal of initial threat determination has been served; or

"(B) a final threat determination has been served.

The Under Secretary or designee must issue either a withdrawal or final threat determination within 60 days of the notification of initial threat determination.

"(2) Revocation.—The Administrator shall issue an order revoking the certificate held by a certificate holder described in subsection (a)(1)(A) or (B) on whom the Under Secretary or designee has served a final determination that the certificate holder poses a threat to civil aviation or national security or that a person who has a controlling or ownership interest in the certificate holder poses a threat to civil aviation or national security by virtue of that interest. The Administrator's order of revocation shall be immediately effective.

"(3) Review of Final Threat Determination and Order of Revocation.—

"(A) A final threat determination by the Under Secretary or designee or an order of revocation issued by the Administrator with regard to a person who is neither a citizen nor permanent resident alien of the United States is not subject to administrative or judicial review.

"(B) A person who is a citizen or permanent resident alien of the United States disclosing a substantial interest in a final threat determination by the Under Secretary or designee under paragraph (1) and an order of revocation issued by the Administrator under paragraph (2) may seek review of those actions by filing a petition for review in the United States Court of Appeals for the District of Columbia Circuit or in the court of appeals of the United States for the circuit in which the person resides. The petition for review must be filed not later than 30 days after the issuance of the order of revocation. The court may allow the petition to be filed after the 30th day only if there are reasonable grounds for not filing by the 30th day. The court's review is limited to determining whether it was arbitrary, capricious, or otherwise not according to law for the Under Secretary to make the final threat determination and for the Administrator to issue the order of revocation.

"(C) In any judicial review of the Under Secretary's determination and the Administrator's order under paragraphs (1) and (2), if the actions were based on classified information (as defined in section 1(a) of the Classified Information Procedures Act) or sensitive security information (as defined in regulations issued under section 40119(b) of this title) such information may be submitted to the reviewing court ex parte and in camera.

"(d) Denial of Certificate.—

"(1) Notification of Threat Determination.—The Under Secretary or designee shall notify the Administrator of the identity of—

"(A) any person on whom the Under Secretary or designee has served an initial or final determination that the person poses a threat to civil aviation or national security; or

"(B) any entity on whom the Under Secretary or designee has served an initial or final determination that a person who has a controlling or ownership interest in the entity poses a threat to civil aviation or national security by virtue of that interest.

"(2) Denial.—The Administrator may not issue a certificate to any person or entity identified in paragraph (1) unless the Under Secretary or designee has withdrawn a determination that the person poses a threat. A denial of certificate based on an initial threat determination is not subject to administrative or judicial review.

"(3) Opportunity to Respond to Initial Threat determination.—The Under Secretary or designee shall afford applicants for certificates and persons with a controlling or ownership interest identified in paragraph (1)(A) or (B) notice and an opportunity to respond to an initial determination that an applicant for a certificate or person with a controlling or ownership interest in an applicant poses a threat to civil aviation or national security prior to the issuance of a final determination of threat assessment.

"(4) Review of Initial Threat Determination.—The initial determination by the Under Secretary or designee that an applicant for a certificate or person with a controlling ownership interest in an applicant poses a threat to civil aviation or national security is not subject to judicial review.

"(5) Review of Final Threat Determination and Certificate Denial.—

"(A) A final threat determination by the Under Secretary or designee and the denial of certificate by the Administrator under this subsection with regard to person who is not a citizen or resident alien of the United States is not subject to administrative or judicial review.

"(B) A citizen or permanent resident alien of the United States may seek review of a final threat determination by the Under Secretary or designee and denial by the Administrator under this subsection by filing a petition for review in the United States Court of Appeals for the District of Columbia Circuit or in the court of appeals of the United States for the circuit in which the person resides. The petition for review must be filed no later than the 30th day after the issuance of the denial. The court may allow the petition to be filed after the 30th day only if there are reasonable grounds for not filing by the 30th day. The court's review is limited to determining whether it was arbitrary, capricious, or otherwise not according to law for the Under Secretary to make the final threat determination and for the Administrator to deny a certificate.

"(C) In any judicial review of the Under Secretary's final threat determination and the Administrator's denial, if the actions were based on classified information (as defined in section 1(a) of the Classified Information Procedures Act) or sensitive security information (as defined in regulations issued under section 40119(b) of this title) such information may be submitted to the reviewing court ex parte and in camera.

"(e) Coordination with the Attorney General—Nothing in this section is intended to alter any provisions in section 44939 of this title. The Under Secretary shall coordinate any request to the Administrator of the Federal Aviation Administration under this section with the Attorney General on matters within the Attorney General's jurisdiction under section 44939.".

SEC. 410. NO STATUTE OF LIMITATIONS FOR TERRORISM CRIMES.

(a) Section 3286(b) of title 18, United States Code, is amended by striking ", if the commission" and all that follows through "person".

(b) The amendment made by this section shall apply to the prosecution of any offense committed before, on, or after the date of the enactment of this section.

SEC. 411. PENALTIES FOR TERRORIST MURDERS.

(a) Chapter 113B of title 18, United States Code, is amended—

(1) in the chapter analysis, by inserting at the end the following:

"2339D. Terrorist offenses resulting in death."; and

(2) by inserting at the end the following:

"2339D. Terrorist offenses resulting in death

"A person who, in the course of an offense listed in section 2332b(g)(5)(B) or of terrorist activities (as defined in section 2510), engages in conduct that results in the death of a person, shall be punished by death or imprisoned for any term of years or for life.".

(b) Section 3592(c)(1) of title 18, United States Code, is amended by inserting "section 2339D (terrorist offenses resulting in death)," after "destruction),".

Subtitle B: Incapacitating Terrorism Financing

SEC. 421. INCREASED PENALTIES FOR TERRORISM FINANCING.

Section 206 of the International Emergency Economic Powers Act (50 U.S.C. § 1705) is amended—

(1) in subsection (a), by deleting "$10,000" and inserting "$50,000".

(2) in subsection (b), by deleting "$50,000" and inserting "$250,000"; and by deleting "ten years" and inserting "twenty years".

SEC. 422. MONEY LAUNDERING THROUGH HAWALAS.

Section 1956 of title 18, United States Code, is amended by adding at the end the following:

"(j)(1) For the purposes of subsections (a)(1) and (a)(2), a transaction, transportation, transmission, or transfer of funds shall be considered to be one involving the proceeds of specified unlawful activity, if the transaction, transportation, transmission, or transfer is part of a set of parallel or dependent transactions, any one of which involves the proceeds of specified unlawful activity.

"(2) As used in this section, a "dependent transaction" is one that completes or complements another transaction or one that would not have occurred but for another transaction.

SEC. 423. SUSPENSION OF TAX-EXEMPT STATUS OF DESIGNATED FOREIGN TERRORIST ORGANIZATIONS.

(a) Section 501 (relating to exemption from tax on corporations, certain trusts, etc.) is amended by redesignating subsection (p) as subsection (q) and by inserting after subsection (o) the following new subsection:

"(p) SUSPENSION OF TAX-EXEMPT STATUS OF DESIGNATED TERRORIST ORGANIZATIONS.

"(1) IN GENERAL. The exemption from tax under subsection (a) with respect to any organization shall be suspended during any period in which the organization is a designated terrorist organization.

"(2) DESIGNATED TERRORIST ORGANIZATION. For purposes of this subsection, the term 'designated terrorist organization' means an organization which

"(A) is designated as a terrorist organization by an Executive Order or under the authority of

"(i) section 212(a)(3) or 219 of the Immigration and Nationality Act,

"(ii) the International Emergency Economic Powers Act, or

"(iii) section 5 of the United Nations Participation Act, or

"(B) is a person listed in or designated by an Executive Order as supporting terrorist activity (as defined in section 212(a)(3)(B) of the Immigration and Nationality Act) or terrorism (as defined in section 140(d)(2) of the Foreign Relations Authorization Act, Fiscal Years 1988 and 1989).

"(3) DENIAL OF DEDUCTION. No deduction shall be allowed under section 170, 545(b)(2), 556(b)(2), 642(c), 2055, 2106(a)(2), or 2522 for any contribution to an organization during the period such organization is a designated terrorist organization.

"(4) DENIAL OF ADMINISTRATIVE OR JUDICIAL CHALLENGE OF SUSPENSION OR DENIAL OF DEDUCTION.

Notwithstanding section 7428 or any other provision of law, no organization or other person may challenge a suspension under paragraph (1), a determination or listing under paragraph (2), or a denial of a deduction under paragraph (3) in any administrative or judicial proceeding relating to the organization's Federal tax liability.

"(5) CREDIT OR REFUND IN CASE OF ERRONEOUS DESIGNATION.

"(A) IN GENERAL. If an erroneous designation of an organization pursuant to 1 or more of the provisions of law described in paragraph (2) results in an overpayment of income tax for any taxable year with respect to such organization, credit or refund (with interest) with respect to such overpayment shall be made.

"(B) WAIVER OF LIMITATIONS. If credit or refund of any overpayment of tax described in subparagraph (A) is prevented at any time before the close of the 1-year period beginning on the date of the determination of such credit or refund by the operation of any law or rule of law (including res judicata), such refund or credit may nevertheless be made or allowed if claim therefor is filed before the close of such period.".

(b) If the tax exemption of any organization is suspended under section 501(p) of the Internal Revenue Code of 1986 (as added by subsection (a)), the Internal Revenue Service shall update the listings of tax-exempt organizations and shall publish appropriate notice to taxpayers of such suspension and of the fact that contributions to such organization are not deductible during the period of such suspension.

SEC. 424. DENIAL OF FEDERAL BENEFITS TO TERRORISTS.

Chapter 113B of title 18, United States Code, is amended—

(1) in the chapter analysis, by adding at the end the following:

"2339C. Denial of federal benefits to terrorists"; and

(2) by adding at the end the following:

"§ 2339C. Denial of federal benefits to terrorists

"(a) In general.—Any individual who is convicted of an offense listed in section 2332b(g)(5)(B) shall, as provided by the court on motion of the government, be ineligible for any or all Federal benefits for any term of years or for life.

"(b) Definition.—As used in this section, 'Federal benefit' has the meaning given that term in section 421(d) of the Controlled Substances Act (21 U.S.C. 862(d)).

SEC. 425. CORRECTIONS TO FINANCING OF TERRORISM STATUTE.

(a) Section 2339C(c)(2) of title 18, United States Code, is amended by—

(1) striking "resources, or funds" and inserting "resources, or any funds or proceeds of such funds";

(2) in subparagraph (A), striking "were provided" and inserting "are to be provided, or knowing that the support or resources were provided,"; and

(3) in subparagraph (B)—

(A) striking "or any proceeds of such funds"; and

(B) striking "were provided or collected" and inserting "are to be provided or collected, or knowing that the funds were provided or collected,".

(b) Section 2339C(e) is amended by—

(1) striking "and" at the end of paragraph (12);

(2) redesignating paragraph (13) as paragraph (14); and

(3) inserting after paragraph (12) the following new paragraph:

"(13) the term 'material support or resources' has the same meaning as in section 2339A(b) of this title; and".

(c) Section 2332b(g)(5)(B) of title 18, United States Code, is amended by inserting ")" after "2339C (relating to financing of terrorism".

SEC. 426. TERRORISM-RELATED SPECIFIED ACTIVITIES FOR MONEY LAUNDERING.

(a) AMENDMENTS TO RICO.—Section 1961(1) of title 18, United States Code, is amended—

(1) in subparagraph (B), by inserting "section 1960 (relating to illegal money transmitters)," before "sections 2251"; and

(2) in subparagraph (F), by inserting "section 274A (relating to unlawful employment of aliens)," before "section 277".

(b) AMENDMENTS TO SECTION 1956(c)(7).—Section 1956(c)(7)(D) of title 18, United States Code, is amended by—

(1) striking "or section 2339A or 2339B or 2339B" and inserting "section 2339A or 2339B";

(2) inserting ", or section 2339C (relating to financing of terrorism)" before "of this title"; and

(3) striking "or any felony violation of the Foreign Corrupt Practices Act" and inserting "any felony violation of the Foreign Corrupt Practices Act, or any violation of section 208 of the Social Security Act (relating to obtaining funds through misuse of a social security number)".

SEC. 427. ASSETS OF PERSONS COMMITTING TERRORIST ACTS AGAINST FOREIGN COUNTRIES OR INTERNATIONAL ORGANIZATIONS.

Section 981(a)(1)(G) of title 18, United States Code, is amended by—

(1) striking "or" at the end of clause (ii);

(2) striking the period at the end of clause (iii) and inserting "; or"; and

(3) inserting the following after clause (iii):

"(iv) of any individual, entity, or organization engaged in planning or perpetrating any act of international terrorism (as defined in section 2331) against any international organization (as defined in section 209 of the State Department Basic Authorities Act of 1956) or against any foreign Government, its citizens or residents, or their property. Where the property sought for forfeiture is located beyond the territorial boundaries of the United

States, an act in furtherance of such planning or perpetration must have occurred within the jurisdiction of the United States.".

SEC. 428. TECHNICAL AND CONFORMING AMENDMENTS RELATING TO THE USA PATRIOT ACT.

(a) TECHNICAL CORRECTIONS.—(1) Sections 5312(a)(3)(C) and 5324(b) of title 31 are amended by striking "5333" each time it appears and inserting "5331".

(2) Section 322 of Pub. L. 107–56 is amended by striking "title 18" and inserting "title 28".

(3) Section 5318(k)(1)(B) of title 31, United States Code, is amended by striking "5318A(f)(1)(B)" and inserting "5318A(e)(1)(B)".

(4) Section 5332(a)(1) of title 31, United States Code, is amended by striking "article of luggage" and inserting "article of luggage or mail".

(5) Section 1956(b)(3) and (4) of title 18, United States Code, are amended by striking "described in paragraph (2)" each time it appears; and

(6) Section 981(k) of title 18, United States Code, is amended by striking "foreign bank" each time it appears and inserting "foreign bank or financial institution".

(b) CODIFICATION OF SECTION 316.—(1) Chapter 46 of title 18, United States Code, is amended—

(A) in the chapter analysis, by inserting at the end the following:

"987. Anti-terrorist forfeiture protection."; and

(B) by inserting at the end the following:

"§ 987. Anti-terrorist forfeiture protection

"(a) Right to contest.—An owner of property that is confiscated under this chapter or any other provision of law relating to the confiscation of assets of suspected international terrorists, may contest that confiscation by filing a claim in the manner set forth in the Federal Rules of Civil Procedure (Supplemental Rules for Certain Admiralty and Maritime Claims), and asserting as an affirmative defense that—

"(1) the property is not subject to confiscation under such provision of law; or

"(2) the innocent owner provisions of section 983(d) apply to the case.

"(b) Evidence.—In considering a claim filed under this section, a court may admit evidence that is otherwise inadmissible under the Federal Rules of Evidence, if the court determines that the evidence is reliable, and that compliance with the Federal Rules of Evidence may jeopardize the national security interests of the United States.

"(c) Clarifications.—

"(1) Protection of rights.—The exclusion of certain provisions of Federal law from the definition of the term 'civil forfeiture statute' in section 983(i) shall not be construed to deny an owner of property the right to contest the confiscation of assets of suspected international terrorists under—

"(A) subsection (a) of this section;

"(B) the Constitution; or

"(C) subchapter II of chapter 5 of title 5, United States Code (commonly known as the 'Administrative Procedure Act').

"(2) Savings clause.—Nothing in this section shall limit or otherwise affect any other remedies that may be available to an owner of property under section 983 or any other provision of law.".

(2) Subsections (a), (b), and (c) of section 316 of Pub. L. 107–56 are repealed.

(c) CONFORMING AMENDMENTS CONCERNING CONSPIRACIES.—

(1) Section 33(a) of title 18, United State Code is amended by inserting "or conspires" before "to do any of the foregoing".

(2) Section 1366(a) of title 18, United State Code, is amended by—

(A) striking "attempts" each time it appears and inserting "attempts or conspires"; and

(B) inserting ", or if the object of the conspiracy had been achieved," after "the attempted offense had been completed".

TITLE V: ENHANCING IMMIGRATION AND BORDER SECURITY

SEC. 501. EXPATRIATION OF TERRORISTS.

Section 349 of the Immigration and Nationality Act (8 U.S.C. 1481) is amended—

(1) by amending subsection (a)(3) to read as follows:

"(3) (A) entering, or serving in, the armed forces of a foreign state if—

"(i) such armed forces are engaged in hostilities against the United States; or

"(ii) such person serves as a commissioned or non-commissioned officer; or

"(B) joining or serving in, or providing material support (as defined in section 2339A of title 18, United States Code) to, a terrorist organization designated under section 212(a)(3) or 219 or designated under the International Emergency Economic Powers Act, if the organization is engaged in hostilities against the United States, its people, or its national security interests."; and

(2) by adding at the end of subsection (b) the following: "The voluntary commission or performance of an act described in subsection (a)(3)(A)(i) or (B) shall be prima facie evidence that the act was done with the intention of relinquishing United States nationality.".

SEC. 502. ENHANCED CRIMINAL PENALTIES FOR VIOLATIONS OF IMMIGRATION AND NATIONALITY ACT.

(a) ENTRY CRIMES.—Section 275(a)(1) of the Immigration and Nationality Act (8 U.S.C. 1325(a)(1)) is amended by—

(1) striking "6 months" and inserting "one year"; and

(2) striking "2 years" and inserting "3 years".

(b) REENTRY AFTER REMOVAL.—Section 276 of the Immigration and Nationality Act (8 U.S.C. 1326) is amended—

(1) in subsection (a), by striking "2 years" and inserting "3 years"; and

(2) in subsection (b)(3), by striking "10 years" and inserting "20 years".

(c) ALIEN SMUGGLING.—Section 274(a)(2)(A) of the Immigration and Nationality Act (8 U.S.C. 1324(a)(2)(A)) is amended by striking "one year" and inserting "3 years".

(d) REGISTRATION OFFENSES.—(1) Section 264(e) of the Immigration and Nationality Act (8 U.S.C. 1304(e)) is amended by striking "be fined not to exceed $100 or be imprisoned not more than 30 days" and inserting "be fined under title 18, United States Code, or imprisoned not more than 90 days".

(2) Section 266 of the Immigration and Nationality Act (8 U.S.C. 1306) is amended—

(A) in subsection (b), by striking "be fined not to exceed $200 or be imprisoned not more than thirty days" and inserting "be fined under title 18, United States Code, or imprisoned not more than six months"; and

(B) in subsection (c), by striking "be fined not to exceed $1000, or be imprisoned not more than six months" and inserting "be fined under title 18, United States Code, or imprisoned not more than one year".

(e) UNLAWFUL VOTING.—Section 611(b) of title 18, United States Code, is amended by striking "one year" and inserting "three years".

SEC. 503. INADMISSIBILITY AND REMOVABILITY OF NATIONAL SECURITY ALIENS OR CRIMINALLY CHARGED ALIENS.

(a) Section 212(a)(3) of the Immigration and Nationality Act, as amended, is amended by adding at the end thereof the following new subparagraphs:

> "(G) An alien whose entry or proposed activities in the United States the Attorney General has reason to believe would pose a danger to the national security of the United States as defined in section 219(c)(2) of the Act is inadmissible.
>
> "(H) An alien whom the Attorney General has reason to believe is charged with or has committed a serious criminal offense in a country other than the United States is inadmissible.".

(b) Section 237(a)(4) of Immigration and Nationality Act is amended by adding at the end thereof the following new subparagraphs:

> "(E) An alien whose presence or activities in the United States the Attorney General has reason to believe pose a danger to the national security of the United States, as defined in section 219(c)(2) of the Act is removable.
>
> "(F) An alien whom the Attorney General has reason to believe is charged with or has committed a serious criminal offense in a country other than the United States is removable.".

SEC. 504. EXPEDITED REMOVAL OF CRIMINAL ALIENS.

(a) The caption of Section 238 of the Immigration and Nationality Act is amended to read as follows: "EXPEDITED REMOVAL OF CRIMINAL ALIENS".

(b) Section 238(b) of the Immigration and Nationality Act is amended to read as follows:

"(b) Removal of Criminal Aliens.—

> "(1) The Attorney General may, in the case of an alien described in paragraph (2), determine the deportability of such alien, and issue an order of removal pursuant to the procedures set forth in this subsection or section 240.
>
> "(2) An alien is described in this paragraph if the alien, whether or not admitted into the United States, was convicted of any criminal offense covered in 237(a)(2)(A)(iii), (B), (C), or (D), without regard to its date of commission.
>
> "(3) The Attorney General in his discretion may at any time execute any order described in paragraph (1), except during the 14 calendar day period after the date that such order was issued, unless waived by the alien, in order that the alien has an opportunity to apply for judicial review under section 242, or if the removal has been stayed under section 242(f)(2) of the Act. Notwithstanding any other provision of law including section 2241 of title 28, United States Code, no court other than a court of appeals pursuant to its jurisdiction under section 242 of this Act

shall have jurisdiction to review or set aside any order, action, or decision taken or issued pursuant to this subsection. Review in the court of appeals shall be limited to determining whether the petitioner (i) is an alien and (ii) is subject to a final judgment of conviction for an offense covered in section 237(a)(2)(A)(iii), (B), (C), or (D).

"(4) Proceedings before the Attorney General under this subsection shall be in accordance with such regulations as the Attorney General shall prescribe. The Attorney General shall provide that—

"(A) the alien is given reasonable notice of the charges and of the opportunity described in subparagraph (C);

"(B) the alien shall have the privilege of being represented (at no expense to the government) by such counsel, authorized to practice in such proceedings, as the alien shall choose;

"(C) the alien has a reasonable opportunity to inspect the evidence and rebut the charges;

"(D) a determination is made for the record that the individual upon whom the notice for the proceeding under this section is served (either in person or by mail) is, in fact, the alien named in such notice;

"(E) a record is maintained for judicial review; and

"(F) the final order of removal is not adjudicated by the same person who issues the charges.

"(5) No alien described in this section shall be eligible for any relief from removal that the Attorney General may grant in the Attorney General's discretion."

(c) Section 238(c) of the Immigration and Nationality Act relating to judicial removal is amended to read as follows:

"(d) Stipulated judicial order of deportation.—The United States Attorney may, pursuant to Federal Rule of Criminal Procedure 11, enter into a plea agreement which calls for the alien to waive the right to notice and a hearing under this section, and stipulate to the entry of a judicial order of deportation from the United States as a condition of the plea agreement or as a condition of probation or supervised release, or both. The United States district court, in both felony and misdemeanor cases, and a United States magistrate judge in misdemeanor cases, may accept such a stipulation and shall have jurisdiction to enter a judicial order of deportation pursuant to the terms of such stipulation."

(d) Section 242(f)(2) of the Immigration and Nationality Act is amended to read as follows:

"(2) Particular cases.—Notwithstanding any other provision of law, no court shall enjoin or stay, whether temporarily or otherwise, the removal of any alien pursuant to a final order under this section unless the alien shows by clear and convincing evidence that the entry or execution of such order is prohibited as a matter of law."

SEC. 505. CLARIFICATION OF CONTINUING NATURE OF FAILURE-TO-DEPART OFFENSE, AND DELETION OF PROVISIONS ON SUSPENSION OF SENTENCE.

(a) Subparagraph (A) of section 243(a)(1) of the Immigration and Nationality Act (8 U.S.C. 1253(a)(1)) is amended to read as follows:

"(A) willfully—

"(1) fails or refuses to depart from the United States within a period of 30 days from the date of the final order of removal under administrative processes, or if judicial review is had, then from the date of the final order of the court; or

"(2) remains in the United States more than 30 days after the date of the final is had, then more than 30 days after the date of the final order of the court,".

(b) Section 243 of the Immigration and Nationality Act (8 U.S.C. 1253) is amended by striking—

(1) paragraph (3) of subsection (a); and

(2) subsection (b).

SEC. 506. ADDITIONAL REMOVAL AUTHORITIES.

(a) Section 241(b)(1) of the Immigration and Nationality Act (8 U.S.C. 1231(b)(1)) is amended by inserting at the end the following:

"(D) OTHER PLACES OF REMOVAL.—

"(i) The Attorney General may direct that the alien be removed to another country or region if the Attorney General determines that removal to any country specified in the preceding subparagraphs is impracticable, inadvisable or impossible.

"(ii) The Attorney General may direct that an alien be removed to any country or region regardless of whether the country or region has a government, recognized by the United States or otherwise."

(b) Section 241(b)(2) of the Immigration and Nationality Act (8 U.S.C. 1231(b)(1)) is amended by inserting at the end the following:

"(G) OTHER PLACES OF REMOVAL.—

"(i) The Attorney General may direct that the alien be removed to another country or region if the Attorney General determines that removal to any country specified in the preceding subparagraphs is impracticable, inadvisable, or impossible.

"(ii) The Attorney General may direct that an alien be removed to any country or region regardless of whether the country or region has a government, recognized by the United States or otherwise.".

ACLU SECTION-BY-SECTION ANALYSIS OF PATRIOT II*

February 14, 2003

To: Interested Persons
From: Timothy H. Edgar, Legislative Counsel
Date: February 14, 2003
Re: Section-by-Section Analysis of Justice Department draft "Domestic Security Enhancement Act of 2003," also known as "Patriot Act II"

The Department of Justice (DOJ) has been drafting comprehensive anti-terrorism legislation for the past several months. The draft legislation, dated January 9, 2003, grants sweeping powers to the government, eliminating or weakening many of the checks and balances that remained on government surveillance, wiretapping, detention and criminal prosecution even after passage of the USA PATRIOT Act, Pub. L. No. 107-56, in 2001.

* * *

Title I—Diminishing Personal Privacy by Removing Checks on Government Intelligence and Criminal Surveillance Powers

Title I amends critical statutes that govern intelligence surveillance and criminal surveillance. Both forms of surveillance are subject to Fourth Amendment limitations. *See Katz v. United States*, 389 U.S. 347 (1967) (criminal surveillance); *United States v. United States District Court ("Keith")*, 407 U.S. 297 (1972) (intelligence surveillance). Yet while traditional searches are governed by warrant procedures largely drawn from the common law, wiretapping and other forms of electronic surveillance are governed by standards and procedures embodied in two federal statutes that respond to *Katz* and *Keith*—Title III of the Omnibus Crime Control and Safe Streets Act of 1968, 28 U.S.C. §§ 2510-22, which governs surveillance of criminal suspects, and the Foreign Intelligence Surveillance Act of 1978 (FISA), 50 U.S.C. §§ 1801-63 which governs surveillance of foreign powers and agents of a foreign power for intelligence purposes.

---

*Reprinted with permission from the American Civil Liberties Union

Making it easier for the government to initiate surveillance and wiretapping, including of United States citizens and lawful permanent residents, through the secret Foreign Intelligence Surveillance Court (Sections 101-111). The draft bill's proposed amendments to FISA attack key statutory concepts that are critical to providing appropriate limits and meaningful judicial supervision over wiretapping and other intrusive electronic surveillance for intelligence purposes. These limits were approved by Congress in 1978 because of a history of abuse by government agents who placed wiretaps and other listening devices on political activists, journalists, rival political parties and candidates, and other innocent targets. These so-called "national security wiretaps" and other covert surveillance were undertaken without any court supervision and without even the slightest suspicion that the targets of such surveillance were involved in criminal activities or were acting on behalf of any foreign government or political organization. This pattern of abuse culminated in the crimes of Watergate, which led to substantial reforms and limits on spying for intelligence purposes.

FISA represented a compromise between civil libertarians, who wanted to ban "national security wiretaps" altogether, and apologists for Presidential authority, who claimed such unchecked intelligence surveillance authority was inherent in the President's Article II power over foreign relations. The Congress chose to authorize intelligence wiretaps without evidence of crime, subject to a number of key restraints. One of these restraints, separating intelligence gathering from criminal investigations, has been significantly weakened by the USA PATRIOT Act. The USA PATRIOT Act abolished the "primary purpose" test—the requirement that FISA surveillance could only be used if the primary purpose of surveillance was gathering of foreign intelligence, and not criminal prosecution or some other purpose.

The draft bill eliminates or substantially weakens a number of the remaining constraints on intelligence surveillance approved by Congress. Taken as a whole, these changes go a long way to undermine limits on intelligence surveillance essential to preserving civil liberties and to preventing a repeat of the wiretapping abuses of the J. Edgar Hoover and Watergate eras.

Authorizing the government to initiate wiretaps and other electronic surveillance on Americans who have no ties to foreign governments or powers (sec. 101). This section would permit the government to obtain a wiretap, search warrant or electronic surveillance orders targeting American citizens and lawful permanent residents even if they have no ties to a foreign government or other foreign power. Under FISA, the government need not show, in many circumstances, probable cause that the target of a wiretap is involved in any criminal activity. FISA requires an alternate showing—probable cause that the target is acting on behalf of a foreign government or organization, i.e., a "foreign power." Section 101 of the draft bill eliminates this requirement for individuals, including United States citizens, suspected of engaging in "international terrorism." It does so by redefining individuals, including United States citizens or lawful residents, as "foreign powers" even if they are not acting on behalf of any foreign government or organization. The "foreign power" requirement was a key reason FISA was upheld in a recent constitutional challenge. See *In re Sealed Case No. 02-001*, slip op. at 42 (Foreign Intelligence Surveillance Ct. of Rev. Nov. 18, 2002) (while FISA requires no showing of probable cause of crime, it is constitutional in part because it provides "another safeguard . . . that is, the requirement that there be probable cause to believe the target is acting 'for or on behalf of a foreign power.'")[1]

Permitting surveillance of the lawful activities of United States citizens and lawful permanent residents if they are suspected of gathering information for a foreign power (sec. 102). United States citizens and lawful permanent residents who are not violating any law should not be subject to wiretapping or other intrusive electronic surveillance. The FISA contains dual standards for non-U.S. persons and for U.S. persons with respect to surveillance of "intelligence gathering activities," i.e., the gathering of information for a foreign government or organization. These standards reflect the judgment of Congress that U.S. persons should not face electronic surveillance unless their activities "involve or may involve" some violation of law (as, for example, would certainly be the case with respect to any activity in furtherance of terrorism or other crime). For non-U.S. persons, this showing does not have to be made, i.e., the gathering of information by foreign persons for foreign powers is enough to trigger FISA. The draft bill (at section 102) applies the lower standard to U.S. persons.

Lawful gathering of information for a foreign organization does not necessarily pose any threat to national security. This amendment would permit electronic surveillance of a local activist who was preparing a report on human rights for London-based Amnesty International, a "foreign political organization," even if the activist was not engaged in any violation of law. By eliminating this need to show some violation of law may be involved before authorizing surveillance of U.S. persons, Congress could well succeed in rendering FISA unconstitutional, by eliminating another key reason FISA was upheld in a recent court challenge. See *In re Sealed Case No. 02-001*, slip op. at 42 (Foreign Intelligence Surveillance Ct. of Rev. Nov. 18, 2002) (holding that FISA surveillance of U.S. persons meets Fourth Amendment standards in part because a surveillance order may not be granted unless there is probable cause to believe the target is involved in activity that may involve a violation of law).

Permitting the government, under some circumstances, to bypass the Foreign Intelligence Surveillance Court altogether (Sections 103, 104). Section 103 gives the Attorney General the power to authorize intelligence wiretaps and other electronic surveillance without permission from any court, including the Foreign Intelligence Surveillance Court, for fifteen days, after an attack on the United States or force authorization resolution from the Congress. Under existing federal statutes, a formal declaration of war by the Congress triggers a host of civil liberties consequences, including authorization by the Attorney General to engage in intrusive electronic surveillance for up to fifteen days without any court order at all. The draft bill expands this power dramatically by eliminating judicial review for any surveillance under FISA for a period up to fifteen days pursuant to (1) an authorization of force resolution by the Congress or (2) a "national emergency" created by an attack on the United States. For surveillance under the latter circumstance, no action by Congress would be required. Once the President has unilaterally decided such an attack has occurred, the Attorney General could unilaterally decide what constitutes an "attack" on the United States, creating an emergency that justifies what would otherwise be plainly illegal wiretaps.

DOJ's rationale for this change is that declarations of war are rare and the statute should be updated to reflect this. This argument fundamentally misconstrues the purpose of this provision. The normal FISA process, including review by the Foreign Intelligence Surveillance Court, was Congress's attempt to impose meaningful limits over national security surveillance conducted without a formal declaration of war and for continuing threats that cannot easily by defined by reference to traditional war powers. To use Congress' grant of surveillance authority following a declaration of war as an argument to permit surveillance even in the absence of such action by Congress is a fundamental intrusion on Congress's war powers.

The draft bill (at section 104) also expands special surveillance authority, available for up to a year with no court order at all, for property "under the open and exclusive control of a foreign power" by permitting eavesdropping on "spoken communications." This expansion of authority leaves intact the current requirement that such surveillance can go forward only if the Attorney General certifies under oath that "there is no substantial likelihood that the surveillance will acquire the contents of any communication to which a United States person is a party." Still, the new authority would plainly involve eavesdropping on communications protected by the Fourth Amendment, as it would inevitably result in listening—without any court order—to the conversations in the United States of anyone who might be using telephones, computers, or other devices owned by a foreign government, political organization, or company owned by a foreign government.

There are serious questions about whether the secret review of surveillance orders by the Foreign Intelligence Surveillance Court, which by its nature can only hear the government's side of the case, is effective in protecting Americans' civil liberties. These amendments would bypass judicial review under FISA altogether.

Sheltering federal agents engaged in illegal surveillance without a court order from criminal prosecution if they are following orders of high Executive Branch officials (Section 106). This section would encourage unlawful intelligence wiretaps and secret searches by immunizing agents from criminal sanctions if they conduct such surveillance, even if a reasonable official would know it is illegal, by claiming they were acting in "good faith" based on the orders of the President or the Attorney General. In order to ensure that FISA was successful in bringing national security surveillance under the rule of law, Congress not only provided a process for legal intelligence surveillance, but also imposed criminal penalties on any government agent who engages in electronic surveillance outside that process. Congress also provided a "safe harbor" for agents who engaged in surveillance that was approved by the Foreign Intelligence Surveillance Court, even if such surveillance was not in fact authorized by FISA. The draft bill (at section 106) substantially undercuts the deterrent effect of criminal sanctions for illegal wiretaps or electronic surveillance by expanding the "safe harbor" to include surveillance not approved by any court, but simply on the authorization of the Attorney General or the President.

Of course, the very spying abuses FISA was designed to prevent were undertaken with the authorization of high-ranking government officials, including the President. For example, President Nixon authorized just such a covert search of the Brookings Institution, whom he and his staff suspected of possessing classified information that had been leaked to the press. As described by Nixon biographer Richard Reeves:

> Nixon sat up. "Now if you remember Huston's plan [to engage in covert surveillance]..."
>
> "Yeah, why?" Haldeman said.
>
> Kissinger said: "But couldn't we go over? Now, Brookings has no right to classified—"
>
> The President cut him off, saying, "I want it implemented.... Goddamit get in there and get those files. Blow the safe and get them."[2]

Any government official acting within the scope of his employment already enjoys "qualified immunity" from charges of violating Fourth Amendment or other constitutional rights—i.e., an official cannot be punished or held civilly liable if a reasonable government official would not have known his or her conduct was illegal. *See Harlow* v. *Fitzgerald*, 457 U.S. 800, 818 (1982). Providing additional protection to government officials who engage in wiretaps or searches without a court order, where a reasonable official would know those wiretaps or searches were clearly illegal, would take away any incentive for such officials to question an illegal authorization by the President, Attorney General or other high official.

Further expanding pen register and trap and trace authority for intelligence surveillance of United States citizens and lawful permanent residents beyond terror-

ism investigations (Section 107). This section allows the government to use intelligence pen registers and trap and trace surveillance devices to obtain detailed information on American citizens and lawful permanent residents, including telephone numbers dialed, Internet addresses to which e-mail is sent or received, and the web addresses a person enters into a web browser, even in an investigation that is entirely unrelated to terrorism or counterintelligence. In so doing, it erodes a limitation on this authority that was part of the USA PATRIOT Act.

The standard for obtaining a pen register or trap and trace order is very low, requiring merely that a government official certify that the information it would reveal is "relevant" to an investigation. Under section 216 the USA PATRIOT Act, the government was given new power to obtain this sensitive information for Internet communications merely by making this certification. This expansion was a serious erosion of meaningful judicial oversight of government surveillance because it expanded the authority to get court orders for pen registers and trap and trace devices in a way that permitted the government to access far more detailed content than was available before such authority was extended to the Internet.

For United States citizens and lawful permanent residents, Congress limited the new authority to terrorism and counterintelligence investigations. This section would remove that limitation, opening the door to expanded government surveillance of United States citizens and lawful permanent residents under controversial government law enforcement technologies like CARNIVORE and the Total Information Awareness Pentagon "super-snoop" program whose development Congress just voted to limit.

Providing cleared, appointed counsel for the Foreign Intelligence Surveillance Court of Review (Section 108). While we welcome the provision providing for an appointed, cleared counsel to argue in favor of a ruling of the Foreign Intelligence Surveillance Court when the government appeals its decisions, it should not substitute for participation, in appropriate cases, by interested civil liberties organizations. The Foreign Intelligence Surveillance Court approves government orders for electronic surveillance and physical searches under FISA. It meets in secret and never hears from anyone other than the government officials seeking its approval. If an order is denied, the government has the right to seek review of that denial in a special three-judge court of appeals, called the Foreign Intelligence Surveillance Court of Review. No one can appeal the approval of a surveillance order, as the target of the surveillance is not notified. Instead, the only challenge to an approved order would occur later, if the information obtained is to be used in a criminal prosecution, in a suppression motion before the district court. If the information is used only for intelligence purposes, there is never an opportunity to challenge the lawfulness of an order approving surveillance.

This section seeks to remedy the problems inherent in a one-sided proceeding, at least with respect to appeals before the Court of Review, by permitting the court to appoint an advocate with security credentials to defend the decision reached in the initial hearing before the Foreign Intelligence Surveillance Court. While the ACLU welcomes this effort to inject an adversary process into the Court of Review's proceedings, it warns that appointing a cleared lawyer should not be a substitute for independent advocacy by civil liberties or other interested organizations. Organizations independent of the government should be permitted to file briefs amicus curiae and, in appropriate cases, to participate in oral argument as interveners on behalf of Americans who may face increased surveillance as a result of an interpretation of FISA being urged by the government. For this reason, Congress should adopt legislation providing clear procedures that require the publication of opinions by the Foreign Intelligence Surveillance Court and the Court of Review, with redactions for classified information.

Providing new contempt powers for Foreign Intelligence Surveillance Court without sufficient due process (Section 109). This section seeks to give the Foreign Intelligence Surveillance Court the power to enforce its judgments through explicit contempt powers. While the ACLU does not object to the enforcement of lawful court orders, the draft bill does not specify a means by which parties seeking to challenge an order of the court can vindicate their rights, such as by a motion to quash. If the court is to be given this authority, both the Fourth Amendment and due process require a mechanism, which currently does not exist, for a party facing a possible contempt sanction to appear before the Foreign Intelligence Surveillance Court and be heard, prior to the imposition of any sanctions.[3]

Using an overbroad definition of terrorism that could cover tactics used by some protest groups as a predicate for criminal wiretapping and other surveillance under Title III (Sections 120, 121). Current law provides, at 18 U.S.C. § 2516, a list of "predicate offenses" that permit the government to conduct wiretaps and other intrusive surveillance. The list is quite lengthy, but reflects the judgment of Congress that electronic surveillance is a particularly intrusive investigative method that is not appropriate for all criminal investigations but should be reserved only for the most serious crimes.

Title 18 already provides that any terrorism crime defined by federal law is a predicate for Title III surveillance. *See* 18 U.S.C. § 2516(q) (providing that any violation of sections 2332, 2332a, 2332b, 2339A, or 2339B is a predicate offense for Title III surveillance). The draft bill, however, extends the predicate even further, to cover offenses that are *not* defined as terrorism *crimes* under federal law, but do fit the definition of either international or domestic terrorism, i.e., they involve acts that are a violation of federal or state law, are committed with the intent of affecting government policy, and are potentially dangerous. *See* 18 U.S.C. § 2331. It is this broad definition that sweeps in the activities of a number of protest organizations that engage in civil disobedience, including People for the Ethical Treatment of Animals and Operation Rescue. Since true crimes of terrorism are already predicates for Title III surveillance, providing this authority is not necessary to listen to the telephone conversations and monitor the e-mail traffic of terrorist groups. To ensure Title III wiretaps are not used to monitor the activities of protest organizations, Congress should reject this provision and should also amend the definition of "terrorism."

Creating a new category of "domestic security surveillance" that relaxes judicial oversight of electronic surveillance of Americans engaged in entirely domestic activity (Section 122). This section authorizes looser standards for judicial oversight of wiretaps of electronic surveillance orders of Americans for entirely domestic activity under a new theory of domestic intelligence gathering. Intelligence-based surveillance and criminal surveillance are conducted under different rationales, but both are subject to Fourth Amendment protections. *See Katz* and *Keith, supra.* Title III, which governs criminal surveillance, provides significantly more robust protections than those afforded for surveillance of foreign intelligence conducted in the United States pursuant to FISA. Title III requires more frequent and continuing supervision of the surveillance order by the authorizing judge, and subsequent notice to the target of the surveillance order unless the government shows adverse results would occur if notice were given.

Title III governs electronic surveillance in domestic criminal and terrorism cases; the looser intelligence standards provided by FISA, including the ability to conduct surveillance in virtually complete secrecy, have always been reserved for "agents of a foreign power." The proposed amendment would fundamentally redefine domestic intelligence gathering through wiretaps and other intrusive surveillance to include entirely domestic security investigations. In so doing, DOJ claims it is accepting the "invitation" of the Supreme Court in *Keith* to devise specific standards for domestic intelligence investigations. It is far from clear the Supreme Court ever issued such an "invitation" because of the ambiguity of the term "domestic intelligence." FISA is, in one sense, a purely domestic intelligence gathering power; it governs gathering of intelligence on United States soil and authorizes surveillance of United States citizens. Under this understanding of "domestic intelligence," Congress has already provided far looser standards for such surveillance than it has for criminal investigations.

In any event, the draft bill's redefinition of intelligence creates what is in essence a twilight zone between the criminal standards provided in Title III and the foreign intelligence standards for targets involved with "foreign powers" in FISA. That twilight zone, as conceived by the draft bill, has significant implications for Americans' right to privacy. Under the DOJ's proposed standards, for domestic terrorism, the normal time period for domestic surveillance orders under Title III would triple from 30 days to 90 days, or, in the case of pen registers and trap and trace devices, from 60 days to 120 days; the judge would be prevented from requiring more frequent reports than once every 30 days, limiting the judge's ability to provide meaningful supervision, and absolute secrecy could be imposed on the government's claim of harm to the "national security," a standard that provides no meaningful judicial check.

Providing for general surveillance orders covering users of high technology devices with multiple functions, thus lowering the bar to surveillance (Section 124). This section would, in some cases, relieve the government from showing probable cause that would justify reading a person's e-mail if it had shown probable cause that a person's telephone conversations would be relevant to criminal activity. It authorizes a general warrant that, in the physical world, would allow officers who could show probable cause to search only one drawer of a desk to obtain a court order allowing a search of the entire building.

The proposed change would erode the privacy rights of users of multi-function devices. Multi-function devices represent an important advance in communications technology. Such devices can combine the functions of a telephone, fax machine and computer with Internet access, or those of a mobile phone and text messaging service. Another example is the popular TiVo video storage device which both records television programs received through a cable or satellite system and communicates a user's preferences through a computer modem.

Unfortunately, the draft bill continues a DOJ trend of using advances in technology to justify eroding privacy standards. While technology is constantly changing, the principles of the Constitution remain constant. Specificity is a basic requirement for any constitutional judicial process permitting government searches or seizures. The Fourth Amendment states that "no Warrants shall issue, but upon probable cause, supported by Oath or affirmation, and particularly describing the place to be searched, and the persons or things to be seized." The fact that the government can show probable cause to monitor e-mail, for example, does not mean that it should also have authority to listen to the target's telephone conversations. Of course, if the government can satisfy the probable cause or other application standard with respect to all of the functions of a device, there is no reason it cannot be granted approval to monitor those functions in a single order. However, the draft bill would make approval for each function automatic, providing that "communications transmitted or received through any function performed by the device may be intercepted and accessed *unless the order specifies otherwise . . .*"

In addition, an order that covers, for example, a personal computer that carries voice or data transmission, also permits "upon a showing as for a search warrant ... the retrieval of other information (whether or not constituting or derived from a communication whose interception the order authorizes)." While somewhat oblique, this language would permit the seizure of any information stored on a computer's hard drive if the government obtains a order to intercept communications through *any* of the computer's communications functions and makes the required showing.

There is no reason that the purchase of new technology should diminish the user's privacy. Whether one owns one device with several communications functions, or separate communications devices, the government's obligations to show probable cause that the monitoring of communications or the seizure of data will provide some evidence of crime should be the same.

Expanding nationwide search warrants so they do not have to meet even the broad definition of terrorism in the USA PATRIOT Act (Section 125). The USA PATRIOT Act gave the government authority to issue nationwide search warrants in terrorism investigations, based on the extremely broad definition of domestic and international terrorism contained in 18 U.S.C. § 2331. This definition covers any violation of law, state or federal, that involves "acts dangerous to human life" and is committed with the requisite intent. The draft bill (at section 125) expands the use of nationwide search warrants to cover any offense listed as a federal terrorism crime under 18 U.S.C. § 2332b(g)(5)(B). In general, this is unlikely to be needed as the crimes listed as terrorism crimes are either violent offenses or at least "involve" dangerous acts. To the extent such offenses do not at least "involve" violence or dangerous acts, they should not be terrorism crimes at all and should not trigger special terrorism powers that are unavailable in order criminal investigations. If Congress grants additional authority for nationwide search warrants for certain offenses listed as terrorism crimes, its authority to get nationwide search warrants under an overbroad definition of international and domestic terrorism should be curtailed, by, for example, eliminating that authority or amending the definition of terrorism.

Giving the government secret access to credit reports without consent and without judicial process (Section 126). This section would allow the government to secretly obtain anyone's credit report without their consent and without any judicial procedure.

The government should not have access to sensitive personal information which has been collected for business purposes on the same basis as businesses, because the government's powers—for example, to compel questioning before a grand jury, arrest, deport, or incarcerate—are far greater than the powers of any business.

In any event, the draft bill does *not*, as the heading states, provide "equal access" for government to such reports; rather, the statute greatly expands access to credit reports by authorizing the government to obtain these reports without consent, notice to the person to whom the credit report pertains, and without a court order. Credit reports are available to business with a "legitimate business need" but only with the consent of the person whose credit report is being examined, such as when that person applies for a loan or a job.

Anyone who has applied for a job or a mortgage and encountered a problem because of a false credit report—which could the result of identity theft, simple error, or malice—knows how difficult it can be to get errors corrected. Under this provision, however, the consequences of an erroneous credit report are far more serious than when credit reports are used for business purposes. Under this provision, because credit reports can be obtained without notice or consent, there is no opportunity for the person to contest an erroneous report.

Creating new terrorism "administrative subpoenas" and providing new penalties for failure to comply with written demands for records that permit the government to obtain information without prior judicial approval (Sections 128 and 129). Under these sections, government can demand—and enforce its demands through civil and criminal penalties—documents and other information from a business, such as an Internet Service Provider, or any individual without prior court approval. Administrative subpoenas provide the government with the ability to compel production of documents or information without obtaining a court order. While such subpoenas can be challenged, after they are issued, through a motion to quash, such a motion must be brought by the party challenging the subpoena, who incurs the trouble and expense of challenging the subpoena.

The draft bill authorizes the use of administrative subpoenas and what the DOJ calls "national security letters" to obtain information in terrorism investigations. These sections reduce judicial oversight of terrorism investigations by relegating the role of the judge to considering challenges to orders already issued, rather than ensuring such orders are drawn with due regard for the privacy and other interests of the target. Furthermore, by granting the government power to compel production of records or other information, such as computer files, without first going to court, the draft bill will likely increase the administrative burden imposed on small businesses, particularly high-technology firms, who are facing ever-increasing demands for records in both civil cases and criminal investigations.

Title II—Diminishes Public Accountability and Due Process By Increasing Government Secrecy

Authorizing secret arrests in immigration and other cases where the detained person is not criminally charged (Section 201). After September 11, 2001, well over a thousand persons whom the government said were connected to its terrorism investigation were detained on immigration charges or material witness warrants without the government revealing who they were or other basic information about their arrests that has always been available to the public and the press. Never before had our government sought to detain persons within the United States in secret; a public process for depriving any individual of liberty is an essential component of the rule of law in a democratic society. As Alexander Hamilton made clear in the Federalist papers more than two centuries ago, a policy that allows "confinement of the person, by secretly hurrying him to jail, where his sufferings are unknown or forgotten" is a "*dangerous engine* of arbitrary government."[4] "The requirement that arrest books be open to the public is to prevent any 'secret arrests,' a concept odious to a democratic society . . . ." *Morrow v. District of Columbia*, 417 F.2d 728, 741-42 (D.C. Cir. 1969).

The government's policy of secret arrests came under fire in both federal and state court in lawsuits brought by the American Civil Liberties Union and other civil liberties and press freedom groups. So far, every court to reach the merits of the argument has agreed that the government's secret arrests policy is not supported by law, is not necessary to protect national security, and violates fundamental principles reflected in state and federal open records laws.[5] When confronted with the ruling in New Jersey state court, the DOJ responded not by complying or appealing the ruling to a higher court, but by issuing a regulation preempting that state's law. It has now chosen to ask Congress to cut short the federal lawsuit in the much the same way.

Threatening public health by severely restricting access to crucial information about environmental health risks posed by facilities that use dangerous chemicals (Section 202). This section would deprive communities and environmental organizations of critical information concerning risks to the community contained in "worst case scenarios" prepared under federal environmental laws. Under section 112(r) the Clean Air Act, 47 U.S.C. § 7212(r), corporations that use potentially dangerous chemicals must prepare an analysis of consequences of the release of such chemicals to surrounding communities. This information is absolutely critical for community activists and environmental organizations seeking to protect public health and safety, and the environment, and by ensuring compliance by private corporations with environmental and health standards and alerting local residents to the hazards to which they may be exposed.

The proposed amendment (sec. 202) severely restricts access to such information, limiting such access to reading rooms in which copies could not be made and notes could not be taken, and excising from the reports such basic information as "the identity or location of any facility or any information from which the identity or location of the facility could be deduced." "Official users" are given greater access, but these users only include *government* officials, and government whistleblowers who reveal any information restricted under this section commit a criminal offense, even if their motivation was to protect the public from corporate wrongdoing or government neglect.

Harming fair trial rights for American citizens and other defendants by limiting defense attorneys from challenging the use of secret evidence in criminal cases (Section 204). This section would inhibit the ability of the accused to defend themselves against criminal charges based in part on classified information. The Classified Information Procedures Act (CIPA), 18 U.S.C. App. 3 §§ 1-16, provides a special procedure to govern an extraordinary situation—where the government seeks to use information in a criminal case which is classified by Executive Order without revealing in open court any more information than is necessary to provide the defendant with a fair trial under the Sixth Amendment.[6]

CIPA entrusts to federal district judges the "gatekeeper" function of determining what classified information can be excluded from open court, what information can be given to the defense in summary form, and what essential information must be disclosed to the defendant to ensure his right to contest the accusations against him and to ensure that evidence the jury or other factfinder considers is reliable, having been tested in an adversarial proceeding. The judge has the power to consider a government request to delete information or substitute a summary in an ex parte proceeding, i.e., without the benefit of hearing from the defense. CIPA does *not* give the government a right to make its case in the absence of the defense; instead, the judge determines how much of the prosecution's submission to examine ex parte and in camera, i.e., in secret. The proposed amendment (sec. 204) would seriously undermine the judge's initial gatekeeping role by compelling a judge, at the request of the prosecution, to determine whether and how to redact classified information without the benefit of an adversary hearing. In other words, the amendment would take away the judge's authority, under current law, to hear defense objections to a prosecution request for authorization to delete specified items of classified information from documents relevant to the defense's case.

CIPA strikes the right balance between the government's national security interests and the defendant's right to see the evidence against him or her. This amendment undermines that balance.

Gagging grand jury witnesses in terrorism from discussing their testimony with the media or the general public, thus preventing them from defending themselves and denying the public information it has a right to receive under the First Amendment (Section 206). This section would gag grand jury witnesses so that they could not publicly respond to false information about them leaked to the press. Rule 6(e) of the Federal Rules of Criminal Procedure imposes a general obligation of secrecy requiring attorneys and grand jurors to refrain from commenting on "matters occurring before the grand jury." In theory, grand jury secrecy is imposed primarily to protect the reputation of individuals who become subject to a grand jury investigation. In practice, such secrecy does not always afford much protection, as law enforcement officials who leak information to reporters in violation of Rule 6(e) are rarely discovered and prosecuted.

Grand jury secrecy is *not* imposed on witnesses, who are free to speak about their testimony to friends, associates or to the media. In practice, this limitation is essential to afford targets of a grand jury investigation the opportunity to defend themselves against leaked accusations and media speculation. Under the proposed amendment (section 206), witnesses in terrorism investigations could be unfairly smeared in the media and be deprived from the ability to defend themselves under pain of a criminal sanction.

Title III—Diminishing Personal Privacy by Removing Checks on Local Police Spying; Undermining Genetic Privacy; Removing Checks on Foreign-Directed Searches and Arrests, Even for Dictatorships; Sharing Sensitive Immigration Information With Local Police

Allowing for the sampling and cataloguing of innocent Americans' genetic information without court order and without consent (Sections 301-306). The proposed bill authorizes collection of genetic information of persons who have not been convicted of a crime for terrorism investigation purposes, and the entering of that sensitive information into a database. At a minimum, such collection should not be permitted on persons who have not be convicted of serious crimes unless a judge decides to permit such collection by issuing a court order on the basis of probable cause to believe the information will assist in a criminal investigation. Furthermore, personal genetic information must be destroyed within a reasonable time, such as when a suspect is cleared, to ensure it is not available for misuse by the government or private industry at a later date.

Drawing a DNA sample involves an intrusion on personal privacy that is far more invasive than simply taking a fingerprint. A fingerprint is useful only as a form of identification. By contrast, a DNA sample includes such intimate, personal information as the markers for thousands of diseases, legitimacy at birth, or (as science advances) aspects of an individual's personality such as his or her temperament. In addition, this personal information is not unique to the individual alone, but also provides clues to the genetic traits of everyone in that individual's bloodline. Genetic discrimination is not merely a distant artifact of the discredited eugenics movement of the first half of the Twentieth Century, but is widespread today among private employers, and is (in most states) perfectly legal.[7]

The potential misuse of DNA information contained in a database requires careful safeguards before such information is collected, and concerning the storage of such information. For example, no forensic purpose is served by saving the DNA itself, as opposed to just the information contained in the DNA that proves identity. The proposed legislation fails to include such safeguards.

Permitting, without any connection to anti-terrorism efforts, sensitive personal information to be shared with local and state law enforcement; opening sensitive visa files to local police (Section 311). This section would authorize the sharing of sensitive consumer credit information and educational records with state and local officials without any limits and without any connection to a terrorism investigation. While sharing of sensitive information in the possession of the federal government should be permitted in some circumstances to accomplish anti-terrorism objectives, such records should not be disseminated broadly for other purposes. The draft legislation contains no requirement that sharing of sensitive information with state and local officials be limited to anti-terrorism investigations; instead, such information can be shared simply "to assist the official receiving that information in the performance of official duties of that official." Special authority to share sensitive personal records should not be granted so blithely.

The draft legislation also provides for sharing of sensitive visa information with state and local officials, including state and local law enforcement, on a broad basis, without requirement that such sharing of information be connected to anti-terrorism investigations. In authorizing such sharing of sensitive immigration files, DOJ is at odds with the views of many state and local police departments, who fear involvement in immigration enforcement matters may undermine their ability to establish the trust and confidence of immigrant communities. Absent such trust, many local and state police are concerned that members of immigrant communities will fear contacting the police if they are a victim of crime or a witness to crime.[8]

DOJ also appears to be at odds with the White House, which has assured the public that the Bush Administration was not interested in expanding the role of state or local law enforcement in immigration matters except with respect to terrorism investigations. As White House Counsel Alberto Gonzalez made clear last year, "Only high-risk aliens who fit a terrorist profile" would be placed in the National Crime Information Center (NCIC) database, which is available to state and local law enforcement officials, and the Administration's conclusion that state and local police had "inherent authority" to arrest such persons was limited to this group of non-citizens.[9] Such a narrow policy would be completely undermined by the adoption of this broad language.

Terminating court-approved limits on police spying designed to prevent McCarthy-style law enforcement persecution based on political or religious affiliation (Section 312). In the name of "intelligence gathering," police departments in many cities spied on innocent members of the public who were active in churches, community groups and political organizations. Federal courts, responding to civil rights lawsuits urging an end to such spying, issued decrees prohibiting this spying absent some reason to believe those individuals were involved in criminal or terrorist activity.

Police spying on political and religious activity is not a relic of some distant past. Recently, citizens in Denver, Colorado, were shocked to learn that the Denver Police Department had kept approximately 3,048 illegal files on peaceful protest groups including Amnesty International and the Nobel Peace Prize-winning American Friends Service Committee. The file on the American Friends Service Committee labeled them a "criminal extremist" group. The files pre-dated September 11, 2001, and were not collected as a response to the terrorist attacks.

The draft bill ends these decrees using language patterned after the Prison Litigation Reform Act. Eliminating these sensible, court-approved limits on local police spying would chill dissent, making Americans afraid to join protest groups and activist organizations, attend rallies, or express their views on controversial policies such as abortion or the war in Iraq.

Loosening sensible protections on police monitoring of political and religious activity will not make us safer from terrorism. During the years the FBI illegally spied on individuals exercising their rights under the First Amendment, including such civil rights leaders as Dr. Martin Luther King, Jr., resources were diverted and not a single instance of violence was prevented. Freeing local police to spy on innocent individuals is not likely to be any more productive. It only makes us less safe as resources are diverted from more productive investigations, and less free, as individuals find themselves entered into a police database for activities that are constitutionally protected.

Granting immunity to businesses that provide information to the government in terrorism investigations, even if their actions are taken with disregard for their customers' privacy or other rights and show reckless disregard for the truth (Section 313). This section would prevent a person harmed by a business's disclosure of information about them, including false information, from holding the business accountable. It would encourage false terrorism tips that could result in ruined reputations, lengthy detentions and even violence. Under this section, a business is given immunity from liability if it shares information voluntarily with the government, based on merely on its "reasonable belief" that its actions would help the government prevent or investigate terrorism.

This section resurrects many of the same problems with Operation TIPS that led Congress to ban that program last year. Enormous controversy was sparked by the Bush Administration's Operation TIPS plan to enlist businesses with access to private homes or otherwise able to obtain sensitive personal information without any court supervision. Under the plan, utility operators or others would be encouraged to report "suspicious activity" through a special federal hotline, where the reports would be placed in a central computer database. The program was rife with potential for abuse, including the reporting of false or erroneous information, and the concern that businesses and private individuals would allow their private prejudices to determine who qualifies as "suspicious." When Congress learned of "Operation TIPS" and considered its potential dangers, it banned the program in legislation creating the new Department of Homeland Security. *See* Homeland Security Act of 2002, § 880, Pub. L. No. 107-296, 116 Stat. 2135, 2245 (2002).

The draft legislation poses many of the same dangers as the government's earlier, more elaborate private spying program. False information can ruin a person's reputation, lead to an erroneous arrest and even to violence. Those who are subject to such false reports should have legal recourse if the business or individual responsible for making the report acted irresponsibly. Defamation is the most likely legal action resulting from a false tip to law enforcement. Further protection for defamation defendants would weaken the incentive for a business to think twice before using a false tip to law enforcement to settle a private score or indulge in invidious discrimination. The proposed language paradoxically would increase the incentive for reports of information of dubious validity, diverting law enforcement from more serious potential crimes.

Granting additional immunity is unnecessary because there is already ample protection in state law against frivolous lawsuits. Truth is always a defense to defamation and states also generally provide a qualified privilege against defamation claims involving reports to law enforcement even where the information proves to be false, protecting a defendant against liability unless malice can be shown. *See, e.g.,* Restatement (Second) of Torts §§ 598, 600.

Permitting searches, wiretaps and surveillance of United States citizens on behalf of foreign governments—including human rights abusers—in the absence of Senate-approved treaties (Sections 321-22). This section would authorize the DOJ to help foreign governments—including those that systematically abuse human rights and do not respect the rule of law—invade Americans' privacy even when the United States Senate has failed or refused to approve a treaty allowing such assistance with such a government. Under current law, the United States does not engage in covert surveillance or issue search warrants on behalf of foreign nations unless the Senate has approved a mutual legal assistance treaty. If a foreign nation with which the United States does not have such a treaty requires information from a United States citizen or resident for its own judicial process, it may still obtain that information by asking the assistance of a United States district court in issuing an order to take testimony or obtain "a document or other thing" under 28 U.S.C. § 1782, but it may not issue search warrants or certain surveillance orders. This limitation ensures that that the Senate consents to more intrusive surveillance on behalf of a foreign nation before Americans' privacy can be invaded at the behest of a foreign government. The draft bill (at section 321) sweeps aside this sensible limitation altogether.

These limitations on foreign-directed searches, wiretaps and surveillance orders do not need to substantially impede the investigation and prosecution of terrorism, as Congress has provided "universal jurisdiction" over many serious terrorism offenses. In other words, such offenses are a crime under United States law and subject to U.S. jurisdiction even if committed in a foreign nation. For such offenses, a United States Attorney could obtain the full panoply of searches and surveillance orders to aid in the investigation of that crime, even if such a crime was also being investigated by a foreign nation under its own laws. Such information could then easily be shared with the foreign nation, under information sharing provisions approved by Congress in the Homeland Security Act. *See* Homeland Security Act of 2002, §§ 891-99, Pub. L. No. 107-296, 116 Stat. 2135, 2252-58.

Permitting arrests and extraditions of United States citizens and other persons to a foreign country in the absence of a Senate-approved treaty and without judicial inquiry into the extraditing country's human rights record (Section 322). Among other things, this section allows, on the determination of the Attorney General, a United States citizen or other person to be sent to a foreign dictatorship to be prosecuted even if an American judge would find that the extradition request was made on account of his or her race, nationality or political opinions. It allows the government to send Americans and others abroad to face foreign criminal charges in foreign criminal courts for a host of charges without any of the protections that normally appear in Senate-approved extradition treaties, and strips any judge hearing an extradition request of the authority to consider the fairness of the requesting country's judicial system or its human rights record.

Section 322 authorizes extradition in the absence of an extradition treaty or in excess of limits imposed by existing extradition treaties. Extradition involves arresting an individual, including a United States citizen, because a foreign government accuses that person of violating a foreign law. It is subject to basic constitutional limitations. *See, e.g., Valentine* v. *United States ex rel. Neidecker*, 299 U.S. 5, 8 (1936) (holding that extradition may take place only in accordance with law because of "the fundamental consideration that the Constitution creates no executive prerogative to dispose of the liberty of the individual"). One important safeguard that protects Americans from facing trial in a potentially unfriendly nation, or in a nation that does not respect fundamental fair trial principles or abuses human rights, is the requirement that such extradition take place where the Senate has, by ratifying an extradition treaty, approved of the practice of a foreign nation sufficiently to permit such extradition.

Another, critical safeguard is the requirement of judicial supervision of extradition requests. This section expressly prohibits the judge from considering any of the following:

- "humanitarian concerns,"
- "the nature of the judicial system of the requesting foreign government," and
- "whether the foreign government is seeking extradition of a person for the purpose of prosecuting or punishing the person because of race, nationality or political opinions of that person."

Under this legislation, an American can be sent abroad to face trial under before the courts of a foreign dictatorship, and an American judge has no ability under the statute to even inquire as to the fairness of that country's court system or the reasons behind its criminal accusations.

Current basic due process and constitutional limits on extradition do not need to substantially impede the prosecution of terrorism, as Congress has provided "universal jurisdiction" over many serious terrorism offenses. In order words, such offenses are a crime under United States law even if committed in a foreign nation. For such offenses, a United States Attorney could charge a person suspected of a terrorism crime committed in a foreign nation if the United States lacked an extradition treaty.

Title IV —Undermining Fundamental Constitutional Rights Of Americans Under Overbroad Definitions Of "Terrorism" And "Terrorist Organization"; Reducing Due Process in Administrative Proceedings for Pilots; Undermining Financial Privacy and Due Process

Further criminalizing association—without any intent to commit specific terrorism crimes—by broadening the crime of providing material support to terrorism, even if support is not given to any organization listed as a terrorist organization by the government (Section 402). Under this section, a person who provides "material support" for "terrorism" as defined under the USA PATRIOT Act, could face a conviction, and lengthy prison terms, even if they did not provide any support for an organization listed as a terrorist organization. The definition of terrorism is not linked to any specific crimes, but covers all dangerous acts that are a violation of any federal or state law and are committed to influence government policy. *See* 18 U.S.C. § 2331. The definition arguably covers some protest activities, such as those used by Operation Rescue or by protesters in Vieques Island, Puerto Rico, as such tactics involve dangerous acts that are a violation of law and are committed to influence the government.

This section modifies the requirement to the crime of providing material support for terrorism, 18 U.S.C. § 2339A, which is a separate crime from providing material support for a designated terrorist organization, 18 U.S.C. § 2339B. Under current law, a person, including an American citizen, can only be prosecuted for providing material support for terrorism if the support is provided with the intent to further one of a list of terrorism crimes. A person can be prosecuted for providing resources to a terrorist organization that is designated by the government under the much broader definition of terrorism that arguably covers some protest groups, but only if such an organization has been designated as an international terrorist organization by the Secretary of State. *See* 18 U.S.C. § 2339B. In each case, the person effectively has some notice that what they are doing is prohibited: either the activity they support is a crime or the group whose lawful activities they would support has been publicly designated a terrorist organization. The amendment takes away this notice by permitting prosecution for providing support for the activities of an undesignated organization.

Groups such as Greenpeace arguably could be designated an international terrorist organization, because of the overbroad definition, but the government has not so designated them. Under this provision, however, the determination of whether to apply the terrorism definition to protest groups belongs not with high Executive Branch officials, but to the prosecutor who chooses to invoke the new criminal definition.

Creating a new, separate crime of using encryption technology that could add five years or more to any sentence for crimes committed with a computer (Section 404). Under this section, any federal felony committed with encryption technology that is now commonly part of computer software could be punished by an additional five years (or more, for a repeat offense.) The criminal conduct will not be any different; the only reason for additional penalties will be that the defendant used a certain technology to commit the offense. Here again, the DOJ's description of the crime differs from the language proposed in the draft text. DOJ says it makes it a separate federal crime for a person to "knowingly and willfully use[] an encryption technology *to conceal* any incriminating communication . . . ." However, the draft text contains no requirement that the defendant intend to conceal anything; the crime is complete if the defendant intentionally uses an encryption technology in the commission of a crime. Thus, a simple fraud crime could, if committed using garden-variety encryption technology available with most standard web browsers, carry an additional jail term of up to five years regardless of whether the defendant intended to conceal his activity by using encryption.

Shifting burden of proof to defendant to obtain pretrial release for a laundry list of terrorism crimes (Section 405). Under this section, the right to bail, protected by the Eighth Amendment, is denied for a host of crimes said to be likely to be committed by terrorists unless the defendant is able to overcome the presumption created by the statute. A major reason for the Constitution's prohibition against excessive bail is that defendants are presumed innocent until and unless they have been convicted in a court of law. Despite this, under certain circumstances, the Constitution permits pretrial detention. In general, the government must establish, by clear and convincing evidence, that no release conditions can adequately ensure the appearance of the defendant at trial or the safety of the community.[10]

There is no reason to exacerbate the constitutional problems posed by the presumption against pretrial release for some drug crimes by expanding that presumption to additional crimes. Before the government imprisons a person who has not been convicted of any crime, the government must bear the burden of establishing that the defendant is a flight risk or a danger to the community. This should not be hard to convince a court with respect to true terrorism defendants; there is no need to apply a pretrial detention presumption to a laundry list of offenses that are simply said to be likely to be committed by terrorists.

Imposing potentially life-long supervision and eliminating statute of limitations for nonviolent crimes listed as terrorism crimes, even where they create no risk of death or serious injury (Sections 408 and 410). Under section 408, a defendant who has served his or her sentence for a nonviolent crime listed as a terrorism crime could face life-long supervision, and possible reincarceration if those supervision conditions are violated, even if the crime for which he or she was convicted posed no risk of death or even serious injury. Likewise, section 410 removes entirely the statute of limitations for such nonviolent offenses. Under the USA PATRIOT Act, certain severe consequences follow from the commission of certain terrorism crimes, including the potential for life-long supervision, even after serving a full criminal sentence. In drafting the USA PATRIOT Act, Congress provided for a modest and very sensible limitation for such consequences—they only follow where the offense results in, or creates a foreseeable risk of, death or serious injury.

Indeed, it is not clear why any offense that would not at least create a risk of serious injury deserves to be labeled terrorism at all. The draft bill (at sections 408 and 410) eliminates this sensible restriction, by applying the severe consequence of lifetime supervision and removal of the statute of limitations even for crimes which do not create even a risk of death or serious injury. While DOJ uses the example of a computer crime causing severe financial damage or the provision of material support to an organization labeled as terrorist, it does not explain why such actions, if they truly were serious enough to be considered terrorism under a common sense rather than a legal definition, would not easily meet the requirement of causing at least a risk of serious injury.

Creating 15 new death penalties, including a new death penalty for "terrorism" under a definition which could cover acts of protest such as those used by Operation Rescue or protesters at Vieques Island, Puerto Rico, if death results (Section 411). The draft bill dramatically expands the death penalty, creating fifteen separate new death penalty crimes by defining a new death sentence that sweeps in the remaining crimes listed as federal crimes of terrorism in 18 U.S.C. § 2332b(g)(5)(B) that do not provide for the death penalty. Among others, these include the provision of material support for the lawful activities of an organization labeled a terrorist organization by the government, 18 U.S.C. § 2339B. While the DOJ labels this provision as providing for the death penalty for terrorist "murders," there is no language in the text that requires any showing by the government of an intent by the defendant to kill; it is sufficient that death results from the defendant's actions.

Even more troubling, the draft bill is not content to create fifteen new death penalties, but also contains language that sweeps in *any* violation of state or federal law that is committed under the definition of domestic or international terrorism contained in 18 U.S.C. § 2331. As a result, activities that (1) involve "acts dangerous to human life," (2) are a violation of any state or federal law, and (3) are committed in order to influence government or the population by intimidation or coercion become death-penalty eligible if death results. Arguably, this definition could fit some protest activities, such as those used by Operation Rescue, People for the Ethical Treatment of Animals, or Greenpeace. For example:

- If protesters at Vieques Island, Puerto Rico, a military bombing range unpopular with local residents, cut a fence to trespass on the military's bombing range, and a bomb killed one of the demonstrators, a prosecutor could charge the survivors with a eligible crime for which the sentence could be death.

- If Greenpeace activists attempted to block an oil tanker entering a port to protest the company's safety record, and a member of the tanker's crew drowned attempting to ward off the activists' boat, the protesters could be charged with a crime for which the sentence could be death.

- If an Operation Rescue anti-abortion demonstration succeeded in blocking a woman seeking follow-up treatment for complications following her abortion, and the woman died, the protestors could be charged with a crime the sentence for which could be death.

Under this provision, protesters could be charged with the death penalty as the result of a tragedy. While dangerous protest tactics can be punished under the law, they are not terrorism and should not be treated as if they were.

Reducing due process for pilots accused of posing a security threat (sec. 409). While the government has authority to revoke a pilot's license on a sufficient showing that the pilot presents a risk to air security, such denials must be accompanied by a fair opportunity for the accused pilot to be heard in an administrative hearing and to have judicial review of any final determination. The draft bill's procedures for revoking pilot licenses are deficient in this respect. They do not clearly provide for an administrative hearing (as opposed to an administrative determination), and judicial review is provided only through a direct appeal to the United States Courts of Appeals, who are unlikely to have the time or resources to conduct a thorough review of the administrative record.

Further undermining privacy in financial transactions and due process in asset forfeiture and other civil proceedings (subtitle B; secs. 421-28). Continued amendment of money laundering and asset forfeiture laws have resulted in a serious erosion of financial privacy and of due process rights in asset forfeiture and other proceedings. These sections continue that trend:

- Section 421 multiplies by five times the maximum civil penalty for violating economic sanctions or trade embargoes from $10,000 to $50,000. This provision would severely penalize the thousands of Americans who travel to Cuba every year (often without fully appreciating that their travel is prohibited). It would also penalize physicians or other activists who wish to protest our sanctions on other countries, such as Iraq, by bringing medicine or other humanitarian aid to those nations in violation of such an embargo.

- Section 422 targets "hawalas"—traditional money transfer systems used for entirely legitimate reasons in many Muslim cultures—by undermining key concepts of the money laundering statutes. Under this provision, money can be deemed "laundered" even if the funds involved are not proceeds of a crime.

- Section 423 further undermines due process for organizations unfortunate enough to be labeled as "terrorist organizations" by the government, by depriving them of the ability to defend their status as legitimate charities in a proceeding to revoke their tax-exempt status.

- Section 427 and 428 expand civil asset forfeiture—a procedure rife with due process problems that the government can use to seize property without proving that the owner is guilty of any crime and without a pre-seizure hearing. Under this provision, the assets of a protest group that arguably fits the USA PATRIOT Act's overbroad definition of terrorism could be more easily seized by the government, and the use of secret evidence is explicitly authorized to permit such seizures.

Title V—Stripping Americans of All Their Rights as U.S. Citizens; Unfairly Targeting Immigrants Under the Pretext of Fighting Terrorism

Stripping even native-born Americans of all of the rights of United States citizenship if they provide support for "terrorism," allowing them to be indefinitely imprisoned in their own country as undocumented aliens. (Section 501). This section would permit the government to punish certain criminal activity by stripping even native-born Americans of U.S. citizenship, thereby depriving them of any nationality at all and potentially relegating them forever to imprisonment as undocumented immigrants in their own country. Among the activities that could be punished this way are providing material support for an organization—including a domestic organization—labeled as a terrorist organization by the government, even if the support was only for the lawful activities of that organization.

The Fourteenth Amendment provides that "All persons born or naturalized in the United States, and subject to the jurisdiction thereof, are citizens of the United States and of the State wherein they reside." While Americans do have the right to give up their citizenship in the United States, the Constitution does not give Congress any power to take away from an American his or her status as a citizen even for participating in crime in time of war. *See Trop v. Dulles*, 356 U.S. 86 (1958) (conviction by court martial of crime of desertion during World War II could not constitutionally lead to loss of citizenship, even though crime was committed voluntarily). Rather, as the Supreme Court has made clear, every citizen of the United States enjoys "a constitutional right to remain a citizen . . . unless he voluntarily relinquishes that citizenship." *Afroyim v. Rusk*, 387 U.S. 253 (1967) (citizenship could not be forfeited merely by voting in foreign election without the requisite intent to abandon U.S. citizenship).

While DOJ is correct to observe that certain voluntary acts, such as serving in a foreign army, can serve to terminate U.S. citizenship, these "expatriating acts" must indicate some desire to show an affinity with a foreign sovereign. Only acts that indicate such a desire to relinquish American nationality can be made the basis for a finding that strips an American of his or her citizenship. *See Vance v. Terrazas*, 444 U.S. 252, 262 (1980).

Moreover, it is the government's burden to establish that the expatriating act was committed with the intent of relinquishing citizenship, a showing this section attempts to short-circuit. *See id.* at 261 (holding that the "trier of fact must . . . conclude that the citizen not only voluntarily committed the expatriating act prescribed in the statute, but also intended to relinquish his citizenship.") Expatriating acts are not defined by reference to how repugnant or offensive they are, or by whether they constitute serious crimes, but by whether they show the individual has an intent to attach himself or herself to another sovereignty. Thus, while serving in a foreign army or voting in a foreign election may indicate an intent to abandon American nationality, the commission of a series of grisly murders, or the control of a vast criminal enterprise plainly do not, although the former are legal while the latter are serious crimes.

Providing support to a terrorist organization, which possesses no sovereignty under international law, is a crime, *see* 18 U.S.C. § 2339A, but plainly does not indicate that the individual desires to attach himself or herself to the allegiance of a foreign nation or to abandon U.S. citizenship in the way that, for example, serving in a foreign army might. Indeed, expatriation in the draft bill is not even limited to providing material support to *foreign* terrorist organizations, as wholly domestic organizations can be designated as terrorist organizations under 8 U.S.C. § 1182(a)(3). In addition, expatriation could result from support of organizations "engaged in hostilities" against the "national security interests" of the United States—which could mean anything—not just against the United States or its people. Finally, the draft bill would allow expatriation even for support of the lawful, humanitarian activities of an organization that the United States has labeled a "terrorist organization," which belies DOJ's analogy of supporting terrorism by serving in a foreign army engaged in hostilities against the United States.

Targeting undocumented workers with extended jail terms for common immigration offenses (Sections 502 and 505). Under the pretext of fighting terrorism, this section—which applies to low-level, garden variety immigration offenses that have nothing to do with terrorism at all—unfairly targets undocumented workers. The United States census revealed that more than seven million undocumented immigrants are living in the United States. At present, the United States is engaged in negotiations with Mexico in part to decide whether to permit greater numbers of temporary workers to come to the United States legally, and whether such a program would also provide a path to legal status for undocumented Mexicans or other undocumented immigrants.

Under the pretext of fighting terrorism, this section short-circuits the national debate over immigration policy by substantially increasing penalties for a number of very common immigration crimes often committed by undocumented immigrants. These include unlawful entry (INA § 275(a)(1)), reentry after removal (INA § 276), and failing to register with the immigration authorities (INA § 264(e)). The draft bill (at sec. 505) also provides that the offense of failing to depart after a deportation order (INA § 243) is a continuing offense—meaning that, in practice, no statute of limitations will apply. Increasing these penalties now would almost certainly not prove an effective deterrent to illegal immigration, as the threat of penalties for illegal immigration has never been sufficient to outweigh the causes of immigration including the pull of economic opportunity and the conditions in the home country, but could frustrate our relations with Mexico and other important U.S. allies seeking to negotiate a new framework for immigration policy.

Providing for summary deportations, even of lawful permanent residents, whom the Attorney General says are a threat to national security (Section 503). Under this provision, any immigrant, including longtime lawful permanent residents, may be expelled from the United States on the unilateral determination of the Attorney General that they are a threat to "national security," which is defined as "the national defense, foreign relations, or economic interests of the United States." INA § 219(c)(2). A person facing removal under this section will be separated from his or her family and community without ever being able to effectively answer the government's true reasons for labeling him or her a security risk.

Immigrants and other non-citizens involved in terrorism are deportable under current law,[11] and suspected terrorists are subject to mandatory detention during any immigration or criminal proceedings.[12] The purpose of this amendment is to eliminate due process entirely for immigrants, including lawful permanent residents, accused of crimes or terrorism by permitting their expulsion merely on the Attorney General's fiat. It is based on the fundamentally flawed notion that non-citizens in the United States do not possess the right to fair treatment under the law, a notion that the Supreme Court has repeatedly rejected. *See Zadvydas v. Davis* 533 U.S. 678, 693 (2001) (reiterating long-standing constitutional rule that "the Due Process Clause applies to all 'persons' within the United States, including aliens, whether their presence here is lawful, unlawful, temporary, or permanent").

The proposal is another DOJ initiative that flies in the face of President Bush's stated opposition to the use of secret evidence in immigration proceedings on the basis that fair treatment should be afforded everyone in America. Under the proposal, a non-citizen, including a lawful permanent resident, accused of posing a risk to national security could be detained and deported without having committed any violation of law and without ever knowing the basis of the accusation against him or her. The provision would essentially authorize a repeat of the "Palmer raids," a discredited episode in the 1920s that involved widespread mass deportations and widespread abuse of the rights of law abiding Russian and other immigrants during a wave of anti-immigrant and nativist hysteria.

DOJ originally asked for this summary deportation power shortly after September 11 in its initial drafts of the USA PATRIOT Act. It was firmly rejected, on a bipartisan basis, by a Congress deeply concerned about the use of secret evidence and core due process in immigration proceedings. It should be rejected again.

Completely abolishing fair hearings for lawful permanent residents convicted of even minor criminal offenses through a retoractive "expedited removal" procedure, and preventing any court from questioning the government's unlawful actions by explicitly exempting these cases from habeas corpus (Section 504). Under this new "expedited removal" provision, any immigrant who was convicted even of a minor criminal offense long ago could be deported under a special procedure that provides for no immigration hearing at all and restricts the federal courts from questioning whether the government's actions are within the law. The expedited removal provision, which currently applies only to some classes of undocumented immigrants, would now apply to all immigrants, including lawful permanent residents. "Expedited removal" would be available for crimes which are called "aggravated felonies" (and other crimes) but can be as minor as a shoplifting offense for which a suspended sentence of one year or more is imposed. No discretionary relief is available, regardless of the compelling humanitarian circumstances of any particular case, and the provision applies retroactively. The provision also unconstitutionally exempts these cases entirely from habeas corpus, 28 U.S.C. § 2241, which protects the right of all persons in custody—including immigrants—to a judicial determination of the legality of the government's actions.

In 1996, Congress adopted harsh laws that greatly expanded the number and types of crimes that could lead to *automatic* deportation—i.e., deportation without any possibility to even apply for discretionary relief from the Attorney General. At that time, DOJ went even further than Congress, arguing that the law applied retroactively, so that even immigrants who had been granted relief for crimes committed years or decades earlier and had turned their lives around would now face automatic deportation. DOJ also argued that its controversial retroactive interpretation of the law could not be questioned by any federal court, including the Supreme Court.

In 2001, the Supreme Court firmly rejected DOJ's position, finding both that Congress had not intended the 1996 immigration laws to apply retroactively and that restrictions on judicial review still left intact the federal court's power to correct unlawful government action through a writ of habeas corpus under 28 U.S.C. § 2241. See *INS v. St. Cyr*, 533 U.S. 289 (2001). ("Judicial intervention in deportation cases is unquestionably required by the Constitution.") At the same time, in Congress, a growing number of members of Congress, on both sides of the aisle, began to reconsider the scope of the 1996 laws, culminating the decision of the House Judiciary Committee in 2002 to approve H.R. 1452, the Family Reunification Act, which would restore discretionary relief for some lawful permanent residents accused of relatively minor offenses, particularly if they had come to the United States at an early age.

The draft bill would seriously undermine fair treatment of lawful permanent residents. It would deny fundamental due process in immigration proceedings by completely eliminating an actual hearing. It would disregard the Supreme Court's *St. Cyr* ruling, stripping the judiciary of its core functions in such cases.

The provision attempts to insulate the Attorney General's "expedited removal" decision from judicial review by taking a step never taken by Congress since the Civil War—expressly denying access to habeas corpus, 28 U.S.C. § 2241, to prevent the federal courts from correcting unlawful actions by the immigration authorities. Because of the jurisdiction provided by by 28 U.S.C. § 2241, the Supreme Court in *St. Cyr* was able to consider the merits and found that Congress had not intended to apply the 1996 laws retroactively. This court-stripping provision violates the Constitution, because the Constitution protects habeas corpus—the Great Writ that keeps detention within the boundaries of the rule of law.[13]

Expanding the Attorney General's authority to designate a country to which an immigrant could be deported, and permitting such deportation even if there is no effective government in such a country (Section 506). This section would authorize the Attorney General to dump immigrants ordered removed in any country in the world, and even to areas which are lawless and have no governing authority whatsoever. This section would have a devastating effect on Somalis and other Africans. While the world's attention is focused elsewhere, a tragedy of extraordinary proportions has been building in Africa, where in Somalia, for example, effective government has broken down as rival armed groups vie for power. For this reason, a federal district court is now entertaining a plea from Somalis to halt deportations to that country. The Immigration and Nationality Act does not provide for forced deportation of anyone to a country or region that lacks any form of government, nor should it. Deportation should not be a death sentence, as such deportation could easily become. Nor is it good foreign policy to simply dump into lawless regions non-citizens ordered removed from the United States because such a policy that will simply exacerbate the severe challenges facing such areas of the world.

ENDNOTES

[1] This and other similarities to criminal wiretap requirements were essential to the review court's holding that "FISA as amended is constitutional because the surveillances it authorizes are reasonable." *Id.* at 56. The ACLU does not agree with that conclusion, but simply notes that even a court with the broadest view of the government's surveillance power has found the requirement that the government show probable cause that a target is acting for a foreign power is constitutionally based.

[2] Richard Reeves, PRESIDENT NIXON: ALONE IN THE WHITE HOUSE 335 (2001). The plan was apparently *not* implemented, despite President Nixon's order, but certainly contributed to the pattern of abuse that finally lead to the Watergate break-in and cover up.

[3] In the absence of such a process, a party could well be barred from challenging the lawfulness of the underlying order in any proceeding to enforce contempt sanctions. *See Walker v. City of Birmingham*, 388 U.S. 307, 317 (1967) (holding civil rights marchers could not challenge the lawfulness of an injunction forbidding a peaceful march in proceedings to enforce contempt sanctions).

[4] THE FEDERALIST No. 84 (Hamilton) (emphasis in original) (quoting 1 Blackstone, COMMENTARIES ON THE LAWS OF ENGLAND 335).

[5] *See American Civil Liberties Union of New Jersey v. County of Hudson*, No. HUD-L-463-02 (N.J. Super. Ct. Law Div. April 12, 2002), *rev'd on other grounds*, 779 A.2d 629 (N.J. Super. App. Div. 2002); *Center for National Security Studies v. United States Dep't of Justice*, 215 F. Supp. 2d 94 (D.D.C. 2002) (appeal pending before D.C. Circuit).

[6] "In all criminal prosecutions, the accused shall enjoy the right . . . to be informed of the nature and cause of the accusation; to be confronted with the witnesses against him; [and] to have compulsory process for obtaining witnesses in his favor . . . ." U.S. Const. amend. 6.

[7] *See* Testimony of Barry Steinhardt, Associate Director of the American Civil Liberties Union, Before the House Judiciary Committee, Subcommittee on Crime, March 23, 2000 (reporting an American Management Association survey in 1997 that reported that six out of ten employers responding use genetic screening information for employment purposes.)

[8] The National Immigration Forum has posted on its website a list of statements by local and state police from across the country, all opposing any attempt to enlist them in the enforcement of immigration laws. *See* Opposition to Local Enforcement of Immigration Laws, updated October 1, 2002, available at: http://www.immigrationforum.org/currentissues/articles/100102_quotes.htm

[9] *See* Letter from White House Counsel Alberto R. Gonzalez to Migration Policy Institute, June 24, 2002, available at: http://www.migrationpolicy.org/files/whitehouse.pdf

[10] *See United States v. Salerno*, 481 U.S. 739, 751 (1987) (holding that pretrial detention is constitutional "[w]hen the Government proves by clear and convincing evidence that an arrestee presents an identified and articulable threat to an individual or the community").

[11] *See* INA § 237(a)(4)(B) ("Any alien who has engaged, is engaged, or at any time after admission engages in any terrorist activity . . . is deportable.").

[12] USA PATRIOT Act, § 412, Pub. L. No. 107-56, 115 Stat. 321 (2001), codified at INA § 236A.

[13] Another court-stripping provision, in Section 504(d), would give the government power to deport people before a federal judge could hear their challenges, even where the law clearly allows judicial review, by posing serious barriers to the judge's ability to stay deportation while considering the case. The provision would overturn rulings of four federal appeals courts that found that the very stringent standard that applies for a judge to grant a request to stop deportation altogether under by INA § 242(f)(2) does not apply to a court's ability to temporarily delay deportation while it considers the case. *See, e.g., Mohammed v. Reno*, 309 F.3d 95 (2d Cir. 2002) (on appeal from habeas review of removal order); *Beijani v. INS*, 271 F.3d 670 (6th Cir. 2001); *Andreiu v. Ashcroft*, 253 F.3d 477 (9th Cir. 2001) (en banc); *Lal v. Reno*, 2000 WL 831801 (7th Cir. June 26, 2000) (unpublished); *but see Weng v. Attorney General*, 287 F.3d 1335 (11th Cir. 2002). As one court noted, in rejecting the interpretation the DOJ is now seeking to enact in this legislation, "This would effectively require the automatic deportation of large numbers of people with meritorious claims, including every applicant who presented a case of first impression." *Andreiu*, 253 F.3d at 48.

THE FOREIGN INTELLIGENCE COURT OF REVIEW DECISION
November 18, 2002

Commentary 297

Amici Curiae Brief filed September 19, 2002 by the ACLU in the United States Foreign Intelligence Surveillance Court of Review Decision 02-001 301

Foreign Intelligence Surveillance Court of Review Decision No. 02-001, November 18, 2002 329

ACLU Petition for Writ of Certiorari to the U.S. Supreme Court of the Foreign Intelligence Surveillance Court of Review Decison 02-001 363

Cover Letters and Written Responses to Questions Regarding the Patriot Act As Submitted by the Department of Justice to the House Judiciary Committee Chairman, May 13, 2003 403

THE FOREIGN INTELLIGENCE COURT OF REVIEW DECISION

November 18, 2002

"Victory" for advocates of controls over governmental initiatives and expanded powers in issuing authority for warrantless electronic surveillance resulting from the Foreign Intelligence Surveillance Court decision of May 17, 2002 was dashed with the swift decision handed down by the Foreign Intelligence Surveillance Court of Review on the 18th of November, 2002. Having heard virtually nothing about these courts over a period of 20 years, the public was suddenly confronted with two decisions in a few short months issued by Courts which had heretofore not issued a denial of a governmental request or had never issued any decision.

Interestingly, at the outset the Review Court indicated it was unwilling to accept that FISA required a barrier between intelligence and law enforcement stating:

> ... it (the lower Court) uses the word "wall" popularized by certain commentators (and journalists) to describe that supposed barrier.

With this, and following further commentary, the Review Court effectively provided the government with the authority it wanted—to obtain authority for electronic surveillance (through the Foreign Intelligence Surveillance Court) when the overall purpose involved in the surveillance is law enforcement rather than intelligence.

The lower court did not refuse to grant the government's original request. Rather, that court approved the government's request for new procedures, *in modified form*, which effectively controlled the government in its endeavor to obtain electronic surveillance authority. The government refused to accept such modifications and appealed to the Review Court which found the modifications unacceptable.

The Review Court found that governmental practice, which had as earlier stated in this work accepted as fact a barrier or "wall" and a requirement that "the purpose" for the surveillance had to be to obtain foreign intelligence information, was incorrect and the new governmental argument saying there was only a need for a "significant purpose" was correct. And the Court found that the Patriot Act did not require meeting anything more than that foreign intelligence be a significant purpose of the request.

The decision distinguished the situation in *United States v. Truong Dinh Hung*, 629 F.2d 908 (4th Cir. 1980) because that case had involved an electronic surveillance prior to passage of the FISA and was predicated on the Presidential executive authority, while FISA did NOT "oblige the government to demonstrate to the FISA court that its primary purpose in conducting electronic surveillance is NOT criminal prosecution . . . " It followed that conclusion with an explanation that the Appeals Court in *Truong* had erred in its assertion that once a government investigation moves from an intelligence to a criminal purpose one is required, under the Constitution, to utilize the normal criminal procedures and not the less stringent methods authorized by FISA.

This landmark decision prompted wide-spread public comment and a precedent breaking request for a Writ of Certiorari to the U.S. Supreme Court filed by the American Civil Liberties Union. Public comment in support was led with predictable enthusiastic support by Attorney General Ashcroft who held a news conference when the decision was issued in which he stated:

> Today's ruling is an affirmation of the will of Congress, a vindication of the agents and prosecutors of the Department of Justice and a victory for liberty, safety and the security of the American people (*Washington Transcript Service*; Landover, Maryland; November 18, 2002).

Ashcroft was quoted further in the foregoing as stating "When implemented, the measures will facilitate cooperation and coordination between law enforcement and intelligence officials in the war on terror . . . "

Others were not so happy. According to an item in *The Washington Post* on November 19, 2002:

> At the Cato Institute, Robert A. Levy, senior fellow in constitutional studies, and Timothy Lynch, director of Cato's project on criminal justice, said the ruling undermines Fourth Amendment privacy protections . . . the new rules could open the door to circumvention of the Fourth Amendment's warrant requirements.

An editorial in *The Washington Post* on November 19, 2002 concluded "The result (of the Court of Review decision) will be subtler than the shrill statements of some civil libertarians . . . The decision does not actually make it any easier for the government to conduct wiretaps or searches. But it grants the government one more sphere in which it gets to unilaterally choose the rules under which it will pursue the war on terrorism." The editorial went on to say such important matters should be constructed after careful scrutiny by legislators, which, it concluded, has not happened to date.

The American Civil Liberties Union and four other organizations, in filing their Petition for a Writ of Certiorari argued that the decision ran counter to the Fourth Amendment and to prior decisions of the court. On March 24, 2003, the U.S. Supreme Court rejected without comment the Petition for a Writ of Certiorari.

The latest Executive Branch information concerning this topic is carried in a detailed set of questions and answers submitted to the House Judiciary Committee Chairman on May 13, 2003 by the Acting Assistant Attorney General, Jamie E. Brown. Included in this carefully crafted document are explanations for actions taken by the Administration, the rationale for amendments to the Patriot Act, and a clear explanation of the Administration view on the "wall" perception which has dominated commentary on intelligence/criminal matters over the past two years. Because this response is timely, and because it provides a unique glimpse into policies and procedures being adopted by the Department of Justice, it is included as a full Document in this Volume.

The filings of the ACLU are also included in their entirety in this work.

AMICI CURIAE BRIEF
FILED SEPTEMBER 19, 2002 BY THE ALCU
IN THE UNITED STATES FOREIGN INTELLIGENCE SURVEILLANCE COURT OF REVIEW DECISION 02-001

IN RE APPEAL FROM JULY 19, 2002 OPINION OF THE UNITED STATES FOREIGN INTELLIGENCE SURVEILLANCE COURT

BRIEF ON BEHALF OF *AMICI CURIAE* AMERICAN CIVIL LIBERTIES UNION, CENTER FOR DEMOCRACY AND TECHNOLOGY, CENTER FOR NATIONAL SECURITY STUDIES, ELECTRONIC PRIVACY INFORMATION CENTER, ELECTRONIC FRONTIER FOUNDATION, AND OPEN SOCIETY INSTITUTE IN SUPPORT OF AFFIRMANCE

ANN BEESON
JAMEEL JAFFER
STEVEN R. SHAPIRO
American Civil Liberties Union
125 Broad Street
New York, NY 10004
Telephone: (212) 549-2601
Facsimile: (212) 549-2651

JAMES X. DEMPSEY
Center for Democracy and Technology
1634 Eye Street, NW, Suite 1100
Washington, DC 20006

Additional Counsel Listed Inside Cover

September 19, 2002

KATE MARTIN
Center for National Security Studies
1120 19th Street, NW, 8th Floor
Washington, DC 20036

DAVID L. SOBEL
Electronic Privacy Information Center
1718 Connecticut Ave., NW, Suite 200
Washington, DC 20009

LEE TIEN
Electronic Frontier Foundation
454 Shotwell Street
San Francisco, CA 94110

Counsel for *Amici Curiae*

TABLE OF AUTHORITIES
CASES:

Abel v. United States, 362 U.S. 217 (1960)

Bartnicki v. Vopper, 532 U.S. 514 (2001)

Berger v. New York, 388 U.S. 41 (1967)

City of Indianapolis v. Edmond, 531 U.S. 32 (2000)

Detroit Free Press v. Ashcroft, No. 02-1437, 2002 WL 1972919, at *1 (6th Cir. Aug. 26, 2002)

Ferguson v. City of Charleston, 532 U.S. 67 (2001)

Franks v. Delaware, 438 U.S. 154 (1978)

Fuentes v. Shevin, 407 U.S. 67 (1972)

Griffin v. Wisconsin, 483 U.S. 868 (1987)

Grosjean v. Am. Press Co., 297 U.S. 233 (1936)

Harris v. United States, 122 S.Ct. 2406 (2002)

Katz v. United States, 389 U.S. 347 (1967)

Richards v. Wisconsin, 520 U.S. 385 (1997)

Skinner v. Railway Labor Executives' Assn., 489 U.S. 602 (1989)

Treasury Employees v. Von Raab, 489 U.S. 656 (1989)

United States ex rel. Attorney General v. Delaware & Hudson Co., 213 U.S. 366 (1909)

United States v. Brown, 484 F.2d 418 (5th Cir. 1973)

United States v. Butenko, 494 F.2d 593 (3d Cir.)

United States v. Cavanagh, 807 F.2d 787 (9th Cir. 1987)

United States v. Duggan, 743 F.2d 59 (2d Cir. 1984)

United States v. Johnson, 952 F.2d 565 (1st Cir. 1991)

United States v. Nicholson, 955 F.Supp. 588 (E.D.Va. 1997)

United States v. Pelton, 835 F.2d 1067 (4th Cir. 1987)

United States v. Robel, 389 U.S. 258 (1967)

United States v. Truong Dinh Hung, 629 F.2d 908 (4th Cir. 1980)

United States v. United States Dist. Court ("Keith"), 407 U.S. 297 (1972)

Vernonia School District 47J v. Acton, 515 U.S. at 653

Wilson v. Arkansas, 514 U.S. 927 (1995)

Zweibon v. Mitchell, 516 F.2d 594 (D.C. Cir.1975)

STATUTES:

18 U.S.C. § 2510 *et seq.*

18 U.S.C. § 2511(3)

18 U.S.C. § 2516(o)

18 U.S.C. § 2518(3)(a)

18 U.S.C. § 2518(3)(d)

18 U.S.C. § 2518(5)

18 U.S.C. § 2518(8)

18 U.S.C. § 2518(8)(d)

18 U.S.C. § 2518(9)

18 U.S.C. § 3013a(b)

18 USC § 2511(3)

50 U.S.C. § 1801 *et seq.*

50 U.S.C. § 1801(b)(2)(A)

50 U.S.C. § 1804(a)(7)(B)

50 U.S.C. § 1805(a)(3)(A)

50 U.S.C. § 1805(a)(3)(B)

50 U.S.C. § 1805(e)

50 U.S.C. § 1806(c)

50 U.S.C. § 1806(e)

50 U.S.C. § 1806(f)

50 U.S.C. §§ 1821-29

50 U.S.C. §1806(k)

Pub. L. 90-351, tit. III, 82 Stat. 211 (1968)

Pub. L. 101-298, sec. 3(b), 104 Stat. 203 (1989)

Pub. L. 104-132, sec. 434, 110 Stat. 1274 (1996)

Pub. L. 99-508, 100 Stat. 1851, 1855-56 (1986)

Pub. L. No. 107-56, 115 Stat. 272 (2001)

S. Rep. 90-1097, at 67 (1968)

MISCELLANEOUS:

The USA PATRIOT Act In Practice: Shedding Light on the FISA Process: Hearing Before United States Senate Committee on the Judiciary, 107th Cong. (Sept. 10, 2002)

I. STATEMENT OF THE CASE

This case of first impression raises the question whether federal law enforcement officials can use the Foreign Intelligence Surveillance Act of 1978 ("FISA"), 50 U.S.C. § 1801 *et seq.*, to initiate, control or direct surveillances for criminal investigation. In the court below, the government sought a judicial ruling that FISA can be used where the primary or even exclusive purpose of surveillance is to gather evidence of criminal conduct. Appropriately, the Foreign Intelligence Surveillance Court ("FISC") rejected the government's attempt to invoke FISA for electronic surveillance that for over thirty years has been governed by an entirely different statute, Title III of the Omnibus Crime Control and Safe Streets Act of 1968 ("Title III"), 18 U.S.C. § 2510 *et seq.*, which applies to wiretaps in criminal investigations. As the FISC noted, the government's construction of FISA would allow an end-run around ordinary Fourth Amendment requirements. Neither the text of FISA as amended by the USA PATRIOT Act ("Patriot Act"), Pub. L. No. 107-56, 115 Stat. 272 (Oct. 26, 2001), nor twenty years of judicial interpretation supports this result. While FISA now allows coordination, consultation and information sharing between intelligence and law enforcement officials, it does not authorize surveillance whose primary or exclusive purpose is law enforcement. Indeed, expanding the scope of secret surveillance under FISA would violate the Fourth Amendment and the Due Process guarantees of the Fifth Amendment, and would jeopardize the First Amendment right to engage in lawful public dissent. Though amici readily acknowledge the need to protect the nation in the current crisis, "[i]t would indeed be ironic if, in the name of national defense, we would sanction the subversion of . . . those liberties . . . which make[] the defense of the Nation worthwhile." *United States v. Robel*, 389 U.S. 258, 264 (1967).[1]

A. The FISA Court's May 17 Order and Opinion

This case arises from the government's attempt to disturb the careful balance wrought by Congress and the courts between individual privacy rights and executive power to obtain foreign intelligence.[2] The government relies on the Patriot Act, which amended FISA after the September 11, 2001 attacks. Prior to the amendments, the government could obtain a FISA surveillance order only upon a certification that "the purpose" of the surveillance was to gather foreign intelligence. The Patriot Act amended this language to require a certification that "a significant purpose" of the surveillance is to gather foreign intelligence. The government argues that this subtle change in language (1) provides it with authority to use FISA orders primarily—or even exclusively—for law enforcement purposes and (2) permits law enforcement officials to initiate, direct and control FISA surveillances to bolster criminal investigations that otherwise would be subject to Title III.

The current controversy arose in March of this year, when the government asked the Foreign Intelligence Surveillance Court to adopt a set of procedures for all FISA cases, past, present and future. Although styled as "Intelligence Sharing Procedures for Foreign Intelligence and Foreign Counterintelligence Investigations Conducted by the FBI," the March 2002 procedures in fact sought to implement the Attorney General's expansive new interpretation of FISA. Under the proposed procedures, FISA surveillance could be initiated, directed, and controlled *by law enforcement officials*. In effect, the government sought to institutionalize an end-run around the Fourth Amendment's ordinary requirements—an end-run that would be available to it in any criminal investigation related to national security.

The FISC correctly rejected the government's audacious reinterpretation of FISA.[3] *See In Re All Matters Submitted to the Foreign Intelligence Surveillance Court*, Memorandum Opinion, May 17, 2002 (hereinafter, "May 17 Opinion"), at 4. Citing the "troubling" history of recent government failures clearly to describe the law enforcement aspects of FISA cases, *id*. at 16, the FISC specifically rejected the section of the proposed procedures that would have allowed law enforcement officials to initiate or control FISA searches, *see id*. at 26-27. The FISC modified that portion of the proposed procedures to substitute two paragraphs concerning consultations between law enforcement officials and intelligence agents. *See id.* In accordance with FISA and the Fourth Amendment, the two substitute paragraphs adopted by the FISC establish objective rules intended to permit coordination and consultation but also to prevent the government from using FISA primarily for law enforcement purposes. The FISC fully approved the government's proposed procedures that allow the FBI to disseminate to law enforcement officers all information collected in intelligence investigations. *See id*. at 26.

The FISC correctly recognized that the Patriot Act's promotion of coordination and information-sharing were not meant to—and constitutionally could not—obviate the distinction between surveillance for law enforcement and intelligence purposes. As the FISC concluded, given the relaxed standards for secret surveillance under FISA, authorization for FISA orders must be based on an assessment of the government's purpose and cannot extend to surveillance controlled by law enforcement officials for law enforcement purposes.

This case does not present the issue whether information collected in FISA surveillances and searches can be used in criminal cases. Nor does it present the issue whether law enforcement officials and intelligence officers can coordinate their efforts in situations where they have overlapping interests in the same target. In the Patriot Act, Congress made changes to FISA and Title III that support essentially unlimited sharing of information between intelligence and law enforcement officers. But those amendments assumed and preserved the distinction between surveillance authorization for criminal investigations and intelligence investigations.

The FISC based its decision on the minimization procedures and its ruling can be affirmed under that reasoning alone. As *amici* explain in detail below, the FISC's ruling is also consistent with FISA's new "significant purpose" language, considered in the context of other Patriot Act changes and the entire statutory scheme for surveillance authorization under Title III and FISA. *See* Section II, *infra*. However if this Court declines to affirm on statutory grounds, the Court must conclude that the significant purpose amendment rendered FISA unconstitutional. As explained below, the Constitution prohibits FISA surveillance where the government's primary purpose is criminal investigation. *See* Sections III and IV, *infra*.

II. FISA DOES NOT AUTHORIZE LAW ENFORCEMENT OFFICIALS TO CONTROL SURVEILLANCE FOR CRIMINAL INVESTIGATIONS

A. The structure of the surveillance statutes reflects a constitutionally based distinction between intelligence gathering and law enforcement

To support its push for expanded surveillance powers under FISA, the government advances in its brief a two-part argument—that law enforcement is a foreign intelligence function within the definition of FISA and that intelligence collection under FISA can be initiated, directed, and controlled by law enforcement officials. Neither argument is supported by the text or history of FISA, Title III, or the Patriot Act. As explained more fully below, this history establishes three principles important to the present dispute: (1) criminal investigation and foreign intelligence gathering are subject to different constitutional and statutory requirements; (2) surveillance whose primary purpose is criminal investigation, including criminal investigation for national security purposes, has always been governed by Title III; (3) to deter abuse, any departure from normal Fourth Amendment requirements for foreign intelligence gathering must be carefully limited.

1. Electronic surveillance poses extraordinary privacy risks, which Congress has addressed through Title III's rigorous requirements

Since the seminal case of *Katz v. United States*, 389 U.S. 347 (1967), the Supreme Court has recognized that electronic surveillance constitutes a search subject to the privacy protections inherent in the Fourth Amendment, *see id.* at 353. Indeed, because of the broad and general scope of electronic surveillance, the Court has stated that "[f]ew threats to liberty exist which are greater than that posed by the use of eavesdropping devices." *Berger v. New York*, 388 U.S. 41, 63 (1967). The privacy threat inherent in electronic surveillance is especially pernicious because of the high likelihood that innocent communications will be intercepted.

> The traditional wiretap or electronic eavesdropping device constitutes a dragnet, sweeping in all conversations within its scope—without regard to the participants or the nature of the conversations. It intrudes upon the privacy of those not even suspected of crime and intercepts the most intimate of conversations.

Id. at 65 (Douglas, J., concurring).

Responding to the Supreme Court's holding in *Katz*, and to widespread reports of abusive government surveillance, *see* S. Rep. 90-1097, at 67 (1968) (noting "the widespread use and abuse of electronic surveillance techniques"), Congress passed Title III in 1968 to implement uniform procedures to govern electronic surveillance in criminal investigations. *See* Omnibus Crime Control and Safe Streets Act of 1968, Pub. L. 90-351, tit. III, 82 Stat. 211, adding 18 U.S.C. § 2510 *et seq.* Title III imposes stringent requirements on electronic surveillance conducted in criminal investigations. One of these requirements, reflecting Fourth Amendment structures, is that law enforcement agents may not conduct such surveillance except on a judge's finding of probable cause that a serious crime has been or is about to committed. *See* 18 U.S.C. § 2518(3)(a) (1994). In passing Title III, Congress clearly sought to "safeguard the privacy of innocent persons" while simultaneously promoting more effective control of crime. *See* Pub. L. No. 90-351, tit. III, 82 Stat. 211 (legislative findings); *see also United States v. United States Dist. Court ("Keith")*, 407 U.S. 297, 302 (1972).

2. Title III has always regulated electronic surveillance in law enforcement investigations undertaken to protect the national security.

From the beginning, Title III procedures have governed criminal investigations for national security purposes. In 1968, espionage, sabotage and treason came at the top of the list of predicate crimes to which the Title III procedures applied. The Senate referred to these as "the offenses that fall within the national security category." S. Rep. 90-1097, at 67 (1968). Over time, as terrorism emerged as a greater concern, Congress added terrorism offenses to the list of Title III predicate crimes, so that now essentially all terrorism crimes are covered by Title III. In the Electronic Communications Privacy Act of 1986, Pub. L. 99-508, 100 Stat. 1851, 1855-56, Congress added to Title III a number of terrorism-related provisions, including section 1203 (relating to hostage taking), section 32 (relating to the destruction of aircraft), section 2284 of title 42 of the United States Code (relating to sabotage of nuclear facilities or fuel), parts of section 1472 of title 49 (referring to aircraft piracy), and the section in chapter 65 relating to destruction of an energy facility. In the Biological Weapons Anti-Terrorism Act of 1989, Congress added section 175 of title 18 (relating to biological weapons) as a Title III predicate. *See* Pub. L. 101-298, sec. 3(b), 104 Stat. 203. In the

Antiterrorism and Effective Death Penalty Act of 1996, Congress added to Title III the visa and passport fraud provisions. *See* Pub. L. 104-132, sec. 434, 110 Stat. 1274, adding 18 U.S.C. § 2516(o).

This process continued in the Patriot Act, which added seven additional terrorism crimes as predicate offenses under Title III. Section 201 of the Patriot added the following to the list of terrorism offenses as predicate crimes under Title III:

> (q) any criminal violation of section 229 [of title 18] (relating to chemical weapons); or sections 2332, 2332a, 2332b, 2332d, 2339A, or 2339B of this title (relating to terrorism); 115 Stat. 278. Congress, even as it amended FISA in the Patriot Act, intended Title III to govern the collection of evidence for prosecuting terrorism offenses threatening national security.

3. FISA governs surveillance for foreign intelligence purposes, and not surveillance to gather evidence of criminal conduct

Congress recognized when it adopted Title III that foreign intelligence collection was distinct from law enforcement. Thus, when Congress enacted Title III, it left untouched the President's claimed authority to gather foreign intelligence information related to national security.[4] This other, exempted sphere of foreign intelligence clearly was *not* meant to govern criminal investigations undertaken to protect national security: Having just created procedures for collecting evidence to prosecute crimes against the national security, Congress would not have said in the same statute that it did not limit the powers of the President to collect evidence to prosecute those crimes. Yet that is what the Attorney General now claims.

The Executive Branch's extremely broad interpretation of its foreign intelligence gathering authority led to widespread and well-documented abuses. *See Zweibon v. Mitchell*, 516 F.2d 594, 616 n.53, 618, 634, 635 n.107 (D.C. Cir.1975); S. Rep. 95-604—Part 1, at 7-9, *reprinted in* 1978 U.S.C.C.A.N. 3904, 3908-10; *The USA PATRIOT Act In Practice: Shedding Light on the FISA Process: Hearing Before United States Senate Committee on the Judiciary*, 107th Cong. (Sept. 10, 2002) (hereinafter, "2002 FISA Hearings") (Statement of Sen. Patrick Leahy) (noting that those illegitimately targeted had "included a Member and staff of the United States Congress, White House domestic affairs advisors, journalists, and many individuals and organizations engaged in no criminal activity but, like Dr. Martin Luther King, who expressed political views threatening to those in power."); *id.* (Testimony of Kenneth C. Bass, III) ("During the Vietnam War [the President's national security power] was invoked to undertake warrantless surveillance of a number of anti-war individuals and groups on a belief that their activities threatened national security. In some cases those surveillance targets were domestic groups with no provable ties to any foreign interest.").

Responding to these abuses, Congress passed FISA in 1978. Like the motivation behind Title III, FISA's purpose was twofold: "Congress sought to accommodate and advance both the government's interest in pursuing legitimate intelligence activity *and the individual's interest in freedom from improper government intrusion.*" *United States v. Cavanagh*, 807 F.2d 787, 789 (9th Cir. 1987) (emphasis added); *see also United States v. Pelton*, 835 F.2d 1067, 1074 (4th Cir. 1987) (FISA passed to create "secure framework . . . [for] electronic surveillance for foreign intelligence purposes within the context of this Nation's commitment to privacy and individual rights" (quoting S. Rep. No. 95-604, at 15, *reprinted in* 1978 U.S.C.C.A.N. 3904, 3916)), *cert. denied*, 486 U.S. 1010 (1988). However, FISA's procedural safeguards are significantly more relaxed than those that Title III established for criminal cases protecting the national security.

4. The procedures of Title III and FISA are substantially different, and FISA was not intended to be an alternative to Title III in criminal cases affecting the national security

Through the enactment of Title III and FISA, Congress created two separate authorization schemes for government surveillance—one for criminal investigation and one for foreign intelligence purposes.[5] In Title III, Congress enacted those standards it believed were necessary to meet Fourth Amendment requirements for using electronic surveillance in criminal investigations. In addition to requiring probable cause to believe that the subject is committing, has committed, or is about to commit one of a list of offenses, *see* 18 U.S.C. § 2518(3)(a), Title III surveillance requires probable cause to believe that the facility to be surveilled is being used by the target "in connection with the . . . offense," *see* 18 U.S.C. § 2518(3)(d). Under Title III, surveillance targets must eventually be notified that their privacy has been compromised, *see* 18 U.S.C. § 2518(8)(d), and targets who later face criminal prosecution can obtain the application under which the interception was approved, *see* 18 U.S.C. § 2518(9). Title III surveillance orders are also normally limited to thirty days, subject to renewal only under the same requirements as govern initial applications. *See* 18 U.S.C. § 2518(5).

As the FISC noted in its May 17 Memorandum Opinion, *see* May 17 Opinion at 9-10, FISA surveillance offers the executive branch significantly greater latitude. *See* Attached Chart (comparing requirements under the two statutes). First, FISA surveillance orders require only probable cause to believe that the target is a foreign power or agent thereof, *see* 50 U.S.C. § 1805(a)(3)(A), and, if directed at a U.S. person, probable cause to believe that the target is, for example, "knowingly engage[d] in clandestine intelligence gathering activities," 50 U.S.C. § 1801(b)(2)(A). Unlike Title III orders, FISA orders do *not* require probable cause to believe that the target is engaging in criminal activity. Second, FISA orders require probable cause to believe that the facility to be surveilled is being used by the target, *see* 50 U.S.C. § 1805(a)(3)(B), but they require no showing that the target is using the facility in connection with a crime. Third, FISA contains no provision for notifying targets—or non-targets whose communications might have been intercepted incidentally—that their privacy has been compromised. Fourth, FISA orders have a term of 90 days which may be extended up to a full year in certain cases. *See* 50 U.S.C. § 1805(e). Fifth, FISA surveillance targets who later face criminal prosecution usually are not provided the application on which the surveillance was based and sometimes cannot even obtain intercepted communications through discovery, and are therefore severely limited in their ability to challenge the legality of the surveillance after the fact. *See* 50 U.S.C. § 1806(f).[6]

Reading the two statutes together, it is clear that Congress intended that Title III's strong standards should govern electronic surveillance whose purpose is to protect national security through criminal prosecutions. It would have been illogical for Congress to have created in FISA separate, *weaker* standards to govern the same government action.[7] Because the rules that govern surveillance under FISA are more relaxed than those that govern Title III surveillance (and, indeed, because FISA does not reflect safeguards that the Fourth Amendment mandates for criminal investigations), it is not surprising that the government seeks to define the foreign-intelligence sphere as capaciously as possible. But the boundaries of the foreign- intelligence sphere must be determined not by executive whim but by statutory and constitutional principle. As discussed below, the USA Patriot Act did nothing to disrupt the longstanding distinction between foreign intelligence and law enforcement surveillance.

B. The Patriot Act confirmed and clarified the boundaries between the foreign intelligence and law enforcement spheres

1. The Patriot Act's "significant purpose" amendment clarified that foreign intelligence need not be the exclusive purpose of surveillance conducted under FISA's authority

Prior to the enactment of the Patriot Act in October 2001, the government could obtain FISA surveillance orders only on a certification that "the purpose" of the surveillance was foreign intelligence.[8] As amended by the Patriot Act, FISA now allows the government to obtain surveillance orders on a certification that "a significant purpose" of the surveillance is foreign intelligence. 50 U.S.C. § 1804(a)(7)(B). Contrary to the government's view, this change was *not* meant to dissolve the boundaries between the foreign intelligence and law enforcement spheres. Rather, the change was intended only to clarify that the government can obtain a FISA surveillance order even if foreign intelligence is not its exclusive purpose.

Congress' amendments to FISA responded to two linked concerns, one relating to FISA authorizations and one relating to coordination and sharing between law enforcement and intelligence officials. The background to these concerns is laid out in a July 2001 GAO report to Congress. *See* United States General Accounting Office, *FBI Intelligence Investigations: Coordination Within*

Justice on Counterintelligence Criminal Matters is Limited, GAO-01-780 (July 2001), available online at <http://www.gao.gov/new.items.d01780.pdf>. The GAO report makes clear that, beginning in the 1990s, there developed considerable confusion and friction within the Justice Department regarding FISA's authorization requirements and the permissible extent of cooperation between intelligence and law enforcement officials. While law enforcement officers wanted intelligence officers to provide them with criminal evidence uncovered in the course of FISA surveillances, intelligence officers had become concerned that providing such information to law enforcement officers would lead the FISC to reject applications to renew surveillance orders on the grounds that foreign intelligence was no longer the primary purpose. *See id.* at 11. The GAO found that, in the view of Criminal Division officials, "the primary purpose test had been, in effect, interpreted by the FBI and Office of Intelligence Policy Review to mean 'exclusive' purpose." *Id.* At 14. Efforts to correct the problem apparently made it worse. Procedures adopted by the Attorney General in 1995 "triggered coordination problems," and some within the Justice Department remained concerned that coordination between intelligence officers and law enforcement officers would either jeopardize criminal prosecutions or lead the FISC to deny applications or renewal requests. *Id.* at 19. To the consternation of the FISC, these conflicts also led to a serious series of incidents in which the government withheld from the court and even misstated to the court information about the extent of law enforcement interest in the targets of FISA surveillance. *See* May 17 Opinion at 16-17.

The Patriot Act responded to these concerns with two amendments: the significant purpose amendment to section 104(a)(7)(B), Pub. L. 107-56, Section 218, 115 Stat. 291, and the coordination amendment to section 106, Pub. L. 107-56, Section 504, 115 Stat. 364, discussed below. The significant purpose amendment clarifies that the government can obtain a FISA order even if foreign intelligence is not its exclusive purpose; the aim of this amendment was to put to rest the mistaken interpretation identified by the GAO as a major source of conflict between the law enforcement and intelligence officers. In addition, the amendment clarifies that applications to renew surveillance orders need not be denied if criminal prosecution becomes one of the government's goals during the course of an investigation.

The Justice Department's July 26, 2002 response to a letter from the House Judiciary Committee confirms that the significant purpose amendment responded mainly to concern with coordination between law enforcement and intelligence investigations:

> The "primary purpose" standard . . . has had its principal impact not with respect to the government's certification of purpose concerning the use of FISA itself, but rather in the FISC's tolerance of increased law enforcement investigations and activity connected to, and coordinated with, related intelligence investigations in which FISA is being used. Given the court's approach in this area, the "significant purpose" amendment has the potential for helping the government

to coordinate its intelligence and law enforcement efforts to protect the United States from foreign spies and terrorists.

Enclosure to Letter to Hon. John Conyers, Jr., from Assistant Attorney General Daniel J. Bryant, dated July 26, 2002, available online at *http://www.fas.org/irp/news/2002/08/doj072602.pdf*. Senators' statements at hearings recently convened by the Senate Judiciary Committee reinforce that the significant purpose amendment was not intended to dissolve the preexisting boundary between authorization for foreign intelligence and law enforcement surveillance. *See* 2002 FISA Hearings (Statement of Sen. Patrick Leahy) ("[I]t was not the intent of these amendments to fundamentally change FISA from a foreign intelligence tool into a criminal law enforcement tool); *id.* (Statement of Sen. Dianne Feinstein) ("I don't believe any of us ever thought that the answer to the problem was to merge Title III and FISA"); *id.* (Statement of Sen. Arlen Specter) ("The word 'significant' was added to make it a little easier for law enforcement to have access to FISA material, but not to make law enforcement the primary purpose").

2. The Patriot Act's significant purpose amendment must be read in conjunction with the Patriot Act's coordination amendment

The Patriot Act's significant purpose amendment must be read in conjunction with the Act's coordination amendment, which authorizes increased coordination and sharing between law enforcement and intelligence officers. The coordination amendment was meant to clarify that intelligence and criminal investigators can and should coordinate and consult with one another to protect against threats to national security, and that such coordination should not in itself prevent the government from meeting the foreign intelligence purpose test. The coordination amendment states:

> (1) Federal officers who conduct electronic surveillance to acquire foreign intelligence information under this title may consult with Federal law enforcement officers to coordinate efforts to investigate or protect against
>
> > (A) actual or potential attack or other grave hostile acts of a foreign power or an agent of a foreign power;
> >
> > (B) sabotage or international terrorism by a foreign power or an agent of a foreign power; or
> >
> > (C) clandestine intelligence activities by an intelligence service or network of a foreign power or by an agent of a foreign power.
>
> (2) Coordination authorized under paragraph (1) shall not preclude the certification required by section 104(a)(7)(B) or the entry of an order under section 105.

115 Stat. 364, adding 50 U.S.C. §1806(k).

Even the mere fact of the amendment shows that Congress did not intend use of FISA for a primary law enforcement purpose. That is, in adopting an amendment entitled "Coordination with law enforcement," Congress was making it clear that FISA surveillances would still be initiated and controlled by intelligence officials. By the text of the amendment, "Federal officers who conduct electronic surveillance to acquire foreign intelligence information under this title" are distinct from "Federal law enforcement officers." 115 Stat. 364. Under the Attorney General's reading of FISA, they would be one and the same, and no coordination would be needed.

Contrary to the government's claim that the FISC ignored the Patriot Act, the FISC language modifying the March 2002 procedures restates the coordination Amendment almost verbatim. To compare, the FISC's May 17 Opinion states: "The FBI, Criminal Division, and OIPR may consult with each other to coordinate their efforts to investigate or protect against foreign attack or other grave hostile acts, sabotage, international terrorism, or clandestine intelligence activities by foreign powers or their agents." May 17 Opinion at 26. Thus, the FISC understood the coordination amendment to address both sides of the equation: what law enforcement officials can do without destroying the intelligence purpose of a search—namely, consult and coordinate, and what they *cannot* do—namely, initiate, control, or direct the investigation.

3. The FISC order contains a set of objective rules that implement the Patriot Act by preventing law enforcement officials from initiating or controlling and directing FISA surveillances

The FISC order contains a set of objective rules that implement the Patriot Act by preventing law enforcement officials from using FISA as an end-run around the Fourth Amendment, as interpreted and enforced via the requirements of Title III and Federal Rule of Criminal Procedure 41:

> (1) law enforcement officials may not turn to the lower standard of FISA as a way of initiating surveillance when they are conducting a criminal investigation.

> (2) law enforcement officials may not take over a properly predicated FISA surveillance and direct and control it for the purposes of a criminal investigation.

The appropriateness of these procedures is illustrated in the case under appeal. In July, the FISC granted a FISA application in a situation where there is both an intelligence investigation and a criminal investigation. The government had asked the FISC to grant the application on the basis of the unmodified March 2002 procedures. The Court refused, instead subjecting the order to the modified procedures. The fact that law enforcement officials and intelligence agents had consulted, coordinated, and will share information did not, it is apparent, lead the court to conclude that the FISA surveillance was improperly predicated. Rather, consistent with the statutory scheme, the procedures correctly establish objective criteria to prevent law enforcement officials from directing and controlling FISA surveillance.

The government concedes in its brief that "the FISC and other courts generally have not interpreted [FISA] to permit electronic surveillance (or physical searches) primarily to obtain evidence for a prosecution." Govt Br. at 25. After the Patriot Act, it remains true that FISA is addressed to foreign intelligence surveillance, and not to surveillance whose purpose is to gather evidence of criminal conduct.

As discussed below, the government's construction of FISA—a construction that would make FISA's lower standards available to the government even in criminal investigations—would render the statute unconstitutional. The canon of constitutional avoidance mandates that a court confronting a statute susceptible of two constructions must adopt the construction that avoids constitutional issues. *See, e.g., Harris v. United States*, 122 S.Ct. 2406, 2413 (2002); *United States ex rel. Attorney General v. Delaware & Hudson Co.*, 213 U.S. 366, 408 (1909). Equally important, *amici* believe it is inappropriate to determine the constitutional issues, and perhaps even the important statutory questions in this case, in a non-adversarial proceeding. Both the proceedings below and the proceedings in this Court have been conducted *ex parte*. While warrant applications are ordinarily considered *ex parte*, there is no rationale for that rule where the questions presented are purely legal ones. If the Court reaches the constitutional issues, which *amici* believe is unnecessary, *amici* urge the Court first to appoint special counsel to argue in opposition to the government in an adversarial proceeding. In any event, a familiarity with the constitutional issues discussed below is vitally important to a full appreciation of the stakes in the statutory dispute.

III. FISA IS UNCONSTITUTIONAL TO THE EXTENT IT AUTHORIZES SURVEILLANCE WHOSE PRIMARY OR EXCLUSIVE PURPOSE IS TO OBTAIN EVIDENCE FOR A CRIMINAL PROSECUTION

The government boldly argues that the USA Patriot Act authorizes a waiver of the Fourth Amendment's usual requirements whenever the government engages in criminal investigations related to "national security." The government should not be permitted to turn the quest for foreign intelligence into a "pro forma justification for any degree of intrusion into zones of privacy guaranteed by the Fourth Amendment," *United States v. Brown*, 484 F.2d 418, 427 (5th Cir. 1973) (Goldberg, J., concurring), *cert. denied*, 415 U.S. 960 (1974). Indeed, "the whole point of Fourth Amendment protection in this area is to avoid . . . Executive abuses through judicial review." *Zweibon v. Mitchell*, 516 F.2d at 636 n.108. As discussed below, eliminating Fourth Amendment protections would also jeopardize other constitutional interests, including the First Amendment right to engage in lawful public dissent, and the warrant, notice, and judicial review rights guaranteed by the Fourth and Fifth Amendments. *See* Section IV, *infra*.

The government's central contention is that FISA "does not discriminate between law enforcement and non-law enforcement protective methods"—that FISA is available even for investigations that are purely criminal, so long as the ultimate purpose of the investigation is to protect against foreign threats to national security. Govt. Br. at 37. The government vaguely suggests that its ability to protect the nation will be compromised if it cannot rely on FISA for investigations whose primary or exclusive purpose is to gather evidence of criminal conduct. Amici of course do not dispute that the government should be able to prosecute spies and terrorists. The government simply misses the constitutional point, however, when it argues that this need justifies use of FISA even for investigations that are purely criminal. As discussed above, the raison d'Ltre of FISA is the collection of foreign intelligence information, and the legitimacy of its departures from the Fourth Amendment's normal requirements rests entirely on the fact that FISA searches and surveillance are directed primarily to the collection of foreign intelligence. If the Government's primary or exclusive purpose in an investigation is the enforcement of criminal law, it must proceed according to the normal strictures of the Fourth Amendment. As the Supreme Court has noted, "it is not asking too much that officers be required to comply with the basic command of the Fourth Amendment before the innermost secrets of one's home or office are invaded." *Berger v. New York*, 388 U.S. at 63.

A. Ordinary Fourth Amendment requirements apply to all searches having law enforcement as their primary or exclusive purpose

Every court that has considered the constitutionality of FISA's lower standards has upheld those standards because the primary purpose of the FISA surveillance is foreign intelligence, not law enforcement. Notably, these courts have emphasized that the Constitution—and not merely statutory law—forecloses the executive branch from invoking FISA in investigations whose primary purpose is law enforcement. In *United States v. Duggan*, for example, the Second Circuit held that FISA's "purpose" language required foreign-intelligence information to be "the primary objective of the surveillance," 743 F.2d 59, 77 (2d Cir. 1984), and noted that FISA's language reflected a "constitutionally adequate balancing of the individual's Fourth Amendment rights against the nation's need to obtain foreign intelligence information," *id*. at 73. Similarly, in *United States v. Johnson*, the First Circuit construed FISA's "purpose" language to mean that "the investigation of criminal activity cannot be the primary purpose of the surveillance," 952 F.2d 565, 572 (1st Cir. 1991), *cert. denied*, 506 U.S. 816 (1992), and rooted its holding in the view that FISA should "not be used as an end-run around the Fourth Amendment's prohibition of warrantless searches," *id.*; *see also United States v. Pelton*in , 835 F.2d 1067 (4th Cir. 1987), *cert. denied* 486 U.S. 1010 (1988). At the very least, these cases stand for the proposition that the government may not rely on a foreign-intelligence exception if the government's primary purpose is law enforcement.

Even before FISA was enacted, it was accepted that any nationalsecurity exception to the Fourth Amendment's usual requirements had to be strictly cabined and could not benefit investigations whose primary purpose was the enforcement of the criminal law. In *Keith*, the Supreme Court held that domestic threats to national security could not justify a departure from the Fourth Amendment's prior judicial authorization requirement. *See Keith*, 407 U.S. at 320. Contrary to the government's assertion, *Keith* did not suggest that procedures appropriate in the intelligence sphere could be used primarily to gather evidence of criminal conduct. Indeed, the government itself argued in *Keith* that lower standards were justified only because "these surveillances are directed primarily to the collecting and maintaining of intelligence with respect to subversive forces, *and are not an attempt to gather evidence for specific criminal prosecutions.*" *Id.* at 318-19 (emphasis added). *Keith* acknowledged the possibility that procedural requirements in the intelligence sphere may be different from those that apply in the criminal sphere:

> Different standards may be compatible with the Fourth Amendment if they are reasonable both in relation to the legitimate need of Government for intelligence information and the protected rights of our citizens. For the warrant application may vary according to the governmental interest to be enforced and the nature of citizen rights deserving protection.

Id. at 322-23. Importantly, however, the Court did *not* suggest that procedures appropriate in the intelligence sphere could be used primarily to gather evidence of criminal conduct.

After *Keith*, several circuit courts considered the status of foreign intelligence surveillance under the Fourth Amendment. *Zweibon v. Mitchell* involved an FBI wiretap of the Jewish Defense League. *See* 516 F.2d at 606. The tap was installed without prior judicial approval and, according to the Attorney General, had been installed to "provide[] advance knowledge of any activities of JDL causing international embarrassment to this country." *Id.* at 609. The court rejected the argument that the wiretap was proper notwithstanding the government's failure to obtain prior judicial approval, basing its argument principally on the finding that a warrant procedure would not fetter the legitimate intelligence-gathering functions of the Executive Branch. *See id.* at 651. The court also noted the risk that expansive and unchecked executive surveillance powers might chill protected speech. *See id.* at 634. Although the surveillance in *Zweibon* was installed under a presidential directive in the name of foreign intelligence gathering for the protection of national security, the targets of the surveillance were neither foreign powers nor their agents. *See id.* at 614. The court opined in *dicta*, however, that "absent exigent circumstances, *all* warrantless electronic surveillance is unreasonable and therefore unconstitutional." *Id.* at 613-14 (emphasis added).[9]

At the time these cases were decided, there was of course no statutory basis for a "primary purpose" requirement; the requirement was rooted not in statutory law but in the Fourth Amendment. In *United States v. Truong*

Dinh Hung, 629 F.2d 908 (4th Cir. 1980), which involved surveillance conducted before FISA was enacted, *see id.* at 915 n. 4, the Fourth Circuit recognized a foreign-intelligence exception to the warrant requirement but limited the exception to cases in which "the surveillance is conducted primarily for foreign intelligence reasons," *see id.* at 915 (internal quotation marks omitted). The court emphasized that this requirement stemmed from the Fourth Amendment:

> [O]nce surveillance becomes primarily a criminal investigation, the courts are entirely competent to make the usual probable cause determination, and . . . importantly, individual privacy interests come to the fore and government foreign policy concerns recede when the government is primarily attempting to form the basis for a criminal prosecution.

Id.

Other pre-FISA cases that recognized a foreign-intelligence exception to the Fourth Amendment's usual requirements similarly cabined the circumstances in which the executive branch may invoke the exception. *See, e.g., United States v. Butenko*, 494 F.2d 593, 606 (3d Cir.) ("Since the primary purpose of these searches is to secure foreign intelligence information, a judge, when reviewing a particular search must, above all, be assured that this was in fact its primary purpose and that the accumulation of evidence of criminal activity was incidental."), *cert. denied*, 419 U.S. 881 (1974); *United States v. Brown*, 484 F.2d at 426; *id.* at 427 (Goldberg, J., concurring) ("The judiciary must not be astigmatic in the presence of warrantless surveillance; rather judges must microscopically examine the wiretaps in order to determine whether they had their origin in foreign intelligence or were merely camouflaged domestic intrusions.").

B. The Supreme Court's "special needs" cases confirm that the Fourth Amendment's ordinary requirements apply to all searches whose primary or exclusive purpose is criminal investigation

The Supreme Court has recognized limited exceptions to the probable cause requirement in a line of cases involving "special needs." Under these cases, Justice Scalia has explained, "[a] search unsupported by probable cause can be constitutional . . . when special needs, *beyond the normal need for law enforcement*, make the warrant and probable-cause requirement impracticable." *Vernonia School District 47J v. Acton*, 515 U.S. at 653 (internal quotation marks omitted and emphasis added). The "special needs" doctrine simply has no application to searches whose primary purpose is law enforcement. Indeed, the Supreme Court clearly reiterated this well-settled rule only last term. *See Ferguson v. City of Charleston*, 532 U.S. 67, 80 (2001) (citing, among other cases, *Skinner v. Railway Labor Executives' Assn.*, 489 U.S. 602 (1989); *Treasury Employees v. Von Raab*, 489 U.S. 656 (1989); *Vernonia School District 47J v. Acton*, 515 U.S. 646 (1995); *Griffin v. Wisconsin*, 483 U.S. 868 (1987)).

Ferguson involved a public hospital's policy of testing pregnant patients for drug use and employing the threat of criminal prosecution as a means of coercing patients into substance-abuse treatment. The Court invalidated the policy. "In other special needs cases," the Court wrote, "we ... tolerated suspension of the Fourth Amendment's warrant or probable cause requirement in part because there was no law enforcement purpose behind the searches in those cases, and there was little, if any, entanglement with law enforcement." *Id.* at 79 n.15; *see also id.* at 88 (Kennedy, J., concurring) ("The traditional warrant requirement and probable-cause requirements are waived in our previous cases on the explicit assumption that the evidence obtained in the search is not intended to be used for law enforcement purposes."). In *Ferguson*, however, "the central and indispensable feature of the policy from its inception was the use of law enforcement." *Id.* at 80.

The government concedes that a general interest in crime control cannot constitute a "special need" sufficient to dispense with the probable cause requirement, but it contends, relying on *City of Indianapolis v. Edmond*, 531 U.S. 32, 41-42 (2000), that "a 'special interest' concerning a particular type of crime" may suffice. Gov't Br. at 73. In fact, *Edmond* only reinforces the rule that any search whose primary or exclusive purpose is law enforcement may proceed only on the basis of probable cause. *Edmond* involved vehicle checkpoints instituted in an effort to interdict illegal drugs.

The government asserted that the drug crimes were a "severe and intractable" problem, and the Court agreed that "traffic in illegal narcotics creates social harms of the first magnitude." *Id.* at 42. The Court also noted that "[t]he law enforcement problems that the drug trade creates likewise remain daunting and complex, particularly in light of the myriad forms of spin-off crime that it spawns." *Id.* Notwithstanding the seriousness of the law-enforcement interest with respect to the particular crimes at issue, however, the Court invalidated the checkpoint policy. "[T]he gravity of the threat alone," Justice O'Connor wrote, "cannot be dispositive of questions concerning what means law enforcement officers may employ to pursue a given purpose." *Id.* The dispositive fact, the Court held, was that the checkpoint policy was instituted "primarily for the ordinary enterprise of investigating crimes." *Id.* at 44. Where the government's "primary purpose ... is to detect evidence of ordinary criminal wrongdoing," *id.* at 38, the Fourth Amendment forecloses the government from conducting searches except based on probable cause.[10]

The "special needs" cases reflect that the Fourth Amendment is particularly concerned with intrusions whose purpose is to gather evidence of crime. There is no support, however, for the proposition—implied by the government's argument—that the Fourth Amendment recognizes a hierarchy amongst crimes. The Fourth Amendment applies to all criminal investigations, not merely those that are concerned with minor crimes. The government's assertion, of course, is not simply that espionage and terrorism crimes are especially serious ones, but that these crimes are special in a *constitutional* sense. Gov't Br. at 73-74. The government does not attempt to locate any support for this audacious assertion in the text of the Fourth Amendment (where there is, in any event, no support to be found); rather it relies on the fact that the prosecution of these crimes serves the ultimate purpose of protecting national security. Gov't Br. at 74. Notwithstanding the government's assertion to the contrary, however, Fourth Amendment requirements do not turn on a criminal investigation's ultimate purpose. As the Court explained in *Ferguson*:

> The threat of law enforcement may ultimately have been intended as a means to an end, but the direct and primary purpose . . . was to ensure the use of those means. In our opinion, the distinction is critical. Because law enforcement involvement always serves some broader social purpose or objective, under respondent's view, virtually any nonconsensual suspicionless search could be immunized under the special needs doctrine by defining the search solely in terms of its ultimate, rather than immediate, purpose.

532 U.S. at 83-84. Indeed, the Supreme Court addressed exactly this issue in *Abel v. United States*, 362 U.S. 217 (1960), which involved the prosecution of a KGB agent for espionage. The Court rejected the argument that a different Fourth Amendment standard should apply merely because the of "the nature of the case, the fact that it was a prosecution for espionage." *Id.* at 219-20. The nature of the case, the Court held, could have "no bearing whatever" on the Fourth Amendment questions at issue. *See id.* (discussing, in particular, questions of evidentiary admissibility).

The Supreme Court's "special needs" cases clearly reaffirm that any search whose primary or exclusive purpose is criminal investigation may proceed only on the basis of probable cause. This basic constitutional protection is not suspended for investigations of crimes that are particularly serious, or for investigations whose ultimate purpose is to protect against threats to national security. Any investigation whose primary or exclusive purpose is to collect evidence of criminal conduct must adhere to the ordinary requirements of the Fourth Amendment.

C. The government's theory would suspend ordinary Fourth Amendment requirements not only in espionage and terrorism investigations but in any investigation related to national security

The government's theory that FISA is available even for investigations that are purely criminal is profoundly troubling in itself, but it is made more so by the government's failure consistently to specify the crimes that in its view are constitutionally "special," let alone point to a constitutional or even statutory basis for such a specification. While the government refers to espionage and international terrorism as crimes that are entitled to special constitutional status, *see, e.g.*, Govt. Br. at 38, it repeatedly asserts the arrant principle that FISA is available to purely criminal investigations so long as the government believes that the prosecution of the crime will protect national security. *See, e.g.*, Govt. Br. at 37 ("[i]t is enough that the government intends to "protect" national security from foreign threats"); Govt. Br. at 38-39 n.13 (legislative history does "not undermine the idea that FISA may used [sic] to obtain evidence for a prosecution designed to protect national security"). The suggestion appears to be that the government could bypass the ordinary requirements of the Fourth Amendment not just in espionage and international terrorism investigations—a disturbing proposition on its own—but that the government could bypass the Fourth Amendment in *any* criminal investigation, however minor the crime being investigated, so long as the government believes that the prosecution is designed to protect national security from foreign threats.

The notion that a search or surveillance may be justified simply because the government invokes the rubric of "national security" flies in the face of the most basic principles of American constitutional democracy. The government's theory would effectively allow the executive branch unilaterally to suspend the ordinary requirements of the Fourth Amendment simply by claiming that a prosecution is designed to address a threat to national security. This Court should not sanction the government's attempt to exploit the rubric of "national security" as a means of avoiding the basic Constitutional requirement that the government stay clear of constitutionally protected areas until it has probable cause to believe that a crime has been committed.

IV. ANY EXPANSION IN FISA SURVEILLANCE AUTHORITY WOULD IMPLICATE NUMEROUS OTHER CONSTITUTIONAL INTERESTS

The government's brief urges this Court to dissolve the constitutional borders that separate intelligence investigations from criminal ones and thereby dramatically to extend FISA's reach. As discussed above, any such extension would effectively institutionalize an end-run around the Fourth Amendment's usual requirements. Given the secrecy that cloaks FISA proceedings, any such extension would also jeopardize a host of other constitutionally protected interests.

Public oversight of foreign intelligence surveillance in the United States is extremely limited. As Senator Leahy testified to the Senate Judiciary Committee,

> Over the last two decades the FISA process has occurred largely in secret. Clearly, specific investigations must be kept secret, but even the basic facts about the FISA process have been resistant to sunlight. The law interpreting FISA has been developed largely behind closed doors. The Justice Department and FBI personnel who prepare the FISA applications work behind closed doors. . . . Even the most general information on FISA surveillance, including how often FISA surveillance targets American citizens, or how often FISA surveillance is used in a criminal case[ ], is unknown to the public.

2002 FISA Hearings (statement of Sen. Patrick Leahy).

While some degree of secrecy may be intrinsic to the very nature of foreign intelligence surveillance, as a general matter such secrecy stands in profound tension with basic democratic values. In a democracy, public scrutiny is the principal check on government misconduct. *See 2002 FISA Hearings* (statement of Sen. Patrick Leahy) ("In matters of national security, we must give the Executive Branch the power it needs to do its job. But we must also have public oversight of its performance. When the Founding Fathers said 'if men were all angels, we would need no laws,' they did not mean secret laws."); L. Brandeis, *Other People's Money* 62 (National Home Library Foundation ed. 1933). ("Publicity is justly commended as a remedy for social and industrial diseases. Sunlight is said to be the best of disinfectants; electric light the most efficient policeman."); *Grosjean v. Am. Press Co.*, 297 U.S. 233, 250 (1936) ("An informed public is the most potent of all restraints upon misgovernment."); *Detroit Free Press v. Ashcroft*, No. 02-1437, 2002 WL 1972919, at *1 (6th Cir. Aug. 26, 2002) ("The Framers did not trust any government to separate the true from the false for us. . . .They protected the people against secret government." (internal quotation marks omitted)). More fundamentally, citizens cannot be said to have chosen their government in any meaningful sense if they are foreclosed from learning what the government's policies are. Even accepting for the moment the necessity of the heavy veil of secrecy that has cloaked FISA proceedings over the past two decades, it must be acknowledged that if secrecy serves the nation, it does so at the expense of democracy. *See Detroit Free Press v. Ashcroft*, 2002 WL 1972919, at *1 ("Democracy dies behind closed doors.").

A. Allowing FISA to be invoked in criminal investigations would raise Fourth Amendment and Due Process concerns because FISA fails to require notice and denies individuals any meaningful opportunity to challenge illegal surveillance

Ordinarily the Fourth Amendment requires that the subject of a search be provided notice that her privacy has been compromised. *See Richards v. Wisconsin*, 520 U.S. 385 (1997) (rejecting blanket exception to knock-and- announce requirement for all felony drug investigations); *Wilson v. Arkansas*, 514 U.S. 927 (1995) (knock-and-announce requirement is "embedded in Anglo-American law"); *cf.* 18 U.S.C. § 2518(8) (requiring notice for electronic surveillance conducted pursuant to Title III); 18 U.S.C. § 3013a(b) (requiring notice in searches executed pursuant to Fed. R. Crim. P. 41, and allowing delayed notice only on individualized showing of necessity). The Fifth Amendment similarly requires that the government provide notice to anyone whom it intends to deprive of property. *See Fuentes v. Shevin*, 407 U.S. 67, 80 (1972) ("Parties whose rights are to be affected are entitled to be heard; and in order that they may enjoy that right they must first be notified."). Yet those targeted for surveillance under FISA are never provided notice that their privacy has been compromised. Even if the absence of any notice requirement in FISA is constitutional as to surveillance conducted until now, expanding FISA's application to surveillance whose primary or exclusive purpose is the enforcement of the criminal law plainly raises new (and significantly more serious) constitutional issues. *See* May 15 Opinion, at 24 (noting that government's proposed minimization procedures would "give the Department's criminal law enforcement officials every legal advantage conceived by Congress to be used by U.S. intelligence agencies to collect foreign intelligence information," including possibility of conducting searches without notice to the target).

FISA's failure to require that surveillance targets eventually be notified that their privacy was compromised raises related Due Process concerns because it denies individuals whose communications were inappropriately intercepted any opportunity to challenge the government's actions. Innocent people whose communications are intercepted will probably never find out about the intercept, and those who somehow find out have no way of holding the government to account. While surveillance targets whom the government ultimately prosecutes do receive notice if the government intends to introduce evidence obtained through FISA, *see* 50 U.S.C. § 1806(c), even in such circumstances the warrant application is not provided to the defendant and even intercepted communications may not be divulged unless the government seeks to introduce them in evidence or they are exculpatory; rather the court reviews the communications *in camera*, *see* 50 U.S.C. § 1806(f).[11] Although the FISC exercises a degree of oversight with respect to FISA surveillance through review of surveillance applications, the executive branch has traditionally been accorded great deference in this area. *See, e.g., United States v. Duggan*, 743 F.2d at 77 (noting that government's "primary purpose" certification is "subjected to only minimal scrutiny by the courts"); *id.* ("The FISA judge ... is not to second-guess the executive branch official's certification that the objective of the surveillance is foreign intelligence information."). In any event, such *in camera, ex parte* review is no substitute for an adversarial hearing.

The Supreme Court recognized in *Franks v. Delaware* that, in the Fourth Amendment context, judicial review is meaningful only if the subject of a search can challenge the propriety of the search in a proceeding that is both public and adversarial. *See* 438 U.S. 154, 168-72 (1978). *Franks* involved a defendant's challenge to a police search; the defendant alleged that the affidavits upon which the search was based were deliberately false. The Supreme Court held that a defendant who makes a preliminary showing that affidavits were deliberately false is entitled to an evidentiary hearing. The Court advanced several rationales for its holding, including that, because the pre-search proceeding is *ex parte*, the prior judicial authorization requirement would "not always ... suffice to discourage lawless or reckless misconduct". *Id.* at 169. "The usual reliance of our legal system on adversary proceedings," the Court noted, "itself should be an indication that an *ex parte* inquiry is likely to be less vigorous." *Id.; see also* 2002 *FISA Hearings* (testimony of Kenneth C. Bass, III) ("[A]ny process that departs from our normal adversary proceedings is subject to increased risk of error. When there is no counsel on 'the other side,' the court finds itself in an uncomfortable position of being critic as well as judge."); May 17 Opinion, at 24 (raising concern that government's proposed minimization procedures would allow Fourth Amendment searches on less than probable cause but preclude "adversarial discovery of the FISA applications and warrants.") The *Franks* Court also noted that the government cannot be relied on to police its own conduct. "Self-scrutiny is a lofty ideal, but its exaltation reaches new heights if we expect a District Attorney to prosecute himself ... for well-meaning violations of the search and seizure clause during a raid [he himself] ordered." 438 U.S. at 169 (internal quotation marks omitted).

B. Any extension of FISA would chill protected speech and therefore raise serious First Amendment concerns

Expanding the circumstances in which the government may invade the individual's protected sphere without probable cause also presents the danger that the government's surveillance power will chill dissent, and indeed that the government may wield its power with the specific intent of chilling dissent. Traditionally, the warrant and probable cause requirements have served as important safeguards of First Amendment interests by precluding the government from intruding into an individual's protected sphere merely because of that individual's exercise of First Amendment rights. The Supreme Court wrote in *Keith*:

> National security cases . . . often reflect a convergence of First and Fourth Amendment values not present in cases of 'ordinary' crime. . . . History abundantly documents the tendency of Government—however benevolent and benign its motives—to view with suspicion those who most fervently dispute its policies. Fourth Amendment protections become the more necessary when the targets of official surveillance may be those suspected of unorthodoxy in their political beliefs.

Keith, 407 U.S. at 313-14; *see also id.* at 314 ("The price of lawful public dissent must not be a dread of subjection to an unchecked surveillance power. Nor must the fear of unauthorized official eavesdropping deter vigorous citizen dissent and discussion of government action in private conversation. For private dissent, no less than open public discourse, is essential to our free society."); *Bartnicki v. Vopper*, 532 U.S. 514, 533 (2001) ("In a democratic society privacy of communication is essential if citizens are to think and act creatively and constructively. Fear or suspicion that one's speech is being monitored by a stranger, even without the reality of such activity, can have a seriously inhibiting effect upon the willingness to voice critical and constructive ideas." (internal quotation marks omitted)); *Zweibon v. Mitchell*, 516 F.2d at 633 ("Prior judicial review is important not only to protect the privacy interests of those whose conversations the government seeks to overhear, but also to protect free and robust exercise of the First Amendment rights of speech and association by those who might otherwise be chilled by the fear of unsupervised and unlimited Executive power to institute electronic surveillances."). Any expansion of the government's authority to conduct electronic surveillance under FISA could easily chill protected speech and implicate serious First Amendment concerns.

CONCLUSION

For the reasons stated above, *amici* urge the Court to affirm the decision of the FISC.

Respectfully submitted,

_____

ANN BEESON
JAMEEL JAFFER
STEVEN R. SHAPIRO
American Civil Liberties Union
125 Broad Street
New York, NY 10004
Telephone: (212) 549-2601
Facsimile: (212) 549-2651

JAMES X. DEMPSEY
Center for Democracy and Technology
1634 Eye Street, NW, Suite 1100
Washington, DC 20006

KATE MARTIN
Center for National Security Studies
1120 19th Street, NW, 8th floor
Washington, DC 20036

DAVID L. SOBEL
Electronic Privacy Information Center
1718 Connecticut Ave., NW, Suite 200
Washington, DC 20009

LEE TIEN
Electronic Frontier Foundation
454 Shotwell Street
San Francisco, CA 94110

Counsel for *Amici Curiae*

Dated: September 19, 2002

ENDNOTES

[1] *Amici*'s interests in this appeal are described in the attached Motion for Leave to File *Amici Curiae* Brief in Support Of Affirmance.

[2] This brief focuses principally on electronic surveillance. Importantly, however, the same arguments that *amici* raise with respect to electronic surveillance apply to physical searches as well, as the FISC's May 17 Opinion recognizes.

[3] The government did not appeal the FISC's May 17 decision. In July, the government submitted an apparently unrelated FISA application. While the FISC (Baker, J.) granted the July application, the FISC denied the government's request that the July application be subject to the *unmodified* March 2002 procedures, instead ruling that the surveillance order would be subject to the March 2002 procedures as modified by the FISC's May 17 Opinion. (The FISC apparently issued an opinion related to the July application that has not been published.) The government now appeals from the FISC's July decision.

[4] The Title III disclaimer provided: "Nothing contained in this chapter . . . shall limit the constitutional power of the President to take such measures as he deems necessary to protect the Nation against actual or potential attack or the hostile acts of a foreign power, to obtain foreign intelligence information deemed essential to the security of the United States, or to protect national security information against foreign intelligence activities." 18 U.S.C. § 2511(3) (as enacted by Title III). Subsection 2511(3) was repealed in 1978 by FISA, which struck § 2511(3) and added § 2511(2)(e) and (f). *See* Pub. L. 95-511, sec. 201(b) and (c).

[5] The focus in this discussion is on the differences between FISA's electronic surveillance provisions and Title III. However, there are similar distinctions between the FISA's physical search provisions, *see* 50 U.S.C. §§ 1821-29, and those that govern physical searches conducted in the course of ordinary law enforcement investigations, *see* Fed. R. Crim. P. 41.

[6] Another provision of FISA, not amended by the Patriot Act, reinforces the conclusion that law enforcement officials cannot initiate FISA surveillances. Section 104(a)(7) of FISA provides that every FISA application shall include a certification from an Executive Branch official "employed in the area of national security." This certification can be made only by the Assistant to the President for National Security Affairs or an executive branch official designated by the President "from among those officers employed in the area of national security or defense." Pursuant to Executive Order 12139, only seven officials have been designated to make that determination: the Secretaries and Deputy Secretaries of State and Defense, and the Director and Deputy Director of Central Intelligence, and the Director of the FBI. The Attorney General is not among them, a clear indication that the FISA authority is to be exercised only when an official other than a prosecutor certifies that there is a intelligence purpose to undertake the surveillance.

[7] The definition of "foreign intelligence information" in FISA is very similar to the exemption language in section 2511(3) of Title III as originally enacted, *compare* 50 U.S.C. § 1801(e) *with* 18 U.S.C. § 2511(3) (as enacted by Title III), which reinforces that foreign intelligence under FISA covers activity *not* governed by Title III—namely, methods of protecting the national security other than through criminal prosecution.

[8] Courts had interpreted the "purpose" language to require that foreign intelligence gathering be the "primary purpose" of surveillance. *See* Section III, *infra*.

[9] The Court also noted that a limitation of warrantless surveillance to agents of a foreign power would "not alter the fact that First Amendment rights of others are likely to be chilled." *Zweibon v. Mitchell, 516 F.2d.* at 635. "Under such a test," the court noted, "a few alien members in a political organization would justify surveillance of the conversations of all members." *Id.*

[10] Justice O'Connor indicated in *dicta* that any departure from this rule could be justified, if at all, only in exigent circumstances. "The Fourth Amendment would almost certainly permit an appropriately tailored road block set up to thwart an *imminent* terrorist attack or to catch a dangerous criminal *who is likely to flee* by way of a particular route." *City of Indianapolis v. Edmond*, 531

U.S., at 44. Such exigencies, however, are "far removed" from ordinary criminal investigation. *Id.* Here, while the government asserts national security interests, it makes no showing of exigency. Indeed, FISA surveillance intended to bring a criminal prosecution would make no sense in the face of an imminent terrorist threat.

[11] Under 50 U.S.C. § 1806(e), "[a]ny person against whom evidence obtained or derived from an electronic surveillance . . . is to be . . . introduced or otherwise used or disclosed in any trial . . . may move to suppress the evidence obtained or derived from such electronic surveillance on the grounds that—(1) the information was unlawfully acquired; or (2) the surveillance was not made in conformity with an order of authorization or approval." However, § 1806(f) requires that, upon the Attorney General's request, the court must review the challenged evidence *ex parte* and *in camera*. The Attorney General makes such requests as a matter of course. *See, e.g., United States v. Nicholson*, 955 F.Supp. 588, 592 (E.D.Va. 1997) ("[T]his Court knows of no instance in which a court has required an adversary hearing or disclosure in determining the legality of a FISA surveillance. To the contrary, every court examining FISA-obtained evidence has conducted its review in camera and ex parte.").

FOREIGN INTELLIGENCE SURVEILLANCE COURT OF REVIEW DECISION NO. 02-001

November 18, 2002

Argued September 9, 2002   Decided November 18, 2002

In re: Sealed Case No. 02-001

Consolidated with 02-002

On Motions for Review of Orders of the United States
Foreign Intelligence Surveillance Court
(Nos. 02-662 and 02-968)

Theodore B. Olson, Solicitor General, argued the cause for appellant the United States, with whom *John Ashcroft*, Attorney General, *Larry D. Thompson*, Deputy Attorney General, *David S. Kris*, Associate Deputy Attorney General, *James A. Baker*, Counsel for Intelligence Policy, and *Jonathan L. Marcus*, Attorney Advisor, were on the briefs.

Ann Beeson, Jameel Jaffer, Steven R. Shapiro, for *amicus curiae* American Civil Liberties Union, with whom *James X. Dempsey* for Center for Democracy and Technology, *Kate Martin* for Center for National Security Studies, *David L. Sobel* for Electronic Privacy Information Center, and *Lee Tien* for Electronic Frontier Foundation, were on the brief.

John D. Cline, Zachary A. Ives, and *Joshua Dratel*, for amicus curiae National Association of Criminal Defense Lawyers.

Before: GUY, *Senior Circuit Judge, Presiding;* SILBERMAN and LEAVY, *Senior Circuit Judges.*

Opinion for the Court filed *Per Curiam.*

Per Curiam: This is the first appeal from the Foreign Intelligence Surveillance Court to the Court of Review since the passage of the Foreign Intelligence Surveillance Act (FISA), 50 U.S.C. §§ 1801-1862 (West 1991 and Supp. 2002), in 1978. This appeal is brought by the United States from a FISA court surveillance order which imposed certain restrictions on the government. Since the government is the only party to FISA proceedings, we have accepted briefs filed by the American Civil Liberties Union (ACLU)[14] and the National Association of Criminal Defense Lawyers (NACDL) as *amici curiae*.

Not surprisingly this case raises important questions of statutory interpretation, and constitutionality. After a careful review of the briefs filed by the government and *amici*, we conclude that FISA, as amended by the Patriot Act,[15] supports the government's position, and that the restrictions imposed by the FISA court are not required by FISA or the Constitution. We therefore remand for further proceedings in accordance with this opinion.

I.

The court's decision from which the government appeals imposed certain requirements and limitations accompanying an order authorizing electronic surveillance of an "agent of a foreign power" as defined in FISA. There is no disagreement between the government and the FISA court as to the propriety of the electronic surveillance; the court found that the government had shown probable cause to believe that the target is an agent of a foreign power and otherwise met the basic requirements of FISA. The government's application for a surveillance order contains detailed information to support its contention that the target, who is a United States person, is aiding, abetting, or conspiring with others in international terrorism. *[approx. 1 page deleted]*[16] The FISA court authorized the surveillance, but imposed certain restrictions, which the government contends are neither mandated nor authorized by FISA. Particularly, the court ordered that

> law enforcement officials shall not make recommendations to intelligence officials concerning the initiation, operation, continuation or expansion of FISA searches or surveillances. Additionally, the FBI and the Criminal Division [of the Department of Justice] shall ensure that law enforcement officials do not direct or control the use of the FISA procedures to enhance criminal prosecution, and that advice intended to preserve the option of a criminal prosecution does not inadvertently result in the Criminal Division's directing or controlling the investigation using FISA searches and surveillances toward law enforcement objectives.

To ensure the Justice Department followed these strictures the court also fashioned what the government refers to as a "chaperone requirement"; that a unit of the Justice Department, the Office of Intelligence Policy and Review (OIPR) (composed of 31 lawyers and 25 support staff), "be invited" to all meetings between the FBI and the Criminal Division involving consultations for the purpose of coordinating efforts "to investigate or protect against foreign attack or other grave hostile acts, sabotage, international terrorism, or clandestine intelligence activities by foreign powers or their agents" If representatives of OIPR are unable to attend such meetings, "OIPR shall be apprized of the substance of the meetings forthwith in writing so that the Court may be notified at the earliest opportunity."

These restrictions are not original to the order appealed.[17] They are actually set forth in an opinion written by the former Presiding Judge of the FISA court on May 17 of this year. But since that opinion did not accompany an order conditioning an approval of an electronic surveillance application it was not appealed. It is, however, the basic decision before us and it is its rationale that the government challenges. The opinion was issued after an oral argument before all of the then-serving FISA district judges and clearly represents the views of all those judges.[18]

We think it fair to say, however, that the May 17 opinion of the FISA court does not clearly set forth the basis for its decision. It appears to proceed from the assumption that FISA constructed a barrier between counterintelligence/intelligence officials and law enforcement officers in the Executive Branch—indeed, it uses the word "wall" popularized by certain commentators (and journalists) to describe that supposed barrier. Yet the opinion does not support that assumption with any relevant language from the statute.

The "wall" emerges from the court's implicit interpretation of FISA. The court apparently believes it can approve applications for electronic surveillance only if the government's objective is not primarily directed toward criminal prosecution of the foreign agents for their foreign intelligence activity. But the court neither refers to any FISA language supporting that view, nor does it reference the Patriot Act amendments, which the government contends specifically altered FISA to make clear that an application could be obtained even if criminal prosecution is the primary counter mechanism.

Instead the court relied for its imposition of the disputed restrictions on its statutory authority to approve "minimization procedures" designed to prevent the acquisition, retention, and dissemination within the government of material gathered in an electronic surveillance that is unnecessary to the government's need for foreign intelligence information. 50 U.S.C. § 1801(h).

Jurisdiction

This court has authority "to review the denial of any application" under FISA. *Id.* § 1803(b). The FISA court's order is styled as a grant of the application "as modified." It seems obvious, however, that the FISA court's order actually denied the application to the extent it rejected a significant portion of the government's proposed minimization procedures and imposed restrictions on Department of Justice investigations that the government opposes. Indeed, the FISA court was clear in rejecting a portion of the application.

Under these circumstances, we have jurisdiction to review the FISA court's order; to conclude otherwise would elevate form over substance and deprive the government of judicial review of the minimization procedures imposed by the FISA court. See *Mobile Comm. Corp. v. FCC*, 77 F.3d 1399, 1403- 04 (D.C. Cir.) (grant of station license subject to condition that is unacceptable to applicant is subject to judicial review under statute that permits such review when application for license is denied), cert. denied, 519 U.S. 823 (1996).

II.

The government makes two main arguments. The first, it must be noted, was not presented to the FISA court; indeed, insofar as we can determine it has never previously been advanced either before a court or Congress.[19] That argument is that the supposed pre-Patriot Act limitation in FISA that restricts the government's intention to use foreign intelligence information in criminal prosecutions is an illusion; it finds no support in either the language of FISA or its legislative history. The government does recognize that several courts of appeals, while upholding the use of FISA surveillances, have opined that FISA may be used only if the government's primary purpose in pursuing foreign intelligence information is not criminal prosecution, but the government argues that those decisions, which did not carefully analyze the statute, were incorrect in their statements, if not incorrect in their holdings.

Alternatively, the government contends that even if the primary purpose test was a legitimate construction of FISA prior to the passage of the Patriot Act, that Act's amendments to FISA eliminate that concept. And as a corollary, the government insists the FISA court's construction of the minimization procedures is far off the mark both because it is a misconstruction of those provisions per se, as well as an end run around the specific amendments in the Patriot Act designed to deal with the real issue underlying this case. The government, moreover, contends that the FISA court's restrictions, which the court described as minimization procedures, are so intrusive into the operation of the Department of Justice as to exceed the constitutional authority of Article III judges.

The government's brief, and its supplementary brief requested by this court, also set forth its view that the primary purpose test is not required by the Fourth Amendment. The ACLU and NACDL argue, inter alia, the contrary; that the statutes are unconstitutional unless they are construed as prohibiting the government from obtaining approval of an application under FISA if its "primary purpose" is criminal prosecution.

The 1978 FISA

We turn first to the statute as enacted in 1978.[20] It authorizes a judge on the FISA court to grant an application for an order approving electronic surveillance to "obtain foreign intelligence information" if "there is probable cause to believe that . . . the target of the electronic surveillance is a foreign power or an agent of a foreign power" and that "each of the facilities or places at which the surveillance is directed is being used, or is about to be used, by a foreign power or an agent of a foreign power" 50 U.S.C. § 1805(a)(3). As is apparent, the definitions of agent of a foreign power and foreign intelligence information are crucial to an understanding of the statutory scheme.²¹ The latter means

> (1) information that relates to, and if concerning a United States person is necessary to, the ability of the United States to protect against—
>
> > A) actual or potential attack or other grave hostile acts of a foreign power or an agent of a foreign power;
> >
> > B) sabotage or international terrorism by a foreign power or an agent of a foreign power; or
> >
> > C) clandestine intelligence activities by an intelligence service or network of a foreign power or by an agent of a foreign power.

Id. § 1801(e)(1).²²

The definition of an agent of a foreign power, if it pertains to a U.S. person (which is the only category relevant to this case), is closely tied to criminal activity. The term includes any person who "knowingly engages in clandestine intelligence gathering activities . . . which activities involve or may involve a violation of the criminal statutes of the United States" or "knowingly engages in sabotage or international terrorism, or activities that are in preparation therefor" Id. §§ 1801(b)(2)(A), (C) (emphasis added). International terrorism refers to activities that "involve violent acts or acts dangerous to human life that are a violation of the criminal laws of the United States or of any State, or that would be a *criminal violation* if committed within the jurisdiction of the United States or any State" Id. § 1801(c)(1) (emphasis added). Sabotage means activities that "involve a violation of chapter 105 of [the criminal code], or that would involve such a violation if committed against the United States" Id. § 1801(d). For purposes of clarity in this opinion we will refer to the crimes referred to in section 1801(a)-(e) as foreign intelligence crimes.²³

In light of these definitions, it is quite puzzling that the Justice Department, at some point during the 1980s, began to read the statute as limiting the Department's ability to obtain FISA orders if it intended to prosecute the targeted agents—even for foreign intelligence crimes. To be sure, section 1804, which sets forth the elements of an application for an order, required a national security official in the Executive Branch—typically the Director of the FBI—to certify that "the purpose" of the surveillance is to obtain foreign intelligence information (amended by the Patriot Act to read "a significant purpose"). But as the government now argues, the definition of foreign intelligence information includes evidence of crimes such as espionage, sabotage or terrorism. Indeed, it is virtually impossible to read the 1978 FISA to exclude from its purpose the prosecution of foreign intelligence crimes, most importantly because, as we have noted, the definition of an agent of a foreign power—if he or she is a U.S. person—is grounded on criminal conduct.

It does not seem that FISA, at least as originally enacted, even contemplated that the FISA court would inquire into the government's purpose in seeking foreign intelligence information. Section 1805, governing the standards a FISA court judge is to use in determining whether to grant a surveillance order, requires the judge to find that

> the application which has been filed contains all statements and certifications required by section 1804 of this title and, if the target is a United States person, the certification or certifications are not clearly erroneous on the basis of the statement made under section 1804(a)(7)(E) of this title and any other information furnished under section 1804(d) of this title.

50 U.S.C. § 1805(a)(5).[24] And section 1804(a)(7)(E) requires that the application include "a statement of the basis of the certification that—(i) the information sought is the type of foreign intelligence information designated; and (ii) such information cannot reasonably be obtained by normal investigative techniques" That language certainly suggests that, aside from the probable cause, identification of facilities, and minimization procedures the judge is to determine and approve (also set forth in section 1805), the only other issues are whether electronic surveillance is necessary to obtain the information and whether the information sought is actually foreign intelligence information—not the government's proposed use of that information.[25]

Nor does the legislative history cast doubt on the obvious reading of the statutory language that foreign intelligence information includes evidence of foreign intelligence crimes. To the contrary, the House Report explained:

> [T]he term "foreign intelligence information" especially as defined in subparagraphs (e)(1)(B) and (e)(1)(C), can include evidence of certain crimes relating to sabotage, international terrorism, or clandestine intelligence activities. With respect to information concerning U.S. persons, foreign intelligence information includes information necessary to protect against clandestine intelligence activities of foreign powers or their agents. Information about a spy's espionage activities obviously is within this definition, and it is *most likely at the same time evidence of criminal activities*.

H.R. REP. NO. 95-1283 (hereinafter "H. REP") at 49 (1978) (emphasis added).

The government argues persuasively that arresting and prosecuting terrorist agents of, or spies for, a foreign power may well be the best technique to prevent them from successfully continuing their terrorist or espionage activity. The government might wish to surveil the agent for some period of time to discover other participants in a conspiracy or to uncover a foreign power's plans, but typically at some point the government would wish to apprehend the agent and it might be that only a prosecution would provide sufficient incentives for the agent to cooperate with the government. Indeed, the threat of prosecution might be sufficient to "turn the agent." It would seem that the Congress actually anticipated the government's argument and explicitly approved it. The House Report said:

> *How this information may be used* "to protect" against clandestine intelligence activities *is not prescribed* by the definition of foreign intelligence information, although, of course, how it is used may be affected by minimization procedures. . . . And no information acquired pursuant to this bill could be used for other than lawful purposes . . . . *Obviously, use of "foreign intelligence information" as evidence in a criminal trial is one way the Government can lawfully protect against clandestine intelligence activities, sabotage, and international terrorism.* The bill, therefore, explicitly recognizes that information which is evidence of crimes involving [these activities] can be sought, retained, and used pursuant to this bill.

Id. (emphasis added). The Senate Report is on all fours:

> U.S. persons may be authorized targets, and the surveillance is part of an investigative process often designed to protect against the commission of serious crimes such as espionage, sabotage, assassination, kidnaping, and terrorist acts committed by or on behalf of foreign powers. *Intelligence and criminal law enforcement tend to merge in this area.* . . . [S]urveillances conducted under [FISA] need not stop once conclusive evidence of a crime is obtained, but instead may be extended longer where protective measures other than arrest and prosecution are more appropriate.

S. REP. NO. 95-701 (hereinafter "S. REP") at 10-11 (1978) (emphasis added).

Congress was concerned about the government's use of FISA surveillance to obtain information not truly intertwined with the government's efforts to protect against threats from foreign powers. Accordingly, the certification of purpose under section 1804(a)(7)(B) served to

> prevent the practice of targeting, for example, a foreign power for electronic surveillance when the true purpose of the surveillance is to gather information about an individual for other than foreign intelligence purposes. It is also designed to make explicit that the sole purpose of such surveillance is to secure "foreign intelligence information" as defined, and not to obtain some other type of information.

H. REP. at 76; see also S. REP. at 51. But Congress did not impose any restrictions on the government's use of the foreign intelligence information to prosecute agents of foreign powers for foreign intelligence crimes. Admittedly, the House, at least in one statement, noted that FISA surveillances "are not primarily for the purpose of gathering evidence of a crime. They are to obtain foreign intelligence information, which when it concerns United States persons must be necessary to important national concerns." H. REP. at 36. That, however, was an observation, not a proscription. And the House as well as the Senate made clear that prosecution is one way to combat foreign intelligence crimes. See *id.*; S. REP. at 10-11.

The origin of what the government refers to as the false dichotomy between foreign intelligence information that is evidence of foreign intelligence crimes and that which is not appears to have been a Fourth Circuit case decided in 1980. *United States v. Truong Dinh Hung*, 629 F.2d 908 (4th Cir. 1980). That case, however, involved an electronic surveillance carried out prior to the passage of FISA and predicated on the President's executive power. In approving the district court's exclusion of evidence obtained through a warrantless surveillance subsequent to the point in time when the government's investigation became "primarily" driven by law enforcement objectives, the court held that the Executive Branch should be excused from securing a warrant only when "the object of the search or the surveillance is a foreign power, its agents or collaborators" and "the surveillance is conducted ,primarily' for foreign intelligence reasons" *Id.* at 915. Targets must "receive the protection of the warrant requirement if the government is primarily attempting to put together a criminal prosecution" *Id.* at 916. Although the *Truong* court acknowledged that "almost all foreign intelligence investigations are in part criminal" ones, it rejected the government's assertion that "if surveillance is to any degree directed at gathering foreign intelligence, the executive may ignore the warrant requirement of the Fourth Amendment" *Id.* at 915.

Several circuits have followed *Truong* in applying similar versions of the "primary purpose" test, despite the fact that *Truong* was not a FISA decision. (It was an interpretation of the Constitution, in the context of measuring the boundaries of the President's inherent executive authority, and we discuss *Truong's* constitutional analysis at length in Section III of this opinion.) In one of the first major challenges to a FISA search, *United States v. Megahey*, 553 F. Supp. 1180 (E.D.N.Y. 1982), aff'd sub nom. *United States v. Duggan*, 743 F.2d 59 (2d Cir. 1984), the district court acknowledged that while Congress clearly viewed arrest and prosecution as one of the possible outcomes of a FISA investigation, surveillance under FISA would nevertheless be "appropriate only if foreign intelligence surveillance is the Government's primary purpose" *Id.* at 1189-90. Six months earlier, another judge in the same district had held that the *Truong* analysis did not govern FISA cases, since a FISA order was a warrant that met Fourth Amendment standards. *United States v. Falvey*, 540 F. Supp. 1306, 1314 (E.D.N.Y. 1982). *Falvey*, however, was apparently not appealed and *Megahey* was. The Second Circuit, without reference to *Falvey*, and importantly in the context of affirming the conviction, approved *Megahey's* finding that the surveillance was not "directed towards criminal investigation or the institution of a criminal prosecution" *Duggan*, 743 F.2d at 78 (quoting *Megahey*, 553 F. Supp.

at 1190). Implicitly then, the Second Circuit endorsed the *Megahey* dichotomy. Two other circuits, the Fourth and the Eleventh, have similarly approved district court findings that a surveillance was primarily for foreign intelligence purposes without any discussion—or need to discuss—the validity of the dichotomy. See *United States v. Pelton*, 835 F.2d 1067, 1075-76 (4th Cir. 1987), cert. denied, 486 U.S. 1010 (1988); *United States v. Badia*, 827 F.2d 1458, 1464 (11th Cir. 1987), cert. denied, 485 U.S. 937 (1988).

Then, the First Circuit, seeing *Duggan* as following *Truong*, explicitly interpreted FISA's purpose wording in section 1804(a)(7)(B) to mean that "[a]lthough evidence obtained under FISA subsequently may be used in criminal prosecutions, the investigation of criminal activity cannot be the primary purpose of the surveillance" *United States v. Johnson*, 952 F.2d 565, 572 (1st Cir. 1991) (citations omitted), cert. denied, 506 U.S. 816 (1992). Notably, however, the Ninth Circuit has refused

> to draw too fine a distinction between criminal and intelligence investigations. "International terrorism" by definition, requires the investigation of activities that constitute crimes.
>
> That the government may later choose to prosecute is irrelevant. . . . FISA is meant to take into account "[t]he differences between ordinary criminal investigations to gather evidence of specific crimes and foreign counterintelligence investigations to uncover and monitor clandestine activities . . . "

United States v. Sarkissian, 841 F.2d 959, 964 (9th Cir. 1988) (citations omitted).

Neither *Duggan* nor *Johnson* tied the "primary purpose" test to actual statutory language. In Duggan the court stated that "[t]he requirement that foreign intelligence information be the primary objective of the surveillance is plain" and the district court was correct in "finding that 'the purpose of the surveillance in this case, both initially and throughout, was to secure foreign intelligence information and was not, as [the] defendants assert, directed towards criminal investigation or the institution of a criminal prosecution.'" Duggan, 743 F.2d at 77-78 (quoting *Megahey*, 553 F. Supp. at 1190).[26] Yet the court never explained why it apparently read foreign intelligence information to exclude evidence of crimes— endorsing the district court's implied dichotomy—when the statute's definitions of foreign intelligence and foreign agent are actually cast in terms of criminal conduct. (It will be recalled that the type of foreign intelligence with which we are concerned is really counterintelligence, see supra note 9.) And Johnson did not even focus on the phrase "foreign intelligence information" in its interpretation of the "purpose" language in section 1804(a)(7)(B). *Johnson*, 952 F.2d at 572.

It is almost as if *Duggan*, and particularly *Johnson*, assume that the government seeks foreign intelligence information (counterintelligence) for its own sake—to expand its pool of knowledge—because there is no discussion of how the government would use that information outside criminal prosecutions. That is not to say that the government could have no other use for that information. The government's overriding concern is to stop or frustrate the agent's or the foreign power's activity by any means, but if one considers the actual ways in which the government would foil espionage or terrorism it becomes apparent that criminal prosecution analytically cannot be placed easily in a separate response category. It may well be that the government itself, in an effort to conform to district court holdings, accepted the dichotomy it now contends is false. Be that as it may, since the cases that "adopt" the dichotomy do affirm district court opinions permitting the introduction of evidence gathered under a FISA order, there was not much need for the courts to focus on the issue with which we are confronted.

In sum, we think that the FISA as passed by Congress in 1978 clearly did *not* preclude or limit the government's use or proposed use of foreign intelligence information, which included evidence of certain kinds of criminal activity, in a criminal prosecution. In order to understand the FISA court's decision, however, it is necessary to trace developments and understandings within the Justice Department post-*Truong* as well as after the passage of the Patriot Act. As we have noted, some time in the 1980s—the exact moment is shrouded in historical mist—the Department applied the *Truong* analysis to an interpretation of the FISA statute. What is clear is that in 1995 the Attorney General adopted "Procedures for Contacts Between the FBI and the Criminal Division Concerning Foreign Intelligence and Foreign Counterintelligence Investigations."

Apparently to avoid running afoul of the primary purpose test used by some courts, the 1995 Procedures limited contacts between the FBI and the Criminal Division in cases where FISA surveillance or searches were being conducted by the FBI for foreign intelligence (FI) or foreign counterintelligence (FCI) purposes.[27] The procedures state that "the FBI and Criminal Division should ensure that advice intended to preserve the option of a criminal prosecution does not inadvertently result in either the fact or the appearance of the Criminal Division's *directing* or *controlling* the FI or FCI investigation toward law enforcement objectives" 1995 Procedures at 2, ¶ 6 (emphasis added). Although these procedures provided for significant information sharing and coordination between criminal and FI or FCI investigations, based at least in part on the "directing or controlling" language, they eventually came to be narrowly interpreted within the Department of Justice, and most particularly by OIPR, as requiring OIPR to act as a "wall" to prevent the FBI intelligence officials from communicating with the Criminal Division regarding ongoing FI or FCI investigations. See *Final Report of the Attorney General's Review Team on the Handling of the Los Alamos National Laboratory Investigation* (AGRT Report), Chapter 20 at 721-34 (May 2000). Thus, the focus became the nature of the underlying investigation, rather than the general purpose of the surveillance. Once prosecution of the target was being considered, the procedures, as interpreted by OIPR in light of the case law, prevented the Criminal Division from providing any meaningful advice to the FBI. *Id.*

The Department's attitude changed somewhat after the May 2000 report by the Attorney General and a July 2001 Report by the General Accounting Office both concluded that the Department's concern over how the FISA court or other federal courts might interpret the primary purpose test has inhibited necessary coordination between intelligence and law enforcement officials. See *id.* at 721-34;[28] General Accounting Office, *FBI Intelligence Investigations: Coordination Within Justice on Counterintelligence Criminal Matters is Limited* (July 2001) (GAO-01-780) (GAO Report) at 3. The AGRT Report also concluded, based on the text of FISA and its legislative history, that not only should the purpose of the investigation not be inquired into by the courts, but also that Congress affirmatively anticipated that the underlying investigation might well have a criminal as well as foreign counterintelligence objective. AGRT Report at 737. In response to the AGRT Report, the Attorney General, in January 2000, issued additional, interim procedures designed to address coordination problems identified in that report. In August 2001, the Deputy Attorney General issued a memorandum clarifying Department of Justice policy governing intelligence sharing and establishing additional requirements. (These actions, however, did not replace the 1995 Procedures.) But it does not appear that the Department thought of these internal procedures as "minimization procedures" required under FISA.[29] Nevertheless, the FISA court was aware that the procedures were being followed by the Department and apparently adopted elements of them in certain cases.

The Patriot Act and the FISA Court's Decision

The passage of the Patriot Act altered and to some degree muddied the landscape. In October 2001, Congress amended FISA to change "the purpose" language in 1804(a)(7)(B) to "a significant purpose." It also added a provision allowing "Federal officers who conduct electronic surveillance to acquire foreign intelligence information" to "consult with Federal law enforcement officers to coordinate efforts to investigate or protect against" attack or other grave hostile acts, sabotage or international terrorism, or clandestine intelligence activities, by foreign powers or their agents. 50 U.S.C. § 1806(k)(1). And such coordination "shall not preclude" the government's certification that a significant purpose of the surveillance is to obtain foreign intelligence information, or the issuance of an order authorizing the surveillance. *Id.* § 1806(k)(2). Although the Patriot Act amendments to FISA expressly sanctioned consultation and coordination between intelligence and law enforcement officials, in response to the first applications filed by OIPR under those amendments, in November 2001, the FISA court for the first time adopted the 1995 Procedures, as augmented by the January 2000 and August 2001 Procedures, as "minimization procedures" to apply in all cases before the court.[30]

The Attorney General interpreted the Patriot Act quite differently. On March 6, 2002, the Attorney General approved new "Intelligence Sharing Procedures" to implement the Act's amendments to FISA. The 2002 Procedures supersede prior procedures and were designed to permit the complete exchange of information and advice between intelligence and law enforcement officials. They eliminated the "direction and control" test and allowed the exchange of advice between the FBI, OIPR, and the Criminal Division regarding "the initiation, operation, continuation, or expansion of FISA searches or surveillance." On March 7, 2002, the government filed a motion with the FISA court, noting that the Department of Justice had adopted the 2002 Procedures and proposing to follow those procedures in all matters before the court. The government also asked the FISA court to vacate its orders adopting the prior procedures as minimization procedures in all cases and imposing special "wall" procedures in certain cases.

Unpersuaded by the Attorney General's interpretation of the Patriot Act, the court ordered that the 2002 Procedures be adopted, *with modifications*, as minimization procedures to apply in all cases. The court emphasized that the definition of minimization procedures had not been amended by the Patriot Act, and reasoned that the 2002 Procedures "cannot be used by the government to amend the Act in ways Congress has not." The court explained:

> Given our experience in FISA surveillances and searches, we find that these provisions in sections II.B and III [of the 2002 Procedures], particularly those which authorize criminal prosecutors to advise FBI intelligence officials on the initiation, operation, continuation or expansion of FISA's intrusive seizures, are designed to enhance the acquisition, retention and dissemination of *evidence for law enforcement purposes*, instead of being consistent with the need of the United States to "obtain, produce, and disseminate *foreign intelligence information*" . . . as mandated in §1801(h) and § 1821(4).

May 17, 2001 Opinion at 22 (emphasis added by the FISA court).[31] The FISA court also adopted a new rule of court procedure, Rule 11, which provides that "[a]ll FISA applications shall include informative descriptions of any ongoing criminal investigations of FISA targets, as well as the substance of any consultations between the FBI and criminal prosecutors at the Department of Justice or a United States Attorney's Office."

Undeterred, the government submitted the application at issue in this appeal on July 19, 2002, and expressly proposed using the 2002 Procedures *without modification*. In an order issued the same day, the FISA judge hearing the application granted an order for surveillance of the target but modified the 2002 Procedures consistent with the court's May 17, 2002 en banc order. It is the July 19, 2002 order that the government appeals, along with an October 17, 2002 order granting, with the same modifications as the July 19 order, the government's application for renewal of the surveillance in this case. Because those orders incorporate the May 17, 2002 order and opinion by reference, however, that order and opinion are before us as well.

* * *

Essentially, the FISA court took portions of the Attorney General's augmented 1995 Procedures—adopted to deal with the primary purpose standard—and imposed them generically as minimization procedures. In doing so, the FISA court erred. It did not provide any constitutional basis for its action—we think there is none—and misconstrued the main statutory provision on which it relied. The court mistakenly categorized the augmented 1995 Procedures as FISA minimization procedures and then compelled the government to utilize a modified version of those procedures in a way that is clearly inconsistent with the statutory purpose.

Under section 1805 of FISA, "the judge shall enter an ex parte order as requested or as modified approving the electronic surveillance if he finds that . . . the proposed minimization procedures meet the definition of minimization procedures under section 1801(h) of this title" 50 U.S.C. § 1805(a)(4). The statute defines minimization procedures in pertinent part as:

> (1) specific procedures, which shall be adopted by the Attorney General, that are reasonably designed in light of the purpose and technique of the particular surveillance, to minimize the acquisition and retention, and prohibit the dissemination, of nonpublicly available information concerning unconsenting United States persons consistent with the need of the United States to obtain, produce, and disseminate foreign intelligence information;
>
> (2) procedures that require that nonpublicly available information, which is not foreign intelligence information, as defined in subsection (e)(1) of this section, shall not be disseminated in a manner that identifies any United States person, without such person's consent, unless such person's identity is necessary to understand foreign intelligence information or assess its importance.

Section 1801(h) also contains the following proviso:

> (3) notwithstanding paragraphs (1) and (2), procedures that allow for the retention and dissemination of information that is evidence of a crime which has been, is being, or is about to be committed and that is to be retained or disseminated for law enforcement purposes. . . .

Id. § 1801(h).

As is evident from the face of section 1801(h), minimization procedures are designed to protect, as far as reasonable, against the acquisition, retention, and dissemination of nonpublic information which is not foreign intelligence information. If the data is not foreign intelligence information as defined by the statute, the procedures are to ensure that the government does not use the information to identify the target or third party, unless such identification is necessary to properly understand or assess the foreign intelligence information that is collected. *Id.* § 1801(h)(2). By minimizing *acquisition*, Congress envisioned that, for example, "where a switchboard line is tapped but only one person in the organization is the target, the interception should probably be discontinued where the target is not a party" to the communication. H. REP. at 55-56. By minimizing *retention*, Congress intended that "information acquired, which is not necessary for obtaining[,] producing, or disseminating foreign intelligence information, be destroyed where feasible" H. REP. at 56. Furthermore, "[e]ven with respect to information needed for an approved purpose, *dissemination* should be restricted to those officials with a need for such information" *Id.* (emphasis added).

The minimization procedures allow, however, the retention and dissemination of nonforeign intelligence information which is evidence of *ordinary crimes* for preventative or prosecutorial purposes. See 50 U.S.C. § 1801(h)(3). Therefore, if through interceptions or searches, evidence of "a serious crime totally unrelated to intelligence matters" is incidentally acquired, the evidence is "*not . . .* required to be destroyed" H. REP. at 62 (emphasis added). As we have explained, under the 1978 Act, "evidence of certain crimes like espionage would itself constitute 'foreign intelligence information,' as defined, because it is necessary to protect against clandestine intelligence activities by foreign powers or their agents" H. REP. at 62; see also *id.* at 49. In light of these purposes of the minimization procedures, there is simply no basis for the FISA court's reliance on section 1801(h) to limit criminal prosecutors' ability to advise FBI intelligence officials on the initiation, operation, continuation, or expansion of FISA surveillances to obtain foreign intelligence information, even if such information includes evidence of a foreign intelligence crime.

The FISA court's decision and order not only misinterpreted and misapplied minimization procedures it was entitled to impose, but as the government argues persuasively, the FISA court may well have exceeded the constitutional bounds that restrict an Article III court. The FISA court asserted authority to govern the internal organization and investigative procedures of the Department of Justice which are the province of the Executive Branch (Article II) and the Congress (Article I). Subject to statutes dealing with the organization of the Justice Department, however, the Attorney General has the responsibility to determine how to deploy personnel resources. As the Supreme Court said in *Morrison v. Olson* in cautioning the Special Division of the D.C. Circuit to avoid unauthorized administrative guidance of Independent Counsel, "[t]he gradual expansion of the authority of the Special Division might in another context be a bureaucratic success story, but it would be one that would have serious constitutional ramifications" 487 U.S. 654, 684 (1988).[32]

* * *

We also think the refusal by the FISA court to consider the legal significance of the Patriot Act's crucial amendments was error. The government, in order to avoid the requirement of meeting the "primary purpose" test, specifically sought an amendment to section 1804(a)(7)(B) which had required a certification "that the purpose of the surveillance is to obtain foreign intelligence information" so as to delete the article "the" before "purpose" and replace it with "a" The government made perfectly clear to Congress why it sought the legislative change. Congress, although accepting the government's explanation for the need for the amendment, adopted language which it perceived as not giving the government quite the degree of modification it wanted. Accordingly, section 1804(a)(7)(B)'s wording became "that *a significant* purpose of the surveillance is to obtain foreign intelligence information" (emphasis added). There is simply no question, however, that Congress was keenly aware that this amendment relaxed a requirement that the government show that its primary purpose was other than criminal prosecution.

No committee reports accompanied the Patriot Act but the floor statements make congressional intent quite apparent. The Senate Judiciary Committee Chairman Senator Leahy acknowledged that "[p]rotection against these foreign- based threats by any lawful means is within the scope of the definition of 'foreign intelligence information,' and the use of FISA to gather evidence for the enforcement of these laws was contemplated in the enactment of FISA" 147 Cong. Rec. S11004 (Oct. 25, 2001). "This bill . . . break[s] down traditional barriers between law enforcement and foreign intelligence. This is not done just to combat international terrorism, but for any criminal investigation that overlaps a broad definition of ,foreign intelligence.'" 147 Cong. Rec. S10992 (Oct. 25, 2001) (statement of Sen. Leahy). And Senator Feinstein, a "strong support[er]" was also explicit. The ultimate objective was to make it

> easier to collect foreign intelligence information under the Foreign Intelligence Surveillance Act, FISA. Under current law, authorities can proceed with surveillance under FISA only if the primary purpose of the investigation is to collect foreign intelligence.
>
> But in today's world things are not so simple. In many cases, surveillance will have two key goals— the gathering of foreign intelligence, and the gathering of evidence for a criminal prosecution. Determining which purpose is the "primary" purpose of the investigation can be difficult, and will only become more so as we coordinate our intelligence and law enforcement efforts in the war against terror.
>
> Rather than forcing law enforcement to decide which purpose is primary—law enforcement or foreign intelligence gathering, this bill strikes a new balance. It will now require that a "significant" purpose of the investigation must be foreign intelligence gathering to proceed with surveillance under FISA.
>
> The effect of this provision will be to make it easier for law enforcement to obtain a FISA search or surveillance warrant for those cases where the subject of the surveillance is both a potential source of valuable intelligence and the potential

target of a criminal prosecution. Many of the individuals involved in supporting the September 11 attacks may well fall into both of these categories.

147 Cong. Rec. S10591 (Oct. 11, 2001).

To be sure, some Senate Judiciary Committee members including the Chairman were concerned that the amendment might grant too much authority to the Justice Department—and the FISA court. Senator Leahy indicated that the change to significant purpose was "very problematic" since it would "make it easier for the FBI to use a FISA wiretap to obtain information where the Government's most important motivation for the wiretap is for use in a criminal prosecution" 147 Cong. Rec. S10593 (Oct. 11, 2001). Therefore he suggested that "it will be up to the courts to determine how far law enforcement agencies may use FISA for criminal investigation and prosecution beyond the scope of the statutory definition of 'foreign intelligence information.'" 147 Cong. Rec. S11004 (Oct. 25, 2001) (emphasis added). But the only dissenting vote against the act was cast by Senator Feingold. *For the Record: Senate Votes*, 59 CONG. QUARTERLY (WKLY.) 39, Oct. 13, 2001, at 2425. Senator Feingold recognized that the change to "significant purpose" meant that the government could obtain a FISA warrant "even if the primary purpose is a criminal investigation" and was concerned that this development would not respect the protections of the Fourth Amendment. 147 Cong. Rec. S11021 (Oct. 25, 2001).

In sum, there can be no doubt as to Congress' intent in amending section 1804(a)(7)(B). Indeed, it went further to emphasize its purpose in breaking down barriers between criminal law enforcement and intelligence (or counterintelligence) gathering by adding section 1806(k):

(k) Consultation with Federal law enforcement officer

(1) Federal officers who conduct electronic surveillance to acquire foreign intelligence information under this title may consult with Federal law enforcement officers to coordinate efforts to investigate or protect against

(A) actual or potential attack or other grave hostile acts of a foreign power or an agent of a foreign power; or

(B) sabotage or international terrorism by a foreign power or an agent of a foreign power; or

(C) clandestine intelligence activities by an intelligence service or network of a foreign power or by an agent of a foreign power.

(2) Coordination authorized under paragraph (1) shall not preclude the certification required by section [1804](a)(7)(B) of this title or the entry of an order under section [1805] of this title.

The FISA court noted this amendment but thought that Congress' approval of consultations was not equivalent to authorizing law enforcement officers to give advice to officers who were conducting electronic surveillance nor did it sanction law enforcement officers "directing or controlling" surveillances. However, dictionary definitions of "consult" include giving advice. See, e.g., OXFORD ENGLISH DICTIONARY ONLINE (2d ed. 1989). Beyond that, when Congress explicitly authorizes consultation and coordination between different offices in the government, without even suggesting a limitation on who is to direct and control, it necessarily implies that either could be taking the lead.

Neither *amicus* brief defends the reasoning of the FISA court. NACDL's brief makes no attempt to interpret FISA or the Patriot Act amendments but rather argues the primary purpose test is constitutionally compelled. The ACLU relies on Title III of the Omnibus Crime Control and Safe Streets Act of 1968, 18 U.S.C. §§ 2510-2522, to interpret FISA, passed 10 years later. That technique, to put it gently, is hardly an orthodox method of statutory interpretation. FISA was passed to deal specifically with the subject of foreign intelligence surveillance. The ACLU does argue that Congress' intent to preclude law enforcement officials initiating or controlling foreign intelligence investigations is revealed by FISA's exclusion of the Attorney General—a law enforcement official—from the officers who can certify the foreign intelligence purpose of an application under section 1804. The difficulty with that argument is that the Attorney General supervises the Director of the FBI who is both a law enforcement and counterintelligence officer. The Attorney General or the Deputy Attorney General, moreover, must approve all applications no matter who certifies that the information sought is foreign intelligence information. 50 U.S.C. § 1804(a).[33]

The ACLU insists that the significant purpose amendment only "clarified" the law permitting FISA surveillance orders "even if foreign intelligence is not its *exclusive* purpose" (emphasis added). In support of this rather strained interpretation, which ignores the legislative history of the Patriot Act, the ACLU relies on a *September 10, 2002* hearing of the Judiciary Committee (the day after the government's oral presentation to this court) at which certain senators made statements—somewhat at odds with their floor statements prior to the passage of the Patriot Act—as to what they had intended the year before. The D.C. Circuit has described such post-enactment legislative statements as "legislative future" rather than legislative history, not entitled to authoritative weight. See *General Instrument Corp. v. FCC*, 213 F.3d 724, 733 (D.C. Cir. 2000).

Accordingly, the Patriot Act amendments clearly disapprove the primary purpose test. And as a matter of straightforward logic, if a FISA application can be granted even if "foreign intelligence" is only a significant—not a primary—purpose, another purpose can be primary. One other legitimate purpose that could exist is to prosecute a target for a foreign intelligence crime. We therefore believe the Patriot Act amply supports the government's alternative argument but, paradoxically, the Patriot Act would seem to conflict with the government's first argument because by using the term "significant purpose" the Act now implies that another purpose is to be distinguished from a foreign intelligence purpose.

The government heroically tries to give the amended section 1804(a)(7)(B) a wholly benign interpretation. It concedes that "the, significant purpose' amendment recognizes the *existence* of the dichotomy between foreign intelligence and law enforcement" but it contends that "it cannot be said to recognize (or approve) its *legitimacy*" Supp. Br. of U.S. at 25 (emphasis in original). We are not persuaded. The very letter the Justice Department sent to the Judiciary Committee in 2001 defending the constitutionality of the significant purpose language implicitly accepted as legitimate the dichotomy in FISA that the government now claims (and we agree) was false. It said, "it is also clear that while FISA states that 'the' purpose of a search is for foreign surveillance, that need not be the only purpose. Rather, law enforcement considerations can be taken into account, so long as the surveillance also has a legitimate foreign intelligence purpose" The senatorial statements explaining the significant purpose amendments which we described above are all based on the same understanding of FISA which the Justice Department accepted—at least until this appeal. In short, even though we agree that the original FISA did not contemplate the "false dichotomy" the Patriot Act actually did—which makes it no longer false. The addition of the word "significant" to section 1804(a)(7)(B) imposed a requirement that the government have a measurable foreign intelligence purpose, other than just criminal prosecution of even foreign intelligence crimes. Although section 1805(a)(5), as we discussed above, may well have been intended to authorize the FISA court to review only the question whether the information sought was a type of foreign intelligence information, in light of the significant purpose amendment of section 1804 it seems section 1805 must be interpreted as giving the FISA court the authority to review the government's purpose in seeking the information.

That leaves us with something of an analytic conundrum. On the one hand, Congress did not amend the definition of foreign intelligence information which, we have explained, includes evidence of foreign intelligence crimes. On the other hand, Congress accepted the dichotomy between foreign intelligence and law enforcement by adopting the significant purpose test. Nevertheless, it is our task to do our best to read the statute to honor congressional intent. The better reading, it seems to us, excludes from the purpose of gaining foreign intelligence information a sole objective of criminal prosecution. We therefore reject the government's argument to the contrary. Yet this may not make much practical difference. Because, as the government points out, when it commences an electronic surveillance of a foreign agent, typically it will not have decided whether to prosecute the agent (whatever may be the subjective intent of the investigators or lawyers who initiate an investigation). So long as the government entertains a realistic option of dealing with the agent other than through criminal prosecution, it satisfies the significant purpose test.

The important point is—and here we agree with the government—the Patriot Act amendment, by using the word "significant" eliminated any justification for the FISA court to balance the relative weight the government places on criminal prosecution as compared to other counterintelligence responses. If the certification of the application's purpose articulates a broader objective than criminal prosecution—such as stopping an ongoing conspiracy—and includes other potential non-prosecutorial responses, the government meets the statutory test. Of course, if the court concluded that the government's sole objective was merely to gain evidence of past criminal conduct—even foreign intelligence crimes—to punish the agent rather than halt ongoing espionage or terrorist activity, the application should be denied.

The government claims that even prosecutions of *non*-foreign intelligence crimes are consistent with a purpose of gaining foreign intelligence information so long as the government's objective is to stop espionage or terrorism by putting an agent of a foreign power in prison. That interpretation transgresses the original FISA. It will be recalled that Congress intended section 1804(a)(7)(B) to prevent the government from targeting a foreign agent when its "true purpose" was to gain non-foreign intelligence information—such as evidence of ordinary crimes or scandals. See supra at p.14. (If the government inadvertently came upon evidence of ordinary crimes, FISA provided for the transmission of that evidence to the proper authority. 50 U.S.C. § 1801(h)(3).) It can be argued, however, that by providing that an application is to be granted if the government has only a "significant purpose" of gaining foreign intelligence information, the Patriot Act allows the government to have a primary objective of prosecuting an agent for a non-foreign intelligence crime. Yet we think that would be an anomalous reading of the amendment. For we see not the slightest indication that Congress meant to give that power to the Executive Branch. Accordingly, the manifestation of such a purpose, it seems to us, would continue to disqualify an application. That is not to deny that ordinary crimes might be inextricably intertwined with foreign intelligence crimes. For example, if a group of international terrorists were to engage in bank robberies in order to finance the manufacture of a bomb, evidence of the bank robbery should be treated just as evidence of the terrorist act itself. But the FISA process cannot be used as a device to investigate wholly unrelated ordinary crimes.

One final point; we think the government's purpose as set forth in a section 1804(a)(7)(B) certification is to be judged by the national security official's articulation and not by a FISA court inquiry into the origins of an investigation nor an examination of the personnel involved. It is up to the

Director of the FBI, who typically certifies, to determine the government's national security purpose, as approved by the Attorney General or Deputy Attorney General. This is not a standard whose application the FISA court legitimately reviews by seeking to inquire into which Justice Department officials were instigators of an investigation. All Justice Department officers—including those in the FBI—are under the control of the Attorney General. If he wishes a particular investigation to be run by an officer of any division, that is his prerogative. There is nothing in FISA or the Patriot Act that suggests otherwise. That means, perforce, if the FISA court has reason to doubt that the government has any real non-prosecutorial purpose in seeking foreign intelligence information it can demand further inquiry into the certifying officer's purpose—or perhaps even the Attorney General's or Deputy Attorney General's reasons for approval. The important point is that the relevant purpose is that of those senior officials in the Executive Branch who have the responsibility of appraising the government's national security needs.

III.

Having determined that FISA, as amended, does not oblige the government to demonstrate to the FISA court that its primary purpose in conducting electronic surveillance is *not* criminal prosecution, we are obliged to consider whether the statute as amended is consistent with the Fourth Amendment. The Fourth Amendment provides:

> The right of the people to be secure in their persons, houses, papers, and effects, against unreasonable searches and seizures, shall not be violated, and no Warrants shall issue, but upon probable cause, supported by Oath or affirmation, and particularly describing the place to be searched, and the persons or things to be seized.

Although the FISA court did not explicitly rely on the Fourth Amendment, it at least suggested that this provision was the animating principle driving its statutory analysis. The FISA court indicated that its disapproval of the Attorney General's 2002 Procedures was based on the need to safeguard the "privacy of Americans in these highly intrusive surveillances and searches" which implies the invocation of the Fourth Amendment. The government, recognizing the Fourth Amendment's shadow effect on the FISA court's opinion, has affirmatively argued that FISA is constitutional. And some of the very senators who fashioned the Patriot Act amendments expected that the federal courts, including presumably the FISA court, would carefully consider that question. Senator Leahy believed that "[n]o matter what statutory change is made . . . the court may impose a constitutional requirement of 'primary purpose' based on the appellate court decisions upholding FISA against constitutional challenges over the past 20 years" 147 Cong. Rec. S11003 (Oct. 25, 2001). Senator Edwards stated that "the FISA court will still need to be careful to enter FISA orders only when the requirements of the Constitution as well as the statute are satisfied." 147 Cong. Rec. S10589 (Oct. 11, 2001).

We are, therefore, grateful to the ACLU and NACDL for their briefs that vigorously contest the government's argument. Both NACDL (which, as we have noted above, presents only the argument that the statute as amended is unconstitutional) and the ACLU rely on two propositions. The first is not actually argued; it is really an assumption—that a FISA order does not qualify as a warrant within the meaning of the Fourth Amendment. The second is that any government surveillance whose *primary purpose* is criminal prosecution *of whatever kind* is *per se* unreasonable if not based on a warrant.

The FISA court expressed concern that unless FISA were "construed" in the fashion that it did, the government could use a FISA order as an improper substitute for an ordinary criminal warrant under Title III. That concern seems to suggest that the FISA court thought Title III procedures are constitutionally mandated if the government has a prosecutorial objective regarding an agent of a foreign power. But in *United States v. United States District Court (Keith)*, 407 U.S. 297, 322 (1972)—in which the Supreme Court explicitly declined to consider foreign intelligence surveillance—the Court indicated that, even with respect to domestic national security intelligence gathering for prosecutorial purposes where a warrant was mandated, Title III procedures were not constitutionally required: "[W]e do not hold that the same type of standards and procedures prescribed by Title III are necessarily applicable to this case. We recognize that domestic security surveillance may involve different policy and practical considerations from the surveillance of, ordinary crime.'" Nevertheless, in asking whether FISA procedures can be regarded as reasonable under the Fourth Amendment, we think it is instructive to compare those procedures and requirements with their Title III counterparts. Obviously, the closer those FISA procedures are to Title III procedures, the lesser are our constitutional concerns.

Comparison of FISA Procedures with Title III

It is important to note that while many of FISA's requirements for a surveillance order differ from those in Title III, few of those differences have any constitutional relevance. In the context of ordinary crime, beyond requiring searches and seizures to be reasonable, the Supreme Court has interpreted the warrant clause of the Fourth Amendment to require three elements:

> First, warrants must be issued by neutral, disinterested magistrates. Second, those seeking the warrant must demonstrate to the magistrate their probable cause to believe that "the evidence sought will aid in a particular apprehension or conviction" for a particular offense. Finally, "warrants must particularly describe the ,things to be seized,'" as well as the place to be searched.

Dalia v. United States, 441 U.S. 238, 255 (1979) (citations omitted).

With limited exceptions not at issue here, both Title III and FISA require prior judicial scrutiny of an application for an order authorizing electronic surveillance. 50 U.S.C. § 1805; 18 U.S.C. § 2518. And there is no dispute that a FISA judge satisfies the Fourth Amendment's requirement of a "neutral and detached magistrate." See *United States v. Cavanagh*, 807 F.2d 787, 790 (9th Cir. 1987) (FISA court is a "detached and neutral body"); see also *Keith*, 407 U.S. at 323 (in domestic national security context, suggesting that a request for prior court authorization could, in sensitive cases, be made to any member of a specially designated court).

The statutes differ to some extent in their probable cause showings. Title III allows a court to enter an ex parte order authorizing electronic surveillance if it determines on the basis of the facts submitted in the government's application that "there is probable cause for belief that an individual is committing, has committed, or is about to commit" a specified predicate offense. 18 U.S.C. § 2518(3)(a). FISA by contrast requires a showing of probable cause that the target is a foreign power or an agent of a foreign power. 50 U.S.C. § 1805(a)(3). We have noted, however, that where a U.S. person is involved, an "agent of a foreign power" is defined in terms of criminal activity.[34] Admittedly, the definition of one category of U.S.—person agents of foreign powers—that is, persons engaged in espionage and clandestine intelligence activities for a foreign power—does not necessarily require a showing of an imminent violation of criminal law. See 50 U.S.C. § 1801(b)(2)(A) (defining such activities as those which "involve" or *"may* involve" a violation of criminal statutes of the United States). Congress clearly intended a lesser showing of probable cause for these activities than that applicable to ordinary criminal cases. See H. REP. at 39-40, 79. And with good reason—these activities present the type of threats contemplated by the Supreme Court in *Keith* when it recognized that the focus of security surveillance "may be less precise than that directed against more conventional types of crime" even in the area of *domestic* threats to national security. Keith, 407 U.S. *at 322. Congress was aware of Keith's reasoning, and recognized that it applies* a fortiori to foreign threats. See S. REP. at 15. As the House Report notes with respect to clandestine intelligence activities:

> The term "may involve" not only requires less information regarding the crime involved, but also permits electronic surveillance at some point prior to the time when a crime sought to be prevented, as for example, the transfer of classified documents, actually occurs.

H. REP. at 40. Congress allowed this lesser showing for clandestine intelligence activities—but not, notably, for other activities, including terrorism—because it was fully aware that such foreign intelligence crimes may be particularly difficult to detect.[35] At the same time, however, it provided another safeguard not present in Title III—that is, the requirement that there be probable cause to believe the target is acting "for or on behalf of a foreign power" Under the definition of "agent of a foreign power" FISA surveillance could not be authorized

> against an American reporter merely because he gathers information for publication in a newspaper, even if the information was classified by the Government. Nor would it be authorized against a Government employee or former employee who reveals secrets to a reporter or in a book for the purpose of informing the American people. This definition would not authorize surveillance of ethnic Americans who lawfully gather political information and perhaps even lawfully share it with the foreign government of their national origin. It obviously would not apply to lawful activities to lobby, influence, or inform Members of Congress or the administration to take certain positions with respect to foreign or domestic concerns. Nor would it apply to lawful gathering of information preparatory to such lawful activities.

H. REP. at 40. Similarly, FISA surveillance would not be authorized against a target engaged in purely domestic terrorism because the government would not be able to show that the target is acting for or on behalf of a foreign power. As should be clear from the foregoing, FISA applies only to certain carefully delineated, and particularly serious, foreign threats to national security.

Turning then to the first of the particularity requirements, while Title III requires probable cause to believe that particular communications concerning the specified crime will be obtained through the interception, 18 U.S.C. § 2518(3)(b), FISA instead requires an official to designate the type of foreign intelligence information being sought, and to certify that the information sought is foreign intelligence information. When the target is a U.S. person, the FISA judge reviews the certification for clear error, but this "standard of review is not, of course, comparable to a probable cause finding by the judge" H. REP. at 80. Nevertheless, FISA provides additional protections to ensure that only pertinent information is sought. The certification must be made by a national security officer—typically the FBI Director—and must be approved by the Attorney General or the Attorney General's Deputy. Congress recognized that this certification would "assure[] written accountability within the Executive Branch" and provide "an internal check on Executive Branch arbitrariness" H. REP. at 80. In addition, the court may require the government to submit any further information it deems necessary to determine whether or not the certification is clearly erroneous. See 50 U.S.C. § 1804(d).

With respect to the second element of particularity, although Title III generally requires probable cause to believe that the facilities subject to surveillance are being used or are about to be used in connection with commission of a crime or are leased to, listed in the name of, or used by the individual committing the crime, 18 U.S.C. § 2518(3)(d), FISA requires probable cause to believe that each of the facilities or places at which the surveillance is directed is being used, or is about to be used, by a foreign power or agent. 50 U.S.C. § 1805(a)(3)(B). In cases where the targeted facilities are not leased to, listed in the name of, or used by the individual committing the crime, Title III requires the government to show a nexus between the facilities and communications regarding the criminal offense. The government does not have to show, however, anything about the target of the surveillance; it is enough that *"an individual"*—not necessarily the target—is committing a crime. 18 U.S.C. §§ 2518(3)(a), (d); see *United States v. Kahn*, 415 U.S. 143, 157 (1974) ("when there is probable cause to believe that a particular telephone is being used to commit an offense but no particular person is identifiable, a wire interception order may, nevertheless, properly issue under [Title III]"). On the other hand, FISA requires probable cause to believe the target is an agent of a foreign power (that is, the individual committing a foreign intelligence crime) who uses or is about to use the targeted facility. Simply put, FISA requires less of a nexus between the facility and the pertinent communications than Title III, but more of a nexus between the target and the pertinent communications. See H. REP. at 73 ("the target of a surveillance is the individual or entity or about whom or from whom information is sought").

There are other elements of Title III that at least some circuits have determined are constitutionally significant—that is, necessity, duration of surveillance, and minimization. See, e.g., *United States v. Falls*, 34 F.3d 674, 680 (8th Cir. 1994). Both statutes have a "necessity" provision, which requires the court to find that the information sought is not available through normal investigative procedures. See 18 U.S.C. § 2518(3)(c); 50 U.S.C. §§ 1804(a)(7)(E)(ii), 1805(a)(5). Although the court's clearly erroneous review under FISA is more limited than under Title III, this greater deference must be viewed in light of FISA's additional requirement that the certification of necessity come from an upper level Executive Branch official. The statutes also have duration provisions; Title III orders may last up to 30 days, 18 U.S.C. § 2518(5), while FISA orders may last up to 90 days for U.S. persons. 50 U.S.C. § 1805(e)(1). This difference is based on the nature of national security surveillance, which is "often long range and involves the interrelation of various sources and types of information" Keith, 407 U.S. at 322; see also S. REP. at 16, 56. Moreover, the longer surveillance period is balanced by continuing FISA court oversight of minimization procedures during that period. 50 U.S.C. § 1805(e)(3); see also S. REP. at 56. And where Title III requires minimization of what is acquired,[36] as we have discussed, for U.S. persons, FISA requires minimization of what is acquired, retained, and disseminated. The FISA court notes, however, that in practice FISA surveillance devices are normally left on continuously, and the minimization occurs in the process of indexing and logging the pertinent communications. The reasonableness of this approach depends on the facts and circumstances of each case. *Scott v. United States*, 436 U.S. 128, 140-43 (1978) (acquisition of virtually all conversations was reasonable under the circumstances). Less minimization in the acquisition stage may well be justified to the extent the intercepted communications are "ambiguous in nature or apparently involve[ ]guarded or coded language" or "the investigation is focusing on what is thought to be a widespread conspiracy [where] more extensive surveillance may be justified in an attempt to determine the precise scope of the enterprise" *Id.* at 140. Given the targets of FISA surveillance, it will often be the case that intercepted communications will be in code or a foreign language for which there is no contemporaneously available translator, and the activities of foreign agents will involve multiple actors and complex plots. *[[4-5 lines deleted]]*

Amici particularly focus on the differences between the two statutes concerning notice.[37] Title III requires notice to the target (and, within the discretion of the judge, to other persons whose communications were intercepted) once the surveillance order expires. 18 U.S.C. § 2518(8)(d). FISA does not require notice to a person whose communications were intercepted unless the government "intends to enter into evidence or otherwise use or disclose" such communications in a trial or other enumerated official proceedings. 50 U.S.C. § 1806(c). As the government points out, however, to the extent evidence obtained through a FISA surveillance order is used in a criminal proceeding, notice to the defendant is required. Of course, where such evidence is not ultimately going to be used for law enforcement, Congress observed that "[t]he need to preserve secrecy for sensitive counterintelligence sources and methods justifies elimination of the notice requirement" S. REP. at 12.

Based on the foregoing, it should be evident that while Title III contains some protections that are not in FISA, in many significant respects the two statutes are equivalent, and in some, FISA contains additional protections.[38] Still, to the extent the two statutes diverge in constitutionally relevant areas—in particular, in their probable cause and particularity showings—a FISA order may not be a "warrant" contemplated by the Fourth Amendment. The government itself does not actually claim that it is, instead noting only that there is authority for the proposition that a FISA order is a warrant in the constitutional sense. See *Cavanagh*, 807 F.2d at 790 (concluding that FISA order can be considered a warrant since it is issued by a detached judicial officer and is based on a reasonable showing of probable cause); see also Pelton, 835 F.2d at 1075 (joining *Cavanagh* in holding that FISA procedures meet constitutional requirements); *Falvey*, 540 F. Supp. at 1314 (holding that unlike in *Truong*, a congressionally crafted warrant that met Fourth Amendment standards was obtained authorizing the surveillance). We do not decide the issue but note that to the extent a FISA order comes close to meeting Title III, that certainly bears on its reasonableness under the Fourth Amendment.

Did Truong Articulate the Appropriate Constitutional Standard?

Ultimately, the question becomes whether FISA, as amended by the Patriot Act, is a reasonable response based on a balance of the legitimate need of the government for foreign intelligence information to protect against national security threats with the protected rights of citizens. Cf. *Keith*, 407 U.S. at 322-23 (in domestic security context, holding that standards different from those in Title III "may be compatible with the Fourth Amendment if they are reasonable both in relation to the legitimate need of the government for intelligence information and the protected rights of our citizens"). To answer that question—whether the Patriot Act's disavowal of the primary purpose test is constitutional—besides comparing the FISA procedures with Title III, it is necessary to consider carefully the underlying rationale of the primary purpose test.

It will be recalled that the case that set forth the primary purpose test as *constitutionally required* was *Truong*. The Fourth Circuit thought that *Keith's* balancing standard implied the adoption of the primary purpose test. We reiterate that *Truong* dealt with a pre-FISA surveillance based on the President's constitutional responsibility to conduct the foreign affairs of the United States. 629 F.2d at 914. Although *Truong* suggested the line it drew was a constitutional minimum that would apply to a FISA surveillance, see *id.* at 914 n.4, it had no occasion to consider the application of the statute carefully. The *Truong* court, as did all the other courts to have decided the issue, held that the President did have inherent authority to conduct warrantless searches to obtain foreign intelligence information.[39] It was incumbent upon the court, therefore, to determine the boundaries of that constitutional authority in the case before it. We take for granted that the President does have that authority and, assuming that is so, FISA could not encroach on the President's constitutional power. The question before us is the reverse, does FISA amplify the President's power by providing a mechanism that at least approaches a classic warrant and which therefore supports the government's contention that FISA searches are constitutionally reasonable.

The district court in the *Truong* case had excluded evidence obtained from electronic surveillance after the government's investigation—the court found—had converted from one conducted for foreign intelligence reasons to one conducted primarily as a criminal investigation. (The defendants were convicted based in part on surveillance evidence gathered before that point.) The district judge had focused on the date that the Criminal Division had taken a central role in the investigation. The court of appeals endorsed that approach stating:

> We think that the district court adopted the proper test, because once surveillance becomes primarily a criminal investigation, the courts are entirely competent to make the usual probable cause determination, and because, importantly, individual privacy interests come to the fore *and government foreign policy concerns recede* when the government is primarily attempting to form the basis of a criminal prosecution.

Id. at 915 (emphasis added).

That analysis, in our view, rested on a false premise and the line the court sought to draw was inherently unstable, unrealistic, and confusing. The false premise was the assertion that once the government moves to criminal prosecution, its "foreign policy concerns" recede. As we have discussed in the first part of the opinion, that is simply not true as it relates to counterintelligence. In that field the government's primary purpose is to halt the espionage or terrorism efforts, and criminal prosecutions can be, and usually are, interrelated with other techniques used to frustrate a foreign power's efforts. Indeed, the Fourth Circuit itself, rejecting defendant's arguments that it should adopt a "solely foreign intelligence purpose test" acknowledged that "almost all foreign intelligence investigations are in part criminal investigations" *Id.* (It would have been more accurate to refer to counterintelligence investigations.)

The method the court endorsed for determining when an investigation became primarily criminal was based on the organizational structure of the Justice Department. The court determined an investigation became primarily criminal when the Criminal Division played a lead role. This approach has led, over time, to the quite intrusive organizational and personnel tasking the FISA court adopted. Putting aside the impropriety of an Article III court imposing such organizational strictures (which we have already discussed), the line the Truong court adopted—subsequently referred to as a "wall"—was unstable because it generates dangerous confusion and creates perverse organizational incentives. See, e.g., AGRT Report at 723-26.[40] That is so because counterintelligence brings to bear both classic criminal investigation techniques as well as less focused intelligence gathering. Indeed, effective counterintelligence, we have learned, requires the wholehearted cooperation of all the government's personnel who can be brought to the task. A standard which punishes such cooperation could well be thought dangerous to national security.[41] Moreover, by focusing on the subjective motivation of those who initiate investigations, the *Truong* standard, as administered by the FISA court, could be thought to discourage desirable initiatives. (It is also at odds with the Supreme Court's Fourth Amendment jurisprudence which regards the subjective motivation of an officer conducting a search or seizure as irrelevant. See, e.g., *Whren v. United States*, 517 U.S. 806 (1996).)

Recent testimony before the Joint Intelligence Committee amply demonstrates that the *Truong* line is a very difficult one to administer. Indeed, it was suggested that the FISA court requirements based on *Truong* may well have contributed, whether correctly understood or not, to the FBI missing opportunities to anticipate the September 11, 2001 attacks.[42] That is not to say that we should be prepared to jettison Fourth Amendment requirements in the interest of national security. Rather, assuming arguendo that FISA orders are not Fourth Amendment warrants, the question becomes, are the searches constitutionally reasonable. And in judging reasonableness, the instability of the *Truong* line is a relevant consideration.

The Fourth Circuit recognized that the Supreme Court had never considered the constitutionality of warrantless government searches for foreign intelligence reasons, but concluded the analytic framework the Supreme Court adopted in *Keith*—in the case of domestic intelligence surveillance—pointed the way to the line the Fourth Circuit drew. The Court in *Keith* had, indeed, balanced the government's interest against individual privacy interests, which is undoubtedly the key to this issue as well; but we think the *Truong* court misconceived the government's interest and, moreover, did not draw a more appropriate distinction that Keith at least suggested. That is the line drawn in the original FISA statute itself between ordinary crimes and foreign intelligence crimes.

It will be recalled that *Keith* carefully avoided the issue of a warrantless foreign intelligence search: "We have not addressed, and express no opinion as to, the issues which may be involved with respect to activities of foreign powers or their agents" 407 U.S. at 321- 22.[43] But in indicating that a somewhat more relaxed warrant could suffice in the domestic intelligence situation, the court drew a distinction between the crime involved in that case, which posed a threat to national security, and "ordinary crime" *Id.* at 322. It pointed out that "the focus of domestic surveillance may be less precise than that directed against more conventional types of crimes" *Id.*

The main purpose of ordinary criminal law is twofold: to punish the wrongdoer and to deter other persons in society from embarking on the same course. The government's concern with respect to foreign intelligence crimes, on the other hand, is overwhelmingly to stop or frustrate the immediate criminal activity. As we discussed in the first section of this opinion, the criminal process is often used as part of an integrated effort to counter the malign efforts of a foreign power. Punishment of the terrorist or espionage agent is really a secondary objective;[44] indeed, punishment of a terrorist is often a moot point.

Supreme Court's Special Needs Cases

The distinction between ordinary criminal prosecutions and extraordinary situations underlies the Supreme Court's approval of entirely warrantless and even suspicionless searches that are designed to serve the government's "special needs, beyond the normal need for law enforcement" *Vernonia School Dist. 47J v. Acton*, 515 U.S. 646, 653(1995) (quoting *Griffin v. Wisconsin*, 483 U.S. 868, 873 (1987) (internal quotation marks omitted)) (random drug- testing of student athletes).[45] Apprehending drunk drivers and securing the border constitute such unique interests beyond ordinary, general law enforcement. *Id.* at 654 (citing *Michigan Dep't of State Police v. Sitz*, 496 U.S. 444 (1990), and *United States v. Martinez- Fuerte*, 428 U.S. 543 (1976)).

A recent case, *City of Indianapolis v. Edmond*, 531 U.S. 32 (2000), is relied on by both the government and amici. In that case, the Court held that a highway check point designed to catch drug dealers did not fit within its special needs exception because the government's "primary purpose" was merely "to uncover evidence of ordinary criminal wrongdoing" *Id.* at 41-42. The Court rejected the government's argument that the "severe and intractable nature of the drug problem" was sufficient justification for such a dragnet seizure lacking any individualized suspicion. *Id.* at 42. *Amici* particularly rely on the Court's statement that "the gravity of the threat alone cannot be dispositive of questions concerning what means law enforcement officers may employ to pursue a given purpose" *Id.*

But by "purpose" the Court makes clear it was referring not to a subjective intent, which is not relevant in ordinary Fourth Amendment probable cause analysis, but rather to a programmatic purpose. The Court distinguished the prior check point cases *Martinez-Fuerte* (involving checkpoints less than 100 miles from the Mexican border) and *Sitz* (checkpoints to detect intoxicated motorists) on the ground that the former involved the government's "longstanding concern for the protection of the integrity of the border" *id.* at 38 (quoting *United States v. Montoya de Hernandez*, 473 U.S. 531, 538 (1985)), and the latter was "aimed at reducing the immediate hazard posed by the presence of drunk drivers on the highways" *Id.* at 39. The Court emphasized that it was decidedly not drawing a distinction between suspicionless seizures with a "non-law-enforcement primary purpose" and those designed for law enforcement. *Id.* at 44 n.1. Rather, the Court distinguished general crime control programs and those that have another particular purpose, such as protection of citizens against special hazards or protection of our borders. The Court specifically acknowledged that an appropriately tailored road block could be used "to thwart an imminent terrorist attack" *Id.* at 44. The nature of the "emergency" which is simply another word for threat, takes the matter out of the realm of ordinary crime control.[46]

Conclusion

FISA's general programmatic purpose, to protect the nation against terrorists and espionage threats directed by foreign powers, has from its outset been distinguishable from "ordinary crime control" After the events of September 11, 2001, though, it is hard to imagine greater emergencies facing Americans than those experienced on that date.

We acknowledge, however, that the constitutional question presented by this case—whether Congress's disapproval of the primary purpose test is consistent with the Fourth Amendment—has no definitive jurisprudential answer. The Supreme Court's special needs cases involve random stops (seizures) not electronic searches. In one sense, they can be thought of as a greater encroachment into personal privacy because they are not based on any particular suspicion. On the other hand, wiretapping is a good deal more intrusive than an automobile stop accompanied by questioning.

Although the Court in *City of Indianapolis* cautioned that the threat to society is not dispositive in determining whether a search or seizure is reasonable, it certainly remains a crucial factor. Our case may well involve the most serious threat our country faces. Even without taking into account the President's inherent constitutional authority to conduct warrantless foreign intelligence surveillance, we think the procedures and government showings required under FISA, if they do not meet the minimum Fourth Amendment warrant standards, certainly come close. We, therefore, believe firmly, applying the balancing test drawn from *Keith*, that FISA as amended is constitutional because the surveillances it authorizes are reasonable.

Accordingly, we reverse the FISA court's orders in this case to the extent they imposed conditions on the grant of the government's applications, vacate the FISA court's Rule 11, and remand with instructions to grant the applications as submitted and proceed henceforth in accordance with this opinion.

ENDNOTES

[14] Joining the ACLU on its brief are the Center for Democracy and Technology, Center for National Security Studies, Electronic Privacy Information Center, and Electronic Frontier Foundation.

[15] Uniting and Strengthening America by Providing Appropriate Tools Required to Intercept and Obstruct Terrorism Act of 2001, Pub. L. No. 107-56, 155 Stat. 272 (Oct. 26, 2001).

[16] The bracketed information is classified and has been redacted from the public version of the opinion.

[17] To be precise, there are two surveillance orders on appeal, one renewing the other with identical conditions.

[18] The argument before all of the district judges, some of whose terms have since expired, was referred to as an "en banc" although the statute does not contemplate such a proceeding. In fact, it specifically provides that if one judge declines to approve an application the government may not seek approval from another district judge, but only appeal to the Court of Review. 50 U.S.C. §§ 1803 (a), (b).

[19] Since proceedings before the FISA court and the Court of Review are *ex parte*-not adversary-we can entertain an argument supporting the government's position not presented to the lower court.

[20] As originally enacted, FISA covered only electronic surveillance. It was amended in 1994 to cover physical searches. Pub. L. No. 103-359, 108 Stat. 3444 (Oct. 14, 1994). Although only electronic surveillance is at issue here, much of our statutory analysis applies to FISA's provisions regarding physical searches, 50 U.S.C. §§ 1821-1829, which mirror to a great extent those regarding electronic surveillance.

[21] Foreign power is defined broadly to include, *inter alia*, "a group engaged in international terrorism or activities in preparation therefore" and "a foreign-based political organization, not substantially composed of United States persons" 50 U.S.C. §§ 1801 (a) (4), (5).

[22] A second definition of foreign intelligence information includes information necessary to "the national defense or the security of the United States" or "the conduct of the foreign affairs of the United States" 50 U.S.C. § 1801(e)(2). This definition generally involves information referred to as "affirmative" or "positive" foreign intelligence information rather than the "protective" or "counterintelligence" information at issue here.

[23] Under the current version of FISA, the definition of "agent of a foreign power" also includes U.S. persons who enter the United States under a false or fraudulent identity for or on behalf of a foreign power. Our term "foreign intelligence crimes" includes this fraudulent conduct, which will almost always involve a crime.

[24] Section 1804(d) simply provides that "[t]he judge may require the applicant to furnish such other information as may be necessary to make the determinations required by section 1805 of this title".

[25] At oral argument before the FISA judges, the court asked government counsel whether a companion provision of FISA, section 1822(c), that gives the court *jurisdiction* over physical searches "for *the purpose* of obtaining foreign intelligence information" obliged the court to consider the government's "primary purpose" We think that language points in the opposite direction since it would be more than a little strange for Congress to require a court to make a searching inquiry into the investigative background of a FISA application before concluding the court had jurisdiction over the application.

[26] Interestingly, the court noted that the FISA judge "is not to second guess the Executive Branch official's certification that the objective of the surveillance is foreign intelligence information" *Duggan*, 743 F.2d at 77.

[27] We certainly understand the 1995 Justice Department's effort to avoid difficulty with the FISA court, or other courts; and we have no basis to criticize any organization of the Justice Department that an Attorney General desires.

²⁸ According to the Report, within the Department the primary proponent of procedures that cordoned off criminal investigators and prosecutors from those officers with counterintelligence responsibilities was the deputy counsel of OIPR. See AGRT Report at 714   n.949. He was subsequently transferred from that position and made a senior counsel. He left the Department and became the Legal Advisor to the FISA court.

²⁹ There are other detailed, classified procedures governing the acquisition, retention, and dissemination of foreign intelligence and non- foreign intelligence information that have been submitted to and approved by the FISA court as "minimization procedures" Those classified minimization procedures are not at issue here.

³⁰ In particular, the court adopted Part A of the 1995 Procedures, which covers "Contacts During an FI or FCI Investigation in which FISA Surveillance or Searches are being Conducted" The remainder of the 1995 Procedures addresses contacts in cases where FISA is not at issue.

³¹ In describing its experience with FISA searches and surveillance, the FISA court's opinion makes reference to certain applications each of which contained an FBI agent's affidavit that was inaccurate, particularly with respect to assertions regarding the information shared with criminal investigators and prosecutors. Although we do not approve any misrepresentations that may have taken place, our understanding is that those affidavits were submitted during 1997 through early 2001, and therefore any inaccuracies may have been caused in part by the confusion within the Department of Justice over implementation of the 1995 Procedures, as augmented in January 2000. In any event, while the issue of the candor of the FBI agent(s) involved properly remains under investigation by the Department of Justice's Office of Professional Responsibility, the issue whether the wall between the FBI and the Criminal Division required by the FISA court has been maintained is moot in light of this court's opinion.

³² In light of *Morrison v. Ison* and *Mistretta v. United States,* 488 U.S. 361 (1989), we do not think there is much left to an argument made by an opponent of FISA in 1978 that the statutory responsibilities of the FISA court are inconsistent with Article III case and controversy responsibilities of federal judges because of the secret, non-adversary process. See *Foreign Intelligence Electronic Surveillance: Hearings on H.R. 5 ,   5,   , and 56 2 Before the Subcomm. on Legislation of the ermanent Select Comm. on Intelligence,* 95th Cong., 2d Sess. 221 (1978) (statement of Laurence H. Silberman).

³³ Furthermore, the Attorney General of Deputy Attorney General must approve the use in a criminal proceeding of information acquired pursuant to FISA. 50 U.S.C. § 1806(b).

³⁴ The term "foreign power" which is not directly at issue in this case, is not defined solely in terms of criminal activity. For example, although the term includes a group engaged in international terrorism, which would involve criminal activity, it also includes any foreign government. 50 U.S.C. § 1801(a)(1).

³⁵ For example, a federal agent may witness a "meet" or "drop" where information is being passed but be unable to determine precisely what information is being transmitted and therefore be unable to show that a crime is involved or what specific crime is being committed. See H. REP. at 39-40; see also S. REP. at 23.

³⁶ Title III requires agents to conduct surveillance "in such a way as to minimize the interception of communications not otherwise subject to interception under this chapter" 18 U.S.C. § 2518(5).

³⁷ *Amici* also emphasize that Title III generally entitles a defendant to obtain the surveillance application and order to challenge to the legality of the surveillance, 18 U.S.C. § 2518(9), while FISA does not normally allow a defendant to obtain the same if the Attorney General states that disclosure or an adversary hearing would harm national security, 50 U.S.C. § 1806(f). Under such circumstances, the judge conducts an in camera and ex parte review to determine whether the electronic surveillance was lawful, whether disclosure or discovery is necessary, and whether to grant a motion to suppress. Id. §§ 1806(f), (g). Clearly, the decision whether to allow a defendant to obtain FISA materials is made by a district judge on a case by case basis, and the issue whether such a decision protects a defendant's constitutional rights in any given case is not before us.

[38] In addition to the protections already discussed, FISA has more extensive reporting requirements than Title III, compare 18 U.S.C. § 2519(2) with 50 U.S.C. § 1808(a)(1), and is subject to close and continuing oversight by Congress as a check against Executive Branch abuses. S. REP. at 11-12. Also, the Patriot Act contains sunset provisions, see Section 224(a) of Patriot Act, Pub. L. 107-56, 115 Stat. 272 (Oct. 26, 2001), thus allowing Congress to revisit the Act's amendments to FISA.

[39] Although the plurality opinion in *Zweibon v. Mitchell*, 516 F.2d 594, 633-51 (D.C. Cir. 1975) (en banc), cert. denied, 425 U.S. 944 (1976), suggested the contrary in dicta, it did not decide the issue.

[40] We are told that the FBI has even thought it necessary because of FISA court rulings to pass off a criminal investigation to another government department when the FBI was conducting a companion counterintelligence inquiry.

[41] The AGRT Report bears this out: "Unfortunately, the practice of excluding the Criminal Division from FCI investigations was not an isolated event confined to the Wen Ho Lee matter. It has been a way of doing business for OIPR, acquiesced in by the FBI, and inexplicably indulged by the Department of Justice. One FBI supervisor has said that it has only been ‚lucky' that a case has not yet been hampered by the rigid interpretation of the rules governing contacts with the Criminal Division. It may be said that in the Wen Ho Lee investigation, luck ran out" Id. at 708 (citation omitted).

[42] An FBI agent recently testified that efforts to conduct a criminal investigation of two of the alleged hijackers were blocked by senior FBI officials—understandably concerned about prior FISA court criticism—who interpreted that court's decisions as precluding a criminal investigator's role. One agent, frustrated at encountering the "wall" wrote to headquarters: "[S]omeday someone will die—and wall or not—the public will not understand why we were not more effective and throwing every resource we had at certain ‚problems.' Let's hope the National Security Law Unit will stand behind their decisions then, especially since the biggest threat to us now, [Usama Bin Laden], is getting the most ‚protection.'" The agent was told in response that headquarters was frustrated with the issue, but that those were the rules, and the National Security Law Unit does not make them up. *The Malaysia Hijacking and September 11th: Joint Hearing Before the Senate and House Select Intelligence Committees* (Sept. 20, 2002) (written statement of New York special agent of the FBI).

[43] The Court in a footnote though, cited authority for the view that warrantless surveillance may be constitutional where foreign powers are involved. *Keith*, 407 U.S. at 322 n.20.

[44] To be sure, punishment of a U.S. person's espionage for a foreign power does have a deterrent effect on others similarly situated.

[45] The Court has also allowed searches for certain administrative purposes to be undertaken without particularized suspicion of misconduct. *See, e.g., New York v. Burger*, 482 U.S. 691, 702-04 (1987) (warrantless administrative inspection of premises of closely regulated business); *Camara v. Municipal Court*, 387 U.S. 523, 534-39 (1967) (administrative inspection to ensure compliance with city housing code).

[46] Amici rely on *Ferguson v. City of Charleston*, 532 U.S. 67 (2001), in arguing that the "special needs" cases acknowledge that the Fourth Amendment is particularly concerned with intrusions whose primary purpose is to gather evidence of crime. In that case, the Court struck down a non-consensual policy of testing obstetrics patients for drug use. The Court stated that "[w]hile the ultimate goal of the program may well have been to get the women in question into substance abuse treatment and off of drugs, the immediate objective of the searches was to generate evidence *for law enforcement purposes* in order to reach that goal" Id. at 82-83 (emphasis in original; footnotes omitted). In distinguishing the "special needs" cases, the Court noted that "[i]t is especially difficult to argue that the program here was designed simply to save lives" in light of evidence that the sort of program at issue actually discouraged women from seeking prenatal care. Id. at 844 n.23. Thus, *Ferguson* does not involve a situation in which law enforcement is directly connected to the prevention of a special harm.

ACLU PETITION FOR WRIT OF CERTIORARI TO THE U.S. SUPREME COURT OF THE FOREIGN INTELLIGENCE SURVEILLANCE COURT OF REVIEW DECISON 02-001

No.

PETITION FOR LEAVE TO INTERVENE AND PETITION FOR A WRIT OF CERTIORARI

In the Supreme Court of the United States

IN RE: SEALED CASE OF THE FOREIGN INTELLIGENCE
SURVEILLANCE COURT OF REVIEW NO. 02-001

AMERICAN CIVIL LIBERTIES UNION, NATIONAL ASSOCIATION OF
CRIMINAL DEFENSE LAWYERS, AMERICAN-ARAB ANTI-DISCRIMINATION
COMMITTEE, *and* ARAB COMMUNITY CENTER FOR ECONOMIC
AND SOCIAL SERVICES, *Petitioners.*

ON PETITION FOR LEAVE TO INTERVENE AND PETITION FOR A WRIT OF CERTIORARI TO THE FOREIGN INTELLIGENCE SURVEILLANCE COURT OF REVIEW

ANN BEESON
Counsel of Record
JAMEEL JAFFER
STEVEN R. SHAPIRO
American Civil Liberties
Union Foundation
125 Broad Street

New York, NY 10004
(212) 549-2601

JOSHUA L. DRATEL
JOHN D. CLINE
TOM GOLDSTEIN
National Association of
Criminal Defense Lawyers
14 Wall Street, 28th Floor
New York, NY 10005
(212) 732-0707

Counsel for Petitioners

PARTIES TO THE PROCEEDINGS

Petitioners are the American Civil Liberties Union, the National Association of Criminal Defense Lawyers, American-Arab Anti-Discrimination Committee, and the Arab Community Center for Economic and Social Services. Respondent is the United States.

CORPORATE DISCLOSURE STATEMENT

In accordance with United States Supreme Court Rule 29.6, petitioners confirm that none of the petitioners have parent companies nor do any publicly held companies own ten percent or more of their stock.

QUESTIONS PRESENTED

(1) Does the USA PATRIOT Act ("Patriot Act"), Pub. L. No. 107-56, 115 Stat. 272 (Oct. 26, 2001), authorize the government to conduct surveillance under the Foreign Intelligence Surveillance Act ("FISA"), 50 U.S.C. § 1801 *et seq.*, even where the government's primary purpose is law enforcement rather than foreign intelligence?

(2) If the Patriot Act authorizes the government to conduct surveillance under FISA even where the government's primary purpose is law enforcement, does FISA as amended by the Patriot Act contravene the First or Fourth Amendment of the United States Constitution?

TABLE OF CONTENTS

Questions Presented

Table of Authorities

Introduction

Opinions Below

Jurisdiction

Constitutional and Statutory Provisions

Statement of the Case

Reasons for Granting the Writ

    I. The Court of Review's Decision Presents an Important Statutory and Constitutional Question Concerning the Scope of Any Foreign-Intelligence Exception to the Fourth Amendment's Usual Requirements

    II. The Court of Review Disregarded the Canon of Constitutional Avoidance By Reaching Difficult Constitutional Questions Unnecessarily

    III. The Court of Review's Decision Conflicts With This Court's Fourth Amendment Jurisprudence

        A. The court of Review's Decision Disregards the Fourth Amendment By Endorsing Warrantless and Unreasonable Searches in Criminal Investigations

        B. The Court of Review's Decision Diregards the Fouth Amendment By Allowing the Government to Conduct Searches for Law Enforcement Purposes Without Providng Notice

        C. The Court of Review's Decision Disregards the Fourth Amendment By Foreclosing Meaningful Judicial Review of FISA Applications

        D. The Court of Review's Decisions Conflicts With This Court's Special Needs Jurisprudence

    IV. The Court of Review's Decision Conflicts With the Decisions of Numerous Lower Federal Courts Which Have Held That Any Foreign-Intelligence Exception Must Be Limited to Investigations Whose Primary Purpose is Foreign Intelligence

    V. The Court of Review's Decision Jeopardizes First Amendment Freedoms By Eliminating Fourth Amendment Safeguards

Conclusion

Appendices A and B [omitted]

Appendix C

TABLE OF AUTHORITIES

Cases

Berger v. New York, 388 U.S. 41 (1967)

Chimel v. California, 395 U.S. 752 (1969)

City of Indianapolis v. Edmond, 531 U.S. 32 (2000)

Dalia v. United States, 441 U.S. 238 (1979)

Ferguson v. City of Charleston, 532 U.S. 67 (2001)

Franks v. Delaware, 438 U.S. 154 (1978)

Gerstein v. Pugh, 420 U.S. 103 (1975)

Halkin v. Helms, 690 F.2d 977 (D.C. Cir. 1982)

Miller v. United States, 357 U.S. 301 (1958)

Payton v. New York, 445 U.S. 573 (1980)

Pennsylvania Bureau of Correction v. United States Marshals Service, 474 U.S. 34 (1985)

Richards v. Wisconsin, 520 U.S. 385 (1997)

Tully v. Mobil Oil Corp., 455 U.S. 245 (1982)

United States ex rel. Attorney General v. Del. & Hudson Co., 213 U.S. 366 (1909)

United States v. Brown, 484 F.2d 418 (5th Cir. 1973)

United States v. Butenko, 494 F.2d 593 (3d Cir. 1974)

United States v. Donovan, 429 U.S. 413 (1977)

United States v. Duggan, 743 F.2d 59 (2d Cir. 1984)

United States v. Johnson, 952 F.2d 565 (1st Cir. 1991)

United States v. Klein, 80 U.S. (13 Wall.) 128 (1872)

United States v. Nicholson, 955 F.Supp. 588 (E.D.Va. 1997)

United States v. Pelton, 835 F.2d 1067 (4th Cir.)

United States v. Truong Dinh Hung, 629 F.2d 908 (4th Cir. 1980)

United States v. United States District Court ("Keith"), 407 U.S. 297 (1972)

Vernonia School District 47J v. Acton, 515 U.S. 646 (1995)

Weeks v. United States, 232 U.S. 383 (1914)

Wilson v. Arkansas, 514 U.S. 927 (1995)

Zweibon v. Mitchell, 516 F.2d. 594 (D.C. Cir. 1975)

Statutes

USA PATRIOT Act ("Patriot Act"), Pub. L. No. 107-56, 115 Stat. 272

Title III of the Omnibus Crime Control and Safe Streets Act of 1968, Pub. L. 90-351, tit. III, 82 Stat. 211

18 U.S.C. § 2518(1)(b)

18 U.S.C. § 2518(2)

18 U.S.C. § 2518(3)

18 U.S.C. § 2518(3)(a)

18 U.S.C. § 2518(3)(b)

18 U.S.C. § 2518(3)(d)

18 U.S.C. § 2518(5)

28 U.S.C. § 1254

28 U.S.C. § 1254(1)

28 U.S.C. § 1254(2)

28 U.S.C. § 1651(a)

Foreign Intelligence Surveillance Act ("FISA"), 50 U.S.C. § 1801 *et seq.*

50 U.S.C. § 1801(b)(2)(D)

50 U.S.C. § 1801(i)

50 U.S.C. § 1803(b)

50 U.S.C. § 1804(a)(4)(A)

50 U.S.C. § 1804(a)(7)

50 U.S.C. § 1804(a)(7)(A)

50 U.S.C. § 1804(a)(7)(B)

50 U.S.C. § 1804(a)(7)(E)

50 U.S.C. § 1805(a)(3)(A)

50 U.S.C. § 1805(a)(3)(B)

U.S.C. § 1805(a)(5)

50 U.S.C. § 1806(f)

50 U.S.C. § 1823(a)(7)(B)

50 U.S.C. §§ 1821-29

50 U.S.C. §§ 1841-46

50 U.S.C. §§ 1861-62

Constitutional Provisions

First Amendment

Fourth Amendment

Legislative Materials

S. 113, 108th Cong. (2002)

S. Rep. 90-1097 (1968)

S. Rep. 94-755 (1976)

S. Rep. 95-604 (1977)

Senate Select Comm. to Study Governmental Operations with Respect to Intelligence Activities, Intelligence Activities and the Rights of Americans, Final Report ("Church Committee Report"), S. Rep. No. 94-755 (1976)

Other Authorities

"What do I have to do to get a FISA?" (Document released by FBI in response to August 21 Freedom of Information Act request submitted by ACLU et al.)

PETITION FOR A WRIT OF CERTIORARI

Petitioners respectfully petition for a writ of *certiorari* to review the judgment of the Foreign Intelligence Surveillance Court of Review in this case.

INTRODUCTION

Petitioners seek this Court's review of the first-ever decision of the Foreign Intelligence Surveillance Court of Review ("Court of Review"), a decision that seriously compromises the privacy and free-speech rights of people living in the United States. In an extraordinary and far-reaching ruling that conflicts with decisions of this Court and a number of lower courts, the Court of Review construed provisions of the USA Patriot Act ("Patriot Act") to allow the government vastly to expand its surveillance of Americans by using the Foreign Intelligence Surveillance Act ("FISA") even in investigations whose primary purpose is law enforcement rather than foreign intelligence. The Court of Review's decision effectively overturned a decision of the Foreign Intelligence Surveillance Court ("FISA Court") that had avoided the constitutional question by interpreting the amended FISA more narrowly, though the Court of Review acknowledged that "the constitutional question presented in this case . . . has no definitive jurisprudential answer." App. 52a. Petitioners urge this Court to grant review in order to clarify that the government cannot constitutionally conduct surveillance under lower foreign-intelligence standards where its primary purpose is law enforcement rather than foreign intelligence.

OPINIONS BELOW

The opinion of the Foreign Intelligence Surveillance Court of Review in *In re: Sealed Case No. 02-001* is reprinted as Appendix A hereto. *See* App. 1a-53a. The opinion of the Foreign Intelligence Surveillance Court is reprinted as Appendix B hereto. *See* App. 54a-86a.

JURISDICTION

The judgment of the Court of Review was entered on November 18, 2002. This Court has jurisdiction under 50 U.S.C. § 1803(b), under 28 U.S.C. § 1254(1), and under the All Writs Act, 28 U.S.C. § 1651(a).

Section 1803(b) of Title 50 creates jurisdiction in this Court to review, on petition of the government for a writ of *certiorari*, any Court of Review decision upholding the denial of a government surveillance application.[1] The statute is silent as to whether a party *other* than the government may petition for a writ of *certiorari* where the government *prevails* in the Court of Review. Petitioners urge the Court to construe the statute generously. A reading that would disallow parties other than the government from petitioning for a writ of *certiorari* would effectively foreclose this Court from reviewing any decision by the Court of Review in favor of the government.

Yet nothing in the statute suggests that Congress intended that result. On the contrary, the apparent intent of the statute is to ensure that this Court will be able to correct the Court of Review when necessary. Congress's failure specifically to authorize parties other than the government to seek this Court's review is easily explained by the fact that, in litigation originating in the FISA Court, the government is ordinarily the only party. If Congress had intended that in certain cases the Court of Review rather than this Court would be the final arbiter of difficult constitutional questions, it would surely have manifested its intent in clear language.

This Court also has jurisdiction under 28 U.S.C. § 1254, which provides that "[c]ases in the courts of appeals may be reviewed by the Supreme Court . . . [b]y writ of *certiorari* granted upon the petition of any party to any civil or criminal case. . . ." The Court of Review is a "court[] of appeals" within the meaning of this provision. *See Tully v. Mobil Oil Corp.*, 455 U.S. 245 (1982) (per curiam) (holding that the Temporary Emergency Court of Appeals was a 'court of appeals' for purposes of § 1254(2)).

Finally, if neither of the provisions cited above provides jurisdiction, this Court has jurisdiction under the All Writs Act, 28 U.S.C. § 1651(a), which provides that "[t]he Supreme Court and all courts established by Act of Congress may issue all writs necessary or appropriate in aid of their respective jurisdictions and agreeable to the usages and principles of law." In *Pennsylvania Bureau of Correction v. United States Marshals Service*, 474 U.S. 34, 43 (1985), this Court stated that "[w]here a statute specifically addresses the particular issue at hand, it is that authority, and not the All Writs Act, that is controlling." It also stated, however, that the All Writs Act "fill[s] the interstices of federal judicial power when those gaps threate[n] to thwart the otherwise proper exercise of federal courts' jurisdiction." *Id.* at 41.

Petitioners submit that the All Writs Act provides jurisdiction here. First, FISA does not "specifically address[]" the question whether a party other than the government may petition for a writ of *certiorari*. Second, if jurisdiction did not exist under the All Writs Act, this Court's authority to review a decision of the Court of Review would depend on whether the decision was favorable or unfavorable to the government. Finally, jurisdiction under the All Writs Act is appropriate in this extraordinary case for a number of other reasons. The FISA Court, sitting *en banc* for the first time in its history, ruled unanimously against the government. The Court of Review, which ultimately reversed the FISA Court, convened for the first time to hear the government's appeal. Both the lower court and the Court of Review recognized the broad impact of their rulings and published their decisions. Though some of petitioners here were permitted to file briefs *amicus curiae* in the lower court proceedings, the government was the only party. The litigation clearly involves important constitutional issues concerning FISA itself and not simply the legal sufficiency of a particular surveillance application.

CONSTITUTIONAL AND STATUTORY PROVISIONS

The First Amendment to the United States Constitution provides in relevant part that "Congress shall make no law . . . abridging the freedom of speech, or of the press." The Fourth Amendment provides that "The right of the people to be secure in their persons, houses, papers, and effects, against unreasonable searches and seizures, shall not be violated, and no Warrants shall issue, but upon probable cause, supported by Oath or affirmation, and particularly describing the place to be searched, and the persons or things to be seized." The pertinent provisions of FISA, as amended by the Patriot Act, are reprinted in Appendix C hereto. *See* App. 87a-105a.

STATEMENT OF THE CASE

This case involves the meaning and constitutionality of certain amendments made by the Patriot Act to FISA. The Court of Review held that the Patriot Act constitutionally authorizes the government to rely on FISA even when the primary purpose of an investigation is law enforcement rather than foreign intelligence.

FISA was enacted in 1978 to govern surveillance of foreign powers and their agents inside the United States. The statute created the FISA Court, a court composed of seven (now eleven) federal district court judges, and empowered the FISA Court to grant or deny government applications for surveillance orders.[2] FISA also set out the conditions that the government is required to satisfy before the FISA Court will issue a surveillance order. These standards are substantially less stringent than those that the Fourth Amendment ordinarily requires. In order to obtain a FISA surveillance warrant, the government must show probable cause to believe that the prospective surveillance target is a "foreign power" or an "agent of a foreign power," 50 U.S.C. § 1804(a)(4)(A), and it must certify, among other things, that "the purpose" (now, "significant purpose") of the surveillance is to obtain "foreign intelligence information," *id.* § 1804(a)(7)(B). The government is *not* required, however, to articulate any suspicion that the target is engaged in criminal activity. It is not required to show (or even to certify) that the facilities to be targeted are being used for the kinds of communications that are sought to be intercepted. It is not required to provide the target with even delayed notice that her privacy has been compromised—even if the target is ultimately determined to have been inappropriately or illegally targeted. In essence, FISA allows the government to conduct electronic surveillance and physical searches without complying with the ordinary requirements of the Fourth Amendment.

According to the government, the Patriot Act dramatically expanded the class of investigations in which FISA is available. Prior to the Patriot Act, the government could invoke FISA only by certifying that "the purpose" of the surveillance was to obtain foreign intelligence information. The Patriot Act replaced "the purpose" with "a significant purpose." 115 Stat. 272, § 218 (amending 50 U.S.C. §§ 1804(a)(7)(B) and 1823(a)(7)(B)). On the government's theory, that change allows it to obtain surveillance warrants under FISA's undemanding standards even where its primary purpose is law enforcement rather than foreign intelligence.

In March of last year, the Attorney General requested that the FISA Court adopt a new set of procedures (the "2002 Procedures") for all FISA investigations concerning United States persons.[3] The 2002 Procedures were to supersede procedures that had been in place since 1995 (the "1995 Procedures"). Although styled as "Intelligence Sharing Procedures for Foreign Intelligence and Foreign Counterintelligence Investigations Conducted by the FBI," the 2002 Procedures in fact sought to implement the Attorney General's expansive interpretation of the Patriot Act's amendments to FISA. Most relevant to this litigation, the 2002 Procedures endorsed the use of FISA in investigations whose primary purpose is law enforcement rather than foreign intelligence. They also stated that FISA surveillance could now be initiated, directed, and controlled by law enforcement rather than intelligence officials.

In a decision dated May 17, 2002, the FISA Court rejected the 2002 Procedures. *See* App. 54a-86a. The court noted that, while the 1995 Procedures "permit[ted] substantial consultation and coordination" between the intelligence and criminal officials, the court had closely supervised such consultation and coordination to ensure that FISA was "not being used *sub rosa* for criminal investigations." *Id.* 68a. Notwithstanding this close supervision, the government had abused its FISA authority in "an alarming number of instances." *Id.*[4] The Court found that the 2002 Procedures, far from addressing the government's history of abuse, would eliminate altogether the safeguards that prevented the government from using FISA as a means of evading ordinary Fourth Amendment requirements in routine criminal investigations. *See id.* 72a. The March 2002 Procedures, the Court wrote,

> mean[ ] that criminal prosecutors will tell the FBI when to use FISA (perhaps when they lack probable cause for a Title III electronic surveillance), what techniques to use, what information to look for, what information to keep as evidence and when use of FISA can cease because there is enough evidence to arrest and prosecute.

Id. 76a. Rather than denying the Attorney General's motion, however, the Court modified the proposed procedures, first by requiring that consultations between criminal and intelligence investigators be monitored by officials of the Office of Intelligence Policy Review, and second by adding a proviso that prohibited law enforcement officials from "directing or controlling the investigation using FISA searches and surveillances toward law enforcement objectives." *Id.* 77a.

The Attorney General appealed the FISA Court's decision to the Court of Review, which convened for the first time in order to hear the appeal.[5] On appeal, the government advanced two arguments. The first of these, which the government had not presented to the FISA Court (and indeed had never before advanced before Congress or any court), was that there had never been any statutory basis for the view—adopted by the Fourth Circuit in *United States v. Truong*, 629 F.2d 908 (4th Cir. 1980), and then by several other courts—that FISA is available only where the government's primary purpose is foreign intelligence. After examining the relevant FISA provisions as they existed before the Patriot Act, the Court of Review agreed. In the Court's view, FISA as originally enacted did not envision a dichotomy between law enforcement and foreign intelligence. Indeed, the Court noted, fi[t]he definition of an agent of a foreign power, if it pertains to a U.S. person (which is the only category relevant to this case), is closely tied to criminal activity." App. 8a. Thus, the Court accepted the government's view that the primary-purpose restriction did not have a statutory basis before the Patriot Act. It proceeded to find, however, that the Patriot Act's "significant purpose" amendment had endorsed the relevance of a judicial inquiry into the government's purpose:

> [E]ven though we agree that the original FISA did not contemplate the "false dichotomy" [between foreign intelligence and law enforcement], the Patriot Act actually did—which makes it no longer false.... [I]n light of the significant purpose amendment... it seems section 1805 must be interpreted as giving the FISA court the authority to review the government's purpose in seeking the information.

Id. 32a.

Having concluded that the "significant purpose" amendment had endorsed the dichotomy between foreign intelligence and law enforcement, the Court could not accept the government's principal argument. It was sympathetic, however, to the government's alternative argument—that the "significant purpose" amendment had been intended to "eliminate[] any justification for the FISA court to balance the relative weight the government places on criminal prosecution as compared to other counterintelligence responses." *Id.* 33a. After the Patriot Act, the Court reasoned, the government meets its statutory obligation as long as "the certification of the application's purpose articulates a broader objective than criminal prosecution ... and includes other non-prosecutorial responses." *Id.* "So long as the government entertains a realistic option of dealing with the agent other than through criminal prosecution, it satisfies the significant purpose test." *Id.* 32a.

The Court thus made clear its view that the Patriot Act amendments license the use of FISA even if the government's primary purpose is law enforcement. Indeed, the Court reasoned that the government may use FISA even for the primary purpose of prosecuting ordinary, *non-*"foreign-intelligence crimes," so long as the crime is not "wholly unrelated" to foreign intelligence. *Id.* 34a.

The Court dedicated the remainder of its opinion to addressing the constitutionality of the Patriot Act amendments.[6] The Court acknowledged the significant differences between FISA's procedural requirements and those of Title III of the Omnibus Crime Control and Safe Streets Act of 1968 ("Title III"), Pub. L. 90-351, tit. III, 82 Stat. 211, the statute that governs electronic surveillance in criminal investigations. The Court wrote, "to the extent the two statutes diverge in constitutionally relevant areas . . . a FISA order may not be a 'warrant' contemplated by the Fourth Amendment," id. 44a, but declined to decide the issue. Instead, it proceeded directly to the question whether FISA searches are reasonable.

The Court expressly rejected *Truong* and other Court of Appeals cases holding that the government cannot constitutionally invoke any foreign-intelligence exception to the Fourth Amendment's usual requirements where its primary purpose is law enforcement. The Court of Review held that these cases were misguided because "criminal prosecutions can be, and usually are, interrelated with other techniques used to frustrate a foreign power's efforts." *Id.* 46a. The Court also rejected *amici*'s reliance on this Court's "special needs" cases. *See id.* 50a-51a. The Court held that these cases were inapposite because, whatever the purpose of any particular FISA investigation, FISA is a statute whose "programmatic purpose" is not law enforcement but foreign intelligence. *Id.* 52a. The Court concluded:

> [W]e think the procedures and government showings required under FISA, if they do not meet the minimum Fourth Amendment warrant standards, certainly come close. We, therefore, believe firmly . . . that FISA as amended is constitutional because the surveillance it authorizes are reasonable.

Id. 53a.

REASONS FOR GRANTING THE WRIT

Although FISA was enacted in 1978, this Court has never considered the statute's constitutionality. The question has become extraordinarily important in light of the Court of Review's interpretation of the Patriot Act. This Court should accept review in order to make clear that the government may not constitutionally rely on any foreign-intelligence exception to the Fourth Amendment's usual requirements in investigations whose primary purpose is law enforcement rather than foreign intelligence.

The Court of Review's decision, which upheld the constitutionality of the relevant Patriot Act amendment, need not have addressed the constitutional question at all, because the statute supports a narrower construction that would avoid the constitutional question altogether. In any event, the Court of Review's answer to the constitutional question was incorrect. The decision conflicts with the clear rulings of this Court by sanctioning warrantless and unreasonable searches in routine criminal investigations, by allowing the government to conduct searches for law enforcement purposes without providing notice or establishing criminal probable cause, and by foreclosing meaningful judicial review of FISA surveillance applications. It also conflicts with decisions of numerous lower federal courts that limited any foreign-intelligence exception to investigations whose primary purpose is foreign intelligence. Finally, it contravenes this Court's jurisprudence by undermining Fourth Amendment safeguards that previously inhibited the government from infringing First Amendment rights.

For these reasons, petitioners urge the Court to grant review in this case.

I. THE COURT OF REVIEW'S DECISION PRESENTS AN IMPORTANT STATUTORY AND CONSTITUTIONAL QUESTION CONCERNING THE SCOPE OF ANY FOREIGN-INTELLIGENCE EXCEPTION TO THE FOURTH AMENDMENT'S USUAL REQUIREMENTS

FISA was enacted to establish a framework within which the Executive Branch may conduct intelligence surveillance of foreign powers and their agents inside the United States. The statute allows the government to conduct surveillance on less demanding standards than are ordinarily required by the Fourth Amendment. Although FISA has now governed foreign-intelligence surveillance for twenty-five years, this Court has never before reviewed the statute's constitutionality.

FISA was enacted in response to rampant abuse of executive surveillance powers. During the Cold War and the McCarthy era, the FBI routinely installed electronic surveillance devices on private property in order to monitor the conversations of suspected communists. *See* S. Rep. 95- 604, at 11 (1977). The FBI's COINTELPRO, authorized by President Nixon in the 1970s, wiretapped Martin Luther King, Jr. and other dissidents and anti-war protesters solely because of their political beliefs. *See generally* 2 Senate Select Comm. to Study Governmental Operations with Respect to Intelligence Activities, Intelligence Activities and the Rights of Americans, Final Report ("Church Committee Report"), S. Rep. 94-755 (1976). The CIA illegally surveilled as many as seven thousand Americans in Operation CHAOS, including individuals involved in the peace movement, student activists, and black nationalists. *See generally Halkin v. Helms*, 690 F.2d 977 (D.C. Cir. 1982). The Church Committee Report, issued in 1976, concluded that "[u]nless new and tighter controls are established by legislation, domestic intelligence activities threaten to undermine our democratic society and fundamentally alter its nature." Church Committee Report, at 2.

While FISA was enacted in part as a response to such abuse, the standards that govern FISA surveillance have always been substantially less stringent than the Fourth Amendment requires in criminal investigations. When FISA was first enacted, however, it applied only to a relatively narrow and strictly delineated class of investigations. This is no longer the case. Since 1978, Congress has amended FISA on numerous occasions, each time adding new surveillance tools to the executive's foreign-intelligence toolbox.[7] As a result, FISA as it exists now bears little resemblance to the statute that Congress enacted in 1978.

The Patriot Act amendments at issue in this case are the most recent in the long list of amendments to FISA, and they are also the most significant changes to FISA since the statute's enactment. While most previous amendments have added to the tools available to the government in FISA investigations, the Patriot Act amendments dramatically expand the *class* of investigations in which FISA is available. Previously, FISA's significance was limited to investigations whose primary purpose was foreign intelligence. The Patriot Act amendments—on the Court of Review's theory, at least—extend FISA's significance even to investigations whose primary purpose is law enforcement. If the Court of Review's theory is correct, the government may now use FISA as a law-enforcement tool in a broad category of criminal investigations.

While FISA as originally enacted raised constitutional questions, the extension of FISA to investigations whose purpose is not primarily foreign intelligence raises constitutional concerns of an entirely different magnitude. What began as a relatively narrow and well-defined exception to the Fourth Amendment's ordinary strictures has now become a license for the executive to ignore the Fourth Amendment altogether in a broad class of criminal investigations.[8] This vast expansion in the foreign- intelligence exception has occurred even though, as indicated above, this Court has never sanctioned even the comparatively narrow exception contemplated by FISA as originally enacted.

This Court should accept review in order to make clear that any foreign-intelligence exception cannot constitutionally apply in investigations whose primary purpose is law enforcement.

II. THE COURT OF REVIEW DISREGARDED THE CANON OF CONSTITUTIONAL AVOIDANCE BY REACHING DIFFICULT CONSTITUTIONAL QUESTIONS UNNECESSARILY

Under the canon of constitutional avoidance, when a "statute [is] susceptible of two interpretations, by one of which it would be unconstitutional and by the other valid," a court's "plain duty is to adopt that construction which will save the statute from constitutional infirmity." *United States ex rel. Attorney General v. Del. & Hudson Co.*, 213 U.S. 366, 408 (1909). The Court of Review disregarded this canon by adopting the constitutionally problematic theory that FISA is available even when the government's primary purpose is law enforcement.

Through the enactment of Title III and FISA, Congress created two distinct authorization schemes for government surveillance.[9] Title III, enacted in 1968, governs electronic surveillance in criminal investigations. FISA, enacted in 1978, governs electronic surveillance for foreign-intelligence purposes. Criminal investigations relating to national security crimes have always been governed by Title III. Thus, Title III as originally enacted included espionage, sabotage, and treason as predicate offenses. The Senate referred to these as "the offenses that fall within the national security category." S. Rep. 90-1097, at 67 (1968). These national-security crimes remain predicate offenses under Title III today.[10]

Congress's decision to retain the national-security crimes as predicate offenses to Title III makes clear that Congress did not intend to make FISA available in criminal investigations. As discussed above, the standards that govern FISA surveillance are substantially less demanding than those that govern surveillance under Title III. Congress cannot have thought that the government would continue to rely on Title III if the less demanding requirements of FISA were also available. The Court of Review inappropriately disregarded a narrow construction of the Patriot Act's amendments in favor of a broader construction that raises difficult constitutional questions.

III. THE COURT OF REVIEW'S DECISION CONFLICTS WITH THIS COURT'S FOURTH AMENDMENT JURISPRUDENCE

The Court of Review's decision contravenes this Court's Fourth Amendment jurisprudence by holding that the government may constitutionally rely on FISA in investigations whose primary purpose is law enforcement. FISA orders are not warrants within the meaning of the Fourth Amendment, and searches conducted on the basis of FISA orders are presumptively unconstitutional. The Court of Review erred in failing to recognize that FISA orders are not warrants in the constitutional sense, and also erred in finding that FISA surveillance is reasonable. First, FISA searches are not based on criminal probable cause and FISA orders do not meet the Fourth Amendment's particularity requirement. Second, FISA targets do not receive notice—even delayed notice—that their privacy has been compromised. Finally, the applications for FISA searches are not subject to meaningful judicial scrutiny.

Even if the statute's procedures are constitutionally adequate with respect to surveillance whose primary purpose is foreign intelligence, the Court of Review erred in finding those procedures constitutional in investigations whose primary purpose is law enforcement. This Court's jurisprudence is clear: surveillance whose primary purpose is law enforcement must be conducted in conformity with the usual requirements of the Fourth Amendment.

A. The Court of Review's Decision Disregards the Fourth Amendment By Endorsing Warrantless and Unreasonable Searches in Criminal Investigations

Although the Court of Review acknowledged that a FISA order "may not be" a warrant within the meaning of the Fourth Amendment, App. 44a, it did not actually decide the issue. The Court of Review erred in failing to recognize that FISA orders are not warrants within the meaning of the Fourth Amendment, and it erred in upholding the reasonableness of FISA searches conducted in investigations whose primary purpose is law enforcement.

FISA orders are not warrants within the meaning of the Fourth Amendment. In order to be constitutionally adequate, a warrant must (i) be issued by a neutral, disinterested magistrate; (ii) must be based on a demonstration of probable cause to believe that "the evidence sought will aid in a particular apprehension or conviction for a particular offense"; and (iii) must particularly describe the things to be seized as well as the place to be searched. *Dalia v. United States*, 441 U.S. 238, 255 (1979) (internal quotation marks omitted). FISA orders do not satisfy two of these three independent requirements.

FISA orders do not require the government to show probable cause that the target is committing, has committed, or is about to commit a particular criminal offense. *See, e.g., Gerstein v. Pugh*, 420 U.S. 103, 113-14 (1975). Rather, the government need only show probable cause to believe that the surveillance target is a foreign power or agent of a foreign power. *See* 50 U.S.C. § 1805(a)(3)(A). The Court of Review understated the differences between FISA's probable-cause requirement and ordinary criminal probable cause. Yet the government itself has frankly acknowledged the significant distance between the two standards. In response to a Freedom of Information Act request filed by Petitioner ACLU and others on August 21, 2002, the FBI released, among other things, a document from the FBI's National Security Law Unit entitled, "What do I have to do to get a FISA?" It states, in relevant part,

> Probable cause in the FISA context is similar to, but not the same as, probable cause in criminal cases. Where a U.S. person is believed to be an agent of a foreign power, there must be probable cause to believe that he is engaged in certain activities, for or on behalf of a foreign power, which activities involve or may involve a violation of U.S. criminal law. The phrase "involve or may involve" indicates that the showing of [nexus to] criminality does not apply to FISA applications in the same way it does to ordinary criminal cases. *As a result, there is no showing or finding that a crime has been or is being committed, as in the case of a search or seizure for law enforcement purposes.* The activity identified by the government in the FISA context may not yet involve criminality, but if a reasonable person would believe that such activity is likely to lead to illegal activities, that would suffice. *In addition, and with respect to the nexus to criminality required by the*

definitions of "agent of a foreign power," the government need not show probable cause as to each and every element of the crime involved or about to be involved.

"What do I have to do to get a FISA?," at 2 (Document released by FBI in response to August 21 Freedom of Information Act request submitted by ACLU et al.) (emphases added).

With respect to the particularity requirement, *see, e.g., Berger v. New York*, 388 U.S. 41, 55-56 (1967), FISA orders do not require the government to have reason to believe that the surveillance will yield information about a particular offense. Rather, the government need only certify that the information sought is foreign intelligence information. *See* 50 U.S.C. § 1804(a)(7)(A). Nor do FISA orders require that the government show probable cause to believe that the facilities to be surveilled will be used in connection with a particular offense, or even that they will be used to communicate foreign intelligence information. Instead, the government need only show probable cause to believe that the facilities are being used or likely to be used by the surveillance target. *See* 50 U.S.C. § 1805(a)(3)(B).

Indeed, FISA orders also fail to meet the standards set out under Title III, the statute that governs electronic surveillance in criminal investigations. *See* 18 U.S.C. § 2518(3)(a) (requiring government to show probable cause that target is engaged in criminal activity); *id.* § 2518(3)(b) (requiring government to show probable cause that surveillance will yield information about particular offense); *id.* § 2518(3)(d) (requiring government to show probable cause that facilities to be monitored are being used in connection with particular offense); *id.* § 2518(5) (limiting term of surveillance orders to 30 days). Nor do FISA orders meet the standards set out under Rule 41 of the Federal Rules of Criminal Procedure, the rule that governs physical searches in criminal investigations. *See, e.g.,* Fed. R. Crim. P. 41(d)(1) (requiring criminal probable cause); Fed. R. Crim. P. 41(e)(2)(A) (requiring that warrant be executed "within a specified time not longer than 10 days").

Because FISA orders are not warrants within the meaning of the Fourth Amendment, searches conducted under FISA are presumptively unconstitutional. *See, e.g., Payton v. New York*, 445 U.S. 573, 586 (1980); *Chimel v. California*, 395 U.S. 752, 762-763 (1969). This Court has repeatedly emphasized that the failure of government agents to obtain a warrant before conducting a search is not "an inconvenience to be somehow weighed against the claims of [government] efficiency." *United States v. United States District Court ("Keith")*, 407 U.S. 297, 315 (1972) (internal quotation marks omitted). Rather, the warrant clause "is an important working part of our machinery of government, operating as a matter of course to check the well-intentioned but mistakenly over-zealous executive officers who are a party of any system of law enforcement." *Id.* at 316 (internal quotation marks omitted).

B. The Court of Review's Decision Disregards the Fourth Amendment By Allowing the Government to Conduct Searches for Law Enforcement Purposes Without Providing Notice

The Fourth Amendment generally requires that the subject of a search be provided notice that the search has taken place. *See Wilson v. Arkansas*, 514 U.S. 927 (1995) (holding that common-law "knock-and-announce" principle informs Fourth Amendment reasonableness inquiry); *Miller v. United States*, 357 U.S. 301, 313 (1958) ("The requirement of prior notice of authority and purpose before forcing entry into a home is deeply rooted in our heritage and should not be given grudging application."). While notice need not necessarily be contemporaneous with the search, *see United States v. Donovan*, 429 U.S. 413, 429 n.19 (1977) (holding that delayed-notice provisions of Title III supply a constitutionally adequate substitute for contemporaneous notice), this Court has never upheld a statute that, like FISA, authorizes the government to search a person's home or intercept his communications without *ever* informing him that his privacy has been compromised.

The non-provision of notice in FISA investigations is particularly problematic because notice is withheld as a categorical rule, and not upon an individualized showing of necessity. *See Richards v. Wisconsin*, 520 U.S. 385, 393-94 (1997) (rejecting categorical exception to knock-and-announce principle for searches executed in connection with felony drug investigations); *Franks v. Delaware*, 438 U.S. 154, 168-72 (1978) (holding that subject of an allegedly illegal search must be afforded an opportunity to challenge the propriety of the search in a proceeding that is both public and adversarial). Except in the few cases that end in prosecutions,[11] FISA targets never learn that their homes or offices have been searched or that their communications have been intercepted. Most FISA targets have no way of challenging the legality of the surveillance or obtaining any remedy for violations of their constitutional rights.

C. The Court of Review's Decision Disregards the Fourth Amendment By Foreclosing Meaningful Judicial Review of FISA Applications

Even if FISA's substantive requirements are constitutional, and petitioners believe they are not, the low level of scrutiny that the FISA Court applies with respect to those requirements is constitutionally inadequate in the context of investigations whose primary purpose is law enforcement. The government satisfies most of FISA's requirements simply by certifying that the requirements are met. *See* 50 U.S.C. § 1804(a)(7) (enumerating necessary certifications); *see also* App. 34a ("the government's purpose as set forth in a section 1804(a)(7)(B) certification is to be judged by the national security official's articulation and not by a FISA court inquiry into the origins of an investigation nor an examination of the personnel involved"); *United States v. Duggan*, 743 F.2d 59, 77 (2d Cir. 1984) (noting that government's "primary purpose" certification is "subjected to only minimal scrutiny by the courts"); *id.* ("The FISA judge . . . is not to second-guess the executive branch official's certification that the objective of the surveillance is foreign intelligence information.").

While certain (but not all) of these certifications must be accompanied by "a statement of the basis for the certification," 50 U.S.C. § 1804(a)(7)(E), the statute makes clear that the FISA Court is not to scrutinize such statements carefully, but rather is to defer to the government's certification unless it is "clearly erroneous on the basis of the statement made under § 1804(a)(7)(E)," *id.* § 1805(a)(5). As the Court of Review acknowledged, "this standard of review is not, of course, comparable to a probable cause finding by the judge." App. 40a (internal quotation marks omitted).

Judicial oversight under Title III is substantially more robust. To obtain a surveillance order under Title III, the government must provide the court with "a full and complete statement of the facts and circumstances relied upon by the applicant[] to justify his belief that an order should be issued." 18 U.S.C. § 2518(1)(b). The court may "require the applicant to furnish additional testimony or documentary evidence in support of the application." *Id.* § 2518(2). The government cannot meet any of the statute's substantive requirements merely by certifying that it has met them. On the contrary, with respect to most of the statute's substantive requirements, the statute requires the court to find probable cause to believe that they are satisfied. *See id.* § 2518(3).

In fact, FISA so limits the FISA Court's review of government surveillance applications that the FISA Court is severely inhibited in fulfilling its Article III obligation to serve as a meaningful check against unconstitutional actions by the executive branch. By requiring the FISA Court to defer to executive certifications, the statute forecloses the FISA Court from determining whether the substantive requirements have in fact been satisfied. The Constitution prohibits Congress from restricting federal courts' authority in this way. *See United States v. Klein,* 80 U.S. (13 Wall.) 128 (1872).

Ironically, the Court of Review suggested that the lower FISA court, in exercising its limited oversight under the statute, "may well have *exceeded* the constitutional bounds that restrict an Article III court." App. 25a (emphasis added); *see also id.* 47a (characterizing the FISA Court's ruling as "quite intrusive"). The accusation is remarkable because the FISA Court has *never* turned down a surveillance application. Indeed, according to the Attorney General's own reports, between 1996 and 2001 the FISA Court approved without modification 5207 of 5209 applications, or 99.96% of the total.[12] At least with respect to searches whose primary purpose is law enforcement, the review contemplated by the statute is constitutionally inadequate.

D. The Court of Review's Decision Conflicts With This Court's "Special Needs" Jurisprudence

The Court of Review upheld the constitutionality of the Patriot Act's amendments in part by reference to this Court's "special needs" cases. Yet the "special needs" doctrine simply has no application to searches whose primary purpose is law enforcement. On the contrary, those cases stand for the proposition that "[a] search unsupported by probable cause can be constitutional . . . when special needs, *beyond the normal need for law enforcement*, make the warrant and probable-cause requirement impracticable." *Vernonia School District 47J v. Acton*, 515 U.S. 646, 653 (1995) (internal quotation marks omitted and emphasis added).

This Court recently reaffirmed this well-settled rule in *Ferguson v. City of Charleston*, 532 U.S. 67 (2001). That case involved a public hospital's policy of testing pregnant patients for drug use and employing the threat of criminal prosecution as a means of coercing patients into substance- abuse treatment. The Court invalidated the policy. "In other special needs cases," the Court wrote, "we . . . tolerated suspension of the Fourth Amendment's warrant or probable cause requirement in part because there was no law enforcement purpose behind the searches in those cases, and there was little, if any, entanglement with law enforcement." *Id.* at 79 n.15; *see also id.* at 88 (Kennedy, J., concurring) In *Ferguson*, however, "the central and indispensable feature of the policy from its inception was the use of law enforcement." *Id.* at 80.

This Court's decision in *City of Indianapolis v. Edmond*, 531 U.S. 32 (2000), is to the same effect. *Edmond* involved vehicle checkpoints instituted in an effort to interdict illegal drugs. The government asserted that the drug crimes were a "severe and intractable" problem, and the Court agreed that "traffic in illegal narcotics creates social harms of the first magnitude." *Id.* at 42. Notwithstanding the seriousness of the law-enforcement interest with respect to the particular crimes at issue, however, the Court invalidated the checkpoint policy. "[T]he gravity of the threat alone," Justice O'Connor wrote, "cannot be dispositive of questions concerning what means law enforcement officers may employ to pursue a given purpose." *Id.* Where the government's "primary purpose [is] to detect evidence of ordinary criminal wrongdoing," *id.* at 38, the Fourth Amendment forecloses the government from conducting searches except based on probable cause.

The Court of Review acknowledged that the special needs cases apply only where the government's primary purpose is not law enforcement, but it contended that in the present case the relevant purpose is FISA's "programmatic purpose." App. 52a. This Court has made abundantly clear, however, that Fourth Amendment requirements do not turn on a criminal investigation's programmatic or ultimate purpose. In *Ferguson*, for example, the government argued that the ultimate purpose of the hospital's policy was not law enforcement but public health. The Court rejected that argument's relevance, writing:

> The threat of law enforcement may ultimately have been intended as a means to an end, but the direct and primary purpose . . . was to ensure the use of those means. In our opinion, the distinction is critical. Because law enforcement involvement always serves some broader social purpose or objective, under respondents' view, virtually any nonconsensual suspicionless search could be immunized under the special needs doctrine by defining the search solely in terms of its ultimate, rather than immediate, purpose.

532 U.S. at 83-84.13 The Court of Review's decision thus directly conflicts with this Court's special-needs cases.

IV. THE COURT OF REVIEW'S DECISION CONFLICTS WITH THE DECISIONS OF NUMEROUS LOWER FEDERAL COURTS WHICH HAVE HELD THAT ANY FOREIGN- INTELLIGENCE EXCEPTION MUST BE LIMITED TO INVESTIGATIONS WHOSE PRIMARY PURPOSE IS FOREIGN INTELLIGENCE

The Court of Review's ruling rejected the well-settled consensus that any foreign-intelligence exception must be limited to investigations whose primary purpose is foreign intelligence. *See, e.g., United States v. Johnson*, 952 F.2d 565, 572 (1st Cir. 1991), *cert. denied*, 506 U.S. 816 (1992) (stating that FISA may "not be used as an end-run around the Fourth Amendment's prohibition of warrantless searches"); *United States v. Pelton*, 835 F.2d 1067 (4th Cir. 1987), *cert. denied* 486 U.S. 1010 (1988); *United States v. Duggan*, 743 F.2d at 77.

Neither this Court nor any other court until now has ever held that the government can waive the usual Fourth Amendment standards when its purpose is criminal investigation. Indeed, it was accepted even before FISA was enacted—that is, even before there was a statutory basis for the primary-purpose limitation—that any intelligence exception had to be restricted to investigations whose primary purpose was foreign intelligence. Thus in *Keith* the government argued for a domestic-intelligence exception to the warrant requirement by assuring the Court that it would not rely on the exception as a means of evading Fourth Amendment requirements in criminal investigations. *Keith*, 407 U.S. at 318-19. Lower courts that addressed the permissibility of a *foreign*-intelligence exception similarly emphasized that any such exception could not constitutionally be used in law enforcement investigations. For example, the Fourth Circuit in *Truong* recognized a foreign-intelligence exception to the warrant requirement but limited the exception to cases in which "the surveillance is conducted primarily for foreign intelligence reasons." *See Truong*, 629 F.2d at 915 (internal quotation marks omitted). The court emphasized that this requirement stemmed from the Fourth Amendment:

> [O]nce surveillance becomes primarily a criminal investigation, the courts are entirely competent to make the usual probable cause determination, and . . . im-

portantly, individual privacy interests come to the fore and government foreign policy concerns recede when the government is primarily attempting to form the basis for a criminal prosecution.

Id. Other pre-FISA cases affirmed the same principle. *See, e.g., United States v. Butenko*, 494 F.2d 593, 606 (3d Cir. 1974) ("Since the primary purpose of these searches is to secure foreign intelligence information, a judge, when reviewing a particular search must, above all, be assured that this was in fact its primary purpose and that the accumulation of evidence of criminal activity was incidental."), *cert. denied*, 419 U.S. 881 (1974); *United States v. Brown*, 484 F.2d 418, 426 (5th Cir. 1973); *id.* at 427 (Goldberg, J., concurring).

The Court of Review disregarded these cases and disagreed with *Truong's* assumption that "foreign policy concerns recede" when the government's principal intent is to prosecute. App. 46a. It then rejected the primary-purpose limitation entirely, reasoning that the limitation inhibits or even forecloses the government from using criminal prosecution as a tool to protect national security. *See id.* 46a- 50a. In fact, the primary-purpose limitation has *never* prevented the government from using criminal prosecution as a tool to protect national security. Its only effect is to dictate which standards the government must meet in order to engage in surveillance whose profound intrusiveness even the government does not dispute. *See Berger v. New York*, 388 U.S. at 63 ("It is not asking too much that officers be required to comply with the basic command of the Fourth Amendment before the innermost secrets of one's home or office are invaded"). The government is always entitled to engage in such surveillance if it can meet the requirements of the Fourth Amendment, and the primary-purpose limitation does not compromise this authority. The Court of Review erred in discounting without discussion the other side of the *Truong* court's reasoning—the principle that privacy concerns come to the fore when the government's intent is to prosecute. *See, e.g., Weeks v. United States*, 232 U.S. 383, 393 (1914) (stating that exclusionary rule is necessary because "[i]f letters and documents can thus be seized and held and used in evidence against a citizen accused of an offense, the protection of the Fourth Amendment ... is of no value").

In summary, the Court of Review's conclusion that FISA searches and surveillance are reasonable when used primarily for criminal investigation finds no support in this Court's or appellate court rulings.

V. THE COURT OF REVIEW'S DECISION JEOPARDIZES FIRST AMENDMENT FREEDOMS BY ELIMINATING FOURTH AMENDMENT SAFEGUARDS

Traditionally, the warrant and probable cause requirements have served as important safeguards of First Amendment interests by preventing the government from intruding into an individual's protected sphere merely because of that individual's exercise of First Amendment rights. Expanding the circumstances in which the government may conduct searches without conforming to those requirements presents the danger that the government's surveillance power will chill activity that is protected under the First Amendment.

This Court has recognized the importance of the Fourth Amendment in protecting First Amendment rights:

> National security cases . . . often reflect a convergence of First and Fourth Amendment values not present in cases of 'ordinary' crime. . . . History abundantly documents the tendency of Government—however benevolent and benign its motives—to view with suspicion those who most fervently dispute its policies. Fourth Amendment protections become the more necessary when the targets of official surveillance may be those suspected of unorthodoxy in their political beliefs.

Keith, 407 U.S. at 313-14; *see also id.* at 314 ("The price of lawful public dissent must not be a dread of subjection to an unchecked surveillance power. Nor must the fear of unauthorized official eavesdropping deter vigorous citizen dissent and discussion of government action in private conversation. For private dissent, no less than open public discourse, is essential to our free society."). The D.C. Circuit made the same point in *Zweibon v. Mitchell*, 516 F.2d. 594 (D.C. Cir. 1975), a case that rejected the constitutionality of a warrantless wiretap of the Jewish Defense League:

> Prior judicial review is important not only to protect the privacy interests of those whose conversations the government seeks to overhear, but also to protect free and robust exercise of the First Amendment rights of speech and association by those who might otherwise be chilled by the fear of unsupervised and unlimited Executive power to institute electronic surveillances.

Id. at 633.

The Court of Review's decision endorses a dramatic expansion of the foreign-intelligence exception, and opens the door to surveillance abuses that seriously threatened our democracy in the past. To protect robust and uninhibited debate by petitioners and all Americans, this Court should accept review and strictly limit surveillance that undermines First Amendment freedoms.

A. CONCLUSION

For the reasons stated above, petitioners urge this Court to grant review in this case.

Respectfully submitted.

>ANN BEESON
>Counsel of Record
>JAMEEL JAFFER
>STEVEN R. SHAPIRO
>*American Civil Liberties Union*
>   *Foundation*
>
>JOSHUA L. DRATEL
>JOHN D. CLINE
>TOM GOLDSTEIN
>*National Association of*
>   *Criminal Defense Lawyers*

February 2003

Appendix C
Excerpts from the Foreign Intelligence Surveillance Act

§ 1801. Definitions

As used in this subchapter:

(a) "Foreign power" means—

(1) a foreign government or any component thereof, whether or not recognized by the United States;

(2) a faction of a foreign nation or nations, not substantially composed of United States persons;

(3) an entity that is openly acknowledged by a foreign government or governments to be directed and controlled by such foreign government or governments;

(4) a group engaged in international terrorism or activities in preparation therefor;

(5) a foreign-based political organization, not substantially composed of United States persons; or

(6) an entity that is directed and controlled by a foreign government or governments.

(b) "Agent of a foreign power" means—

(1) any person other than a United States person, who—

(A) acts in the United States as an officer or employee of a foreign power, or as a member of a foreign power as defined in subsection (a)(4) of this section;

(B) acts for or on behalf of a foreign power which engages in clandestine intelligence activities in the United States contrary to the interests of the United States, when the circumstances of such person's presence in the United States indicate that such person may engage in such activities in the United States, or when such person knowingly aids or abets any person in the conduct of such activities or knowingly conspires with any person to engage in such activities; or

(2) any person who—

(A) knowingly engages in clandestine intelligence gathering activities for or on behalf of a foreign power, which activities involve or may involve a violation of the criminal statutes of the United States;

(B) pursuant to the direction of an intelligence service or network of a foreign power, knowingly engages in any other clandestine intelligence activities for or on behalf of such foreign power, which activities involve or are about to involve a violation of the criminal statutes of the United States;

(C) knowingly engages in sabotage or international terrorism, or activities that are in preparation therefor, or on behalf of a foreign power;

(D) knowingly enters the United States under a false or fraudulent identity for or on behalf of a foreign power or, while in the United States, knowingly assumes a false or fraudulent identity for or on behalf of a foreign power; or

(E) knowingly aids or abets any person in the conduct of activities described in subparagraph (A), (B), or (C) or knowingly conspires with any person to engage in activities described in subparagraph (A), (B), or (C).

(c) "International terrorism" means activities that—

(1) involve violent acts or acts dangerous to human life that are a violation of the criminal laws of the United States or of any State, or that would be a criminal violation if committed within the jurisdiction of the United States or any State;

(2) appear to be intended—

(A) to intimidate or coerce a civilian population;

(B) to influence the policy of a government by intimidation or coercion; or

(C) to affect the conduct of a government by assassination or kidnapping; and

(3) occur totally outside the United States, or transcend national boundaries in terms of the means by which they are accomplished, the persons they appear intended to coerce or intimidate, or the locale in which their perpetrators operate or seek asylum.

(d) "Sabotage" means activities that involve a violation of chapter 105 of Title 18, or that would involve such a violation if committed against the United States.

(e) "Foreign intelligence information" means—

(1) information that relates to, and if concerning a United States person is necessary to, the ability of the United States to protect against—

(A) actual or potential attack or other grave hostile acts of a foreign power or an agent of a foreign power;

(B) sabotage or international terrorism by a foreign power or an agent of a foreign power; or

(C) clandestine intelligence activities by an intelligence service or network of a foreign power or by an agent of a foreign power; or

(2) information with respect to a foreign power or foreign territory that relates to, and if concerning a United States person is necessary to—

(A) the national defense or the security of the United States; or

(B) the conduct of the foreign affairs of the United States.

. . .

(h) "Minimization procedures", with respect to electronic surveillance, means—

(1) specific procedures, which shall be adopted by the Attorney General, that are reasonably designed in light of the purpose and technique of the particular surveillance, to minimize the acquisition and retention, and prohibit the dissemination, of nonpublicly available information concerning unconsenting United States persons consistent with the need of the United States to obtain, produce, and disseminate foreign intelligence information;

(2) procedures that require that nonpublicly available information, which is not foreign intelligence information, as defined in subsection (e)(1) of this section, shall not be disseminated in a manner that identifies any United States person, without such person's consent, unless such person's identity is necessary to understand foreign intelligence information or assess its importance;

(3) notwithstanding paragraphs (1) and (2), procedures that allow for the retention and dissemination of information that is evidence of a crime which has been, is being, or is about to be committed and that is to be retained or disseminated for law enforcement purposes; and

(4) notwithstanding paragraphs (1), (2), and (3), with respect to any electronic surveillance approved pursuant to section 1802(a) of this title, procedures that require that no contents of any communication to which a United States person is a party shall be disclosed, disseminated, or used for any purpose or retained for longer than 72 hours unless a court order under section 1805 of this title is obtained or unless the Attorney General determines that the information indicates a threat of death or serious bodily harm to any person.

(i) "United States person" means a citizen of the United States, an alien lawfully admitted for permanent residence (as defined in section 1101(a)(20) of Title 8), an unincorporated association a substantial number of members of which are citizens of the United

States or aliens lawfully admitted for permanent residence, or a corporation which is incorporated in the United States, but does not include a corporation or an association which is a foreign power, as defined in subsection (a)(1), (2), or (3) of this section.

§ 1804. Applications for court orders

(a) Submission by Federal officer; approval of Attorney General; contents

Each application for an order approving electronic surveillance under this subchapter shall be made by a Federal officer in writing upon oath or affirmation to a judge having jurisdiction under section 1803 of this title. Each application shall require the approval of the Attorney General based upon his finding that it satisfies the criteria and requirements of such application as set forth in this subchapter. It shall include—

(1) the identity of the Federal officer making the application;

(2) the authority conferred on the Attorney General by the President of the United States and the approval of the Attorney General to make the application;

(3) the identity, if known, or a description of the target of the electronic surveillance;

(4) a statement of the facts and circumstances relied upon by the applicant to justify his belief that—

(A) the target of the electronic surveillance is a foreign power or an agent of a foreign power; and

(B) each of the facilities or places at which the electronic surveillance is directed is being used, or is about to be used, by a foreign power or an agent of a foreign power;

(5) a statement of the proposed minimization procedures;

(6) a detailed description of the nature of the information sought and the type of communications or activities to be subjected to the surveillance;

(7) a certification or certifications by the Assistant to the President for National Security Affairs or an executive branch official or officials designated by the President from among those executive officers employed in the area of national security or defense and appointed by the President with the advice and consent of the Senate—

(A) that the certifying official deems the information sought to be foreign intelligence information;

(B) that a significant purpose of the surveillance is to obtain foreign intelligence information;

(C) that such information cannot reasonably be obtained by normal investigative techniques;

(D) that designates the type of foreign intelligence information being sought according to the categories described in section 1801(e) of this title; and

(E) including a statement of the basis for the certification that—

(i) the information sought is the type of foreign intelligence information designated; and

(ii) such information cannot reasonably be obtained by normal investigative techniques;

(8) a statement of the means by which the surveillance will be effected and a statement whether physical entry is required to effect the surveillance;

(9) a statement of the facts concerning all previous applications that have been made to any judge under this subchapter involving any of the persons, facilities, or places specified in the application, and the action taken on each previous application;

(10) a statement of the period of time for which the electronic surveillance is required to be maintained, and if the nature of the intelligence gathering is such that the approval of the use of electronic surveillance under this subchapter should not automatically terminate when the described type of information has first been obtained, a description of facts supporting the belief that additional information of the same type will be obtained thereafter; and

(11) whenever more than one electronic, mechanical or other surveillance device is to be used with respect to a particular proposed electronic surveillance, the coverage of the devices involved and what minimization procedures apply to information acquired by each device.

§ 1805. Issuance of order

(a) Necessary findings

Upon an application made pursuant to section 1804 of this title, the judge shall enter an ex parte order as requested or as modified approving the electronic surveillance if he finds that—

(1) the President has authorized the Attorney General to approve applications for electronic surveillance for foreign intelligence information;

(2) the application has been made by a Federal officer and approved by the Attorney General;

(3) on the basis of the facts submitted by the applicant there is probable cause to believe that—

(A) the target of the electronic surveillance is a foreign power or an agent of a foreign power: *Provided,* That no United States person may be considered a foreign power or an agent of a foreign power solely upon the basis of activities protected by the first amendment to the Constitution of the United States; and

(B) each of the facilities or places at which the electronic surveillance is directed is being used, or is about to be used, by a foreign power or an agent of a foreign power;

(4) the proposed minimization procedures meet the definition of minimization procedures under section 1801(h) of this title; and

(5) the application which has been filed contains all statements and certifications required by section 1804 of this title and, if the target is a United States person, the certification or certifications are not clearly erroneous on the basis of the statement made under section 1804(a)(7)(E) of this title and any other information furnished under section 1804(d) of this title.

(b) Probable cause

In determining whether or not probable cause exists for purposes of an order under subsection (a)(3), a judge may consider past activities of the target, as well as facts and circumstances relating to current or future activities of the target.

§ 1806. Use of information

(c) Notification by United States

Whenever the Government intends to enter into evidence or otherwise use or disclose in any trial, hearing, or other proceeding in or before any court, department, officer, agency, regulatory body, or other authority of the United States, against an aggrieved person, any information obtained or derived from an electronic surveillance of that aggrieved person pursuant to the authority of this subchapter, the Government shall, prior to the trial, hearing, or other proceeding or at a reasonable time prior to an effort to so disclose or so use that information or submit it in evidence, notify the aggrieved person and the court or other authority in which the information is to be disclosed or used that the Government intends to so disclose or so use such information.

· · ·

(e) Motion to suppress

Any person against whom evidence obtained or derived from an electronic surveillance to which he is an aggrieved person is to be, or has been, introduced or otherwise used or disclosed in any trial, hearing, or other proceeding in or before any court, department, officer, agency, regulatory body, or other authority of the United States, a State, or a political subdivision thereof, may move to suppress the evidence obtained or derived from such electronic surveillance on the grounds that—

(1) the information was unlawfully acquired; or

(2) the surveillance was not made in conformity with an order of authorization or approval.

Such a motion shall be made before the trial, hearing, or other proceeding unless there was no opportunity to make such a motion or the person was not aware of the grounds of the motion.

(f) In camera and ex parte review by district court

Whenever a court or other authority is notified pursuant to subsection (c) or (d) of this section, or whenever a motion is made pursuant to subsection (e) of this section, or whenever any motion or request is made by an aggrieved person pursuant to any other statute or rule of the United States or any State before any court or other authority of the United States or any State to discover or obtain applications or orders or other materials relating to electronic surveillance or to discover, obtain, or suppress evidence or information obtained or derived from electronic surveillance under this chapter, the United States district court or, where the motion is made before another authority, the United States district court in the same district as the authority, shall, notwithstanding any other law, if the Attorney General files an affidavit under oath that disclosure or an adversary hearing would harm the national security of the United States, review in camera and ex parte the application, order, and such other materials relating to the surveillance as may be necessary to determine whether the surveillance of the aggrieved person was lawfully authorized and conducted. In making this determination, the court may disclose to the aggrieved person, under appropriate security procedures and protective orders, portions of the application, order, or other materials relating to the surveillance only where such disclosure is necessary to make an accurate determination of the legality of the surveillance.

(g) Suppression of evidence; denial of motion

If the United States district court pursuant to subsection (f) of this section determines that the surveillance was not lawfully authorized or conducted, it shall, in accordance with the requirements of law, suppress the evidence which was unlawfully obtained or derived from electronic surveillance of the aggrieved person or otherwise grant the motion of the aggrieved person. If the court determines that the surveillance was lawfully authorized and conducted, it shall deny the motion of the aggrieved person except to the extent that due process requires discovery or disclosure.

§ 1823. Application for order

(a) Submission by Federal officer; approval of Attorney General; contents

Each application for an order approving a physical search under this subchapter shall be made by a Federal officer in writing upon oath or affirmation to a judge of the Foreign Intelligence Surveillance Court. Each application shall require the approval of the Attorney General based upon the Attorney General's finding that it satisfies the criteria and requirements for such application as set forth in this subchapter. Each application shall include—

(1) the identity of the Federal officer making the application;

(2) the authority conferred on the Attorney General by the President and the approval of the Attorney General to make the application;

(3) the identity, if known, or a description of the target of the search, and a detailed description of the premises or property to be searched and of the information, material, or property to be seized, reproduced, or altered;

(4) a statement of the facts and circumstances relied upon by the applicant to justify the applicant's belief that—

(A) the target of the physical search is a foreign power or an agent of a foreign power;

(B) the premises or property to be searched contains foreign intelligence information; and

(C) the premises or property to be searched is owned, used, possessed by, or is in transit to or from a foreign power or an agent of a foreign power;

(5) a statement of the proposed minimization procedures;

(6) a statement of the nature of the foreign intelligence sought and the manner in which the physical search is to be conducted;

(7) a certification or certifications by the Assistant to the President for National Security Affairs or an executive branch official or officials designated by the President from among those executive branch officers employed in the area of national security or defense and appointed by the President, by and with the advice and consent of the Senate—

(A) that the certifying official deems the information sought to be foreign intelligence information;

(B) that a significant purpose of the search is to obtain foreign intelligence information;

(C) that such information cannot reasonably be obtained by normal investigative techniques;

(D) that designates the type of foreign intelligence information being sought according to the categories described in section 1801(e) of this title; and

(E) includes a statement explaining the basis for the certifications required by subparagraphs (C) and (D);

(8) where the physical search involves a search of the residence of a United States person, the Attorney General shall state what investigative techniques have previously been utilized to obtain the foreign intelligence information concerned and the degree to which these techniques resulted in acquiring such information; and

(9) a statement of the facts concerning all previous applications that have been made to any judge under this subchapter involving any of the persons, premises, or property specified in the application, and the action taken on each previous application.

§ 1824. Issuance of order

(a) Necessary findings

Upon an application made pursuant to section 1823 of this title, the judge shall enter an ex parte order as requested or as modified approving the physical search if the judge finds that—

(1) the President has authorized the Attorney General to approve applications for physical searches for foreign intelligence purposes;

(2) the application has been made by a Federal officer and approved by the Attorney General;

(3) on the basis of the facts submitted by the applicant there is probable cause to believe that—

(A) the target of the physical search is a foreign power or an agent of a foreign power, except that no United States person may be considered an agent of a foreign power solely upon the basis of activities protected by the first amendment to the Constitution of the United States; and

(B) the premises or property to be searched is owned, used, possessed by, or is in transit to or from an agent of a foreign power or a foreign power;

(4) the proposed minimization procedures meet the definition of minimization contained in this subchapter; and

(5) the application which has been filed contains all statements and certifications required by section 1823 of this title, and, if the target is a United States person, the certification or certifications are not clearly erroneous on the basis of the statement made under section 1823(a)(7)(E) of this title and any other information furnished under section 1823(c) of this title.

(b) Probable cause

In determining whether or not probable cause exists for purposes of an order under subsection (a)(3), a judge may consider past activities of the target, as well as facts and circumstances relating to current or future activities of the target.

(c) Specifications and directions of orders

An order approving a physical search under this section shall—

(1) specify—

(A) the identity, if known, or a description of the target of the physical search;

(B) the nature and location of each of the premises or property to be searched;

(C) the type of information, material, or property to be seized, altered, or reproduced;

(D) a statement of the manner in which the physical search is to be conducted and, whenever more than one physical search is authorized under the order, the authorized scope of each search and what minimization procedures shall apply to the information acquired by each search; and

(E) the period of time during which physical searches are approved; and

(2) direct—

(A) that the minimization procedures be followed;

(B) that, upon the request of the applicant, a specified landlord, custodian, or other specified person furnish the applicant forthwith all information, facilities, or assistance necessary to accomplish the physical search in such a manner as will protect its secrecy and produce a minimum of interference with the services that such landlord, custodian, or other person is providing the target of the physical search;

(C) that such landlord, custodian, or other person maintain under security procedures approved by the Attorney General and the Director of Central Intelligence any records concerning the search or the aid furnished that such person wishes to retain;

(D) that the applicant compensate, at the prevailing rate, such landlord, custodian, or other person for furnishing such aid; and

(E) that the Federal officer conducting the physical search promptly report to the court the circumstances and results of the physical search.

(d) Duration of order; extensions; review of circumstances under which information was acquired, retained, or disseminated

(1) An order issued under this section may approve a physical search for the period necessary to achieve its purpose, or for 90 days, whichever is less, except that (A) an order under this section shall approve a physical search targeted against a foreign power, as defined in paragraph (1), (2), or (3) of section 1801(a) of this title, for the period specified in the application or for one year, whichever is less, and (B) an order under this section for a physical search targeted against an agent of a foreign power as defined in section 1801(b)(1)(A) of this title may be for the period specified in the application or for 120 days, whichever is less.

(2) Extensions of an order issued under this subchapter may be granted on the same basis as the original order upon an application for an extension and new findings made in the same manner as required for the original order, except that an extension of an order under this chapter for a physical search targeted against a foreign power, as defined in section 1801(a)(5) or (6) of this title, or against a foreign power, as defined in section 1801(a)(4) of this title, that is not a United States person, or against an agent of a foreign power as defined in section 1801(b)(1)(A) of this title, may be for a period not to exceed one year if the judge finds probable cause to believe that no property of any individual United States person will be acquired during the period.

(3) At or before the end of the period of time for which a physical search is approved by an order or an extension, or at any time after a physical search is carried out, the judge may assess compliance with the minimization procedures by reviewing the circumstances under which information concerning United States persons was acquired, retained, or disseminated.

§ 1825. Use of information

(d) Notification by United States

Whenever the United States intends to enter into evidence or otherwise use or disclose in any trial, hearing, or other proceeding in or before any court, department, officer, agency, regulatory body, or other authority of the United States, against an aggrieved person, any information obtained or derived from a physical search pursuant to the authority of this subchapter, the United States shall, prior to the trial, hearing, or the other proceeding or at a reasonable time prior to an effort to so disclose or so use that information or submit it in evidence, notify the aggrieved person and the court or other authority in which the information is to be disclosed or used that the United States intends to so disclose or so use such information.

• • •

(f) Motion to suppress

(1) Any person against whom evidence obtained or derived from a physical search to which he is an aggrieved person is to be, or has been, introduced or otherwise used or disclosed in any trial, hearing, or other proceeding in or before any court, department, officer, agency, regulatory body, or other authority of the United States, a State, or a political subdivision thereof, may move to suppress the evidence obtained or derived from such search on the grounds that—

(A) the information was unlawfully acquired; or

(B) the physical search was not made in conformity with an order of authorization or approval.

(2) Such a motion shall be made before the trial, hearing, or other proceeding unless there was no opportunity to make such a motion or the person was not aware of the grounds of the motion.

(g) In camera and ex parte review by district court

Whenever a court or other authority is notified pursuant to subsection (d) or (e) of this section, or whenever a motion is made pursuant to subsection (f) of this section, or whenever any motion or request is made by an aggrieved person pursuant to any other statute or rule of the United States or any State before any court or other authority of the United States or any State to discover or obtain applications or orders or other materials relating to a physical search authorized by this subchapter or to discover, obtain, or suppress evidence or information obtained or derived from a physical search authorized by this subchapter, the United States district court or, where the motion is made before another authority, the United States district court in the same district as the authority shall, notwithstanding any other provision of law, if the Attorney General files an affidavit under oath that disclosure or any adversary hearing would harm the national security of the United States, review in camera and ex parte the application, order, and such other materials relating to the physical search as may be necessary to determine whether the physical search of the aggrieved person was lawfully authorized and conducted. In making this determination, the court may disclose to the aggrieved person, under appropriate security procedures and protective orders, portions of the application, order, or other materials relating to the physical search, or may require the Attorney General to provide to the aggrieved person a summary of such materials, only where such disclosure is necessary to make an accurate determination of the legality of the physical search.

(h) Suppression of evidence; denial of motion

If the United States district court pursuant to subsection (g) of this section determines that the physical search was not lawfully authorized or conducted, it shall, in accordance with the requirements of law, suppress the evidence which was unlawfully obtained or derived from the physical search of the aggrieved person or otherwise grant the motion of the aggrieved person. If the court determines that the physical search was lawfully authorized or conducted, it shall deny the motion of the aggrieved person except to the extent that due process requires discovery or disclosure.

ENDNOTES

[1] Section 1803(b) provides, in relevant part, "If [the Court of Review] determines that the application was properly denied, the court shall immediately provide for the record a written statement of each reason for its decision and, on petition of the United States for a writ of *certiorari*, the record shall be transmitted under seal to the Supreme Court, which shall have jurisdiction to review such decision."

[2] In its current form, FISA comprises four Subchapters. The first and second address electronic surveillance and physical searches, respectively. The third addresses "pen register" and "trap and trace" devices. The fourth addresses government access to certain business records and other tangible things. Only the first and second of FISA's Subchapters are at issue in this litigation.

[3] "United States person" is defined in 50 U.S.C. § 1801(i). *See* App. 91a.

[4] For example, the government came forward in September 2000 "to confess error in some 75 applications related to major terrorist attacks directed [against] the United States." App. 69a. In November 2000, after "a special meeting to consider the troubling number of inaccurate FBI affidavits in so many FISA applications," the FISA Court barred one FBI agent from appearing before it as a FISA affiant. *Id*. In March 2001, the government reported further abuses in a different series of applications. "In virtually every instance," the Court noted, "the government's misstatements and omissions in FISA applications and violations of the Court's orders involved information sharing and unauthorized disseminations to criminal investigators and prosecutors." *Id*. 70a.

[5] The Attorney General did not appeal the FISA Court May 17 order directly, presumably because that decision did not pertain to a specific surveillance order. Instead, the Attorney General submitted a surveillance application on July 19, proposing the 2002 Procedures without modification. The FISA judge hearing that application granted the order but modified the proposed procedures in accordance with the FISA Court's May 17 order. The Attorney General then appealed the July 19 order, along with an October 17 order granting, with modifications, the government's application for renewal of the July 19 surveillance order. *See* App. 22a.

[6] The Court recognized at the outset that "some of the very senators who fashioned the Patriot Act amendments" had expressed concern that the "significant purpose" amendment would give rise to serious constitutional questions. App. 35a. For example, Senator Leahy stated that "[n]o matter what statutory change is made . . . the court may impose a constitutional requirement of ,primary purpose' based on the appellate court decisions upholding FISA against constitutional challenges over the past 20 years." *Id*. (internal quotation marks omitted).

[7] For example, the statute was amended in 1995 to allow the government to obtain FISA orders for physical searches as well as electronic surveillance. *See* 50 U.S.C. §§ 1821-29. The statute was amended again in 1998 to allow the government to install "pen registers" and "trap and trace" devices, *see id*. §§ 1841-46, and to allow the government access to certain business records of private individuals and organizations, *see id*. §§ 1861-62. The statute was amended yet again in 1999 to expand the definition of "agent of a foreign power." *See id*. § 1801(b)(2)(D). The Patriot Act made numerous amendments to FISA in addition to those at issue in this case.

[8] A recent proposal would broaden this class even further by removing the "foreign power or agent of a foreign power" requirement in investigations not involving United States persons. *See* s. 113, 108th Cong. (2002).

[9] The focus in this discussion is on the differences between FISA's electronic surveillance provisions and those of Title III. However, there are similar differences between FISA's physical search provisions, *see* 50 U.S.C. §§ 1821-29, and those that govern physical searches conducted in the course of ordinary law enforcement investigations, *see* Fed. R. Crim. P. 41.

[10] Section 201 of the Patriot Act added "any criminal violation of section 229 [of title 18] (relating to chemical weapons); or sections 2332, 2332a, 2332b, 2332d, 2339A, or 2339B of this title (relating to terrorism)." 115 Stat. 272, § 201.

[11] Not even FISA targets who are prosecuted are afforded a meaningful opportunity to challenge the surveillance's legality. When a defendant contests the legality of FISA surveillance, the Attorney General may file an affidavit in the district court stating that "disclosure or an adversary hearing would harm the national security of the United States." 50 U.S.C. § 1806(f). The district court must then review the surveillance application and order *ex parte* and *in camera*, unless disclosure is "necessary to make an accurate determination of the legality of the surveillance." *Id.* In practice, the Attorney General files such affidavits as a matter of course. *See United States v. Nicholson*, 955 F.Supp. 588, 592 (E.D.Va. 1997) ("[T]his Court knows of no instance in which a court has required an adversary hearing or disclosure in determining the legality of a FISA surveillance. To the contrary, every court examining FISA-obtained evidence has conducted its review *in camera* and *ex parte*.").

[12] The Attorney General's annual reports to Congress regarding the Foreign Intelligence Surveillance Act are available at < http://www.usdoj.gov/04foia/readingrooms/oipr_records.htm>.

[13] The Court of Review, App. 51a, also relied on the following dictum from *Edmond*: "The Fourth Amendment would almost certainly permit an appropriately tailored road block set up to thwart an imminent terrorist attack of to catch a dangerous criminal who is likely to flee by way of a particular route." *City of Indianapolis v. Edmond*, 531 U.S. at 44. This Court specifically recognized, however, that such exigencies are "far removed" from ordinary criminal investigation. App. 51a. Here, the government makes no showing of exigency. Indeed, FISA surveillance intended to bring a criminal prosecution would make no sense in the face of an imminent terrorist threat.

COVER LETTERS AND WRITTEN RESPONSES TO QUESTIONS REGARDING THE PATRIOT ACT AS SUBMITTED BY THE DEPARTMENT OF JUSTICE TO THE HOUSE JUDICIARY COMMITTEE CHAIRMAN

May 13, 2003

U.S. Department of Justice

Office of Legislative Affairs

Office of the Assistant Attorney General   *Washington, D.C. 20530*

May 13, 2003

The Honorable F. James Sensenbrenner, Jr.
Chairman
Committee on the Judiciary
U.S. House of Representatives
Washington, D.C. 20515

Dear Mr. Chairman:

Thank you for your letter of April 1, 2003, co-signed by Ranking Member Conyers, which posed several questions to the Department on USA PATRIOT Act implementation and related matters. An identical response will be sent to Congressman Conyers.

Pursuant to your request, on April 9, 2003, we notified the Committee that we had forwarded questions number 18, 19, 22, 23, 24, 31, 32 and 26, relating to the authority or operations of the Immigration and Naturalization Service, to the Department of Homeland Security for response. With this letter, we are pleased to transmit responses to the remaining questions.

While we have made every effort to answer each question thoroughly and in an unclassified format, four of the questions will require the submission of classified information. The answer to a portion of question 16(a), and questions 30 and 37 are classified and will be delivered to the Committee under separate cover. In accordance with the direction provided in the Committee's letter of April 1, 2003, and the longstanding Executive branch practices on the sharing of operational intelligence information with the Congress, the classified answers to question 1(c), and a further portion of question 16(a), will be delivered to the House Permanent Select Committee on Intelligence.

We appreciate the opportunity to provide the Committee with information on the Department's efforts in the war on terrorism. If we may be of further assistance on this, or any other matter, please do not hesitate to contact this office.

Sincerely,

Jamie E Brown

Jamie E. Brown
Acting Assistant Attorney General

Enclosures

U.S. Department of Justice

Office of Legislative Affairs

Office of the Assistant Attorney General   *Washington, D.C. 20530*

May 13, 2003

The Honorable John Conyers, Jr.
Ranking Minority Member
Committee on the Judiciary
U.S. House of Representatives
Washington, D.C. 20515

Dear Congressman Conyers:

    Thank you for your letter of April 1, 2003, co-signed by Chairman Sensenbrenner, which posed several questions to the Department on USA PATRIOT Act implementation and related matters. An identical response will be sent to Chairman Sensenbrenner.

    Pursuant to your request, on April 9, 2003, we notified the Committee that we had forwarded questions number 18, 19, 22, 23, 24, 31, 32 and 26, relating to the authority or operations of the Immigration and Naturalization Service, to the Department of Homeland Security for response. With this letter, we are pleased to transmit responses to the remaining questions.

    While we have made every effort to answer each question thoroughly and in an unclassified format, four of the questions will require the submission of classified information. The answer to a portion of question 16(a), and questions 30 and 37 are classified and will be delivered to the Committee under separate cover. In accordance with the direction provided in the Committee's letter of April 1, 2003, and the longstanding Executive branch practices on the sharing of operational intelligence information with the Congress, the classified answers to question 1(c), and a further portion of question 16(a), will be delivered to the House Permanent Select Committee on Intelligence.

    We appreciate the opportunity to provide the Committee with information on the Department's efforts in the war on terrorism. If we may be of further assistance on this, or any other matter, please do not hesitate to contact this office.

Sincerely,

Jamie E Brown

Jamie E. Brown
Acting Assistant Attorney General

Enclosures

USA PATRIOT Act

1. Section 215 of the Act amended 50 U.S.C. § 1861 to allow the FBI Director or his designee (who must hold the rank of Assistant Special Agent in Charge or higher) to apply for an order from the Foreign Intelligence Surveillance Court for "the production of tangible things (including books, records, papers, documents, and other items) for an investigation to protect against international terrorism or clandestine intelligence activities. . . ." Such an investigation may only be conducted under guidelines approved by the Attorney General under Executive Order 12333 (or a successor order). 50 U.S.C. § 1861(a)(2)(A).

   A. What guidelines has the Attorney General approved under Executive Order 12333 or a successor order for the conduct of such investigations?

   Answer: These investigations are conducted under the Attorney General Guidelines for FBI Foreign Intelligence Collection and Foreign Counterintelligence Investigations, which were approved pursuant to Executive Order 12333.

   B. Before such an order can be sought, do the guidelines require that the FBI have already established probable cause that a person under investigation is an agent of a foreign power? What is the Department's definition of "probable cause" and how has it changed since September 11, 2001?

   Answer: The Department does not have the authority to define "probable cause"; it is a statutory and constitutional term. Except where a statute has been amended, the term has not changed meaning since September 11, 2001.

   Section 215 of the USA PATRIOT Act (Act) added the current version of 50 U.S.C. § 1861 to the Foreign Intelligence Surveillance Act (FISA). In order to obtain business records, section 1861(b)(2) requires the Department to demonstrate to the Foreign Intelligence Surveillance Court (FISC) that the records are sought "for an investigation to obtain foreign intelligence information not concerning a United States person or to protect against international terrorism or clandestine intelligence activities, provided that such investigation of a United States person is not conducted solely upon the basis of activities protected by the first amendment to the Constitution." The Guidelines do not impose a probable cause requirement over and above the requirements Congress set forth in the statute.

   Congress did not authorize a new innovation with section 215. Grand juries investigating ordinary crimes traditionally have had the power to issue subpoenas to all manner of businesses, including libraries and bookstores. For example, in the so-called Unabomber investigation of the mid-1990s, federal grand juries subpoenaed library records at Brigham Young University, the University of Utah, Northwestern University, the University of California, the University of Montana, and the Missoula County Library in order to determine who had checked out the four books cited in the "Unabomber Manifesto." Section 215 simply provided that this investigative tool is also available for foreign intelligence and terrorism investigations.

Importantly, section 215 of the USA PATRIOT Act imposes more restrictions on its use than a federal grand jury subpoena for the same records. First, a court must explicitly authorize the use of section 215 to obtain business records. By contrast, a grand jury subpoena is issued on the authority of the district court and clerk of the court but without any prior judicial review or approval. Second, section 215 contains explicit safeguards for activities protected by the First Amendment, unlike federal grand jury subpoenas. And, third, as noted above, section 215 requires, for an investigation relating to a U.S. person, that the information be sought in an investigation to protect against international terrorism or clandestine intelligence activities. By contrast, a federal grand jury can obtain business records whenever such records are relevant to a grand jury investigation of any federal crime. *See generally United States v. R. Enterprises., Inc.*, 498 U.S. 492 (1991).

C. Please produce all guidelines approved under Executive Order 12333 or a successor order for the conduct of such investigations.

Answer: These guidelines are classified at the Secret level. Under section 3.3 of Executive Order 12333, the Guidelines "shall be made available to the congressional intelligence committees." As required, we have provided the House Permanent Select Committee on Intelligence (HPSCI) with the Guidelines, and, pursuant to the Committee's April 1, 2003, letter, we will provide HPSCI with another copy for the review of the House Committee on the Judiciary.

2. Such investigations also may not be conducted of a United States person solely on the basis of activities protected by the First Amendment to the Constitution of the United States. 50 U.S.C. § 1861(a)(2)(B). Other authorities under the Foreign Intelligence Surveillance Act ("FISA") are also subject to the limitation that an investigation of a United States person in which those authorities are used may not be conducted solely on the basis of activities protected by the First Amendment to the U.S. Constitution. See, e.g., 50 U.S.C. § 1842 (regarding pen register and trap and trace orders under FISA).

A. In seeking such orders, does the government make an explicit certification that an investigation of a United States person is not being conducted solely on the basis of activities protected by the First Amendment to the Constitution of the United States?

> **Answer:** 50 U.S.C. § 1842(c)(2) requires that an application for a pen register or trap and trace device include a certification "that the information likely to be obtained is foreign intelligence information not concerning a United States person or is relevant to an ongoing investigation to protect against international terrorism or clandestine intelligence activities, provided that such investigation of a United States person is not conducted solely upon the basis of activities protected by the First Amendment to the Constitution." Accordingly, applications concerning United States persons made under this section include a certification by a Department attorney that the investigation of a United States person is not being conducted solely upon the basis of activities protected by the First Amendment.
>
> 50 U.S.C. § 1861(b)(2) requires that each application for access to certain business records "shall specify that the records concerned are sought for an authorized investigation in accordance with subsection (a)(2) to obtain foreign intelligence information not concerning a United States person or to protect against international terrorism or clandestine intelligence activities." Section 1861(a)(2)(B) requires that an investigation under this section of a United States person not be conducted solely upon the basis of activities protected by the First Amendment to the Constitution. Section 1861 does not require that an application concerning a United States person make an explicit certification that the investigation is not being conducted solely on the basis of activities protected by the First Amendment.

B. In issuing such orders, does the court make an express finding that an investigation of a United States person is not being conducted solely on the basis of activities protected by the First Amendment to the Constitution of the United States?

> **Answer:** With respect to orders for a pen register or trap and trace device, 50 U.S.C. § 1842(d)(1) states that "[u]pon application made pursuant to this section, the judge shall enter an ex parte order as requested, or modified, approving the installation and use of a pen register or trap and trace device if the judge finds that the application satisfies the requirements of this section." The statute does not require the FISC to make an express finding that the investigation of a United States person is not being conducted solely on the basis of activities protected by the First Amendment of the Constitution of the United States. However, the judge may approve the application only if he or she finds that the application satisfies all the requirements of the section 1842, and—as noted above—section 1842(c)(2) provides that the application shall include a certification that investigation of a

United States person is not being conducted solely upon the basis of activities protected by the First Amendment.

With respect to orders for access to certain business records, 50 U.S.C. § 1861(c)(1) provides that "[u]pon application made pursuant to this section, the judge shall enter an ex parte order as requested, or as modified, approving the release of records if the judge finds that the application meets the requirements of this section." The statute does not require the FISC to make an express finding that the investigation of a United States person is not being conducted solely on the basis of activities protected by the First Amendment of the Constitution of the United States. However, the judge may approve the application only if he or she finds that the application satisfies all the requirements of the section 1861, and as noted above—section 1861(a)(2)(B) requires that an investigation not be conducted of a United States person solely upon the basis of activities protected by the First Amendment to the Constitution of the United States.

3. The Department has increased the use of "national security letters" that require businesses to turn over electronic records about finances, telephone calls, e-mail and other personal information.

A. Please identify the specific authority relied on for issuing these letters.

<u>Answer</u>: Congress has authorized the issuance of National Security Letters in 12 U.S.C. § 3414(a)(5) (the Right to Financial Privacy Act); 15 U.S.C. §§ 1681u and 1681v (the Fair Credit Reporting Act); 18 U.S.C. § 2709 (the Electronic Communications Privacy Act); and 50 U.S.C. § 436(a) (relating to records of persons with authorized access to classified information, who may have disclosed that information to a foreign power).

B. Has any litigation resulted from the issuance of these letters (i.e. challenging the propriety or legality of their use)? If so, please describe.

<u>Answer</u>: There has been no challenge to the propriety or legality of National Security Letters.

4. Has any administrative disciplinary proceeding or civil action been initiated under section 223 of the Act for any unauthorized disclosure of certain intercepts? If so, please describe each case, the nature of the allegations, and the current status of each case.

<u>Answer</u>: There have been no administrative disciplinary proceedings or civil actions initiated under section 223 of the Act for unauthorized disclosures of intercepts.

5. In the Administration's 2004 Budget Request, DOJ is requesting $22 million to establish an automated cross-case analytical system to facili-

tate sharing case specific information through the agencies that belong to the Organized Crime Drug Enforcement Task Force Program. These include law enforcement agencies in DOJ, the Department of Homeland Security, and the Department of Treasury. Is this system also intended to facilitate implementation of the authority to share criminal investigative information with intelligence officials under Section 203 of the Act? Will it be used for that purpose?

> **Answer**: The Department's 2004 budget request is specifically intended to establish and support a central warehouse for drug investigative information and to enable the Organized Crime Drug Enforcement Task Force (OCDETF) and its member agencies to undertake cross-case analysis of that drug information. However, the system may indirectly facilitate or enhance efforts to share investigative information with intelligence officials. In particular, the proposed system would be co-located with the Foreign Terrorist Tracking Task Force (FTTTF), not only enabling OCDETF to leverage FTTTF's existing technology and analytical tools, but also enabling FTTTF, as appropriate, to extract relevant drug investigative information. To the extent such information included foreign intelligence information, FTTTF would certainly ensure that the information was shared in accordance with the Act and the Attorney General's September 23, 2002, Guidelines Regarding Disclosure to the Director of Central Intelligence and Homeland Security Officials of Foreign Intelligence Acquired in the Course of a Criminal Investigation. In addition, the proposed system will likely utilize the Special Operations Division (SOD) as a clearinghouse for the distribution of tips and leads to the field. Given that SOD already has established protocols for the identification and dissemination of foreign intelligence information, such protocols certainly would be applied to any intelligence gained from the data warehouse.

6. **What has been the role of the Department in establishing standards or procedures regarding implementation of the authorities provided in Section 358 (Bank Secrecy Provisions and Activities of United States Intelligence Agencies to Fight International Terrorism)? Please provide any written guidance regarding the requirements of that section that the Department has either issued or approved.**

> **Answer**: The Department of Justice has not been involved in establishing standards or procedures regarding implementation of the authorities provided in section 358. Nonetheless, criminal investigations of terrorism violations in which the Department is involved—such as violations of 18 U.S.C. §§ 2339A and 2339B, which prohibit providing material support or resources either to terrorists or to designated foreign terrorist organizations—have substantially benefitted from section 358, which allows financial regulators to

share certain financial information related to terrorism with intelligence and criminal investigators.

7. What are the dollar amounts that have been paid under the reward authorities provided in Section 501 of the Act or the terrorism related awards under the newly enacted 28 U.S.C. § 530(C)(b)(1)(J)? How many non-U.S. citizens have received rewards under these authorities?

Answer: As of April 30, 2003, the Department of Justice has provided a total of $245,000.00 in reward payments, as tracked in its accounting records (1997-2002). Current financial data does not capture these reward payments by a particular statute, nor does it delineate the citizenship of the recipients. The information that is currently available can only provide us the amount paid, and the time period in which it was paid. However, the financial data indicates that there have been no reward payments made in the last 2 years and hence the data tells us that there are currently no known rewards paid under the newly enacted 28 U.S.C. § 530C(b)(1)(J).

8. The Administration's Office of Justice Programs 2004 Budget request includes a $12 million increase for Regional Information Sharing System (RISS) improvements. The request refers to Section 701 of the USA PATRIOT Act and states that the requested increase will be used to expand RISS's accessibility to state and local public safety agencies to share terrorism alerts and related information. Please provide the Committee with a description of the management oversight process by which DOJ will ensure that the proposed expenditures will accomplish improvements in the U.S. information infrastructure and the specific improvements that are envisioned. Please provide copies of any guidance issued to state and local agencies with respect to the further dissemination of such materials.

Answer: Currently, 84 United States Attorneys Offices (USAOs) are using the Regional Information Sharing Systems Program (RISS.net) as a method to communicate with the Department's state and local law enforcement partners. In the USAOs, there are nearly 600 "Access Officers" of RISS.net. These users typically include the Anti-Terrorism Task Force Coordinators, Counterterrorism Attorneys, OCDETF Attorneys, Intelligence Analysts, and Law Enforcement Coordinating Committee Coordinators. Additionally, in many districts the United States Attorney, First Assistant United States Attorney, and Criminal Chief also utilize the RISS System. The Department expects the remaining USAOs to be fully vetted for RISS in the very near future.

The RISS Program is funded, managed and monitored by the Bureau of Justice Assistance (BJA) of the Office of Justice Programs (OJP).

Each of the six projects is monitored on an annual basis by BJA program staff and the OJP Office of General Counsel (OGC). The OGC monitoring focuses on compliance with the "Criminal Intelligence Systems Operating Policies," which are designed to ensure that information in the system is relevant, updated, and based on a reasonable suspicion of criminal activity.

While this level of monitoring and oversight will continue, we intend to refine our focus to ensure that the enhancements to the RISS.net system are responsive to the need for expansion, both with respect to terrorism and to the broader public safety audience envisioned in the USA PATRIOT Act. We are working very closely with the Department of Homeland Security (DHS), both at the Chief Information Officer level and with the Information Analysis and Infrastructure Protection Directorate (IA&IP), to ensure that the RISS infrastructure enhancements are consistent with the statutory authorities and responsibilities of DHS.

In addition, BJA's overall information technology (including RISS) is, in large measure, guided by the Global Justice Information Sharing Initiative, a Federal Advisory Committee made up of State and local constituency organizations that reports to the Attorney General, and Global's Intelligence Working Group, comprised of Federal, State and local intelligence officials and information sharing specialists. Specifically, RISSATIX is the improvement to the U.S. information infrastructure envisioned in this regard, and we are already working with DHS to provide an architecture that will provide for an effective two-way exchange of information between State and local law enforcement, public safety and other first responder agencies, and organizations and officials at DHS.

9. Under section 213 of the USA PATRIOT Act, a court may order a delay in any notice of the execution of a search warrant if "the court finds reasonable cause to believe that providing immediate notification of the execution of the warrant may have an adverse result," which is defined as (1) endangering the life or physical safety of an individual; (2) flight from prosecution; destruction or tampering with evidence; (3) intimidation of potential witnesses; or (4) otherwise seriously jeopardizing an investigation or unduly delaying trial. Please respond to the following questions regarding the use of this authority:

A. How many times has the Department of Justice sought an order delaying notice of the execution of a warrant under this section?

Answer: Whenever Justice Department personnel execute a court-issued search warrant, they always provide required notice to the person whose property has been searched. But in some cases—*e.g.*, when it is necessary to protect human life, or to avoid compromising an investigation—federal law authorizes the Department to delay giving notice for short periods of time.

The Department has had the legal authority to delay giving notice that a warrant had been executed since before the USA PATRIOT Act. But the law was a mix of inconsistent rules, practices, and court decisions that varied widely from jurisdiction to jurisdiction across the country. This lack of uniformity hindered terrorism cases and other complex nationwide investigations.

Section 213 of the USA PATRIOT Act resolved this problem by establishing a uniform statutory standard. Now, a court can delay the required provision of notice if it finds "reasonable cause" to believe that immediate notification may have an adverse result as defined by 18 U.S.C. § 2705 (including endangering the life or physical safety of an individual, flight from prosecution, evidence tampering, witness intimidation, or otherwise seriously jeopardizing an investigation or unduly delaying a trial). The section requires that notice be provided within a "reasonable period" of a warrant's execution, and a court can further extend the period for good cause.

Section 213's "reasonable cause" standard is in accord with prevailing caselaw for delayed notice of warrants before the USA PATRIOT Act. *See, e.g., United States v. Villegas*, 899 F.2d 1324, 1337 (2d Cir. 1990) (government must show "good reason" for delayed notice of warrants). It also is consistent with the exceptions to the general rules that agents must "knock and announce" before entering, and that warrants must be executed during the daytime. *See Richards v. Wisconsin*, 520 U.S. 385 (1997) (no-knock entry to execute warrant is justified when the police have "reasonable suspicion" that knocking and announcing their presence would be dangerous or futile or would inhibit the effective investigation); Fed. R. Crim. P. 41(c)(1) ("The warrant shall be served in the daytime unless the issuing authority, by appropriate provision of the warrants, and for reasonable cause shown, authorizes its execution at times other than daytime.").

As of April 1, 2003, the Department of Justice has requested a judicial order delaying notice of the execution of a warrant under section 213 forty-seven times, and the courts have granted every request.

B. How many times has a court ordered the delay in such notification?

<u>Answer</u>: As of April 1, 2003, courts have ordered the delay in such notification each of the forty-seven times requested by the Department.

10. That same section allows the notice to be delayed when the warrant prohibits the seizure of among other things, any tangible property, unless "the court finds reasonable necessity for the seizure." 18 U.S.C. § 3103a (b)(2).

> **A. Since the enactment of that section, how many times has the government asked a court to find reasonable necessity for a seizure in connection with delayed notification under this section?**
>
> <u>Answer</u>: Whenever Justice Department personnel execute a court-issued warrant authorizing the seizure of property, the Department provides required notice to the person whose property was seized. In some highly sensitive cases, however, it is necessary that courts be able to authorize a temporary delay in giving that notice.
>
> Section 213 of the USA PATRIOT Act is designed primarily to allow courts to authorize delayed notice of *searches*. But it also enables courts, in certain narrow circumstances, to authorize delayed notice of *seizures*. Section 213 expressly requires that any warrant issued under it must prohibit the seizure of any tangible property, any wire or electronic communication, or (except as expressly provided in chapter 121) any stored wire or electronic information. Courts can waive this requirement only if they find "reasonable necessity" for the seizure.
>
> As of April 1, 2003, the government has asked a court to find reasonable necessity for a seizure in connection with delayed notification under this section fifteen times, and the courts have granted fourteen of the requests.
>
> **B. On what grounds has the government argued that seizure was reasonably necessary under a warrant for which the government also asked for delayed notification?**
>
> <u>Answer</u>: The government has argued that seizure was necessary: (1) to prevent jeopardizing the investigation by protecting the safety of confidential informants; (2) to prevent compromising an investigation by preventing the removal or destruction of evidence; and/or (3) to seize controlled substances that are inherently dangerous to the community.
>
> **C. How often has a court found "reasonable necessity for the seizure" in connection with a warrant for which it also permitted delayed notification?**
>
> <u>Answer</u>: As of April 1, 2003, a court has found reasonable necessity for the seizure in connection with a warrant for which it also permitted delayed notification fourteen times.
>
> **D. How often has a court rejected the government's argument that a seizure was reasonably necessary in connection with a warrant for which the government sought delayed notification?**

>**Answer:** As of April 1, 2003, a court once has rejected the government's argument that a seizure was reasonably necessary. In that one instance, the government requested a delayed-notice warrant to permit federal agents to check a storage unit that was believed to contain information concerning credit card fraud, false identification documents, and other such material. The government also sought authority to seize the items discovered to prevent their possible destruction or removal. The court authorized the warrant but did not authorize seizure because it believed that photographs of relevant items in the storage unit would be sufficient.

> **E. On what grounds have the courts found that the seizures were reasonably necessary in connection with warrants for which delays in notification were granted?**

> **Answer:** The courts have found that the seizures were necessary: (1) to prevent jeopardizing the investigation by protecting the safety of confidential informants; (2) to prevent compromising an investigation by preventing the removal or destruction of evidence; and/or (3) to seize controlled substances that are inherently dangerous to the community.

> **F. What grounds have the courts rejected as establishing reasonable necessity for a seizure in connection with a warrant for which the government sought delayed notification?**

> **Answer:** In the one instance, the government requested a delayed-notice warrant to permit federal agents to check a storage unit that was believed to contain information concerning credit card fraud, false identification documents, and other such material. The government also sought authority to seize the items discovered to prevent their possible destruction or removal. The court authorized the warrant but did not authorize seizure because it believed that photographs of relevant items in the storage unit would be sufficient.

11. That same section allows a court to order delayed notice when "the warrant provides for the giving of such notice within a reasonable period of its execution, which may be extended for by the court for good cause show." 18 U.S.C. § 3103a(b)(3).

> **A. What are the shortest and longest periods of time for which the government has requested initial delayed notice?**

> **Answer:** The most common period of delay authorized by courts is seven days. Courts have authorized specific delays of notification as short as one day and as long as ninety days; other courts have permitted delays of unspecified duration lasting until the indictment was unsealed.

B. On what grounds has the government argued that the period of delayed notification was reasonable?

<u>Answer</u>: The government has argued that the delay period was reasonable in light of the need: (1) to protect the physical safety of cooperators, confidential sources and informants; (2) to prevent the harassment or intimidation of witnesses; (3) to prevent compromising an investigation, which may cause the subject to flee; and/or (4) to prevent the removal or destruction of evidence by avoiding disclosure of the scope and nature of the investigation.

C. How often has the government sought an extension of the period of delayed notice?

<u>Answer</u>: As of April 1, 2003, the government has sought an extension of the period of delayed notice 248 times. This number includes multiple extensions for a single warrant. For example, if a court authorizes a delay of notification for seven days and the investigation lasts one month, the government might seek four renewals.

D. On what grounds has the government asked for an extension of the period of delayed notice?

<u>Answer</u>: The government has sought extensions of the delayed notice period: (1) to permit the imminent arrest of subjects; (2) to protect the physical safety of confidential sources and informants; (3) to prevent the harassment or intimidation of witnesses; (4) to prevent jeopardizing undercover investigations; (5) to prevent compromising an investigation, which may cause the subject to flee; and/or (6) to prevent the removal or destruction of evidence by avoiding disclosure of the scope and nature of the investigation.

E. How often has a court rejected the government's request for delayed notification on the ground that the period for giving delayed notice was unreasonable?

<u>Answer</u>: As of April 1, 2003, a court has never rejected the government's request for delayed notification on the ground that the period for giving delayed notice was unreasonable.

F. On what grounds have the courts rejected the government's position that the period for giving delayed notice was reasonable?

<u>Answer</u>: As of April 1, 2003, no court has rejected such a request.

G. How often has a court rejected the government's request for an extension of the period of delayed notification?

<u>Answer</u>: As of April 1, 2003, no court has rejected such a request.

H. On what grounds have the courts rejected the government's argument that an extension of the period for delayed notice was reasonable?

Answer: As of April 1, 2003, no court has rejected such a request.

12. On January 21, 2003, the Wall Street Journal published an article entitled "New Powers Fuel Legal Assault on Suspected Terrorists." That article claims that the Department of Justice is using information that was "previously largely unavailable" and that had been obtained from FISA surveillance to support criminal prosecutions. According to the article, this information is now available to prosecutors as a result of the FISA Review Court's decision regarding the meaning of the Act's amendment to FISA permitting the government to obtain a surveillance order when "a significant purpose," (rather than "the purpose") of the surveillance is to collect foreign intelligence.

A. Prior to the FISA Review Court's decision, as long as surveillance was properly ordered for "the purpose" of collecting foreign intelligence, was there any legal impediment to prosecution of a crime using evidence obtained under FISA?

Answer: Prior to the Foreign Intelligence Surveillance Court of Review's decision in *In re Sealed Case*, 310 F.3d 717 (2002), there was no legal impediment to the use of evidence obtained pursuant to FISA in a criminal prosecution. Under 50 U.S.C. §§ 1806 and 1825 as originally enacted, information properly obtained or derived from a lawful FISA search or surveillance could be used in a proceeding, including a criminal proceeding, with the approval of the Attorney General. There are published decisions of the federal Courts of Appeals in which such information was used in a criminal prosecution. *See, e.g., United States v. Duggan*, 743 F.2d 59 (2d Cir. 1984).

While there was no *legal* impediment to introducing in a criminal prosecution evidence obtained through FISA before the USA PATRIOT Act and the decision of the Court of Review, as a *practical* matter such evidence was unavailable because of the metaphorical "wall" between law enforcement and intelligence activities. This wall—which derived from certain court decisions and administrative practice by the Department—prevented the sharing of information between, and coordination among, law enforcement and intelligence officials, thereby interfering with a comprehensive and effective defense of the national security against international terrorism and other threats. The wall—and how it was affected by the USA PATRIOT Act, revised Department guidelines issued in March 2002, and the Court of Review's decision—are described in the answer to Question 12(C).

B. Please identify all cases brought since the FISA Review Court's decision that use information that was previously unavailable under FISA procedures.

Answer: After enactment of the USA PATRIOT Act, and even prior to the Court of Review's decision, the Attorney General instructed all United States Attorneys to review intelligence files to determine whether there was a basis for proceeding criminally against subjects of intelligence investigations. This substantial effort represented an enhanced level of review by criminal prosecutors of national security investigative matters. The overall goal of the effort was to protect the Nation from further terrorist attacks by identifying evidence of felonies that had been, or were about to be, committed.

On October 1, 2002, the Attorney General addressed the United States Attorneys and instructed each of them to develop a plan to monitor terrorism and intelligence investigations, and to ensure that information regarding any individual who poses a threat of terrorism to America is shared with other agencies and that appropriate criminal charges are considered.

Almost 4,500 intelligence files were considered as part of the review process and most of these files have been now been reviewed by a criminal prosecutor pursuant to the Attorney General's directive. Evidence or information from this review has been incorporated in numerous cases.

C. Please explain why such information was unavailable and why it became available following the FISA Review Court's decision.

Answer: Before the USA PATRIOT Act, the metaphorical "wall" between the intelligence community and federal law enforcement often precluded effective and indeed vital information sharing, perversely creating higher barriers in the most serious cases. This wall, which derived from certain court decisions, was established in written Department guidelines in July 1995. Sections 218 and 504(a) of the Act—as implemented by Department guidelines issued in March 2002 that were approved by the Court of Review in November 2002—finally permitted the coordination between intelligence and law enforcement that is vital to protecting the Nation's security.

The wall between intelligence and law enforcement resulted from perceived differences between legal authorities that permit the Federal Bureau of Investigation (FBI) to engage in electronic surveillance in the course of its foreign counterintelligence function, on the one hand, and its law enforcement function on the other. These perceived differences created an artificial dichotomy between intelligence gathering and law enforcement, and FISA and Title III (which authorizes electronic surveillance in criminal cases).

As enacted in 1978, FISA required that "the purpose of electronic surveillance is to obtain foreign intelligence information," a term that was (and still is) defined to include information necessary to the ability of the United States to "protect" against espionage or international terrorism. *See* 50 U.S.C. §§ 1804 (a)(7)(B), 1801(e). Courts interpreted "the purpose" to mean "the primary purpose," and they interpreted "foreign intelligence information" to include information necessary to the ability of the United States to protect against espionage or international terrorism *using methods other than law enforcement*. Thus, according to this judicial interpretation of FISA, that statute could be used only if the primary purpose of surveillance or a search was the protection of national security using non-law enforcement methods; gathering evidence to support the prosecution of a foreign spy or terrorist could be a significant purpose of the surveillance or search, but only if that prosecutorial purpose was clearly secondary to the non-law enforcement purpose. As a practical matter, courts determined the government's purpose for using FISA by examining the degree of coordination between intelligence and law enforcement officials: the more information and advice exchanged between these officials, the more likely courts would be to find that the primary purpose of the surveillance or search was law enforcement, not intelligence gathering. This legal structure created what the Court of Review termed "perverse organizational incentives," expressly discouraging coordination in the fight against terrorism. *In re Sealed Case*, 310 F.3d at 743.

To maintain the ability to present viable FISA applications under this perceived legal standard, the Justice Department issued written guidelines in July 1995 that limited the contacts between Department personnel involved in foreign intelligence collection and those involved in law enforcement. This wall between intelligence and law enforcement allowed for intelligence information—including information developed from FISA-approved methods—to be shared with prosecutors and criminal investigators only where such information established that a crime "has been, is being, or will be committed." In such circumstances, the intelligence officials could seek approval to "throw information over the wall." The decisions on when to take this action, however, resided *solely* with intelligence officials.

This policy proved to be wholly unworkable, as it entrusted the decision whether to share information with those who were not best positioned to apply the applicable standards. Only the law enforcement agents and prosecutors pursuing a particular criminal investigation can determine what evidence is pertinent to their case. In contrast, intelligence officials, who focus on the development of foreign intelligence for national security purposes rather than collecting and reviewing information for a particular criminal investigation, rarely consider the potential evidentiary value of a particular piece of information, unless such information self-evidently proves that a crime has been, or may be, committed. Thus, as a matter both of perceived legal imperative and of Department culture, it was impossible to permit full coordination between intelligence and law-enforcement personnel and to combine foreign intelligence and law enforcement information into a seamless body of knowledge. Indeed, law enforcement and intelligence personnel could not speak openly to each and share information beyond the piecemeal sharing envisioned by the previously existing rules. As a result, sharing under these guidelines was relatively rare and generally not meaningful.

The reexamination of these perceived standards became more urgent after the September 11 attacks, when the Attorney General clarified that the Department's primary mission was the prevention of terrorist attacks before they occur. This goal could not be achieved where personnel needed for key preventative tools (including criminal investigation and prosecution and immigration enforcement) did not have the full range of actionable intelligence, including information developed through FISA methods. The USA PATRIOT Act addressed this problem by making two changes to FISA. First, section 218 displaced the "primary purpose" standard, permitting the use of FISA when a "significant purpose" of the search or surveillance was foreign intelligence. Second, section 504(a) clarified that coordination between intelligence and criminal personnel was not grounds for denial of a FISA application.

Following enactment of the USA PATRIOT Act, the Department promulgated new procedures dated March 6, 2002, that expressly authorized—and indeed required—coordination between intelligence and law enforcement. These revised procedures were rejected in part by the FISC on May 17, 2002, but were approved in full by the Court of Review on November 18, 2002. (The decisions of both courts are attached.)[1] In addition to confirming that the Department's revised procedures were valid under FISA, as amended by the USA PATRIOT Act, the Court of Review also noted that the judicial decisions and administrative actions that established the wall between intelligence and law enforcement were not even required by FISA *prior to* the amendments enacted by the USA PATRIOT Act. *See In re Sealed Case*, 310 F.3d at 723-27, 735. In December 2002, the Department issue field guidance with respect to the March 2002 procedures and the Court of Review's decision. (A copy of the field guidance is attached.)[2]

The enhanced ability to coordinate efforts and share information—permitted as a result of sections 218 and 504(a) of the USA PATRIOT Act, the Department's March 6, 2002 procedures, and the Court of Review's decision—has allowed the Department of Justice to investigate cases in a more orderly, efficient, and knowledgeable way, and has permitted all involved personnel, both law enforcement and intelligence, to discuss openly legal, factual, and tactical issues arising during the course of investigations. These substantive and procedural improvements have maximized the prospects that the option best calculated to protect the national security and the American people will be chosen in any individual case. In sum, the Department has developed counterterrorism tools and methods that plainly would not have been possible under the previous standards.

The recent indictment of Sami Al-Arian and other alleged members of a Palestinian Islamic Jihad (PIJ) cell in Tampa, Florida, illustrates a case that benefitted from the new standards. The allegations contained in the conspiracy indictment were based largely on electronic surveillance authorized pursuant to FISA and conducted prior to the USA PATRIOT Act. Before the Act, the Department was required to submit repeated certifications that the primary purpose of the proposed surveillance methods was intelligence, as opposed to criminal law enforcement. Moreover, special handling procedures were imposed in this investigation on intelligence officials to guard against information sharing that was believed to be improper. On several occasions, information developed through FISA surveillance was identified as potentially relevant to a criminal case against Al-Arian and others, and the FBI's intelligence personnel notified the Criminal Division of this information. The Criminal Division duly disseminated this information to the U.S. Attorney in Tampa, as envisioned by the July 1995 rule. However, the existing protocols denied criminal prosecutors and investigators full access to information obtained through FISA, and they prevented criminal and intelligence personnel from coordinating their parallel investigations.

The USA PATRIOT Act's amendments to FISA and the new rules adopted by the Department pursuant to those amendments enabled criminal investigators in Tampa finally to obtain and systematically consider the full range of evidence of the alleged conspiracy. After the Court of Review's decision confirmed the Department's understanding of the Act, this information, which existed in the FBI's intelligence—but not criminal—files, became available and was examined. Armed with the entire intelligence yield, prosecutors for the first time were able to consider the comprehensive history of the surveillance of Al-Arian and others, to understand the context of their communications, and to document the decade-long conspiracy that is alleged. Such a comprehensive review and evaluation would not have been possible under the old rules. Thus, the USA PATRIOT Act was critical to the Department's ability to safeguard the Nation's security by bringing criminal charges against Al-Arian and others in February 2002.

In order to ensure that—as with the Al-Arian case—criminal investigators benefit from now-available intelligence information, after enactment of the USA PATRIOT Act the Attorney General directed that prosecutors review existing intelligence files to determine whether they contained evidence of crimes. This process, which is almost completed, involved the detailed review of almost 4,500 files. The Attorney General also directed, in October 2002, that each United States Attorney know fully the FBI's intelligence cases in their Districts. These efforts, along with coordination between law enforcement and intelligence personnel in ongoing investigations, have been made possible by the USA PATRIOT Act and are essential to preventing terrorism before it occurs and locating and prosecuting terrorists.

13. The FISA Review Court's decision permits enhanced coordination between law enforcement and intelligence officials.

A. What FISA-related training is currently being planned or conducted?

B. What topics will it address?

C. Who will give the training?

D. Who will receive the training?

E. Is the training going to be coordinated with the Intelligence Community in general and/or the Director of Central Intelligence?

Answer to A through E: In the past year, the Department's Office of Intelligence Policy and Review (OIPR) has conducted FISA training for FBI and/or US Attorney's Office personnel in various cities, including San Diego, Portland, Denver, Houston, Detroit, Chicago, New York, Washington, and Boston, and at the FBI Academy in Quantico.

Between May and September 2003, eight training sessions are planned for FBI and US Attorney's Office personnel. Approximately 100 FBI agents and prosecutors are expected to attend each session. Most of the sessions will occur at the National Advocacy Center in South Carolina, while others are expected to occur in Washington, DC. In addition to FISA, topics covered by these sessions will include an overview of the intelligence community; information sharing and coordination between the intelligence community and law enforcement agencies; FBI intelligence investigations; law enforcement investigations and collection tools; litigation involving classified information; training on sections 203 and 905 of the USA PATRIOT Act, and training as required by section 908 of that Act; and the handling of classified information. OIPR, the FBI, the Criminal Division, the Executive Office for U.S. Attorneys, the Central Intelligence Agency, the Department of Homeland Security and other entities have been planning the training, and will conduct it jointly. Additional training also will be conducted for FBI personnel involved in national security investigations who are unable to attend one of these eight training sessions.

14. How many emergency FISA surveillance orders did the Department of Justice process between FISA's enactment and September 11, 2001? How many has it processed since September 11, 2001? Has the change from 24 to 72 hours in 50 U.S.C. 1805(f) and 1824(e) facilitated the use of FISA emergency searches and surveillance, and if so, how?

Answer: From the enactment of FISA in 1978 through September 11, 2001, available records indicate that Attorneys General issued 47 emergency authorizations for electronic surveillance and/or physical searches under FISA. Between September 11, 2001 and September 19, 2002, the Attorney General made 113 emergency authorizations for electronic surveillance and/or physical searches under FISA. Of course, following September 11, 2001, the Department conducted the most extensive investigation in the history of the United States, with the overriding goal of preventing another catastrophic terrorist attack occurred against the American people and the United States homeland. FISA was the critical investigative tool in that effort.

The change from 24 to 72 hours in the pendency of the Attorney General's emergency approval authority under FISA before review by the FISC has enabled the Department to respond more quickly, and therefore more effectively, to threats against our national security. By lengthening the time before approval is sought from the FISC, the Department has been able to use the emergency authority to obtain information that otherwise might well have been unavailable. Moreover, by providing additional time, the Department has been able to submit more thoroughly vetted applications originating in Attorney General emergency approvals to the FISC for its review.

15. Since enactment of the USA Patriot Act, what procedures have been implemented to improve the efficiency of processing FISA applications?

Answer: On April 15, 2002, the Counsel for Intelligence Policy—who is responsible for OIPR—reported to the Deputy Attorney General on actions taken at that time to improve the FISA process. These reforms included:

A requirement that, to improve the prioritization of FISA applications, renewal applications to the FISC were to be made at the FISC's regular sessions, in the absence of exigent circumstances. This new requirement has enforced a more orderly preparation of renewal applications and limited the more labor-intensive "special" sessions to higher priority initiations and other, operationally driven exigencies.

Refined procedures for the vetting and requesting of emergency Attorney General approvals under FISA. In order to ensure that requests from the FBI for emergency approvals reflected the priorities of Bureau management, such requests are now made only by the Assistant Directors for Counterintelligence or Counterterrorism or their Deputies.

Establishment of regular meetings between OIPR and FBI managers to set and review priorities under FISA.

Expanded OIPR presence at FBI field offices on a continuous basis. Specifically, OIPR has placed one of its line attorneys in New York on a temporary basis to work with the New York field office, has hired an attorney to begin work on a permanent basis in San Francisco, and plans to hire attorneys permanently assigned to New York, possibly Chicago, and with other key field offices as budgets permit.

Appointment of an Assistant Counsel in OIPR to establish, with FBI attorneys, a joint FISA training program for all FBI foreign counterintelligence agents.

Adjustments by the Counsel and his Deputy for Operations, on a continuing basis, to improve the workloads, procedures, substance, and flow of the FISA process. To accommodate multiple emergency and other requests that at times may overpower OIPR duty officers, for example, the Counsel or Deputy for Operations has adjusted workloads, called for volunteers, or taken other management action to keep OIPR line attorneys productive and effective.

On January 27, 2003, the Counsel for Intelligence Policy reported on the status of additional steps taken by the FBI and the Department to improve the efficiency of the FISA application process. These steps include:

Revised filing procedures with the FISC that enable it to review, adjudge, and issue orders more efficiently.

Procedures enabling FBI field offices to submit FISA requests directly to OIPR, rather than just through FBI headquarters, to accelerate the application process.

Standardization of requests from the FBI for FISA authorities that will enable faster preparation of applications.

A major reorganization approved by the Director of FBI of the units and process for handling FISA within FBI headquarters that will enable the Bureau to handle and track applications to the FISC, and to distribute its orders, more efficiently. Specifically, in November 2002, the FBI created the FISA Unit within the Office of General Counsel to perform the administrative support functions for the FISA process. The FISA unit (1) ensures that all FISA applications move expeditiously through the FISA process, coordinating with the field divisions, FBI headquarters substantive units, the National Security Law Unit (NSLU), and OIPR, (2) is overseeing the development and implementation of an automated tracking system that will electronically connect the field divisions, FBI headquarters, NSLU, and OIPR, and (3) distributes all FISA court orders and warrants to the field divisions, telecommunications carriers, Internet service providers, and others.

An affirmation of the need for regular meetings between OIPR and Bureau managers to review priorities and dockets for applications to the FISC.

Approval by the Attorney General of OIPR's assigning attorneys to work in the field at FBI field offices to improve the preparation and handling of FISA applications and to facilitate the sharing of intelligence information between Department components in a manner consistent with FISA and applicable Court orders.

Moreover, the Department has increased the capacity of OIPR by increasing the hours and workloads of OIPR attorneys, detailing lawyers from other components of the Department to OIPR, and hiring additional attorneys. In particular, since September 11, 2001, 16 lawyers have been detailed to OIPR from elsewhere in the Justice Department, and OIPR has hired 15 new attorneys. The FBI is making similar adjustments to increase the staffing of the NSLU.

Finally, the Department has, in coordination with the FBI, undertaken a substantial training program outlined in the answer to Question 13.

16. In testimony presented to the Senate Judiciary on March 4, 2003, FBI Director Robert Mueller stated that:

The FBI's efforts to identify and dismantle terrorist networks have yielded major successes over the past 18 months. We have charged over 200 suspected terrorists with crimes—half of whom have been convicted to date. The rest are awaiting trial. Moreover, our efforts have damaged terrorist networks and disrupted terrorist plots across the country. In the past month alone, the FBI has arrested 36 international and 14 domestic suspected terrorists.

A. What authorities under the USA PATRIOT Act were used in identifying and dismantling terror networks and were relied upon to prevent terrorist plots?

Answer: The Department of Justice and the FBI have used numerous authorities provided by the USA PATRIOT Act in the investigation of the September 11 terrorist attacks, and the continuing efforts to detect and prevent terrorism before it occurs and to arrest and prosecute terrorists. The Department and FBI have used, among others, investigative authorities provided in the following sections of the Act:

201: Adds certain terrorism crimes to the list of offenses for which wiretap orders are available.

- These provisions have proven to be beneficial to law enforcement officials, as several wiretap orders have used this expanded list of terrorism offenses.

203: Permits law enforcement to share grand jury and electronic, wire, and oral interception information containing foreign intelligence or counterintelligence with federal law enforcement, intelligence, protective, immigration, national defense, or national security officials.

- The Department has made disclosures of vital information to the Intelligence Community and other federal officials under section 203 on dozens of occasions.

- On September 23, 2002, the Attorney General issued guidelines that establish procedures for the disclosure to the Intelligence Community of grand jury and electronic, wire, and oral interception information that identifies a United States person, as defined by federal law. These guidelines include important privacy safeguards. For example, they require that all such information be labeled by law enforcement agencies before disclosure to intelligence agencies and be handled by intelligence agencies pursuant to specific protocols designed to ensure its appropriate use.

205: Authorizes the FBI to expedite employment of translators in the fight against terrorism.

- The Bureau has hired 264 new translators to support counterterrorism efforts, including 121 Arabic and 25 Farsi speakers.

- The Bureau also is working to implement its Law Enforcement and Intelligence-agency Linguist Access system (LEILA), which will store data regarding the proficiency and security clearance levels of linguists available to the Bureau and its partner agencies. LEILA will work across agency lines to maximize the use and availability of the intelligence community's language resources.

207: Increases authorization periods for FISA searches and electronic surveillance.

- While the details of FISA operations are classified, the FISA court has authorized operations under section 207. The USA PATRIOT Act has not only provided additional time to government investigators targeting potential terrorist activity, but has also helped the government and the FISC to focus their efforts on more far-reaching terrorism-related cases.

209: Allows voice mail stored with a third party provider to be obtained with a search warrant (upon a showing of probable cause), rather than with a more time-consuming wiretap order.

- Since the USA PATRIOT Act was passed, such warrants have been used in a variety of criminal cases to obtain key evidence, including voice-mails in the accounts of foreign and domestic terrorists.

210: Clarifies the types of records that law enforcement can subpoena from electronic communications providers to include the means and source of payment, such as bank accounts and credit card numbers.

- Prosecutors in the field report that this new subpoena authority has allowed for quick tracing of suspects in numerous important cases, including several terrorism investigations and a case in which computer hackers attacked over fifty government and military computers.

211: Clarifies that statutes governing telephone and Internet communications (and not the burdensome provisions of the Cable Act) apply to cable companies that provide Internet or telephone service in addition to television programming.

- Cable companies that provide telephone and Internet services are now subject to search warrants, court orders, and subpoenas to the same extent as all other communications carriers, ensuring that terrorists and other criminals are not exempt from investigations simply because they choose cable companies as their communications providers.

212: Allows computer-service providers to disclose communications and records of communications to protect life and limb; clarifies that computer-hacking victims can disclose non-content records to protect their rights and property.

- Section 212 has been used to disclose vital information to law enforcement on many occasions, including one case where such records enabled agents to trace kidnappers' communications. This provision also proved invaluable in the investigation of a bomb threat against a school. An anonymous person, claiming to be a student at a high school, posted on an Internet message board a bomb death threat that specifically named a faculty member and several students. The owner and operator of the Internet message board initially resisted disclosing to law enforcement any information about the suspect for fear that he could be sued if he volunteered that information. Once agents explained that the USA PATRIOT Act created a new provision allowing the voluntary release of information in emergencies, the owner turned over evidence that led to the timely arrest of the individual responsible for the bomb threat. Faced with this evidence, the suspect confessed to making the threats. The message board's owner later revealed that he had been worried for the safety of the students and teachers for several days, and expressed his relief that the USA PATRIOT Act permitted him to help.

216: Amends the pen register/trap and trace statute to clarify that it applies to Internet communications, and gives federal courts authority to authorize the installation and use of pen registers and trap and trace devices in other districts.

- The Department has used the newly-amended pen/trap statute to track the communications of (1) terrorist conspirators, (2) at least one major drug distributor, (3) thieves who obtained victims' bank account information and stole the money, (4) a four-time murderer, and (5) a fugitive who fled on the eve of trial using a fake passport.

- This new authority was employed in the investigation of the murder of journalist Daniel Pearl to obtain information that proved critical to identifying some of the perpetrators.

- The Deputy Attorney General has issued a memorandum to field offices clearly delineating Department policy regarding the avoidance of "overcollection," the inadvertent collection of "content" when using pen/trap devices. This guidance will help protect the privacy of Internet users by ensuring that only addressing information, and not the content of their communications, is collected and used pursuant to section 216. (A copy of this memorandum is attached.)[3]

217: Allows victims of computer-hacking crimes to request law enforcement assistance in monitoring trespassers on their computers.

- This provision has been used on several occasions. Computer security officials and law enforcement investigators around the country universally have praised this provision, and the Department is committed to implementing it fully.

218: Allows law enforcement to conduct FISA surveillance or searches if "a significant purpose" is foreign intelligence.

- As explained in the answer to question 12, this change has allowed increased coordination between intelligence and law enforcement personnel in foreign counterintelligence investigations in which FISA is being used.

219: Permits federal judges, in terrorism investigations, to issue search warrants having effect outside the district.

- This provision has been used on at least three occasions. One noteworthy example occurred during the ongoing anthrax investigation, when FBI agents applied for a warrant to search the premises of America Media, Inc., in Boca Raton, Florida—the employer of the first anthrax victim. Because of section 219, agents were able to obtain a search warrant from the federal judge in Washington, D.C., overseeing the wide-ranging investigation. This saved investigators from wasting valuable time on petitioning another judge in another district for that authority.

220: Permits a court with jurisdiction over the offense to issue a search warrant for electronic evidence in possession of an Internet service provider located in another district.

- This provision has dramatically reduced the unnecessary administrative burdens in the court districts that are home to large Internet providers, such as the Northern District of California and the Eastern District of Virginia. The enhanced ability to obtain this information quickly has proved invaluable in several time-sensitive investigations, such as one involving the tracking of a fugitive, and another involving a hacker who stole a company's trade secrets and then extorted money from the company.

319: Permits the forfeiture of funds held in United States interbank accounts.

- On January 18, 2001, a federal grand jury indicted James Gibson for various offenses, including conspiracy to commit money laundering, and mail and wire fraud. Gibson, a lawyer, had defrauded his clients, numerous personal injury victims, of millions of dollars by fraudulently structuring settlements. Gibson and his wife, who was indicted later, fled to Belize, depositing some of the proceeds from their scheme in two Belizean banks. The Department's efforts to recover the proceeds initially proved unsuccessful. Although Belize's government initially agreed to freeze the monies, a Belizean court lifted the freeze and prohibited the government from further assisting American law enforcement agencies. Efforts to break the impasse failed, while the Gibsons systematically looted their accounts in Belize, purchasing yachts and other luxury items. Following the passage of the USA PATRIOT Act, a seizure warrant was served on the Belizean bank's interbank account in the United States pursuant to section 319, and the remaining funds were recovered.

- In December 2001, the Department also used section 319 to recover almost $1.7 million in funds. This money will be used to compensate the victims of the defendant's fraudulent scheme.

373: Makes it unlawful to run an unlicensed foreign money transmittal business; eliminates prior requirement that the defendant have known about the state licensing requirement.

- On April 30, 2002, a federal jury in Boston convicted Mohamed Hussein on two charges of running a foreign money transmittal business (Barakaat North America, Inc.) without a license in violation of section 373. The al-Barakaat network was affiliated with and received funding from al Qaeda. In 2000 and 2001, after Hussein ignored Massachusetts's warning that his business needed to be licensed, nearly three million dollars was wired from his Boston bank account to the United Arab Emirates. On July 22, 2002, Hussein was sentenced to one and a half years in prison, to be followed by two years of supervised release.

402: Appropriates funds to triple the number of INS agents on the northern border and allocates monies to the INS and the Customs Service to make improvements in technology for monitoring the northern border and acquiring additional needed equipment.

- The INS has rapidly implemented section 402, and committed to hiring 245 new agents and assigning them to the Canadian border by December 2002. The INS has arranged recruitment visits by over 300 trained border patrol agents to colleges, universities, and military installations. Since September 2001, the INS has received over 65,000 applicants for agent positions, and the agency is making selections at the rate of 1,000 per month (these selections are in various stages of the pre-employment process). The INS has also added five additional border agent basic training classes to its training schedule.

- The INS also has worked to quickly install the Integrated Intelligence Surveillance System (ISIS) at 55 northern border sites. When it is completed in approximately 18-24 months, ISIS, a computer-aided detection system, will provide 24-hour/7-day border coverage through ground-based sensors, fixed cameras, and other technology. The INS further has enhanced border security by deploying three new single-engine helicopters and 500 infrared scopes for border agents at northern border stations. These scopes significantly increase agents' night-vision capability while on patrol.

403: Requires the FBI to share information in its National Crime Information Center (NCIC) files with INS and the State Department for purposes of adjudicating visa applications.

- On April 11, 2002, the Attorney General issued a major directive on the coordination of terrorism-related information. That directive requires all of the Department's investigative components, including the FBI, to include in the NCIC database the names, photographs, and other identifying data of all known or suspected terrorists.

- Since the USA PATRIOT Act was passed, the FBI has given the State Department over 8.4 million records from NCIC databases. The FBI also has provided to the INS 83,000 comprehensive records of key wanted persons in the NCIC databases, as well as information regarding military detainees in Afghanistan, Pakistan, and Guantanamo Bay. The INS has been working with the FBI and United States Customs Service to provide to INS officers at airports NCIC data on alien passengers. An information system to permit such NCIC searches is on schedule to be deployed by the end of fiscal year 2003.

414: Encourages the Attorney General to expedite the implementation of the integrated entry and exit data system authorized by Congress in 1996.

- The INS has established a multi-agency office to ensure that the system is swiftly put into operation. On December 31, 2003, the system should be operational for all travelers to the U.S. at all air and sea points of entry. The system should be up and running at the 50 largest land points of entry one year later, and at all points of entry for all travelers by December 31, 2005.

416: Requires the Attorney General to implement and expand the foreign student visa monitoring program authorized by Congress in the 1996 Illegal Immigration Reform and Immigrant Responsibility Act.

- The INS began enrolling schools for SEVIS on July 1, 2002. On May 16, 2002, the INS published a proposed regulation that set a January 30, 2003 deadline for all schools and programs to use SEVIS for all of their foreign students. The INS has set up an outreach program for eligible schools demonstrating the benefits of SEVIS, developed training program materials, set up training sessions, begun a competitive process to select contractors to assist with the certification of schools prior to enrollment, and published a variety of guidelines and memoranda concerning SEVIS implementation.

801: Makes it a federal offense to engage in terrorist attacks and other acts of violence against mass transportation systems.

- The Department attempted to use section 801 in against "shoebomber" Richard Reid, who has been convicted of attempting to ignite a bomb hidden in his shoes during an international flight. A federal judge dropped the charge, concluding that airplanes do not fall within the meaning of "mass transportation vehicle." Congress subsequently closed this loophole in section 609 of the "Prosecutorial Remedies and Tools Against the Exploitation of Children Today Act of 2003," or "PROTECT Act."

805: Enhances the ban on material terrorist support by making it apply to experts who provide advice or assistance to be used in preparing for or carrying out terrorism crimes, and to acts occurring outside the United States. The section also adds to the list of underlying terrorism crimes for which provision of material support is barred, makes it clear that prohibited material support includes all types of monetary instruments, and enhances penalties for material support.

- On October 21, 2002, six United States citizens who live near Buffalo, New York were indicted on charges of providing support or resources to terrorists. In the early summer of 2001, these men allegedly participated in weapons training at a terrorist training camp in Afghanistan known to be used by al Qaeda. At a safehouse on the way to the camp, they are alleged to have seen a video on suicide bombing that featured the attack on the USS Cole, in which 17 U.S. sailors were murdered. The indictment alleges that the defendants also were trained in the use of assault rifles, handguns, and long range rifles. While they were at the camp, Osama bin Laden visited and delivered a speech instructing the approximately 200 trainees in anti-American and anti-Israeli sentiment as well as general al Qaeda doctrine.

- On October 30, 2002, two Pakistani nationals and one United States citizen were charged with conspiring to provide Stinger anti-aircraft missiles to anti-U.S. forces in Afghanistan. Syed Mustajab Shah, Muhammed Abid Afridi and Ilyas Ali were charged with conspiracy to distribute heroin and hashish and conspiracy to provide material support to al Qaeda. The defendants allegedly arranged to exchange 600 kilograms of heroin and five tons of hashish for cash and four Stinger missiles, and stated that they intended to sell the missiles to al Qaeda forces in Afghanistan.

- On November 1, 2002, four men, including a United States citizen and a U.S. resident, were charged with conspiracy to distribute cocaine and conspiracy to provide material support to a foreign terrorist organization in a drugs-for-weapons plot to deliver $25 million worth of weaponry to the United Self-Defense Forces of Colombia (known by its Spanish language acronym, "AUC"). The AUC—whose leader, Carlos CastaZo-Gil, was charged with five counts of drug trafficking in September 2001—is an 8,000-member Colombian paramilitary group listed on the State Department's Foreign Terrorist Organization List. The two U.S.-based defendants allegedly sought to broker a deal between an undercover law enforcement officer and the other two defendants, who are high-ranking AUC leaders. The charges assert that, under the agreement, the AUC would have exchanged cocaine for five shipping containers full of Russian- and Eastern European-made weaponry, including shoulder-fired anti-aircraft missiles, 9,000 assault rifles, and 3,000 grenades.

Section 905: Requires federal law enforcement agencies to disclose expeditiously to the Director of Central Intelligence any foreign intelligence acquired by the Department in the course of a criminal investigation, except when disclosing such information would jeopardize an ongoing investigation.

- On September 23, 2002, the Attorney General released guidelines that formalize the procedures and mechanisms already established for the Department of Justice and other federal law enforcement agencies that acquire foreign intelligence in the course of a criminal investigation.

Whether the Department has used the surveillance techniques and other amendments authorized by sections 204, 206, 214, and 215 is classified. Accordingly, the answer relating to the Department's use of sections 204, 214 and 215 will be delivered to the Committee under separate cover. The answer relating to the Department's use of section 206 will be provided to the House Permanent Select Committee on Intelligence (HPSCI) pursuant to the direction in the Committee's letter of April 1, 2003, and in keeping with the longstanding Executive branch practice on the sharing of operational intelligence information with Congress.

B. In your judgment, how many of those investigations would have been much more difficult or impossible without the authorities available under the Act?

Answer: In our judgment, the Government's success in preventing another catastrophic attack on the American homeland in the 20 months since September 11, 2001, would have been much more difficult, if not impossibly so, without the USA PATRIOT Act. The Department's overall experience is that the authorities Congress provided in the Act have substantially enhanced our ability to prevent, investigate, and prosecute acts of terrorism.

Some of the authorities provided in Title II of the Act substantially eased administrative burdens and increased the efficiency of law enforcement without changing the underlying substantive legal standards—for example, sections 219 and 220. In such cases, the USA PATRIOT Act's authorities made available resources that otherwise would have been devoted to administrative tasks, thereby maximizing the law enforcement personnel available to investigate terrorists. In other instances, the Act in fact allowed the Department to access information that previously had been unavailable, as a legal or practical matter, or simply more difficult to obtain. For example, the Department's response to question 12, *supra*, explains how section 218 of the Act facilitated the terrorism investigation of Sami Al-Arian and other alleged members of a Palestinian Islamic Jihad cell in Tampa, Florida.

17. The Act supplemented the government's authority to freeze and forfeit assets of suspected terrorists and terrorist organizations. Please provide the Committee with information related to the freezing or confiscation of such assets since the enactment of the Act.

   A. Please identify all suspected terrorists or terrorist organizations whose assets the federal government has frozen or forfeited?

   Answer: Since September 11, 2001, the United States has frozen over 600 bank accounts and $124 million in assets around the world. We have conducted 70 investigations into terrorist financing with 23 convictions or guilty pleas to date.

   The Department of Justice has not been given the responsibility of freezing terrorist assets held in the United States. Such freezing results from the designation of terrorist-related groups and individuals under Executive Order 13224 and the International Emergency Economic Powers Act (IEEPA), both of which are enforced by the Treasury Department's Office of Foreign Assets Control (OFAC). However, Justice Department lawyers have successfully defended in court a number of these freezings—for example, on December 31, 2002, the Seventh Circuit upheld Treasury's freeze on the assets of Global Relief Foundation, which is believed to have supported Osama bin Laden, al Qaeda, and other known terrorist groups. *See Global Relief Found. v. O'Neill*, 315 F.3d 748 (7th Cir. 2002).

   In most terrorism cases, it has not been necessary for the Justice Department to seek forfeiture of U.S.-based terrorist assets under the USA PATRIOT Act's new authorities, because the assets had already been frozen by OFAC. "Forfeiture," unlike freezing, enables a court to transfer to the United States the ownership of assets which are the proceeds of or are related to a particular crime. Section 806 of the USA PATRIOT Act expanded the government's authority to forfeit terrorist-related assets; this change was codified at 18 U.S.C. § 981(a)(1)(G). After September 11, 2001, the Department of Justice filed a seizure warrant on a New Jersey bank account suspected of containing assets belonging to one or more of the 19 dead hijackers. The Department also included a forfeiture count in the Texas indictment of Hamas leader Musa Abu Marzook, *United States v. Elashi*, CR No. 3:02-CR-052-R (N.D. Tex. filed Dec. 17, 2002). Each of these actions, however, were based on pre-USA PATRIOT Act authority.

B. Please identify the specific authority, whether or not under the Act, that the federal government has asserted in freezing or forfeiting the assets of suspected terrorists or terrorist organizations.

Answer: The judicial forfeiture action in the Marzook case was predicated on money laundering. Assets of terrorists and terrorist organizations, and those who act for or on behalf of, provide financial or other support for, or are otherwise associated with them, can also be frozen pursuant to Executive Order 13224 (Global Terrorism) and Executive Order 12947 (Individuals and Groups who Threaten Middle East Peace Process).

C. Have any seizures or forfeitures been challenged in court?

Answer: The Civil Division of the Justice Department has been involved in judicial challenges to the OFAC designation and freezing actions of terrorist-related entities that have a U.S. presence. These challenges involved two Illinois-based charities suspected of being associated with al Qaeda (Benevolence International Foundation and Global Relief Foundation), a Texas entity believed to be a Hamas front (Holy Land Foundation for Relief and Development) and two entities affiliated with an al Qaeda-connected Somalian financial network known as al-Barakaat (Global Service International, Inc. and Aaran Money Wire Service).

D. What have been the results of any such challenges?

Answer: The United States was successful in defending the Holy Land Foundation challenge in district court, and the case is now on appeal to the D.C. Circuit. One issue remains in the district court and has been stayed. The Seventh Circuit affirmed the district court's denial of a preliminary injunction in Global Relief Foundation and ruled in favor of the government on all of the statutory and constitutional claims raised in the appeal. The government has moved to dismiss the remaining issues in the case on the grounds that the administrative record amply supports Global Relief's designation under Executive Order 13224. Although the designations of certain Barakaat-related entities have been withdrawn, their challenge has not yet been dismissed.

E. Has any court, pursuant to section 316 of the Act (codified at 18 U.S.C. § 983 note), admitted evidence that would otherwise be inadmissible in a forfeiture proceeding? If so, on what circumstances justified admitting such evidence in such cases?

Answer: Because no forfeiture cases have yet been brought pursuant to 18 U.S.C. § 981(a)(1)(G), there has been no occasion to invoke the tool provided in section 316 of the Act. To the extent that section 316 also applies to freezing orders and confiscations under IEEPA, the

Department of Justice is unaware of any instances where the evidentiary rules discussed in section 316 were invoked.

18. Section 402 authorizes appropriations to triple the number of INS Border Patrol Agents and Inspectors in each state along the Northern Border, and also authorizes appropriations to provide necessary personnel and facilities to support such personnel.

A. How many additional Inspectors has the INS hired at the Ports of Entry along the Northern Border?

B. How many of those hires are working as Inspectors along the Northern Border at this time?

C. By how many Inspectors has the total staffing at the ports along the Northern Border increased since September 11, 2001?

Answer: Pursuant to the Committee's April 1, 2003, letter, in light of the transfer of the Immigration and Naturalization Service (INS) to the Department of Homeland Security (DHS), we have referred these questions to DHS for a response. We previously provided the Committee with a copy of this referral.

19. What technology improvements have been completed and what additional technology improvements are planned for FY2003 expenditures to improve Northern Border security?

Answer: Pursuant to the Committee's April 1, 2003, letter, in light of the transfer of the INS to DHS, we have referred this question to DHS for a response. We previously provided the Committee with a copy of this referral.

20. Subtitle B of Title IV of the USA PATRIOT Act gives the Attorney General additional authority to detain certain suspected alien terrorists, and improves systems for tracking aliens entering and leaving the United States and for inspecting aliens seeking to enter the United States. Section 411 amends the Immigration and Nationality Act (INA) to broaden the scope of aliens ineligible for admission or deportable due to terrorist activities, and defines the terms "terrorist organization" and "engage in terrorist activity."

A. Has the INS relied upon the definitions in section 411 of the Act to file any new charges against aliens in removal proceedings? If so, how many times has it used each provision?

Answer: Prior to the transfer of the INS to DHS, the INS had not relied upon the definitions in section 411 of the Act to file any new charges against aliens in removal proceedings.

Despite the fact that this authority has not yet been used, each case is reviewed for the potential use of the section 411 amendments to the immigration law. The options in reviewing the case of a suspected alien terrorist range from continuing an ongoing intelligence-gathering operation to criminal prosecution to removal, including both conventional removal under Title II of the Immigration and Nationality Act (INA) to removal before the Alien Terrorist Removal Court under Title V of the INA. Cases are reviewed with the goal of taking the appropriate action to protect the national security.

In the past, decisions have been made to forego filing security-related charges (that would include the amendments made by section 411 of the USA PATRIOT Act) for a variety of reasons, including: (1) the fact that the underlying evidence on the security-related removal charge is classified and cannot be declassified; (2) there was a clear non-security-related charge of removability that would result in a more expeditious removal since security-related charges of removal may generate more litigation; (3) aliens charged with security-related grounds of removal have asserted claims for asylum based on the fact that they have been labeled as "terrorists" by the United States government, thus prolonging the proceedings.

B. In your July 26, 2002 response, you stated that one alien had been denied admission under these new provisions. Have any aliens been denied admission under these grounds since that response?

Answer: Prior to the transfer of the INS to DHS, at least three aliens had been denied admission under these new provisions.

C. What effect have the amendments to the INA in section 411 of the Act had on ongoing investigations in the United States?

Answer: Since passage of the Act and before transfer of INS to DHS, INS and the Department's Criminal and Civil Divisions issued field guidance and undertook numerous training efforts to familiarize INS field attorneys and officers, Assistant U.S. Attorneys, FBI officials, and other federal personnel with the new provisions. This guidance is being employed in pending investigations.

D. Section 212(a)(3)(F) of the INA, as amended by section 411 of the Act, renders inadmissible any alien who the Attorney General determines has been associated with a terrorist organization and intends while in the United States to engage solely, principally, or incidentally in activities endangering the United States. Has the Attorney General made such a determination with respect to any alien thus far?

Answer: The Justice Department had not made use of this provision prior to the transfer of INS to DHS.

The security-related cases we have encountered at ports-of-entry in the recent past have involved aliens subject to removal on other grounds. Due to the time sensitivity of such cases, it was more expeditious to deny admission based on other charges than to refer the cases to the highest levels of the Departments of Justice and State. Nevertheless, we believe that this authority is an important tool to maintain in current law for use in appropriate cases.

> E. Have there been any challenges to the constitutionality of the charges added to the INA by section 411 of the Act? If so, please identify the case(s) and the status of the proceedings.
>
> **Answer:** Because, prior to the transfer of the INS to DHS, the INS had not relied upon the definitions in section 411 of the Act to file any new charges against aliens in removal proceedings, this question is inapplicable.

21. Section 412 of the Act provides for mandatory detention until removal from the United States (regardless of relief from removal) of an alien certified by the Attorney General as a suspected terrorist or threat to national security. It also requires release of such alien after seven days if removal proceedings have not commenced, or if the alien has not been charged with a criminal offense. In addition, this section of the Act authorizes detention for additional periods of up to six months of an alien not likely to be deported in the reasonably foreseeable future if release will threaten our national security or the safety of the community or any person. It also limits judicial review to habeas corpus proceedings in the U.S. Supreme Court, the U.S. Court of Appeals for the District of Columbia, or any district court with jurisdiction to entertain a habeas corpus petition, and limits the venue of appeal of any final order by a circuit or district judge under section 236A of the INA to the U.S. Court of Appeals for the District of Columbia.

> A. At the time of your July 26, 2002 response, you had not used the authority in Section 412. Have you used the authority since that response? If so, please state:
>
> > i. How many of the aliens for whom certifications have been issued have been removed?
> >
> > ii. How many aliens for whom the Attorney General issued certifications are still detained? At what stage of the criminal or immigration proceedings are each of those cases?
> >
> > iii. How many of the aliens who were certified have been granted relief? How many of those aliens are still detained?
> >
> > iv. Have any challenges to certifications under section 236A(a)(3) of the INA been brought in habeas corpus proceedings in accordance with section 236A(b)? If so, please identify the case(s) and the status of each proceeding.

> v. Has the Attorney General released any aliens detained under section 236A because the alien was not charged with a criminal offense or placed into removal proceedings within seven days?
>
> vi. How many non-certified aliens have received relief from removal and remain detained longer than 6 months since such relief was ordered?
>
> <u>Answer to i through vi:</u> Prior to the transfer of INS to DHS, the Attorney General did not use the authority provided by section 412 of the USA PATRIOT Act for the mandatory detention of certified aliens. Numerous aliens who could have been considered for section 236A certifications have been detained since September 11, 2001 and the enactment of the USA PATRIOT Act. It has not been necessary, however, to use the new certification procedure in these particular cases because traditional administrative bond proceedings have been sufficient to detain these individuals without bond. We believe that this authority should be retained for use in appropriate situations.

22. On September 20, 2001, the INS issued an interim rule amending the period of time that an alien may be detained while the agency assesses whether to issue a Notice to Appear (NTA), placing the alien in immigration proceedings. Prior to amendment, the INS was required to issue an NTA within 24 hours of the alien's arrest. As amended, the INS has 48 hours after an alien is arrested to decide whether to issue an NTA, "except in the event of an emergency or other extraordinary circumstance in which case a determination will be made within an additional reasonable period of time."

> A. What is the authority for the INS to detain an alien for longer than 48 hours without filing charges?
>
> B. How many aliens have been detained for more than 48 hours without being charged under the authority in this regulation?
>
> C. What is the longest period that an alien has been detained without being charged under the authority in this regulation?
>
> D. Have any challenges to this regulation been brought in judicial proceedings? If so, please identify the case(s) and the status of each proceeding.
>
> <u>Answer:</u> Pursuant to the Committee's April 1, 2003, letter, in light of the transfer of the INS to DHS, we have referred these questions to DHS for a response. We previously provided the Committee with a copy of this referral.

23. Since September 11, 2001, the government has required that certain non-citizens from certain Middle Eastern countries register with the INS (or its successor agency).

> A. How many terrorists or suspected terrorists have been investigated and/or detained as a result of the requirement that non-citizens register with the federal government?
>
> B. What is the government's policy regarding whether non-citizens are able to have counsel present during the registration process, specifically during the interview?
>
> C. If counsel are not permitted at any point, what is the government's authority for denying such right to counsel?
>
>> **Answer:** Pursuant to the Committee's April 1, 2003, letter, in light of the transfer of the INS to DHS, we have referred these questions to DHS for a response. We previously provided the Committee with a copy of this referral.

24. Since September 11, 2001, how many individuals have been deported from the United States? To what countries were those individuals deported? What was the racial and ethnic background of such individuals? For what reason were these individuals deported?

> **Answer:** Pursuant to the Committee's April 1, 2003, letter, in light of the transfer of the INS to DHS, we have referred this question to DHS for a response. We previously provided the Committee with a copy of this referral.

Attorney General's Investigative Guidelines

25. On May 14, 2002, the Department issued revised investigative guidelines that established procedures for the initiation of investigations by the Federal Bureau of Investigation ("Bureau").

> A. Why were the guidelines for General Crimes and Domestic Security Investigations revised when the apparent threat against the United States is a threat from foreign terrorist groups? Do these guidelines apply only to investigations of U.S. citizens? Are U.S. citizens not subject to the foreign intelligence investigative guidelines?
>
>> **Answer:** In May 2002, the Attorney General issued a revised version of the Attorney General's Guidelines on General Crimes, Racketeering Enterprise and Terrorism Enterprise Investigations (the Guidelines). The previous version of the Guidelines also governed criminal investigations of domestic and international terrorism. The revision of the Guidelines was critical in providing the FBI with the appropriate tools to combat terrorism, because foreign terrorists often engage in conduct that violates the criminal laws of the United States. These guidelines apply to criminal investigations of citizens and non-citi-

zens alike. Similarly, both citizens and non-citizens are subject to the classified foreign intelligence guidelines, though in certain instances standards in those guidelines are different for U.S. persons and non-U.S. persons.

B. The new guidelines allow FBI agents to attend a public event, such as a political demonstration or a religious service, and to use data mining services, provided doing so is for the purpose of preventing or detecting terrorism. How will it be determined that the purpose of attending the event or using the service is to prevent or detect terrorism? How does the amount of evidence establishing that predicate differ from the amount of evidence that would be sufficient to check out leads or open a preliminary inquiry? What level of predication is required to permit FBI agents to attend public events or to use data mining services?

Answer: The revised Attorney General's Guidelines were designed to afford FBI agents the same degree of access to publicly available information as all other members of the general public enjoy. The old Guidelines did not clearly authorize agents to gather information for counterterrorism or other law enforcement purposes—for example, by visiting public places, or researching publicly available information—unless they were looking into particular crimes or criminal enterprises. In effect, agents had to wait for terrorist plots to develop, and for some lead or evidence to come from others, before they could begin gathering information. The revised Guidelines were designed to enable law enforcement to proactively gather intelligence that could be useful to detecting and preventing terrorist attacks, by attending public events or collecting publicly available information.

Agents can do so, however, only to the extent that such events or information are available to any other member of the general public. Part VI.A.2 of the Attorney General's Guidelines specifically provides that "[f]or the purpose of detecting or preventing terrorist activities, the FBI is authorized to visit any place and attend any event that is open to the public, on the same terms and conditions as members of the public generally." The Guidelines specifically mandate that "[n]o information obtained from such visits shall be retained unless it relates to potential criminal or terrorist activity" and prohibit the FBI from "maintaining files on individuals solely for the purpose of monitoring activities protected by the First Amendment or the lawful exercise of any other rights secured by the Constitution or laws of the United States."

The Guidelines also authorize the FBI to operate and participate in identification, tracking, and information systems for the purpose of identifying and locating terrorists, excluding or removing from the United States alien terrorists and alien supporters of terrorist activity as authorized by law, assessing and responding to terrorist risks and threats, or otherwise detecting, prosecuting, or preventing terrorist activities.

The Guidelines authorize the FBI to engage in these activities (subject to certain limitations, including those mentioned above) in the absence of a pre-existing lead or specific predication. This authority is designed to enable the FBI to draw proactively on available sources of information in order to prevent acts of terrorism. The determination whether a proposed use of this authority is for the purpose of preventing or detecting terrorism is made by the relevant FBI field office, and an agent who attends a public event when unrelated to preventing or detecting terrorism is subject to sanction for violating the Guidelines.

The Guidelines also recognize three levels of investigative activity: (1) the prompt and extremely limited checking out of initial leads; (2) preliminary inquiries (which are undertaken when there is information or an allegation that indicates the possibility of criminal activity and the responsible handling of which requires some further scrutiny beyond checking initial leads); and (3) full investigations (which may be initiated where facts or circumstances reasonably indicate that a federal crime has been, is being, or will be committed).

C. Since the issuance of these guidelines, how many religious sites (mosques, churches, temples, synagogues, etc.) have federal authorities entered in an official capacity without disclosing their identities? Please provide the total number of such sites and a breakdown of how many were affiliated with each particular type of site (mosque, church, temple, synagogue, etc.).

When agents visit religious sites pursuant to AG guidelines, what investigative tools are they permitted to use (i.e., wearing a wire, placing a listening device in the site)? If the information obtained from such visits is found unrelated to any criminal or terrorist investigation, when is such information destroyed and in what manner? Have, and if so provide details, any terrorism-related investigations or prosecutions resulted from such visits?

Answer: The revised Attorney General's Guidelines clarify that agents who are investigating individuals with ties to religious groups may use the same techniques they would use when investigating any other person. Individuals affiliated with religious entities are not singled out for special scrutiny. But neither will they have effective immunity from lawful investigations.

The old Guidelines did not clearly state that FBI agents could investigate terrorists with ties to mosques in the same way they could investigate suspects with ties to other sorts of entities. As a result, agents were reluctant to follow suspected terrorists into mosques—even when those facilities were held open to all members of the general public. The lack of clear authority to proactively collect terrorismrelated information may have hampered the FBI's investigation of Sheik Omar Ahmad Rahman, who was convicted for his role in the 1993 World Trade Center bombing. According to one media account:

> Although the FBI placed Rahman's bodyguard and driver under loose surveillance, Rahman himself was never questioned or put before a grand jury. Nor were his offices bugged, according to a former senior FBI official. Records of Rahman's mosques in Brooklyn and Jersey City were never subpoenaed, and no wiretaps were put on the mosques' phones, the official said.

FBI Wary of Investigating Extremist Muslim Leaders, WASH. POST, Oct. 29, 2001, at A04.

The new Guidelines simultaneously enhance the FBI's ability to visit public places and attend public events, and impose significant limitations designed to safeguard the civil liberty and privacy of law-abiding citizens. The new Guidelines allow FBI agents, like any community police officer, to visit public places and attend public events, but only "on the same terms and conditions as the general public." In addition, the Guidelines prohibit agents from retaining any information from such visits unless it relates to potential criminal or terrorist activity.

Because the FBI only retains from such visits information about potential terrorist attacks or other criminal conduct, it does not keep records or statistics reflecting the number of occasions that agents have visited public places. However, in response to numerous requests, officials in the FBI's Office of the General Counsel recently conducted an informal survey of the FBI's field offices. Their discussions with approximately 45 field offices indicate that fewer than ten of those offices have conducted investigative activities at mosques since September 11, 2001. All but one of those visits were conducted pursuant to, or were related to, open preliminary inquiries or full investigations. In the one reported instance where a visit was conducted pursuant to the Guidelines provision authorizing agents to visit public places and attend public events, no information relating to potential terrorism or criminal activity was found and, therefore, no substantive information from the visit was retained in FBI records.

D. Since the issuance of these guidelines, how many public meetings, and what types of such meetings (rallies, town halls), have federal authorities entered in an official capacity without disclosing their identities?

When agents visit public meetings pursuant to FBI guidelines, what investigative tools are they permitted to use (e.g., wearing a wire, placing a listening device in the meeting area)? If the information obtained from such visits is found unrelated to any criminal or terrorist investigation, when is such information destroyed and in what manner? Have, and if so provide details, any terrorism-related investigations of prosecutions resulted from such visits?

> **Answer:** The new Guidelines allow the FBI to proactively visit public places and attend public events to detect or prevent terrorist activities prior to developing evidence of the possibility of criminal activity or a specific lead. Use of this tool is explicitly limited to the detection and prevention of terrorist activities. If an agent desires to collect evidence of non-terrorism crimes by visiting public places and attending public events, he or she must first be within one of the categories of authorized investigative activity—either the prompt and extremely limited checking out of leads, a preliminary investigation, or a full investigation.
>
> The investigative techniques that are authorized during attendance at public places depend upon the stage of the investigation when the public visit occurs. For example, the Guidelines bar the use of non-consensual electronic surveillance except during a full investigation. Moreover, all constitutional, statutory, and regulatory restrictions on the use of any investigative technique must, of course, be observed.
>
> FBI agents who visit public places and events may not retain any information unless it relates to terrorism or other criminal activity. As a result, the Department has not maintained centralized statistics on how many times agents attend public meetings.

E. Are FBI agents required to record in writing—before they use data mining techniques or attend a public event under the guidelines—how such activity is for the purpose of detecting or preventing terrorism?

> **Answer:** There is currently no requirement that agents record in writing the purpose for which they use information systems. The determination whether a proposed use of this authority is for the purpose of preventing or detecting terrorism is made by the relevant FBI field office, and an agent who attends a public event when unrelated to preventing or detecting terrorism is subject to sanction for violating the Guidelines.

F. The changes to the preliminary inquiry procedures extended the period that such an inquiry can remain open and allowed extensions for up to a year without notice to FBI Headquarters. In considering this change, did you find that your field agents had been reluctant to conduct preliminary inquiries because they could not keep them open

long enough without burdensome approval requirements? What other problems did the 90-day limit present to agents? What other problems did requiring approval from Headquarters to continue a preliminary inquiry present to agents? How does Headquarters conduct important analysis of information generated by a preliminary inquiry if Headquarters is unaware of the inquiry for a year?

> **Answer:** The revised Guidelines extend the period to complete the preliminary inquiry to 180 days. Additional extensions of time may be granted for 90-day periods. The first two extensions may be granted by the Special Agent in Charge (SAC), upon a statement of reasons why further investigative steps are warranted when no "reasonable indication" of criminal activity exists. All extensions following the second extension may only be granted by FBI Headquarters, upon receipt of a written request and the statement of such reasons.
>
> The prior 90-day limit did not always afford a sufficient period within which to make an appropriate analysis of the value of continuing the investigation.
>
> Finally, agents are required to share foreign intelligence collected during criminal investigations—including during preliminary inquiries—with the intelligence community pursuant to the Attorney General's Guidelines Regarding Disclosure to the Director of Central Intelligence and Homeland Security Officials of Foreign Intelligence Acquired in the Course of a Criminal Investigation, adopted on September 23, 2002.

G. The Guidelines now permit a Special Agent in Charge to open a terrorism enterprise investigation without obtaining approval from FBI Headquarters. Instead, Headquarters must only be notified. What is contained in the required notice? Does the notice provide enough of a description of the evidence to permit FBI Headquarters to make an evaluation of the evidence and determine whether the investigation should continue or is it simply a formal notification that such an investigation has been opened and/or is continuing? Will the information in the notification be sufficient to use it to coordinate that investigation with others?

> **Answer:** As part of the initiation of a Terrorism Enterprise Investigation (TEI), field offices are required to submit to FBI Headquarters a communication setting forth a factual description describing how the predication standards for the initiation of the TEI have been satisfied. Additionally, a Section Chief within the Counterterrorism Division must concur with the initiation of the TEI. FBI Headquarters must also submit to the Department of Justice a memorandum justifying the initiation of the TEI. These procedures are described in Part III.B of the Attorney General's Guidelines on General Crimes, Racketeer-

ing Enterprise and Terrorism Enterprise Investigations. (A copy of the Guidelines is attached.)[4]

Finally, with respect to coordination of terrorism investigations, field agents are required to share foreign intelligence collected during criminal investigations with the intelligence community pursuant to the Attorney General's Guidelines Regarding Disclosure to the Director of Central Intelligence and Homeland Security Officials of Foreign Intelligence Acquired in the Course of a Criminal Investigation, adopted on September 23, 2002. Such sharing does not ordinarily occur through FBI Headquarters.

H. Who at the Bureau is responsible for making and approving the decision for a field agent to enter a public place, and must such approval be in writing prior to entering the public place?

> **Answer:** The Guidelines do not require supervisory approval before an agent enters a public place on the same terms and conditions as members of the public generally.

I. After a field agent visits a public place or event, are any notes or other records of what he or she observed retained? If so, under what circumstances, for what reasons, and for how long are they retained? Under what circumstances is information related to protected 1st Amendment activity retained in FBI or DOJ files? Are any records retained if a preliminary inquiry is never opened?

> **Answer:** No substantive information obtained from the visit may be retained unless it relates to potential criminal or terrorist activity. If information obtained during the visit rises to the level of a lead, such information must be properly documented, including a statement describing how the information is related to potential criminal and/or terrorist activity, and then filed accordingly. If the visit does not develop information relating to potential criminal or terrorist activity, an agent must note in the file the date, time and place visited and that the visit had negative results.

J. Who has access to any records and how does the FBI keep them secure?

> **Answer:** The FBI is subject to numerous laws, regulations, and policies regarding access to and the security of FBI systems and records. Safeguards include maintaining records in limited access space and password protections on computerized data. All FBI personnel are required to pass an extensive background investigation. Information is accessed only by authorized FBI personnel or by non-FBI personnel properly authorized to assist in the conduct of an agency function related to the information.

K. **Given the transfer of a substantial number of agents into terrorism investigations, what training did those agents receive on the use of the Guidelines?**

Answer: One hundred of the agents transferred to counterterrorism squads have received training on the Guidelines at the Basic Counterterrorism Operators In- service at the FBI Academy in Quantico, Virginia; 160 more agents will receive this training at the same course that started April 21, 2003. In January 2003, training on the revised Guidelines was given at the annual Chief Division Counsel (CDC) conference. The goal was to enable the CDCs to provide subsequent training to agents stationed in their respective field offices. In addition, instruction on the revised Guidelines was given during a recent Joint Terrorism Task Force conference.

L. **With the FBI's authority to "data mine" under the Guidelines, many fear that the FBI will have too much information and that the Bureau does not currently have the tools necessary to make good use of intelligence or to keep vast amounts of information secure. What has been done and is being done to improve the Bureau's ability to interpret all of this new data? What security measures have been implemented to prevent unauthorized access to such data?**

Answer: The Secure Counterterrorism Operational Prototype Environment (SCOPE) and Investigative Data Warehouse constitute the FBI's programs to provide current technologies to investigators and analysts and to collaborate with its law enforcement and intelligence partners. SCOPE will allow the FBI to use a number of specialized tools to identify and present hidden relationships found in data. The FBI is also utilizing software products that allow for the search, retrieval, and categorization of information. In addition, the CIA and NSA are helping to upgrade the FBI's analytic tradecraft by training and co-locating their personnel with FBI analysts.

With respect to security, please see the answer to question (J), *supra*. The same FBI security measures apply for preventing unauthorized access to law enforcement data. It is restricted to those with a need to know and is limited to official duties. Access to all data is logged and recorded. Specifically, the FBI Special Technologies Applications Section (STAS) implements user-access- control by issuing a user-ID and password to every authorized user. It implements role-based security by assigning every user to roles that are required for their position, and labels every record in the database with necessary tags to protect the confidentiality of the data. Distribution procedures require that all reports be vetted through an FBI agent who reviews the dissemination list and report produced.

M. Since the Guidelines permit the use of "publicly available" information, what efforts are going to be made to verify the accuracy of the data retrieved? Will agents be required to attempt to independently verify retrieved information for accuracy?

Answer: Safeguards to ensure the accuracy and reliability of information are essential components of any effective information system. Pursuant to a directive of the Director of the FBI, Reports Officers are being assigned to Headquarters and Field Offices to vet information provided to law enforcement, intelligence, and policy entities and to ensure its accuracy.

In collecting information for law enforcement purposes, it is impossible to determine in advance what specific information is relevant, timely, and complete. With the passage of time information may acquire new significance as further investigation brings new details to light. Trained investigators and analysts exercise due diligence to verify information through links, relationships, and other interpretations discovered during investigative efforts.

N. What type of supervision will be required when agents use data mining? Will field agents be able to initiate data mining on their own or will they be required to obtain approval from a supervisor?

Answer: Since all FBI personnel using information systems will have the proper security clearance, access and need to know, general supervision guidelines will apply. Agents are able to access information systems based on their own investigative need and authorization, and the system will keep track of where and what is accessed. Supervisors can review this information as necessary.

O. What data mining services has the FBI used? How long will data obtained through data mining be retained and how will it be indexed?

Answer: The FBI does not use a data mining service but typically uses search engines, queries and indexing programs in order to collate and access its information systems. Search results from such information systems will be maintained in accordance with the Federal Records Act and applicable records disposition schedules. Data is indexed in accordance with FBI Indexing Guidelines.

P. In its May 2002 Report on Financial Privacy, Law Enforcement, and Terrorism, the Prosperity Task Force on Information Exchange and Financial Privacy outlined many problems with sharing too much information with too many countries and without proper controls. How has the FBI protected against the wide distribution of information to too many countries without proper controls?

Answer: The FBI, Department of Justice, and Intelligence Community have substantial controls on dissemination of information to foreign countries. These controls are extensive and complex in nature and are applied according to the manner in which information is obtained and disseminated. For example, any dissemination of information first depends upon the means by which it was collected/obtained—*e.g.*, via federal grand jury or other subpoena process, court authorized criminal search warrants and Title III electronic surveillance orders, consent searches, FISA-authorized searches and surveillance collections, National Security Letters, and other sensitive and classified intelligence collection methods and sources.

Dissemination of information obtained via criminal court authorized processes is subject to controls imposed by various court orders, statutes, and the Federal Rules of Criminal Procedure. Dissemination of information obtained or derived from FISA is likewise subject to controls imposed by the FISA and the Foreign Intelligence Surveillance Court. Furthermore, the FBI's National Security Law Unit and the Department's Office of Intelligence Policy and Review are consulted on and provide appropriate advice on dissemination of FISA and foreign intelligence information. Information obtained or derived from the FISA process is always appropriately marked as such to ensure any dissemination complies with relevant procedures and controls. With regard to foreign intelligence information, the Director of Central Intelligence formulates policy concerning relationships between the U.S. Intelligence Community and foreign intelligence services. Classified information is designated by established classification levels and marked according to established classification standards which include appropriate controls over dissemination of the information. As is the case with information obtained or derived from grand jury subpoenas and Title III orders, the USA PATRIOT Act removed many barriers to the timely sharing of information between counterintelligence and counterterrorism intelligence operations and criminal investigations. While many barriers have been removed, extensive controls over dissemination of information still remain. With regard to information obtained or derived from other than the means addressed above, dissemination to foreign governments is carefully scrutinized and evaluated according to a number of factors ranging from the sensitivity and potential importance of the information to the status of the country to which the information is to be provided, and is evaluated in context with the reason the information was requested and the intended use of the information. In short, the FBI does not and cannot haphazardly disseminate information to foreign countries without proper controls and careful evaluation.

Q. Since Syria, Cuba, Libya, Iran, Iraq, China, and others are members of Interpol and share in the international information exchange system, what procedures prevent these countries from receiving information on terrorist suspects who may be supported by participating countries?

Answer: The information provided by an Interpol Member Country remains the Member Country's information and that Member Country controls the distribution and use of that information and can ask for the information to be deleted or adapted. For example, when a Member Country, providing information to the Interpol General Secretariat (IPSG), asks for database checks to be completed or queries other Member Countries and provides a copy to the IPSG, the Member Country provides information regarding any further distribution of this information. The Member Country may advise that the information cannot be released without prior authorization, may specifically state which countries, regions or zones can receive the information, or may designate that the information can be provided to all Interpol Member Countries. Most Member Countries utilize a mixture of all three options, depending on the sensitivity of the investigation and the specific information. Many Member Countries also have a routine rule regarding most police information, including or excluding specific countries or regions. As such, information provided by the United States remains U.S. information, and the U.S. controls the distribution and use of that information.

R. The Guidelines permit acceptance and retention of information "voluntarily provided by private entities." What will the FBI do to ensure the accuracy of the information received from such sources? To what extent have such "private entities" been third parties as opposed to the specific individuals to whom the information pertained? How does the Department interpret "voluntarily" (e.g., does it mean the information was unsolicited, was provided pursuant to a government request, or was provided pursuant to a government subpoena?)?

Answer: Evaluation of source information has always been a fundamental component of FBI investigations. Historically, agents have received information from various sources, including criminal informants, anonymous callers, or other sources of information. The decision to take action based on such information, its use in obtaining investigative tools such as search warrants and electronic surveillance court orders, and ultimately the use of such information in a criminal prosecution have always required an assessment of the reliability of the information provided by the source and/or the credibility of the source of information.

The FBI does not have readily available data indicating to what extent private entities voluntarily providing information have been third parties, as opposed to specific individuals to whom the information pertained.

The FBI interprets "voluntarily" as meaning the information was provided other than in response to compulsory process (*e.g.*, a grand jury or other subpoena).

S. Where and how is information obtained through data mining stored? Is access to data obtained through data mining limited to those involved in a particular investigation? How is erroneous information corrected or purged, if at all? Has the Department issued written policies to provide guidance in this area? Does it plan to issue such policies?

> <u>Answer</u>: To the extent that Department activities in the collection, use or dissemination of records are subject to Privacy Act restrictions, the Department must comply with these restrictions, regardless of the medium involved.
>
> Information obtained by the FBI is stored in appropriate FBI systems in both hard copy and electronic format. Access to data is governed by applicable legal restrictions, including the Privacy Act. Amendment or correction of data is conducted in accordance with the Privacy Act. Sections 16.40 to 16.55 of Title 28, Code of Federal Regulations, contain Department of Justice Privacy Act rules.

Has, and from what companies, the Department purchased information or entered into contracts with data mining companies? To what extent and how will persons listed in such information be able to correct errors or inaccuracies?

> <u>Answer</u>: The Department has purchased information or entered into contracts with companies that warehouse public source information. Persons listed in those data collections should seek to correct errors or inaccuracies with source agencies. The FBI has access to Lexis/Nexis news, public source and financial data on a query basis; however, it is currently not aggregated with any other data. Commercial data from Choicepoint and iMap is also available for our unclassified users and its use is based on acceptable DOJ privacy constraints. The FBI also has access to a number of other databases from non-DOJ components of the intelligence community at the classified level that are currently being used for data-mining and pattern recognition. A listing of all the classified databases that are available through Intelink, Intelink-S, and CT-Link should be addressed to the Director of Central Intelligence. Additionally, the FBI has access to a number of unclassified sources from non-DOJ components such as the State Department VISA application database and INS data, as well as unclassified data from the Open Sources Information System (OSIS) as part of the intelligence community.

T. Is retained information reviewed at reasonable intervals to determine its continuing relevance to antiterrorism efforts? If so, who is responsible for performing such reviews?

Answer: Yes, retained information is reviewed at reasonable intervals to determine its relevance. Reviews may be routinely performed by analysts, case agents, task force members, supervisors, and legal counsel. In the course of an investigation, trained investigators and analysts exercise due diligence to verify information through links, relationships and other interpretations discovered during the use of information systems and other investigative efforts.

Miscellaneous Authorities

26. There have been numerous reports that the Department of Justice has detained individuals as material witnesses, presumably pursuant to judicial orders under 18 U.S.C. § 3144, in connection with terrorism investigations. Please provide the Committee with the following information with respect to each such detainee since September 11, 2001: (1) the length of detention of each detainee; (2) the number of such detainees who either sought review of or filed an appeal from a detention order under 18 U.S.C. § 3145; and (3) the results of such review or appeal.

A. Were these individuals given access to legal counsel? If not, why not?

Answer: Every single person detained as a material witness as part of the September 11 investigation has been represented by counsel. Indeed, material witnesses have the right to a lawyer who can assist them in challenging the legality of the detention at any time. The witnesses get counsel at their first appearance before a judge. The court will appoint free counsel for material witnesses who are financially unable to obtain adequate representation. See 18 U.S.C. § 3006A(a)(1)(G) ("[r]epresentation shall be provided for any financially eligible person who . . . is in custody as a material witness"). Other witnesses may retain counsel of their choice.

Every single person detained as a material witness as part of the September 11 investigations was found by a federal judge to have information material to the grand jury's investigation. An individual may be detained under the material witness statute, 18 U.S.C. § 3144, only when a federal judge concludes that (1) his testimony is "material in a criminal proceeding," (2) it may become impracticable to secure his presence by subpoena, and (3) he meets the criteria for detention under the Bail Reform Act, 18 U.S.C. § 3142. These witnesses also all have the right to be presented promptly before a judge to have bond set and to argue that they should be released on bond. In some cases, the Government has agreed to release individuals on bond, and courts have released witnesses on bond in a few additional cases. *See, e.g., United States v. Awadallah*, 202 F. Supp. 2d 55 (S.D.N.Y. 2002). Material witnesses have status hearings in court, when requested by their counsel or scheduled by the judge, regarding the length of their detention and progress toward obtaining their testimony.

We note that Rule 6(e) requires secrecy of everyone involved in the grand jury process *except* the witness. Thus, each of the detained material witnesses is free to identify himself publicly. The fact that few have elected to do so suggests they wish their detention to remain non-public.

With respect to the request for details about material witnesses detained during terrorism investigations, the Department of Justice has consistently taken the view that Federal Rule of Criminal Procedure 6(e) and court orders in individual cases prohibit it from revealing the exact numbers of material witnesses who are detained pending their testimony before a grand jury. The Department also cannot reveal the details of cases, as that would reveal the direction and focus of secret grand jury proceedings. In addition, disclosing such specific information would be detrimental to the war on terror and the investigation of the September 11 attacks. Thus, it continues to be imperative that the specific number of material witnesses detained as part of the September 11 investigation, the districts and investigations to which they relate, and the length of their detention not be released.

Likewise, the Department cannot provide the number of detainees who may have appealed their detention orders, or the results of such appeals, except where they have been made public by the courts. *See, e.g., United States v. Awadallah*, 202 F. Supp. 2d 55 (S.D.N.Y. 2002); *In re the Application of the United States for a Material Witness Warrant*, 213 F. Supp. 2d 287, 288 n.1 (S.D.N.Y. 2002) (neither the witness's name nor identifying facts are set forth in the opinion because the matter was sealed as proceedings ancillary to grand jury proceedings). We note that the use of the material witness statute is rarely challenged on appeal, probably because the use of the statute in grand jury proceedings is an appropriate law enforcement technique authorized by Congress, routinely used by the Department, and repeatedly approved by federal courts nationwide. *See Bacon v. United States*, 449 F.2d 933 (9th Cir. 1971), *In re the Application of the United States for a Material Witness Warrant*, 213 F. Supp. 2d 287 (S.D.N.Y. 2002).

There have been some misconceptions in the public about the number of material witness warrants that the Government issued as part of its September 11 investigation, as well as the circumstances, length, and terms of these detentions. Notwithstanding the restrictions noted above on releasing specific information about material witnesses, the Department is able to provide some general information about these material witnesses:

> As of January 2003, the total number of material witnesses detained in the course of the September 11 investigation was fewer than 50.
>
> Approximately 90% of these material witnesses were detained for 90 days or less.
>
> Approximately 80% of these material witnesses were detained for 60 days or less.
>
> Approximately 50% of these material witnesses were detained for 30 days or less.
>
> The few individuals detained for more than 90 days were detained for an extended period of time in part because they pursued litigation that precluded obtaining their testimony, made efforts to proffer or seek immunity before testifying, or took other actions that delayed the proceedings. While such actions are legitimate, they often take time to resolve and can result in longer detention. Moreover, some detainees facing deportation did not pursue efforts to provide prompt testimony.

B. What is the percentage breakdown for the detainees in terms of national origin, race, and ethnicity?

> **Answer:** We do not maintain data on these characteristics of detained material witnesses.

C. Please list the charges that the Department has brought against each such detainee.

> **Answer:** We can only provide information about those material witnesses whose status has been made public in court proceedings. In this regard, Osama Awadallah was charged with perjury; Abdallah Higazy was charged with lying to federal agents; Mohammed Osman Idris was charged with false statements on a passport application; Mohammed Hassan El-Yacoubi was charged with false statements on a passport application; Saleh Ali Almari was charged with conspiracy to commit mail and wire fraud; Earnest James Ujaama was charged with conspiracy to provide material support to Al Qaeda and with using, carry, possessing and discharging a firearm during a crime of violence; and Zacarias Moussaoui was charged with conspiracy to commit acts of terrorism transcending national boundaries, conspiracy to murder United States employees, conspiracy to commit aircraft piracy, conspiracy to use weapons of mass destruction, conspiracy to destroy aircraft, and conspiracy to destroy property. Most

material witnesses remain witnesses and have not been charged with a criminal offense.

D. Please provide the legal basis for detaining those individuals who have been cleared of any connection with terrorism beyond the date of such clearance.

<u>Answer</u>: When a material witness has satisfied his warrant by providing the relevant information he possesses, the warrant is dismissed and the witness is then released *unless* he is transferred to custody on another legal basis, such as immigration charges or federal or state criminal charges.

E. Please provide a list of all requests by the government to seal proceedings in connection with any of the detainees and copies of any orders issued pursuant thereto.

<u>Answer</u>: We are prohibited by court orders from providing any information regarding specific sealed material witness proceedings, including copies of sealing orders. We routinely move to seal *all* grand jury material witness proceedings pursuant to Rule 6(e) of the Federal Rules of Criminal Procedure.

27. On October 31, 2001, the Department of Justice promulgated an interim rule, with provision for post promulgation public comment, that requires the director of the Bureau of Prisons to monitor or review the communications between certain inmates and their lawyers for the purpose of deterring future acts that could result in death or serious bodily injury to persons or substantial damage to property that would entail the risk of death or serious bodily injury to persons. 66 Fed. Reg. 55062, 55066 (2001).

A. How many inmates have been subject to the interim rule?

<u>Answer</u>: The Attorney General has ordered the monitoring of attorney communications for a single inmate: Sheik Omar Ahmad Rahman, who was convicted for his part in the 1993 plot to bomb the World Trade Center. He is confined in the Administrative Maximum United States Penitentiary in Florence, Colorado.

A federal grand jury has indicted Rahman's lawyer, Lynne Stewart, for helping him communicate with his terrorist associates outside of prison. According to the indictment, Stewart distracted prison guards while Rahman and his translator discussed whether to continue to comply with a cease-fire in terrorist activities against Egyptian authorities.

Rahman and his attorneys were notified that their communications were subject to monitoring. No monitoring has occurred, however, because the inmate and his attorneys thus far have chosen not to communicate further with each other.

B. The interim rule required prior written notification to an inmate and any attorneys involved "[e]xcept in the case of prior court authorization. 66 Fed. Reg. at 55066. Under this exception to the required notification, how many cases were there/are there where inmates and their attorneys were not notified that their communications were monitored?

> **Answer:** In our interpretation, the requirement that prior written notification be given to an inmate and attorneys involved "[e]xcept in the case of prior court authorization" refers to a court-authorized interception. While there may have been cases where inmates have been targeted and conversations have been intercepted between such inmates and their attorneys, Title III requires that those conversations be minimized, *i.e.*, not listened to after initial identification of the parties involved, due to the attorney-client privilege. There also may have been cases where attorneys have been the subject of an investigation and, as a result, had their conversations intercepted. Such conversations would have also been minimized under established procedures. Neither the Department, nor any federal law enforcement agency to our knowledge, maintains any records that track the number of attorneys and/or inmates whose communications were intercepted and/or monitored by prior court authorization.

C. The interim rule prohibited disclosure of information prior to approval of disclosure by a federal judge, except where the person in charge of the monitoring determines that acts of violence or terrorism are imminent. How many times did the person in charge of the monitoring disclose information after approval by a federal judge? After a determination that acts of violence or terrorism are imminent?

> **Answer:** As indicated in the answer to question 27(A), *supra*, no monitoring has occurred under the interim rule. Thus, there have been no occasions in which information obtained through monitoring has been disclosed.

D. How many post-promulgation comments were received by the Department of Justice?

> **Answer:** The Bureau of Prisons received thousands of form letters and approximately 30 substantive comments on the interim rule during the comment period.

E. Is the Department of Justice considering any revisions to the interim rule?

> **Answer:** The Department of Justice is considering the comments and is in the process of preparing the final rule.

28. The Department of Defense has detained two United States citizens in military prisons in the United States as enemy combatants. These

detentions have been challenged in court, where the Department of Justice has represented the Department of Defense. Has the Department of Justice received any information regarding the detention by the Department of Defense within the United States or abroad of any other United States citizens? Does the Department of Justice have any agreement, arrangement, or understanding, formal or informal, with the Department of Defense regarding the detention of United States citizens as enemy combatants?

> **Answer:** At this time, the Department of Justice is aware of the detention by the Department of Defense (either within the United States or abroad) of no United States citizens as enemy combatants besides Yaser Hamdi and Jose Padilla.
>
> As the question notes, the Department of Justice has represented officials of the Department of Defense who have been named respondents in habeas corpus actions brought on behalf of detained enemy combatants. The Department of Justice is assigned that role by statute. *See* 5 U.S.C. § 3106. Thus, at least to this extent, the Department of Justice has a "formal" "arrangement" with the Department of Defense regarding the detention of U.S. citizens as enemy combatants and litigation surrounding such detentions. The Department of Justice and Department of Defense also maintain lines of communication to ensure that intelligence concerning persons who may properly be deemed enemy combatants (a category that might, from time to time, potentially include U.S. citizens) is shared in a timely manner in order to permit each department to carry out its functions.

29. FBI Director Robert Mueller announced the formation of "flying squads" that would be prepared to be deployed on short notice into terrorism investigations.

> **A. Have these "flying squads" been formed?**
>
> **Answer:** Yes, the Flying Squads were created in June 2002.
>
> **B. How many agents are assigned to a flying squad?**
>
> **Answer:** Two flying squads have been formed within the FBI's Counterterrorism Division, with a total of 24 agents. Both flying squads are managed by a Unit Chief and supported by a Supervisory Special Agent for administrative deployment matters. Each of the two flying squads is led by a Team Leader (Supervisory Special Agent), an Assistant Team Leader (Term-Supervisory Special Agent), and is staffed with nine Special Agents.
>
> **C. What kind of training have the flying squad agents received?**
>
> **Answer:** Flying squad agents have received training in post-blast investigations and personal safety while working in an overseas envi-

ronment. In the near future, they will receive specialized training in the following: major case management, basic statement analysis, effective interrogation and negotiation techniques, crisis management, FISA, weapons of mass destruction, advanced overseas security awareness, U.S. Embassy operations, U.S. intelligence community operations and issues, and other specialty areas.

D. Have they been deployed into investigations?

Answer: Yes, the flying squads have been deployed into investigations.

E. If so, how many times?

Answer: Since their establishment, the flying squads have deployed 23 times (12 domestically and 11 internationally).

F. Did they prove to be a useful addition to the investigation to which they were deployed?

Answer: Yes. Flying squads have been used to very good operational effect. They have been deployed at the direction of FBI Headquarters executive management, field office management and Legal Attaches. The flying squads, as necessary, have been accompanied by an array of FBI operational and supporting assets, including terrorist financial operations and analysis, intelligence, laboratory/forensics and substantive investigative specialists. The flying squads have proved useful in assisting FBI field offices and Legal Attaches in their terrorism investigations, to determine the whereabouts of all subjects, assess their involvement in terrorist activities, determine links to others, and to fully exploit all investigative techniques (*e.g.*, FISA). The flying squads have provided guidance, strategies, and analytical support to the requested field offices or Legal Attaches and have recommended various courses of action. Such assistance has been very beneficial to the terrorism investigative efforts of field offices and Legal Attaches.

30. Does the FBI use, as one of its terrorism investigative tools, aircraft to conduct surveillance of various persons or locations? What type of information is sought using such surveillance?

Answer: The answer to this question is classified and, accordingly, will be delivered to the Committee under separate cover.

31. Has the DOJ through any of its agencies formulated a policy position regarding criteria for establishing the authenticity of foreign govern-

ment-issued identity cards since the passage of the USA PATRIOT Act? If so, please produce a copy of that position.

> **Answer:** Pursuant to the Committee's April 1, 2003, letter, in light of the transfer of the INS to DHS, we have referred this question to DHS for a response. We previously provided the Committee with a copy of this referral.

32. Has the DOJ through any of its agencies, including especially the INS, prepared or issued a policy with regard to security standards and acceptance of "Matricula Consulars" identity cards issued by foreign governments to persons who are residing in the United States but who may not be lawfully present in the United States.? If so, has that policy been provided in writing to the Office of Management and Budget, the Secretary of State, or the Secretary of the Treasury? If such a policy has been prepared, please provide a copy to the Committee.

> **Answer:** The Department of Justice is currently participating in an interagency process to develop an Administration policy regarding consular identification cards. We refer you to DHS for information related to the former INS on this issue.

33. Regarding the FBI's National Crime Information Database, has the Department lifted a requirement that the FBI ensure the accuracy and timeliness of information about criminals and crime victims before adding it to the database? Please provide a copy of any memoranda pertaining to the requirement that was lifted.

> **Answer:** The FBI recently obtained a limited Privacy Act exemption for the National Crime Information Center (NCIC) database but the exemption does not change any of the requirements for entry, audit, validation, and hit confirmation of NCIC records as provided for in the Criminal Justice Information Services (CJIS) User Agreement and the NCIC 2000 Operating Manual.
>
> Paragraph (j)(2) of the Privacy Act permits the head of any agency to promulgate rules to exempt any system of records within the agency from certain provisions of the Privacy Act. When an agency claims an exemption, it must publish reasons for the exemption in the Federal Register and afford the public an opportunity to comment.
>
> Paragraph (e)(5) of the Privacy Act states that agencies shall maintain all records used by the agency in making any determination about any individual "with such accuracy, relevance, timeliness, and completeness as is reasonably necessary to assure fairness to the individual in the determination."
>
> On January 31, 2003, the FBI published a proposed rule in the Federal Register exempting the NCIC (JUSTICE/FBI-001) from paragraph (e)(5) of the Act. *See* 68 F.R. 4974 (Jan. 31, 2003). No comments were re-

ceived regarding the proposed rule. Accordingly, after the close of the public comment period, on March 24, 2003, the FBI published a final rule exempting NCIC from paragraph (e)(5) of the Act. *See* 68 F.R. 14141 (Mar. 24, 2003).

34. Is the FBI ordering its field offices to ascertain the number of mosques and Muslims in their areas? Is the government seeking membership lists from mosques? If so, why? From how many mosques is the government seeking such lists? How, if at all, has the agency reassigned its agents as a result? How many investigations of or prosecutions for terrorism as a result of these activities?

<u>Answer</u>: The FBI has undertaken a broad demographic assessment for the primary purpose of providing FBI Executive management with a snapshot of each field office's working environment and of the communities they serve. As a relatively small part of that broad assessment, information concerning the number of mosques and the approximate size of the Muslim population in a given geographic area was collected, mostly from publicly available sources.

If the FBI is to perform effectively its primary mission of detecting and preventing acts of terrorism, our field offices need to reach out to the overwhelmingly law-abiding and patriotic members of these communities to help us locate terrorists and their supporters who may reside among them in an effort to avoid detection. The demographic survey has facilitated the FBI's efforts in knowing where these communities are concentrated and where to turn for assistance.

For example, the FBI has reached out to these communities to assure them that, despite the emphasis on counterterrorism, investigating civil rights remains a high priority of the FBI. The FBI field offices have been tasked to contact Muslim leaders for the purpose of establishing a dialogue and discussing procedures for alerting the local FBI office to such issues. Over 500 such meetings have occurred since September 11, 2001.

35. Is the Department assisting in the implementation of the Computer Assisted Passenger Prescreening System (CAPPS I or II), which would be used to screen airline passengers?

A. To what extent is the Department, or any of its components, providing information about specific persons for inclusion in CAPPS?

<u>Answer</u>: CAPPS I and CAPPS II are projects of the Transportation Security Administration (TSA), which is part of DHS. CAPPS II is currently under development and will function as a server that, when operational, will examine and check passenger identification with associated information in airline passenger name records. Following this check, CAPPS II will then match the individual passenger name

characteristics against numerous government databases and other criminal and public databases.

One of the databases that CAPPS II, when operational, proposes to access is the Violent Gang Terrorist Organization File (VGTOF) that is maintained by the FBI. The VGTOF is the FBI's primary list of suspected terrorists. An individual may be entered into VGTOF by FBI field offices if there is an open terrorism case in the field office. In addition, even if no case has been opened by a field office, an individual's name may also be entered into VGTOF by the FBI's Terrorist Watch and Warning Unit if the individual is of special interest to the Counterterrorism Division at FBI Headquarters.

B. From what databases or other sources, including companies, does such information come from?

<u>Answer</u>: As previously mentioned, FBI field offices, based on an open terrorism case, and the FBI's Terrorist Watch and Warning Unit may enter an individual's name into VGTOF. Information regarding an individual to be entered in VGTOF may come from but is not limited to: leads developed during an open terrorism case in FBI field offices, human intelligence sources, court authorized electronic surveillance sources, and information shared with the FBI by other law enforcement, intelligence, and homeland security agencies.

C. What checks are in place to ensure that the information is accurate and does not constitute inappropriate profiling?

<u>Answer</u>: TSA can provide additional information regarding the accuracy of the information accessed by CAPPS II.

D. In what manner are individuals afforded an opportunity to correct erroneous or inaccurate information?

<u>Answer</u>: TSA can provide additional information regarding the correction of erroneous or inaccurate information found in CAPPS II.

36. "Operation Liberty Shield" involves stopping cars at airports, checking the identification of truckers who transport hazardous material on the highway, and monitoring Internet and financial transactions.

A. Please identify the specific authority on which "Operation Liberty Shield" was created and implemented.

B. What level of predication is required before an agent may monitor the Internet and financial transactions?

C. What terrorism-related investigations and/or prosecutions have resulted from Operation Liberty Shield?

<u>Answer</u>: Pursuant to the Committee's April 1, 2003, letter, in light of the transfer of the INS to DHS, we have referred these questions to

DHS for a response. We previously provided the Committee with a copy of this referral.

37. There have been three successive FBI sweeps since September 11, 2001, to monitor, question, arrest, detain, or deport various immigrants. The first sweep focused on young Arab and Muslim males and occurred in the months following September 11, 2001. The second sweep occurred in March 2002 and centered on thousands of individuals of Middle Eastern and South Asian heritage. The third sweep occurred in March 2003 as part of "Operation Liberty Shield." Please provide information on each of these operations.

A. When were the plans for such operations first considered by the Department?

B. What guidance was provided to U.S. Attorney's Offices and/or FBI offices with respect to questions that should be asked of such immigrants?

C. What has been the outcome of each of these plans? Please provide details such as how many were monitored, questioned, arrested, detained, or deported for each operation. Please provide details as to the number and types of terrorism-related investigations and prosecutions that have resulted from these sweeps.

D. Please identify the specific authority relied on to create and implement these plans, including the monitoring, questioning, arrests, detentions, and deportations.

<u>Answer</u>: The answers relating to these questions are classified, and, accordingly, will be delivered to the Committee under separate cover.

38. In August 2002, a Justice Department rule went into effect giving authority to state and local police to enforce immigration laws.

A. Which state and local governments are using this new authority and to what extent?

B. How many immigration violations were found as a result of state and local law enforcement participation under this new authority?

C. Have any persons or groups affected by this new authority (e.g. immigrants, civil rights organizations) submitted any formal complaints to the Department (including the Inspector General) regarding this authority. If so, please provide details.

<u>Answer to A through C:</u> The only rule that went into effect in August 2002 giving authority to state and local police to enforce immigration laws was the Mass Influx Rule, published at 67 F.R. 48354 (July 24, 2002). This rule, which implements authority given the Attorney General in section 372 of the Illegal Immigration Reform and Immi-

grant Responsibility Act of 1996 (IIRIRA), Pub. L. No. 104-208, Div. C., 110 Stat. 3009-46, gives state and local police the authority to assist federal immigration officers in the event of a mass influx of aliens as declared by the Attorney General (now the Secretary of DHS). This rule requires the signing of a Memorandum of Understanding with the state or local government and requires training, although under a rule published on February 26, 2003, the training requirement may be abbreviated or waived in unanticipated situations requiring an expeditious response to protect the public safety, public health, or national security. To date, there has been no declaration that a situation of a mass influx of aliens exists. Consequently, no state or local government has exercised this authority, and therefore no immigration violations were found as a result of state and local law enforcement participation under this new authority. We are not aware of any complaints regarding this authority (other than comments received during the rule-making process).

This question may be referring to the inherent arrest authority that is possessed by States. This power is not the creation of the federal government. However, the Attorney General did cite this authority on June 5, 2002, in announcing the development of the National Security Entry-Exit Registration System (NSEERS). He stated the following:

> When federal, state and local law enforcement officers encounter an alien of national security concern who has been listed on the NCIC [National Crime Information Center] for violating immigration law, federal law permits them to arrest that individual and transfer him to the custody of the INS. The Justice Department's Office of Legal Counsel has concluded that this narrow, limited mission that we are asking state and local police to undertake voluntarily—arresting aliens who have violated criminal provisions of Immigration and Nationality Act or civil provisions that render an alien deportable, and who are listed on the NCIC—is within the inherent authority of the states.

With respect to the legal authority of state and local law enforcement officers to arrest such aliens, the Justice Department's Office of Legal Counsel (OLC) previously had opined that states possess inherent authority to arrest aliens for criminal immigration law violations generally. In April 2002, OLC additionally opined that states also possess inherent authority to arrest aliens whose names have been entered into the NCIC database because they have both (1) violated *civil* provisions of the federal immigration laws that render them deportable and (2) been determined by federal authorities to pose special risks, either because they present national security concerns or because they are absconders who have not complied with a final order of removal or deportation. The federal government has never preempted this authority; the only barriers to executing such arrests are statutes or policies that states or municipalities may have imposed upon themselves.

This authority is crucial to the success of the absconder initiative. Although every absconder has potentially committed a criminal immigration violation because ignoring a final order of removal is a criminal act, the crime occurred only if the act was "willful." As of February 2003, 1,141 absconders had been apprehended, with 545 removed from the United States, 391 in the custody of federal immigration authorities awaiting removal, and 44 under criminal prosecution by the United States Attorneys for various crimes. Some of the apprehensions involved local law enforcement officials. Others did not. We do not have a statistical breakdown indicating which of these arrests involved civil immigration violations or which local law enforcement agencies, if any, were involved.

The exercise of this arrest authority in the context of the absconder initiative has not generated any formal complaints by arrested aliens. However, there has been one highly-speculative lawsuit on the issue, *Tejeda-Delgado, et. al., v. City of Los Angeles*, in which several removable plaintiffs (who were not arrested) claim that the INS conspired to have the Los Angeles Police Department wrongfully arrest them for civil deportation purposes by posting their names in the NCIC database.

ENDNOTES

[1] Attachments A and B. [Omitted]

[2] Attachment C. [Omitted]

[3] Attachment D. [Omitted]

[4] Attachment E. [Omitted]

Printed in the United States of America/BNB